HOLLIS F. FAIT, Ph.D.

Professor of Physical Education,
University of Connecticut

Illustrated by Janis Fait

Special Physical Education

Adapted, Corrective, Developmental

Fourth Edition

W. B. SAUNDERS COMPANY

PHILADELPHIA • LONDON • TORONTO

W. B. Saunders Company: West Washington Square
Philadelphia, Pa. 19105

1 St. Anne's Road
Eastbourne, East Sussex BN21 3UN, England

1 Goldthorne Avenue
Toronto, Ontario M8Z 5T9, Canada

Library of Congress Cataloging in Publication Data
Fait, Hollis F

   Special physical education.

   Includes bibliographies.
   1. Physical education for handicapped children.
I. Title.
GV445.F32 1978   613.7′042   77-78568
ISBN 0-7216-3503-2

Special Physical Education: Adapted, Corrective, Developmental   ISBN 0-7216-3503-2

Last digit is the print number: 9   8   7   6   5   4   3

Foreword

If we are to succeed in providing an important educational dimension to any area of inquiry we must keep the body of knowledge in perspective. Advancement in any field comes with a solid foundation upon which we launch our inquiries, research, and teaching. The move with the flow of progress must be tempered with the wisdom of the past.

The impact of a text is often congruent with the strength and vitality of the author as well his ability to express in comprehensible language the rhetoric of his topic.

Hollis Fait in this edition has looked closely at the prevalence of handicapping conditions among school age children and addresses the needs of physical educators in providing appropriate motor activities for these youngsters. By focusing on a child centered approach and the child's motor needs he avoids the trap of orienting the book on the disability and enhances the thrust of helping the child toward a higher level of physical, social, emotional, and educational functioning.

In this fourth edition of *Special Physical Education: adapted, corrective, developmental* the author has continued the saga initiated almost two decades ago of reflecting the concerns, needs, and advances that the educator faces in providing physical education for the individual with a handicapping condition.

The strengths of this book are many and too numerous for a list to be all-inclusive but some of the major attributes appear to be

- Orientation toward prevalent problems of school age children
- Limited but concise discussion of etiology and pathology
- Presentation of developmental patterns of normal growth and maturation, which is essential in assessing motor skill behavior of the handicapped child
- Discussion of theoretical base of motor learning and perception
- Inclusion of evaluation procedures and instruments
- Description of assistive devices most commonly utilized
- Inclusion of subjects related closely to the present acceptable approaches in educating the handicapped child

Basically the book in its organizational plan presents a very consistent approach to physical education planning and activities that makes it useful to not only physical educators but to other professionals, such as special educators, recreators, corrective therapists, regular educators, and administrators. By bringing together those disorders that produce similar motor problems in the handicapped individual, one can view these students from the perspective of their abilities in motor performance rather than their limitations. This emphasis on the more positive elements reduces to some extent the labeling and categorizing that is so often detrimental to the individual child.

Dr. Fait has again succeeded in capturing the essence of the body of knowledge in physical education for the handicapped individual, which will enable further development of the professions in best serving handicapped children and youth of today.

WILLIAM A. HILLMAN, JR.
Project Officer,
Division of Personnel Preparation,
Bureau of Education for the
Handicapped,
Department of HEW

Preface

This edition, like the three previous ones, is designed for use as a basic text in physical education for the handicapped. The educational concept of serving all children who have special needs and are able to attend public school is now reinforced by judicial decree and legislative mandate. Thus, it is imperative that physical educators have the knowledge to understand and provide for the special needs, interests, and abilities of students with various physical, mental, and emotional handicaps. It is the objective of this book, as it was of its predecessors, to provide that information by drawing upon the related fields of medicine, psychology, rehabilitation, therapeutic recreation, and special education to form a body of knowledge that is effectively integrated with educational theories and special methods and techniques for teaching the handicapped.

To keep the book to a size that allows reasonable coverage in a semester, it was necessary to make choices among the handicapping conditions to be covered. The criterion applied was that the disorder must be sufficiently prevalent among elementary and secondary school-age children so that teachers of physical education would need to know about the condition in order to plan an appropriate program for these students. Hence, conditions such as cystic fibrosis and muscular dystrophy have been added, and others, such as poliomyelitis and tuberculosis of the bone, which are no longer prevalent among children, have been eliminated. Likewise, disorders found exclusively among the middle-aged and elderly have been omitted. In keeping with the criterion, the presentation of the pathology and etiology of the disorders has been limited to information that is pertinent to physical education activities or is generally considered to be part of the knowledge of special physical education.

This edition has been organized in such a way as to bring together those disorders that produce similar motor limitations. This method of organization encourages prospective teachers to think of handicapped students in terms of their abilities in motor performance rather than to view them as persons with a certain type of handicap that requires specific adaptations and modifications to be made in order for them to engage in physical education activities. Such positive emphasis is highly desirable because it reduces the possibility of the student's being labeled and categorized to the detriment of regard for him as an individual.

The new chapters in this edition are "Developmental Patterns," "Motor Learning and Perception," "Evaluation," "Assistive Devices," and "Relaxation." The discussion on developmental patterns was included to provide the necessary background for assessing the influence of the handicapping condition on growth and maturation, so that the areas of motor skill development that require special attention can be more easily identified. The chapter on motor learning and perception presents a balanced discussion of the theories on the relationship of perception and motor learning. The objective of this chapter is to provide a sound basis for selecting the teaching techniques and tools that will most effectively serve the handicapped child. The evaluation chapter represents a significant and timely expansion of evaluation procedures and instruments previously treated, in other chapters. The chapter on assistive devices is the first of its kind to appear in any textbook on physical education for the handicapped. It was developed in response to a need expressed by physical education teachers to know about the function and operation of the devices and to understand the possibilities for extending their use in physical education. The placement of relaxation as a separate chapter permits a more complete development of information about organizing and conducting a program in this now widely accepted component of physical education.

In addition, the discussion of integration (mainstreaming) and dual scheduling, concepts advocated in earlier editions, has been expanded to re-emphasize the procedures by which integration can readily be accomplished in physical education. Also, a clear and concise discussion of the development of the Individualized Education Plan (IEP) is included with special attention given to the role of the physical educator in the planning process.

The text has been updated as well as expanded. Much of the material has been developed by the author from his research and experiences in working with the handicapped; this continues the pioneering effort of the previous editions to present new ideas and practices that have been tested in work with the handicapped. It has been immensely satisfying to the author to have the original suggested adaptations, evaluation tools, philosophical concepts, and terminology that appeared in the earlier editions so widely accepted by teachers and utilized by other authors that they are now the common property of those who work with the handicapped in physical education. It is hoped that the present edition will serve the profession equally well.

HOLLIS F. FAIT

Acknowledgments

The author acknowledges with gratitude his indebtedness to the many people who have offered advice and assistance during the preparation of the manuscript for this revised edition. Special recognition is given to **Dr. John Dunn**, assistant professor of physical education, Oregon State University, author of the revised chapter on mental retardation; and to **Dr. Patrick DiRocco**, assistant professor of physical education, University of Connecticut, author of the revised chapter on cerebral palsy. The author also wishes to give special recognition to those colleagues who authored or co-authored sections of certain revised chapters: **Dr. Leon Johnson**, professor of physical education, University of Missouri, on the role of the handicapped in society; **Dr. Roosevelt Holmes**, Head of the Department of Physical Education and Recreation, Fayetteville State University, on the deaf-blind; **Dr. John Billing**, associate professor of physical education, University of Connecticut, on the graded exercise program; and **Walter Davis**, graduate assistant in physical education, University of Connecticut, on spina bifida.

Appreciation is also expressed to various authors whose contributions added so greatly to the quality of the earlier editions. Much of their original work has been revised and updated in this edition, and any errors or omissions that may appear in the text are the responsibility of the author, not of the original contributors.

To the individuals, schools, organizations, and publications that loaned photographs, illustrations, and materials go sincere thanks for their courtesy and generosity. Special acknowledgment is made of the contribution by past and present graduate students, in the training program for special physical educators, who designed and constructed items of equipment described in the book. Finally, heartfelt thanks are expressed to Mrs. Gladene Hansen Fait for her careful editing of the manuscript and for the performance of numerous other tasks which so greatly facilitated its preparation.

Contents

Section 2.   ORGANIZING AND CONDUCTING THE PROGRAM

Section 3. CONDITIONS RESULTING IN ENERVATED AND IMPAIRED MOVEMENT

chapter 9

ORTHOPEDIC HANDICAPS

chapter 10

CEREBRAL PALSY

chapter 11

DISORDERS RESULTING IN MUSCULAR WEAKNESS

Section 4. ACTIVITIES AND PROGRAMS

Section 1

Fundamentals

This section is designed to promote an understanding of the role of physical education in providing a special education service to the handicapped by presenting certain basic information about historical background, general patterns of growth and development, the nature of motor learning, and the psychology of the handicapped.

Chapter 1

Historical Background

Among our population are large numbers of children and adults who differ so markedly in mental, physical, emotional, or behavioral characteristics from their normal peers as to require special help in realizing their optimum potential. Recognition by educators and laymen alike of the special needs of these children and adults has resulted in a number of programs designed to give appropriate assistance in a variety of ways. On the educational level, this has taken the form of provisions to serve handicapped children in the regular classes of the school or to provide instruction appropriate to their abilities in separate classes if this serves their needs more effectively.

Various terms have been used to designate children whose characteristics interfere with their achieving optimum development through the regular education offerings of the school, but the term currently in most common usage is handicapped. The term is descriptive of the circumstances of the person who is at a disadvantage in displaying the reactions and patterns of behavior of the normal segment of society because of physical, mental, or emotional disability, or any combination of these. Accordingly, one who has such a disability but has overcome it to the extent that he is no longer at a disadvantage is not considered to be handicapped.

Not all physical educators working with children who have special educational needs approve the designation of all such individuals as handicapped. Some professionals believe the appellation should be limited to those persons who are adversely affected psychologically, emotionally, or socially by their disability. In this way, they explain, the word would properly reflect "an attitude of self-pity, feeling sorry for one's self, and despair" demonstrated by some individuals who have physical, mental, and emotional problems. Other terms, impaired and disabled, are then applied only to those who have a physical disorder but who have made a satisfactory adjustment. Impaired is further defined as referring to those with "identifiable organic or functional disorders" and disabled as referring to those "who because of impairments are limited or restricted in executing some skills, performing tasks, or participating in certain activities."[1] Substitution of the words inconvenienced or exceptional for handicapped is advocated by others in the field as having a less derogatory connotation.

Since some term must be used to facilitate communication, the author's preference is for the word handicapped, used in the customary sense of the medical and

---

[1]AAHPER: *Guidelines for Professional Preparation Programs for Personnel Involved in Physical Education and Recreation for the Handicapped.* Washington, D.C., American Association for Health, Physical Education and Recreation, 1973, p. 3.

paramedical fields to indicate a disadvantage imposed by physical, mental, or emotional characteristics. As a consequence of this disadvantage, the individual is unable to display normal reactions and behavior patterns, normal being defined as that most prevalent and widely accepted by our society.

It is interesting to note in this connection that the word handicap has its origin in an ancient Anglo-Saxon game of chance, "hand in the cap." In the game, one player challenged another for possession of his cap in exchange for a cap of his own. A certain amount of money was placed with the hand in the cap of lesser value, as determined by an impartial judge, to equalize the chances of the two players. The practice of equalizing the opportunities in certain games is still current in the awarding of a handicap to a participant of lesser strength or ability so that he will not be at so great a disadvantage. It would seem particularly appropriate for physical educators to use a word derived from the name of a game to describe those students whom they are helping, through motor activity, to overcome the disadvantages imposed by their conditions.

A number of different names are also given to the special educational provisions made in the physical education curriculum for those unable to profit from the offerings made to the student body. Among the terms used are corrective, developmental, and adapted physical education. The choice of names is determined largely by the emphasis and approach of the special program. The basic intent of all the programs is the same: the development of total well-being with specific emphasis upon the improvement of posture and general physical condition through motor activity.

Corrective physical education is a program that emphasizes the change or improvement in function or structure by means of selected exercises. *Developmental* physical education stresses the development of motor ability and physical fitness in those who are below the desired level. *Adapted* physical education programs are those which have the same objectives as the regular physical education program, but in which adjustments are made in the regular offerings to meet the needs and abilities of exceptional students. It should be explained here that *adapted* has also been widely used as a general term for all the programs directed toward students with deficiencies and disabilities. It is desirable, however, to avoid using the word in this all-inclusive sense, because it creates confusion with the more delimiting use of the term. A better umbrella term is *special physical education,* a term developed by the author which has won wide acceptance in this country and abroad. Special physical education is a particularly appropriate appellation because of its connotation of serving all students, meeting their individual needs through special provisions in the physical education program.

THE ROLE OF THE HANDICAPPED IN SOCIETY

Education for all is a basic tenet of our democratic faith, and the opportunity for each individual to develop his potential is a guiding principle of our educational system. In the progress toward equalized educational opportunities for all, the handicapped have not always received due consideration. The development of special programs and methods of instruction and the integration of the handicapped into the regular school programs have had to wait largely upon enlightened public opinion regarding the handicapped and their special needs.

The first real public awareness of the problem of the disabled in the United States came in the early years of this century, growing out of the tragic consequences of disease and war. In 1916 our country experienced an epidemic of infantile paralysis, and within the next few years the wounded and disabled returned from World War I. An aroused public's desire to help the victims of paralysis and the disabled soldiers forged a new attitude toward the handicapped which spurred legislative and educational assistance.

Early Attitudes. To appreciate fully the new attitude and its ramifications, one must leaf back through the pages of history and appraise the prevailing attitude toward the handicapped in other times and places. In primitive societies defective children generally perished at an early age as a consequence of their inability to withstand the rigors of primitive man's strenuous existence. Even in the civilized societies of early Greece, the Spartan father of a crippled child was expected to carry the babe to the hills to be left to perish, while the Athenians, whom we generally consider more humanitarian than their Spartan neighbors, permitted such babies to die of neglect. During the days of the Roman Empire, crippled babies suffered a like fate.

Although some handicapped individuals found social acceptance as court jesters during the Middle Ages, the prevailing attitude was one of superstition and fear. Physical and mental disabilities were believed to have been caused by Satan, and the afflicted were held to be sinful and evil. Hence, the handicapped were either harshly treated or carefully avoided.

The humanistic philosophy which flowered in the period of the Renaissance undoubtedly softened the general attitude toward the physically handicapped, but the gain in understanding of their problems did not extend to include treatment, care, and education. Some legislation to prevent conditions which might produce crippling injuries was passed during the Industrial Revolution, but beyond this the conditions of the handicapped were lost sight of in the tremendous technical advancement of the age.

Thus it was not until the 1900s that social awareness of the problems of the handicapped gained momentum in this country. This awareness resulted in the organization of conferences on the welfare of the crippled child and in the opening of schools for crippled children and clinics and centers for their treatment.

World Wars I and II gave impetus to the development of the techniques of orthopedic surgery, which had already made important gains through the treatment of crippled children. From the treatment of war casualties, care was gradually expanded to include physically disabled civilians. Accompanying the physical reconditioning of crippled soldiers and civilians came a movement to rehabilitate the handicapped, to help them become useful, self-sufficient citizens again. There developed after World War I what were known at the time as curative workshops, in which patients were taught purposeful activities for their therapeutic value. This type of program is now known as occupational therapy, and it has as its goal the rehabilitation of the patient through the teaching of skills by which he may become at least partially, if not totally, self-sustaining. Today there are also programs of physical therapy, therapeutic recreation, corrective therapy, and art, dance, and music therapies which endeavor to help the disabled reach maximum potential.

Funds for most early efforts to provide rehabilitation services for the disabled came from charity and fraternal organizations, private philanthropy, and community service organizations. A great deal was accomplished through the efforts of these groups, not the least of which was helping to arouse public concern for the needs and rights of the crippled, the blind, the deaf, and the otherwise handicapped. As a result, states began to pass the legislation needed for a more nearly complete program of care and rehabilitation of a heretofore largely neglected segment of our population. Today, states own and support hospitals and institutions at which adults and children can secure the kind of professional care and treatment their disabilities require. The states also assume a share of the responsibility for the educational and vocational needs of the handicapped.

Federal legislation had been enacted following World War I to provide certain benefits to disabled veterans; these were supplemented by further legislation in 1943 to increase the scope of aid to the veterans of World War II. The legislation provided for the rehabilitation of soldiers with war disabilities under the supervision of the Veterans Administration.

The first law providing for assistance to civilians with disabling injuries was passed in 1920. Under its provisions civilians injured in industrial accidents and from certain other causes were entitled to vocational rehabilitation: they were to be returned to employment where possible. A subsequent law in 1943 provided for physical restoration as well as vocational rehabilitation.

From the 1940s to the present there has been a steady growth of services to the handicapped as the result of private, state, and federal assistance. Examples of the expanded services include research into the cause and cure of mentally and physically crippling diseases; better facilities and increased knowledge in detecting, diagnosing, and treating disabling conditions; vocational rehabilitation and training; job placement or replacement; and, in the case of veterans and the industrially disabled, compensation or disability allowances and pensions. Also during this time special hospitals and schools for certain kinds of handicaps were established throughout the country. These included hospitals or special homes for the crippled, convalescent, and aged; institutions for the mentally ill and emotionally disturbed; and schools for the blind, deaf, and mentally retarded. A service of a different kind, but nonetheless important, was the legislative mandate that all new and remodeled public buildings must be made accessible to the handicapped. Features such as ramps and elevators to replace stairs and corridors, and toilet facilities large enough to accommodate wheelchairs, enable the handicapped to function much more independently.

Recent Changes. Of special note is the emphasis during the 1960s on support for measures to improve education for the handicapped. The creation of the Bureau of Education for the Handicapped during this time is of singular importance. For the first time there existed at the federal level an agency with the sole purpose of administering programs and projects related to the education of the handicapped. Another milestone of the period was the passage of an amendment to the Elementary and Secondary Education Act that provided funds to support research and demonstration projects in physical education and recreation for the handicapped.

The decade of the 1970s has seen the development of a different emphasis from that of the '60s, this one focusing on restatement by the courts of the scope of the rights of all handicapped individuals. Various civil and human rights, long denied them, were sought for handicapped people in state and district courts across the country. An example is the "right of treatment," desperately needed on behalf of children in institutions for the mentally ill and mentally retarded, where a humane physical and psychological environment for habilitation is often lacking. By and large, the courts have upheld the plaintiffs' quest to ensure equality under the law for the handicapped in all areas of human endeavor.

Education of All Handicapped Act. Another critical area of rights pertains to professional standards that are applied in the assignment of children to special education programs in public schools. To ensure that all handicapped children are secure in their right to quality education, Congress in the Fall of 1975 approved passage of Public Law 94–142, the "Education of All Handicapped Act." The law sets forth specific steps required of schools to establish an Individualized Education Program (IEP) for each handicapped child. This individualized program must be written specifically for the handicapped child by a team composed of parents, the child's teacher, a representative of the school, and, when appropriate, the child and other personnel as needed. Such planning not only serves to improve the educational services for the handicapped population but also carries over to general curriculum planning to effect improvement in education for all children.

The implications of the movement to ensure the rights of handicapped individuals will continue to manifest themselves in major changes for years to come. Some significant changes are already being implemented in this country's educational system. One very noticeable change can be seen in the move away from special classes for the handicapped toward the concept called mainstreaming. In mainstreaming, handicapped children are integrated into the regular educational programs, with the teachers operating as a team to achieve the educational goals and to provide the programs' needs.

An important effect of the various legislative acts and judicial decisions has been to stimulate educational programs that make it possible for the handicapped to become economically contributing members of society. This is of tremendous importance to them and to society, for as they become self-sufficient the cost of their care is removed from society. Changes in attitude toward the employment of the handicapped over the years have helped to improve their economic status. Once, only a few of the most skilled could find employment, and then sometimes even they found it difficult to convince employers that they were capable of doing the same job as those without handicaps. For a period of time there was a movement to give partial employment or part-time jobs to the handicapped. Favorable experiences in employing handicapped workers have helped to foster a growing attitude that the handicapped deserve to be given equal consideration when seeking employment and equal compensation for performing the same work as their fellow employees.

Figure 1–1. In mainstreaming, handicapped students are integrated into the regular school program.

In the foregoing paragraphs we have attempted to understand the handicapped individual and his position in society. We have seen how the attitude toward the disabled has changed from complete disregard to a consideration of him as a potentially productive member of his culture who differs from his fellows only in the extent of his disability. The change in attitude has motivated and in turn been given impetus by the work of numerous service and philanthropic organizations and by the legislation of state and federal governments and the decisions handed down by their courts.

SPECIAL PHYSICAL EDUCATION

Although the special physical education program is a relatively recently developed service for the handicapped, it is interesting to note that the basic concept of the program – the correction and improvement of motor functions of the body through exercise – is an ancient one. Pictures and records dating back three thousand years before Christ have been found in China depicting the therapeutic use of gymnastics. In more recent times a system of medical gymnastics was developed in Sweden, by Per Henrick Ling, which was introduced in this country in 1884 and had a wide vogue. It was a system of calisthenics of precise, definite movements designed to produce a healthier body and improve posture. Because it was believed that exercise of this nature would be highly beneficial to school children, programs of calisthenics were widely introduced in the public schools of that period.

Corrective Physical Education. A department of corrective physical education was first established by Dudley Sargent at Harvard in 1879 with the objective of correcting certain pathological conditions. The idea of physical education as corrective exercise for bad postural habits and for the general improvement of health persisted until about the time of World War I. Then, following the development of successful physical therapy techniques for paralyzed and convalescent soldiers, the idea of corrective exercises for students with physical handicaps took hold. Soon, a number of colleges had established corrective classes for students who were unable to participate in the regular physical education program. Corrective physical education for the improvement of posture was de-emphasized generally, but a few schools continued to stress corrective exercises in their physical education classes. The trend today is to provide a corrective physical education program for those who need to improve their posture and body awareness.

Adapted Physical Education. Adapted physical education grew out of the early corrective classes that were established specifically for those with disabilities. Gradually, over the years following World War I, the practice grew of assigning handicapped students to corrective courses in order to protect their condition from possible aggravation. As yet little consideration was given to the idea that the handicapped student could be taught to play modified forms of sports or games or that he might possibly be integrated into regular classes for part of his instruction. During the 1940s fundamental changes were initiated in physical education for handicapped students in some universities and colleges. A recognition of the value of play as an educational tool to implement social, mental, and physical development became the philosophical basis of course offerings to the handicapped. Calisthenics, gymnastics, and corrective exercise were supplanted in the course content by games, sports, and rhythmic activities modified to meet the individual needs of the students. In some schools special classes of adapted activities were developed for the handicapped students; in other schools those who could participate with safety in some activities of the regular physical education classes began to receive as much instruction as their cases warranted in these regular classes.

Programs for the Physically and Mentally Handicapped. Although physical education programs for the handicapped were limited in number during the years from 1940 to 1960, a slow but steady increase was discernible. Almost all of the programs developed at this time were for the physically handicapped. Youngsters with mental disabilities and with abnormal behavior problems were generally not provided for unless they were in one of the few institutions that recognized the need of the residents for a special kind of physical education program. Even in these institutions physical education was directed primarily toward those with adequate motor skills for sports participation.

Physical education for the mentally retarded began to receive attention early in the 1960s. The publication of the first textbook to discuss the need of the mentally retarded for adapted physical education, Fait's *Adapted Physical Education,* while not responsible for the upsurge of interest in providing for the special needs of the retarded in physical education, did chart the direction for the future development of such programs. Interest in the movement was fostered by the attention focused on it by the family of former President John F. Kennedy; their concern for the welfare of the mentally retarded was expressed by their active support of a number of projects to enhance the motor experiences of the retarded.

In 1965, the American Association for Health, Physical Education, and Recreation (AAHPER), with the financial assistance of a grant from the Joseph P. Kennedy, Jr., Foundation, created the "Project on Recreation and Fitness for the Mentally Retarded" for the promotion of the recreational skills and physical fitness of mental retardates. Later the project developed into an organizational unit of the AAHPER called the Unit on Programs for the Handicapped. The new unit expanded the scope of its efforts to include all handicapping conditions. Under the direction of Julian Stein, the unit has been very influential in increasing interest in and providing information about physical education for the total special population.

The greatest impetus to the movement to provide quality physical education to serve the needs of the handicapped has come from the establishment of federal funding for the promotion of research and training in physical education in colleges and universities. By the most recent count, over 50 institutions of higher learning receive grants either for research and demonstration projects related to the motoric needs of the handicapped or for programs to prepare personnel to work with the handicapped in physical education or recreation.

The effect of the increase in knowledge and understanding that has resulted from these programs has been a commendable expansion in the number and quality of public school physical education programs for the handicapped. New and more sophisticated methods and procedures for evaluating, planning, and teaching handicapped students are replacing the "watered down" adaptations of physical education programs of the past. The benefits to handicapped students who have had the advantage of a good physical education experience that served their special needs supply the best possible indication of the importance and value of the federally funded programs.

SELECTED READINGS

AAHPER: *Education of All Handicapped Children Act: Implications for Physical Education. IRUC Briefings.* Washington, D.C., American Alliance for Health, Physical Education and Recreation, 1976.
AAHPER: *Guidelines for Professional Preparation Programs for Personnel Involved in Physical Education*

and Recreation for the Handicapped. Washington, D.C., American Association for Health, Physical Education and Recreation, 1973.

AAHPER: *Physical Education and Recreation for Impaired, Disabled and Handicapped Individuals . . . Past, Present and Future.* Washington, D.C., American Alliance for Health, Physical Education and Recreation, 1976.

Sherrill, Claudine: *Adapted Physical Education.* Dubuque, Iowa, Wm. C. Brown Co., Pub., 1976.

U.S. Department of Health, Education, and Welfare: *Basic Education Rights for the Handicapped.* Washington, D.C., U.S. Government Printing Office, 1973.

Van Dalen, Deobold B., and Bennett, Bruce L.: *A World History of Physical Education,* ed. 2. Englewood Cliffs, N.J., Prentice-Hall, Inc., 1971.

Chapter 2

Developmental Patterns

In the growth of children from infancy to adolescence, certain discernible patterns of development occur roughly at each year of age. Consequently, at a certain chronological age a large majority of children demonstrate much the same physical development and similar intellectual and social traits. An understanding of the patterns of physical, intellectual, and social developments that are characteristic of each age group is extremely useful to teachers of children from nursery school to secondary school. Beyond the period of adolescence, development becomes so highly individualized that patterns characteristic of specific ages are no longer easily identifiable. During the early years, however, definite patterns in development are readily observed and awareness of them will help the teacher serve the individual student more effectively; this is particularly true if the student is handicapped.

The patterns of development common to the chronological age can be used by the teacher as criteria to evaluate the degree to which a handicapping condition is affecting normal growth and development. In some instances, the handicap will be seen to have interfered with the development of certain motor skills that most other children of the same age have developed; or it may be determined by a comparison with the pattern of social development typical of the age group that a handicapped child's social growth has been retarded by his attitude toward his condition.

It should be noted at this point that significant differences in development can be expected among the students in any classroom where children are approximately the same age. Although children of a given age follow the same general developmental patterns, some progress at a faster or slower rate. The various aspects of physical development, such as height, weight, strength, and endurance, are generally, but not always, accelerated or retarded to the same degree. It is also usually true, but not always, that the rate of intellectual and social development parallels physical development. The exceptions can be found among handicapped as well as non-handicapped children. Account must be taken of the existence of the possible differences in rate of development when evaluating the effects of a handicap upon development.

If, then, it is determined that a handicapping condition is negatively influencing development, special steps can be taken to help the child improve. These might include selective exercises and activities to promote physical development if this is where the deficiency occurs; or if help is needed to overcome poor social development, attention can be directed toward increasing the opportunities for social interaction in group play. These are only two examples of the numerous ways in which the teacher can meet the special needs of handicapped students whose development has not kept pace with that of their peers; the subject of serving special needs is explored more fully in later chapters.

Familiarity with the developmental patterns also provides the teacher with a means of assessing progress toward achieving the degree of development that is common at a given age. This is particularly helpful with young children who are difficult to test with standardized tools of evaluation. Although the comparison of a child's status of development with patterns that are generally characteristic of his age group is highly subjective and open to errors of misinterpretation, it is nevertheless a useful means of determining if and how much improvement has been made. It can be said of the method that its accuracy increases with experience in its use, thereby increasing its usefulness.

It is often difficult to determine if handicapped children are ready to learn a new skill. Readiness is that state of development in which the child has acquired the physical, mental, and emotional capacity to comprehend the requirements of a task and to execute them. Since a handicapping condition may so alter the responses of the child as to cause misdiagnosis of his readiness for new learning experiences, teachers need other means of making the determination. The patterns of development can provide one of the means, since they indicate the abilities and potentialities that are usually evident in those of the same chronological age and may well be present in the handicapped student as well.

When studying the developmental patterns that are presented on the following pages, it should be kept in mind that no single description of the characteristics of chronological age will fit every child of that age. It is not likely that very many children will exhibit all of the patterns ascribed to their age group; it is possible that very few will evidence a particular pattern. Each child does, after all, grow and develop at his own individual rate, a rate that is influenced by factors such as inheritance, socioeconomic background, and educational environment.

DEVELOPMENTAL PATTERNS*

Three Year Olds (Nursery School)

Physical

Most three year old children have mastered the upright position and evidence very little sway and weave in walking. They are likely to be somewhat knock-kneed, but this tendency will disappear before the age of four.

Three year olds can balance on one foot for a brief moment, and some are able to walk upstairs, alternating the feet. They can jump from objects 12 to 14 inches high, landing on both feet, and jump down from higher distances, landing on one foot. They can also jump upward, using both feet. Most have developed enough muscular strength and coordination to be able to ride a tricycle. Also, they have begun to develop fine motor skills and are able to make controlled marks for the first time.

They can catch a large ball with the arms fully extended but their arms do not recoil in catching. In throwing they chiefly use the arm and shoulder; they generally do not put one foot in front of the other while throwing, but they do turn the body by stepping forward on one foot.

There will be a tendency in some children toward handedness. The visual acuity is about 40/100 to 20/40.

---

*This material was developed by the author and associates from many sources and first appears in expanded form in the author's textbook, *Physical Education for the Elementary School Child.* 2nd edition, published by the W. B. Saunders Company.

Social

Three year olds are eager to try new experiences on their own, but they slip back under the protection of parents or teachers when they encounter any difficulty. They have begun to cooperate with others to some degree and to understand the nature of taking turns. They are able to put off immediate gratification for later success if the period between the two is relatively short.

Children of this age are developing a desire to please others and are very concerned with gaining approval for their actions. Although they are beginning to take an interest in playing with others, they spend a large share of the time playing alone or engaging in parallel play alongside other children. Three year olds have a keen interest in imitating and will often, when asked, do little tasks that they have seen others do. However, they frequently rebel at such requests, and sometimes this rebellion takes the form of violent reaction. They usually get over these rebellious moments very quickly.

Intellectual

At the age of three, youngsters can talk in sentences. They have developed an understanding of shape and form, and so they are able to match simple shapes but cannot yet distinguish colors. They are able to translate simple directions into actions and are most willing to do so. Eagerness to learn and continual questioning are characteristic.

Imagination is developing at a very rapid rate. Hence, the children are very curious and greatly attracted to objects that are new and strange. There is considerable experimentation with toys and other objects in the environment to determine what they are like, how they feel to the touch, whether they come apart.

Three year olds are constantly attempting new movements — walking up and down stairs, climbing over and under objects, crawling through holes, and maneuvering into empty spaces. There is also much imitation of movement — of other persons, animals, and moving objects.

Four Year Olds (Nursery School)

Physical

The four year olds' leg musculature and coordination have strengthened and improved so that these children are much better runners at age four than at age three. They can change stride patterns and are beginning to learn to skip but as yet cannot hop. Balance has improved considerably; they are now able to balance on one foot for several seconds and can walk on a wide balance beam easily. They can run smoothly at different speeds, turn sharply, and stop and start quickly.

They now attempt to catch a ball by giving with their arms and by using their hands more frequently than their arms. Although they will attempt to catch a ball with one hand, they have difficulty in doing so. When they grasp a small ball to throw, they now use thumb and fingers but favor the use of the medium finger rather than the index finger. Body and arm movements are combined in throwing. Boys throw the ball with a horizontal motion from above their shoulder, while girls throw the ball from above the shoulder with a downward sweep.

Four year olds are able to lace their shoes but still cannot tie them. They can dress and undress themselves with reasonable ease and have no difficulty in self-care at the toilet.

Many four year olds no longer nap during the day. If they do, they have a tendency to sleep longer during their nap than do three year olds.

Vision has improved since the age of three and is generally somewhere between 20/40 and 20/20.

Social

Four year olds prefer to play in small groups of two or three. While they do share with others, they do not do so consistently. Many times they become just as possessive about playthings as they were when they were three. In fact, it often appears that they purposely evoke social reaction by being overly possessive with playthings or bossy with playmates.

By the age of four, children have become aware of the opinions and attitudes of other people; their criticism of others and their opinions of themselves also have social implications. Four year olds have difficulty making clear distinctions between truth and fiction, which is a natural process of development in youngsters of this age. Unreasonable fears, such as fear of the dark, are slowly being overcome as children progress toward the fifth year.

Intellectual

Four year olds are continually practicing their language skills. They chatter on and on. They ask questions incessantly, doing so more to test their own concepts than to learn new facts. There is a beginning of abstract reasoning in their thought processes; they can place certain things in categories, for example, this is big or this is little; they can also distinguish between one and many.

At this age imagination is keenly developed. These children have insatiable curiosity and enthusiasm for learning. They learn about adult activity through role playing, experimenting with different roles in the imaginative play.

Five Year Olds (Kindergarten)

Physical

The overall growth of five year olds is relatively slow. A rapid increase in muscle tissue increases the potential for the production of energy for movement, especially gross motor activities. Improved coordination is becoming evident, with improved control and ease of body movement. However, large muscle control is still more advanced than small muscle control. Some improvement in the coordination of small muscles will be noticeable. Boys tend to be superior to girls in motor skills, and they generally perform with more vigor and forcefulness.

These children are extremely flexible, because there is more space between the joints and the relatively longer and less firmly attached ligaments than in older children. Their immature bones have proportionately more water and protein substances and less minerals, and so have less resistance to pressure and muscle pull.

At five years, the skills of walking, running, and climbing have been learned and, as opportunity is offered, will be improved and extended. Children of this age show continued improvement in power and form while running and are therefore able to control to a considerable extent the start, stop, and turn.

Jumping and hopping can be performed successfully by most five year olds.

Figure 2-1. Alternate foot ascent and descent may be a recent accomplishment in the developmental pattern of five year olds. (Courtesy of Childcraft Education Corp.)

Although most of them can do a gallop step and some can skip, few can give a skillful performance of these steps until later.

Climbing and descending stairs (the alternate foot descent may be a recent accomplishment) are established skills, as is the climb and descent of a ladder. However, the child will associate the height of the climb with the difficulty of the ascent; even children who climb well show cautious all-fours movement when the height is increased. At five years of age, boys and girls display equal ability in the skill. Children of this age enjoy climbing fences, and onto and under chairs and tables.

Some elements of mature throwing action are becoming evident, although most children at this stage still employ the off-balance step forward on the right foot as the ball is delivered with the right hand. The majority of the children will show improvement at an increasing rate, both in throwing for accuracy and in throwing for distance.

Five year olds have short stubby fingers that make it difficult for them to catch objects in the hands. They are, therefore, not successful in attempts to catch small balls.

As with the other skills, there is a wide range of individual ability. This is shown in the bouncing of a ball. The size of the ball in relation to the size of the hand is important; although younger children may successfully bounce a large ball, the majority will be six years or older before they can bounce a small ball. Ball bouncing is the only skill in which girls are likely to perform better than boys.

There is fairly marked improvement in dynamic balance. Children are able to stand on one foot, and most can balance on the toes. Some improvement is shown in a kicking action, but the necessary controlled body balance and rhythmic leg swing have not yet been attained.

Although some five year olds can swim, most will not learn to swim at this age. They can handle a sled and a tricycle and may attempt to ride a bicycle.

Social

Kindergarten age children play together for short periods in groups of three or four, with frequent shifting of the composition of the groups. Much of the time the children engage in parallel play alongside other children rather than actually participating in play together. The attention span of this age group is relatively short. These children both need and want supervision of their activities. They want approval but do not seek it as actively as those who are younger. They are less self-centered and less boastful than a year or two earlier.

Intellectual

Five year olds are able to learn to count and read to a limited extent. They learn to print their names, and they know right from left. Imaginative play is intellectually stimulating for them. Imitating actions, acting out stories, and exploring movement are favorite activities.

Ability in role playing has decreased since four years of age. Also, attempts by the children to do what is expected of them tend to decrease their search for new and unique ways of doing things.

Six Year Olds (First Grade)

Physical

Six year olds are very active. They are boisterous and rough in play; at the same time, performance is more deliberate. Frequently, they appear to be clumsy as they overdo or overextend an action. Motor control is much improved, and they become frustrated with failures in tasks involving fine motor skills. However, six year olds tend to show more interest in the actual performance of stunts and activities than in the level of their achievement.

Children of six have acquired most of the basic motor skills, and are now concerned with perfecting and combining the skills. Their running, in particular, has improved since they were five, and they are able to use this skill effectively in their play.

The steady increase in climbing ability is continued, with the majority of six year olds being proficient in this skill. Boys may tend to be slightly superior to girls in climbing skills.

Skill in jumping is well established by the time children are six, but it is not until they reach this age that they are able to hop with skill. Even at this age, there is a wide range of ability in hopping. Girls from six to nine years of age tend to be superior to boys of the same age in controlled hopping. Also, they show a more graceful action, hopping on the balls of their feet rather than using the flat-footed action generally employed by boys.

By the age of six, the majority of the children can skip (with variations in the level of performance). Although children can do a gallop step by the time they are four or five, most are six and a half years old before they accomplish this activity with skill.

Once the skills of jumping, hopping, skipping, and galloping are accomplished, children tend to experiment with variations, to improvise, and to incorporate the skills in other activities. Six year olds have developed the level of balance, control, range of movement, and arm-foot opposition necessary to perform a skilled kicking action.

There is a continued increase in the proficiency of throwing a ball; but even at six years there is a wide range of skill level from very awkward to highly proficient. By six and a half years, most boys are using a mature throwing action and are able to throw farther than girls.

Between the ages of five and six years there is a significant increase in the ability to catch a ball. Many six year olds use a hand catch with the elbows at the side when catching a large ball but are not able to perform this skill when catching a small ball.

The ability to bounce a ball and to strike a ball is similar to that shown by five year olds; the degree of progress is relative to the opportunity to practice these skills. The batting stance of the six year old child tends to be stiff, and the batting action is a type of swat.

There is an increase in dynamic balance ability between six and eight years. There is also a steady increase in static balance. An awareness of balancing the body in space is evident. Consequently, six year olds can handle a small bicycle, roller skates, bobsled, toboggan, and skis.

Many children at this age will learn to swim if exposed to swimming.

Social

First graders enjoy group play, although they show preference for small groups. The composition of the groups is likely to change frequently, as the groups break up because of a quarrel, and members leave and others take their places. Boys and girls play together readily. Boys begin to fight and wrestle to demonstrate their masculinity or to express emotions which they cannot otherwise express. A sudden shift from good to bad behavior is to be expected. Taking turns, which was fairly well mastered during kindergarten, now appears to have been forgotten.

Intellectual

Because they are being introduced to the mysteries of letters and numbers, these children delight in using their new reading and arithmetic skills. They are immensely curious and eager to handle different kinds of materials. They have vivid imaginations for the most part and enjoy using them in creative play activities. At this stage, children are aware that simple rules must govern cooperative play, and they are willing to apply these and are able to do so with reminders from the teacher.

First graders like to use large blocks and other equipment that they can push and pull around for climbing on and in, and for building. They enjoy active games with singing and are able to join in the singing. Other favorite activities are skipping to music, crawling on all fours, playing tag, and swinging.

Children at six are able to identify and produce many possible combinations or new relationships among objects, sounds, movements, and ideas; they respond well to encouragement to add, subtract, and mix these together to determine what will happen as a result.

Seven Year Olds (Second Grade)

Physical

Second graders are significantly more accomplished in motor skills and eye-hand coordination than first graders. There is evidence of the beginning of patterns common to middle and later childhood, in which consolidation of growth, perfection of known skills, and rapid learning take place.

Activity tends to be variable with seven year old children; sometimes they are very active, and at other times they are inactive. Movements and postures tend to be more tense than those of the six year olds. There is more and better coordinated use of both the large and small muscles of the body.

Social

These children are less boisterous than they were as first graders, and they tend to be more cautious in their approach to activities. Their attention span has increased, but sitting still for long periods is still difficult. Their actions are more self-directed and less impulsive. Second graders begin, for the first time, to observe differences among their classmates. Some element of competition is usually observable in their social relationships.

Intellectual

Most second graders are fairly facile with simple printed materials and enjoy using their reading skills. They have acquired basic addition and subtraction facts and like to make use of these. They are capable and willing to accept increased personal responsibilities. They welcome opportunities to act on their own.

While they tend to engage in fewer new activities and ventures, they do show intense interest in certain activities for a period of time. They are able to produce increasingly more complex combinations in movements and in the manipulation of objects.

Eight Year Olds (Third Grade)

Physical

Eight year olds may show a high level of skill in activities such as skating, swimming, and cycling. Coordination of small muscles begins to be evident, and there is a growing interest in games requiring this type of skill. Skills of team games can be learned. However, small muscle work, such as writing, is still difficult and tiring.

Awareness of their own body increases, and posture changes become more adaptive. Their movements show more control than previously, as the total pattern of body movements becomes rhythmical and graceful.

There is a marked improvement in throwing, catching, dodging, kicking, and striking a ball. A leveling off in ability in dynamic balance is evident, and there will be a slight decrease in flexibility, unless the proper physical activities are provided to prevent it.

Girls become increasingly skillful in the ability to skip with a rope. They learn to run in and out of a moving rope, although they still have difficulty in varying the step while working in the rope.

Social

Group play in the third grade is maintained for a longer period without being dissolved as the result of disagreement. By the time children are eight years old, they are able to resolve their differences in play to a considerable degree. But, while they are able to work together for a common goal, such as winning a relay, they are not yet equal to the demands of more competitive play.

Both boys and girls are adventurous, but the play of the former tends to be considerably rougher and more challenging. Consequently, the sexes tend to separate into their respective groups during free play.

Intellectual

At eight years of age children enter a more sophisticated quest for explanations. The questions of why expand into questions of how, who, when, and where. Eight year olds begin to develop a concept of the order of a sequence and willingly experiment and explore possible changes in the order by adding to or subtracting from the sequence to develop a completely new pattern.

Third graders usually become very interested in the world beyond their local environment; they enjoy their introduction to history. The intellectual development is such that group discussions and projects can be conducted with considerable success.

Children at this age particularly enjoy rhythms of a spontaneous and dramatic nature. They demonstrate a fairly wide variety of play interests.

Nine Year Olds (Fourth Grade)

Physical

Prior to pre-adolescent changes, sex differences are slight, and there is little difference in physique between boys and girls.

Nine year olds are at an intermediate age — between childhood and youth. Some of the girls will have commenced the accelerated growth spurt of the pre-adolescent period. They will also be at the start of a corresponding period of the greatest gain in strength.

A sequence of change in the rate of increase in height, body breadth, and body depth and in heart size, lung capacity, and muscle strength, in addition to changes in other structures and functions, becomes evident in girls between the ages of eight and 12 years and in boys between the ages of nine and 13 years.

Self-motivation is a characteristic of nine year olds, who both work and play hard. They have a great deal of energy and tend to stay with an activity until exhausted. They may have difficulty in calming down after strenuous and exciting activities. They are often so active that it is necessary to provide extra rest periods for them.

The interest of the previous year in posture has been abandoned as the nine year olds show preference for careless or awkward postures.

An increase in ability in dynamic balance is evident.

Gross motor activity is still prominent as previously acquired skills are combined and integrated. The children are becoming aware of specific skills and are interested in practicing skills in order to improve performance. There is improved eye-hand coordination, and fine motor activities are becoming more skillful.

Between the ages of nine and 12 years, particularly on the part of boys, there is evidence of the sequence of development in the mechanics of the long jump. Boys progress toward a more mature and efficient manner of jumping. Improvement shown with age is greater for boys than girls, but there is a great deal of overlap.

Although nine year olds have better control of their own speed, they may show some timidity of involvement in fast movement, such as sliding or skiing. They are interested in their own strength, and in their ability to lift things. Boys still engage in rough-and-tumble play, such as informal wrestling and tumbling.

Figure 2–2. At nine years of age, children become aware of, and are interested in practicing, specific skills. (Courtesy of Town of Vernon Schools, Rockville, Conn.)

Social

Antagonism toward the opposite sex may become evident, particularly if there is overt or subtle encouragement from the school or community. Fourth graders are less spontaneous in their relationships with adults, and tend to move in exclusive groups. Gangs and clubs are formed to promote this exclusiveness.

Intellectual

During the fourth grade students demonstrate a real interest in how things are made and in the cause and effect relationship. Reading skill is developed sufficiently to enable them to pursue special interests and hobbies on their own, with little or no assistance from adults. The pursuit of these activities may become so dominant an interest among some children that they will not participate in vigorous play as much as they should. Others develop a keen interest in motor activity and show a great desire to perform finely coordinated activities with speed and skill. These youngsters will also begin to show an interest in team games and in learning the skills of these games.

Ten Year Olds (Fifth Grade)

Physical

There is a further increase in proficiency in motor performance during the tenth year. Boys, on an average, are superior to girls; but many girls are as physically skilled as some of the boys. Batting action has improved markedly since the initial attempts. There is now a good swing action and the footwork is more appropriate. Practice has made some contribution to this improvement, but the progressive growth changes of the total neuromuscular system are also involved.

The overall pattern of organization displayed by 10 year olds is more flexible than that shown when they were nine year olds. Although alert, 10 year olds tend to be more relaxed and casual than nine year olds. Their performance of activities is carried out with skill and speed.

With the steady increments that have taken place in body size and strength, there is a corresponding consistent improvement in the basic skills, such as running, jumping, and throwing.

There is an increase in skills relevant to team sports and to future motor activities of adulthood. Ten year olds are also beginning to concentrate on the development of selective motor skills.

Skill shown in fine motor activities is approaching the adult level. Sex differences are shown in the superiority of girls in manual dexterity and in the superiority of boys in gross muscle movements that involve strength, speed, and coordination.

Social

The gang spirit continues into the fifth grade. Children at this age are organized and competitive. They are adventurous and enjoy an element of danger in their activities. They are also likely to show signs of a desire for greater independence. Their dependability is increasing when they are given responsibility. There is a broadening interest in team games, especially those that demand vigorous activity.

Intellectual

Fifth graders are interested in the ideas and achievements of others, particularly in motor skills. They are capable of evaluating and of learning to express their own points of view adequately. At the age of 10, children are developing the ability to plan ahead and are consequently capable of handling fairly long-range assignments.

Eleven Year Olds (Sixth Grade)

Physical

There is a wide range of individual difference in the rate at which children mature, and at 11 years of age this factor is becoming obvious. The rapid growth of the early maturer is contrasted with the slower, less intense growth of the later maturer; and, particularly with boys, there is a difference in body proportions between the two extremes. Girls between 11 and 14 years of age are generally taller than boys of the same age. After 11 years the ratio of sitting height to standing height tends to rise for girls.

At the age of 11, boys are entering the accelerated growth period of pre-adolescence, which is preceded by a brief leg-length growth spurt. The earlier rapid growth rate of girls was accompanied by a widening of the hips, whereas the rapid growth rate of boys is marked by a broadening of shoulder width.

At 11 years, boys are twice as strong as when they were six years old. Girls are not as strong as boys but, relative to the strength of boys, they are stronger in the legs than in the arms and hands. Both sexes appear to follow a sequence of strength development — first leg power, then biceps and back, and later forearm.

The increase in muscle growth and the increasing sex differences in the relationship of muscles to body weight and in the development of skeletal structures have a marked effect on the skill performances of boys and girls after 11 or 12 years of age. Such sex differences are most apparent in skills involving jumping, running, and throwing. In addition to these biological factors, cultural expectations are involved in the increased sex differences in motor performance.

Boys demonstrate greater physical endurance than girls. Girls tend to have greater control over hands and fingers, and so display fine muscle movement superior to that of boys, particularly between the ages of 10 and 13 years. However, research indicates that, even in cases in which there are significantly different levels of performance between the sexes in fine muscle movement and in eye-hand coordination, these differences are less than the range of variation that exists within either sex.

Some researchers find little improvement in balance after 11 years, which would indicate that a peak period has been reached. However, others claim that boys, especially, continue to improve through 14 years of age.

At all age levels, boys are superior to girls in throwing for distance, and this difference in ability increases with age. The superiority of boys in this skill is thought to be due partly to their more mature throwing pattern and partly to their mechanical advantage in propulsion of an object for distance brought about by greater length, girth, and strength of the forearm. There is not a marked sex difference in throwing for accuracy, although boys do tend to show superiority.

Social

A desire for recognition is prevalent among 11 year olds. Being a member of a club or gang helps to fulfill this need. Sixth graders are increasingly independent in thought and action, and are genuinely interested in being helpful to others. Interest in team play is high, and these children respond well to organized games. They are both willing and able to practice motor skills to improve their playing ability.

Intellectual

By their eleventh year, youngsters are capable of dealing with fairly complex ideas. They have an understanding of the interrelationships of cause and effect. Assessment of their own capacities and abilities is greater than ever before. Ability to organize and to assume responsibility for doing a job is also greatly improved.

At this age, there is less restlessness than was exhibited at an earlier age, and the children are able to give sustained attention to mental activity. Children at 11 years of age will try almost anything for experience but tend to lack confidence if the results of their efforts are to be made public.

Twelve Year Olds (Seventh Grade)

Physical

At 12 years, individual differences become even more marked, with a great amount of overlapping in characteristics and skills between age levels. Differences in body proportions between early and late maturing girls are not as pronounced as between early and late maturing boys.

Many 12 year old children reach adult maturity in some eye-and-hand coordination skills. Girls tend to show superiority in fine motor and manual dexterity skills, whereas boys are superior in activities that involve muscular strength, speed, and coordination of gross movements.

At pubescence there is a slackening in the rate of increase in motor ability. This slackening precedes the period of greatest growth.

Those 12 year olds who are physically more developed will demonstrate superior athletic skills, and the majority of those who excel in team sports will be those who are pubescent or post-pubescent.

During a girl's twelfth year there occurs a peak in her body's flexibility. Generally, there is an increase in flexibility to 12 years, then there is a decline. The exceptions to this trend appear in the shoulder, knee, and thigh, where girls show a gradual decline from six years to 18 years. Of all measures of flexibility, that of the ankle is the most constant.

Social

Seventh graders are unsure of their relationships with the group and with those in authority, and this gives rise to feelings of insecurity and frustration. The choice of activities in which these youngsters will participate is based more upon individual preference than any other consideration. Self-consciousness about learning new skills is evidenced.

Intellectual

Increasing self-control is demonstrated by seventh graders. They are more and more capable of solving intellectual problems, and can deal fairly capably with abstract ideas. There is likely to be considerable intellectual concern about the moral code of their society.

Girls of this age tend to find partner and individual activities more appealing than team or large group activities. Boys maintain a high interest in the more vigorous games and activities.

Thirteen Year Olds (Eighth Grade)

Physical

The changes in body proportions that occur during the years of 13 to 16 contribute to "adolescent awkwardness," but this will be less obvious in those who are becoming sexually mature at a slow rate and in those who had reached a high level of motor proficiency during childhood.

Anatomically, the girl has certain mechanical disadvantages in comparison to boys; and as she approaches maturity, these become more obvious — the oblique angle of the attachment of the femur to the pelvis, the shorter arms and legs in proportion to the trunk, and the broader pelvis. Girls are larger than boys in girth of the thigh, and boys are larger than girls in thoracic circumference and girth of the forearm.

The rate of functional growth in strength is greater than the rate of anatomical growth in the cross section of muscle during adolescence. Boys reach approximately 50 per cent of their 17 year old shoulder strength in both thrusting and pulling actions at 13½ years, which is about one year later than the equivalent development of manual strength. With girls, pulling strength is developed at the same rate as manual strength, whereas thrusting strength matures more rapidly, particularly in the year preceding menarche. The girl may reach an approximate of her adult level of strength as early as 13 years.

A distinct relationship between strength measures and motor performance is shown in boys, but no such relationship is apparent in girls. The development of muscle power following growth in muscle size will not alone guarantee muscular skill. Training, practice, environment, and motivation are all important contributory factors.

The motor performance of boys is positively and significantly related to all measures of maturity (chronological, anatomical, and physiological); there is no such correlation in the motor performance of girls. However, body build may show some significant relationship in the case of a girl with an exceptional performance level.

A typical characteristic of the pubescent child is muscular fatigue. Endurance, as measured by the 600-yard run, shows continued improvement from six to 13 years. After this age, boys continue to improve, but girls show a loss in efficiency. Girls of 13 will score less in sit-ups than 10 to 12 year old girls.

Boys show increasing superiority in motor performance as they grow older, and this superiority is especially marked in skills of agility. As they grow older, girls tend to improve in balance, control, and strength, but they decline in agility.

Girls show a steady increase until they are 15 or 16 in skill in throwing events, both those involving distance and those involving accuracy. Performance by boys in these events, although not as marked in throws at targets, is superior and will increase at a steady rate.

Social

Embarrassment and lack of confidence in the performance of new skills appear at this age. As a consequence, many of these students are likely to take spectator roles unless encouraged to do otherwise. Any antagonism toward the opposite sex that developed in earlier years has disappeared and has been replaced by a growing interest in boy-girl relationships. Individual friendships are important, but group membership is very desirable.

Intellectual

These students have acquired a considerable body of knowledge, which they are becoming increasingly capable of using in the process of logical reasoning. Ability to deal with abstract ideas is more in evidence, and a wide variety of interests is characteristic. An intelligent response to frustrating situations is more likely than an excessively emotional one. However, escape from undesirable experiences is often sought in identification with the real or imaginary idols of movies, television, and adventure fiction.

SELECTED READINGS

Fait, Hollis F.: *Experiences in Movement: Physical Education for the Elementary School Child,* Ed. 3. Philadelphia, W. B. Saunders Co., 1976.

Flinchum, Betty: *Motor Development in Early Childhood.* St. Louis, The C. V. Mosby Co., 1975.

Gallahue, David, *et al. A Conceptual Approach to Moving and Learning.* New York, John Wiley and Sons, Inc., 1975.

McGraw, Myrtle B.: *The Neuromuscular Maturation of the Human Infant.* New York, Hafner Publishing Co., 1969.

Rowan, Betty: *The Children We See.* New York, Holt, Rinehart and Winston, Inc., 1973.

Stone, L. Joseph, and Church, Joseph: *Childhood and Adolescence.* New York, Random House, 1973.

Chapter 3

Motor Learning and Perception

Motor learning refers to the acquisition of skills involving muscular movement. The skills of movement with which physical educators have been traditionally concerned are gross motor in nature, gross motor movements being defined as those requiring vigorous action and big muscle group contraction, for which a fairly large amount of space is needed. This definition is not meant to imply that fine motor skills are not utilized in physical education activities; fine motor skills are nearly always involved, but usually as part of a larger body movement that is predominantly gross motor. In the gross motor skill of throwing, this is illustrated by the involvement of the fine motor movement of the fingers to grasp the ball as part of the total movement.

The acquisition of gross motor skills has undoubtedly been a concern of man from his earliest days. However, it was not until the latter part of the 19th century that muscular movement became the subject of scientific investigation. Physical educators have been actively involved in research related to motor movement only since World War II. In the years since such research began, there has been a slow but steady increase in experimental work and publication of research related to the learning of motor movements.

The first textbook on the psychology of motor learning written for physical educators appeared in 1928; it was written by Coleman Griffith and was entitled *Psychology of Coaching*. It helped to create an awareness of the need for physical educators to understand the nature of motor learning and how individuals learn motor skills. The first comprehensive textbook on the subject of the psychology of motor learning to be widely used in the preparation of physical education teachers was Cratty's *Movement Behavior and Motor Learning,* published in 1964. The publication of this book was quickly followed by others; and with the increased attention to motor learning, there occurred extensive expansion of courses in the subject in colleges and universities. Today the study of motor learning is, as it should be, an integral part of the training of physical educators. Knowledge of how, when, and why children learn motor skills is particularly important in developing good programs for handicapped students.

Motor Skill Tenets. The research and empirical evidence produced by the serious study of the phenomenon of movement have established certain tenets that are useful to the physical educator in teaching motor skills. Those most relevant to the purpose of this book are reviewed in the following paragraphs.

The ability to learn a motor skill is influenced by growth and maturation.

A child can learn a specific motor activity only when he has achieved the actual physical growth required to accomplish the movement. Motor readiness is affected not only by physical size but also by the level of maturation of the neuromuscular system. Maturation occurs as a result of experience and of physiological changes that are produced naturally as age increases.

To determine the readiness of a handicapped child to learn, the teacher must be very sensitive to the child's reaction to the learning of motor movement. Pressuring the child to learn an activity when it is not possible for him to do so is detrimental to his well-being. On the other hand, it is necessary to encourage the child to explore his motor potential by trying to achieve various motor feats. The teacher must work out a procedure that will encourage but not pressure the child. Toward this end, it is useful to evaluate the motor achievements of the handicapped child by making a comparison of his or her motor development with that of normal youngsters in the same age group (described in Chapter 2) and by careful assessment of the child's mental, emotional, and physical limitations.

The best way to perform any given skill is dictated by mechanical and physiological principles of movement.

Application of the principles of movement ensures the most effective performance, regardless of anatomical and physiological differences in body structure. When a handicapped child's physical structure deviates markedly from normal, the most acceptable means of performing a skill is usually not appropriate. The handicapped child will need to be encouraged to explore so that he or she can find the best way to perform the skill in question, using the principles of movement as a guide.

A new skill is learned through reinforcement and repetition.

Reinforcement refers to any condition or event following a response that increases the probability that the response will be repeated. The instructor must determine the type of reinforcement that produces the best learning in any situation and then utilize that reinforcement. It should be noted that the child's knowledge that certain effort by him produces a desired result is also a type of reinforcement, and the one that in the long run is probably the most effective. However, because many mental retardates are unable to understand the final consequence of any act, immediate goals must be stressed and reinforcement must be immediate and extrinsic (such as awarding a piece of candy upon completion of the task); mastery of several parts of the whole is too abstract a concept for most of these children.

Repetition of motor movement tends to establish that movement as part of an individual's repertoire of movements. Therefore, repeated performance of the new skill should be encouraged by the teacher. However, to effect and establish improvement in the quality of the movement, the performer must be aware of what he is working toward and how he can achieve it and, in general, be motivated to improve.

A child progresses in the learning of movement at a specific rate that is uniquely his own.

The teacher should determine as early as possible the learning pace of the student and take that into consideration in setting goals for him. It must be kept in mind that individuals may learn different activities at different rates; for example, a child may rapidly learn to throw but have a more difficult time learning to kick a ball. The rate of motor learning for those with normal intelligence shows very little relationship to intelligence as measured by an IQ test. However, there is a fairly high relationship between speed of learning and intelligence when the IQ falls below 70, particularly if it is lower than 60. Some relationship also exists, although it is relatively limited, between motor ability and intelligence below the IQ of 70.

Emotion affects the process of learning motor skills.

Extreme emotional reactions are known to be detrimental to learning. Even though emotional responses to anxiety, fear, and humiliation may not be expressed overtly, these responses may be a strong deterrent to learning. It is incumbent upon the teacher to create an emotional atmosphere that is conducive to learning, taking into consideration that individuals may respond differently to the same situation. The teacher must be alert to the characteristic emotional responses of each student in order to develop the best possible "climate" for learning.

Confusion often exists concerning the effects of emotions upon the learning of motor skills, arising from the fact that ability to perform physically is increased under stress in an emotional situation. The reaction of the body to a highly emotional situation that permits the exertion of great physical effort is one that occurs after a skill has been learned. During the time that a skill is being learned, extreme emotion is actually detrimental to the learning process.

Motor behavior is specific; that is, the learning of one skill does not necessarily improve performance in another.

Transfer of the learning of one skill to the learning of another skill can occur but is not automatic. The transfer occurs only under certain circumstances: (1) when two activities have identical elements and the performer is aware of the similarities of the two, and (2) when a principle learned in one situation can be generalized and applied in another situation.[1] The teacher can help students make a transfer in learning by:

> creating opportunities for the development of meaningful generalizations;
> providing practice in applying the generalizations in actual situations;
> pointing out the likenesses between activities in which transfer can occur;
> providing a variety of different kinds of motor activities so that the possibility
> of transfer from one activity to another is increased.

Cratty and Martin[2] believe that when children are informed about how skill ability in one motor task may be transferred to performance in another, a greater transfer may be expected to occur more often in the tasks of the handicapped child than in those of the non-handicapped child.

A performer's learning ability is enhanced when he succeeds at his task.

"Nothing succeeds like success" is as true for motor skill performance as for any other endeavor. Hence, the teacher should choose activities for the handicapped student that can be achieved with some degree of success. A complex task may be broken down into parts to encourage quick success in the learning of one or more segments before they are combined in the performance of the whole task. The student should be kept informed of his or her progress and be praised for any improvement, regardless of how small or unimpressive it is.

The kind and amount of praise given must be in keeping with the child's maturation and level of ability. For a child who has much success, the praise may be minimal for small successes or may be reserved entirely for greater achievements. But a child whose improvement is slow and whose achievement is small needs to know that he has been successful when he does something well and be assured that others recognize and appreciate his accomplishment.

A performer learns faster when practice sessions are separated by adequate periods of rest.

Children learn faster when their interest is high. Long practice sessions tend to dull this interest. To prevent the detrimental effect of loss of interest, the teacher should

[1]Hollis F. Fait: *Experiences in Movement: Physical Education for the Elementary School Child.* Philadelphia, W. B. Saunders Co., 1976, p. 19.

[2]Bryant J. Cratty and Sister Margaret Mary Martin: *Perceptual-Motor Efficiency in Children.* Philadelphia, Lea and Febiger, 1969, p. 47.

Figure 3-1. Activities should be chosen that provide a degree of success, regardless of motor limitations.

keep instructional periods short, and change activities frequently, stopping for periods of rest when interest begins to wane.

Fatigue detracts from the learning process. Physically handicapped children often tire more easily than the non-handicapped, and the teacher must be continuously alert to signs of fatigue during the teaching of a physical activity to the physically handicapped. Fatigue is also a factor in learning for mentally retarded youngsters. If, as is often the case, these children are in poor physical condition, they will tire easily from physical exertion. In addition, they usually exhibit short attention spans. Therefore, the teacher will need to provide frequent periods of rest and to change the type of activity often to achieve peak learning potential.

A motor skill that is over-learned will be retained for a longer period of time.

Over-learning can be defined as the process of repeating a task until its performance is automatic; that is, without conscious effort being exerted to accomplish the task. When a motor skill is over-learned, the length of retention time is very high, sometimes lasting a lifetime. A good example is bicycling, a skill that is over-learned by youngsters through constant repetition during the years when bicycling is most popular. In their adult years, these people can, after many years of not riding, mount a bike and ride without any loss of skill.

The point at which skill is over-learned varies with each individual. Mentally retarded children will require many more repetitions in performing a skill to reach the point of over-learning than will non-retardates.

Retention of movement is greater when it has a natural relationship to other movements.

The movements of skipping provide a good illustration. Although the hop is often taught to youngsters as a component of the total movement, the ability to perform the hop will be retained longer if it is related to and practiced with the other movements of the skip. Many physical skills have this kind of interrelationship of movements that form a definite rhythmic pattern of performance. Teaching the movements in their natural pattern ensures longer retention than teaching them in isolation.

PERCEPTUAL-MOTOR LEARNING

In the 1960s, a number of men and women in the physical education profession directed their attention to an aspect of motor learning that had not been previously emphasized or thoroughly examined: the perceptual process that occurs while performing a motor skill. The interest was triggered by the earlier publication of the theories and experimental work in perceptual-motor learning by two men: Getman, an optometrist; and Kephart, a psychologist. The book by Getman, *Improve Your Child's Intelligence,* appeared in 1952, and eight years later Kephart published *The Slow Learner in the Classroom.* In the decade after their publication, both books were widely read, and they had tremendous influence upon the development of perceptual-motor programs in the physical education curriculum. The books were followed by works by such eminent perceptual-motor theorists and practitioners as Ayres, Barsch, Frostig, and Vallett, and by some who are lesser known.

Although differences of opinion existed among these people about other aspects of perceptual-motor learning, they were in agreement that perception is the recognition and interpretation of stimuli received by the brain from the sense organs in the form of nerve impulses, and that a motor response to the interpretation is perceptual-motor. Today this definition is accepted universally.

Movement and Perception

There was also agreement among the early theorists that movement is an important key in the development of perception; that understanding the concept of left and right (laterality) was vital to the process of moving the eyes left to right in reading; and that improvement in eye-hand coordination is related to the perceptual concept involved in eye-hand coordination and is critical in learning to write. Kephart considered movement the basis of intellectual development. Others of this group believed that the learning involved in perceiving and interpreting perception in movement is automatically transferred to perceptual learning in academic activities, particularly reading and writing.

Physical educators concerned with methods and techniques of teaching motor movements were quick to incorporate the perceptual-motor concepts established by Kephart and others into their practices and procedures. Programs of perceptual-motor skills were rapidly established in schools, particularly at the elementary level, or were incorporated into the existing physical education curricula. It is understandable that many practitioners were drawn to the theories espoused by the perceptual-motor advocates, because the importance placed on motor development greatly enhances the role of physical education—does, in fact, make the teaching of physical education activities basic to the learning of many fundamental academic skills.

Many of the concepts that served as the bases for these perceptual-motor programs are in serious question today.[3] Since the concepts were largely unsubstantiated by objective research, some ran counter to conclusions from research evidence that were

---

[3]Bryant J. Cratty: *Physical Expression of Intelligence.* Englewood Cliffs, N. J., Prentice-Hall, Inc., 1972, pp. 70–74.

even then well-established. Others of these concepts have been refuted by recent research findings.

Research has established that the learning of motor skills is specific. This applies also to perceptual-motor movement, since perception is involved in all voluntary muscular movement except reflex action. There is very little evidence to indicate a direct relationship between learning specific perceptual-motor skills and learning to read and write.

Although researchers have found that many of the motor activities that were devised to improve perception in academic endeavors are not successful in this purpose, they are useful in developing the motor skills involved in the activities. Perception and interpretation of stimuli in the performance of the particular skills may also be improved. Although transfer of neither the motor skills nor the perceptual-motor responses to other activities occurs, the capacity of the child in both areas is improved and is thus likely to enhance his future performances.

There is little doubt that perception is of vital importance to volitional movement. Emphasis in teaching directed toward perception in movement is of value in improving faulty perception in movement.

Terminology

It is well for the physical education teacher to have some familiarity with the vocabulary of the specialists concerned with perceptual-motor problems. The words and phrases most meaningful and useful in the work of the physical educator are defined below.

For visual perception the terms are as follows:

> visual discrimination—the ability to note or observe differences between forms, sizes, colors, textures, distances, and speeds;
>
> visual figure–ground sensation—visualizing a specific figure isolated from other figures around it and in its background;
>
> depth–perception, or stereopsis—perceiving three dimensions in proper perspective, having awareness of distance between objects or points; and
>
> visual agnosia—partial or total inability to recognize objects through vision.

The common terms of auditory perception are as follows:

> auditory discrimination—the ability to discriminate between different tones and frequencies of sound;
>
> auditory figures–ground phenomenon—the ability to distinguish a specific sound or sound pattern from other noises occurring at the same time;
>
> directionality of sound—distinguishing the direction from which the sound is coming; and
>
> auditory temporal perception—the ability to distinguish between rhythm patterns and the speed at which various sounds are made, and to distinguish the accent given each individual sound.

The terms frequently associated with kinesthesis and touch and pressure are as follows:

> vestibular sense—pertaining to the sensation provided by the semicircular canals of the inner ear that register the location and movements of the head;
>
> proprioceptors—sense receptors located in the muscles, joints, and tendons that provide information about the location of the body and its parts and whether or not they are in motion;
>
> laterality—an inner sense that one side of the body is different from the other;
>
> directionality—an awareness of direction;

body image—a personal conception of one's own body;

body awareness—cognizance of the body in space, relationship of body parts to each other and to external objects, relationship of the body to gravitational forces, and the quality, quantity, and direction of movement; and

apraxia—a disorder of the nervous system characterized by the inability to perform purposeful movement, not due to paralysis.

Development of Perception

The Gestalt psychologists of the early 1900s felt that perception was not learned but was instead a factor of maturation. It was reasoned that perception matured at a predetermined rate and experiences had little influence upon the development. However, research accomplished since the early 1900s provides sufficient evidence to reject that theory. Today's evidence does support the concept that the process of perceiving can be improved through certain educational procedures. However, perception does not necessarily improve automatically as the result of engaging in a given activity. Some children, through participation in an activity that involves the utilization of a specific sense, learn by themselves through trial and error to make an appropriate motor match with the sensory input. Others, because of learning disabilities, do not; they require specific assistance in interpreting sensory input and reacting to it with a suitable motor response.

The human body perceives through different sense modalities. Each modality is different in function, providing a specific type of stimulation. The modalities that are usually involved in increasing the sensitivity and in improving the interpretation and reaction to the interpretation are sight, hearing, touch and pressure, and kinesthesis (the sensation of the location of body parts and of movement in muscles, tendons, and joints).

Children with learning disabilities cannot organize a sufficiently great amount of sensory information at one time to enable them to make an effective motor response. The amount of sensory stimuli directed at learning disabled children must be reduced to that which the child is able to absorb. The task at hand may be made simpler by breaking it down into its components, thereby reducing the inputs of many different sensory stimuli at one time. This does not mean that various methods of providing sensory information should not be utilized. If the teacher finds that the student is not assimilating the information from one source of sensory input, other sources should be tried. For example, a child may not learn how to perform a skill by watching a demonstration, but may get the idea when manual kinesthesis is used to lead him through the required movements.

Although it is not clearly established how sensory interpretation and response to interpretation can be improved, it is generally conceded that practice in utilizing the senses and responding to the interpretation of the sense perceptions has value in effecting improvement of the process. The practice has to include cognition or conceptualization of the process of perception–interpretation; that is, there has to be an analysis of the deficient perception supplemented by analysis of the perception of the normally functioning senses to arrive at an interpretation that will produce the desired result. For example, a child with problems of visual discrimination in size must use the normal perceptions from senses other than sight to evaluate the size of the object he is looking at. He then compares the result with the visual input he receives ordinarily and makes the necessary adjustments to achieve agreement between the visual input and the input from the other senses. Much practice in simple repetitive exercises designed specifically for the deficiency is required to improve the interpretation of the stimuli.

Much the same procedure is utilized with a child who has problems in reacting with appropriate motor movement to a sensation. For example, a child who cannot balance well on the balance beam must first analyze the sensations he receives just before he loses his balance. Then through experimentation he must discover the movements of his body that eliminate those sensations. Practice in consciously substituting these for the unsatisfactory movements will eventually result in an automatic response of the muscles to maintain balance when a fall is imminent.

Impairment of Perception

Research has not supplied the educator with all the answers concerning the nature of perception and its relationship to movement. It is postulated that the perceptual difficulties discussed above may be caused by brain injuries or by malfunction of the portion of the nervous system that interprets perception.

It is possible that such injury or malfunction occurs in one phase of perception but that other phases may be unimpaired. Training the malfunctioning phase of perception or substituting another sensory organ for the one that is not functioning properly may help to overcome the motor problem that the perception problem creates. However, in cases where no specific problem exists but where there is a non-specific form of poor motor function, can the cause be placed upon any one perceptual area of malfunctioning? Probably not; it is reasonable to expect that the quality of motor ability fits a normal bell-shaped curve the same way as it is supposed that intelligence does. If this is the case, it can be assumed that low general motor ability, or a large portion of it, is not caused by an organic lesion or malfunctioning of the nervous system, but that the ability to learn motor movement is inherent within the neuromuscular system. The author feels that a large number of non-specific awkward children fall into this category.

The Awkward Child. Children who demonstrate characteristics of non-specific awkwardness do not necessarily respond positively to perceptual–motor activities designed for children with perceptual disabilities. Motor awkwardness appears to be general in nature; however, in close observation of awkward children it can usually be noted that the awkwardness occurs in some specific movements and not in others. The awkwardness may, for example, appear in the skills of jumping, hopping, and skipping but not in throwing and catching.

To effect remediation of motor awkwardness in the specific skills in which it occurs, the first step is to determine the reason for the awkwardness. To make such a determination in the case of awkwardness in running, for example, the teacher observes the child making a run and watches for such faults as (1) failure to coordinate the arm and leg movements, (2) failure to swing the leg straight forward in each stride, and (3) twisting of the trunk from side to side with each stride. (For description and techniques of such an evaluation see Chapter 7). After identification of the movement fault or faults that produce awkwardness in performing the skill, the child is taught how to overcome his problem and achieve a well-coordinated performance. Such instruction is much the same as that used to help any child break the habits of ineffective skill performance and achieve more efficient and graceful movement.

SELECTED READINGS

AAHPER: *Foundations and Practices in Perceptual Motor Learning—A Quest for Understanding.* Washington, D.C., American Association for Health, Physical Education and Recreation. 1971.

Arnheim, Daniel D., and Sinclair, William A.: *The Clumsy Child*. St. Louis, The C. V. Mosby Co., 1975.
Bell, Virginia Lee: *Sensorimotor Learning from Research to Teaching*. Pacific Palisades, Calif., Goodyear
    Publishing Co., 1970.
Corbin, Charles B. (Editor): *A Textbook of Motor Development*. Dubuque, Iowa, William C. Brown Co.,
    1973.
Cratty, Bryant J., and Martin, Sister Margaret Mary: *Perceptual-Motor Efficiency in Children*. Philadelphia,
    Lea and Febiger, 1969.
Cratty, Bryant J.: *Teaching Motor Skills*. Englewood Cliffs, N. J., Prentice-Hall, Inc., 1973.
Singer, Robert N. (Editor): *Readings in Motor Learning*. Philadelphia, Lea and Febiger, 1972.

Chapter 4

Understanding the Handicapped

Success in working with those who are handicapped is dependent upon understanding their special problems. It is significant that for most disabled people* the major problems are psychological in nature rather than physical. Ways have been found to reduce, if not actually eliminate, the physical pain of a disability. Many mechanical devices have been created and methods of rehabilitation developed to assist the handicapped person in achieving more normal use of his body. Medical treatment and the careful regulation of diet and activity enable many victims handicapped by functional diseases to lead normal lives in many respects. But regardless of how nearly normal body function and physical performance may be, the presence of the disability creates many psychological problems. Anxieties and fears are created about the condition itself or its effects upon the future. Frustrations are commonly experienced, and the individual's sense of security and self-confidence is threatened. Feelings of guilt are also sometimes aroused by the disability, as when the victim believes that he is being punished by the affliction. Because these problems are frequently more difficult to alleviate than the physical problems arising from the incapacitating illness or injury, their solution often constitutes the major obstacle in the total education of the handicapped.

FACTORS AFFECTING ADJUSTMENT

Satisfactory solutions are achieved through the process of adjustment, a term used to describe the changes which an individual undergoes so that he may adapt to his environment. Adjustment begins at the moment of birth and is a continuous process throughout life. Certain innate factors, the result of inheritance, influence the kind of adjustment that is made in response to the stimuli of the environment. These factors are intelligence, physical appearance, and temperament.

Intelligence. The degree of native intelligence determines the amount and quality of the direction and control of behavior. The more intelligent the child, the better able he will be to direct and control his behavior. His greater ability to reason enables him to anticipate the results of certain actions, and he acts accordingly. Because he understands more, he is less likely to resort to undesirable behavior to achieve his ends.

---

*Mentally ill and socially maladjusted persons are not included in this discussion. Their problems are discussed in Chapter 19, Behavioral Disorders.

Children who are mentally retarded are often able to learn socially acceptable behavior, but in new and unexpected circumstances they are unable to apply the learned behavior.

Physical Appearance.   Physical appearance is an important factor in the development of behavior tendencies because of the responses of others to physical characteristics such as body build, facial features, and obvious deformities. We are aware that even such slight deviations as more-than-average height or weight cause others to respond with a certain amount of teasing or even ridicule. Greater deviations from normal cause more intense responses, even to the extent of casting the one who deviates in an inferior social role. The adjustment of a handicapped individual is often greatly influenced by the nature of the responses to him of those in his social environment and his responses to them.

Temperament.   Behavior tendencies are also influenced by what is generally called temperament, but which scientific evidence indicates is actually glandular function. Although the precise functioning of all the glands is not presently known, it is known that the personality of an individual is affected if certain imbalances or malfunctions occur in the various glands. For example, less than normal activity of the thyroid gland influences certain metabolic changes that produce laziness, dullness, and depression while, in contrast, an overactive thyroid causes an individual to be very active, tense, and restless.

ENVIRONMENTAL INFLUENCE

A continual interplay exists between the conditions arising from these innate factors and the conditions of the environment — the attitudes and responses of others. Society tends to react in definite ways to any deviation from the norm. Sometimes the reaction is one of ridicule, curiosity, or maudlin sympathy; in the case of those close to the handicapped person, the reaction is often one of indulgence or overprotectiveness. The combined reactions of those in the social environment toward the one who deviates mentally or physically from the norm greatly influence his adjustment.

Because of his physical appearance or his inability to participate normally in the activities of his contemporaries, the handicapped individual is set apart. If the disability has been present since infancy, the child may live for a time in a fairly normal environment. For the first year or two of childhood, the play activities of the child are self-centered. The very young child plays side by side with other children, but the activities are not usually cooperative ones. Because this is true, he is not required to perform his play activity in the same way as his playmates, and he calls no particular attention to his "adapted" method of play. The methods and mannerisms which are necessitated by his particular disability do not come as markedly to the attention of his playmates during this period of self-centered play as they will when, as a slightly older child, play becomes a more cooperative and competitive venture requiring normal competence in motor performance and verbalization.

Even before the child begins to feel isolation from his peers, he may sense the attitude of his parents and other adults in his environment. Overprotective and solicitous parents and relatives may promote an awareness of being different. If the disability is one which elicits shock or pity from adults and curiosity from older children, the child begins to wonder about himself. As he grows older, he becomes more acutely aware of the reactions of others to him. His inability to compete successfully in the play activities of others in his age group sets him increasingly apart from them. His drives for success, recognition, and approval are thwarted. His self-confidence and self-esteem are shaken. A satisfactory adjustment becomes increasingly difficult with the development of the child's negative self-concept.

We have been speaking of the child whose disability has been present from his earliest years, perhaps even from birth. Many other youngsters, adults, and aged people find themselves confronted suddenly with a disability which prevents them from participating in their former life. A sudden accident in the home, at school or work, or on the highway has changed the course of life for many thousands of those whom we number among the handicapped. Many thousands more find themselves handicapped as the result of crippling diseases such as muscular dystrophy or heart attack. Additional thousands are the tragic victims of warfare. For all of these, the problems of adjustment are thrust upon them with abruptness and sharp intensity. But like the child who comes gradually to recognize his situation, they too must make adjustments.

When a person is disabled by injury or illness after his personality traits and patterns of adjustment have been established, the new adjustments which must be made to his handicapping condition will be largely of the same nature as previous adjustments. If his previous psychological adjustments have been good, he will likely, after a time, work out satisfactory solutions to the emotional problems presented by his new circumstances. Maladjusted personalities will probably resort to the same unacceptable means of solving problems which they employed prior to this time.

Nearly everyone confronted with a sudden debilitating illness or injury experiences a period of emotional upheaval upon realizing that the former mode of living must undergo considerable change and adjustment. The independence of action which a whole healthy body makes possible may be reduced to partial or total dependence upon others for even the necessities of daily living. This realization coupled with the negative responses of family and friends to the patient's condition may be particularly injurious to self-esteem. Initial responses to these circumstances may be ones of fear, anxiety, despondency, and self-pity. However, as the rehabilitation begins and the patient is reassured of his adequacy in the performance of many of his former skills and pleasures, he begins to make a better psychological adjustment. The more difficult it is to make satisfactory substitutions for the lost motor skills or sensory perceptions, the greater is the adjustment problem.

WAYS OF MAKING ADJUSTMENTS

Adjustment to the problems presented by a handicapping condition may be made in several recognized ways. The mechanisms employed are not relegated to the handicapped alone; they are used by everyone in seeking satisfactory adjustment. There is, however, a tendency for the handicapped to resort to the use of certain of these mechanisms more frequently and with greater intensity; as a consequence, they become unacceptable means of adjustment. Some of the mechanisms are given:

1. *Sublimation*—the replacement of a desire or impulse that cannot be satisfied with one which can be fulfilled.

2. *Compensation*—an attempt to offset some shortcoming or limitation by developing some special talent or ability.

3. *Identification*—the conscious or unconscious assuming of the attitudes, manners, etc., of another admired individual or group.

4. *Projection*—placing the blame on others for one's own shortcomings.

5. *Escape*—an attempt to avoid reality by escaping from it in daydreams or fantasy.

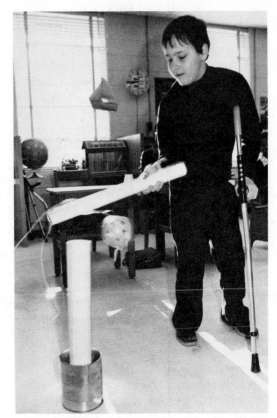

Figure 4-1. Improvised equipment may help a child find satisfying substitute motor skills and thereby aid his adjustment.

6. *Rationalization*—the substitution of reasons other than the real ones for a certain act.

7. *Repression*—the unconscious inhibition of unpleasant memories.

Sublimation.   Most people realize that not all desires and impulses can be satisfied in their original form, perhaps because of social disapproval, personal limitations, or other restrictions; then the original desire or impulse is replaced by another which is capable of being fulfilled. In other words, the mechanism of sublimation is used to achieve adjustment. The handicapped person must necessarily make many more such substitutions than the non-handicapped. His problem is further complicated if his handicap restricts the choice of substitutes.

Compensation.   Everyone uses compensation as an adjustment mechanism, either consciously or unconsciously, to build up or maintain self-esteem. Physically handicapped individuals often develop special talents or abilities to offset their limitations in physical performance. A partially sighted boy, for example, may work very hard to develop a musical talent for playing the piano to compensate for his inability to perform the athletic skills which win esteem for his peers.

Identification.   Identification is a frequently employed mechanism, particularly by children and adolescents, who like to identify themselves with teachers, adult friends, movie stars, and athletic heroes. The handicapped child is particularly likely to identify himself with an individual who represents all the things he is not and cannot be. The danger in overuse of identification is that the activity and achievements of the one who is the object of the identification will provide the identifier with so much satisfaction that he will not attempt to achieve anything himself.

Projection. Projection might be said to be a negative application of the identification mechanism, for here the individual attributes to others activities and attitudes for which he is himself responsible but which he will not accept. An example of the operation of the projection mechanism in a normal youngster is his offering as a reason for his being late for class the excuse that his mother forgot to set his alarm clock. Projection is essentially a means of adjustment in which others are blamed for one's personal failures. A handicapped person unable to make satisfactory progress in mastering locomotion with crutches or prosthesis may lay the blame on the doctors, for fitting him poorly, rather than accept his responsibility for the failure.

Escape. Avoiding difficult situations or problems by escaping into daydreams or fantasy is fairly common in all youngsters, not just the handicapped; however, the latter are likely to resort to this kind of escape more frequently. A handicapped person—one who is deaf, for example—finding the demands of his environment too great and his failure to meet them too frequent, is likely to withdraw from social contacts and to escape to a dream world to gain the satisfaction he cannot otherwise achieve.

Rationalization. Rationalization is another commonly employed mechanism. When the real reasons for certain behavior cannot be expressed because they are not socially acceptable, other reasons which will be accepted are substituted. The need to substitute a more acceptable explanation for the action usually indicates a self-dissatisfaction with the action and the adjustment. Environmental demands on the individual which exceed his physical and mental capabilities often cause the individual to find excuses for his limiations. Thus, the handicapped person who does not measure up often resorts to rationalization.

Repression. Repression of unpleasantness, of places and people which are feared or disliked, is not a conscious act. It does, however, prompt peculiar behavior, because the individual tries to avoid things, places, and people which call forth an association with the repressed memory. The mentally or physically defective child who was ridiculed at the beach may thereafter exhibit great fear of going into the water. He will attribute his fear and dislike of the water to something tangible, such as the water being too cold, but the actual reason, his unpleasant experience with those who teased and laughed at him, will be repressed in his subconscious mind.

A person does not usually make a conscious selection of a special adjustment mechanism; rather, he is confronted by a situation and he attempts to make an adjustment which is satisfying to him. If he succeeds, he is likely to use the same mechanism when confronted by a similar situation. If the mechanism does not actually solve the problem, it is, of course, not an acceptable means of adjustment. It may actually become harmful if it is used so frequently that the individual ceases to try to find a more satisfactory mechanism.

THE EFFECTS OF SPECIFIC HANDICAPS

The nature of the handicap or the extent of disability appears to have no significant influence on the adjustment mechanism which is used. Observations of the handicapped have revealed no definite personality traits inevitably arising from a particular handicap, with the possible exception of cerebral palsy (discussed in Chapter 10). However, subjective observations of handicapped groups have led some authorities to conclude that the problems presented to individuals by a major disability such as blindness, deafness, or severe crippling are so similar for each person that certain common behavior tendencies are observable. Undoubtedly, the innate personality factors influence a difference in adjustment even among those similarly afflicted. An individual who is by temperament an active, aggressive person is more likely to seek adjustment through action and to achieve it in a satisfactory way such as compensation, whereas one who is by temperament quiet and retiring is more likely to seek adjustment in less active ways such as, perhaps, in daydreaming.

THE ROLE OF THE TEACHER

The environment of the handicapped individual does, as was suggested, play an important role in adjustment. Because any handicap reduces the social interaction between the person and his environment, the environment cannot make the same contribution that is possible with normal people. Nevertheless, the help and understanding of those in the handicapped person's environment make a tremendous difference in the quality of his adjustment. No one develops a socially acceptable personality and becomes well adjusted entirely by his own efforts; he must have the help of family, friends, teachers, and classmates.

It is in the role of teachers that we are here primarily concerned with the promotion of a good environment for the wholesome personality development of the handicapped. Any educational endeavor to help the handicapped make a more satisfactory adjustment must include the promotion of better understanding among the children with whom the handicapped child comes in daily contact in the classroom and on the playground. These children constitute the greater portion of his social environment. If they can be given a fuller understanding of the role which society forces on the handicapped, if they can acquire respect for a handicapped person as an individual rather than as a deviate, many of the difficulties imposed by his handicap can be alleviated.

In developing a favorable climate in the classroom for the acceptance of those who are handicapped, the teacher may discuss with the students the reasons for liking and disliking certain people. The importance that is sometimes attached to attractive physical appearance may be pointed out and contrasted with more meaningful personal attributes. The teacher might emphasize that performing the best one is capable of is just as admirable and worthy of respect as being the most outstanding performer. Attention should be directed toward the concept that one does not have to excel in the popular spectator sports such as football and basketball; success, according to one's ability, in an adapted game of corner ping pong or loop badminton is of no less significance than success in the more popular games.

In addition to helping others understand and accept the handicapped, an educational program should be directed toward helping these youngsters develop skills and abilities to offset their shortcomings, and to find satisfactory substitutes for the desires they cannot fulfill and the activities they cannot perform. In these ways the handicapped may overcome the fear, shame, and social inadequacies which cause them to seek refuge in escape and projection and other unacceptable behavior. The special physical education program can make particularly significant contributions to the total educational program by helping the handicapped to develop better motor skills, improve body mechanics, increase physical fitness, and enhance body image. The special contributions of various kinds of physical education activities will be presented in the chapters dealing with the specific types of disabilities.

SELECTED READINGS

Bolton, Brian: *Psychology of Deafness for Rehabilitation Counselors.* Baltimore, University Park Press, 1976.

Garrison, Karl G., and Magoon, Robert A.: *Psychology: An Interpretation of Psychology and Educational Practices.* Columbus, Ohio, Charles E. Merrill Pub. Co., 1972.

Kirtley, Donald D.: *The Psychology of Blindness.* Chicago, Nelson-Hall Pub., 1975.

Lindgren, Henry: *Psychology of Personal Development.* New York, American Book Co., 1969.

Sherrick, Carl E., *et al.: Psychology and the Handicapped Child.* Washington, D.C., U.S. Dept. of Health, Education, and Welfare, 1974.

Section 2

Organizing and Conducting the Program

The chapters in this section are concerned with the practical aspects of providing a good physical education program to handicapped students. Ideas are suggested for effective planning and operation of the program and for instructional and evaluative procedures that foster motor learning.

Chapter 5

Organization and Administration of Special Physical Education

When organizing a special physical education program for handicapped students in the regular school, it is useful to have a rough estimate of the number of children (and the nature of their disabilities) expected to take part in the physical education program and of the number with low physical fitness and poor posture for whom special work must also be planned. In a school system with an established special physical education program, the figures available from previous years can be used as a guide in estimating the number to be enrolled. Where there are no such records, estimates can sometimes be made from information gathered by the school system for projected enrollments. Generally, it can be expected that between 10 and 12 per cent of the school-age population will have some type of physical, mental, or emotional disability requiring special educational consideration.

Identifying in the group the specific students who have disabilities and who need special educational consideration is the concern of those with a direct involvement in school-related services for the handicapped. Among these may be the school physician and nurse, special education teachers, the principal, the teacher of physical education, and in the elementary school, the classroom teacher. They supply data for the identification process from such sources as medical diagnoses, formal tests of perceptual learning disability, school records, and teacher evaluations and observations. Information from the physical educator may consist of an analysis of motor ability and physical condition based on certain motor ability tests, physical fitness tests, and posture screening tests.

INDIVIDUALIZED EDUCATION PROGRAM

For each child identified as having special educational needs, an individualized program of instruction must be prepared. The guidelines from the Bureau of Education for the Handicapped for developing individualized education programs require that each school organize a curriculum team made up of a representative of the school, the child's teacher, a parent, and, if appropriate, the child for whom the program is being planned. Other school personnel may be added to the team as deemed desirable, and it is extremely important that the teacher of special physical education be a member of the team. Because physical education is concerned with motor skills that receive attention nowhere else in the curriculum, only the physical educator is prepared to contribute an assessment of current motor abilities and to develop short and long term physical education goals with appropriate evaluation procedures for measuring achievement of the goals.

The curriculum team analyzes all the available data on the individual child, utilizing the information collected in the identification process together with input from the child and parents. Together, the team plans a complete curriculum that will best serve the needs of the child and prepares a written statement documenting the decision made about objectives, content, implementation, and evaluation of progress.

The physical education teacher, then, may expect to teach individualized education programs to a number of students who have conditions that have restricted their motor development or denied them opportunities to develop socially in play. In addition to these students, there will be, in every school, some students who require special consideration in physical education because of a handicapping condition that places them at a disadvantage in gross motor activities but does not affect their performance in other areas of the school curriculum. Examples are children who are convalescing from injury or illness, who have mild heart or kidney disorders, or who exhibit extreme nonspecific awkwardness or low physical fitness. For these students an individualized program should be planned by the physical education teacher based upon the recommendations of the student's physician.

Good communication should be established between the physical education teacher and the student's doctor. The doctor should be advised of the physical education requirement for all students and informed of the nature of the special physical education program. An excellent means of accomplishing this is by using an examination form, like the one in Figure 5–1, that is to be completed by the doctor. The form briefly describes the requirement in physical education and the special provisions that can be made in the program to allow all those with some tolerance for exercise to participate successfully and to their benefit. The form also provides for indication by the doctor of the functional capacity of the student and of the body areas that need special protection in activity.

Forms that require the doctor to check the physical education activities in which the student cannot participate force the doctor to make judgments about the nature of various activities for which he may not have sufficient background to make appropriate decisions. The form in Figure 5–1 avoids this difficulty by requesting the kind of information from the doctor that enables the physical educator to select suitable activities and make the necessary adaptations.

Parents of handicapped students should also receive a form letter (Fig. 5–2) explaining the special program, its objectives, and the activities that are offered. The policy for exempting students should be explained and the parents urged to discuss the program with their physicians and with the physical education teacher. With their questions answered and their reservations eliminated, the parents can give wholehearted support to the physical education of their children.

MAINSTREAMING

Mainstreaming is a term that has come to be used to describe the integration of handicapped students into regular school classes — into the "mainstream" of education. When handicapped children first began to be served in the public schools, separate

Referral Form

Dear Doctor:

The State Board of Education requires every pupil to participate in some form of physical education. The range and latitude of the Health and Physical Education Program in any city is so varied that every pupil able to be in school can derive benefit from some phase of the program. Special classes have been organized for those pupils who are not able to participate safely or successfully in the unrestricted activities of the regular program. These classes offer a diversified program of developmental activities, games, sports, and rhythms suitable to the capacities and limitations of pupils with disabilities. Daily classes of approximately 55 minutes, with about 16 minutes of undressing, showering, and dressing leave around 39 minutes for actual activity. Please complete this form to assist us in planning a program best suited to the pupil's needs.

_____(name)_____   _____(name)_____
                                                     Supervisor
Director, School Health Department   Department of Health and Physical Education

NAME _____   SCHOOL _____

ADDRESS _____   GRADE & SECTION _____

TELEPHONE NUMBER _____

Diagnosis or Description of the Condition

Severity of the Condition ☐-chronic; ☐-acute; ☐-permanent; ☐-temporary;
  Other (specify)

Anticipated Date Pupil May Return to Unrestricted Activity _____, 19___

Date Pupil Should Return for Reexamination _____, 19___

FUNCTIONAL CAPACITY

☐-Unrestricted - no restrictions need be placed on the pupil relative to vigorousness
                  or type of activity

☐-Restricted - pupil's condition is such that the intensity and type of activity
                 need to be limited (check one category below)

        ☐-Mild-ordinary physical activity need not be restricted, but
            unusually vigorous efforts need to be avoided

        ☐-Moderate-ordinary physical activity needs to be moderately
            restricted and sustained strenuous efforts need to be avoided

        ☐-Limited-ordinary physical activity needs to be markedly restricted

Figure 5-1. Sample referral form. (Courtesy of American Alliance for Health, Physical Education, and Recreation.)

Illustration continued on following page

ANATOMICAL ANALYSIS

Indicate body areas in which physical activity
should be minimized or eliminated - -

Remarks:

	Minimized	Eliminated	Both	Left	Right
Neck					
Shoulder Girdle					
Arms					
Hands and Wrists					
Abdomen					
Back					
Legs					
Knees					
Feet and Ankles					
Other (specify)					

/__/-REMEDIAL - Pupil's condition is such that defects or deviations can be improved
or prevented from becoming worse through the use of carefully selected
exercises. The following are types of exercises recommended for this
pupil's condition: (Please be specific)

_____

_____

_____

_____

_____

_____

_____

_____

Signed_____, M.D.

Address_____

_____

Telephone Number_____

Date_____, 19____

Figure 5-1. *Continued*

_____ School

                                                    Date _____

Dear Parents:

   The program of health and physical education at our school has a wide
variety of activities to offer to all students. The activities are adapted to fit
the special needs of each pupil regardless of his physical attributes. After
receiving the recommendations of your family physician, it was found that
your child could participate in the following activities which are being
offered in physical education this year:

_____
_____
_____

   By giving your child an opportunity to participate in these physical
activities, we hope to achieve these objectives:
   develop his physical fitness and health to optimum potential;
   develop skills in the basic motor movements of sports and everyday living;
   develop a variety of sport skills for use in worthy leisure time activity;
   promote a desire for continuous physical improvement;
   promote an understanding of his physical limitations and potentialities;
   provide opportunities to play and participate socially with others.

   We hope that our plans meet with your approval. If you wish to discuss
the program further, please call me at _____.

                                          Yours truly,

Figure 5-2. Sample form letter to parents.

classes were created in which instruction was adapted to serve their special needs. The
classrooms in which these children were taught were generally self-contained so that all
instruction the students received, including physical education, was segregated from
that of the general population of the school. It was soon realized, however, that this
arrangement denied certain benefits to handicapped and non-handicapped students
alike.

   Integrating handicapped students into regular classes has the advantage of calling
less attention to the student's difference than segregation might. Also, the student is
given additional opportunity to adjust to normal society. At the same time, the
non-handicapped students in the class can be guided to a better understanding and
appreciation of those who, unlike themselves, cannot fully participate in life's activities.

   It should be understood that these beneficial outcomes of the integrated class do
not manifest themselves automatically; they may not even occur in the majority of
situations. Good results depend upon a number of satisfactory conditions: the
leadership of the instructor, the personality adjustment of the handicapped student, and
the attitude of his or her peers.

   Obviously, some handicapped students, because of the nature of their condition or
adjustment to it, cannot be provided with the best environment for educational
achievement in integrated classes. Such students must still receive part or all of their
instruction in special classes. This holds true for physical education as well as for
academic classes.

SCHEDULING CLASSES

The ideal method of scheduling the classes of special physical education activities is to present them at the same hour as the regular physical education classes. This has the desirable advantage of making it possible for the handicapped students to shift from the special class into the regular class when the activities being offered are such that they can participate with success. The separate special class will need a teacher who can take charge during the time that another instructor is directing the activities in the regular class. It also requires that space be available for the special class, although, if space is at a premium, the class can be accommodated on the gymnasium floor with the regular class. This, of course, calls for careful coordination and planning between the two instructors.

The school situation may be such that it is not practical to create a special class for the disabled under the supervision of a special teacher. Many schools faced with ever increasing school populations and lack of finances cannot provide all the services that they would wish to. Nevertheless, it is possible to give the handicapped an excellent program of physical education within the regular class. This places great demands upon the ingenuity of the teacher and requires careful organization of the two programs which will run simultaneously under his direction, but these challenges can be met and with good results.

To the advantage of this dual program is the ease with which the handicapped are motivated. Most handicapped students want to take a more active part of the play activities of their peers and are eager to expand their limited skills. Given direction and encouragement, they can be relied upon to work to their capacity to achieve the desired goal. With these favorable circumstances, the physical educator can instruct the two programs at the same time with minimum hardships and maximum results.

The organization and supervision of the dual program may follow any one of several possible patterns. All the students, the handicapped and the non-handicapped,

Figure 5–3. A special physical education class may meet in the classroom for some types of activities.

may meet in the gymnasium for roll call and for instructions on the class procedures for that period. Those in the special class may then be excused to go to their activity area and begin their assigned activity, while the instructor starts the activity in which the regular class is participating for the period. When the activity is under way, he can give his attention to the special class. Depending upon the specific circumstances, it may be more advantageous to the program for the instructor to meet with the handicapped students during a free period to explain the nature of the program being planned for them, and to brief them on a procedure for conducting the class largely on their own responsibility.

Physical Fitness and Posture Program.   As has been indicated, a large percentage of any regular physical education class will be likely to need special work in physical fitness and posture. Consequently, a considerable portion of the total class time may profitably be devoted to exercises and activities for developing physical fitness and for improving body mechanics and body image.

How much work is needed by individual students can be determined by posture evaluations (Chapter 28) and physical fitness tests (Chapter 27). If the scores of the class fall in such a way as to make grouping easy, the students can be divided into groups, with each group working on the exercises it is most in need of. Another possibility for presenting exercises to the entire class is to establish stations around the gymnasium at which equipment is available for a certain type of exercise. Students rotate from station to station, doing the exercise at each station for a specified number of repetitions.

Students with extremely low physical fitness or very poor posture will probably need work beyond that which is offered in the regular class. Such students may be placed in the special physical education class or, if the students' attendance there is not feasible, the teacher will need to work out a program of exercises for the students to follow on their own, with as much assistance and encouragement from the teacher as is possible.

EXEMPTION FROM PHYSICAL EDUCATION

As a general rule, it may be stated that a student should be enrolled in physical education when he can participate in physical activity to his advantage. It would be difficult to imagine a situation in which a student with a handicap could not benefit from some type of physical education. Unless the program of physical education cannot make adequate provision for all students, some exemptions will necessarily have to be given to students unable to participate satisfactorily in the class situation. The more varied the program and the greater the provisions for special physical education activities, the fewer will be the number of necessary exemptions from physical education.

PERSONAL DATA SHEETS AND HEALTH RECORDS

Most schools now keep a cumulative health record for each student. These can be a very valuable aid to the special physical education teacher. They provide a history of the disability and the nature of the disability. Many schools keep the health records through all 12 grades. Although the records do not follow the student to college, they could be very valuable to the instructor of the college special physical education program. Secondary teachers should perhaps make a practice of encouraging handicapped students to have their health records sent to the colleges in which they enroll.

Not all school health records include a description of the limitations of the student in physical education. The value of such information to the teacher of the special program is evident. If the school does not include this information, it should be encouraged to begin to do so, including the physical education activities in which the student has participated.

The teacher of the special physical education program will find it extremely helpful to keep his own files on the students enrolled in the program (see Figure 5–4). The record on each individual might include a brief description of the disability, physician's recommendations, special safety controls, a summary of the progress toward the desired objectives, and the special problems and needs of the student with which the teacher may be of help.

Information that is kept in the files should be only that which is useful in improving the instruction for the individual student. Unsubstantiated observations and opinions of a derogatory nature should not be placed in the student's file. Official files of students must be made available to parents and to students of legal age upon request. However, notes, forms, and records made by the individual teacher that are not part of the permanent file and are used only for instructional purposes are exempt from the legal requirement.

In situations in which the students in the special program are assigned to the

RECORD OF STUDENT IN SPECIAL PHYSICAL EDUCATION CLASS

Name _____ Class _____ Section _____ Date _____

Physician's recommendations _____

_____

_____

_____

Limitations _____

_____

Recommendations for participation _____

_____

_____

Physical fitness test results _____

_____

Motor ability test results _____

_____

Postural screening results _____

_____

Past experience in physical education _____

_____

Special problems _____

_____

_____

Specific objectives _____

_____

_____

Figure 5–4. Sample record of student in special physical education.

```
TEMPORARY TRANSFER OF SPECIAL STUDENT TO REGULAR
                PHYSICAL EDUCATION CLASS

Name _____ Class _____ Section ____ Date _____
Limitations _____
_____
_____

Recommendations _____
_____
_____
_____

Date student will report to class _____
Date student will return to special class _____
```

Figure 5–5. Sample temporary transfer of special student to regular physical education class.

regular class for activities being presented there in which they can participate, the teacher of the special class must supply certain essential information about the students to the teacher in charge of the regular class. This information should include the limitation on their participation and description of their personal needs. A sample form is shown in Figure 5–5.

ABSENCES FROM THE SPECIAL PHYSICAL EDUCATION CLASS

The action which the physical education teacher takes regarding absences from class must be partially dependent upon the school's policy in the matter of absences from school. In general such policies are not concerned with the matter of making up the actual time lost but with making up the work which has been missed, so that the student can be better assured of fulfilling the objectives of the course. In regular physical education classes on the high school level, it is often the practice to require students to make up within a given period the class time they have missed. This means that the students will participate in more than the usual amount of physical activity until they have made up the work missed. Such practice for make-up will probably not be applicable in the special class. These students will, for the most part, be exerting physical effort up to their tolerance level in the scheduled activities, and to increase their expenditure of energy by requiring additional work equivalent to the hours of class time missed would most certainly be disadvantageous, if not actually detrimental, to their health. Consequently, some other method of making up the work must be devised that will help the student to achieve the objectives of the course without undue exertion on his part. To accomplish this, the student may be assigned to become familiar with the rules and regulations or to investigate the history of the sport or some similar assignment which is consistent with the overall objectives of the course.

Cases in which the students are absent from physical education classes but are not absent from school also plague the physical educator. Frequently, students or their parents believe they are well enough to attend classes but not well enough to participate in physical education. There are circumstances in which this is undoubtedly true, but in the great majority of cases it is not. If a student is well enough to be in school, he is well enough to participate in physical activity. On the other hand, if he doesn't feel well enough to attend physical education, it is questionable if he should be in school at all. Cases of slight fever and colds are examples of conditions when students shouldn't be in school much less in physical education.

An explanation of this to students and to parents will cut down the number of requests for excuses from physical education by students attending their other classes. Rigidly enforcing the concept that anyone too ill for physical education is too sick to be in school is, moreover, a good health measure because it helps to ensure that an ill student gets the rest he needs and it safeguards against spreading of colds and other communicable diseases.

SPECIAL HEALTH AND SAFETY NEEDS OF THE HANDICAPPED

The special class presents certain problems in health and safety which are not found in the regular classes of physical education. Many students in the class lack endurance and strength, particularly in the early months of the class, and must be protected from overexertion. Students should be made aware of their tolerance levels and educated to exercise caution for their own protection. Although some of the enrolled students will shun physical activity because of the sheltered life they have led as handicapped children, others will be so enthused with the opportunities to participate in the activities which are being taught them that they will fail to regard the safety precautions. They will require supervision and direction until they become fully aware of the importance of taking the necessary precautionary measures. The poorly coordinated ones will not be adept at avoiding accidents, and they may be more prone to falling and stumbling and less adroit at catching and dodging thrown objects.

Certain students are highly susceptible to infection. Even a small cut or scratch can be potentially serious to a diabetic, for example. Other students may have other hygienic problems. For still others the problems will be related to dietary needs; the obese, the poorly coordinated, and the chronically fatigued may have problems essentially dietary in nature. All of these must be given consideration in planning the program for a class of handicapped students.

The handicapped should be taught to assume responsibility for their own health and safety. The teacher must, of course, provide the best possible environment for learning the necessary protective measures. This will include not only good program planning and superior teaching methods but also safe, clean equipment and facilities.

There is always some hazard for handicapped students who engage in play with normal peers. They may not be able to move quickly enough to avoid collision, or they may not see a thrown ball until it is too late to dodge it. Then, too, in their desire to compete successfully, they may overexert themselves or take unnecessary risks that result in accidents. Every precaution should be taken to reduce the possibilities of accidental injuries by removing all physical hazards, such as unessential playing equipment and unnecessary barriers and obstructions, from the playing area. Specific safety measures which should be observed for each kind of handicapping condition will be suggested in subsequent chapters. In addition to these, however, the teacher should instill in the class respect for the playing courtesies of the game and a sportsmanlike regard for the abilities and limitations of others.

Liability.   It is not only the moral responsibility but the legal responsibility of the special physical education teacher to exercise all precautions necessary to avoid accidents and injury, and to protect the welfare of the students involved. Statistics indicate that more accidental injuries occur in physical education classes than in any other area of school life. There are also more damage suits involving injury in physical education classes than there are in other classes or school activities. Although statistics are incomplete concerning the frequency of accidental injury in special physical education programs, there is evidence to indicate that the percentage of injuries is considerably less than in the regular physical education program. This is probably due to the greater precautions exercised by teacher and students alike.

Regardless of the fact that injuries in the special program are less likely to occur, the teacher must remember that he or she is liable for damage if negligence is shown to be the cause of injury. State laws governing negligence vary from state to state, but generally, negligence is said to occur when the teacher has not fulfilled his duty or when actions which were obviously wrong or were not those of a reasonably prudent person directly contributed to the injury.

A prudent person is considered to be one who is able to see the harmful consequences of a specific situation and who makes adjustments to prevent them from occurring. Common situations that frequently cause accidents are as follows: (1) defective equipment and unsafe facilities; (2) allowing or encouraging students to take unreasonable risks; (3) inadequate supervision and poor instruction; and (4) poor selection of activities in relationship to the student's limitations.

The teacher should be constantly aware of the state of repair of all equipment and facilities. He or she should refrain from using potentially hazardous equipment and facilities until proper repairs can be made. Care should be taken not to allow students to take unnecessary risks in performance or to encourage them in excessive effort that may result in injury to them. Students in competitive situations should be closely observed for signs of overexertion in the effort to win. Extreme fatigue may lead to injury, and the teacher should watch constantly that the student does not exceed his tolerance level to exercise or that he does not become so fatigued that he no longer has control over his movements.

Accidents frequently occur when there is inadequate supervision and poor instruction. A teacher is considered legally responsible for the improper conduct of his students when such conduct leads to an accident during physical education instruction and also for the injury of one member of the class by another. Inadequate preparation of the student for motor performance is another frequent cause of accidental injury. Failure to prepare the student with appropriate lead-up skills prior to performance of a complex skill is evidence of negligence.

THE ORGANIZATION OF PHYSICAL EDUCATION IN SPECIALIZED INSTITUTIONS

The organization and administration of physical education in private and public institutions established specifically for handicapped students are in many respects similar to the school situation. Any difference is usually one necessitated by the nature of the institution.

In all special residential or day schools, such as schools for the blind, the deaf, and the emotionally disturbed, where an educational program similar to that in a regular school is carried on, the administration of the physical education program will not differ greatly from that in the regular school. However, the entire physical education program will be organized to fit the needs of the students enrolled in the school; that is, the entire program consists of activities adapted to meet the special needs of the students. The same will hold true of programs in schools for the mentally retarded. The specific organization and methods of teaching in these school situations will be discussed in separate chapters. It should be pointed out here that certain students may have more than one kind of handicap; for example, the blind boy may also have diabetes. Certain adjustments or further adaptation of the activities may be necessary to meet the additional limitations of such students.

The administration and organization of physical education in institutions for those who exhibit abnormal behavior (the mentally ill and socially maladjusted) are determined by the organization of the institution itself. If an educational program is part of rehabilitation, physical education may be included in the curriculum following a pattern similar to that of regular schools. The physical education activities in these institutions take on added significance because recreational outlets are necessarily limited, and the planning of the program must take this into consideration. In penal institutions security is one of the chief problems of the program, and the instructor must exercise care that play equipment is not smuggled away for use as escape weapons or in revolt against authority.

Physical education programs for children who are long-term patients in special children's hospitals are under the guidance of medical personnel. The chief responsibility of these institutions is therapy, not education; in no way must the physical education program take precedence over or hinder therapy. A definite line must be drawn between therapy and physical education. Therapy is concerned with the scientific application of prescribed physical movement activity or exercise for specific corrective purposes such as restoring normal alignment or function, while physical education refers to the learning of sport and physical recreational skills and their concomitant learnings. Physical education is a complement to therapy rather than a substitute.

SELECTED READINGS

Bucher, Charles A.: *Administration of School and College Health and Physical Education Programs,* ed. 6. St. Louis, The C. V. Mosby Co., 1972.

Frost, Reuben B., and Marshall, Stanley J.: *Administration of Physical Education and Athletics: Concepts and Practices.* Dubuque, Iowa, Wm. C. Brown Co., Pub., 1977.

Gearheart, B. R.: *Organization and Administration of Educational Programs for Exceptional Children.* Springfield, Ill., Charles C Thomas, Pub., 1974.

Johnson, Marion L.: *Functional Administration of Physical and Health Education.* Boston, Houghton Mifflin, 1977.

NAPECW and NCPEAM: *Mainstreaming Physical Education, Briefings 4.* (np), The National Association for Physical Education of College Women and The National College Physical Education Association for Men, 1976.

Zeigler, Earle F., and Spaeth, Marcia J. (Editors): *Administrative Theory and Practice in Physical Education and Athletics.* Englewood Cliffs, N.J., Prentice-Hall, Inc., 1974.

Chapter 6

Teaching Special Physical Education

It is the function of the teacher to provide a good learning situation. As a consequence, certain changes occur in the student. In physical education the most obvious changes will undoubtedly be the improvement of motor skills and a higher level of physical fitness. This will be evident not only in the success with which the student participates in games and physical education activities but also in general improvement in movement patterns. Another desirable change that will occur, but which is likely to be less obvious to an untrained observer, is the student's increased understanding and appreciation of his personal limitations and attributes. This manifests itself in an improved attitude toward himself and toward others. For many handicapped individuals who suffer serious personality maladjustments, this is the first long step toward better adjustment and the development of more wholesome personality traits.

In order to provide the kind of learning situation which makes these desired results possible, the teacher needs both knowledge and training and certain special qualities of character and personality. Because of the specific problems which a physical or mental handicap creates for the individual who is so afflicted, a teacher of the handicapped must possess certain attributes in excess of those generally required of the teacher of normal individuals.

ATTRIBUTES OF THE TEACHER OF SPECIAL PHYSICAL EDUCATION

Perhaps the single most important attribute the teacher of handicapped students can possess is emotional maturity. Emotional maturity is the ability to solve problems and adjust to the circumstances without undue emotional involvement. The teacher of the handicapped must be a stabilizing influence, must represent to the students the ultimate in successful adjustment. A teacher who is himself unable to resolve his own psychological problems is not likely to be able to assist his students in the solving of their problems. If his behavior is particularly immature, he may even contribute to the maladjustment of his students rather than help them make satisfactory adjustments to their handicaps.

Patience and a sense of humor are indispensable qualities in any good teacher. Those who work with the handicapped need to be endowed with a generous portion of each, for progress often proceeds very, very slowly. When the results of long hours of work do manifest themselves, however, they are extremely rewarding to the student and to the teacher.

Creativity is yet another desirable quality in the teacher of those who deviate from the norm, for it may be necessary for him to improvise equipment as well as techniques for performing skills. When facilities and equipment for the teaching of adapted activities are limited, the imaginative teacher adjusts and modifies the available facilities and equipment to fit the requirements of his program. He meets the challenge of an unusual handicap by devising suitable adaptations of the activities to meet the needs of the particular individual. Moreover, the teacher who is imaginative and creative is far better able to encourage and promote creativity in those whom he teaches. Creativity can be so easily stifled in physical education because of the tendency to enforce conformity in order to impress patterns in skill performance upon children.

Organizational ability is essential in the good physical education teacher. Regardless of the method of teaching used, carefully planned class procedures and well-organized class activities are time and energy savers. They make achievement of the desired goal easier and more certain. Class instruction left entirely, or even partially, to chance results in wasted time and motion, in poor learning, and in poor teaching.

Finally, a good teacher of adapted physical education has great enthusiasm for teaching physical education to all, regardless of their capabilities in the performance of physical skills. He is convinced of the contributions he can make to the lives of the handicapped and has developed numerous methods and techniques to implement his program. He has acquired the gift of insight, he knows when a technique is applicable, and he is willing and able to adjust his methods to meet the specific needs of the moment.

PROFESSIONAL QUALIFICATIONS OF THE TEACHER OF SPECIAL PHYSICAL EDUCATION

As regards the qualifications that a teacher should have to instruct adapted activities, it should be said that the background subject areas are essentially the same as those for physical education. A thorough knowledge of sport and recreational game skills is very important, as is a sound understanding of the nature of the human body and its response to exercise. Training in methods of teaching and the psychology of learning, including motor learning, is very necessary.

In addition to knowledge pertaining to physical education generally, the teacher should acquire some specific information about the causes, nature, and psychological implications of the various handicapping disabilities. It is necessary to understand the effects of exercise upon these conditions and how sports and games may be utilized to improve the social and emotional as well as the physical well-being of handicapped individuals. The teacher must also have a basic knowledge of emergency treatment of minor injuries and, most particularly, the practices that are applicable to certain handicaps such as the emergency care to be administered to an epileptic in a seizure or a diabetic in insulin shock.

OBJECTIVES OF THE SPECIAL PROGRAM

The aim of the special physical education program is to help the student achieve optimum physical, mental, and social growth through a carefully planned program of selected activities. To accomplish it, general or curriculum objectives are identified.

They may include the following:

(1) develop optimum physical fitness;

(2) develop skills in the basic motor movements;

(3) develop a variety of sport skills for participation in sports as a worthy leisure-time activity;

(4) develop a desire for continuous physical improvement;

(5) improve body awareness;

(6) promote an understanding in the student of the nature of his handicap and its limitations while emphasizing the potentialities which may be developed;

(7) give the student a feeling of value and worth as an individual, regardless of his handicap.

Physical fitness is just as necessary and important to the handicapped boy or girl as it is to the normal child. Although the fitness level that is possible for the handicapped may be lower, body efficiency can be improved by a program of regulated activities within the tolerance level of the student. Strength, endurance, flexibility, and recovery from exercise are all important factors of fitness. An optimum increase in these factors results in a more efficient body and is the outcome of a well regulated program of physical activities.

Exercise serves also as a prophylaxis of certain diseases. There is evidence to indicate that coronary diseases, diabetes, and duodenal ulcer are more frequent in those who are sedentary than in those who are active. A tension syndrome produced by an insufficient outlet for aroused emotions and anxieties provides a basis for certain orthopedic difficulties such as stiff neck, painful back and shoulders, and tension headaches. The handicapped individual who has not been guided into a program of vigorous physical activities in which he can participate with success may be more prone than others to these conditions.

Increasing the skills in basic motor movements such as running, changing direction, and falling correctly are tremendously important to the handicapped child. These skills are fundamental to everyday movement, and an improvement in them enables the handicapped individual to work and play more efficiently and with greater pleasure.

Improved basic motor skills also increase the ability to perform certain sport skills with greater success. As he becomes more skilled in the execution of motor skills in game situations, the handicapped student begins to feel less set apart from others; he approaches normalcy. Skills in a wide variety of sports and games also provide the student with increased recreational opportunities, which can, in turn, promote further physical development and social growth.

Body awareness is defined as a consciousness of the positions the body occupies in space and of how the body moves in the environment to occupy new space. Such awareness requires the development of a kinesthetic sense (knowing where certain parts of the body are in relation to other parts), coordination (moving the correct parts of the body in order to accomplish a certain movement), and depth and space perception (comprehending the size of the space the body is moving through and the distance from the body to the space it is moving toward). Improving body awareness enables the handicapped child to gain a better idea of the basic concepts of movement so that he will be better able to select the movements that he can perform most efficiently and effectively in any given situation.

The handicapped, more often than not, are acutely aware of their limitations. A well-organized program of physical activities helps such students to recognize their potential for doing many things they have always thought were restricted for them. The psychological implications of this are tremendous: the student's entire appraisal of himself may improve.

Analyzing and Applying Principles of Movement. In teaching motor skills to the handicapped, the teacher must understand and develop the ability to analyze the movements made by the student and to apply the mechanical principles of movement to achieve the most effective performance possible for the particular student. Analysis of movement consists of determining which essential parts of the body are involved in a given movement and how these parts relate to each other in the performance of the movement. Knowledge of anatomy and kinesiology is, of course, extremely useful in making an accurate analysis.

Every individual differs from every other anatomically, physiologically, and neurologically; therefore, the best way to perform a movement varies to some extent for each person. The handicapped person, because his difference is increased by his particular condition, will usually vary to a much greater extent. Consequently, the best way for him to perform a particular skill can be most effectively determined by analyzing his movements in order to understand how he moves and then, by applying the principles of movement, to discover the most efficient and effective way to utilize the movements in the performance of the skill.

All movements, including human movements, are regulated by the laws of motion. In human movements, the chief elements are those related to maintaining equilibrium and stability.

Principles of Stability. The ability to achieve stability is important in all action as well as in all stationary positions. The successful performance of such activities as standing, sitting, running, jumping, and bouncing requires some degree of stability. In maintaining stability, the body is governed by certain principles:

1. When the center of gravity is lowered, greater stability is achieved.
2. The larger or wider the base of the support, the greater the stability.
3. When the center of gravity is over the base, stability is greater.

When the body is lowered, as in bending the knee, the center of gravity is lowered, thereby providing more stability. In activities in which force must be received, such as catching a fast ball, greater stability can be created by lowering the body, thereby making it more capable of receiving the force without losing balance. Balance is more easily maintained in a sitting position than standing; hence, one who is on crutches may increase his stability by sitting to play some types of games, such as bowling or shuttle badminton, rather than trying to balance with his crutches in the erect position.

A larger base allows a greater range of body movement before the center of gravity moves beyond the base to cause the loss of balance. This is particularly evident in walking a narrow beam; maintaining balance in this kind of activity is difficult because the base of support is relatively small. In movement that requires a stable base, spreading the feet creates a larger base. A case in point is one in which a person balances himself with a cane; the triangle made by the feet and the cane affords more support as the size of the triangle is increased.

It should be noted that a wide base does not always create the most efficient position. If the stance is so wide that the legs are at an extreme angle to the ground, muscular efficiency is decreased so that actually any advantage created for maintaining balance by a wide base is nullified by the decrease in the muscular efficiency of the legs used in maintaining balance.

When the center of gravity is near the center of the base, greater stability is created. Many directions for performing skills include a suggestion to distribute the weight evenly in order to give better balance to the body. Such distribution brings the center of gravity to the center of the base. If the participant must make a quick move or start in a specific direction, he or she leans the body in that direction so that the balance is easily disturbed by the shifting of weight. In starting a race, the body is leaned forward and the center of gravity falls near the front of the base. In running rapidly, the center of gravity falls in front of the base so that, in a sense, the body falls forward and the "legs run up under the body." When slowing from a fast pace, the body is straightened so that the center of gravity is brought back near the center of the base.

Principles of Moving the Body. The movement of the human body or any part of it is governed by these laws of motion:

1. An object which is at rest will remain at rest, or if in motion will remain in motion at the same speed in a straight line unless acted upon by a force.

2. When a body is acted upon by a force, its resulting change of speed is directly proportional to the force and inversely proportional to the mass.

3. For every action, there is an equal and opposite reaction.

The tendency of the body to remain either stationary or in motion is known as inertia. The more the object weighs, the more force is required to overcome its inertia. Also, the faster the movement of the object, the greater the difficulty of overcoming its inertia. In initiating movement, the inertia is overcome by use of force. Once an object is moving, less force is required to keep it moving. In pushing a car, for example, less energy is required to push it after it is moving than to bring it into motion. The same is true of the body. An individual attempting to move from a sitting position to a standing position will find it much easier to complete the movement entirely than to stop half way and then continue rising.

If unequal forces are applied to two objects of equal mass, the object to which the greater force is applied will move at a greater speed. If equal forces are applied to two masses of different size, the larger mass will move at a slower rate. For example, if two boys are batting balls and one of the boys consistently hits the ball with more force, his ball will travel much farther; however, if the boys are hitting with equal force but one has a heavier ball, the heavier ball will travel less distance than the lighter ball.

The equal and opposite reaction is perhaps most easily illustrated by the swimmer pushing backward against the water—the water moves backward as the swimmer moves forward. This reaction is not so obvious when the performer pushes against a large solid object, such as a wall or the ground, because of the large size of the object in relation to the performer who is exerting force against it; movement of the large object is insignificant in relation to the movement of the performer and, therefore, is not noticed. When the body is not supported by a surface but is in the air, the equal and opposite reaction occurs within the body itself; for example, when one jumps from a diving board and swings one arm, which has been extended to the side, to the front of the body, the entire body will turn in the direction opposite to that in which the arm is moving. The speed of the turn is increased if the extended arm is bent as it is brought to the front. The rotary motion of turning is accelerated by shortening the radius of the body when the arm is brought close to the body. Conversely, the rotary motion is decreased when the radius of the moving body is increased. Application of this principle is, as should now be apparent, very important in diving and tumbling activities.

Still another factor that must be considered when absorbing force is the relationship of the force to the size of the area which bears the brunt of the impact. Force concentrated on a small area of body surface is likely to cause more serious injury than the same amount of force spread over a larger area. For this reason, injury is more likely in a fall in which the weight is taken on one foot than equally on both feet.

In catching an object, both factors (absorbing the force over a longer time and spreading the force over a larger area while receiving it) are important for the safety and success of the performer in catching the object. Consequently, to catch a ball that has

Figure 6-1. A portable net may be utilized in learning the principles of movement that apply to catching a ball when mobility is restricted.

been thrown hard, the elbows are bent to help absorb the force; to catch large balls, the body is leaned backward as the ball is caught. A baseball glove helps to disperse the impact of the ball over a large area of the hand as well as to lengthen the time it takes the ball to slow down. The padding acts as a cushion as the force is reduced over a longer period of time.

In many instances the handicapped, especially the orthopedically and neurologically handicapped, will not be able to perform the movements described in the principles of absorbing force. In these cases, it is necessary to first determine if participation in the movements is contraindicated. If not, an analysis of those movements that can be performed should be made in order to determine what movements may be substituted for the lost movements. For example, a person who lacks the ability to bend his knees to lower his body closer to the ground while falling may use his arms to help absorb the force of the fall. The arms are slightly bent to take the force of the fall, and the body is lowered quickly to the ground to increase the distance over which kinetic energy is lost.

Principles of Imparting Force to an Object. Many of the activities in physical education require the projection of a ball or an object into the air. In throwing a ball there are three main concerns: (1) the speed of the throw, (2) the distance, and (3) the direction in which the ball will travel.

The speed and the distance that the ball is thrown are dependent upon the speed at which the hand was traveling at the moment of release. The speed that the hand can acquire depends upon the distance it travels before the ball is released. Therefore, it is advantageous to make the backswing of the throwing movement as long as possible by rotating the body, shifting the weight, and taking a step. The use of these movements to create distance is effective only if they are synchronized so that each one is added to the preceding movement to take advantage of the momentum already created.

The distance that the ball will travel depends not only upon the force exerted in the throwing but also on the angle at which it is released. As soon as the ball leaves the hand, gravity has a tendency to pull it downward. The pull of gravity becomes more noticeable as the ball is slowed by the resistance of the air. A greater distance can be obtained if the ball is thrown upward as well as forward because the ball will stay in the air longer and, hence, travel farther. The throwing angle which gains the most distance is approximately 45 degrees.

The follow-through is an important part of the throw. Stopping the movement immediately after the release of the ball tends to produce a short, jerky movement throughout the total throw and affects the direction and distance of the throw. Furthermore, stopping the throw abruptly may cause injury to the arm because the muscles that must contract for the throw may be damaged by the tremendous force exerted in the opposite direction.

The direction in which the ball travels depends upon the direction in which the force was applied at the moment of release. In most throwing, the hand describes an arc in the throwing process; when the ball is released, it goes off at a tangent to the arc described by the hand. The release of the ball must be timed so that the tangent is in the desired direction. It is easier to release the ball at the correct time when the hands are moved in a flatter arc at the time of the release. A ball which is too large to hold in the fingers and must be held in the palm is more difficult to release at the right time than one held in the fingers. Keeping the palm of the hand directly behind the ball as it moves in the desired direction will keep the ball moving in that direction.

The direction of flight may be influenced by winds as well as by any spin that is placed on the ball when it is released. A spin to the right causes the ball to curve to the right; a spin to the left causes it to curve to the left.

When an implement such as a bat or a racket is used to apply force to an object, the implement becomes an extension of the arm. The arm in throwing or batting is a lever; with the addition of an implement, the resistance arm of the lever becomes longer. Hence, greater momentum can be created. When a bat is swung in an arc, the end of the bat is moving much faster than the hands that are holding it. Consequently, when the ball rebounds, it does so at a much faster rate than if the bat were only moving at the speed of the hands.

The direction the ball travels is even more difficult to control when using an implement than when throwing. The angle of the ball as it leaves the striking surface is determined by the angle at which it hit the surface. The ball will bounce from the object at an angle opposite to that at which it struck; so, in batting a ball the bat must strike the ball at an angle opposite the direction of the intended flight of the ball. To cause the ball to rebound in the same direction that it came from, it must strike the implement at right angles.

Teaching Movement Principles to Participants. There is no agreement among teachers on the value of teaching the principles of movement to participants before they engage in performance of skills. Research studies[1] have not helped to clarify the issue. Some studies have indicated that students perform better when they are taught the mechanical principles before attempting performance; other studies have shown that students perform better without having been exposed to such knowledge. Whether participants profit from instruction in principles of movement appears to be dependent upon how the information is presented. The following suggestions are offered as ways in which maximum benefit may be gained from the teaching of the principles to students before their participation in motor activities:

1. Select the principles to be taught in relation to the ability of the students to understand them.

2. Simplify the presentation, when necessary, to fit the situation and the ability of the students to comprehend.

---

[1]Robert N. Singer: *Motor Learning and Human Performance.* New York, The Macmillan Co., 1968.

3. Avoid belaboring the obvious—do not offer explanations when the concept is already well understood by the participants.

4. Avoid lengthy sessions of discussion.

5. Integrate the teaching of principles with the teaching of a skill or movement.

In the author's work with the physically handicapped, he has found that they are usually more capable of experimenting intelligently to find the best kind of movement to fit their needs and abilities if they have some understanding of movement principles; this is particularly true of the orthopedically handicapped. Consequently, it is recommended that the principles be taught to handicapped students with close adherence to the above suggestions.

MOTIVATING THE HANDICAPPED STUDENT

Highly motivated students learn more quickly and retain more of the learning than those who are not motivated. Some handicapped students are highly motivated by their own desires and goals and will present no problem to the teacher. They will be driven by their wish to acquire the same skills as the non-handicapped, or by their desire to develop body physique or to increase the strength and proportions of certain areas of the body. Other students, however, have no such self-motivating goals. They will have given up the struggle to keep up with the normal world. They have no desire to improve themselves or to compensate for their disabilities. Perhaps, because of overindulgence and overprotection by well-intentioned adults and peer companions, there will exist an apathy toward the need for making any effort which requires physical exertion. This is not a condition peculiar to the handicapped. It is fairly prevalent in regular physical education classes, but is probably not as deeply rooted in the normal child as in the handicapped. The teacher will need to help these students set up desirable objectives and arouse an enthusiasm for working to achieve them.

Motivation of the student requires insight, the ability to visualize the chain of events and causes which have produced a certain effect or behavior. To exercise this ability in the interest of properly motivating the individual student, the teacher must know and understand him well. He must know the student's abilities, interests, ambitions, and potential.

RECOGNIZING INDIVIDUAL DIFFERENCES

Good motivating techniques cannot be developed without a recognition of individual differences. The difference from others created by the physical or mental disability of an individual is obvious. If he is not actually different in appearance, he moves in a different fashion because of the restrictions of his disability. It is fairly obvious, also, that this individual experiences problems in adjustment which also set him apart. There is a tendency to think of these apparent differences as constituting the only "individual differences" of a handicapped person. This is, of course, inaccurate, for he possesses assorted abilities, traits, and characteristics which make him the person he is. He differs from others in certain aspects of these qualities just as ordinary individuals differ from each other. The teacher should never be blinded to these less obvious personal differences, for in understanding the *total individual* lies the soundest basis for good educational practices and procedures.

ACQUIRING INFORMATION ABOUT THE STUDENT

The more a teacher knows about his handicapped student, the better able he is to teach him. Medical knowledge about the student's condition is necessary and is usually fairly easy to obtain from health records or in consultation with medical personnel who have served the patient. There are, however, other facts which are invaluable to the physical educator in planning his program and which he may secure best in personal conversation with the student himself. Such facts have to do with the student's acceptance of his handicap, his attitude toward activity and toward showering and dressing with others, the type of activities he aspires to take part in, and his fears and his emotional disturbances.

For students beyond the elementary school age, a conference of an informal nature can be arranged with each student individually. For younger children an actual conference is not necessary to obtain the desired information. Indirect questions to the youngsters while they are under the instructor's supervision will reveal a good deal about their attitudes towards themselves and others. The observations of other teachers and conversations with the parents will supply additional information.

It is not always easy for the teacher to gather reliable and useful information from the conference. The student may be uncooperative or inattentive, or so eager to please that he will say whatever he thinks the teacher wishes to hear. The teacher should not become distressed over these "failures"; much more has probably been accomplished than surface evidence indicates. The important thing is for the student to know of the teacher's genuine interest in him and his welfare.

Actual observation of the student in the physical education class will reveal things about him which have not been brought out in the conference. A comparison of the statements made by the student about his limitations with actual observation and with the medical record will give a truer indication of the student's capacities and limitations than any one of these can give by itself. This is not to be interpreted to mean that the medical record is not reliable; just that it does not tell the whole story. The medical report is largely a factual record of the disability and does not purport to present the psychological implications.

In the conference the teacher may be able to pave the way for acceptance of the values of the special program and the creation of favorable attitudes toward physical activity. If the student can be convinced of the values of his wholehearted participation in the program, his aid can be enlisted in working out a tentative program of adapted activities determined by his needs and interests. The conference may also afford the teacher the opportunity to establish the controls necessary for protecting the condition from aggravation.

Additional knowledge can be provided by other school personnel as well as by the handicapped student's parents. The curriculum teams within the school that are charged with developing the individualized education programs will also be able to provide information important to the physical education teacher in developing the program.

TEACHING METHODS

A method of teaching is a general procedure used by the teacher to help the student understand and apply the information that is being presented. In physical education, the methods most commonly used are the direct or traditional method, the indirect or problem-solving method, or a synthesis of both. The direct method has been most frequently utilized by teachers in the past. The problem-solving method has come into use fairly recently and is rapidly gaining popularity. A synthesis of the two is not generally recognized as a method although it is widely practiced; for this reason and for others that will be discussed later, the author includes it as one of the methods of teaching physical education.

Techniques of teaching may be defined as special ways the teacher employs to handle instructional problems efficiently and to deal effectively with the varied responses of different children. Teaching techniques used by physical education teachers are of three general types: verbalization, visualization, and kinesthesis. Any of the techniques may be used with any method of teaching. Before examining how they are used with a specific teaching method, the various techniques will be described to provide the necessary background for understanding the use of the terms in the later discussion.

Verbalization.   Verbalization refers to the use of the spoken word in the process of teaching. Describing a skill or explaining the strategy of a play vocally is an example of the use of the technique. The oral presentation of a motor problem to be solved is included in this category. Oral reports and class discussions are other examples of utilizing verbalization in classroom teaching, although their use is more limited in the teaching of physical education than in other types of classes.

Some concepts can only be put across to students by means of verbalizing them: their presentation cannot be clearly made in any other way. For example, in the demonstration of a skill, verbalization is frequently employed to clarify a concept which could not be clearly identified without the use of a descriptive oral explanation.

Visualization.   Visualization is a technique that employs the visual attention of the students. Included under this general heading are demonstrations, motion pictures, filmstrips, posters and pictures, diagrams, and the printed word.

Demonstration is a most effective tool, particularly when used with the traditional method of teaching. In a good demonstration, the skill is executed in perfect form one or more times, depending upon its complexity. The students then attempt to execute the skill by duplicating the movements they have observed. The teacher may need to simulate the handicap of the student he is teaching in order to give a meaningful demonstration. Even if it proves impossible for the teacher to duplicate exactly the adjustment that must be made by the student, the demonstration is still useful to the handicapped student because it will help him to identify the objective of the movement and by doing this will provide the insight he needs into how he may best achieve similar results for himself through experimentation.

Movies and filmstrips are effective for showing the proper techniques of performing skills. Most of these have a certain limitation for use in the special class, however, since they show how the skills are performed by normal individuals without the handicaps that these students must circumvent in their performances. But if the teacher is prepared to describe possible adaptations of the skills for the students watching the film, a very effective teaching situation can be developed. Alert students with active minds and imaginations may also be assigned to watch the films and plan possible adaptation of the skills. These can then be discussed with the teacher and tried out under his supervision, or they can be set up as problems to be solved by the student.

Showing films often constitutes a considerable problem because they must be shown in a darkened room. Then, too, setting the film up takes time so that if the film is lengthy, most or all the period is taken up with watching the film and discussing it at its conclusion. This means that the students are denied valuable active participation for that period. Consequently, films should be used judiciously in the special program.

If the special class is held in a separate classroom rather than within the gymnasium, there is the possibility that the room can be sufficiently darkened for the showing of movies or filmstrips. The showing could be kept brief enough to permit practice of the demonstrated skills immediately afterward in the same room. Given sufficient time, the films may be shown again after the practice session to emphasize the correct techniques.

Still pictures, posters, and diagrams may be used effectively to illustrate correct skill techniques. Pictures of non-handicapped performers executing the skills are less desirable than ones in which an adapted technique is illustrated, but they are nevertheless extremely useful. Diagrams of plays on the blackboard are used to good advantage in teaching handicapped students who may be more unfamiliar with the strategy of games than would normal students who have participated in sports more widely.

The use of *the printed word* is a technique that has been largely overlooked as an effective teaching tool in physical education. Textbooks, pamphlets, and other written materials can be particularly advantageous in the special class in a dual program situation. Depending upon their reading level, students in the special class can use the written materials to answer questions which may arise when the teacher is busy with the regular class. Handicapped students who know little about a particular activity may be assigned to read about it before work in that activity begins, so they will be familiar with the terminology and the general performance of the activity.

There are many textbooks available, some designed especially for a comprehensive activity course in physical education and others devoted entirely to the skills and strategy of a particular sport or recreational activity. Most of these are suitable for use by high school students. They are directed chiefly toward the non-handicapped, but the student in the special class may still utilize much of the instruction. For example, in teaching weight-lifting to a student who suffers a chronic dislocation of the shoulder, the instructor might direct the student to read about all the lifts except those which bring the arms higher than the shoulders, as a student with this disability can perform all the lifts except these.

Textbooks designed for service classes usually offer a brief history of the game and stress the care of equipment and the playing courtesies, all of which are essential if the student is to attain the fullest possible understanding and appreciation of the activity. While an effective and well organized teacher can manage to bring this additional information to his class, his job is made considerably easier by the use of a textbook. Moreover, by assigning the students to acquire this information from books, a little more time is gained for working with individual students.

Worksheets are helpful when the student is working by himself. An example of the kind of worksheet which may be used is given in Figure 6–2. A mimeographed form sheet such as this will aid the student in determining the cause of his skill faults and also show his progress.

Kinesthesis. The use of kinesthesis refers to the involvement of muscular activity in the teaching-learning situation. When a student attempts to perform a skill and must make an adjustment in his stance or grip because it doesn't feel right to him, he is making use of kinesthesis. Of course, in the case of beginners, the student will not know how the correct form feels. In fact the correct form may feel more awkward than the incorrect. This is often the case in assuming the grip of a golf club or in making an overhand throw. It is only after the student begins to associate the desired result with the correct form that he will begin to "feel right" about his performance.

In a sense, the adjustment which the student makes when his muscular movements have not achieved satisfactory results is a phase of kinesthesis. Adjusting the serve in table tennis after the ball has fallen short of the net is a learning related to kinesthesis.

PRACTICE GUIDE		
TECHNIQUES	COMMON ERRORS	MY ERRORS
Grip	Gripping too high up on the handle	
Serve	Failure to watch the bird while serving Failure to use the wrist in stroking Serving to the same spot repeatedly Moving the feet during the serve Holding the bird too close to the body; this causes the bird to go into the net Setting up the bird for the opponent which may be caused by holding the bird away from the body or by not using enough or too much wrist in the stroke	
Strokes in General	Standing too close to the bird while stroking Failure to use the wrist in the stroke Failure to place the shot away from the opponent Telegraphing shots or using strokes in a specific pattern	
Overhead Stroke	Allowing the bird to drop too low before stroking	
Forehand Stroke	Failure to hit the bird up when it has dropped lower than the net	
Backhand Stroke	Failure to abduct the wrist in the backswing and snap the wrist forward as the swing comes forward	
Net Shots	Hitting net shots too high	
Drives	Hitting up on the bird	
Court Positions	Failure to return to the proper position after stroking the bird Encroaching on partner's court area Backing up for deep shots instead of pivoting and running back	

Figure 6-2. Practice guide for badminton.

Of course, the player's eyes tell him that his serve was no good, but the adjustment in the muscular movement made to perform the skill more accurately is kinesthetic in nature.

When a student performs a skill and then attempts to correct his own errors in order to achieve a more satisfactory performance, he is engaging in what is called exploratory kinesthesis. Such exploration is an integral phase of the learning of any new activity and is particularly to be fostered among students who are handicapped.

Still another phase of teaching which employs kinesthesis is that of actually leading the student's hand, arm, or part of the body involved in the activity through the performance of the skill. This technique is called manual kinesthesis. It is extremely helpful to students who have failed to grasp the fundamentals through exploration, visualization, or verbalization. With students who have sensory deviations, as in the case of blindness, the technique is invaluable. It would be practically impossible, for example, to teach a blind boy to catch or throw a ball unless his hands were led through the movements by his instructor.

Direct or Traditional Method.   Basically in the direct method the teacher selects the activity or skill to be learned and instructs the participants by describing the skill or by using one of the visual techniques to show how the skill is performed. The participants then attempt the skill, and the teacher assists each student in making the adjustments in movement necessary to perform the skill according to the prescribed standards.

Figure 6–3. Manual kinesthesis is helpful to a student who is unable to grasp the fundamentals of performing a skill. (Courtesy of Enrico Fermi High School.)

The procedure is often described as consisting of the 3 D's: Demonstration, Diagnosis, and Direction. The 3 D's are discussed in the following paragraphs as they apply to the teaching of the handicapped.

Various techniques of *demonstration* have already been described. To present to handicapped students the best method of performing a skill will require considerable insight and imagination on the part of the instructor. He must try to put himself in the place of the awkward child who has difficulty learning to skip or the blind student who desires to become a wrestler. At times it may be helpful to the teacher to attempt the skill simulating the handicap, as, for example, attempting the side stroke in swimming without using one of the legs so as to demonstrate more clearly for the student who has lost a leg. Not all handicaps can be simulated successfully: loss of both arms, for instance, seriously affects the balance of the body, and while the instructor can attempt to perform a skill without the use of his arms, he will not be confronted with the same problem of balance as his armless student. Consequently, his demonstration will be limited in its value to the student except as it gives him insight into the movement. The demonstration must, therefore, be supplemented with analysis of the student's movements as he attempts the skill.

We have just spoken of the need for *diagnosis* of the skill performance in the case of a handicapped student for whom a demonstration is not entirely satisfactory. Diagnosis goes beyond this, however; it is an integral factor in teaching skill improvement. Every good physical educator becomes an expert in diagnosing or analyzing learning difficulties and in giving clear explicit directions to the student to enable him to acquire a new pattern of movement.

It is not enough for the teacher to show a learner how to do the skill and to diagnose his learning difficulties, he must also direct the student in overcoming his difficulties. *Direction* is extremely important in the teaching of students with handicaps, for these students want intensely to succeed in performing the skill, and the more quickly any learning difficulties can be overcome the sooner the skill can be mastered.

The techniques that are utilized by the teacher are dependent upon the circumstances and the objectives which are sought. The beginning teacher must choose his techniques on the basis of what he knows about the needs of the handicapped and on his prediction of the success a particular technique will have in accomplishing the changes he hopes will be effected in the students. In addition, he may utilize the suggestions for performing sports skills in Chapters 22 to 26 as a springboard for exploration and experimentation to determine the best teaching techniques for each individual handicapped student.

Problem-solving or Indirect Method.   In the problem-solving method, the teacher presents a motor task in the form of a problem to be solved by the individual students in the class. Basically, the problems are offered as a guide to the student to help him discover the movements his body is capable of and how he may control these movements to accomplish a specific goal. The method is very effective in teaching sports skills to the handicapped, particularly those who are orthopedically and neurologically handicapped, because it necessitates experimentation with movement to determine the best way to perform the skill within the limitations imposed by the handicap.

The nature of the problem to be solved by the students is determined by their level of maturation, past experiences, and the medical limitations established by the physician. It is very important that both the teacher and the student understand the kinds of activities and specific movements that are contraindicated by a student's handicap so that he will not attempt anything (as he explores various movements in response to the problem that he is attempting to solve) that may be harmful to him.

To use the problem-solving method effectively, the teacher must decide not only the general area of motor learning to be examined but the kind of problem that will evoke most effectively the exploration of the selected area. Problems in motor movement may take two forms:

1. A SINGLE PROBLEM.   The single problem consists of a simple motor task to be solved by the individual student. For example, the boy on crutches could be given the problem: Can you balance your body with the use of only one crutch? All problems should be organized and stated in such a way that, when the student solves it, he will have gained a fuller understanding of how his body can be controlled in movement and the extent and kinds of movement his body is capable of performing.

2. SEQUENCE OF SUBPROBLEMS LEADING TO THE ANSWER OF A MAJOR PROBLEM. This approach has been described as guided discovery or independent discovery depending upon the role the teacher plays.

In guided discovery, the teacher presents the major problem to the participant and then guides him toward a solution by posing subproblems that, when solved, will provide answers that lead to the resolution of the major problem. An example that illustrates the procedure follows:

Major problem: (For students who have the use of only one arm.) How can a golf ball be stroked most effectively by using one arm to hold the club?

Subproblems:

1. How should the grip be taken on the club to get the firmest hold?

2. Where on the club should the grip be taken to achieve the best leverage and the best control?

3. Which movement produces the most power in hitting the ball, a forward or a backward movement?*

---

*The teacher should be aware that when using the right arm to stroke the ball with a backward movement, a left-handed club is used; when making a forward stroke, a right-handed club is used.

4. Is it now necessary to adjust the grip to execute the stroke with optimum power and control?

Effectively conducted guided discovery should lead to independent discovery. Independent discovery, as the name implies, is a form of problem-solving that requires the student to work independently in the search for the solution to the motor problem. The major problem is divided into subproblems by the student himself, and he develops them so they will lead to the solution of the major problem. He then experiments with each subproblem until he has worked out a satisfactory solution to each one. The solutions are then combined to provide the answer to the major problem.

In many situations involving a handicapped student, independent discovery will need to be a cooperative endeavor between the student and the teacher. For example, solving the problem of how a student with an amputated hand can swim the crawl stroke will require the student to try various positions and movements. The teacher will observe and, applying his knowledge of mechanical analysis, suggest additional variations with which the student may experiment. Following this pattern of cooperative effort between student and teacher, a solution will eventually be discovered.

Synthesis of Methods. In actual practice, many physical education teachers combine the problem-solving and traditional methods of teaching. The author believes such a synthesis is a highly effective way of teaching handicapped youngsters. It unites the best of each method and permits flexibility so that the teacher can choose the method best suited to a specific situation and to his own special talents and abilities.

A synthesis of the two methods is likely to be more effective in helping handicapped students to achieve the objectives of the program than the exclusive use of either method may be. It allows the child to be creative and experimental and impresses upon him the possibilities of movement of which his body is capable. It will encourage him to think reflectively and to apply the process of logical reasoning in solving the problem. But if, at any time, the teacher should sense a lack of security among the students with the problem-solving method, or confusion arising from failure to solve the motor task, he can shift to the more direct approach. When time is a factor in developing a phase of the program, certain aspects of the motor problem being considered can be taught with the traditional techniques, since they generally require less time. Review of formally learned skills and evaluation of performance may also generally be more efficiently handled by traditional methods.

SELECTED READINGS

Burton, Elsie C.: *The New Physical Education for Elementary School Children.* Boston, Houghton Mifflin, 1976.

Fait, Hollis F.: *Experiences in Movement: Physical Education for the Elementary School Child,* Ed. 3. Philadelphia, W. B. Saunders Co., 1976.

Heitaman, Helen M., and Kneer, Marion E.: *Physical Education Instructional Techniques: An Individualized Humanistic Approach,* Englewood Cliffs, N.J., Prentice-Hall, Inc., 1976.

Siedentop, Daryl: *Developing Teaching Skills in Physical Education.* Boston, Houghton Mifflin, 1976.

Singer, Robert N., and Dick, Walter: *A Systems Approach.* Boston, Houghton Mifflin, 1976.

Vannier, Maryhelen, and Fait, Hollis F.: *Teaching Physical Education in the Secondary Schools,* Ed. 4. Philadelphia, W. B. Saunders Co., 1975.

Chapter 7

Evaluation

Implicit in the term special physical education is the mandate to provide every child with a physical education experience that is of greatest benefit to him as an individual. Good decisions concerning how to provide the best possible physical education program to each child are based on sound evaluation of his needs and abilities. Periodically, evaluation must also be made to determine the amount of improvement that has occurred and to discover the kinds of activities and kinds of procedures and techniques of teaching that are proving most effective.

Both written and motor tests are utilized in physical education. However, because fundamentals of developing, administering, and interpreting such tests are established in courses of measurement and evaluation required of physical education majors, written tests will not be discussed and only such information as is germane to evaluating motor ability of the handicapped will be presented in this chapter.

NORM-REFERENCED TESTS

In the past most physical education tests of motor ability were of a kind now called norm-referenced tests. Basically, such a test is developed by selecting certain items that are considered to be the most representative of the components that make up a certain motor skill. The test is then administered to a random sample group to determine its discriminatory value. (The test has the highest discrimination when 50 per cent of the sample group fails to respond correctly to each item.) All items at the extremes of the number of correct and incorrect responses are then eliminated. Further refinement is accomplished by eliminating items that do not correlate highly with other items of the test, since such items are assumed not to evaluate the same area. The test is then checked for reliability by giving it once more to the sample group to determine if the results are similar on the two trials. Finally, the validity is determined by comparing it to another test that evaluates the same motor skill. If there is no existing comparable test, a body of experts is asked to rate the performances of those taking the test and to correlate the results with the test results. The concept guiding the construction of a normative test is the development of an evaluation tool that will fairly, representatively, and reliably assess a given distribution of children so that it may be determined how each stands in relationship to the others.

Heavy reliance on the norm-referenced tests to assess academic ability, particularly when used in the placement of school children in special classes, caused concern among parents, teachers, and public opinion makers about the way in which such evaluation was used in assigning children to roles in our society. In response to these concerns educators, particularly those working with handicappped children, have developed other types of referenced evaluation that are not based upon the performance of others but upon the performance of the individual being tested. With the development of the individualized education program (IEP), discussed on page 43, tests that provide an evaluation based on performance as related to a special level of achievement rather than the performance of others have become widely accepted as useful and important evaluation instruments.

CRITERION-REFERENCED TESTS

Other types of referenced evaluation are the criterion-referenced and domain-referenced tests, both of which are well suited to evaluation in physical education. In the criterion-referenced test, a criterion or level of mastery of certain information or skills is arbitrarily established for each item of the test or for the test as a whole. The score achieved by the test taker, then, describes how well the criterion was met. A domain-referenced test, because it also utilizes a criterion, is often thought to be the same as the criterion-referenced test; however, there is a basic difference. The process of establishing a domain is distinctly different from setting a criterion. For example, to establish a domain in a motor activity the teacher must visualize a pattern of movement rather than a specific isolated movement. In the activity of running, the total pattern of movement is the domain; the movement of picking up one foot and putting it in front of the other foot is a vital part of the domain but not the domain itself. After the domain has been determined, the test maker must decide which components of the domain or pattern are to be examined. For each of these a criterion is set, and the evaluation of how well the pattern is performed is based on the level of mastery of the components. A domain need not be limited to a pattern of movement; it may be any general skill, that is, one that is composed of more than one component.

Most good written tests made by teachers for their own use are of the criterion-referenced type: a standard is set up for the information that is expected to have been acquired about a specific subject, and questions are developed to determine if the knowledge has been learned. Many motor skill evaluation procedures are also criterion-referenced; fewer are domain-referenced. Generally the evaluation is made from observation, watching a performance to assess whether or not the student moves correctly as determined by comparison to a criterion of good performance. If judgment is also made of how well specific movements are integrated into the total pattern of movement, the evaluation becomes domain-referenced. The criterion in either situation is one formulated in the mind of the teacher from training and experience in motor movement.

Most physical education teachers rely heavily on close observation of the performance of students to provide evidence by which to determine the ability of the students and to evaluate their progress. Coaches of athletic teams utilize this technique almost exclusively in assessing weaknesses and strengths of players. However, physical educators who teach handicapped students have not used it as widely and not as successfully. This is due chiefly to the difficulty of setting the criterion for the handicapped and to the problems associated with identifying the components of a domain and selecting appropriate measurements.

MOTOR ABILITY TESTS

Since many types of motor behavior are specific, the learning that occurs in one skill transfers to the learning of another skill only under specific circumstances (see page 27. Therefore, in selecting a component, the teacher must be aware of how the skill that is to be measured contributes to the evaluation of the domain. For example, eye-hand coordination used in connecting dots or figures on paper with a pencil does not transfer to, and so provides very little information about, eye-hand coordination in striking a ball. Since this is the case, a test of connecting lines is not an appropriate evaluation of the domain of striking a ball.

Extreme care must also be exercised to avoid the assumption that measured ability in one motor skill demonstrates comparable ability in another. For example, the ability to do a handstand does not provide an indicator of the ability to balance the body while standing on one foot with the eyes closed. To assume that an evaluation of either skill measures the other is incorrect, as is the assumption that a measurement of either evaluates total balancing ability.

The difficulty of setting the criterion for a given skill in evaluating handicapped students can be overcome by becoming very familiar with the way in which the skill is best performed by the non-handicapped. Books that describe the techniques of playing games and sports are helpful. More valuable, however, to the teacher is the ability to do the skill well himself, because this enables him to simulate performance of the skill with the limitations of the physically handicapped student and so work out an effective way of performing the skill. With the knowledge of the best way to perform the skill as a basis, it is possible to make a movement analysis that will result in a suitable criterion for performance by a handicapped student. In some instances, the criterion developed for the non-handicapped will only need to be appropriately modified. These suggestions presume that the potentiality of the handicapped student has been previously assessed.

There is a place for both norm-referenced and criterion- and domain-referenced testing in the evaluation of physical education students. In situations where information is needed about the relative performance of individual students or groups, norm-referenced testing is probably more useful. On the other hand, when information is needed to make day-by-day instructional decisions for individual students, the criterion- and domain-referenced tests are preferable.

Self-evaluation.   Self-evaluation is an important skill and every student should be encouraged to develop the ability to evaluate his or her own progress toward achieving the objectives of the program. Self-evaluation of the kind involved in problem-solving can, and should, be more widely used by teachers of the handicapped regardless of the method of teaching used. To institute self-evaluation in a more traditional program, the teacher must be certain that the objectives are clearly recognized by the students; involving them in setting up the objectives is an especially good way of accomplishing this.

There have been various tests developed to measure motor ability. Since motor skills are relatively specific in nature, the better of these tests include a wide variety of motor skills. The greater variety provides a more complete profile of the overall motor ability, since there is no one skill (or even several) representative of all the rest.

Tests of motor performance developed prior to 1960 were usually called tests of motor ability, motor proficiency, motor performance, or motor coordination. Some of the more recent tests are labeled perceptual-motor tests because they purportedly measure perceptual-motor efficiency. (Since all voluntary movement involves perception, all tests of motor ability measure perceptual-motor ability indirectly.)

Perceptual-motor Tests.   Many of the perceptual-motor ability tests were developed by special educators, while the older motor performance tests were developed by people with training in physical education. The two groups frequently use different constructs and different groupings of skills in developing their tests. Vocabularies differ as does the use of terms. Special educators often use a single term to encompass several components that have traditionally been identified by two or more terms by physical educators. For example, bilateral integration, a term popularized by Ayres (a special educator) to describe a smooth working together of the right and left sides of the body, includes the traditional physical education concepts of agility and specific kinds of coordination.

Unfortunately, the tests developed by the special educators have often ignored the research performed by those in physical education that provides evidence of the specificity of motor skills and, hence, special educators have made greater claims for the validity of their tests as measurements of perceptual-motor ability than evidence would warrant. The perceptual-motor tests are valuable educational tools, but they do not provide the overall measurement of motor ability that is often claimed. Rather, they offer information concerning the ability to perform a specific motor skill. The best known of the perceptual-motor tests used to measure motor skills are the Developmental Test of Visual Perception (Frostig, 1963), Purdue Perceptual Motor Survey (Kephart-Roach, 1966), and Southern California Perceptual Motor Tests (Ayres, 1959–69). Table 7–1 gives a summary by Sherrill,[1] of the motor skills that each test measures and the domain that each purportedly measures.

Behavioral Objectives. An entirely different evaluation instrument is the use of behavioral objectives as test items to assess ability in different types of motor skills. In her development of one such instrument, Sherrill[2] has included identification of specified body parts, determining right-left of the body, changing position in space as directed, specific types of static (stationary) and dynamic (while moving) balance, moving objects in space in a specific manner, and visual tracking (following an object with the eyes). Such a test provides information as to whether or not the skill can be performed and, at the same time, it establishes a teaching objective. The test item can actually be used to teach so that the skill is learned.

Balance Tests. Motor ability tests that measure balance are currently in vogue, particularly in perceptual-motor programs. In interpreting the results of balance tests, one must consider that contributions to achieving and maintaining balance are made by the eyes, the inner ears, and the proprioceptors (nerve endings that supply information about movements of the body). The eyes are involved in most balancing feats when the balancing is performed with the eyes open, in which instance the eyes provide feedback to the central nervous system so adjustments may be made in the muscles to maintain equilibrium. Information about the movement of muscles is also provided by the proprioceptors. The inner ear, which includes the semicircular canal, supplies information concerning the movement of the head. Ability to balance the body depends upon proper interpretation of the feedback from all three sources.

Balance is of two kinds: static and dynamic. To secure a complete assessment of the total ability to balance, performance of both kinds should be measured. Balance tests should include items that evaluate the three different sense modalities involved in balance. The author suggests six test items that isolate, in part, the use of the senses in balance.

1. Stand on one foot with eyes open (evaluates the use of all three senses in one position of static balance).

2. Stand on one foot with eyes closed (evaluates the use of proprioceptors and the inner ear in one position of static balance).

3. Balance a book on the head with eyes closed (evaluates chiefly the use of the inner ear in holding the head in one position of static balance).

---

[1]Claudine Sherrill: *Adapted Physical Education and Recreation.* Dubuque, Iowa, Wm. C. Brown Co. Pub., 1976, p. 162.
[2]*Ibid.,* pp. 164–69.

Table 7–1. PERCEPTUAL–MOTOR TESTS AND THE FACTORS
THEY PURPORT TO MEASURE

Frostig Developmental Test of Visual Perception (1963)	Kephart-Roach Purdue Perceptual-Motor Survey (1966)	Ayres Southern California Perceptual-Motor Tests (1965–69)
1. Eye-Motor Coordination a. Keeping pencil between two horizontal or curved lines b. Connecting dots or figures	1. Balance and Posture a. Walking board b. Hopping and jumping	1. Imitation of Postures Reproduction of 12 arm and hand movements
2. Figure-Ground a. Overlapping outlines b. Embedded figures	2. Body Image and R-L Dis- crimination a. Identification of body parts b. Imitation of movement c. Obstacle course d. Kraus-Weber e. Angels-in-the-snow	2. Crossing Midline of Body Using right or left hand to touch designated ear or eye
3. Form Constancy Over- lapping and Embedded Forms	3. Perceptual-Motor Match a. Chalkboard activities b. Rhythmic writing	3. Bilateral Motor Coordi- nation Rhythmic tapping using palms of hands on thighs
4. Position in Space Figures like stars, chairs, ladders in different positions in space	4. Ocular Control Ocular pursuits	4. Right-Left Discrimination Identification of right and left dimensions of various objects
5. Spatial Relations Reproducing designs or figures by connecting dots appropriately	5. Form Reproduction Drawing simple geometric figures on blank paper	5. Standing Balance Eyes open
		6. Standing Balance Eyes closed

4. Balance a flat object on the lower leg while lying on the back in the hook position with eyes closed (evaluates the ability of proprioceptors in one position of static balance). The test may be made to evaluate one position of dynamic balance by attempting to move the leg while balancing the flat object.

5. Balance a book on its edge on the palm of the hand with eyes closed (evaluates the ability to balance an object on the palm of the hand using the proprioceptors in one position of static balance). The test may be made to evaluate one position of dynamic balance by having the hand move while balancing the book.

6. Balance while moving from one block to the next, as indicated in Figure 7–1 (evaluates the ability to achieve dynamic balance while walking in a straight line, jumping forward and backward, hopping forward and backward, and turning in the air while jumping). The footsteps may be drawn in chalk on the floor as a guide.

In interpreting the results of these tests one must remember that motor skills are specific, that learning to move the muscles appropriately to maintain balance in one position does not necessarily ensure the ability to balance in another position, even if the same sense modalities are involved.

Tests for Mental Retardates. The Lincoln-Oseretsky Motor Development Scale is a test, commonly used in the past, for assessing the motor ability of the mentally retarded. The test includes 36 items, covering these general categories: body balance, balancing of objects, kinesthesis (sense of movement), finger speed and dexterity,

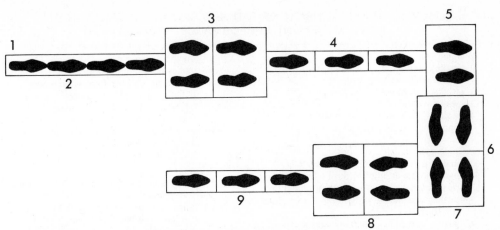

Figure 7–1. Hopscotch balance test. 1. Start; 2. Step one foot in front of the other; 3. Hop forward on both feet; 4. Hop forward on one foot; 5. Hop and half turn; 6. Hop and full turn; 7. Hop and half turn; 8. Hop and full turn; 9. Hop backward on one foot.

rhythm as expressed by foot or hand and finger movements, jumping, and catching. Of the 36 items, 21 evaluate some type of finger speed and dexterity, seven are tests in balancing the body, and the other eight are distributed among the remaining categories.

In interpreting the results of this test, the fact of its being heavily weighted in finger speed and dexterity and in body balance must be taken into consideration. When the test is given in its entirety, the results tell more about the ability of the student in these two skill domains than in any of the others.

A test found to be very appropriate in evaluating basic motor skills of the severely and profoundly retarded is the Texas Revision of Fait's Basic Motor Skills Test: Basic Movement Performance Profile (Table 7–2). The original test was designed to measure basic skills appropriate for teaching to severely and profoundly mentally retarded children, with measured IQs from 0 to 34, who had no physical handicaps. In the revision the test items were expanded and refined and placed in order of difficulty of performance by profoundly mentally retarded subjects. The revision has a reliability coefficient of .94. It has been found that a mean score for most groups of severely and profoundly retarded subjects is between 35 and 45, with a score of 2 representing an "average" in the majority of items.

A motor fitness test specifically for use with the moderately mentally retarded is that developed by Johnson and Londeree.[1] The test is composed of 13 items; however, the authors suggest that a satisfactory motor fitness profile of moderately mentally retarded subjects can be secured with a battery of six of the items: flexed arm hang, situps, standing long jump, softball throw for distance, 50 yard dash, and 300 yard run-walk. Percentile scoring tables are available for comparing individual scores.

Evaluation of Awkward Children. A motor skill test developed by Fait is useful in evaluating the motor ability of awkward children (See Table 7–3 for examples of test items.) The test measures the specific motor skills most needed by children to function efficiently in everyday life; hence, the skills are referred to as basic skills. Rationale for the test is the fact that coordination is specific in nature; that is, coordination in one skill does not necessarily transfer to another skill. Consequently, many different skills are to be measured to obtain an adequate profile of a child's motor ability.

Each basic skill selected was examined to determine its components; that is, the

---

[1]Leon Johnson and Ben Londeree: *Motor Fitness Testing Manual for the Moderately Mentally Retarded.* Washington, D.C., American Alliance for Health, Physical Education and Recreation, 1976, passim.

Table 7-2. TEXAS REVISION OF FAIT'S BASIC MOTOR SKILLS TEST*
BASIC MOVEMENT PERFORMANCE PROFILE**

1. Walking
   - 0 — makes no attempt at walking
   - 1 — walks while being pulled
   - 3 — walks with toe-heel placement
   - 3 — walks with shuffle
   - 4 — walks with heel-toe placement and opposite arm-foot swing

2. Pushing (wheelchair)
   - 0 — makes no attempt to push wheelchair
   - 1 — makes some attempt to push wheelchair
   - 2 — pushes wheelchair once with arms only
   - 3 — pushes wheelchair with continuous motion for 10 ft.
   - 4 — pushes wheelchair carrying adult occupant continuously for 10 ft.

3. Ascending Stairs (up 4 stair steps)
   - 0 — makes no attempt to walk up stairs
   - 1 — steps up one step with assistance
   - 2 — walks up 4 steps with assistance
   - 3 — walks up 4 steps; two feet on each step
   - 4 — walks up 4 steps; alternating one foot on each step

4. Descending Stairs (down 4 stair steps)
   - 0 — makes no attempt to walk down stairs
   - 1 — steps down one step with assistance
   - 2 — walks down 4 steps with assistance
   - 3 — walks down 4 steps, two feet on each step
   - 4 — walks down 4 steps, alternating one foot on each step

5. Climbing (4 rungs; 1st choice, ladder of slide, 2nd choice, step ladder)
   - 0 — makes no attempt to climb ladder
   - 1 — climbs at least one rung with assistance
   - 2 — climbs 4 rungs with assistance
   - 3 — climbs 4 rungs, two feet on each rung
   - 4 — climbs 4 rungs, alternating one foot on each rung

6. Carrying (folded folding chair)
   - 0 — makes no attempt to lift chair from floor
   - 1 — attempts but not able to lift chair from floor
   - 2 — lifts chair from floor
   - 3 — carries chair by dragging on the floor
   - 4 — carries chair 10 ft.

7. Pulling (wheelchair)
   - 0 — makes no attempt to pull wheelchair
   - 1 — makes some attempt to pull wheelchair
   - 2 — pulls wheelchair once with arms only
   - 3 — pulls wheelchair with continuous motion for 10 ft.
   - 4 — pulls wheelchair carrying adult occupant continuously for 10 ft.

8. Running
   - 0 — makes no attempt to run
   - 1 — takes long walking steps while being pulled
   - 2 — takes running steps while being pulled
   - 3 — jogs (using toe or flat of foot)
   - 4 — runs for 25 yds., with both feet off the ground when body weight shifts from the rear to front foot

9. Catching (bean bag tossed from 5 ft. away)
   - 0 — makes no attempt to catch bean bag
   - 1 — holds both arms out to catch bean bag
   - 2 — catches bean bag fewer than 5 of 10 attempts
   - 3 — catches bean bag at least 5 of 10 attempts
   - 4 — catches bean bag at least 8 of 10 attempts

10. Creeping
    - 0 — makes no attempt to creep
    - 1 — will assume hands and knees position
    - 2 — creeps with a shuffle
    - 3 — creeps alternating hands and knees
    - 4 — creeps in a crosslateral pattern with head up

11. Jumping Down (two foot take-off and landing from 18 in. folding chair)
    - 0 — makes no attempt
    - 1 — steps down from chair with assistance
    - 2 — steps down from chair
    - 3 — jumps off chair with two foot take-off and landing with assistance
    - 4 — jumps off chair with two foot take-off and landing while maintaining balance

12. Throwing (overhand softball, 3 attempts)
    - 0 — makes no attempt to throw
    - 1 — grasps ball and releases in attempt to throw
    - 2 — throws or tosses ball a few feet in any direction
    - 3 — throws ball at least 15 ft. in air in intended direction
    - 4 — throws ball at least 30 ft. in the air in intended direction

13. Hitting (volleyball with plastic bat)
    - 0 — makes no attempt to hit ball
    - 1 — hits stationary ball fewer than 3 of 5 attempts
    - 2 — hits stationary ball at least 3 of 5 attempts
    - 3 — hits ball rolled from 15 ft. away fewer than 3 of 5 attempts
    - 4 — hits ball rolled from 15 ft. away at least 3 of 5 attempts

*Items are listed in order of difficulty for profoundly retarded subjects.

**From Richard Ness: "The Standardization of the Basic Movement Performance Profile for Profoundly Retarded Institutionalized Residents." Unpublished Dissertation, North Texas State University, Denton, Texas, 1974.

Table 7–2. TEXAS REVISION OF FAIT'S BASIC MOTOR SKILLS TEST
BASIC MOVEMENT PERFORMANCE PROFILE (*Continued*)

14. Forward Roll
    0 — makes no attempt to do forward roll
    1 — puts hands and head on mat
    2 — puts hands and head on mat and pushes with feet and/or knees in an attempt to do roll
    3 — performs roll but tucks shoulder and rolls to side
    4 — performs forward roll

15. Kicking (soccer ball)
    0 — makes no attempt to kick stationary ball
    1 — pushes stationary ball with foot in attempt to kick it
    2 — kicks stationary ball several feet in any direction
    3 — kicks stationary ball several feet in intended direction
    4 — kicks ball rolled from 15 ft. away in direction of roller

16. Dynamic Balance (4 in. beam with shoes on)
    0 — makes no attempt to stand on beam
    1 — stands on beam with assistance
    2 — walks at least 5 steps with assistance
    3 — walks at least 5 ft. without stepping off beam
    4 — walks at least 10 ft. without stepping off beam

17. Hanging (2 hands on horizontal bar)
    0 — makes no attempt to grasp bar
    1 — makes some attempt to hang from bar
    2 — hangs from bar with assistance
    3 — hangs from bar for at least 5 seconds
    4 — hangs from bar for at least 10 seconds

18. Dodging (a large cage ball rolled from 15 ft. away)
    0 — makes no attempt to dodge ball
    1 — holds up hands or foot to stop ball
    2 — turns body to avoid ball
    3 — dodges ball at least 5 of 10 attempts
    4 — dodges ball at least 8 of 10 attempts

19. Static Balance (standing on one foot with shoes on)
    0 — makes no attempt to stand on one foot
    1 — makes some attempt to stand on one foot
    2 — stands on one foot with assistance
    3 — stands on one foot for at least 5 seconds
    4 — stands on one foot for at least 5 seconds with 5 lbs. weight in the same hand as elevated foot

20. Jumping (standing long jump, 3 attempts)
    0 — makes no attempt to jump
    1 — jumps with a one-foot stepping motion
    2 — jumps from crouch with two foot take-off and landing at least 1 ft.
    3 — jumps from crouch with two foot take-off and landing at least 2 ft.
    4 — jumps from crouch with two foot take-off and landing at least 3 ft.

Table 7–3. UNIVERSITY OF CONNECTICUT AND MANSFIELD TRAINING
SCHOOL BEHAVIORAL RATING SCALE*

	Never	Some-times	Fairly Often	Frequently	Most of the Time	Unknown
Overly aggressive in relationship with others	4	3	2	1	0	
Belligerent: strikes, hits, attacks others	4	3	2	1	0	
Alert to happenings around him	0	1	2	3	4	
Destructive to equipment and facilities	4	3	2	1	0	
Destructive to himself	4	3	2	1	0	
Loud and boisterous	4	3	2	1	0	
Withdraws from situations	4	3	2	1	0	
Attempts a task even when difficult for him	0	1	2	3	4	
Participates in meaningful movement on his own initiative	0	1	2	3	4	
Takes simple directions	0	1	2	3	4	

*Developed for the Department of Physical Education, Mansfield Training School, Mansfield Depot, Connecticut.

Table 7–4. BASIC SKILLS EVALUATION CHART

Ratings

Meets Criterion	1
Some Correction needed	2
Much Correction Needed	3

Running Rapidly	1	2	3	Comments
1. Synchronizes arms movements with leg movements (elbows bent).				
2. Holds arms and trunk muscles in relaxed manner.				
3. Holds head in natural position (head isn't held to one side or doesn't move from side to side).				
4. Bends knee and lands on ball of foot while knee of non-supporting leg is bent at 90° angle (side-view).				
5. Leans body forward at a slight angle.				
6. Brings weight over lead foot as it contacts ground.				
7. Places toes straight ahead (does not toe in or out).				
8. Brings leg straight forward after pushing off from foot.				
9. Other.				

Change of Direction and Dodging	1	2	3	Comments
1. Shortens stride and breaks with lead foot.				
2. Lowers body by bending at knees and leans body in direction of movement.				
3. Widens stance in last step before turning.				
4. Slows speed and changes center of gravity of body to permit movement of desired part of body.				
5. Other.				

Throwing Overhand	1	2	3	Comments
1. Turns dominant shoulder away from direction of throw as hand is brought back behind head and turns dominant shoulder forward as ball is thrown.				
2. Cocks wrist as it is brought behind head and snaps it forward when ball is released.				
3. Brings upper arm parallel with ground and points elbow away from body as ball is brought back behind head.				
4. Changes body weight and steps forward with correct foot.				
5. Follows through.				
6. Other				

*From Hollis F. Fait: *Tasks and Resource Book*. Philadelphia, W. B. Saunders Company, 1978.

movements that have to be made to accomplish the skill. A criterion of the most effective way to perform each movement was established, and a scale of three levels of performance was set, based on the criterion. The three levels are 1, meets criterion; 2, some correction needed; and 3, considerable correction needed. The level at which the child being examined performs provides a guide for teaching movements that will enable the child to execute the basic skill more effectively.

The test serves as an example of the procedures discussed above for establishing domains, isolating components, and setting criteria. The teacher can develop an evaluation tool to measure other specific motor skills using the test as a guide. Or, following the procedure used in developing the test, the teacher can develop a measuring device for use in evaluating students with a physical handicap. For example, to make an instrument for evaluating the ability of a paraplegic to make an overhand throw, the first step is to assess the motor potential of the student through observation of his attempts to throw a ball overhand. Of the five items in the section entitled Throwing Overhand, the student will probably be able to perform all except the fourth and fifth items. These items, then, can be modified to reflect a criterion of effective performance within the limitations imposed by the handicap. Item four might be changed to read: Twists shoulder in direction of throw as the arm is brought forward; and item five to read: Follows through with the arm.

Assessment of Behavioral Changes

The question frequently arises as to the effects on the handicapped of participation in an organized motor activities program. The concern is particularly great with respect to those who are severely and profoundly mentally retarded. To assist in making an evaluation of the influence of the physical education program on such participants, the author has developed a behavior rating scale, shown below. The scale is designed to give some indication of observable behavioral changes in the totally dependent child that reflect the learning to which he has been exposed in physical education class. (It should be noted that physical education is not the only experience the child has during the day. Any behavioral changes, positive or negative, will reflect his total experience.) It is recommended that ratings be made before and after the student's exposure to an extensive program of physical education activities. The ratings should be made by the physical educator and the supervisor in the residence where the student lives and by others who have close contact with the student. The validity of the rating is generally increased when more than one rater is used and an average (mean) is taken. In addition to providing information about behavioral changes, the test, when administered as suggested, promotes rapport between the physical educator and those who care for the student.

SELECTED READINGS

AAHPER: *Testing for Impaired, Disabled and Handicapped Individuals*. Washington, D.C., American Alliance for Health, Physical Education, and Recreation, (nd).

Baumgartner, Ted A., and Jackson, Andrew S.: *Measurement and Evaluation in Physical Fitness Education.* Boston, Houghton-Mifflin, 1975.

Clarke, Harrison: *Application of Measurements to Health and Physical Education,* ed. 5. Englewood Cliffs, N.J., Prentice-Hall, Inc., 1976.

Hively, Wells, and Reynolds, Maynard C. (Editors): *Domain-Referenced Testing in Special Education.* Minneapolis, Leadership Training Institute, Special Education, University of Minnesota, 1975.

Matthews, Donald K.: *Measurement in Physical Education,* ed. 5. Philadelphia, W. B. Saunders Co., 1977.

Chapter 8

Assistive Devices

Natural arm and leg movements that have been lost through injury or illness can often be compensated for, to some degree, by the use of assistive devices. The term assistive devices is applied to a variety of contrivances that assist, substitute for, or facilitate movement of the limbs. These devices range in complexity from the simple cane, which provides support in balancing the body, to artificial hands, the fingers of which are powered by small concealed batteries, enabling the user to duplicate many actions of the real hand.

Among the handicapped children for whom the special physical education teacher must plan an appropriate program will be some who use assistive devices. Consequently, some information about the devices and their operation is important. Knowledge of the function of the specific device is helpful in understanding the movement problem imposed by the disability and in understanding the way and extent to which the device helps to overcome the problem. This insight facilitates analysis of the motor skills that are possible with the device so that appropriate physical education activities can be more readily selected and successfully presented.

Acquaintance with the operation of assistive devices is useful when the user requires assistance in transferring to or from the device as, for example, in moving from the wheelchair to a gymnasium mat on the floor. Understanding the techniques of effecting the transfer increases the efficiency and safety of the operation. Lack of such knowledge may, in addition to decreasing the effectiveness of the transfer, actually bring about fear or pain in the one being moved.

Information about the operation of assistive devices is also useful when assistance is required in removing and replacing them. The various braces and harnesses that are used to support the trunk or to hold artificial limbs in place are usually removed for certain types of physical activity. Safe, painless assistance in taking off and putting on the device is more likely to occur if the techniques of the operation are understood.

Locking mechanisms are provided on some devices to create stability or immobility when such is desired. An understanding of these and of how they function is important so that one may properly assist a user of such a device who doesn't understand how to operate the lock.

AMBULATORY DEVICES

The most common of the assistive devices are those used to aid in ambulation and will, in this discussion, be referred to as ambulatory devices. They include canes, crutches, walkers, scooters, leg and trunk braces, and leg prostheses.

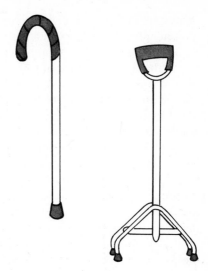

Figure 8-1. Common straight cane and quad cane.

The simplest of these ambulatory devices is the cane. It is used primarily to help maintain body balance while standing or walking. The cane achieves this function by widening the base of support, thereby providing greater stability. Pressure on the cane reduces the weight-bearing strain on the involved limb; that is, the disabled leg, foot, or both of these.

The cane may be of the straight wooden variety with a curved handle seen commonly in usage. For safety's sake, the cane should have a rubber tip that prevents slipping. Proper length is important to effective and comfortable use: the cane should be long enough to allow the elbow to be flexed slightly when the tip is resting on the ground about six inches away from the side of the foot.

Those who have severe problems in balance may need more assistance than the common straight cane offers. For such individuals there is a metal cane with four feet at its base, hence its name of quad cane (Fig. 8-1). Quad canes vary in width and in style of handle. While somewhat awkward to use, these canes do provide substantial stability and permit ambulation by those who would experience great difficulty in walking with a regular cane.

For most efficient use, the cane is held in the hand opposite the involved limb and is brought forward as this limb is moved forward. The cane must be held close enough to the body to prevent leaning the body toward it, as this adversely affects balance. For the same reason, the cane should be advanced the same distance as the involved limb.

To ensure against accidents on the floor of the playroom or gymnasium occurring to those using canes, care must be taken to remove obstacles and to keep the floor dry and skid-proof. Concern to avoid collision with those using canes must be instilled in players whose mobility is unencumbered.

Crutches

Crutches are ambulatory devices that offer more stability than canes. Several types of crutches are currently available. The most common and most simple are made of wood with double uprights, underarm bar, and hand piece, which is adjustable to the length of the arm. In use, the crutches are placed under the arms, and the hands on the hand pieces, where pressure is exerted to move the body. The top of the crutch is placed approximately two inches short of the axilla (armpit) and should be well padded to avoid injury to the radial nerve of the arm.

Other types of crutches are made of metal and consist of a single vertical upright with a support for the forearm. Adjustment of these is accomplished by depressing a button on the lower part of the crutch. Three of the commonly used metal crutches are the Löfstrand, or Canadian, crutch; the Canadian elbow-extensor crutch, which extends farther up the arm than the Löfstrand crutch; and the forearm support crutch (Fig. 8–2 *A* and *B*). In using the former two, weight is taken by the hands, while in the latter, as the name implies, the weight falls on the forearm.

All crutches, whether wooden or metal, should be equipped with broad rubber tips to prevent slipping. Since the tips become worn with use, they should be inspected frequently and replaced promptly, when necessary. The safety precautions recommended for participants using canes on the playing floor also apply to those with crutches. Assistance may be given to a weak or unskilled user of crutches by grasping his belt at the back with one hand.

As an additional safety measure, as well as for program planning purposes, it is desirable for the special physical educator to have an understanding of the various gaits used in crutch walking. The placement of the feet and crutches for each of four crutch walking gaits is illustrated in Figure 8–3 *A* to *D*. The gait is determined by the individual's physical condition and ability to take steps. The speed at which the crutch user wishes to move is another factor in determining the choice of gait, provided he has the strength and endurance for faster speed. With this information, the teacher can select suitable activities and make appropriate adaptations with the assurance they can be performed safely and effectively by participants on crutches.

Walkers

A walker is a four-legged stand with a hand railing that extends across the front and to the sides of the body (Fig. 8–4 *A* and *B*). It offers a wide base of support and affords greater security than do either canes or crutches. Hence the walker is greatly preferred by aged persons, who often have poor vision as well as lack of strength and balance.

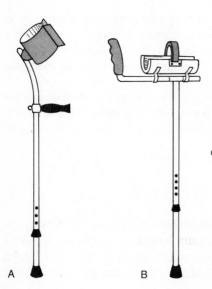

Figure 8–2. *A.* Löfstrand crutch. *B.* Forearm support crutch.

A   B

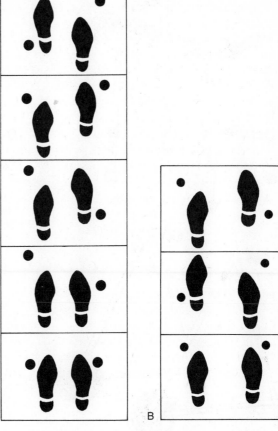

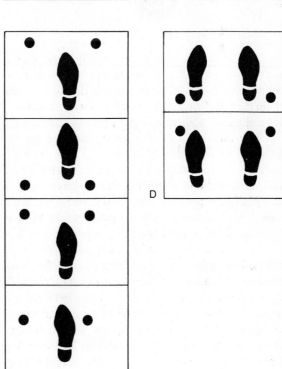

Figure 8–3. *A*. Four point gait. *B*. Two point gait. *C*. Three point gait. *D*. Swing through gait.

Figure 8–4. *A.* Pick-up walker. *B.* Rolling walker.

The two types of walkers shown in the illustration are the basic styles, the pick-up and the rolling walker. The techniques for using either are similar. The user grasps the railing, which should be at a height that allows the elbows to be slightly flexed, and lifts or pushes the walker forward a short distance. Then, one or more steps are taken, depending on ability, and the process is repeated.

The pick-up walker is recommended for those who need more support than is provided by the quad cane but who lack the balance required for the successful use of crutches. Individuals who do not have the strength to lift the pick-up walker or who have arm or hand problems that interfere with lifting employ the rolling walker. To accommodate persons who cannot stand but are able to use their feet, there is a rolling walker with a seat. Such a walker might be used by someone during convalescence from hip surgery until the hip is permitted to bear weight.

Several safety measures need to be observed in the use of both kinds of walkers. The rolling walker should be equipped with a hand brake to prevent unexpected rolling and loss of balance. If there is no brake, the walker should be stabilized by backing it against a wall. When moving the body between a chair and walker, the arms of the chair should be used for support; an uneven distribution of weight on the walker may cause it to move or tip. A pick-up walker should be set down so that all the legs touch the surface at the same time. It should be lifted using the arms, with the body's weight forward rather than by bending and straightening the back, which may cause so much backward lean that the body loses its balance.

Wheelchairs

The wheelchair provides a means of locomotion to those who are so severely immobilized by their condition that they cannot stand or walk even with the aid of the ambulatory devices described in the preceding section. There are many types of wheelchairs available; they are commonly constructed with two large wheels in back and two smaller caster wheels in front. Attached to the larger wheels are slightly smaller wheels that are not in contact with the ground: these are called hand rims and are used for propelling the wheelchair by hand. Other equipment may include adjustable foot rests, movable leg rests, brakes to lock the large wheels, arm rests that may be detachable, and handles for use by a helper in pushing the wheelchair.

One type of wheelchair is lightweight and collapsible for easy transportation in the car by those who are able to drive. For wheelchair users who lack the strength for, or whose condition prevents, arm movement for self-propulsion, there are motorized wheelchairs powered by a large battery. Simple controls on the armrests respond to the slightest touch by the operator.

In the physical education class, when the wheelchair user is engaged in any activity in which his safety might be jeopardized by sudden rolling of the chair, the brake must be set. The teacher should always check to see that this is done.

Help is usually needed to negotiate curbs and stairs of one or two steps (more steps should not usually be attempted). To give safe assistance in going up, the teacher should stand behind the chair with the front of the chair toward the curb or steps and tilt the chair until the small wheels rest on the level surface when the wheelchair is pushed forward. The procedure is reversed when going down the curb or steps. The chair is turned so the person seated in it faces away from the curb or steps. The rear wheels are pulled back until the front wheels reach the edge of the step or curb and then the chair is slowly lowered to the surface. The backward pull continues until the front wheels can be lowered. The wheelchair can also be moved down with the person seated in it facing forward rather than backward. This requires more skill to ensure the occupant's safety. If the tilt of the chair is not maintained so the rear wheels touch ground first, the occupant will be dumped out of the wheelchair.

Since many wheelchairs have detachable armrests to facilitate movement in and out of the chair, assistance given by grabbing this part of the chair will usually result only in pulling the chair arms off. Instead, the hold should be taken on the leg or wheel.

When going down or up a hill or ramp, the one who is helping to move the wheelchair should always be below the chair. Thus, in moving down the incline, the chair is turned and slowly pulled backward. It is tilted to place the weight on the large wheels. If the person being moved has sufficient strength and the incline is steep, he may assist by exerting pressure on the hand rims to help retard the speed of movement. In moving up the incline, the chair is pushed forward and tilted to bring the weight onto the large wheels. If he is capable, the occupant of the chair can assist by pushing on the hand rims to aid the forward movement.

When lifting someone who cannot move himself from the chair to a mat for activity, the following procedure is suggested. The wheelchair is moved close to the edge of, or even onto, the mat. The wheels are locked and checked to see if they are secure. If the person being assisted is able to get to his feet, the arms of the chair are not detached but the foot and leg rests are moved aside. The helper stands to one side of the chair and lifts up on the torso under the arms of the person in the chair, who assists by pushing on the armrests. The helper then reaches down with one hand to release the lock on the side where he is standing and swings the chair away so that he can move behind the

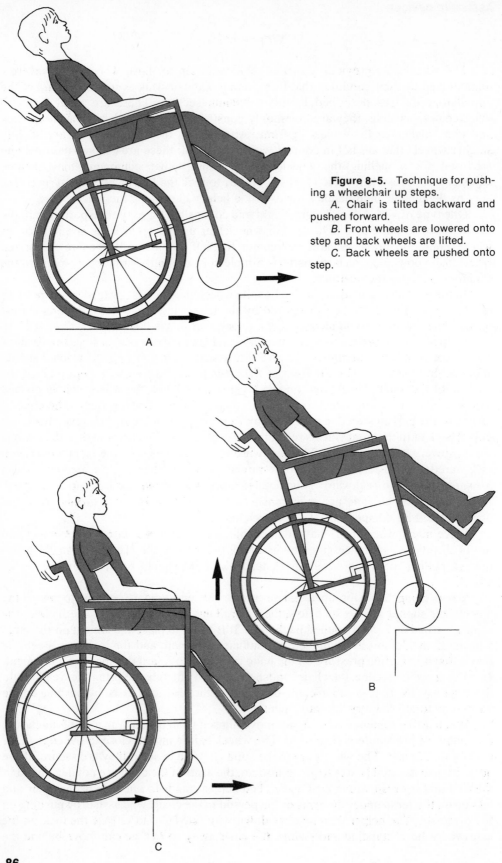

Figure 8–5. Technique for pushing a wheelchair up steps.

A. Chair is tilted backward and pushed forward.

B. Front wheels are lowered onto step and back wheels are lifted.

C. Back wheels are pushed onto step.

Figure 8–6. Technique for moving a wheelchair down steps while occupant faces forward.

A. Chair is tilted backward and pushed slowly forward.

B. Back wheels are lowered slowly to the floor, followed by lowering the front wheels.

A

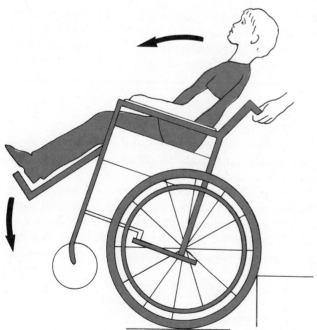

B

wheelchair's occupant to give support to the occupant's torso while lowering him to the mat. The process is reversed to place him back in the chair.

If the person in the chair is unable to assist in any way, two helpers will be needed to move him to the mat. One stands on each side of the wheelchair, from which the armrests have been removed, and slides the hand that is nearer the front under the thighs of the occupant of the chair. The hands grasp each other under the thighs. The other hands are gently pushed behind his back and clasped together at about the level of the lumbar area. The occupant is then lifted up and forward from the wheelchair and lowered to the mat. If the person in the wheelchair is small, one helper can manage the lift by using the same points of support. To return the wheelchair user to his chair, the procedure is reversed.

Scooter Boards

The scooter board is a flat board to which four caster wheels are attached for easy movement. Either a sitting or prone lying position may be taken on the board; propulsion is created by pushing the hands against the floor. Commercial scooter boards are usually approximately 14 by 18 inches in size, but longer ones can be easily constructed in the home or school workshop.

Scooter boards, particularly those of longer length, are excellent means of providing mobility to the handicapped youngster who cannot stand or who is unable to move about with any degree of speed and security. If the youngster is unable to sit on the board, he may lie. Use of the scooter board greatly extends the opportunities for participation in physical education activities for those with disabilities of the lower extremities. In many games movement on the scooter can be substituted for walking and running.

The chief safety precaution in the use of scooter boards during physical education activities is to avoid injuries to the fingers. Participants should be warned to remove their hands from the floor and to not grasp the edge when other scooters approach them to avoid the possibility of the fingers and hands being run over or crushed between colliding scooters.

PROSTHESES

An artificial substitute for any part of the body is called a prosthesis. The development of prosthetic devices has made enormous progress in recent years so that it is now possible to provide artificial parts that closely resemble the actual body segment in function and in cosmetic appearance. There are prostheses for various parts of the body, but the most important to this discussion are those for the lower and upper limbs. The loss of all or part of a limb is most often due to surgical amputation required by injury or disease. A less frequent cause is congenital amputation, a term meaning that a segment is missing at birth.

Leg Prostheses

The type of prosthesis provided for a lower limb depends upon the level of amputation; that is, the place on the leg where the amputation occurs. If the level of amputation is below the knee joint but above the ankle, either a conventional below the

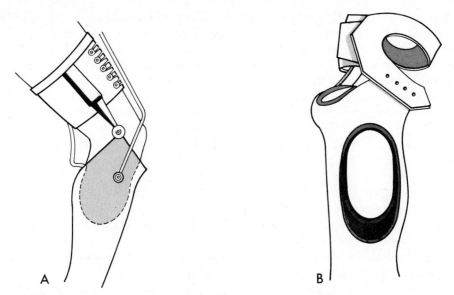

Figure 8–7. *A.* Conventional below-knee prosthesis. *B.* Patella tendon bearing prosthesis.

knee prosthesis or the new PTB (patellar tendon bearing) prosthesis is used. The former type has a tight corset that is laced around the thigh just above the knee (Fig. 8–7 *A*). With the PTB the stump is encased in a thin-walled plastic shank and is held in place by a strap secured above the knee (Fig. 8–7 *A* and *B*). The artificial foot may have a simulated ankle joint or it may be a solid foot device with a rubber heel that creates the appearance of ankle action in movement.

In amputation of the foot at the ankle, called Syme's amputation, the usual prosthesis is the Canadian-type Syme prosthesis, shown in Figure 8–8. It does not have an ankle joint and is constructed so that the socket will bear the weight either on the distal portion (end) of the stump or on the distal and proximal rim (sides of the stump). It is held in place by the contour of the leg when the leg is in the prosthesis after the door on the side of the prosthesis has been strapped shut.

A leg that has been amputated above the knee can be equipped with a prosthesis

Figure 8–8. Canadian-type Syme prosthesis.

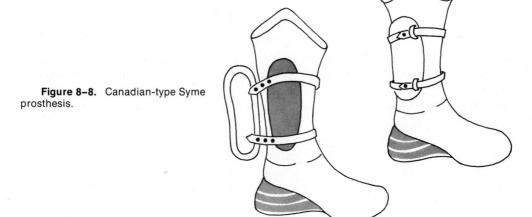

that has an artificial knee joint and a socket for insertion of the stump. Mechanical aids that operate either manually or automatically to lock the knee for standing may be added, if required, to stabilize the knee. The prosthetic device can be held in place in several possible ways. One of these ways is suction; the socket is so constructed in relationship to the stump that, when the stump is inserted, suction is created to hold it securely in the socket while walking. Special valves control the amount of suction. A sock, which is usually worn over the stump, is omitted with this type of prosthesis. The prosthesis may also be held in place by a Silesian bandage, a light webbing attached to each side of the socket near the crotch area that holds the leg in the socket. The prosthesis can also be held in place by means of suspenders or a pelvic belt. The suspenders pass over the shoulder to hold the prosthesis on the stump. The pelvic belt encircles the pelvic area to secure the prosthesis.

If the level of amputation is such that no thigh remains, a more elaborate prosthetic device that resembles a tilt table is used. The hip is fitted into the socket and held in place by a harness that resembles a girdle. The socket in articulation with the lower part of the device creates a table-like hip joint with a lock that stabilizes the hip for standing and walking and unlocks for sitting.

To ensure safety and enjoyment in physical education activities by students wearing leg prostheses, the teacher must understand the leg and trunk movements necessary to achieve locomotion. With this in mind, it is possible to analyze the total movements required to perform a skill and to determine the modifications or adaptations that will be necessary for successful participation by the student.

The teacher should also learn how the locking mechanism of the student's prosthesis operates and how to remove and put on the prosthetic device. Then, if assistance is needed, the teacher will know how to proceed. Small children, mental retardates, and those with cerebral palsy are particularly likely to need such help.

It is important to remember that the artificial limb should not get wet, because this causes deterioration of rubber and leather parts. If the prosthesis does become wet, it should be removed and thoroughly dried with a cloth. A stump sock that has become damp from perspiration should be changed.

The skin at the stump's surface is very susceptible to injury and slow to recover due to poor circulation in the area. Consequently, any blisters, calluses, or sores noted by the teacher while helping a child with his or her prosthesis should be reported to the proper personnel so that medical attention and adjustment of the prosthesis can be secured, if necessary.

Arm Prostheses

Arm prostheses are of two types: a cosmetic prosthesis, which is a dress hand or arm designed for appearance and not for use, and a work prosthesis, which is designed to enable the wearer to perform various tasks. The work prosthesis is usually fitted with a split utility hook that substitutes effectively for the hand in the performance of various jobs. When the fingers or thumb is missing, a prosthesis is utilized that substitutes only for the missing digits.

Some arm prostheses are rigged with steel cables and a shoulder harness so that the wearer, by moving the shoulder, can manipulate the utility hook constructed for grasping. A similar arrangement is used with a prosthesis designed to enable the shoulder to flex and the artificial elbow joint to extend, in the case of amputation above the elbow.

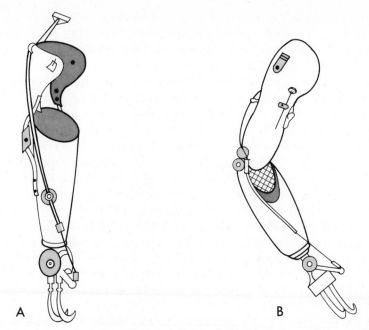

Figure 8–9. *A.* Long below-elbow prosthesis. *B.* Standard above-elbow prosthesis.

When amputation of the arm occurs below the shoulder, one of two different kinds of prostheses is used: the long below-elbow prosthesis (Fig. 8–9 *A*) designed for use with long stumps, and the standard above-elbow prosthesis for shorter stumps (Fig. 8–9 *B*). In disarticulation at the shoulder, the prosthesis is constructed to encase the shoulder area; the simulated upper arm has joint action at the shoulder and at the elbow, and the split hook attaches to the simulated lower arm (Fig. 8–10). Operation is made

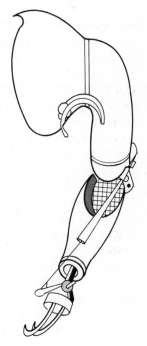

Figure 8–10. Arm prosthesis for disarticulation at the shoulder.

possible by an electric device powered by a small battery. A similar device is used for manipulation of joints and utility hooks in other prostheses. The devices are activated by movement of the shoulders or, in some cases, by controls inserted in the shoe that respond to pressure from the heel and toes.

In recent years a surgical procedure, known as kineplasty, has been developed for control of the movement of the arm prostheses: in this procedure the muscle is connected to the prosthesis to provide a force to operate a utility hook that grasps. Although the operation is still controversial, there is general consensus that it is most effective for below-the-elbow amputations where the insertion is made into the biceps. Regardless of the location of the insertion, there is always some danger of irritation and infection, and for this reason the technique has not won full acceptance.

Students with arm prostheses are trained by specialists in the use of the device. Once the basic skills have been established, the amputee may be interested in extending the possible uses of his prosthesis to include the motor skills of games and sports. Some possibilities that have been worked out by physical education teachers are described in detail in Section 4 of this book; others can be developed by the teacher working with the individual student. The chief precaution that must be exercised is the prevention of misuse that will damage the prosthesis, as would be the case if it became wet and was not dried properly or if excessive force were exerted with it.

Recent amputees may need remedial posture exercises, which can be provided as part of their physical education program. After the loss of an arm or leg, the body tends to compensate for the lost weight by realignment that distributes the weight more evenly over the remaining segments of the body. This often results in a poor posture that is usually less efficient and that is likely to cause other problems, such as back pain. Students with misalignment due to arm or leg amputation will profit from a posture improvement program appropriate to their individual needs, as discussed in Chapter 28.

Orthotic Devices for Lower Limbs

An orthesis is a device that is applied to a segment of the body for support or immobilization, to prevent or correct a deformity, or to assist or restore function. The need for its use is indicated by pain, weakness, or paralysis in the particular part of the body. Ortheses can be applied to the spinal column and to both upper and lower limbs. Our concern here is with ortheses used as braces on the lower limbs to give support to body weight, to decrease pain, or to aid ambulation. Braces are referred to as supportive, corrective, protective, or dynamic, according to their function. A supportive brace stabilizes a specific part of the body, such as a painful joint. A corrective brace encourages changes in the structure, position, or function of the body, as would be the case when a brace is applied in the treatment of a clubfoot. Protective bracing affords protection from further injury to the body or prevents greater deformity. Dynamic bracing is utilized when there is a need to mobilize a body part or to aid weakened muscles, as in the loss of leg muscle strength due to poliomyelitis. Such braces utilize springs and cables or elastic bands to provide the required force to assist movement.

A full leg brace commonly consists of a shoe, a stirrup to which the uprights to the shoe are attached, uprights that support the total brace and run parallel to the length of the brace, knee joints in the upright to allow movement of the knee, and a weight-bearing band or ring at the top of the brace which comes to the very top of the thigh. Knee joints may operate freely or be provided with locks. There are many different types of locks in use. One of the most common is the drop ring lock, which locks automatically when the brace is straightened but which must be unlocked manually. Another commonly used locking device is the automatic lock. It locks when the knee is straightened, and holds against a moderate amount of force but unlocks when the knee is bent forcefully.

Another orthesis is the abduction leg brace, used in the treatment of Legg-Calvé-Perthes disease (discussed in Chapter 9). It consists of a brace on both legs with a bar between them that holds the legs apart. One type of leg abduction brace allows no flexion of the knee; another permits knee flexion. The most common of the former type is the Newington ambulatory splint, shown in Figure 8–11. Both legs are encased so that no knee action is possible. An abduction bar between the legs at the ankles keeps the legs apart and slightly rotated inward. The brace is used at any time the legs must bear weight. It may be removed for swimming. Walking is possible while wearing the brace with the use of Canadian crutches; the technique is to twist the body to move one leg forward with the help of the crutches and then repeat the action on the other side.

Of the abduction braces that allow knee action, the two most commonly used are the Craig bar and the Toronto brace. The former is an abduction bar attached to high-top shoes to keep the legs apart. The Toronto brace is similar to the Newington splint except that it has a pivotal hinge in the center of the abduction joint that allows a step to be taken forward without pivoting on the opposite foot and also enables the bending of the knees. Both kinds of braces are removed for swimming.

Wearers of braces who are able to attend school will have been taught the care and use of their devices by the medical personnel involved with their treatment. So, unless the student is very young or unable to communicate effectively, as may be the case with mental retardates and those with cerebral palsy, the teacher will not need to give much assistance to those with braces. Nevertheless, it is well to be familiar with the locking mechanism and the way in which the brace comes off and is put on in order to be of help if aid is needed. Awareness of the movement possibilities with the brace is essential to the development of suitable physical education activities for the student with a brace.

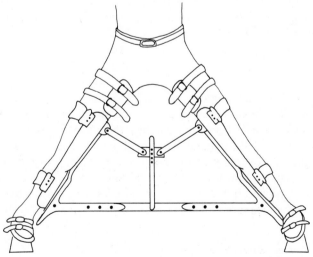

Figure 8–11. Newington ambulatory splint.

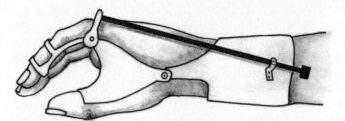

Figure 8–12. Hand opponens orthesis.

Orthotic Devices for Upper Limbs

The type of orthotic device used for the arms and hands varies according to the purpose it serves and the part of the limb involved. Some devices or braces for the upper limbs that the physical educator will likely encounter and will need to know about to develop special programs for those who wear them are discussed in the paragraphs that follow.

Hand Opponens Orthesis

Hand opponens is the name given to any of several muscles of the hand that bring the fingers together in such a way as to form a cup in the palm of the hand. The hand opponens orthesis is designed to maintain correct thumb and palm position (Fig. 8–12) in a hand that is paralyzed. Attachments can be added to the brace to provide wrist support and better prehension (grip).

Reciprocal Wrist-Extension Finger-Flexion Orthesis

This is a device used by quadriplegics (those with paralysis of all four limbs) who have some movement of the wrist extensor muscles. The orthotic device is fitted to the wrist and hand to enable greater control and movement. Basically, the brace functions to hold the fingers partially flexed with the thumb in the grasping position. A connective device from the fingers to above the wrist aids the fingers and thumb in grasping when the wrist is extended. With the orthesis the quadriplegic is able to work the lever of a motorized wheelchair, which he might not otherwise be capable of doing. He may even be able to write with the aid of the device.

Feeders

Feeders are devices that support the hand and lower arm to allow the user to feed himself. There are two basic types of feeders, suspension and supportive. With the former, the arm is supported by an overhead bar; the latter consists of a swivel arm with ball bearings. Both types have a metal arm trough in which the arm rests. The design is such that the slightest movement of the body or shoulder will result in useful motion, enabling the person using the device to extend and flex his arm and so feed himself. Feeders have been utilized by physical educators to enable students who require the devices to achieve the arm movements needed to play a modified form of table tennis.[1]

---

[1]Adams, *et al.: Games, Sports, and Exercises for the Physically Handicapped.* Philadelphia, Lea and Febiger, 1975. p. 132.

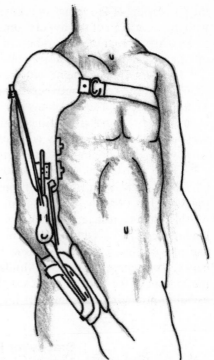

Figure 8-13. Shoulder suspension device with a forearm cuff.

With adaptations, light batting activities as well as those in which a light object is propelled forward may also be done.

Cable-controlled Hook Brace

This assistive device for those with flaccid or paralyzed hand muscles consists of a split hook positioned on a brace attached around the wrist. The split hook is located in the palm of the hand between the thumb and the index finger. A cable is connected to a shoulder harness so that the hook can be opened or closed by movement of the shoulder.

Shoulder Suspension Device

The shoulder suspension device is designed to support a weakened shoulder girdle. The device holds the arm up so that the shoulder joint is not required to support the weight of the arm. It is often used with other devices needed to enable the arm to function; one such device is the forearm cuff shown in Figure 8-13. In the illustration, the shoulder suspension device is used with a cuff that encircles the forearm and with a movable elbow unit. Rubber bands attach to the cuff and shoulder suspension device to aid in elbow flexion.

Back Braces

There are numerous kinds of back braces but all are designed chiefly to support the back and relieve pain, to protect the back from further injury, or to effect correction of the positioning of the spine. In relieving back pain the main purpose of the back braces, with the exception of the hyperextension braces, is to compress the abdominal area and to decrease lumbar lordosis (abnormal curve in the small of the back). The braces most often used for this purpose are corsets, rigid braces, belts, and molded jackets.

The corset is a garment with longitudinal metal stays. It is worn around the trunk, generally at the region between the groin area and ribs, chiefly to treat low back pain. The rigid brace is used for pains in various areas of the back. It is sometimes called the chair-back brace because it has a rigid brace in the back. Although there are many variations, the brace usually consists of a hip band and a chest band joined together with two metal uprights on each side of the spinal column.

There are several different kinds of belts. The trochanteric belt is a two to three inch wide band worn around the pelvis. It is often used for support after a pelvic fracture. The sacroiliac and lumbosacral belts are also bands, but they are larger in width. The sacroiliac belt ranges in width from four to six inches, while the lumbrosacral belt is eight to 16 inches wide. Both belts are worn around the lower back and are useful in preventing low back pain associated with spinal disc (cartilage between vertebrae) disorders. Molded jackets are constructed of heavy material to fit the contour of the body. The jacket provides equal pressure through the trunk and so is useful in providing back support for very old or debilitated persons.

Braces for Repositioning the Spine

Various types of braces are used to place pressure on the spine in order to increase or decrease the anterior-posterior curves or to straighten the lateral curvature of the spine. Bracing for scoliosis is utilized more frequently than is other bracing for repositioning the spine.

One of the most common and apparently most effective braces used in the treatment of scoliosis (discussed in Chapter 9) is the Milwaukee brace. It consists of pads, straps, and metal strips designed to place pressure to the scoliotic curve at the neck and hip in one direction and at the convex side in the other (Fig. 8–14). The neck

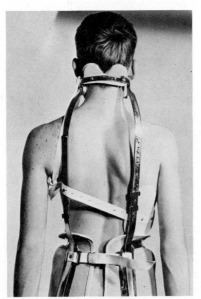

Figure 8–14. Milwaukee brace.

pad and neck ring exert pressure on the neck; the ring is hinged in front and fastens in the back. One of the posterior (back) uprights is attached to the thoracic pad by a snap and exerts force against the curve. The uprights are attached anteriorly to the pelvic girdle. A strap tightens and holds the pelvic girdle securely.

The Milwaukee brace must be worn at all times, except for swimming or special exercise. Youngsters wearing the brace can participate in vigorous play, including such games as basketball, tennis, and soccer.

SELECTED READINGS

Department of Medicine and Surgery, Veterans Administration: *Bulletin of Prosthetic Research.* Washington, D.C., U.S. Government Printing Office, 1975.

Christopherson, Victor A., *et al.: Rehabilitation Nursing Perspectives and Applications.* New York, McGraw-Hill Book Co., 1974.

Gilbert, Arlene E.: *You Can Do It From a Wheelchair.* New Rochelle, N.Y., Arlington House, Pub., 1973.

Kamenetz, Herman L.: *The Wheelchair Book.* Springfield, Ill., Charles C Thomas, Pub., 1969.

Krusen, Frank H., *et al.* (Editors): *Handbook of Physical Medicine and Rehabilitation,* ed. 2. Philadelphia, W. B. Saunders Co., 1971.

Larsen, C., and Gould, M.: *Orthopedic Nursing.* St. Louis, The C. V. Mosby Co., 1970.

Stryker, Ruth P.: *Rehabilitative Aspects of Acute and Chronic Nursing Care.* Philadelphia, W. B. Saunders Co., 1977.

Section 3

Conditions Resulting in Enervated and Impaired Movement

Discussed in this section are disorders that occur so commonly in school-age children that physical educators are very likely to find students with these conditions in their classes. So that physical education teachers will be prepared to offer appropriate programs for these students, the chapters on the various kinds of disorders briefly describe the etiology and pathology, discuss special considerations in planning the program, and suggest kinds of activities that may be offered.

Chapter 9

Orthopedic Handicaps

Orthopedic is derived from the Greek words meaning "to straighten the child," and in modern usage is applied both to a specific type of disability and to the branch of medicine concerned with its prevention and treatment. An orthopedic handicap is one that does not allow the patient to perform properly the motor and locomotor functions of his body and limbs. Such disabilities affect the functions of the bones, joints, and tendons.

The public attitude toward individuals handicapped by orthopedic disabilities has changed immensely since the Middle Ages, when the only hope of acceptance in his society of one so handicapped was to become a court jester. Today the individual with an orthopedic handicap has opportunities for treatment, rehabilitation, gainful employment, and social acceptance far beyond the dreams of even the most imaginative court jester. While much remains to be done, especially in equalizing social and employment opportunities, those with orthopedic disabilities have, over the years, generally suffered less from a lack of public understanding of their needs and problems than have most other kinds of handicapped people.

Care for children crippled by orthopedic disorders was extremely limited until the 19th century, when the work of several prominent orthopedic surgeons in England, continental Europe, and in the United States began to direct attention to the prevention and remedial treatment for the crippling conditions. Concern about the plight of crippled children remained almost entirely medical until the closing years of the century, when the increasing number of such children aroused interest in adequate educational provisions for them. Special schools for crippled children were established, as were special classes within the public schools. Currently, orthopedically handicapped children are mainstreamed into the regular classes of the public schools including, whenever possible, the classes in physical education. A number of hospitals for crippled children exist throughout the country, and these provide educational instruction as well as medical and therapeutic treatment. However, advanced treatment techniques and the desire to return children to their homes as quickly as possible have greatly reduced the actual time the children spend in the hospital. The result is that more children receive their education in the public schools than in the hospitals.

Because of the lack of uniformity in defining the conditions of crippling and orthopedic handicaps, statistics of incidence are neither very meaningful nor very accurate. The number can be doubled or cut in half by the inclusion or exclusion of certain conditions. It is consequently not possible to determine how many cases of orthopedically handicapped youngsters there are currently or how many of these may be expected to be found in the regular school, the special school, or the hospital.

The orthopedically handicapping conditions presented in this chapter are those most commonly found among school-age children. The discussion is divided into three sections: Disorders that Immobilize Lower Limbs, Disorders that Limit Ambulation, and Disorders that Affect Other Body Movements. This organization allows specific orthopedic disabilities that cause similar movement problems to be brought together under one heading, permitting emphasis to be placed on the movement potential of handicapped students with similar limitations rather than on the disabilities and restrictions imposed by each type of orthopedic handicap.

NEEDS AND ADJUSTMENTS OF THE ORTHOPEDICALLY HANDICAPPED

When a normally active human being finds his usual movements restricted by disease or accident, he faces the necessity of changing many of the patterns of his daily life. The degree to which he is able to make these changes determines to a large extent how satisfactory his adjustment will be. The age at which and the suddenness with which the incapacitating disability strikes appear to have considerable effect upon the adjustment which the individual makes. Very intense emotional reactions usually follow a sudden loss of limb by amputation, but these usually subside as the patient discovers that he is still capable of many of the activities of his former life. He is likely to make a satisfactory adjustment as he acquires compensatory motor skills. A child with a limb missing from birth or early infancy may have a deep-seated but less easily detected emotional disturbance as the result of the continual frustration he experiences in attempting to do the things which normal children do. On the other hand, he may have made an entirely adequate adjustment as the result of having acquired such satisfactory compensatory skills that he and those with whom he associates do not think of his being different. If the child has not made this kind of adjustment, he needs help in overcoming his fears and frustrations so that better adjustment will be possible.

The incapacitation produced by an infectious disease like spondylitis is usually much less sudden than that resulting from amputation. Nevertheless, a strong emotional reaction is usually evidenced during the early stages of the disease, which increases as the disease progresses and the crippling becomes more evident. It is likely to continue even after the disease has been terminated if the limitation to normal locomotion remains. The most common emotional reactions are withdrawal, hostility, and aggressiveness.

The age of the patient presents certain other problems in adjusting to the disability. Children and adolescents are particularly susceptible to the reaction of others to the cosmetic appearance of their disabilities. They may worry unduly about how they look and become overly sensitive to the responses of others to their appearance. The anxieties thus aroused are not easily relieved.

Orthopedic crippling occurring early in life frequently limits the child's opportunities for play and other social contacts and greatly restricts the development of satisfactory social growth. Courage, resourcefulness, and initiative fostered in the vigorous exchanges of childhood play activities are commonly deficient in physically disabled children who do not engage in normal play.

These desirable characteristics are also frequently lacking in orthopedically handicapped adults, stemming from their inability to participate in the normal patterns of living. In addition, many of them have inferiority feelings or have excessive anxieties usually related to their inability to support themselves economically. On the whole, a change of any kind is more difficult as age advances, owing to the force of daily habits. Consequently, unless the adult is given a good deal of help, satisfactory adjustment is very difficult.

The lack of active play in the lives of these youngsters and adults has detrimental physiological, as well as psychological, results. General body fitness is lacking. Coordination is poor. There is increased susceptibility to injury and hypokinetic diseases.

To achieve satisfactory adjustment, the orthopedically handicapped person must compensate for his lack of success in physical performance or he must seek satisfying substitutions. Some people compensate by achieving superiority in intellectual endeavors, in the development of musical, artistic, or literary talents, or in the creativity of crafts. Some measure of compensation can be achieved by nearly everyone, but compensation is not enough — satisfactory substitutions for the loss of motor skills must also be found.

Physical education can make one of its most significant contributions to the welfare of the handicapped in the teaching of substitute motor skills which will enable them to take pleasure in active participation in games and sports. This is, of course, only part of the role of physical education for the orthopedically handicapped. Play provides the incentive for the improvement in motor skills, and as locomotion increases morale receives a needed lift. When more complex game skills are achieved or former skills are reacquired, the youngster's self-esteem reestablishes itself and he looks forward with greater confidence and reassurance to achieving satisfactory substitutions for his lost skills.

As participation becomes more active, physical fitness is increased and body mechanics are improved. The individual becomes more skilled in the use of previously unused portions of the body and in the use of his assistive device, if one is required. Because he can play better and longer, owing to the improved conditioning and better playing skills, he enjoys himself more and others enjoy playing with him. In such an atmosphere of social acceptance, the first steps may be taken toward a more satisfactory adjustment.

PLANNING THE PROGRAM

The physical educator employed in a special school or hospital for crippled children which provides physical education as well as therapeutic exercises must clearly understand the division between the physical therapy and physical education. His program in this situation must be limited to those big-muscle activities used for leisure-time play and the promotion of body conditioning, but not specifically concerned with correction of the handicap for the purpose of increased motor function. The activities should not, of course, detract in any way from the physical therapy; they can and should complement the therapeutic exercises. Consequently, the program should be carefully planned in consultation with the medical authorities so that muscles will not be used incorrectly, thus negating the therapeutic treatment.

The Hospital or Special School.   During the hospital stay or active treatment stage, the physical education teacher must consider the medical problems that are related to specific types of disabilities. Weakened muscles must not be strained by overwork; the muscles of the set antagonistic to the weaker ones must be protected from overdevelopment, which would produce muscular imbalance; the hip joints in Legg-Calvé-Perthes disease must bear no weight; an injured joint in the spinal column must be protected from all movement. In most cases of crippling diseases, after the disease is arrested and muscular re-education is nearly complete, the physical education activities need be limited only by the structural limitations of the student.

One of the important objectives of the physical education program for children in special schools and hospitals is to provide play opportunities which encourage them to try the motor skills which they are acquiring or relearning under the care of the physical therapist. Consequently, the program must be carefully planned to provide good progression of skills and experiences. When the very simple skills are satisfactorily mastered, more complex ones can be introduced, and finally very complex skills can be taught. The variety of skills required by the games should be as wide as possible.

The students should be prepared for the great amount of practice which may be necessary to accomplish a skill. If they understand this, they will not become discouraged when they compare their present rate of skill acquisition with their rate before they were afflicted. Words of encouragement and praise should be spoken often by the instructor. If the students are in special schools for the mentally retarded or emotionally disturbed, they will need extra encouragement in overcoming the limitations in movement imposed by their orthopedic handicap. They must be helped in setting realistic goals for themselves and in accepting the fact that improvement in motor skill, however small, is very worthwhile.

The Regular School.   A student returning to school after hospitalization with an orthopedic disability may display no apparent after-effect, while others may exhibit a mild or even severe crippling condition. Although there may be no visible debility, the physical education teacher should not immediately include the student in the regular physical education class. Possible muscular weakness or lack of endurance may not be observable. The teacher should not attempt to include the student in the activities until he has received medical recommendations as to the amount of activity in which the student should engage and the kinds of activities which will prove most beneficial, as well as those which should be restricted. With this knowledge the teacher will be able to plan the kind of program which will help the student increase his general level of fitness and motor efficiency so that he will be better able to meet the physical demands of daily life.

The returning student who has a moderate or severe disability may need considerable help in achieving maximum physical efficiency. Upon receipt of the medical report, the teacher should work out a carefully planned, graduated program of exercises and activities to meet the special needs of the student. It is advisable to secure medical approval of the planned program. The student who has considerable residual paralysis or a limb amputation is also likely to need a great deal of help in making a satisfactory adjustment to his handicap. Because of his possible concern about his appearance and his inabilities to perform motor skills, he may experience more anxieties about physical education class than about other phases of his school life. The teacher can help alleviate his fears by helping him to find a solution which is satisfying to him about dressing and showering in the presence of others, and by preparing him to meet the challenges of his restriction with good humor rather than with fear of embarrassment or ridicule.

Many students who have had their orthopedic disability for much of their lives achieve a high level of motor efficiency by the time they enroll in physical education. Special instruction for them may need only be directed toward refinement of movement patterns and the introduction of new skills. Other youngsters, however, require the same kinds of physical education programming considerations as those with recently acquired orthopedic handicaps.

The specific activities of the special program for the orthopedically handicapped will be determined by the nature and extent of the handicap and the general debility. The early phases of the program for the returning student will be largely exercises and games, approved by the doctor to increase physical fitness and improve posture and body awareness. As the physical condition and motor performance improve, modified games, dances, and team sports can be introduced into the adapted program. Specific suggestions are made following the discussion of the orthopedically handicapping conditions in each of the three sections of this chapter. When the situation warrants it, the handicapped student should be included in the activities of the regular class.

DISORDERS THAT IMMOBILIZE LOWER LIMBS

Many types of orthopedic disorders can cause such severe paralysis of the lower limbs that the use of a wheelchair or similar device is required to achieve locomotion. The two types of such disorders the physical educator most frequently encounters are traumatic spinal cord injuries and spina bifida. The two conditions are similar in that

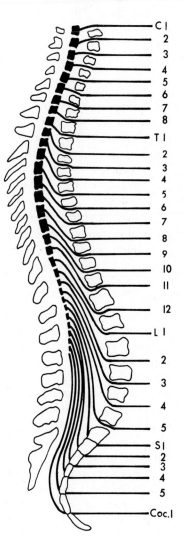

Figure 9–1. Nerves emerging from different levels of the column.

they both produce lesions in the spinal cord and result in subsequent paralysis of the lower limbs.

The spinal cord is housed in the spinal or vertebral column. It is cylindrical in shape, but it does flatten out at certain segments of the spinal column. Its circumference is approximately the same throughout the length of the cord, except for an enlargement in the area giving rise to the nerves that innervate the upper limbs. Another enlargement occurs at the lumbar (small of the back) segment of the spine where nerves leave to innervate the lower limbs. The spinal cord begins where the skull and spinal column meet; it terminates between the last thoracic (upper back) vertebra (T-12) and the second lumbar vertebra (L-2). (See Fig. 9–1). Nerves from the spinal cord pass down into the lumbar and sacral (tail bone) segments of the spinal column.

Sensory and motor nerves emerge from the spinal cord and exit the spinal column through foramina (openings) in the vertebrae. Motor nerves emerging from different levels of the spinal column innervate different muscles.

Injury to the spinal cord in turn affects the innervation of muscles. The higher the level of injury, the less will be the amount of muscle movement available to the affected person. Because groups of muscles are innervated from nerves emerging at particular levels of the spinal column, it is possible to specify the limits of muscle action remaining to individuals who suffer cord injury at a specific vertebra.

Injury to the Spinal Cord

Injury to the cord in which it is severed at or above the third cervical vertebra results in death. Partial lesion in this area creates weakness over the entire body. Complete severance of the cord above the second thoracic vertebra (T-2) results in involvement of the upper and lower limbs; the term for this condition is quadriplegia, meaning all limbs are affected. Complete severance at the second thoracic vertebra (T-2) or below results in paraplegia, a term used to indicate involvement of only the lower trunk and legs. In both conditions, the degree of paralysis may vary from partial to complete.

Fourth Cervical Level (C-4). The person with injury just below the fourth cervical vertebra has use of only the neck muscles and the diaphragm (the main muscle of respiration). Upper limb function is possible only with an electrically powered assistive device, described in the previous chapter, that moves the arm and opens and closes the hand. Complete assistance is needed in transferring to and from the wheel-chair.

Fifth Cervical Level (C-5). Those who sustain injury below the fifth cervical vertebra retain use of the neck muscles, diaphragm, deltoid muscles of the shoulder, and biceps of the arms. The arms can be raised but gravity must be relied upon to lower them; likewise the elbow can be flexed but gravity must be utilized to extend it. A substitute is required for the non-functioning hand and wrist musculature and may be either a fixed support of the wrist and fingers or the electrical device described earlier. A person with this type of injury can perform many activities with his arms; for example, he is able to groom himself, help apply his braces, and push his wheelchair for short distances if it is equipped with a special projection on the rims of the wheels. He will need complete assistance in transferring to and from his wheelchair.

Sixth Cervical Level (C-6). A person with a functional sixth cervical vertebra has the use of the wrist extensors in addition to the movements retained by those with higher levels of injury. With the ability to extend the wrist and with the use of gravity for flexion, considerable utilitarian movement is possible. Small instruments can be attached to a leather cuff worn on the arm. Wrist extension is possible through use of a special mechanism that makes the finger flex, providing a grip and release.

Those with injuries at this level can, in addition to all the activities performed by those with higher lesions, push the wheelchair for long distances and make use of the overhead trapeze (a bar hung overhead to be grasped with the hands as an aid in moving the body). A person injured at this level can also transfer his or her body by holding the extended arms close to the body and adducting the shoulders to stabilize the elbows. Some very adroit individuals are able to drive a car with hand controls.

Seventh Cervical Level (C-7). When the injury is below the seventh cervical vertebra, the major additional functions that remain are extension of the elbow and flexion and extension of the fingers. Movement of the hand is not completely normal because the intrinsic muscles of the hand do not function. The person with this level of injury can do pull-ups, push-ups, and grasp and release. Consequently, he can be fairly independent in manipulating the wheelchair and in transferring from one place to another.

Upper Thoracic Levels (T-1 to T-9 inclusive). Individuals with lesions in the first through the ninth vertebrae have total movement capacity in the arms but none in the legs; the term given to this condition is paraplegia. Control remains of some of the muscles of the upper back, the abdominal muscles, and muscles of the ribs. Complete control of the wheelchair is possible, as are self-feeding and grooming. Although standing is possible by use of long leg braces with pelvic bands, ambulation is very limited.

Lower Thoracic Levels (T-10 to T-12 inclusive). Victims of a separation of the spinal cord in the lower thoracic upper lumbar level have the movement potential of all types described above and possess complete abdominal muscle control as well as control of all the muscles of the upper back. Complete innervation of the abdominal muscles makes walking feasible with the support of long leg braces.

Lumbar Levels (L-1 to L-5 inclusive). The lumbar levels one through three innervate the muscles of the hip joint that flex the thigh. The fourth level of the lumbar also innervates the muscles of flexion of the hip and, together with the fifth level, innervates all the muscles of the lower leg and the muscles that extend the hip.

Those with the lesion at the upper lumbar levels have fairly good walking ability. The hip can be flexed but it is necessary to depend on gravity to extend it. With injuries below the fifth level, the voluntary muscles of the lumbar region are not affected.

Sacral Levels (S-1 to S-5 inclusive). The sacral level supplies nerves to the muscles of the pelvic floor, the bladder, the anal sphincter (muscle that controls the anus), and the external genitals (organs of sex). Those with the lesion in this area or at any level above it do not have bladder or bowel control.

Traumatic Spinal Cord Injuries

When one first encounters traumatic spinal cord injuries, the tendency is to assume that the major consequence of the injuries is lack of motor movement. Unfortunately, many other serious problems are brought about by destruction of the spinal cord. Most of these are not noticeable to the casual observer, but they are of important consequence and should be understood by the physical education teacher working with students who have spinal cord injuries.

A condition called hyperreflexia (exaggeration of reflexes) occurs when the spinal column is severed. It is more common in quadriplegics than in paraplegics. The symptoms vary, ranging from whitening of the area around the mouth and mild sweating to severe hypertension, excruciating headaches, profuse sweating, and feelings of impending doom. It is thought that hyperreflexia is caused by the indiscriminate release of a hormone into the body, the result of the sympathetic nervous system's no longer being under the control of the spinal cord. The release of the hormone is stimulated by a full bladder.

A condition called contractures (abnormal shortening of muscles) occurs frequently. It is the result of allowing joints to remain in one position for long periods of time. Contractures can be avoided by periodically moving and stretching the muscles around the joints.

Still another problem that may occur is heterotopic bone formation. This is a laying down of new bone in soft tissue around joints, especially at the hip joints. During the process of formation, the area may become inflamed and swollen. It is not known what causes the problem or how it can be prevented. Such formation is usually self-limiting; and if the condition interferes with joint movement, removal by surgery is possible.

Urinary infections are common among those who have spinal cord injuries. All persons with separated spinal cords lack bladder control and must use a catheter and bag, which are worn at all times, even while swimming. The most frequently used catheter is a tube inserted into the urethra (the canal conveying urine from the bladder to the exterior) that empties into the bag attached to the leg. The presence of the catheter and the difficulty of excreting the urine create conditions in which infection is very likely to occur. Also, since the bag may cause irritation to the skin, it must be moved from one leg to another at least once a day. Another type of catheter, used especially by males, is not inserted into the urethra; rather it covers the external genital organs. Drainage flows directly into the bag. The possibility of urinary infection is less with the use of this catheter.

For many paralyzed individuals, defecation is difficult; however proper scheduling of bowel movements and ingestion of sufficient bulk in the diet can usually alleviate the problem. If the problem is severe, a surgical procedure known as ileostomy or colostomy is necessary to create an opening in the small or large intestine through which the fecal matter can move into an attached bag. Like the urine bag, the ileostomy bag must be moved from leg to leg to avoid irritation. It is removed for swimming; a water-tight bandage is placed over the stoma (opening) to retain the fecal material and to prevent infection.

Because their condition requires them to remain seated or lying on the back for long periods of time, persons with spinal cord injuries commonly develop decubitus ulcers on the back and buttocks. The major cause is pressure of the body weight on these areas. Pads placed to relieve the pressure help to prevent the ulcers from developing.

Almost all persons who have spinal cord injuries become spastic; that is, they experience spasms of the muscles, to some degree. The condition may last for years or may gradually disappear over the course of time. Spasticity is a problem because it prevents any effective movement in those parts of the body over which partial control is possible.

Spasms can occur at any time and can be violent enough to awaken the person from sleep or even throw him from his wheelchair. The condition can be controlled to some extent by medication. In some cases, surgery is necessary. All muscles that are spastic must receive daily passive stretching to maintain full range of motion in all involved joints and to prevent contracture.

A weight control problem is also likely to plague those with spinal cord injuries. Low expenditure of energy due to lack of physical activity results in fat being stored rather than burned. Consequently, unless they are very careful to avoid foods high in calories and to remain as active as possible, paralyzed individuals tend to become obese relatively easily, exposing them to the serious problems commonly associated with obesity.

Spina Bifida

Spina bifida is a congenital anomaly (deviation from normal) resulting from nonfusion of the dorsal arch in one or more vertebrae. The lumbar vertebrae are the most often affected, but incomplete development can occur at any level of the spine.

The exact cause or causes of this neural tube development failure have not been identified. Both environmental and hereditary factors have been cited. The occurrence risk for spina bifida and related anomalies in siblings and offspring of spina bifida victims is slightly higher than the expected occurrence in the general population; also, the incidence is higher among the Welsh and Irish and lower in Mongoloid and Negroid groups. A relationship between the occurrence of the disease and maternal age, socioeconomic, seasonal, and other environmental factors has been noted in some surveys.[1] Environmental factors probably interact with multifactorial genetic determinants to produce spina bifida.

Classification. Classification and terminology regarding spina bifida will vary with authors. The classification and definitions offered by Freeman will be utilized in this discussion. Essentially there are two clinical forms: spina bifida occulta (no external manifestations or signs) and spina bifida manifesta (a demonstrable abnormality). Spina bifida cystica is a term often applied to the most common anomalies found under spina bifida manifesta.

Spina bifida occulta is a common abnormality in which incomplete formation of the vertebral column occurs without external manifestations. In the great majority of cases there is no disability associated with the bony maldevelopment, and treatment is not required. Occasionally, a clump of dark hair or a dimple may appear on the infant's back: in these cases the condition is referred to as spina bifida occulta with skin manifestations.

There are two types of spina bifida cystica; in both, a lesion and herniation (protrusion) are present on the back of the newborn infant at the location of the defective vertebra. The protrusion, or sac, varies in size and appearance. It may be covered by skin or a transparent membrane. In one type, meningocele, the sac contains the meninges (membranes that envelop the brain and spinal cord) and spinal fluid but does not involve the spinal cord. This type, which is rare, is generally not accompanied by motor or sensory deficiencies. The only necessary procedure is surgical operation to reduce the herniation, close the lesion, and prevent infection. Prognosis is excellent.

When the neural tissue of the spinal cord is attached to the sac, the condition is called meningomyelocele or myelomeningocele. This type is much more common than meningocele, thus subsequent discussion primarily concerns this type.

Myelomeningocele

Myelomeningocele is a very severe anomaly in which some degree of neurological impairment is inevitable. The extent of involvement depends on the location of the

---

[1]Lewis B. Holmes, Shirley G. Driscoll, and Leonard Alkins: "Etiologic Heterogeneity of Neural-Tube Defects." *New England Journal of Medicine*, Vol. 29, 1976, p. 365.

lesion and the degree of spinal cord damage. Sacral lesions may cause only muscular flaccidity (weakness or softness) in the lower legs and feet. The abdominal and leg muscles will be involved in patients with lesions located in the third to fifth vertebrae. Complete paraplegia will generally occur from lesions located in the first and second lumbar and thoracic vertebrae. Lesions located on the cervical region are often meningoceles and will generally show no paralysis, though some have involvement of the arm muscles. The loss of sensation invariably accompanies paralysis.

Muscle imbalance occurs and joint deformities may result when there is partial or unequal paralysis in the lower limbs. Most frequent is the unopposed action of the hip flexor and adductor muscles, causing hip dislocation. Knee joint deformities (recurvation, or backward bending) occur but are less common. Pes cavus and equinovarus (see Figure 9–3) are often present. Scoliosis, lordosis, kyphosis, or a combination of these may be present at birth or may appear later as a result of rapid growth accompanied by the absence of a complete vertebral column.

Innervation of the muscles concerned with micturition (urinating) comes from the sacral level of the spine; therefore, bladder paralysis is almost universal in myelomeningocele victims. This means incontinence (lack of control) may occur, with resultant urine build-up in the bladder that eventually reaches the kidneys and causes hydronephrosis (cystic enlargement of the kidney). Anal sphincter muscles may become paralyzed so that bowel incontinence also occurs.

Myelomeningocele lesions predispose the meninges to immediate and serious infections. Urinary tract and renal (kidney) infections due to urine build-up and stagnation constitute serious and continuous hazards. Repeated infections are most often the causes of fatalities in spina bifida.

The most common and most serious complication associated with myelomeningocele is hydrocephalus. It is present in over 80 per cent of myelomeningocele victims and is caused by the accumulation of excessive amounts of cerebrospinal fluid within the cranial cavity. When present with spina bifida, it is generally brought about by obstruction of the cerebrospinal canal. Unchecked, hydrocephalus may cause brain damage and subsequent mental retardation.

Myelomeningocele patients are, as are all those paralyzed, very susceptible to skin ulcerations (sores) because of the loss of sensation in the skin. Obesity may also become a problem, and the incidence of congenital heart disease seems to be higher in spina bifida children.

Treatment.   Prior to the 1950s, myelomeningocele infants were left untreated and the vast majority died within a few months. Today improved surgical techniques and drug treatments can lead to prolonged life in many patients. Unfortunately, however, paralysis and other serious problems present at birth are not reversible and treatment is not completely ameliorative. Extensive and continuous medical treatment of a child with poor prognosis places heavy emotional, social, and economic burdens on the family. Thus, even today, selective treatment is advocated.[2] Complete evaluation is made and a decision for treatment is reached based on economic, social, familial, and medical factors.

Because of the number of complications and the diversity of clinical manifestations, each patient must be treated individually and only general procedures are outlined. Most infants are taken to myelomeningocele clinics where a team of specialists can give intensive care. Immediate and vigorous treatment is necessary for

---

[2]John Lorber: "Selective Treatment of Myelomeningocele: to Treat or Not to Treat?" *Pediatrics,* Vol. 53, 1974, p. 307.

optimal success. Prompt surgical closure of the skin defect is performed to prevent infection. Hydrocephalus is treated by surgical drainage, with the insertion of a shunt to provide a permanent drainage system. A shunt consists of a plastic tube with a valve that runs from the ventricle in the brain to the heart or abdomen.

Correction of skeletal deformities, especially in the hip and spine, is extremely difficult. Orthopedic surgery may be required but must be performed in conjunction with other operations. Deformities of the foot and knee are more easily treated, and braces or casts may be used.

There are two important urological considerations. One is the prevention of infection and renal dysfunction and the other is the prevention of socially unacceptable incontinence. Controversy exists as to which is the best of the several treatment methods available. As yet, none seems to be satisfactory in all cases. Treatment varies with the individual, and depends on urinary tract involvement, the sex and age of the patient, and the preference of the family and physician.

Successful micturition may be brought about by manual pressure on the lower abdomen (Credé maneuver) for some patients or by a catheter from the bladder for others. For boys, a urinal bag with penile attachment may be used. When progressive upper urinary tract damage is evident, surgical diversion is recommended. The most common is the ileal loop. In this diversion the ureters are brought into a loop of the bowel, which is opened to the outside through the abdominal wall, thus eliminating the bladder as a collection bag. Antibiotic drugs are used to combat infections.

Bowel management through diet, medication, and the use of suppositories and enemas when necessary is relatively successful. Further treatment is generally not necessary.

Prognosis for the myelomeningocele infant is not encouraging in spite of advances in treatment. A recent report shows mortality rates to be as high as 50 per cent.[3] Those who survive may still face paralysis, continued threats of infection, and genitourinary problems. Continued advancement in treatment will result in more survivors, hopefully with improved changes of successful adjustment. Concurrent with improved treatment practices are new methods of screening and detection of spina bifida during the fetal period which provide the possibility of prevention through early identification and selective abortion. Genetic counseling is available for parents in danger of producing spina bifida offspring.

Suggested Activities

The kinds of motor activities in which a student who is restricted to a wheelchair can engage depend upon the specific nature of the handicap. For those with spinal injuries, including spina bifida, the activity choices depend on the severity and level of the lesion. (It will be recalled from the discussion of the nature of such injuries that complete destruction of the cord at a given level paralyzes all muscles below that level, and injury or partial severance creates partial paralysis below the level at which it occurs.) The physical educator will need to assess the movement potential of each student, utilizing his knowledge of the level of injury and his actual observation of the student. Careful attention in the observation of the ways in which the student manipulates his body to perform his daily routine will provide possible clues as to his potential for movement.

---

[3]Alexander S. Cass: "Urinary Tract Complications in Myelomeningocele Patients," *The Journal of Urology,* Vol. 115, 1976, p. 102.

Paraplegics, after recovery from the initial injury, can perform most physical education activities from the wheelchair. For younger children, catching and throwing games are easily devised; target games using bean bags are also readily developed. Bouncing balls off walls is another activity possible for the child in a chair. Even a game of modified handball is possible; the child bats the ball so that it returns to him or to a partner, who in turn bats it to the wall. A ball suspended from the ceiling with a heavy cord makes an excellent piece of equipment for teaching catching and throwing skills to the child confined to the wheelchair. In addition, the suspended ball can be used for various activities, such as throwing at a target drawn on a board or at empty milk cartons or plastic bottles standing on a table.

The child in a wheelchair can also take part in parachute play. There is no reason why he or she cannot engage in all of the common activities of parachute play, including exchanging places with another player while the parachute is in the air, by substituting locomotion of the chair for walking and running. The same substitution is possible in most basic skill games.

Older children can be offered many of the activities included in the regular program, with only such modifications as are necessitated by the need to remain in the chair. The way in which the skills are performed usually requires some adaptations; specific suggestions for these are made in the chapters on various activities. In some instances, the regulations and equipment must also be modified. The playing area for games and sports is usually reduced in size, playing equipment is lighter, and frequently the handles of rackets and mallets are extended to increase the range of the reach. In team games, the area that each player must cover is reduced, the assignment of duties is made on the basis of the players' abilities, or two people with different abilities share an assignment. For rhythm and dance activities, the size of the formations is increased to accommodate the wheelchair in the maneuvers.

For paraplegics and quadriplegics, special attention should be given to providing

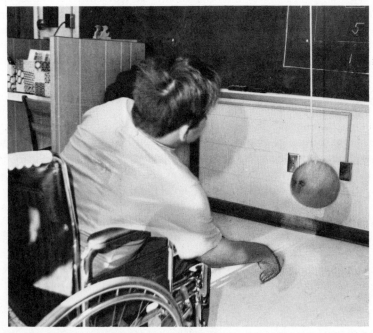

Figure 9–2. The suspended ball returns to the player in the wheelchair after each throw, eliminating problems of retrieval.

exercises to achieve and maintain physical fitness. Especially important for the paraplegic are activities that strengthen the arms and shoulder girdle, because optimal strength in these muscles will make propelling the wheelchair and transferring to and from it easier and less exhausting. Emphasis should also be given to activities that encourage a full range of motion in the spastic muscles to aid in the prevention of contracture.

Swimming is an especially good activity for total physical conditioning. For the paraplegic, weight training can be used to develop muscular strength. Quadriplegics can also engage in conditioning with weights if certain adaptations are made. In total quadriplegia, a head harness attached to wall pulleys is supplied. For partial quadriplegics with some arm movement, special weight resistance exercises are possible (see Chapter 26, Weight Training).

Several organizations* promote competition on local, national, and international levels for paraplegics and quadriplegics. Events include archery, bowling, basketball, table tennis, racing in wheelchairs, and the discus, shot, and javelin throws. Classification systems, based on the levels of injury, have been developed so that no player or team will have an unfair advantage over another. The system used in the United States is as follows:

I. All those with cervical injuries
A. who are without use of the triceps or have very weak triceps;
B. who have the use of the triceps.

II. Those with injury below the first through fifth thoracic level.

III. Those with injury below the fifth through tenth thoracic level.

IV. Those with injury below the tenth thoracic level through the second lumbar level.

V. Those with injury below the second lumbar level.

DISORDERS THAT LIMIT AMBULATION

Many orthopedic disorders affect ambulation, the ability to walk. This section includes a discussion of the disabilities that make walking difficult. However, these disabilities may, in severe cases or cases of multiple handicaps, confine the person to a wheelchair.

Tuberculosis of the bone, rickets, osteomyelitis, and poliomyelitis were once very common causes of orthopedic handicaps in children; this is no longer true, owing to the effectiveness of prevention and treatment methods. Congenital hip dislocation, talipes, certain types of osteochondrosis, epiphysiolysis, and leg amputation are still relatively prevalent disorders affecting ambulation.

Congenital Hip Dislocation

Congenital dislocation of the hip refers to a partially or completely displaced femoral head (in relation to the acetabulum of the hip) that is present at birth. Defective development of the acetabulum accompanies the condition and is termed dysplasia of the hip. Because the acetabulum is much shallower than normal, it allows easy displacement of the head of the femur. In time, with continued dislocation, the

---

*Addresses of groups that conduct national and international competition can be obtained from the American Alliance for Health, Physical Education and Recreation, Washington, D.C.

acetabulum changes in shape, becoming triangular or oval rather than flat, and may become filled with fibrous tissue.

Congenital hip dislocation occurs more commonly among girls than boys. It is more often unilateral than bilateral, and the left hip is affected more often than the right.

Prolonged malpositioning of the hip joint produces a chronic weakness of the leg and hip muscles. If the condition is left untreated, ambulation becomes difficult; however, if adequate medical treatment, consisting of bracing and surgery, is received early in life, the prognosis for normal locomotion is very good.

Talipes

Talipes (commonly called clubfoot) is a deformity in which the foot is twisted out of shape or position. In most cases, the condition is congenital, but it can be acquired as the result of certain neuromuscular diseases — spastic paralysis, for example.

The limitations and capabilities of anyone with talipes depend upon the extent of derangement of the foot or feet. With only moderate derangement, one can perform with minimum limitation. In more severe cases, walking may be very difficult, and standing for any length of time impossible.

Braces when used in the early years are effective in remedying talipes in which deformity is mild. Surgery is necessary when the foot is extremely malformed.

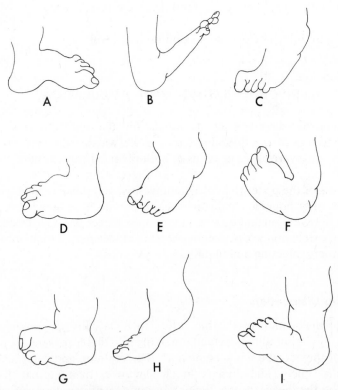

Figure 9-3. Talipes. *A*, Cavus — hollow foot. *B*, Calcaneus — heel lower than toes. *C*, Equinus — toes lower than heel. *D*, Valgus — toes and sole of foot turned out. *E*, Equinovarus — combination of talipes varus and talipes equinus. *F*, Calcaneovarus — combination of talipes calcaneus and talipes varus. *G*, Varus — toes and sole of foot turned in. *H*, Equinovalgus — combination of talipes valgus and talipes equinus. *I*, Calcaneovalgus — combination of talipes calcaneus and talipes valgus.

Osteochondrosis

Osteochondrosis, also known as osteochondrosis deformans juvenilis, is a disorder of the epiphysis (growth center) of the bone. The exact cause is not known. Some authorities suspect that trauma to the bone that interferes with the normal blood supply to the epiphysis may be the basic reason for development of the disorder. The bone area around the epiphysis becomes softened and undergoes partial necrosis (death), and is consequently liable to deformity if pressure is applied to the bone. In time, new bone replaces the dead tissue and the bone returns to normal. The bone retains its original shape unless it has come under stress or strain such as occurs in weight-bearing. The period of time from the beginning of the disease until the dead tissue is replaced varies according to the bone involved.

Two of the most common forms of osteochondrosis are Legg-Calvé-Perthes disease and Osgood-Schlatter disease. (Some authorities do not classify the latter as a type of osteochondrosis but as a form of osteochondritis, since there is some question about the way the epiphysis is involved.)

Legg-Calvé-Perthes Disease. Legg-Calvé-Perthes disease, usually referred to simply as Perthes disease, is a condition in which the capitular epiphysis (growth center of the head of the bone) of the femur is affected. The condition is most commonly found in boys between the ages of five and 10. Very seldom does it occur in girls. The cause of the disease has not been definitely established, but it has been postulated that the probable cause is a circulatory disturbance arising from strain on or trauma to the hip area.

In Perthes disease, the epiphysis of the femoral head disintegrates and is absorbed and replaced by other bone tissue. Collapse of the head of the femur may occur, causing it to flatten. In this case, when the new bone is formed, the shape of the normal epiphysis is not regained. Treatment consists of attempting to prevent the collapse of the femoral head by limiting the strain of bearing weight. This is achieved by utilizing ambulation and non-weight-bearing devices, such as the Newington ambulatory splint, during the later stages. If weight-bearing is prevented during the acute stages of the disease, function may return to normal. However, in many cases a slight limp persists and there is some restriction of hip motion.

The first signs of Perthes disease in a child are often a slight limp and complaints of pain along the inner side of the thigh or knee. As the disease progresses, the limp becomes more noticeable. Usually the limp is not severe and there is no extensive limitation of motion in the hip area. Examination by x-ray will verify the presence of the disease.

Osgood-Schlatter Disease. Osgood-Schlatter disease is manifested by the separation of the tibial tubercle (a prominence on top of the tibia to which the kneecap is attached) from the tibia. It frequently occurs in boys between the ages of 10 and 15, but is rare in girls. The occurrence is more common among boys who are very active, particularly those who ride bicycles.

The disease responds well to treatment. Usually, vigorous use of the leg is contraindicated for a period of six to nine months. In the early stages, the knee may be immobilized by a cast. There is a tendency for the disease to recur following trauma or irritation to the area.

Epiphysiolysis

Epiphysiolysis (slipped epiphysis) is a condition in which there is a separation of the epiphysis from the bone itself. As the separation occurs, the epiphysis slips to the side of the shaft of the bone. Slipping epiphysis may occur at any bone growth center.

However, by far the most common location is in the head of the femur and, unless otherwise designated, the term epiphysiolysis is assumed to refer to a slipped epiphysis in the femur.

When slipping occurs in areas other than the femur, the probable cause is acute trauma. Although some of the cases that involve the femur are caused by trauma, the vast majority are not. In these cases the cause of the slipping is not known, but a very large percentage of them also have Frölich's syndrome, a condition associated with endocrine dysfunction, marked by obesity and underdevelopment of the genitals.

Epiphysiolysis begins with a widening of the epiphyseal line, the space between the bone and epiphysis. At this time mild pain is experienced in the groin area. As the slip progresses, a change occurs in the relationship of the femur to the pelvis that causes the thigh to rotate outwardly; the hip becomes slightly flexed and the leg shortened. As this occurs, the child develops a slight limp. The limp becomes more prominent and the pain may increase as the epiphysis slips downward.

The course of the disorder from the active through the healing stage is one to three years. If not treated, the deformity becomes fixed. In a few cases, the limp may disappear, but usually it becomes progressively worse. The bones of the hip may atrophy, and later osteoarthritis may develop.

The treatment usually requires surgery. Pins are inserted across the epiphyseal line to help correct the displacement. After surgery, the child is usually allowed, if involvement is unilateral, to walk using crutches to keep the weight off the affected hip. In a case of bilateral involvement, the child is restricted to a wheelchair for a time.

Leg Amputation

Amputation is the loss of part or all of a limb by surgery or accident. A small but significant number of babies are born without limbs or with deformed limbs that require amputation. Other reasons for amputation are tumor, trauma, and disease. Amputation may be performed to arrest a malignant condition. Traumatic amputation may occur as the result of accident, or the damage may be so extensive as to require surgical removal of the limb. The diseases responsible for most amputations are those, like diabetes and arteriosclerosis, that cause circulatory problems. Such problems occur more often in the legs than in other parts of the body.

The leg amputee can be readily fitted with a prosthesis. The problems of ambulation will vary with the specific level of amputation. Those with below-knee amputations can readily learn the use of the prosthesis in locomotion. Many young amputees learn to use their prostheses so well that walking effectiveness is altered very little.

Those with amputations above the knee but below the hip may have difficulty in developing a proper walking gait, since the gait pattern is drastically changed because of the loss of the knee joint. Steps are shortened to prevent a movement that would tend to flex the artificial knee as it is swung forward. The individual must lean forward at the hips and when the foot strikes the ground, the hip must be extended to prevent bending of the knee. As the weight passes over the artificial leg, the thigh is flexed and the artificial limb flexes at the knee, owing to the weight of the lower part. The hip is then extended to bring the body weight over the artificial foot as it is planted on the ground.

A common fault in walking for the above-the-knee amputee is the abduction or rolling gait. As the weight is borne on the good leg, the opposite side of the body is raised, elevating the hip and causing the prosthesis to swing out from the body as well as forward.

Amputation of both lower extremities obviously adds serious problems. However, the basic technique in walking is approximately the same. The chief difference is the need to manipulate two artificial limbs rather than one.

Suggested Activities

A student with an orthopedic disorder affecting ambulation may or may not be using an assistive device to aid locomotion. If the assistive device is a cane or crutches, few problems arise to hinder participation in physical education. Many of the activities suitable for students in wheelchairs are also appropriate for these children. The chief difference is that those with canes or crutches need to learn to balance themselves in such a manner as to free one hand for use (see Fig. 9–4). The kind of crutches as well as the manner of use will vary from one situation to the next. In most cases it is easier to use the arms in activity if Löfstrand crutches are used. The balance can be maintained by one crutch while the other arm is free. The crutch does not fall to the ground because it is anchored to the forearm. Activities such as volleyball, throwing a ball, and striking with one hand can all be readily accomplished.

All children whose ambulation is impaired are at a disadvantage when speed of locomotion is required. Such activities should be adapted so that the distance the player has to travel is limited. For example, in badminton the regulations can be changed so that the objective becomes to hit the bird back to the disabled opponent rather than to place it where he cannot return it. Decreasing the speed needed to move from one place to another also allows more efficient participation by these students. Using a balloon for

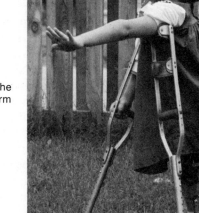

Figure 9–4. By appropriate propping of the crutch, balance can be achieved to free an arm for activity. (Courtesy March of Dimes.)

a ball in a game of toss is an example of a way in which the requirement for fast movement can be modified, since a balloon when thrown moves at a slower rate through the air than does a ball.

Activities for young children can be adapted from some of the basic skill games described in Chapter 20. For example, children who have difficulty moving can participate in games such as Circle Ball, Wonder Ball, or Target Toss from a sitting position in a chair. Children with some degree of functional leg movement can play Driving Pig to Market, Softball Bowling, Partner Toss, and similar games in which leg agility is not essential. These children can also participate in singing games like Here We Go Over the Mountain, Rig-a-Jig, and Way Down Yonder in the Paw-Paw Patch by substituting walking for skipping.

The student with a leg prosthesis has a problem in maintaining balance. The unilateral amputee should practice maintaining his balance on his prosthetic limb so as to be able to use his sound foot for other purposes in game situations; for example, kicking a football or trapping in soccer. Balance on stairs is easier to maintain if the sound limb leads when ascending and if the prosthesis leads when descending.

Certain devices can be used to help leg amputees to perform various skills. Poles of wood or metal to lean against can be erected in playing areas for players who require support while using their hands. Tables that permit the disabled player to stand by supporting himself within recessed areas are available but are better suited to indoor than outdoor play. Children who cannot stand but are able to sit unsupported in a straight chair can perform many activities while so seated.

In most cases, single leg amputees with prostheses can develop balance and other locomotion skills so that they are able to participate in all physical education activities. Many become active in athletic competition such as football or baseball, both as amateurs and as professionals. These athletes usually train in the same manner as others. Strengthening exercises are done while wearing the prosthesis, thus strengthening the muscles that control the device.

The prosthesis is not worn in the water, and a missing leg will cause a change in the center of gravity in swimming. Consequently, the swimmer experiences difficulty in maintaining a prone or back position because the body tends to turn in the water toward the heavier side (away from the missing limb). Proper stroking can eliminate the problem (see Chapter 25, Swimming).

The child with an orthopedic handicap enjoys movement in the water that is not possible out of the water. Even children with Legg-Calvé-Perthes disease, who are denied participation in so many activities, can enjoy the pleasures of swimming. While not encouraged to stand erect in the water, they can do so without much risk because the buoyancy of the water reduces the pressure of body weight on the head of the femur. For others, the water buoyancy makes control of the body easier by minimizing the effects of weak muscles and the lack of balance and stability which hinders or restricts movement out of the water. Assistive devices that must always be worn otherwise can usually be removed for swimming.

Many unilateral leg amputees have been very successful in skiing. Those with below-the-knee amputations can usually wear regular skis with their prosthesis. Skiers who have a single above-the-knee amputation employ a three track ski technique, in which one regular ski and two handheld outriggers are used. The outrigger consists of a Löfstrand crutch attached by a hinge to a short ski (shown in Fig. 9-5). The outrigger is constructed to allow only limited movement at the hinge. A moveable spike is inserted at the rear of the ski. The spike is lifted when skiing downhill, and can be lowered to sink into the snow when skiing over flat terrain or moving uphill.

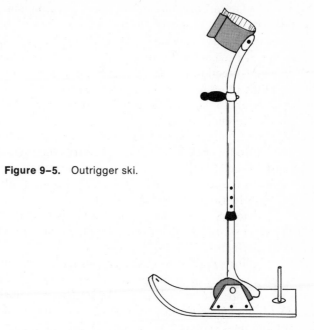

Figure 9–5. Outrigger ski.

DISORDERS THAT AFFECT OTHER BODY MOVEMENT

The first two sections of this chapter have been directed toward orthopedic handicaps that prevent or impede ambulation. This section will discuss other orthopedic disorders that affect body movement but do not necessarily impose limitations on locomotion to any great extent; included are wryneck, scoliosis, spondylitis, spondyloses, and arm amputation. Under certain conditions, some of these disabilities indirectly affect walking gait because the resultant deformity causes problems in body balance which, in turn, disturb the normal gait.

Wryneck

Wryneck is also called torticollis. In this disorder the neck is persistently held at a tilt, with the chin pointing in the opposite direction. This is caused by contracted cervical muscles. This disorder may be congenital or hysterical, or it may be caused by pressure on the nerves, by muscle spasm, or by inflammation of the glands in the neck. Treatment is symptomatic; that is, it differs depending on the symptoms.

Scoliosis

With a normal spinal column, when the body is viewed from the back, the right and left sides of the body are symmetrical, both shoulders and both hips are at the same level, and the spinal column is straight. Most individuals will show a very slight deviation in the spinal column. A slight deviation is usually not noticeable to casual observation and, if it does not become progressively worse, is of no consequence. However, a lateral curvature that is obvious must be considered an abnormal condition.

The lateral curvature of the spine is accompanied by a twisting of the vertebrae and takes its name, scoliosis, from the Greek word *skolios,* meaning twisting or bending. The lateral curve may be to the right or left or a combination of both. If it is to the right or left, it is called a C curve. An S curve is one in which the lower part curves in the opposite direction. In the latter condition, one of the curves is usually the primary curve while the other is a secondary curve developed to compensate for the first in restoring equilibrium to the trunk as a whole. An uncorrected C curve will eventually encourage the development of an S curve.

The C curve takes its name from the direction of convexity of the curve. A left C curve is to the individual's left and causes the right shoulder to be lowered and right hip to be raised (Fig. 9–6*A*). The reverse is true of the right C curve. A condition of convexity of the curve, present at birth, is usually a left C curve. A curve that develops after birth is usually to the right.

In most S curves the primary curve is to the left, in the upper portion of the spine. The right shoulder will be held lower than the left, while the left hip will be raised higher than the right (Fig. 9-6*B*).

Scoliosis may be functional or structural in nature. If the curve tends to disappear when a hanging or prone position is assumed, it is probably functional. The causes of scoliosis are varied. A shortened leg, disease, injury, congenital conditions, and faulty postural habits often due to hearing and vision problems are the most frequent causes. Seldom does scoliosis in its early stages cause pain or noticeable fatigue. However, in the later stages the muscular pull necessitated by the abnormal condition of the spine may cause back fatigue and frequent pains. It is, moreover, a definite cosmetic handicap.

Treatment consists of bracing and muscle re-education. Among the commonly used orthopedic devices are corsets, adjustable frames, and casts. However, one of the most effective devices is the Milwaukee brace (shown in Fig. 8–14).

Muscle re-education is vitally important in the treatment of scoliosis. It is carried out only after careful examination by a doctor. Actual exercises, other than asymmetrical (exercise of both sides, see Chapter 28), should be under the direct supervision of medical personnel. Basically, the exercises consist of stretching the muscles that have pulled the spinal column into the curve and strengthening those muscles that straighten the column, along with general physical fitness exercises.

Figure 9–6. Diagrammatic illustration of the slant of shoulders and hips in scoliosis. *A.* C curve to left. *B.* S curve to left.

A   B

Learning which muscles to contract and to relax to straighten the spine is effected through constant repetition of using the muscles that straighten the spine. Appropriate exercises also contribute to the prevention of scoliosis. (For special exercises that help to strengthen muscles that maintain efficient posture, refer to Chapter 28.)

Spondylitis and Spondylolisthesis

Spondylitis and spondylolisthesis are disorders of the spinal column. The latter is a deformity, usually inherited, in which a vertebra slips forward over another vertebra, usually the fourth or fifth vertebra. As a result, motion in bending forward is restricted and often painful. The pain may be aggravated by lordosis (swayback). Treatment consists of maintaining proper posture. In more advanced cases, surgery is usually performed to stabilize the joint.

Spondylitis is an inflammation of the vertebrae. It is almost always serious and is frequently associated with infectious diseases such as tuberculosis of the bone and brucellosis. The infection may destroy the affected vertebrae, resulting in permanent stiffening of the back. Drugs are used to control the inflammation. If the cause is an infectious disease, the disease must be treated. Surgery is often used to fuse the affected vertebrae.

Arm Amputation

Arm amputation may occur at various levels (refer to Chapter 8, Assistive Devices). Causes of upper limb amputations are the same as those discussed earlier in this chapter under the heading Leg Amputation. The arm amputee's prosthesis does not substitute as well as does the leg prosthesis for the leg amputee. It is almost impossible to develop a mechanical device that substitutes for the human hand and fingers in both function and appearance. Nevertheless, it is possible to achieve considerable dexterity with the utility arm and split hook in performing manual tasks, including racquet and paddle games in physical education.

The motor limitations of a person who has lost his arm(s) are obvious. However, a problem that is not readily apparent until the amputee attempts certain kinds of activities is that of balance. Maintaining an erect position both in everyday activities and in games and sports is difficult because of the body imbalance created by the missing segment(s). Attempts to maintain proper balance in the erect position often result in lateral spinal curvature. In the water, the body imbalance creates difficulty in maintaining effective positions for the various strokes.

SUGGESTED ACTIVITIES

Physical education activities for those with orthopedic disorders that affect other body movements must be selected to meet their special needs and limitations, with consideration for their interests and movement potential.

Students with wryneck and scoliosis are usually not greatly restricted in movement. Those with wryneck are able to perform all activities except those that place an undue stress upon neck muscles. Some, because of spasms in the neck muscles or limited movement in the neck, cannot participate in the forward roll, the headstand, or similar activities.

Scoliosis does not interfere with the normal performance of motor activities unless there is extreme deformity. Locomotion may be affected to some degree, as may movements of the body that require extreme flexibility, such as tumbling. Activities that place undue stress on the spinal column, such as football, may be contraindicated.

Weightlifting programs for those with scoliosis should be initiated only with the approval of the doctor. All exercise that affects the muscles on only one side of the spinal column should not be attempted without approval by the doctor. Most asymmetrical exercises can be participated in without adding further to the imbalance of the body. Chin-ups, passive hanging from a bar, and pushing or pulling equally with both hands are examples of suitable exercises.

Activities for those who have spondylitis should be suspended until the inflammation is brought under control. If there is no permanent damage to the spinal column, the student can resume normal activity. If damage does occur, the activities selected must not cause undue twisting or stress and strain on the spinal column.

The congenital arm amputee or student who has had a single arm since early life has usually made sufficient motor adaptation by the time he reaches school to require little assistance in making adaptations in motor skill performance. The student with a recent amputation, in contrast, will need to relearn some skills before he is able to participate in most activities. Also, he must adjust to his handicap. Many children after losing a limb become self-conscious and tend to withdraw from activity. The physical education teacher can be of great assistance to such a student by encouraging him to try the suggested modifications of the activities. When he finds that he can perform many skills that he thought he could never engage in again, he is very likely to begin to accept his loss and adjust more successfully.

Those who have lost a single arm, if it is not the dominant arm, can play most basic skill games and participate in more advanced physical education activities without significant modifications, except in the technique of catching. If the dominant hand is lost, the patient can learn to use his other hand. Performing the skill with this hand will at first seem extremely awkward, but practice will overcome this. The development of arm dexterity should be initiated with simple throwing activities such as throwing beanbags or darts at a target. Devices can be specially built by an orthotist to fit into the arm prosthesis to hold sports equipment such as gloves. Patients having difficulty in learning to catch with one hand may wish to have such a device made. How to catch a ball with a glove and one arm is described in Chapter 24, in the section on softball.

Most racquet games are not affected by single arm amputation. In the case of the double arm amputee with sufficient stump, a paddle or racquet can be attached to the stump to enable play of many racquet games (see Chapter 23). Swimming, as mentioned previously, is a good activity for single or double amputees and others with orthopedic disorders affecting body movement.

Of course, the student who has use of his feet can participate in activities that chiefly require foot action, such as soccer, goal kicking, and various running events.

It is possible for the double arm amputee to play volleyball by using parts of the body to play the ball; the head and knee are the most effective for this.

Soccer handball, a game developed at the University of Connecticut for those with limited use of their arms, can be played by participants who have upper limb involvement in both arms. It is played in a handball court with a soccer ball. The ball is kicked against the wall. The serve, to be good, must be kicked against the front wall and must return behind the service line. The ball is allowed to bounce once. It may hit any wall or combination of walls and remain in play. The ball may be played with any part of the body.

SELECTED READINGS

Adams, Ronald C., *et al.: Games, Sports, and Exercises for the Physically Handicapped,* ed. 2. Philadelphia, Lea and Febiger, 1975.

Bauer, Joseph J.: *Riding for Rehabilitation.* Toronto, Ontario, Canadian Stage and Arts Pub. Ltd., 1972.

Bleck, Eugene E., and Nagel, Donald A.: *Physically Handicapped Children: A Medical Atlas for Teachers.* New York, Grune and Stratton, 1975.

Cratty, Bryant J.: *Developmental Games for Physically Handicapped Children.* Palo Alto, Calif., Peek Publications, 1976.

Dibner, Susan, and Dibner, Andrew: *Integration or Segregation for the Physically Handicapped Child.* Springfield, Ill., Charles C Thomas, Pub., 1973.

Freeman, John M. (Editor): *Practical Management to Meningomyelocele.* Baltimore, University Park Press, 1974.

Krusen, Frank H.: *Handbook of Physical Medicine and Rehabilitation.* Philadelphia, W. B. Saunders Co., 1972.

Stryker, Ruth P.: *Rehabilitative Aspects of Acute and Chronic Nursing Care.* Philadelphia, W. B. Saunders Co., 1972.

Winters, Jim: *National Amputee Ski Technique.* Carmichael, Calif., San Juan School District, (n.d.).

Chapter 10

Cerebral Palsy

Based on what we know today about the causes and prevalence of cerebral palsy, it would be safe to say that this condition has probably afflicted man since the beginning of his existence. However, until relatively recently, cerebral palsy has received little significant attention from those in medicine, education, or the social services. The great strides of medical science over the past century have been largely responsible for stimulating attention to and concern about the lot of those afflicted with cerebral palsy.

W. J. Little, an English orthopedic surgeon, is credited with being the first physician to document and analyze the condition of cerebral palsy. His published reports on 63 children, describing the manifestations of their condition, appeared in the early 1860s, and the disorder became known as Little's disease. The term was changed to spastic paralysis in the 1930s and finally to cerebral palsy in the 1940s.

In spite of improved medical treatment, those with cerebral palsy face many difficulties. Lack of public understanding of the condition hinders opportunities for personal development. Because of the distortion of speech and facial expressions the disorder may cause, many misconceptions and stigmas attach to the victim, producing social isolation. Other physical manifestations of the various cerebral palsy conditions make movement difficult, giving rise to problems in performing even the skills of daily living.

Through the efforts of such groups as The United Cerebral Palsy Association and The National Foundation, the educational, occupational, and social opportunities for persons with cerebral palsy are continually improving. The extent to which individuals with cerebral palsy can avail themselves of these new opportunities will depend, in part, on the amount of independence they can attain in their motor behavior. It is in the achievement of this objective that the physical educator's expertise is needed.

THE NATURE AND CAUSES OF CEREBRAL PALSY

Cerebral palsy is a condition resulting from brain damage that is manifested by various types of neuromuscular disabilities. These disabilities are characterized by the dysfunction of voluntary motor control. The lesion causing the brain damage is found in the upper motor neurons of the cerebrum and brain stem, thus affecting the functions of the central nervous system.

To date, cerebral palsy is incurable. However, the condition is amenable to therapy and training, and the motor functions of those afflicted can be improved. In addition, cerebral palsy is nonprogressive; that is, the extent of the lesion will not increase, thus the condition will not worsen or result in death.

A major characteristic of this condition is that it interferes with the development of the central nervous system. The degree of this interference is related to the extent of the lesion and the age at which it occurs. Generally, the earlier the occurrence, the more extensive will be the interference. Thus, because approximately 90 per cent of all those afflicted contract cerebral palsy early, either at birth or during the prenatal period, many victims of cerebral palsy are multiply handicapped.

Cerebral palsy may be incurred before or during birth or at any time in later life. Approximately 30 per cent of all cerebral palsy cases have a prenatal cause, while 60 per cent have a natal and 10 per cent a postnatal cause. Major causes of cerebral palsy before birth are maternal infection such as rubella (German or three day measles), metabolic malfunctions, toxemia (toxic products in the blood), or anoxia (deficiency of oxygen). During the birth process cerebral palsy is usually caused by anoxia or trauma to the head. Postnatal occurrences are caused chiefly by severe head injuries or infections such as encephalitis (inflammation of the brain) or meningitis (inflammation of the covering of the brain and spinal cord).

Estimates of the incidence of cerebral palsy range from 1 to 3.5 cases per 1000 births. Cerebral palsy does not appear to be related in any way to socioeconomic structures; however, it is more prevalent among Caucasians, the firstborn, and males. Of those afflicted, about 10 per cent will be so severely handicapped that they will require custodial care for the rest of their lives. The remaining 90 per cent can be found in various educational settings, ranging from the public schools to hospital schools.

Types of Cerebral Palsy Conditions

There are five major types of conditions: (1) spasticity, (2) athetosis, (3) ataxia, (4) ridigity, and (5) tremor. Various combinations of these conditions can be found in many cases. The physical education instructor should know the manifestations of each condition so that he can better understand the effect each type has upon the movement capabilities of the afflicted.

Spasticity

Spasticity results from a lesion in the motor cortex. The motor cortex is the area in the central nervous system composed of motor neurons grouped together to form tracts. These tracts originate in the upper central portion of the cerebrum and proceed downward through the brain into the spinal column. It is in this area that voluntary motor actions originate.

Spasticity is the most prevalent type of cerebral palsy, occurring in between 50 to 60 per cent of all cases. It is characterized by a persistent and increased hypertensity of muscle tone. The continuous hypertensity results in contractures (abnormal shortening) of the afflicted muscles, usually leading to postural deviations.

Voluntary control of movements in the afflicted limbs is limited in the spastic cerebral palsy victim. Movement is usually restricted, jerky, and uncertain. Inconsistent control of movements is also present. On any given occasion, a movement may be very slow and deliberate or very explosive. In addition, the spastic individual tends to respond to the slightest stimulation, be it visual, verbal, or tactual, with a muscular reaction.

Another common characteristic of the spastic person is a hyperactive stretch reflex. The stretch reflex, which is monosynaptic (passing through a single nerve junction), serves as a protective agent for the skeletal muscles. When a muscle is stretched too quickly, the reflex causes the antagonist muscles to contract to prevent the stretching muscle from being injured by a violent overstretch. This reflex is elicited by muscle spindles located throughout the skeletal muscles. The proper stimulation of these spindles is controlled by various motor centers in the brain.

When the normal neurologic controls of a healthy muscle are greatly reduced, the stretch reflex is disturbed both in timing and in strength. Any sudden stretch will result in a strong contraction. A frequent result of the hyperactive stretch reflex is a sudden contraction followed by repeated jerks. This reaction is known as clonus.

Spasticity tends to affect the flexor muscle groups; thus, the maintenance of proper posture becomes very difficult. In addition, the spastic victim may have pathological reflex problems that also affect movement ability. If the lower limbs are spastic, they may be rotated inward and flexed at the hip joint, and the knees may be flexed and adducted, while the heels are lifted from the ground. These characteristics force a crossing of the legs through the midline during the walking gait, producing a scissors-type movement called the scissors gait. When the upper limbs are involved, the victim may have pronated forearms with flexion at the elbows, wrists, and fingers. Mental impairment is more frequently associated with spasticity than with any other type of cerebral palsy.

Athetosis

Athetosis is caused by a lesion in the area of the basal ganglia called the globus pallidus. This area is composed of large masses of neurons located deep within the center of the cerebrum. It is this part of the brain that controls purposeful movement.

Athetosis, the second most prevalent type, is seen in approximately 30 per cent of all individuals afflicted with cerebral palsy. The condition is characterized by constant involuntary movements that are uncontrollable, unpredictable, and purposeless. At times the movements are slow and rhythmical, while on other occasions they are jerky and fast. In addition, the athetoid individual is hampered by a problem known as overflow. This is manifested by extraneous movements that accompany voluntary motion. The combination of overflow and involuntary movement produces a situation in which the athetoid's body position is constantly in a stage of change.

The muscles of the head and upper limbs are commonly affected. Frequently seen movements of the upper limbs include constant flexion and extension of the fingers, wrists, and elbows, plus the drawing of the arms backward while palms are held downward. Lack of head control is a major problem. In many cases the head is continually drawn back and the face turned to one side. Accompanying this are facial contortions in which the mouth is frequently open; this produces drooling and makes eating and speaking very difficult. Other individuals may be affected by inward rotation of their feet.

There are several clinical types of athetosis, the most common being characterized by rotary movements. The amount of athetoid-type movements is reduced when the person is relaxed and calm and increased when the person is nervous and tense. Athetosis is not commonly characterized by mental retardation.

Ataxia

A third type of cerebral palsy, ataxia, is the result of a lesion in the cerebellum, the area located below the cerebrum and posterior to the brain stem. The cerebellum acts as the feedback mechanism of the brain and organizes the information to coordinate muscular functions.

The major manifestations of ataxia are a reduced sense of balance, which results in frequent falls, and a reduced sense of kinesthesis, which produces uncoordinated movements. Examples of ataxic problems are inconsistent foot placement in locomotion, overshooting when reaching for objects, and a general loss of manual dexterity. The person with ataxia usually exhibits a very awkward gait.

Although this is the third most common type of cerebral palsy, ataxia accounts for less than 10 per cent of the cases. The condition is usually acquired rather than congenital.

Rigidity

Rigidity is the most severe type of cerebral palsy, accounting for 2 to 5 per cent of cases. It is characterized by hypertensity of both agonist and antagonist muscles, making movement very difficult. Because of the relative absence of the stretch reflex, hyperextension of body parts is common.

The muscles of the affected limbs usually atrophy, and postural defects are present. Rigidity is a result of a diffused brain lesion that affects both the motor cortex and the basal ganglia. Severe mental retardation is usually present.

Tremor

Of the five major types of cerebral palsy, tremor occurs least frequently. It results in uncontrolled, involuntary, rhythmic motions. The motions may appear only upon attempting movement, or they may be present at all times. This condition can be caused by a lesion of the cerebellum or basal ganglia.

If the damage is to the cerebellum, the tremor is usually manifested in the arms. The tremor is accentuated during movement and reaches its peak as the body part approaches the end of the movement. If the basal ganglia is damaged, the symptoms are less severe and may disappear during sleep or relaxation. The cranial and digital muscles are the most affected.

Major Reflex Problems

Many of the movement problems of the victim of cerebral palsy are reflexive in nature. These movements depend solely upon the proper stimulus and cannot be controlled. For the purpose of developing a better understanding of the motor behavior of persons with cerebral palsy, a brief discussion of the commonly seen reflex behavior is in order.

All individuals are born with certain reflex patterns, which are the foundations upon which motor behavior is developed. These reflexes are present within the first few months of life and then are suppressed by higher brain centers as the infant develops control of his movements. In many persons afflicted with cerebral palsy, several reflex patterns persist for a longer than normal period and, in effect, retard motor development. Following is a description of the major pathological reflexes.

Grasp Reflex

This reflex is present at birth and usually disappears by the fourth month, when the infant has developed voluntary grasping and releasing movements of the hands. The reflex causes the hand to close in a grasping pattern and is elicited by pressure on the palms or by hyperextension of the wrists. The persistence of the grasp reflex retards the child's development of the releasing patterns of the hands.

Symmetrical Tonic Neck Reflex

This reflex is elicited by extension and flexion of the head and is characterized by two distinct patterns. When the head is flexed, the arms go into flexion and legs into extension. When the head is extended beyond the midline, the arms go into extension and the legs into flexion. The symmetrical tonic neck reflex is also present at birth and its primary function is to help the infant develop extension patterns. It normally is repressed between the fourth and sixth months. The persistence of this reflex greatly hampers the individual's movements when the head is not held in the midline. Since many persons afflicted with cerebral palsy have great difficulty in developing head control, this reflex pattern is a major problem.

Asymmetrical Tonic Neck Reflex

This reflex is present at birth and disappears between the fourth and sixth months. The apparent purpose of the reflex is to aid in the development of extension patterns. The asymmetrical tonic neck reflex is elicited by rotation of the head to either side. When the head is turned, the arm and leg on the side of the body to which the face is turned are extended and the limbs on the opposite side are flexed. The reflex is much stronger in the child with cerebral palsy than that usually seen in normal infants, and, unlike its characteristic in normal children, it does not disappear. Again, it can readily be seen how the lack of control of this reflex can be very detrimental to the cerebral palsy victim's motor development.

Tonic Labyrinthine Reflex

This reflex is present in normal infants until about the fourth month. Because it is elicited by trunk position, the reflex has two possible reactions, depending on whether the infant is in a supine or prone position.

When the infant is in a supine position, extensor tone dominates. Consequently, it is difficult for the child to flex at the shoulder, elbow, hip, and knee joints. When the infant is in a prone position, flexor tone dominates. Thus, it is difficult for the child to extend at those same joints. The persistence of the tonic labyrinthine reflex makes it very difficult for the child to obtain freedom of movement and locomotor patterns in the horizontal position.

Topographical Classification

Since cerebral palsy affects different parts of the body, a topographical classification is used to describe the portion of the body involved:

1. Monoplegia: only one limb is involved.
2. Paraplegia: only the legs are involved.
3. Diplegia: primarily, legs are involved; arms are slightly affected.
4. Hemiplegia: limbs on one side of the body are involved.
5. Triplegia: three limbs are involved; usually the legs and one arm.
6. Quadriplegia: all four limbs are involved.

Quadriplegia is more frequently found in athetotic cerebral palsy, while the other types occur more often in the spastic condition. Spastic hemiplegia is the most common involvement.

Treatment

Treatment to help alleviate the motor dysfunction of cerebral palsy is conducted primarily by physicians and physical therapists. It is upon the ability level developed through the treatment that the physical educator will attempt to build motor patterns to be utilized in play and leisure activities. Some understanding of the medical treatment and of the techniques utilized by the physical therapist in the muscular treatment of cerebral palsy is important to the physical educator because such knowledge enables him to plan a better program of supplementary skills.

Medical Treatment. Medical treatment for the motor dysfunction of cerebral palsy is conducted by orthopedic surgeons and, when applied, usually involves bracing or surgery, or both. Over the past quarter century, physicians have become more conservative in their treatment, and the use of these medical procedures has greatly decreased. However, some individuals are still given medical treatment, and physical educators should understand its purpose.

When bracing is used it is almost exclusively done in the lower limbs. There are two major objectives in the use of braces: (1) to keep spastic muscles stretched to prevent contractures and structural deviations, and (2) to give support to weak muscles. A person wearing a brace should probably keep the brace on during physical education (swimming not included); however, it is advisable to check with the physician.

The objectives in performing surgery fall into three categories: (1) as a cosmetic procedure to improve the appearance of the individual, (2) to reduce contractures and prevent structural deviations, and (3) to improve the performance of a movement pattern. The procedure will involve muscle transfers, tendon lengthenings, or neurectomies (severing of nerves). Surgery is usually performed on young children and is done only after a thorough evaluation suggests a reasonable amount of improvement can be expected.

Many surgical procedures involve improving the function of the lower limbs. There are three common procedures utilized in this area: (1) lengthening of the Achilles tendon to allow the heel to rest on the ground: (2) the Eggars procedure, which involves transferring the insertion of the hamstrings to the femur to reduce the flexion deformity of the knee and to help extend the hip; and (3) the Sharrod procedure, which involves transferring the insertion of the iliopsoas (muscle of the thigh) through a hole in the ilium (hip bone) to the greater trochanter of the femur, a point near the head of the upper leg, for the purpose of improving abduction at the hip joint. When instructing students who have had these operations, the physical educator should consult with the physician to develop a thorough understanding of the movement potentials and limitations of the body parts involved.

Physical Therapy. Without question, physical therapy is the primary source of movement education for the individual who suffers from cerebral palsy. There are many different theories and methods employed, but in a generic sense they can be divided into those methods developed to treat spasticity and those to treat athetosis. Today, many physical therapists do not adhere to a pure system, but use procedures from various methods in order to accomplish their objectives. Physical educators working with victims of cerebral palsy should become familiar with current procedures. For athetosis, it is recommended that the procedures of conductive education (by Peto, Hungary)[1] and sensory training (by Frederic Harris, U.S.A.)[2] be investigated; for spasticity, sensory stimulation (by Margaret Rood, U.S.A.)[3] and neurodevelopmental treatment (by Karl and Bertha Bobath, England)[4] should be reviewed.

Until the past decade, many physical therapists followed what has become known as the traditional approach in the treatment of spasticity. In this approach, spastic cerebral palsy was viewed as predominantly a muscular problem that manifested itself in the muscle imbalance of opposing groups. Treatment involved the following: (1) conscious relaxation of spastic muscles, (2) passive stretching of spastic muscles, (3) strength-building exercises for the antagonistic muscles, and (4) motor pattern training for afflicted segments. Now that the neurological basis of cerebral palsy has become known, new therapeutic treatment methods have been developed.

Of the new methods developed, the one originated by the Bobaths will be of the most interest to physical educators. Not only does their description of the method explain the neurological basis of the cerebral palsy condition but it also provides a very good explanation of motor development during infancy.

The Bobaths view cerebral palsy as a neurological problem and the spastic condition as one that produces a retardation of normal development with a retention of primitive motor behavior along with the manifestation of abnormal motor patterns. The Bobaths believe that the spastic cerebral palsy victim should be helped to attain proper postures in order to develop more efficient movement. They recommend that the afflicted individual start receiving treatment in the first few months of life and that this training be continued until adolescence. Their treatment involves reducing the effects of the pathological reflexes by manipulation and proper positioning, followed by teaching motor patterns for everyday life and self-help.

In concluding this section, the discussion of Harold Frost[5] concerning treatment for the spastic condition should be considered. Dr. Frost, a noted orthopedic surgeon, contends that no treatment has been developed that can totally alleviate the problems of spasticity. Thus, he believes that, although motor training for those afflicted with this condition is important, the primary goal in the treatment and education of the spastic cerebral palsied individuals should be the development of the total person. Physical education can definitely contribute to this goal by offering quality programs to help the spastic child to develop motor patterns that can be used in play and leisure activities.

NEEDS AND ADJUSTMENTS OF THE INDIVIDUAL WITH CEREBRAL PALSY

Besides having motor dysfunction, many victims of cerebral palsy have concomitant problems. These multiple disabilities greatly restrict the individual's attempts at satisfactory social adjustment. Thus, a comprehensive training program from an early preschool period through adulthood is a vital need of the cerebral palsy victim.

---

[1]Ester Cotton and Margaret Parnwell: "From Hungary: The Peto Method." *Special Education,* 1967, Dec., pp. 7–11.

[2]Frederic Harris: "Inapproprioception: A Possible Sensory Basis for Athetoid Movements." *Physical Therapy,* 1971, Vol. 51, No. 7, pp. 761--770.

[3]Margaret Rood: "Neurophysiological Reactions as a Basis for Physical Therapy." *Physical Therapy Review,* 1954, Vol. 34, No. 9, pp. 444–449.

[4]Karl Bobath: "The Neuropathology of Cerebral Palsy and Its Importance in Treatment and Diagnosis." *Cerebral Palsy Bulletin,* 1959, Vol. 1, No. 8, pp. 13–33.

[5]Frost, Harold. *Orthopedic Surgery in Spasticity.* Springfield, Illinois: Charles C Thomas, 1972.

The incidence of mental retardation in the cerebral palsy population has been estimated to be as high as 60 per cent. The highest incidence of retardation appears in the spasticity and rigidity conditions. Because of the problems in accurately measuring the I.Q. of these individuals, estimates of the incidence of mental retardation are not totally reliable; however, the academic performance of many is below the level of their peers.

Perceptual deficits are another problem of the victim of cerebral palsy. Some of these deficits are a result of delayed development due to an inadequate foundation of motor functions, while others are probably neurological. Many of their perceptual problems are in the visual or haptic (tactile) modalities.

A majority of cerebral palsied individuals have sensory deficiencies, with a major portion of these being visual problems. Convulsions and learning disabilities also occur. In addition, nearly all of these individuals have speech defects caused by their inability to control the muscles of speech. Their problems in communicating are a great barrier to social and academic adjustments. The need for speech therapy by this population must not be minimized.

In spite of the movement and learning problems the cerebral palsied individuals must cope with, probably their greatest adjustment needs have to do with their emotional well-being. Because of their motor inadequacies, communication problems, and, in many cases, unpleasant appearance, they often experience social rejection or excessive sympathy. The acceptance that all persons seek is often denied them. Many must also deal with the rejection and shame of their parents and relatives. Without a proper atmosphere of acceptance, these individuals have a very difficult time developing a good self-concept and consequent feelings of adequacy and contentment. Instead, tremendous frustration, which may be coupled with excessive fears, is a common occurrence.

A number of professionals in the field believe that some of the emotional problems observed in the cerebral palsied are a result of specific brain damage. This opinion is substantiated to some extent by the observance of several pronounced behaviors in certain types of cerebral palsy. For example, those with spastic cerebral palsy often exhibit withdrawal traits and are not usually overresponsive to affection. However, regardless of the influence of structural damages on their emotional stability, it can reasonably be assumed that most of their emotional problems are environmentally related.

Planning the Program

The program for cerebral palsied students should be governed by two primary objectives: (1) to enhance physical development and muscular control, and (2) to assist psychosocial development. The primary needs of each student will determine where the emphasis should be placed. If the student is receiving adequate physical therapy and displaying satisfactory motor improvement, the greater contribution can be made in the psychosocial realm. Development in this area can be accomplished not only by encouraging social interaction but also by promoting acquisition of sport and leisure activity skills that can add enjoyment to life and provide an avenue for further social endeavors. If the individual's greater need is to develop basic motor skills, then the program should emphasize the first objective. Through consultation with the physical therapist or physician, or both, the teacher can discover which skills need additional work. Activities can then be planned within the program that require the student to practice these skills. For example, if there is a need to develop some skill in manual

Figure 10-1. This adaptation of running the obstacle course has the objective of walking with crutches between closely placed furniture without touching, to develop skill in moving through small spaces.

manipulation, activities such as placing objects in a container, rearranging blocks, and striking with rackets can be offered.

A thorough evaluation of the facilities and equipment must also be made as part of the comprehensive planning of the program. Ramps to help the student reach elevated teaching stations should be provided. Lockers should be assigned that will not require the student to maneuver a narrow aisle. Certain areas of the shower facilities must be equipped with benches and hand supports under the shower heads to make safe showering available. In addition, the equipment should be investigated to determine its appropriateness. When possible, special equipment should be purchased. Many times, special equipment can be constructed by the teacher or other school personnel. This is an excellent alternative when budgets are restricted. As with all other programs, the scope of the program that can be offered is, to a large extent, dependent upon the facilities and equipment available. Thus, adequate attention to these factors will greatly enhance the program.

Two additional items that must be considered in planning the program are scheduling and placement. Whenever possible, these students should be integrated with their peers, even when they are frequently unable to participate in activities with their classmates. If a student is not able to benefit from an integrated situation, because of limitations in staff, facility, or skill, he or she should be placed in a special class.

Special classes should be scheduled in facilities that can be utilized adequately by the students. Consideration should also be given to the extra time needed by the students to prepare for class, to change afterward, and to move to and from the facilities.

It is important to ensure that the program is challenging and offers a genuine learning experience. Individuals afflicted with cerebral palsy can learn, and it is the responsibility of the physical education teacher to recognize their motor potentials and to develop these abilities through physical education.

Suggested Activities

Because programming for cerebral palsied students is individualistic, the activities selected should be determined by the type and severity of the disability, the amount of muscular training that has occurred, and the interest level of the student. Thus, the physical educator looks at what the student *can* do and builds the program from there. Facts that are important to learn are as follows:

1. What body parts are affected and what is the type of affliction?
2. What surgery has been performed and what are the effects of these operations?
3. What reflex problems are present?
4. What is the person's level of emotional stability?
5. What medication is being used and what are the effects of drugs?

In addition, the physical educator should attempt to learn if there are any perceptual-motor deficits or any mental deficiencies. The physical educator should also know the verbal ability of the student and the kind of physical education and recreation experiences he has had.

The type of cerebral palsy will determine the adaptations that are needed. When working with spastic individuals, activities requiring a lot of agility and fast moving actions should be avoided. The environment should be structured to minimize external stimuli (loud noises and sudden movements will cause the person to become tense). If the student has reflex problems, movements that elicit the unwanted responses must be avoided. When instructing those with athetosis, the emphasis must be on creating a relaxed atmosphere; they need to remain calm, since body tension and excitement tend to increase the athetoid symptoms. To reduce tension, frequent rest periods should be planned.

An important aid in the performance of motor skills is apparatus that can be utilized to create distal stabilization, which is the stabilization of an opposite limb during the performance of a movement. This procedure tends to reduce involuntary movements. For those with ataxia, adjustments must be made for severe balance and coordination problems; for example, (1) conducting balance activities on the floor instead of on a balance beam, (2) using very soft balls to reduce the possibility of injuries in catching, and (3) creating wider space between objects in the agility run.

Carryover leisure activities are an important aspect of the program. Community activities that the individual can engage in should be taught. Examples of activities that have been successfully taught to these students include bowling, table tennis, horseshoes, and swimming.

Swimming is an excellent activity. The buoyancy of the water allows the victim of cerebral palsy to have a freedom of movement that he cannot have out of water. The water also provides a superb environment for the student to practice walking. Special techniques for the teaching of swimming skills to cerebral palsied students are presented in Chapter 25.

It is also recommended by some authorities that muscular relaxation training be given to these students. There is considerable disagreement, however, as to the effects of such training. More research is still needed to determine its appropriate use. Chapter 29 explains the techniques of such training.

SELECTED READINGS

Benda, Clemens: *Developmental Disorders of Mentation and Cerebral Palsies.* New Yrok, Grune & Stratton, Inc., 1970.

Crabbe, W.: *Orthopaedics for the Undergraduate.* Philadelphia, Lea and Febiger, 1969.

Cruickshank, William: *Cerebral Palsy: A Developmental Disability,* ed. 3. Syracuse, Syracuse University Press, 1976.

Edgington, Dorothy: *The Physically Handicapped Child in Your Classroom.* Springfield, Ill., Charles C Thomas, Pub., 1976.

Finnie, Nancy: *Handling the Young Cerebral Plasied Child at Home.* Hew York, E. P. Dutton and Company, Inc., 1975.

Frost, Harold: *Orthopedic Surgery in Spasticity.* Springfield, Ill., Charles C Thomas, Pub., 1972.

Levy, Janine: *The Baby Exercise Book.* New York, Pantheon Books—Division of Random House, 1973.

Chapter 11

Disorders Resulting In Muscular Weakness

There are several serious diseases that, although they differ in many respects, share the common effect of bringing about abnormal weakness in the muscles. The four most common of these diseases affecting young people are muscular dystrophy, multiple sclerosis, myasthenia gravis, and polymyositis. They occur most frequently during the late teens and early adult years; however, children of younger ages do get the diseases. One type of muscular dystrophy, unfortunately the most common type, affects only young children, often in their second or third year of life.

In the usual course of the disease the affected youngster becomes progressively weaker and more restricted in his movements. Although many victims eventually become severely incapacitated, most will be able to attend school for some years. Youngsters with milder cases are generally able to be in regular attendance throughout their years of education. During the time they are in school, these youngsters are usually able to participate in some physical education activities. Hence, it is essential for the physical education teacher to understand the disorders and the special needs of the young people who are afflicted.

MUSCULAR DYSTROPHY

The term muscular dystrophy applies to a group of related muscle diseases that are progressively incapacitating because the muscles gradually weaken and eventually atrophy. Muscular dystrophy, or the propensity for the disease, is inherited. Females who may not themselves have the disease transmit the sex-linked trait to their children, particularly to their sons. Consequently, the incidence of muscular dystrophy is much higher among males than among females. It is estimated that there are more than a quarter of a million cases of the disease in this country.

The exact cause of the disease has not been fully determined. It is known that muscle protein is lost and is gradually replaced by fat and connective tissue, causing increasing degeneration of the voluntary muscle system.

Childhood Muscular Dystrophy

The most prevalent type of muscular dystrophy, accounting for about 65 per cent of all dystrophies, affects young children. It is known as Duchenne, or progressive,

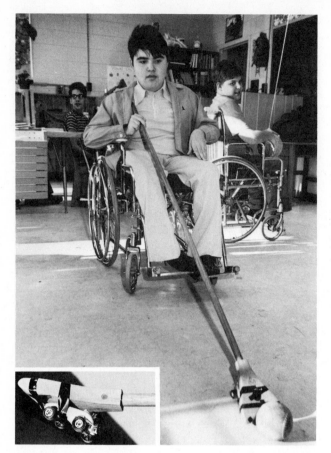

Figure 11–1. The child with muscular dystrophy is characteristically weak and needs modifications to be made in activities, such as this attachment of wheels to the cue and the substitution of a tennis ball for the puck to play a game of shuffleboard.

muscular dystrophy. The disease is also called pseudohypertrophic muscular dystrophy, because the hypertrophy of the muscles, particularly of those in the calves of the legs, produced by replacement of lost protein with fat, creates the deceptive appearance of a healthy well developed musculature.

The symptoms make their appearance in the second or third year of life. Prominent among the early signs are difficulty in running, climbing stairs, and rising from a sitting position. The walking gait resembles a side-to-side waddle. Falls are frequent, and regaining the feet is performed in abnormal fashion by placing the hands and feet on the floor to raise the hips to a forward lean position and then elevating the trunk by pushing the hands against the legs along the length of the legs. This method of rising is called Gowers' sign.

As the disease progresses, contractures form in the muscles of the legs and hips and the early symptoms become more pronounced. Within a few years, the dystrophic child becomes so weakened that he must rely on a wheelchair for locomotion. Later, he will be confined to bed for much of the time. Death frequently occurs before the age of 20, and results from a secondary cause, usually respiratory or cardiac in nature.

Other Types

Another type of muscular dystrophy occurs most fequently during the teens and twenties, although it sometimes appears in younger children. Unlike progressive muscular dystrophy, this type affects girls as frequently as boys. The disease can take one or both of two forms that closely resemble one another.

One form is called limb-girdle, deriving its name from the area of the body in which the symptoms first manifest themselves. Difficulty is experienced in the use of the thigh and hip muscles and is caused by weakness in the musculature of the pelvic girdle. The shoulder girdle muscles are involved less frequently. The rate of deterioration varies, but severe crippling occurs in most cases.

Another form of the disease, known as facioscapulohumeral, afflicts the muscles of the face, shoulder, and upper arm. Its first symptom is a very slight weakening of the facial muscles followed by subsequent involvement of the muscles of the shoulder and upper arm. The degree of weakening varies among individuals; in some it is very slight. The disease progresses slowly over many years and may be arrested at any time.

Characteristic of the disease in its more advanced stages are sagging cheeks, pouting lips, inability to close the eyes completely, and a lack of facial expression caused by weakness of the muscles of the face. Lack of strength and awkwardness in movements of the shoulder and arm muscles are other symptoms. Less frequently affected are the muscles of the thigh and hip: symptomatic of the presence of the disease, when these areas are involved, are frequent falling and a waddling gait.

Other types of muscular dystrophy have been identified, but they occur so rarely that discussion of them here is not warranted. Sometimes a patient may have two or more forms of the disease.

To date, no treatment has been discovered to halt the progress of the disease. However, some hope is held out as the result of recent experiments with medications that help to build up protein in the muscle cells or that prevent the loss of excessive protein from the cells. Secondary infections, which so often cause complications and lead to death, can be largely controlled by the use of antibiotics. Physical therapy that includes stretching exercises and deep breathing exercises can, in some cases, retard muscle shortening. Braces worn to compensate for muscle weakness sometimes help to delay confinement to a wheelchair.

MULTIPLE SCLEROSIS

Multiple sclerosis is one of our country's most common chronic diseases of the nervous system, affecting about 500,000 people. The disease attacks females more frequently than males. The peak period of onset is approximately the age of 30, but youngsters of high school age do contract the disease; young children are very seldom affected. Multiple sclerosis does not cause early death. Those who are afflicted may live up to 75 per cent of the normal life span; deaths of younger people are almost always due to the complications of secondary infections to the lungs or bladder.

During the course of the disease, hardened patches of varying size appear in random areas of the brain and spinal cord, interfering with the function of the nerves in these areas. The patches are actually scar tissue resulting from the disintegration of the thick white covering of the nerve fibers. The covering is called myelin and the process of its disintegration is known as demyelination.

The effects of multiple sclerosis vary according to the portion of the nervous system in which the patches appear; consequently, symptoms differ considerably among victims of the disease. Often, however, an early indication of the presence of the disease is a problem with vision, such as double vision or reduction of the field of vision. Unusual weakness, fatigue, and numbness are other common early symptoms. Slurred or monotonous speech, stiff or staggering gait, and tremors or shaking of the limbs may occur as the disease progresses. Eventually there may be paralysis.

The frequency of the attacks varies in different individuals. During the course of the disease, especially in the early stages, attacks are followed by periods of remission during which the symptoms largely disappear. These are followed by periods of exacerbation in which the symptoms return. As the scar tissue proliferates on the central nervous system, the symptoms become more prominent and the periods of remission occur less frequently and finally cease to occur. However, in some cases, even after several attacks, the symptoms permanently disappear.

The cause of the demyelination from which the symptoms of multiple sclerosis rise is not known. Much of the search for the cause has centered on environmental factors, since the disease occurs most frequently in the temperate zones and very seldom in the tropics. Investigation is also being made of such causative possibilities as malfunctioning of the biochemistry of the myelin virus, and the presence of an autoimmune disease in which antibodies attack the normal tissue of the myelin.

The treatment of multiple sclerosis includes the use of drugs. However, their benefits have been found to be limited to the first few weeks of treatment. After that, the symptoms return as before.

Adherence to good health practices is important in the treatment, since multiple sclerosis appears to become worse after any illness. Emotional distress also seems to have an adverse affect on the disease, so promotion of good mental health is important. Physical therapy for those afflicted usually includes massage and exercise to retard weakening of the affected muscles to the extent possible.

MYASTHENIA GRAVIS

Myasthenia gravis is a relatively common chronic disease characterized by progressive muscular weakness. Onset can occur at any age, although young children incur the disease less frequently than do other age groups. The incidence is highest in females between the ages of 14 and 35 and in males between the ages of 40 and 70. Obviously, then, the physical education teacher may expect to encounter some students, particularly high school age girls, who are afflicted with myasthenia gravis.

Specific symptoms vary depending upon the muscles involved; all of the voluntary muscles can be affected. The onset of the disease seldom occurs all at once; rather, the symptoms are more likely to appear over a long period of time and go unrecognized initially. Muscular contraction becomes gradually less forceful; but for a time, rest after muscular exertion restores the former strength of the muscles. The muscles do not become painful as they do in physiological fatigue.

The disease may begin with a characteristic weakness in a single set of muscles or in several sets. Most commonly, the muscles that are initially affected and most severely involved are those of the face and throat, causing difficulty in chewing and swallowing. Other symptoms produced by the weakness of muscles in this area are a drooping of the upper eyelids and a nasal quality of the voice. As the disease progresses, the back, abdomen, arms, and legs may be affected. In advanced cases, the muscles used in respiration may be involved, producing complications that are often fatal.

The cause of myasthenia gravis is not known. It has been postulated that a block occurs, owing to formation of an abnormal chemical compound, that hinders the nerve impulses at the end-plates (terminal ends of a nerve that contract a muscle fiber).

Recent advances in the treatment of myasthenia gravis have effected a reduction in the death rate and in the severity of the disease. Among the improvements in treatment have been such emergency and support measures as the utilization of tracheotomy to open the windpipe, the use of respirators to assist breathing, and the administration of antibiotics to prevent infection. The symptoms can be fairly well controlled with drug treatment. According to the National Institute of Neurological Diseases and Stroke, myasthenia gravis is one of the most successfully managed neuromuscular disorders.

It has been noted that the disease may worsen suddenly when there is emotional stress or when a cold or other infection is present. Consequently, treatment is also directed toward maintaining good physical and mental health.

POLYMYOSITIS

There are several types of polymyositis. All are characterized by inflammation of the voluntary muscles, resulting in diminished muscular strength and reflex action. Both children and adults may be afflicted with the disease; the incidence is higher among females than among males.

The disease may be acute or chronic. In its acute form, the symptoms are high fever and weakness and severe pain in the muscles. The attacks frequently result in death. Symptomatic of the chronic form is a progressive weakening of the muscles. All of the voluntary muscles may be affected, but most frequently the involvement is in the muscles of the legs and trunk. Disturbance of the walking gait and of other movements utilizing the muscles of the legs and trunk can be observed. Muscle contractures occur in both the acute and chronic forms, but are more common in the latter.

Polymyositis may also involve other systems. The most frequently involved of these is the skin; the disorder in this case is called dermatomyositis. It is characterized not only by muscular weakness but also by scaling, atrophy, and a pinkish discoloration of the skin.

Some types of polymyositis are remittent. Periods when the health of the affected person improves are followed by periods of attack. Between the attacks the weakened and contracted muscles do not regain their functional efficiency.

The exact cause of the disease is unknown. Based on various data on the disease, medical investigators have hypothesized that it is allergic in nature, which refers to the body's characteristic response to invasion by a foreign substance.

Treatment involves the administration of drugs; however, their effect on the course of the disease is difficult to assess, since spontaneous remission does occur. General systemic measures, such as a well-balanced diet high in protein and prompt attention to infectious and respiratory ailments, are important in the treatment. Braces may be used to support the body and assist in movement.

NEEDS AND ADJUSTMENTS OF THOSE WITH DISORDERS CAUSING MUSCULAR WEAKNESS

Maintenance of the best possible physical and mental health is, as we have seen, important in the treatment of those afflicted with any of the diseases characterized by muscular weakness. Since exercise plays an essential role in physical conditioning, a logical assumption would be that participation in selected physical education activities is highly recommended by physicians who specialize in the treatment of these disorders. This is not entirely the case. Various kinds of exercise are prescribed for those who have muscular dystrophy, and these can be supplemented with appropriate physical education activities. For patients with multiple sclerosis, complete bed rest is recommended by some doctors; but other doctors, actually a large majority, believe that inactivity leads to secondary complications and so they advocate exercises that help to retard incapacitation and loss of fitness. These exercises can be supplemented in the physical education program. With respect to myasthenia gravis and polymyositis, the value of special exercises in the treatment program has not been given significant attention by the medical profession. Consequently, there is little information to guide the physical education teacher who has students with these disorders. More frequent communication with the doctors of these students will be necessary to develop a suitable program to serve their special needs.

In helping students with muscular weakness to maintain a level of physical fitness consistent with their capacity to engage in physical activity, the physical eduction teacher is likely to encounter apathy or resistance. Students who are experiencing considerable muscular weakness and pain usually prefer not to exert the effort required to do even mildly taxing motor activities. They see little value in working to delay the general deterioration and incapacitation that they know, or suspect, is their inevitable fate.

Motivating such students requires planning and patience. Discovering and utilizing their interests to make participation appealing will help to provide the basis for acceptance of the program. Praise and encouragement are essential in motivating effort; it may be necessary to offer extrinsic rewards as well. Goals must be short term so that results can be seen as immediate benefits.

The debility that is characteristic of the diseases discussed in this chapter is distressing to those affected. Inability to perform physical tasks with the same vigor and control as previously is frustrating and bewildering. Disturbances in walking gait and of the facial features are particularly distressing because they create problems of social acceptance and often give rise to ridicule.

When a youngster becomes so incapacitated that he must use a wheelchair to move about, the difficulty in adjusting is increased. While others in his peer group are expanding their activities and experiences, his world is becoming more restricted. He is denied the adventure and excitement that accompany each new stage of growth and development in the years of childhood and young adulthood. Awareness of his present state and of the unlikelihood of future improvement produces feelings of depression and anxiety.

Perhaps the greatest contribution the physical education teacher can make to these children is to serve their need to feel part of the group. In physical education more than in any other school situation, the children can be brought into activities from which they would otherwise be excluded. Since the activities in which they are able to participate are limited, the teacher must exercise great ingenuity in modifying activities to allow some types of participation with the group. When muscular weakness is extreme, it may be necessary that the student's contribution be no more than beating a drum for a rhythmic activity or coaching the base runners in a softball game. Whatever the level of participation, the youngster must feel he is part of the group, that he is making a worthy contribution.

Program Planning for Those With Muscular Disorders

Probably no two students, even with the same disorder, will have the same kind and degree of limitations, so the activity program will need to be planned on an individual basis. The selection of appropriate motor activities requires careful preliminary analysis of the movement potential of the student. Consultation with the student's physician is recommended to ensure that the activities and planned modifications will have no adverse effects and that they will complement the student's physical therapy program.

In general, the activities selected should provide moderate exercise to the unaffected muscles. Such exercise is needed not only to maintain physical efficiency but also to consume calories to assist in weight control, almost always a difficult task for the sedentary person. The use of specific exercises to increase the strength of the affected muscles appears to be of unproved value and may even accelerate the degeneration.

Care should be taken that no strain is exerted to perform the exercise. Generally, no resistance other than gravity should be used to involve the affected muscles. At the first sign of strain or fatigue, the exercise should be terminated. All types of motor activity are contraindicated when the student is tired.

If the student is mature enough to understand the principles of movement, the teacher should describe these to him. Preferably such discussion would occur in connection with the learning of movements to which the principles apply. The purpose is to give the student enough information and insight into movement to enable him to make the necessary adjustments to perform the skills of other activities on his own; or if he is going to become progressively weaker, so that he can accommodate his skill technique to his diminishing capability.

Suggested Actvities

Activities for students who are only mildy affected or whose conditions are not yet advanced may be chosen from among the less vigorous of the regular physical education sports, games, and dances. Possibilities are the basic skill games, shuffleboard, table tennis, archery, softball, and volleyball. Modification of these and other activities will be required for students who suffer greater deterioration of muscular strength and reflex action. The kind of adaptation made is largely determined by the degree of mobility of the participant.

The activities described below are generally suitable for those who are very restricted in locomotion or who are confined to wheelchairs. They may be used in the form in which they are presented or modified to meet special needs. Similar games or activities can be readily developed by the teacher after his initial experience with students who have progressive muscular weakness.

1. The children form a circle to pass the ball to one another. The ball may be passed in various ways — one hand, two hands, overhand, or underhand. Balls of different sizes may be used, and more than one ball may be used at one time. Another possibility is the assignment of numbers at random around the circle; the ball is then passed in numerical order. Reassignment of numbers should be made frequently to keep interest high.

2. A ball suspended from the ceiling affords several activity possibilities. It may be batted with a plastic bat, thrown to a target on the wall, or used for a game of catch by two or more children.

3. An inflated balloon of heavy rubber may be used for catching and throwing by students who are too weak to handle the heavier weight of a regular ball.

4. The attachment of a long cord to a bean bag enables its easy retrieval by students with restricted movement. The bean bag can be used for throwing at a target or for throwing between students. In both situations, the thrower retains a hold on the cord after the bean bag leaves his hand.

5. A bowling game is simulated with plastic bowling pins and a heavy ball. Milk cartons that have been filled with beans to give them weight may be substituted for the pins. The ball is rolled toward the pins to knock down as many as possible. Score may be kept if desired. If the player is unable to roll the ball, a cue may be used. A player in a wheelchair may need to use a special ramp on which the ball is placed and guided toward the pins.

6. A game may be made of bouncing a ball beside the wheelchair for the student who is confined to the chair. A basketball or lighter rubber ball is used. The student explores different heights of the ball in the dribble, various ways of striking the ball with the hand, and so forth. He may also dribble the ball while moving the wheelchair.

7. Batting activity is possible from a sitting or standing position with the use of a batting tee and a ball attached with a string to the tee. The ball is retrieved by pulling on the string.

8. With a special paddle that hangs from a frame (Fig. 11-2), the student can engage in a game of hitting a table tennis ball over the net, to the left or right court. A modified game of table tennis is also possible.

9. Exploration of motor movements in unaffected parts of the body provides suitable activity. For example, the student whose leg is not involved may explore to discover how slowly and how rapidly he can move it and the various heights to which he can raise it.

10. Exercises of contraction and relaxation (described in Chapter 29, Relaxation) are other possible activities, as are rolling, crawling, and similar movements performed on a mat. The choices of relaxation exercises and movements on the mat are dictated by the areas of the body affected by the disease.

Since physical therapy to retain flexibility is usually prescribed for those with muscular dystrophy early in the course of the disease, complementary exercises can be offered in the physical education program. Examples of these are given:

Throwing—encourage full range of motion from the ready position to the follow-through.

Reaching for and picking up objects—encourage the extension of the body as far as possible in the bend and reach.

Batting and striking—encourage a full swing.

Kicking—encourage full extension of the leg in the kick.

Stepping up and over objects—encourage taking the longest possible step consistent with good balance.

Swimming is an appropriate activity for most individuals with muscular weakness, regardless of the lack of muscle action. Extremely weak muscles can often function

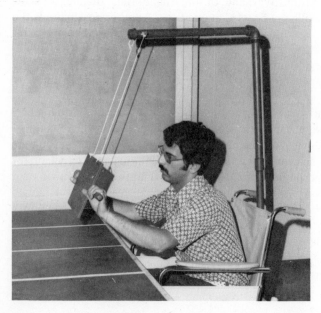

Figure 11-2. A paddle with a large playing surface, suspended by cords from a frame, reduces the strenuousness of table tennis for an extremely weak player.

when they are free from the pull of gravity by the buoyancy of the water It has been found that those with muscular weakness can master the elementary back stroke more easily than other strokes and, therefore, it is recommended that this be the first swimming stroke taught. Flotation devices are extremely helpful in supporting a segment of the body that is completely restricted in movement. (See Chapter 25, Swimming, for further discussion.)

There is a special technique for assisting the youngster with muscular dystrophy to rise from a sitting position. The helper stands facing the youngster and puts his arms around the lower back and locks his hands. The helper lifts up so that the youngster's trunk can sway backward and his hips be pulled forward to a balanced position. The lift should not be made under the arms.

SELECTED READINGS

Downey, John A. and Low, Niels L.: *The Child With Disabling Illness*. Philadelphia, W. B. Saunders Co., 1974.

Greenblatt, M. H.: *Multiple Sclerosis and Me*. Springfield, Ill., Charles C Thomas, Pub., 1972.

Krusen, Frank H., *et al.: Handbook of Physical Medicine and Rehabilitation,* ed. 2. Philadelphia, W. B. Saunders Co., 1971.

Swaiman, K. F., and Wright, F. S.: *Neuromuscular Diseases of Infancy and Childhood*. Springfield, Ill., Charles C Thomas, Pub., 1970.

Walton, J. N.: *Disorders of Voluntary Muscles*. Boston, Little, Brown, and Co., 1969.

Chapter 12

Sensory Impairments

The term sensory impairment describes a condition in which one or more of the senses are diminished in their effectiveness to respond to stimuli. Such a condition may be present from birth or may develop at any time during life as the result of injury or disease. The lack of sensory response to stimulation may be total or partial. Difficulties for the person involved are created by any sensory impairment regardless of the time of incurrence or the degree of severity. However, the educational problems arising from loss of sight or hearing are incomparably more difficult than those brought about by deficiencies in taste, smell, and touch.

For this reason, the discussion in this chapter will be limited to visual and auditory handicaps and to a combination of the two, referred to herein as dual sensory impairment. Much of the information presented concerning the causes, special needs, and adjustment problems of persons with either of the handicaps also applies to those with dual impairment and can serve as a foundation for a fuller understanding of the presentation of the dual sensory disability.

VISUAL HANDICAPS

Physical education for the sightless has a long and interesting history. In the 1830s three schools for blind children were founded in the United States, providing the first educational opportunities for such children. One of these schools, Perkins Institute in Boston, had as its director a medical doctor who was an enthusiastic advocate of the benefits of physical exercise. He organized a program of vigorous physical activity for the blind students in his school which included playing outdoors, swimming in the ocean, and work on gymnastic apparatus. His program was far in advance of the physical education in the public schools of his day.

Gradually, other schools for the blind were established. Some of these made provisions for physical training classes in which gymnastics constituted the chief activity. Military training, which received emphasis in the public schools following the Civil War, displaced gymnastic training in schools for the blind. The consequence was that marching and military exercise or formal gymnastics have formed the core of physical education for blind students in many schools until very recent times. In other schools, the play movement which swept the country in the early part of this century encouraged administrators to begin athletic programs in wrestling and track and field. Intramural teams in these sports became prevalent, and soon varsity teams entered into interschool competition.

Today physical education programs at the special schools offer a balanced variety of activities, including intramural and interscholastic sports. Many visually handicapped students who in former years would have been enrolled in special schools now attend public schools where they participate in regular physical education or special physical education as their needs require.

The Nature and Causes of Visual Handicaps

Approximately one child out of every four or five has some significant deviation from the accepted norm of good vision. A large majority of these have such slight deviations that they are not extremely detrimental to the child or are remediable either medically or by wearing prescribed lenses. For these children no special educational provisions need be made. However, about one out of every 1500 have such severe deviations from normal vision that they cannot read books printed in regular type and so require materials printed in large type or Braille.

Visual acuity is commonly measured by the use of a chart having several lines of progressively smaller letters or symbols. The person being tested reads the chart from a specific distance. His visual acuity, as determined by the number of lines he is able to read, is expressed in a numerical ratio, for example, 20/200. In the ratio, the first number indicates the distance in feet that the person being tested had to be from the chart in order to see what someone with normal vision can see at the distance indicated by the second number, which in this case is 200 feet.

The degree to which the child is handicapped is determined largely by how greatly his vision deviates from normal. Although for purposes of classification those with visual acuity of 20/200 or less with glasses are considered blind, most of those so classified have some useful sight. They may be able to perceive light, form, or movement and are, consequently, considered to be partially seeing (see Table 12–1). The partially seeing have traditionally been enrolled in schools for the blind along with the totally blind because their visual handicaps require special educational methods and equipment. However, the enrollment of partially seeing students in regular school systems, with some special arrangements made for their needs, is now an increasingly common practice. Sometimes their instruction is provided in special classes with a teacher trained in methods of instructing the partially seeing and with equipment designed especially for their needs. In other situations they are accommodated in the regular classroom.

The age at which the individual became blind has as much bearing on his educational needs as the degree to which his sight is affected. Blindness at birth is more handicapping than blindness which occurs later in life, because it prevents the individ-

Table 12–1.   DEGREES OF VISUAL ACUITY

Legal Blindness. Visual acuity of 20/200 or less or a field of vision less than 20°. Students' so designated are eligible to receive special assistance from state and Federal sources.

Travel Vision.   Visual acuity from 5/200 to 10/200 inclusive. Enough sight is present to allow moving or walking without extreme difficulty.

Motion Perception.   Visual acuity from 3/200 to 5/200 inclusive. Movement can be seen but usually not the still object.

Light Perception.   Visual acuity less than 3/200. A bright light can be distinguished at a distance of three feet or less but movement cannot.

Total or Complete Blindness. Inability to see light.

Tunnel Vision. A field of vision of 20° or less. The field of vision is so drastically narrowed that the person sees as though looking through a tube.

ual from establishing visual concepts of any kind. The most common causes of blindness are diseases, accidents, and heredity. Conditions of a hereditary nature that produce blindness are cataract, atrophy of the optic nerve, and retinitis pigmentosa (deposits of pigment on the retina of the eye). Accidental injuries on farms and in industry produce numerous incidents of blindness among adults, while playing with sharp instruments and hazardous toys causes many vision accidents among children.

Infectious diseases cause many cases of vision loss. The secondary infection of a contagious disease which has attacked the body, such as smallpox, scarlet fever, or typhoid fever, may cause eye difficulties, or they may be caused by infectious diseases which affect the eyes primarily.

Gonorrhea, once a common cause of prenatal blindness, has been brought under effective control by state legislation requiring doctors delivering babies to use silver nitrate or other effective medicinals in the eyes of newborn babies. Another cause of blindness, occuring in premature infants, is also being successfully controlled. This is a condition known as retrolental fibroplasia, which was discovered to be related to the administration of oxygen to premature babies.

Among the infectious diseases which affect the eyes and frequently cause loss of sight are trachoma and ophthalmia. Trachoma is a chronic inflammation of the conjunctiva believed to be conveyed mechanically to the eye through the use of common washcloths, towels, and handkerchiefs or by the fingers. Ophthalmia is an inflammation of the conjunctiva occurring most often during the first two weeks of a baby's life. It is the result of infection by any one of several pathogenic organisms contracted by the baby during birth, or from the presence of contaminated objects near the eyes.

Another cause of visual impairment in infants is the infection of the mother by rubella (German or three-day measles) during the first trimester of pregnancy. During the rubella epidemic of 1963–65, a large number of children were born with vision problems as the result of their mothers' having contracted the disease in early pregnancy. Since that time a vaccine to prevent rubella has been discovered and marketed. With the widespread use of the vaccine, rubella, like gonorrhea and retrolental fibroplasia, may cease to be a major factor in the development of childhood vision impairments.

Glaucoma, a disease of the eye characterized by increased intraocular (within the eye) pressure that leads to total blindness, is a very common disorder. Even though nearly one half of all cases of blindness result from glaucoma, the condition rarely occurs in anyone under the age of 40.

Needs and Adjustments of Those With Vision Impairment

Children with impaired vision have the same needs for physical activity as other children, but the fact that they are unable to see normally does in numerous instances restrict their play activities to such an extent that they are noticeably retarded in their physical development. Fear of injury instilled in them by protective parents reduces their natural interest in big-muscle movements such as running, climbing, and jumping which are an inherent part of the normal child's play and contribute to his muscular growth and the development of coordination. As a result, physical vitality and resistance to certain diseases are low and overweight is often a problem. Posture may be poor both because of the lack of strength in the postural muscles and because of the lack of visual examples of good posture to emulate.

Because the urges of a child who is blind to move and play are frustrated, he often develops certain mannerisms known as blindisms.* These are physical movements through which, it is thought, the blind child seeks to fulfill the need for muscular movement without moving about through space. Rocking back and forth, twitching of the head, and jerking of the limbs are characteristic blindisms. It is desirable to overcome these mannerisms, since they set the blind child apart from his seeing peers. Moreover, in working to eliminate the blindisms a greater sense of security in moving about in space will be developed.

Those who are blind are likely to have personality problems as well as physical incapacities. Because of their fears of activity, the blind tend to pursue solitary and sedentary occupations. This limits their social contacts, which may in turn feed a feeling of inferiority. Frustrations experienced in attempting normal activity or normal social relations contribute to maladjustment. Fantasies and daydreaming are common among the blind who have made unsatisfactory adjustments to their circumstances. The age at which the blinded individual lost his sight has considerable effect upon his social adjustment. Children who have been without sight since birth have more difficulty in social adjustment than those who had achieved some degree of social maturity before losing their sight. However, the latter may experience anxieties and fears about their future, resulting in extreme cases of despondency and depression.

The age at which the impairment occurs also influences the movement patterns. These are also governed by the degree to which the person can see. Those who have gained assurance from previous experiences or from their ability to see slightly will move about with less awkwardness and with more confidence than others whose fears are heightened by lack of such assurance.

The blind tend to develop their other senses to a higher degree than normal people to compensate for their lack of sight. Some believe the blind to have a "sixth sense" because they have developed such an awareness of their environment that they appear to perceive things which their normal associates cannot perceive. There is no evidence to support the concept that the blind have an unnatural or mystical gift which enables them to perform activities which would seem possible only for the seeing. The adroitness with which a blind person walks down the crowded sidewalk avoiding other walkers and obstacles, negotiates the curb, and crosses with the light seems almost superhuman to the fully visioned, who cannot conceive of doing this themselves without the use of eyes. Behind the skill of the blind walker are a highly developed kinesthetic sense, the ability to listen closely to auditory clues, and experience in the interpretation of the various stimuli to his other senses. His "sixth sense" is actually the acute development of the other senses.

Planning the Special Program in the Regular School

There are several effective teaching procedures that may be utilized to integrate students with visual handicaps into the regular physical education class. Before these procedures can be used, of course, the teacher must ascertain the degree to which the students can perceive and how well they have developed compensatory skills. With this knowledge about the students, the teacher can make simple modifications in the activities to accommodate the youngsters in the games of the class. An example should suggest many more similar possibilities to the physical education teacher. Assuming that a student with partial vision is able to distinguish a white covering over

---

*These mannerisms also develop among sighted persons who are mentally retarded or emotionally disturbed.

the bases but cannot see well enough to bat a pitched ball, someone may be appointed to bat for him and he will do his own base running. The worn path between the bases will help to guide him around the bases because it will feel different to his feet from the grass.

It is a sensible procedure to have the partially seeing students equally divided between the teams. In this way no team will feel at a disadvantage, and the normal team members will tend to think of these students as teammates who can help them be successful if they all work together. In this matter, as in all classroom situations, the teacher will set the tone with which the problem is solved. If he is overly protective and solicitous of the handicapped students in the class, such will be the general attitude displayed by the class. Acceptance of the students for what they are with an appreciation of the talents and abilities they display will be the response of the class if this is the attitude demonstrated by the instructor.

The student who wears glasses for corrected vision presents a safety problem in vigorous participation in sports. If he cannot remove the glasses during play, he should wear either the special type of rugged glasses made to withstand rough treatment or he should wear glass guards. In lieu of either of these measures, if they are impractical for one reason or another, the student may be removed from the more strenuous types of activities and placed in the special program. It may be necessary to give the glasses protection and support in some instances by placing adhesive tape over the stems of the glasses at the temples.

Another problem with which the teacher must be concerned is a condition of retinal detachment. Partially seeing individuals who suffer from progressive myopia sometimes have this condition, in which there is a partial detachment of the retina from the choroid. It will be necessary to safeguard such individuals from situations which might produce a blow to the head, as such a jar may cause further detachment which can result in total blindness. Contact sports and diving are contraindicated for them. However, according to Dr. Rachun of Cornell University, persons with corrected myopia can participate in contact sports with safety.[1]

Planning the Program in the Special School

The discussion which follows concerns the teaching of physical education in a special school for the blind; however, the presentation has many recommendations which can be used by the physical educator in the regular school system to provide a better program for the partially seeing students who are enrolled in his classes.

Play Areas.   The play area, indoors and out, should be a large, uncluttered space. As a safety precaution the play area should be free of nonessential equipment and unnecessary obstructions. For outdoor playing fields, hedges and shade trees are considered desirable boundaries rather than walls or fences, which present a certain element of danger. Boundaries for games can be indicated by varying the composition of the court as, for example, having the in-bounds area composed of concrete and the out-of-bounds area of sand or grass. Players will then be able to tell by foot sensitivity when they have stepped out of bounds.

Boundaries in the indoor playing area should be painted in white for the benefit of those students able to distinguish white. The gymnasium should be well lighted to present the best possible seeing conditions for those who are able to perceive light. A

[1]Medicine in Sports. "Athletes with Ocular Defects Need Careful Handling." *Newsletter,* Vol. 9, No. 2, March 1969, p. 1.

contrast in playing surfaces in the gymnasium can be achieved with wood and concrete.

The blind should be thoroughly introduced to an unfamiliar playing area before they are allowed to play. They should know the size and shape of the area and the nature of the boundaries before they engage in activity in the area. To orient the students the teacher should walk with them around the area, describing the essential details. A few simple games or contests might be played to help the students gain familiarity with the playing area before engaging in strenuous play.

To guide blind children in running activities and to give them greater security, hanging ropes and rings which are grasped in the hands may be suspended from wires strung across the gymnasium well above the heads of the participants. For outside running events wires can be placed along the path of the runner to guide him. The runners will need some type of warning at the finish line; this may be a knotted cord hanging from a suspended crossbar which will brush against the runner as he passes the finish line, or some sort of auditory signal such as a whistle may be sounded.

Equipment. Playground equipment for younger children may be the same type found on any playground, including swings, jungle gyms, and teeter-totters; however, greater care must be exercised in locating them to avoid possible injury to the nonseeing participants. Swings should be constructed with no more than two swings on the stand; a third swing in the center is difficult to reach without danger when the other two swings are occupied. The use of guard rails or ground markers is a necessary safety precaution to prevent youngsters from bumping into equipment or being hit by flying swings.

It is recommended that balls to be used by the blind be larger in size and softer than regulation balls and that they be painted yellow or white to make them more easily seen by those with some vision. Bells or rattles inside the balls help to indicate the location to the blind.

A portable aluminum rail is a useful aid to the blind in bowling. The rail may be used on bowling alleys or on the gymnasium floor when plastic bowling sets are being

Figure 12–1. A special rail that helps the blind player to determine direction when releasing the ball can be used for practice in the gymnasium or for play at a regular bowling alley.

used. Stationary bicycles, common equipment in physiology or exercise laboratories, are excellent for use by the blind in physical conditioning. Information concerning the purchase of the above-mentioned special equipment for the blind can be obtained by writing to the American Foundation for the Blind, Inc., Aids and Appliances Division, 15 West 16th Street, New York, N.Y. 10011.

Only such playing equipment as is actually in use should be permitted in the playing area to ensure maximum safety. Blind children can memorize the location of the permanent fixtures but cannot avoid superfluous equipment which has been left in their way. The youngsters can also memorize the place in the storage closets where each item of equipment is kept and are capable of securing the needed items and returning them at the end of the play period.

Class Organization. Class organization may be determined by the schedule of other classes and activities for the students in the school; that is, the physical education class may have to be organized on the basis of the students who are available at the hours when physical education is offered. If the schedule permits, the best procedure for organizing classes is on the basis of general strength and coordination rather than chronological age. If the students are all of about the same general physical ability, the class activities can be more easily planned to meet the specific needs of the group. However, if the problem-solving method is utilized, a wide range of ages and abilities can be accommodated.

Proper Approach. The introduction of new skills requires a kinesthetic approach. The teacher and perhaps a few of the students who have learned the skill may demonstrate it while the sightless examine the parts of the body involved with their hands. (An inspection of people and objects with the hands is called "brailling," in the vernacular of the blind). At times it may be helpful to the student for the teacher to place the student's hands and feet and other parts of the body into the desired positions. Lengthy verbal explanations should be avoided. However, clear concise descriptions which accompany the kinesthetic approach may be used with great effectiveness. In planning the teaching of a skill, a sighted instructor may gain greater insight into the problems which the skill will present to his sightless students if he closes his eyes while performing the skill.

A whistle is an essential piece of equipment for the instructor of visually handicapped students, and it may be blown to identify for the students the location of the teacher, to signal for attention, or for other purposes. A meaningful set of signals may be worked out with the students. A megaphone is useful to the teacher in making his voice heard to the players. The players will need to be given a great many details of the progress of the game which would be naturally observed by players with normal vision. For example, if a kick ball game is in progress, the players will need to be told which players are on which bases; who will kick next; the placement of players on the field; when an out or a score is made. Here again, if the teacher will try to put himself in the position of the blind player and try to think of the game information that he would want to know as the game progresses, this will guide him in selecting the most useful information to give the players.

Nearly all the varieties of activities offered to normal children in the physical education curriculum can be presented to blind children. Some require more adaptation than others, but blind children enjoy and need participation in the same games, sports, and physical activities as other children. In addition, the activities can help them overcome some of the problems, physical and emotional, which are the direct result of the visual handicaps.

Free Play. Although children should be encouraged to use the playground equipment on their own during the leisure hours, they should be given explicit instruction in the use of the play equipment for their own safety and for that of others. All children should be taught the skills involved in the use of the apparatus and the safety measures which must be observed. This is most especially true of children with visual handicaps.

The teacher may find some hesitancy on the part of some blind children to play on the equipment. This is most likely to be true of those who have led extremely sheltered lives. The teacher must begin with the children at their level of motor skill development and their level of self-confidence and strengthen both by encouraging participation at the tempo they will accept. In very young children and very timid ones, it may be necessary to inspire a desire for carefree play on the equipment.

Chair seats on swings and teeter-totters require less balancing skill and promote confidence and security. In introducing these pieces of equipment, the teacher should tell the children something about how they look and how they are used while the children explore them with their hands. Each child may be assisted in sitting on the equipment and trying it with the help of the teacher. A reassuring grasp on the shoulders or arm promotes confidence during the first attempts. When a certain amount of confidence has been developed, mounting and dismounting and safety precautions can be taught to the children.

The safe and enjoyable use of the slide requires careful instruction by the teacher. The children must be taught to wait their turn at the bottom of the ladder and not to climb the steps until the one who is having his turn claps his hands to let everyone know that he is going down the slide. When he reaches the bottom, he must inform the one who is waiting at the top that the slide is clear. The one who is waiting at the top signals by clapping to the one who is waiting to climb up.

To encourage a reluctant child the teacher may first have to help him sit on the slide near the end and hold him as he slides down. This may be done several times at increasing heights. The child should be shown how he may slow down the speed of the slide by forcing his feet against the sides.

Jungle gyms and parallel ladders are dangerous if improperly used by either sighted or nonsighted children. Children often have sufficient confidence to get on the bars but do not have sufficient skills and strength to perform with safety. A low single bar can be utilized to develop sufficient arm and hand strength and to develop skill in hanging or swinging the body through space. Or a child may be started out very low on the jungle gym where the danger of falling would be minimal. On the parallel ladders a thick board may be placed between the rungs of the two upright ladders of a very high ladder. This lessens the distance of the drop and the board can also be used as a jouncing board to spring up and down on, which is an excellent exercise in itself.

Suggested Activities

Primary Grade Activities. In the primary grades physical education activities and games are often utilized as tools in the learning of reading, number concepts, and other areas of study. There are many methods of doing this, and each primary school teacher has worked out numerous ways of her own which might be employed in teaching the blind. Many activities suggest themselves, and the suggestions made below are given only as a foundation from which other ideas will spring.

For teaching number concepts, the turns taken in certain activities may be counted, such as the number of times a ball is bounced or the steps taken on a balance beam. In developing reading readiness the background of meaningful experience is expanded, and toward this end numerous physical activities may be utilized. Exploration of the surrounding areas, following paths and sidewalks, going up and down hills, and climbing trees are a few possibilities.

Many of the singing games and mimetic games of the primary grade level need no adaptation for the blind. A game such as London Bridge or mimetic activity such as a measuring worm race does not need any modification. Other games may need only slight modifications to offset the disadvantage of being unable to see the other players. In the game Red Light and Green Light, which is recommended for blind children because it encourages them to run freely and swiftly, the teacher should name those who are moving on the call of "red light," since the children will not be able to tell which runners should be brought back.

Because blind persons need to develop greater spatial awareness, activities in physical education should promote learning to move the body through space and to relate the body's location to other people or objects that share the space. Motor exploration activities are an excellent vehicle for such learning. In motor exploration the student is not trying to find the most effective way to make a movement; rather he is experimenting with a number of different ways of moving to discover the one that is most efficient for and most satisfying to him. In the process he learns a great deal about moving the body through space. Suggested motor activities for exploration of space are as follows:

Movement while Stationary.   The objective in these activities is to learn how the body can be moved without locomotion.

1. With the arms at the sides, move them up and down. (If the arms are bare, the wind currents created by the movements can be felt on the arms.)

2. Move any part of the body except the arms but do not move from the original space.

3. Lift up one leg and then try to lift up the other. (Because this is impossible to do, it teaches the concept of motor limitations.)

Exploring Locomotion.   Elementary skills of locomotion are rolling, crawling, walking, running, jumping, and variations of these. Exploration of these skills helps children to learn the variety of ways the body can be moved from place to place.

1. Move from one place to another, not allowing the feet to touch the floor.

2. Move about the play area, trying to create an impression of being tall, small, wide, flat, round, and so on.

Communication through Movement.   In this phase of exploratory movement, children learn the ways in which the body may be used to communicate emotions and ideas.

1. Move like, and make noises like, a dog. (Previous to this activity, children will need to have an opportunity for brailling a dog and listening to it bark and to have been given an idea of how it moves.)

2. Move in a manner to show fear, anger, happiness, and so on.

3. Move to depict a gentle rain, a hot sunny day, and a snowstorm.

Manipulation of Objects.   Having discovered movements that can be made with the body, the blind child is ready to explore the use of the body in the manipulation of objects. The ball is the most common object of manipulation in physical education and so it will be used in the sample activities.

1. Make the ball move, using the hand, foot, head, shoulders, and so on.

2. Move the ball so that it makes different sounds.

3. Throw a ball (suspended from the ceiling by a cord) at different speeds.

Relaxation.   Muscular relaxation is another activity that lends itself to exploration. Learning to relax is not always easy, and participation in the exploratory activities helps to develop an understanding of the process. Suggestions for such activities are made in the discussion of relaxation in Chapter 29.

Spatial Awareness. Excellent activities for teaching spatial awareness can also be presented by the direct or traditional method. Possibilities include the following:

1. Walk in a straight line. (Blind children have a tendency to veer to the side of their dominant hand or weave back and forth.)

2. Follow sounds; for example, drum beat, voice, footsteps.

3. Slide a hand along a rope that encloses a small area while walking around it; retrace the steps without touching the rope.

4. While walking, turn on command to make a 90 degree turn, a 45 degree turn, and so on.

5. Follow a cord stretched between two points. At the farther point, release the hold on the cord and return to the starting point.

Activities for Older Children.* There are many games suitable for elementary, junior high, and senior high school students which need no modification. Many dual competitive games such as arm wrestling or Indian leg wrestling can be presented without modification. In tag games and other games in which the players need to make their location known to the one who is "It," the players may make vocal sounds. When partially or totally visioned players are participating in the game, these students may join hands with a blind player and play as a couple. Certain games with balls such as dodge ball and wall ball are easily modified by slight rule changes which prevent seeing players from having undue advantage and which provide for the calling out by players so that blind opponents can locate them by the sound of their voice.

Some games lend themselves more easily than others to adaptation for playing by blind and partially seeing students. As a guide for the selection of those games which can be readily used without much modification, Charles E. Buell suggests these eight characteristics:[2]

1. Blindfolding one or two players.
2. Sounds whereby the sightless know what is happening.
3. Different duties for the blind and partially seeing.
4. Running to a goal easily found by the totally blind.
5. Limited playing area such as gymnasium or tennis court.
6. Direct contact as in wrestling.
7. Line or chain formations.
8. The possibility of players pairing up in couples.

Because the blind rely so much on sound to receive their impressions, they are particularly receptive to the rhythm not only of music but also of the human activities which surround them. The knowledge thus gained of rhythm patterns is a valuable asset in learning to dance. All types of dance may be taught to the blind: musical games, folk dances, modern dance, and social dancing. The musical games such as Farmer in the Dell are limited to young children. All other types of dance can be taught at almost any age level as soon as children have learned to move freely, with confidence and skill, through space.

Sports. Team sports most frequently played by the blind and partially seeing are football, softball, and volley newcomb. Basketball can be played by the partially seeing, but the blind cannot usually participate with success.

Individual sports such as wrestling, swimming, gymnastics, and tumbling need

---

*For descriptions of basic skill games see Chapter 20.

[2]Charles E. Buell: *Physical Education for Blind Children.* Springfield, Illinois, Charles C Thomas, Publisher, 1974, p. 102.

very little modification. Blind children will usually learn more slowly because the teaching process is necessarily slower.

In training for running events in track, the totally blind can run with a partially seeing partner and be guided by his footsteps. Overhead wires with drop cords which slide along the wire that the runner can grasp in his hand will aid him in keeping a steady course. Guide wires about hip high along one side of the track which the student can slide his hand along as he runs is good for the training period. Later, as confidence and skills develop, another wire is placed on the other side so that the runner runs between and is guided by them without placing his hands on the wires. This permits greater speed in running and, if he swerves off the course, the wires brush against him and remind him to adjust his position.

Bowling is a very popular individual sport in blind schools, and a large majority of the schools have bowling facilities. Blind bowlers orient themselves by feeling the sides of the alley or using the rail if it is provided. Golf is another individual sport much favored by blind players. The only adaptation is the necessity of playing with a sighted person who locates the ball.

Interscholastic Athletics.   There is some difference of opinion regarding participation by the blind in interscholastic athletics. There is no substantial evidence to indicate that either the values or evils which appear in the competitive sports programs for normal youngsters are greater or less great for blind players. Because of the wide acceptance of interscholastic sports in the regular schools, it would seem desirable to provide the same opportunities for blind students.

What activities should be included in the interscholastic program? An answer to this is partly dependent upon the offerings in the physical education and intramural programs, for it is considered good policy for the interscholastic program to be an outgrowth of the other two. Another factor which will determine the sports to be offered is the availability of competition. Since there will be few blind schools near enough to make travel feasible, competition may present a difficult problem. Competition in some sports can be arranged with regular schools, and this does, of course, supply a fine opportunity for players and student bodies to build a mutual respect and regard for each other.

Wrestling is perhaps the sport most commonly utilized in the interscholastic sports program because it offers the least disadvantage to the blind. Wrestling has been highly developed in schools for the blind but remains a relatively minor sport in public schools. This makes possible competition with large schools and college freshman teams. Blind wrestlers without much experience may be at a disadvantage when starting the match from a standing position. Starting from a referee's position overcomes this disadvantage. The crowd may be asked to remain as quiet as possible so that the blind wrestler may use his auditory acuity to locate his opponent. However, experienced blind wrestlers have learned to compensate and will not be at a disadvantage under regular rules and crowd situations.

Track and field constitutes another popular activity for interscholastic sports competition. In competition with other blind schools the events usually included are the 50- and 100-yard dashes; the mile and two mile runs; the standing high jump and broad jump; the triple jump; and the throwing events. Competition with regular schools in certain events has been found satisfactory. The dashes and shot-put are the usual events. However, sometimes the regular school can be persuaded to participate in all of the events listed above.

Gymnastics also lends itself well to interscholastic competition, but gymnastic teams have not been widely developed on the secondary level in either regular schools or schools for the blind. Football and basketball can also be included in the interscholastic athletic program, although basketball is restricted to the partially seeing. Swimming offers an unusually fine interscholastic activity. Blind swimmers can participate in all of the various strokes and dives used in competition and can compete successfully against sighted as well as other blind swimmers.

AUDITORY HANDICAPS

Auditory handicaps of varying degrees of severity constitute as a group one of the most common disabilities affecting children and adults. Statistics show that 35 out of every 1000 adults experience some hearing impairment, while 8 out of every 1000 children to the age of 20 have an auditory handicap. These hearing handicaps range from slight deviation from normal hearing to total loss of sound perception. Less than 10 per cent of the children enrolled in schools for the deaf are totally devoid of residual hearing.

Too often in the past a hearing loss has been considered to be handicapping in much the same way as the loss of sight and to affect the victim in much the same way psychologically. Such thinking was to be expected in view of the fact that both handicaps arise from a complete or partial loss of one of the senses. However, this tendency to regard the two conditions as similar has retarded a true consideration of the psychological implications of hearing loss. In recent years, the problems of those with hearing disabilities have been approached with new insight into the effects they may have upon the lives of those whose hearing is partially or totally destroyed. It is extremely important for those who are teaching children with auditory handicaps not only to understand the kinds of hearing difficulties and their causes but also to comprehend the depth of the personality problems which may accompany hearing loss.

The Nature and Causes of Hearing Disabilities

The term deaf is commonly used to describe partial hearing loss as well as total loss. However, Ross and Calvert[3] point out that a definite distinction should be made between hard-of-hearing and deaf. These authors are concerned that labeling a hard-of-hearing child as deaf or reacting to him as if he were deaf will produce a situation that may prevent potential development of hearing ability. Modern educational methods for the student with impaired hearing make the maximum use of the residual hearing that he still possesses. Consequently, it is important that educators teach students with partial hearing losses more nearly like hearing students than like students who are totally deaf.

Hearing disabilities are usually structural in origin. There are two basic kinds of structural disorders: conductive hearing loss and sensorineural hearing loss.

Conductive hearing loss is caused by a physical obstruction to the conduction of the sound waves to the inner ear, such as impacted wax or a middle ear infection. Although the nature of the obstruction may be severe and the hearing seriously impaired, deafness is never total. Impacted wax can be readily removed by a physician, and infection can be treated medically with relatively good chances for arresting or

---

[3]Mark Ross and Donald R. Calvert: "The Semantics of Deafness," Reprint No. 892, Washington, D.C., The Alexander Graham Bell Association for the Deaf, Inc., 1967, *passim*.

improving it, particularly in its early stages. A hearing aid is very useful in improving a hearing loss due to conduction difficulties.

Sensorineural hearing loss is usually a more serious condition and less likely to be improved by medical treatment. It is caused by damage to the cells or nerve fibers that receive and transmit the sound stimuli. The loss of hearing may range from mild to total disability. Some degree of sensorineural deafness is common among the aging. A certain amount of high-tone nerve deafness appears to be part of the natural process of aging in many people, just as many of advanced years suffer hardening of the arteries and deterioration of eyesight. This condition is in fact so prevalent that the commonest cause of nerve deafness is attributed to senility.

In children and young adults the most frequent cause of sensorineural deafness is congenital, the nerve having been injured or destroyed before or during birth. The term congenital indicates that the child was born deaf or inherited the tendency for the hearing to deteriorate at an early age. However, researchers into the causes of deafness in children have discovered that a number of cases heretofore classified as hereditary were actually associated with certain contagious diseases which the mother contracted during the early months of pregnancy. Rubella, mumps, and influenza have all been indicated as causes of deafness in infants whose mothers were afflicted during early pregnancy.

Cases of sensorineural deafness which have a noncongenital origin are classified as acquired deafness. Among the common causes are brain infections such as meningitis, brain fever, and sleeping sickness and communicable diseases such as scarlet fever, measles, influenza, and others.

At one time it was considered that hearing aids were of little value to those with sensorineural hearing loss, but with the improvement of the quality of hearing aids, it has become possible to fit successfully more and more of the victims of this type of hearing loss.

Prolonged loud sounds of any spectra can produce a temporary threshold shift (auditory fatigue); recovery usually takes place within a day. The more intense the sound, the shorter the exposure time necessary before a temporary fatigue takes place. Continual exposure eventually produces a permanent hearing loss. As a general rule, the ears should not be exposed to sounds over 130 decibels* longer than momentarily. There is some evidence to suggest that prolonged listening to amplified music is causing hearing losses in young men and women, especially among the musicians themselves. In these cases, the hearing loss occurs in the higher frequency ranges. The combined sounds of the environment, such as street noises in a city, often reach levels of intensity that may cause hearing loss.

Classification of Hearing Loss.   Hearing loss is measured in terms of decibel loss. Decibel loss refers to the increase of units of sound that are required for a hard-of-hearing person to hear at the same level as the normal person hears. To illustrate, for a person with an auditory loss of 20 decibels to hear a sound at the same level as someone with normal hearing an increase of 20 decibels in the sound is necessary.

Degrees of hearing loss are classified differently by different authorities, but the classification most frequently used in educational circles divides the losses into five categories. These are (1) mild, 20 to 30 decibel loss; (2) marginal, 31 to 40 decibel loss; (3) moderate, 41 to 60 decibel loss; (4) severe, 61 to 75 decibel loss; and (5) profound, over 75 decibel loss.

Some children in the mild category need a hearing aid. Speech is usually normal

---

*For purposes of comparison, a loud shout at a foot distance is measured at 110 decibels, while ordinary conversation is about 60 decibels.

even without special instruction. These children will experience no disadvantage in physical education class caused by hearing disability.

Those with marginal hearing loss cannot hear normal speech from a distance of three feet. If the loss is near 40 decibels, the children show some signs of speech impediment.

Moderate hearing loss produces a condition in which the individual can hear only loud sounds, of 90 decibels or more, from a distance of three feet. In most cases faulty speech develops, requiring special speech training.

Children with severe hearing loss can hear loud sounds but not loud conversational tones. Special training is required to develop adequate speech.

Children with a decibel loss of 75 or more are, for all practical purposes, deaf. Some may hear loud sounds at very close range, but they are unable to distinguish differences in sounds and so the sounds are meaningless to them. Special training is required to learn to develop speech.

Needs and Adjustments of Those With Auditory Handicaps

The most obvious adjustment to their handicap which those with a severe hearing disability must make is to the loss of the normal means of communication. A new way of receiving messages must be found if the disability is acquired after speech has been learned, usually lip reading. If the loss of hearing is congenital or acquired before speech has been learned, a means of conveying as well as receiving communications must be learned. Deaf persons who could not speak were once taught signing as the sole means of communication, but deaf children are now being taught to speak by the technique of properly utilizing the mouth and vocal cords in the production of sounds. They also receive lip-reading and usually signing instruction.

Considerable controversy exists among those who work with the deaf as to the extent to which deaf people should be taught to communicate by speech, lip reading, and signing. One faction contends that signing should not be taught at all and that the educational effort should be directed entirely toward learning to lip read and to speak because such communication skills are closer to normalcy. This approach is known as the oral method. Opponents say that signing, lip reading, and speech should all be taught to give the deaf child the widest possible communication skills. Their approach is referred to as the total method.

In addition to their loss of the usual conversational method of communication with others, those with severe hearing handicaps experience other losses that cause difficult problems of adjustment. One of these is being deprived of the warnings which exist in sound. The honking of the auto horn or the raised voice which warns of impending danger cannot reach the deaf. Until they have learned to adjust to this and compensate for the loss satisfactorily, they experience more than usual anxieties and fears.

The deaf hear nothing of the sounds of life and activity which fall continually upon the normal ear and form a background of noises which those who hear are generally not even conscious of. Many recently deafened people have been reported as describing the loss of this auditory background as "living in a dead world." This extraordinary loss has a deep psychological impact upon the victim, and to it is attributed the severe depression experienced by most people who lose their hearing after years of living in a world of sound.

The noises and sounds which constitute the auditory background of daily life produce, in those who hear, muscular tensions which are largely involuntary and unobserved. One who is recently deafened characteristically substitutes body movement for the missing sensations of movement and sound which formerly surrounded him. These continuous purposeless movements must be understood by the teacher so that he may plan more worthwhile motor movements as substitutions.

Without the orientation of the auditory background and the symbols and warnings which are customarily provided by sound perception, the deaf are prone to frustrations and anxieties. This is more particularly true in cases where hearing is impaired in adolescence or adulthood. The longer a person has had full powers of hearing, the more difficult is his adjustment to a severe hearing loss. The loss of background sounds contributes also to inacurracy in the recognition of space and motion, and, as a consequence, the movements of the deaf are often vague and distorted.

Isolated in his "dead world," the individual with a severe auditory handicap often becomes withdrawn and inactive. The attempt to communicate with others may be so unsuccessful even for those with mild handicaps that they withdraw from social contacts. Children with hearing losses often find they are unable to participate with success in games and sport activities which demand communications and direction and so avoid playing with others. A failure to participate in normal childhood play has been shown to have far-reaching consequences. Not only may such children be deprived of the social maturation which results from the common interchange of play, but also their physical growth and motor skill development may be retarded.

Planning the Program in the Regular School

It is estimated that approximately 4 to 5 per cent of the school population actually experience some hearing loss. The child with a slight auditory deficiency will not be readily noticed in the classroom; or, if noticed because of his behavior, his actions may not be attributed to hearing loss. The child may be inattentive, fail to answer questions, require frequent repetition of directions. He may watch those who are speaking very closely in order to grasp something of the meaning of the speech from the movements of the mouth or gestures of the body, or he may incline his head when spoken to so his ear is directed toward the speaker. Evidence of such mannerisms or behavior patterns may be more quickly revealed in the physical education class than in the regular class, for in the vastness of the gymnasium or playing field the student is even less likely to hear directions and explanations, particularly when these are given in game situations and he is some distance away or has his head turned away from the instructor. Consequently, the teacher should be alert to the possibility that a child who fails to grasp his directions or fails to respond well may have a hearing loss and should take steps to see that the child is adequately tested.

A considerable number of children with hearing defects are being enrolled in the regular schools, and generally speaking, such children can be successfully included in the regular physical education class. However, if the child's impairment has kept him from normal participation in play activities so that he has marked physical needs or personality problems, the teacher should consider his case more carefully to determine if he could profit more from participation in the special class. Children who have experienced recent hearing loss and are still in a period of adjustment may well profit from individualized instruction in the special physical education program, as may those with subnormal strength and coordination.

Many hard-of-hearing students wear hearing aids which may be removed during physical education classes for some types of activities. Without this assistance to his auditory perception, the student will again be handicapped in the amount of verbal direction he can comprehend. The teacher must anticipate this and be prepared to help the student make the necessary adjustment.

For calling roll or giving preliminary instruction to the class before the class activity begins, the teacher should placed the students with auditory handicaps where they will be in the best position to watch his face. During actual play, when the teacher wishes to make comments, he may move close to those students who cannot hear well before speaking. Or the student may be granted "roving" privileges so that he may move about freely to a position where he is better able to hear the speaker.

Other students in the class are usually very cooperative in helping those who cannot hear to make the right responses in game situations once they understand their difficulty. As long as they are unaware that a certain student responds the way he does because of a handicap and not because he's odd, they often ignore or ridicule him. Consequently, the physical education instructor must set the pattern for the class. His kindness and patience in directing and explaining the class activities to the student with a hearing disability will be imitated by the others. Soon the teacher will find that when such a student has muffed a play by being out of position, a couple of his teammates will quietly step over to him and show him what was wrong.

Students with impaired hearing may demonstrate a lack of cooperation in class activities and undesirable behavior in competitive play. Such tendencies are related largely to their failure to have understood the directions or rules of the game. In the lower grades where the play is less dependent upon vocal directions and rulings, the handicapped child is usually a considerably more successful participant than in later years when games become more dependent upon the comprehension of spoken words. Displays of anger and aggressiveness and other unsportsmanlike conduct increase as the child feels more and more inadequate in the increasingly complex games offered in the physical education program at advanced grade levels. Clear explanations directed at the student and careful demonstrations of the skill to be performed should do much to alleviate the misunderstandings which prompted the undesirable behavior.

Students with hearing losses need to be taught more factual information about a game than a normal child whose ears as well as his eyes have given him insight into the activity. The vocabulary of the game as well as the rules and playing strategy must be conveyed with greater care and exactness than is necessary for the student who can hear. Well described and illustrated written materials may be used to good advantage for this purpose with students who read.

Visual aids have greater significance as a teaching technique in the instruction of the hard of hearing and deaf than in perhaps any other situation. Their use can substitute for considerable amounts of verbal instruction. Both movie films and slides can be used to good advantage, although slides will frequently require more explanation than moving pictures. However, the required explanation can be shown on the screen in written form if the students are old enough to be good readers. The films chosen should show performances of the skills in such a way that they are largely self-explanatory. Frequently, reruns of the demonstration will help to make it more clear to those who are trying to learn the correct techniques from the picture.

A blackboard is an indispensable aid in the physical education class which contains students with auditory handicaps. The blackboard can be used to introduce the playing court of a new game with its service and boundary lines, to demonstrate the strategy of many different games, and to outline a problem for problem solving.

Planning the Program in the Special School

Children who have had extreme hearing impairment or have been totally deaf since birth or early infancy are usually enrolled in special residential schools for the deaf. Schools directed entirely toward the education of the deaf are located in nearly every state, and many of them provide special daily instruction to children who have less severe handicaps but can profit from the speech training, language instruction, and lip reading offered to the students in residence. The physical education teacher employed by these special schools will, then, find students in his classes who have considerable sound perception in addition to those who have very little hearing, or none.

The students are best instructed in relatively small groups of perhaps seven to ten. The instructor should place himself so that his face can be well seen by all the students in the group. A circular or straight-line formation is undesirable because not all the students will be able to face the instructor. A staggered line formation or informal grouping is very effective.

Some type of signal will need to be arranged to assemble the class. Many students even with very limited hearing are able to hear very low tones, so that some type of percussion instrument producing low tones might be sounded as a signal. Those who cannot hear it will take their cue from watching the others. The switching on and off of lights is another signal that can be used to attract the attention of the students.

Children with hearing problems are reluctant to leave the old games in which they are comfortable and confident to learn new games and activities. Small children enjoy solitary play on playground apparatus such as swings and bars and usually prefer this to the seeming hazards of group play. But deaf children of every age need the socialization and physical exercise provided by group games and competitive play. With careful and patient instruction they can learn new activities and experiences with the same pleasures as any other children.

SUGGESTED ACTIVITIES

There are few restrictions on the activities which may be offered to students with auditory handicaps in the regular or special physical education class in the usual school or in the physical education program of the special school. The limitations imposed on these students by their disability are of a social rather than physical nature. To help these students in their adjustment to their handicap and in their relationship with others takes precedence in planning the program to meet their greatest need.

Students who have sustained damage to the semicircular canal of the ear will have poor balance and experience dizziness. Certain limitations in activities are necessary for the safety of these students: activities which require climbing on high equipment or demand acute balancing are usually prohibitive.

Games and Sports.   All the individual and team sports may be learned by the deaf and hard-of-hearing. Many special schools are fielding basketball, baseball, and football teams which compete successfully against teams of hearing players. Deaf students enjoy competitive play and play to win, but more important than the winning or losing are the social contacts provided by the game and the acceptance of their worth by opponents with good hearing.

There are, of course, some hazards to the safety of those with auditory handicaps in competitive play because they are unable to hear signals and other warning sounds. As a precautionary measure, certain visual signals such as the waving of colored flags should be arranged. The instructor should be sure that each participant understands the meaning of each signal before play begins. If the opponents are also nonhearing, the signals should be agreed upon and understood by both teams. If the opponents can hear, they should be alerted to the need for the visual signals and for their cooperation in preventing accidents to hard-of-hearing players.

Fencing, archery, bowling, tennis, golf, and badminton are other sports with demonstrated appeal both for students in deaf schools and in regular schools. Activities such as archery and bowling which can be participated in without others have great value as leisure-time activities for those who cannot hear, for whom many avenues of recreation are closed because of their handicap. Because listening to records, radio, concerts, and similar recreational pursuits which require normal hearing are lost to them, many deaf and hard-of-hearing people do not have adequate recreational outlets and their leisure hours are boring and depressing as a consequence. They should be taught some individual sports which they can participate in during leisure time; however, these should not be emphasized to the detriment of team play, which encourages the give and take of social intercourse so extremely vital to these students.

Swimming. Water play and swimming are enjoyed by those with hearing impairments as much as by other active people. Although some may experience balancing difficulties in the water, nearly all can make satisfactory progress in learning the swimming skills. A modified stroke which permits the head to remain above water will be necessary for those who must not get water in the ears or who become disoriented when their heads are submerged.

Rhythmic Activities and Dance. Children of all ages with auditory handicaps take pleasure in rhythmic movement, even though their hearing of the rhythm in music is totally or partially restricted. For successful performance in musical games and dancing, the students must be taught the pattern of movement, with emphasis upon the length of time each phase of the movement is held before it is changed. To students with hearing this is evident in listening to the musical accompaniment, but for those who cannot hear adequately the teacher must accentuate the rhythm with hand movements so that the student can perceive visually what he cannot perceive by hearing. Some students will, of course, hear some of the music, and even those who do not hear melody experience musical vibrations. For this reason a percussion instrument is helpful in establishing rhythms.

Students should be taught simple tap or folk dances first. The basic steps may be presented in demonstration with the back to the students so they will not become confused as to which foot is being used, as is often the case when the teacher faces the class. Dances and musical games which are performed in circles or squares and involve complex formations are best taught in a straight-line formation and in short parts which are later put together in the required formation.

Motor Exploration. Motor exploration and the use of problems in motor movement to be solved through experimentation help the deaf and hard-of-hearing to lose their fears and inhibitions about moving freely in space. Because each student proceeds at his own pace and his own level of competence in motor movement, he is relieved of the pressures that he usually experiences in more formal activities. With each small gain of confidence in his ability to move his body and to control it will come an increased willingness to expand his movement experience. Eventually, his fears and inhibitions will diminish entirely.

Physical Fitness. Those with auditory handicaps may be underdeveloped physically, owing to their withdrawal from vigorous play activities; they may also be poorly coordinated and purposeless in their movements because of their lack of sound orientation. The physical education program at all levels should include a variety of activities for well-rounded physical development as well as specific exercises which develop cardiorespiratory endurance, coordination, flexibility, and muscular tonus.

Balance.   Although their value is questioned by some, balancing stunts and activities should be included for those students who have difficulty maintaining good balance because of damage to the semicircular canal. Such dysfunction is irreversible, but the kinesthetic sense can be developed and the eyes trained through practice to aid in maintaining body balance in compensation for the loss of semicircular canal control. Young children will enjoy such stunts as walking a line and performing the stork stand (standing on one foot). For older children, work on the pogo stick or on a low balance beam is effective in improving balance. Training in all sport activities encourages the development of better balance in those who lack it.

DUAL SENSORY IMPAIRMENT

Children with dual sensory impairment suffer from loss of both sight and hearing. The Bureau of Education of the Handicapped defines the deaf-blind child as one "who has both auditory and visual impairments, the combination of which causes severe communication and other developmental and educational problems so that he cannot be properly educated in special education programs for the hearing impaired child or the visually impaired." The degree of loss of visual and auditory acuity that cannot be accommodated in special educational programs varies from situation to situation. However, a child with a visual ratio of less than 20/200 or a field of vision of 20 degrees or less who has a hearing loss of 25 decibels or more is usually unable to be educated in such programs and so is considered deaf-blind.

Concern for the education of the deaf-blind has been relatively slow in developing despite the well publicized success in teaching Helen Keller to read and speak. Prior to the 1950s, education of the deaf-blind was confined to a very small and select group; most other such children were given little more than custodial care. During the 1950s interest in and efforts to provide for the educational needs of the deaf-blind gradually gained momentum. The endeavors were given impetus by the sudden increase in the number of children born with dual sensory impairments during the 1963–1965 rubella epidemic. In the wake of this disaster, many schools for the blind expanded their curricula to include programs directed toward the education of deaf-blind children. In 1968, 10 original centers were established, each serving from one to seven states, to provide educational services for the deaf-blind. In 1975 a conference of physical educators and recreationists convened at the University of Iowa to assess needs and recommend recreation programs for the deaf-blind, giving considerable attention to physical recreation.

The Nature and Causes of Dual Sensory Impairment

The most common causes of dual sensory impairment are congenital defects. Other causes are linked to accidents and infectious diseases such as meningitis (inflammation of the membrane covering the brain and spinal column). Of the congenital causes, a large percentage of the cases are the result of the pregnant mother's infection by rubella during the first trimester of pregnancy. Until the 1963–1965 rubella epidemic, the number of cases of dual sensory impairment due to rubella amounted to less than one third of the total number of cases; the figure rose to one half with the widespread outbreak of rubella.

Unfortunately children who are deaf-blind as the result of rubella often have other disabilities as well. Among these are other physical disorders and mental and emotional problems.

Needs and Adjustments of Those Who Are Deaf-blind

The deaf-blind child has problems similar to those of blind children and those of deaf children. However, the negative effects of dual sensory deprivation are multiplicative rather than additive. The effects of both blindness and deafness are much more detrimental than the effects of either deafness or blindness alone, for where these disabilities occur separately, the healthy sense organs can be trained to compensate for the deficient one.

One of the great problems for the deaf-blind person is that very little foundation exists for the development of communication skills. The deaf individual is able to see communications between people, and the blind person is able to hear them, but the deaf-blind person has only limited resources for even knowing that people do communicate.

There is, of course, a great need to develop a means of communication for the deaf-blind. Residual hearing, residual sight, or both can be the basis for communication if the child retains either or both. If there is no residual sight or hearing, communication will depend upon body contact using touch signs, signing in the hands, or both of these. In the former the person who is teaching works with the student to establish certain interpretations of specific touches made on the body. Signing in the hands refers to the use of a manual alphabet in which words are spelled out on the hand of the receiver. Many deaf-blind persons also learn to talk by use of the vibration technique, in which the hands are placed on the face and mouth of the talker to feel the vibrations created by the voice, the movements of the mouth, the control of the breath, and to some extent the placement of the tongue.

Like the blind and the deaf, the deaf-blind child needs to develop the unimpaired senses as well as learn to utilize fully any residual sight or hearing. The deaf-blind child must rely heavily on his tactile, kinesthetic, vestibular (inner ear balance), and olfactory sensations as stimuli for movement. The educational environment should provide opportunities for experiences that encourage such use.

Without the ability to communicate, a child who neither sees nor hears is isolated from the world around him. In his isolation he experiences little of the social interaction required to develop a sense of well-being and to fulfill the basic need of belonging. Consequently, the child urgently needs assistance in learning to relate to others, especially to his peers.

The formation of a positive self-concept is important to normal social development. Knowledge of one's physical self, the body image, is necessary for the development of a concept of the self. Because he has great difficulty in learning to move about in his world, the deaf-blind child has limited opportunities to develop an awareness of his body and to integrate his observations with other information to form a concept of himself as a person. One of his most essential needs, therefore, is to have greatly expanded opportunities to utilize his body in movement.

Experiences that create tactile and social awareness and control of the body in gross and fine motor movements need to be provided. The total movement experience for the deaf-blind child must be varied enough to help him understand his potential in movement and to provide the means to realize this potential.

PROGRAM PLANNING

The physical education activities that can be presented to the deaf-blind child depend upon his age and also upon the degree of deafness and blindness and the extent to which movement has been learned. Movements that are taught should be presented in such a manner that they contribute to the communication skills of the child. To accomplish this the physical education teacher must learn body signs for general communication from the teacher who works with the child so that the same signs can be used in physical education. Other signs will need to be developed to convey certain concepts of movement peculiar to physical education. The signs developed for this purpose should be used consistently, and additional signs should be introduced only when the previously learned signs are inadequate in instructing the child in a new motor movement.

The teacher must also develop a daily routine so that the deaf-blind student will know what to expect each day. The lesson should begin with the teacher identifying himself to the child. A watch or ring that is normally worn every day is useful for this purpose; the child can feel it and know which person he is being taught by. Following the introduction, a review of previously taught movements is desirable. The same order should be used in each review. After practice of the previously taught movements, a new movement can be introduced and the child allowed to experiment and practice it. The lesson may end with a familiar activity or game that the child particularly enjoys.

Suggested Activities

Sample activities and teaching suggestions are given below. Each should be given a specific body sign. The teacher should give the sign each time before an activity starts, so that the student can become aware that this sign refers to the activity that follows. The activities are listed in order of difficulty of performance for most children. However, because of past experience or interest, some children may perform the most difficult skills more easily than the skills preceding them. The order also reflects the increased communication skill that will be developed as the activities progress.

Angels in the Snow.   Place the child in a prone position on the floor. Touch his arms, legs, and head one at a time, helping the child to move the parts touched.

Walking.   Help the child to a standing position. Lead him gently forward by the hands until a step is taken (a helper may be needed to push against the legs).

Rocking in a Chair.   Seat the child in the chair. Help him to rock, indicating the need to shift his weight.

Rocking on Back.   Lay the child on his back. Raise the child's legs to a pike position (knees to chest). Arrange your hands to clasp him around the knees. Lift his head and rock his body gently back and forth. Help him shift his weight so that he rocks by himself.

Rocking on Stomach.   Place the child on his stomach. Raise his legs and indicate that he is to hold them up. Elevate his head and shoulders and indicate that he is to hold them up. Help the child to shift his weight so that he rocks by himself.

Crawling.   Help the child assume the position for crawling. Move his limbs in the proper order to move forward in a crawl (a helper is generally needed).

Kneeling.   Help the child take a position on his knees with his buttocks resting on the back of the legs. Lift his buttocks off the legs to raise the trunk to the upright position.

Finger Play.   Move the fingers of the child into various positions; for example, cross one finger over another, touch the thumb to each finger on the same hand, squeeze and release soft objects.

Rolling Down.   Place the child on an incline mat and move his body so that it rolls forward and down the incline. Help him to shift his weight so that his body rolls without assistance.

Rolling on the Level.   Help the child to take a prone position. Move one leg over the other. Cross the arm on the same side over the body. Push the child over onto his stomach. Move the leg that was moved when the child was on his back over the other leg; pull the same arm across his back until the body turns onto the back.

Pushing and Pulling.   Put the child's hands on the object to be pushed or pulled (for pulling, the fingers are placed around the object). Push or pull the student's arms until the object moves.

Rolling over a Medicine Ball.   Place the ball on the mat. Position the child to lie across the ball on his stomach. Push on his body to start the ball moving forward. Tuck his head so that the back of his head will land on the mat as the ball moves forward. Lift his hips and push them over the ball, lowering the hips to the mat.

Running.   Pull the child along by the hand at a slow run. As the child gains confidence, run with him while each holds opposite ends of a short length of rope.

Running Unaided.   The child holds the guide rope while running (see discussion of this technique in the section on suggested activities for the blind).

Rebounding.   Help the child to balance on an inner tube or a jouncing board. Bounce him by lifting at the waist or under the shoulders. Move his legs from flexion to extension in coordination with the lift and return (a helper will be needed).

Jumping.   Put the child in a standing position and indicate that he is to flex his knees. Lift him up and down, simultaneously helping the legs to flex or extend as in rebounding (a helper will be needed).

Tossing.   Place the child's fingers in a grip around an object to be thrown (a bean bag is the simplest to handle). Lead his arm through tossing movements with one hand; with the other hand pull the object from his grasp. When he begins to release the object without aid, move his arm through the toss more vigorously to achieve forward movement of the object.

Striking.   Set a large ball on a batting tee. Place a bat in the child's hands with the proper grip. Move the bat to within a few inches of the ball. Move the arms through the batting motion to strike the ball. As skill improves, move the bat farther from the ball.

Catching.   Place the child's hands in the proper position for catching. Drop a ball onto his hands and immediately bring his arms up to entrap the ball between the arms and chest.

Moving to Drum Beat.   Place a large drum near enough to the child to enable him to feel the vibrations. Beat the drum with one hand and move parts of the child's body in time to the beat.

Children with more advanced communication and motor skills will be able to participate in more complex activities than those just described. Possibilities are pull-ups, scooter board riding, hula hoop play, bean bag tossing at various targets, rebound tumbling on the trampoline, bouncing a ball, catching and rolling a ball, goal kicking, fungo batting, and moving through an obstacle course.

Older students with good communications skills will be able to participate with assistance in many activities, among them bowling, golf, shuffleboard, archery, weight training, track and field events, rhythms, dance, wrestling, and swimming. Adaptations of these are described in the chapters in which the activities are discussed.

SELECTED READINGS

Birch, Jack: *Hearing Impaired Children in the Mainstream.* Reston, Va., The Council for Exceptional Children, 1975.

Buell, Charles E.: *Physical Education and Recreation for the Visually Handicapped.* Washington, D.C., American Alliance for Health, Physical Education, and Recreation, 1974.

Corbett, Edward E., Jr. (Editor): *The Future of Rubella—Deaf/Blind Children Proceedings.* Dover, Delaware, Department of Public Instruction, 1975.

Horsley, June L. (Editor): *The Role of Physical and Occupational Therapy in Meeting the Needs of the Deaf-Blind Child.* Denver, Colorado, Department of Education, 1972.

Kratz, Laura E.: *Movement Without Sight.* Palo Alto, Calif., Peek Publications, 1973.

Lowenfeld, Berthold: *The Visually Handicapped Child in School.* New York, The John Day Co., 1973.

Nesbitt, John, and Howard, Gordon: *Proceedings of the National Institute on Recreation for Deaf-Blind Children, Youth, and Adults.* Iowa City, Iowa, University of Iowa Press, 1975.

Project Staff, East San Gabriel Valley School: *An Educational Program for Multi-Handicapped Children.* Los Angeles, Office of the Los Angeles County Superintendent of Schools, 1972.

Chapter 13

Cardiopathic Conditions

Long before man understood the physiological function of the heart, he was concerned with its influence upon the body. The ancients at various times considered the heart the source of love, courage, and kindness; and the association of the heart with these virtues still fills our present-day language with such descriptive phrases as stouthearted, queen of my heart, sweetheart, and kindhearted. Actual knowledge of the heart dates from the early 17th century, when William Harvey, an English medical doctor, through animal experimentation and observation of his patients, determined its true function. He recorded his findings in a book, which is today acknowledged as the first accurate description of the heart's function.

With the discovery of the x-ray, a fairly generally held belief that excessive exercise was injurious to the heart appeared to be substantiated. Through the use of x-rays it was determined that pathological hearts were frequently enlarged hearts; it was also determined that athletes had larger hearts than nonathletes. From this evidence the conclusion was made that strenuous exercise worked to the disadvantage of the heart. It was many years before this theory was completely invalidated by physiologists investigating the effects of exercise upon the heart. They discovered that the heart subjected to strenuous exercise over a period of years probably did become larger, but this increase in size resulted from increased strength of the heart muscle rather than from a pathological condition.

Recently, some investigators have found that athletic histories are common among those who experience coronary heart disease early in life. However, the increased incidence of heart disease is found also among those of mesomorphic body build. It has consequently been postulated that body build may be the predisposing factor in the increase of heart disease among athletes, since the majority of athletes are mesomorphic.

Other recent studies have found a relationship between a lack of muscular activity and heart disease. It has been shown that those engaging in sedentary occupations are more prone to heart disease than those whose jobs require muscular activity. Although evidence is not complete, most experts are inclined to agree that a certain amount of exercise throughout one's life is to the advantage of the heart.[1]

Increased participation by junior high schools in varsity athletics during the 1940s gave rise to considerable concern about possible damage which might be inflicted on the immature heart by the strenuous activity of competitive play. Many physical educators and medical personnel voiced the opinion that excessive strenuous activity

[1]American College of Sports Medicine: *Guidelines for Graded Exercise Testing and Exercise Prescription*. Philadelphia, Lea and Febiger, 1975, *passim*.

could affect the young heart detrimentally. However, the preponderance of evidence accumulated since then indicates that, if the heart of the young participant is not predisposed to cardiac disturbance, strenuous activity cannot injure it.

THE NATURE AND CAUSES OF HEART DISEASE

Although the number of deaths due to heart disease is no longer increasing, more than 50 per cent of all deaths in the United States are caused by heart disorders. This high percentage is attributed chiefly to the increase in the number of people who reach the age when heart trouble is most likely to occur. Heart disorders are the primary cause of death of all those over the age of 30.

Most heart disorders which occur in the younger age group are of a congenital nature or are caused by rheumatic fever. It has been estimated that there are about 500,000 children in this country suffering from rheumatic fever. Approximately 18,000 to 20,000 new cases are added each year. Of these, approximately two-thirds show some sign of cardiac damage. About three-fourths of these young heart victims will be able to attend school; the other one-fourth will suffer heart damage severe enough to require home instruction.

Heart disorders are of two classifications — organic and functional. In an organic disorder a definite lesion exists in the heart or other parts of the cardiovascular-renal system. No lesion is present in a functional heart disorder, but there is some disturbance in function. The symptoms are: irregular or accentuated heart beat, weakness after physical effort, shortness of breath, dizziness, fatigue, and considerable concern and anxiety. Some authorities believe the disturbance is chiefly psychogenic in origin, arising, for example, from an imagined heart condition. Treatment along psychiatric lines is indicated in this situation.

Medical research has discovered many different kinds of organic heart diseases. Of these the most commonly occurring and consequently the most important health problems are rheumatic heart disease, hypertensive heart disease, coronary heart disease, and congenital heart diseases.

Rheumatic Heart Disease.   Rheumatic heart disease begins most often in children between the ages of six and 12 as the result of rheumatic fever. Early signs of the rheumatic fever, which may occur singly or in combination, are pain in joints and muscles, twitching of muscles, frequent nosebleeds, pallor, poor appetite, fever, and present or recent streptococcal infection. Evidence of these symptoms does not necessarily mean that a child has rheumatic fever; a period of medical observation and special tests may be necessary to determine the presence of rheumatic fever.

Rheumatic heart disease is the result of an attack of rheumatic fever, but the exact cause is not known. Two factors appear to be involved in its development: allergy and a particular kind of streptococcus infection. Rheumatic fever develops only in certain people who have suffered infection of the throat, respiratory tract, or middle ear caused by hemolytic (blood-destroying) streptococcus organisms and who have developed an allergic and inflammatory reaction to the infection. The rheumatic reaction usually occurs a few weeks after the initial attack of the infection but may not be evident until some time later. Rheumatic fever is not communicable, and there is no danger of contracting it by exposure to one who has it.

Rheumatic fever does not always cause heart disease, and the heart is the only organ which may be seriously affected. During the course of the disease the valves of the heart may become inflamed, and subsequent scarring of the valves and surrounding tissue may result. The valves most frequently affected are the mitral and aortic.

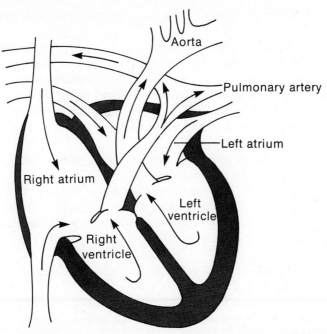

Figure 13–1. Blood enters the right atrium and passes into the right ventricle, where it is pumped to the lungs. Returning from the lungs, the blood enters the left atrium and passes into the left ventricle. It is then pumped through the body by way of the aorta.

The scars may prevent their proper function. When the valves cannot close correctly, a back flow of blood is permitted; this is called regurgitation. If the valves do not open correctly to allow the blood to flow easily, the condition is called stenosis.

Immunity from rheumatic fever does not develop from an attack; on the contrary, the disease tends to recur. Repeated attacks are more likely to damage the heart. For as long as the disease is active and for a period of convalescence it is important to spare the heart unnecessary work. A child with the disease must remain in bed for a given time after which he may participate in motor activity at a gradually accelerated pace.

Hypertensive Heart Disease. Hypertension, or high blood pressure, and changes in the arteries are often associated with heart disease affecting both young people and adults. When the blood pressure is consistently high, the heart is forced to work harder. Arteriosclerosis (hardening of the artery walls) frequently accompanies hypertension, further increasing the work of the heart. When the heart begins to show the effects of this strain, hypertensive heart disease develops.

The causes of arteriosclerosis are not clearly understood. Some authorities feel that an upset in cholesterol (fat) metabolism is a contributing factor; others attribute the disease to hereditary factors. Still others are inclined to blame a mode of living in which excessive anxiety, worry, and fear, and insufficient amounts of rest and relaxation, as well as too much eating and smoking, are common. Such factors are known to increase the work of the heart, thereby placing an added burden on it. Some hardening of the arteries does occur as one grows older as part of the natural process of aging. In males, arteries begin to harden about 10 to 15 years before the process begins in women. The reason for this is not known.

Coronary Heart Disease. Coronary heart disease is most prevalent in middle and old age but sometimes occurs in school-age children. The most serious accident which may occur in coronary heart disease is occlusion (closure) of a coronary artery or a rupture of one of the blood vessels which hemorrhages into the muscle tissue of the heart.

Severe pain in the chest often, but not always, accompanies a heart accident or attack. Weakness, pallor, and sweating may also be present. This condition is known as angina pectoris and is due to anoxia of the myocardium (lack of oxygen to the heart). Excitement, fear, and effort make the condition worse. Bed rest of from two to four weeks is usually advised for a moderately damaged heart before convalescent exercises are begun. A longer bed rest is needed if there has been more extensive damage to the heart.

Other Conditions.   Other causes of heart disease, not as frequent as rheumatic fever, coronary accidents, and hypertensions, are as follows:

OVERACTIVE THYROID.   An overactive thyroid can damage the heart because of increased metabolic activities that may place an excessive burden upon the heart.

ANEMIA.   Severe anemia may injure the heart by placing an undue burden upon it to supply oxygen and by causing a deficiency of oxygen to the heart muscles as well.

Congenital Heart Disease.   This refers to a condition existing at birth which interferes with proper heart function.

Three common congenital heart disorders account for over 50 per cent of all congenital heart defects. These are ventricular septal defects, patent ductus arteriosus, and tetralogy of Fallot.

In ventricular septal defect, lesion occurs, in the septum (center wall) of the ventricles of the heart, that allows the venous blood to mix with the arterial blood. This defect can be repaired by open heart surgery in which the sides of the opening are sutured together or in which a plastic patch is placed over the opening.

Patent ductus arteriosus is a failure of an opening between the aorta and the pulmonary artery to close prior to birth. This opening, the ductus arteriosus, is open during prenatal life, allowing most of the blood of the fetus to bypass the lungs, but normally it closes shortly before birth. When the ductus arteriosus remains open, an undue stress is placed upon the heart. In early life, the symptoms often go undetected. As he becomes older and more active, symptoms of dyspnea (shortness of breath) are noticed when the child exerts himself. Surgery can correct the defect and is usually performed when the child is four to 10 years old. Prognosis is excellent, and the child can often participate in activities without restrictions.

Tetralogy of Fallot is the disorder that occurs in so-called "blue babies." It combines four structural abnormalities: narrowing of the pulmonary artery, ventricular septal defect, enlarged right ventricle, and an abnormal positioning of the root of the aorta that causes it to receive blood from both the right and left ventricles. This, the most serious of the congenital heart disorders, does respond well to surgery in a large number of cases. Without corrective surgery the prognosis is extremely poor.

INFECTION.   Heart disease may be brought about by infection of the inner lining of the heart. This infection is called endocarditis. If the outer covering of the heart, or pericardium, is infected, it is called pericarditis. Another condition, called myocarditis, is an inflammation of the heart muscle, or myocardium.

DISEASE.   The heart can be affected by several of the childhood diseases, notably diphtheria. Tuberculosis and syphilis are other diseases causing heart disease.

Symptoms of Heart Disease

A normal heart makes certain characteristic sounds, which can be heard when the ear or stethoscope is placed in a specific area over a person's chest. There are definite variations in these sounds that accompany certain pathological conditions of the heart. These sounds are known as murmurs. Some murmurs are caused by a structural deviation such as valvular incompetence (leaky valves). Frequently, however, adolescents have functional heart murmurs not caused by a structural deviation. Such a murmur has little significance and should not become the focus of worry and concern. It will very likely disappear as the youngster grows older. Restriction of activity is not necessary.

The important danger signals of heart disease are related to the failure of the heart to perform properly. The following symptoms may indicate heart disease: pain in the chest; shortness of breath; edema (swelling) in the feet, ankles, or abdomen; dizziness; fatigue; indigestion; and double vision. People who experience a disturbance in heart rhythm (skipping a beat) often become greatly concerned, but there is usually no reason for concern, as a very large percentage of these cases show no presence of heart disease. Chest pain may result from many different causes. A sharp pain accompanying deep breath inhalation is very seldom due to heart disease. The pain that accompanies heart disease is of a stifling, crushing nature. Dizziness, fatigue, indigestion, double vision, and shortness of breath also frequently come from other causes than heart disease. No one should assume he has heart disease because he has any, or even all, of the symptoms until he has had a thorough medical examination; in many instances the symptoms are not related to heart diseases.

Emergency Care for Heart Cases

Cardiac crises occur most frequently in older people. However, they do happen in school-age children. The steps in emergency care which should be familiar to the teacher are:

1. Let the person assume the most comfortable position—this will usually be a sitting position.
2. Loosen tight clothing.
3. Give him plenty of air but avoid drafts.
4. Call the doctor immediately. Reassure the patient. The teacher's manner will affect the entire class as well as the patient, so he should strive to remain calm and unemotional.

Classification of Patients with Cardiac Conditions

The physical limitations imposed by cardiac conditions vary depending upon the degree and amount of malfunction of the heart. Patients with heart diseases are classified according to their tolerance to exercise by the American Heart Association as follows:

Mild. Patients with cardiac disease resulting in slight limitation of physical activity. They are comfortable at rest. More than ordinary physical activity results in fatigue, palpitation, dyspnea, or anginal pain.

Moderate. Patients with cardiac disease resulting in moderate limitation of physical activity. They are comfortable at rest. Less than ordinary activity causes fatigue, palpitation, dyspnea, or anginal pain.

Limited. Patients with cardiac disease resulting in inability to carry on any physical activity without discomfort. Symptoms of cardiac insufficiency or of the anginal syndrome are present even at rest. If any physical activity is undertaken, discomfort is increased.

Needs and Adjustments of Those with Cardiopathic Conditions

Youngsters who have had heart disabilities since early childhood do not usually have the same emotional problems as those who are suddenly afflicted. They are, however, likely to find their normal urges frustrated. Because active play with other children is restricted, the young cardiac may be socially immature. If his feeling of being left out of things is very great, he may become withdrawn and harbor feelings of resentment or inferiority. High-school-age youngsters often give evidence of severe frustrations arising from their inability to participate fully in the active games and social activities of their age group. Particularly emotionally distressing to some boys is the thwarting of athletic ambitions. Such a youngster may react with an attitude that, since he is going to die anyway, there is no need to practice care. On the other hand, he may withdraw entirely from social contacts. While this is not as dangerous physically, it can be very damaging psychologically.

Such children need to be counseled into a better course of adjustment, one which recognizes the restrictions as essential but points up the effective and enjoyable life which is possible within the limitations. Direct counseling is usually in the province of other school personnel, but the physical education teacher can do a great deal to reinforce the importance of exercising the necessary controls. If the cardiac student is part of a special class, he will soon become aware that others must also live with certain restrictions. The adapted activities which he learns to play will not only help him to observe the necessary controls in regard to physical exertion, they will also give him the skills to fill his leisure hours with recreational activities which he can participate in with his own age group.

Muscular activity is valuable not only in maintaining the fitness of the heart, but also in promoting total body fitness. A certain amount of muscular activity is necessary to maintain strength and endurance of the skeletal muscle system. Moreover, exercise is an important factor in digestion and the elimination of wastes, as well as a factor in the feeling of well-being.

Many cardiac children can take part in many of the regular physical education activities. Whenever they can be permitted to do so, they should take part in the regular class. No limitations or restrictions need be imposed unless they have been advised by the doctor, as will be the case with students who have been placed on a graded exercise program.

Graded Exercise Program. A graded exercise program is sometimes recommended by physicians to increase the efficiency of the cardiorespiratory system of patients with heart problems. Before the program is set up, an evaluation of the individual's tolerance for exercise is made; for this purpose, a stress or graded exercise test is administered. Basically this test consists of the application of a gradually increased workload over a short period of time during which the heart is monitored by an electrocardiograph. The test provides information about the functional capacity of the heart and about its reaction to exercise. The functional capacity of the heart is expressed in the number of pulse beats per minute.

The graded exercise program is then established with the objective of providing a workload that will produce a pulse rate of approximately 70 per cent of the functional capacity. As the individual becomes conditioned by the exercise, his pulse rate decreases when performing the same amount of work. When this occurs, the workload is increased to again bring the pulse rate up to 70 per cent of the functional capacity. Activities included in the graded exercise program are those that allow great control over intensity; that is, they are self-paced and performed in a stable environment. Examples are walking, jogging, cycling, swimming, and calisthenics.

PLANNING THE PROGRAM

In planning the program for those with cardiac conditions the tolerance level for exercise of each student must be established. If his condition has been classified in one of the categories described on page 171, the physical educator may make suggestions for each student based upon his knowledge of the necessary limitations. The program must, of course, have the approval of the doctor.

When selecting activities, it must be kept in mind that the strenuousness of an activity is not determined solely by its type but by how vigorously and how long it is performed. Some individuals may play table tennis at such a rapid pace that the activity might be classified as moderate, whereas other patients may play much more slowly and deliberately so that the activity would be only mild in nature.

Age, personality, drives, and attitudes all determine the strenuousness with which a person performs an activity. Some may be more tense and work harder under the pressure of the learning situation with a teacher, while in free play they are much more relaxed. There are also those players, particularly among children, who in free play without the guidance of the instructor will not set a wise course in their play. There is a general tendency for children to overwork in muscular activity, while adults are generally too sedentary. All such factors must be given consideration in planning the program.

Competitive play with its emphasis on winning is contraindicated for most heart patients. The emotions involved may speed the action of the heart so that the over-all work of the activity is beyond the tolerance level for the patient. Moreover, when there is an overemphasis on winning there is always a possibility that the participant may ignore safety precautions which he would otherwise heed.

The physical education teacher must be sure that he has all the medical information needed to provide suitable activity at the appropriate level of intensity for those students who have been placed by their doctors on a graded exercise program. Frequent monitoring of the pulse is necessary to enable the participant to adjust the exercise level. Older students are capable of taking their own pulse or may have learned from experience to predict the level of intensity from subjective feelings. The teacher may need to take the pulse count of younger participants. This is readily done by counting the palpitations at the brachial (wrist) or carotid (neck) pulse points. Exercise heart rate can be determined with reasonable accuracy by making either 10 or 15 seconds pulse counts immediately upon the completion of exercise and multiplying by either 6 or 4, respectively, to obtain the per minute count.

The student's exercise tolerance level should be discussed with him, and he should have a clear understanding of his capacity and the amount of activity that constitutes an adequate work load. A guide to help the participant keep within his tolerance level is that as long as he can perform the activity without breathing through the mouth or without forced breathing through the nose he is not overexerting. Activity should stop at once if any cardiac distress or shortness of breath is evidenced.

Short periods of activity are usually best. Rest periods should be provided about halfway through an activity and should equal in length the time devoted to activity.

Some special consideration will need to be given to the influence weather conditions and certain features of the facilities may have on the planned program. In extremely hot weather or on damp rainy days, special precautions may be required for the cardiacs. If activity is to take place on rough or hilly playing areas, the expenditure of energy is likely to be greater, and consideration of this fact should be made in regard to the cardiac patient.

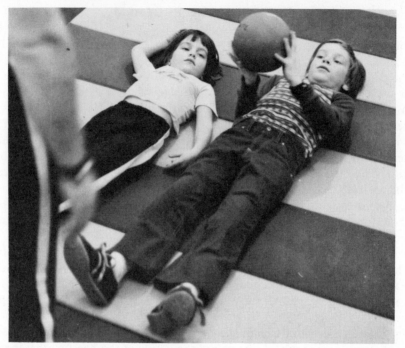

Figure 13–2.   The strenuousness of throwing and catching can be modified by lying down to play.

Flexibility exercises designed to extend the range of movement in the various joints of the body are desirable for total fitness and do not appear to tap the cardiovascular system greatly. They should be included in an exercise program because they maintain complete movement potential. In general, slow stretching with a short period of holding at the extreme range appears to be the best way to develop flexibility with minimal risk of muscle pulls.

Suggested Activities

The following activities are suggested for each class of heart patients; they are intended as a guide for the physical education teacher from which he can develop a program for the approval of the medical doctor.

Mild: Most activities may be offered, including swimming. The participation should not extend over long periods of time. Long-distance running should be avoided; participation in varsity athletic competition and other highly competitive play in which there is great emphasis upon winning is contraindicated.

Badminton and handball may be played as doubles to reduce the strenuousness of the activity, and tennis may be played with the court width cut in half and with the elimination of the drop shot to modify the demands on physical exertion. Other activities which may be employed without modification are:

Softball	Swimming
Paddle ball	Tetherball
Tumbling	

Moderate: These activities are moderately active; players should be warned against making the game strenuous by becoming highly competitive or overactive while playing:

Bowling	Table tennis
Croquet	Bag punching
Bowling on the green	Hiking
Archery	Fly/bait casting and spinning
Horseshoes	Volleyball
Shuffleboard	Interpretative dances
Waltzing	Horseback riding
Folk dancing	Rope spinning

Limited: Activities suggested for this group are:

Walking	Fly/bait casting and spinning
Shuffleboard	Exercises for increasing flexibility
Rifle shooting	

For very young children, many of the basic skill games described in Chapter 20 are applicable, depending upon the classification of the child. Singing games may be used but, if the child is joining in the singing, he should not attempt to perform at the same time, as this may be too strenuous. The teacher or the others in the class may sing while he performs. Games that do not require sustained periods of running, such as Red Light and Call Ball, are very good for children with moderate functional capacity, as they enable the player to rest for short periods between action. Games such as Wonder Ball and Circle Ball, which utilize body activities other than running, are fine exercises. The work load for heart patients may be further minimized by having the children seated to pass the ball around, or the children may lie down in line and a balloon may be substituted for the ball. Another popular activity is modified volleyball. For this game a badminton net is stretched across the playing area three or four feet above the floor; the students sit on each side of the net and volley a balloon back and forth as in volleyball.

SELECTED READINGS

American College of Sports Medicine: *Guidelines for Graded Exercise Testing and Exercise Prescription.* Philadelphia, Lea and Febiger, 1975.

American Heart Association: *If Your Child Has a Congenital Heart Defect.* New York, American Heart Association, 1970.

Burch, George E.: *A Primer of Cardiology,* ed. 5. Philadelphia, Lea and Febiger, 1977.

Fletcher, Gerald, and Cantwell, John: *Exercise and Coronary Heart Disease.* Springfield, Illinois, Charles C Thomas, Pub., 1974.

Morse, Robert L. (Editor): *Exercise and the Heart.* Springfield, Illinois, Charles C Thomas, Pub., 1972.

Ross, John, and O'Rourke, Robert: *Understanding the Heart and Its Diseases.* New York, McGraw-Hill Book Co., 1976.

Chapter 14

Respiratory Disorders

The respiratory disorders discussed in this chapter will be those that prevent adequate ventilation of the lungs, a condition that leads to an insufficient supply of oxygen and the retention of carbon dioxide in the body. The causes of respiratory disorders may be the loss of elasticity of the breathing mechanism, muscular weakness, increased resistance to the flow of air through the connecting tubes of the respiratory system, increased thickness or destruction of the air sacs of the lungs, or a combination of the above.

As a background for understanding the nature of respiratory disorders, a brief review of the anatomy of the respiratory system is useful. The respiratory system may be thought of as having an upper and a lower level. The upper level includes the head and throat, and is made up of the nasal cavity, pharynx, and trachea. These act chiefly as passages for the air, allowing the air to warm before entering the lungs. The diaphragm and the two lungs, which lie on either side of the heart, make up the lower level (Fig. 14–1). The left lung has two lobes (divisions); the right lung has three. The lungs consist mainly of bronchi, bronchioli, and alveoli. The bronchi are tubes branching from the trachea; the bronchioli are branches of the bronchi that transport the air to the alveoli, which are small saclike structures where oxygen and carbon dioxide are exchanged.

Various muscles are also involved in the work of the respiratory system. The most important of these, because it is the primary muscle used in breathing, is the diaphragm, a dome-shaped muscle separating the chest and abdominal cavities. In contraction it flattens and loses it domed appearance, thereby enlarging the chest cavity and allowing expansion of the lungs. This results in inspiration of air into the lungs. When the diaphragm relaxes, the chest cavity diminishes in size and air is forced out of the lungs.

Certain muscles of the neck, chest, and abdomen assist the diaphragm in the breathing process; they also have other functions. If weak, these muscles can be strengthened by exercises of the trunk. The muscles* referred to are the iliocostalis lumborum and iliocostalis dorsi (both are located under the ligamentous band, which is the tissue at the small of the back into which the latissimus dorsi inserts); the external and internal oblique muscles (the internal lies beneath the external); and the rectus abdominus.

The most familiar and most commonly occurring disorders of the respiratory system are asthma, hay fever, emphysema, chronic bronchitis, and cystic fibrosis.

---

*The location of the muscles below the surface are identified by their relationship to the surface muscles. See Figure 26–3 in Chapter 26 for location of the surface muscles of the body.

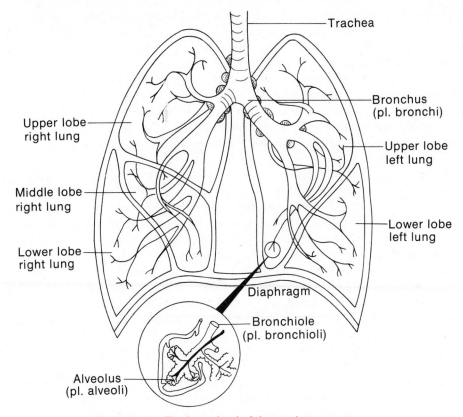

Figure 14–1. The lower level of the respiratory system.

(Tuberculosis, although well known, is no longer a common disease, owing to the effectiveness of treatment and preventive measures.) Asthma, hay fever, and cystic fibrosis affect both children and adults. Emphysema is much more prevalent among adults. There are two types of bronchitis, acute and chronic. The acute form attacks both children and adults, but the chronic form is more common among adults. Even though chronic bronchitis and emphysema primarily affect adults, and, therefore, do not meet the criterion for discussion in this book, we will discuss these diseases briefly, because the basis for their development is laid during childhood and youth. It is generally agreed in the medical profession that these two disorders are insidious; that is, they develop over a long period of time, as the result of inhalation of irritants such as smoke in the heavy use of tobacco, dust, and fumes. Because the kind of air that is breathed in earlier years affects the possibility of incurring chronic bronchitis and emphysema at a later date, educators have a responsibility to make young people aware of the latent dangers of air pollution and smoking, and to teach them the means of prevention. Handicapped students, particularly, need to know how to avoid adding another health problem to the difficulties they are already experiencing.

ASTHMA

Asthma is the common term used for the condition of bronchial asthma. It is a disease of the bronchi characterized by swelling of the mucous membrane lining the bronchial tubes, excessive secretion of mucus, and spasms of the bronchial tubes.

Symptoms of asthma are dyspnea (breathlessness), coughing and wheezing, and a feeling of constriction in the chest. Typically an attack of asthma is characterized by a coughing stage, followed by dyspnea and wheezing. The attack usually terminates with the coughing up of a large amount of thick sputum.

People afflicted with asthma tend to overuse the intercostal muscles in breathing at the expense of the diaphragm. Also, there is a tendency to tighten the abdominal muscles during inspiration, which further reduces the action of the diaphragm. The reduction in action causes a decrease in the amount of air that is inhaled. Continual reliance on the upper chest muscles for breathing results in a gradual loss of flexibility of the diaphragm.

Asthma is a chronic disease in which periodic attacks are followed by periods of remission of the symptoms. Attacks vary greatly in severity and duration; they may range from a slight period of wheezing to a prolonged period of coughing accompanied by severe dyspnea. An attack that persists for days is referred to as status asthmaticus. Attacks are frequently triggered by breathing very cold air or air that has a high content of moisture, or by respiratory tract infections.

Extrinsic asthma is caused by the reaction of the body to the introduction of a foreign substance to which the body is sensitive. Usually this substance, called an allergen, is suspended in inhaled air; however, the offending substance may also be ingested in the form of food or drugs. The most common allergens are plant pollen, dust, molds, and animal fur.

Asthmatic attacks may be induced by exercise. Fatigue and emotions are also factors in attacks. The tolerance level for exercise of those subject to exercise-induced asthma varies from person to person but is related to physical condition; those who are in good physical condition usually have a higher tolerance than those who are not. Attacks also strike different people at different times. In some people, the symptoms occur during exercise; in others, the symptoms manifest themselves several minutes after the end of the activity.

An as yet undefined relationship exists between asthma and the emotions. Some cases are thought to be due chiefly to emotional stress, since they have no extrinsic causes and the symptoms disappear when the emotional tension subsides. Because extrinsic asthmatic cases often become worse in times of emotional distress, this type of asthma is generally considered to be psychosomatic.

Asthmatic attacks that are neither extrinsic in nature nor primarily caused by emotional reaction are thought to be related in some way to a deficient cellular function that affects the sympathetic nervous system, which, in turn, alters the tonus of the bronchial tube linings.

The greatest incidence of asthma occurs among young children, many of whom no longer have asthmatic attacks after puberty. It has been estimated that 2 or 3 per cent of the population of the United States are asthmatic. The incidence of asthma is slightly higher among males than among females.

Treatment. The treatment of asthma begins with attempts to determine the cause. The cause may be an allergen, which must be identified so that it can be avoided. If avoidance is not possible, medication is administered.

There is no permanent cure for asthma. However, certain drugs have been very effective in decreasing the number and severity of attacks. Drugs that enlarge the bronchioli and thin the secretion help the affected person to cough up the mucus blocking the air passage.

Appropriate physical fitness exercises to improve the condition of the body have been found to be helpful to victims of exercise-induced asthma. The asthmatic response to exercise can also be fairly well controlled by the use of drugs. Persons with status asthmaticus are very seriously ill and must be under the care of a physician. They must exercise extreme caution to avoid excessive strain on the heart and lungs.

A person having an asthmatic attack should, in most instances, be placed in the charge of a physician as soon as possible. However, there are some emergency care measures that can be helpful. Relief from breathing difficulties can be given by supporting the victim in a sitting position during the attack. Calming the person is also beneficial because of the influence of the emotions on the severity and frequency of attacks.

HAY FEVER

Hay fever is an allergic disease caused by a sensitivity to specific substances in the air. The most common allergens are pollen and the spores of mold. Spores of mold are not commonly found in the air; however, pollen, especially ragweed pollen, is frequently present, depending upon the geographic area and the time of year when plants release their pollen.

A milder disorder than asthma, hay fever, involves only the upper level of the respiratory system. It is characterized by sneezing, watery eyes, and a runny nose. Often these symptoms are accompanied by a burning sensation in the throat and the roof of the mouth.

Hay fever often interferes with sleep and appetite and can lower the body's resistance to disease. It may lead to inflammation of the ears, sinuses, throat, and bronchi. In some cases it may even be a precursor of asthma.

There is no permanent cure for hay fever, although the symptoms may be relieved. Avoiding the allergen is the most effective preventive measure. Desensitizing injections given in a series have proved to be a helpful preventive for many sufferers. The severity of attacks can be effectively reduced by the use of antihistamines and other drugs.

CYSTIC FIBROSIS

Cystic fibrosis is also called mucoviscidosis. It is inherited as a mendelian or recessive trait; both parents must carry the trait. Although not clearly established, the cause is generally assumed to be an abnormality or inadequacy of some hormone or enzyme of the body that affects the excretion of mucus, saliva, and perspiration. The disease is characterized by the excretion of excessively thick mucus and abnormal amounts of sweat and saliva.

The most serious effect of cystic fibrosis is caused by the production of extremely thick mucus that interferes with breathing and digestion. Mucus of normal consistency flows easily, carrying with it foreign substances, bacteria, wastes, and dirt that will be eliminated from the body. The mucus of the person affected with cystic fibrosis does not flow readily but adheres to surfaces with which it comes in contact. As the mucus adheres to the lungs, it creates breathing problems because it blocks the bronchioli. Infection follows, causing damage to the lung tissue. Also, the thick mucus can block the ducts of the pancreas, a gland whose excretion is vital to digestion. When this blockage occurs, digestion is hindered because the pancreatic excretion cannot reach the small intestine. Fats become especially difficult to digest. Consequently, a child with cystic fibrosis may have a good appetite and eat well and yet fail to grow or gain weight. The most marked symptom of a blocked pancreas duct is the production of bulky, fatty, foul smelling feces.

The presence of the disease can be confirmed by use of a sweat test in which the perspiration is analyzed for concentration of sodium and chlorides (constituents of salt). Chlorides and sodium are released in perspiration; the detection of a large amount of either in the perspiration indicates the presence of the disease.

It is estimated that the incidence of cystic fibrosis is about one in every 1000 births. As high as 3 to 4 per cent of the population of the United States may carry the gene that produces the disease. The frequency of the disease is greater among Caucasians than among Negroes; it is rare among Orientals.

The prognosis of cystic fibrosis is unpredictable. Over 60 per cent of children with the disease die before they reach puberty, and over 75 per cent die before the age of 18; but some live well into adulthood.

Treatment. Treatment involves procedures to aid in the removal of the thick mucus from the lungs and the manipulation of the diet to avoid fatty foods and to ensure ingestion of large amounts of proteins. In addition, extracts of animal pancreas are given with meals to compensate for the pancreatic deficiency.

Various procedures utilized to aid the drainge of thick mucus in the lungs are use of a mist tent to dilute the secretion in the lungs, aerosol therapy in which medication is introduced directly into the lungs, oral expectorants that induce ejection of the mucus, and postural drainage, in which different lying postures are assumed to encourage the draining of the lobes of the lungs so that the mucus will be coughed up and expelled. To help dislodge mucus, the technique of clapping on and vibration of the chest may be applied while the individual is in the drainage position.

BRONCHITIS

Bronchitis is an inflammation of the bronchi of the lungs. The condition may be either acute or chronic. It is possible for acute bronchitis to develop into chronic bronchitis.

Acute bronchitis, which is common among small children, also occurs frequently among adults. In mild cases the disease is sometimes referred to as a cold in the chest. However, acute bronchitis can be a serious disease if it progresses downward into the bronchioli. In its milder form the disease is not a serious concern to the physical education teacher, since it usually runs its course in about 10 days. Children returning to school after severe acute bronchitis should be given the same considerations in physical education as are given the convalescent. (See the section on convalescence, in Chapter 16.)

Chronic bronchitis is a serious disease that interferes with breathing, resulting in dyspnea. Along with shortening of the breath, the sufferer coughs and frequently expels phlegm from the bronchial tubes. The disease may follow a series of attacks of acute bronchitis, or it may appear abruptly or insidiously with no apparent cause. Its chief cause is the long-term inhalation of irritants, such as dust and tobacco fumes. The "smoker's cough" is, in most cases, chronic bronchitis.

Chronic bronchitis usually affects older adults. The incidence is greater among men than among women; however, with the increasing prevalence of smoking among women, the difference in the number of cases is diminishing. Also, as the age of becoming a smoker decreases, the frequency of the disease in young people increases.

Administration of antibiotics and medications to loosen the phlegm in the bronchi is the chief treatment of the disease. Postural drainage, referred to in the discussion of cystic fibrosis, is also effective with chronic bronchitis.

EMPHYSEMA

Like chronic bronchitis, emphysema is a disease more common among adults than among children. In the course of the disease destruction of the alveolar walls occurs. Small holes appear in the alveolar membrane, and the lungs as a whole lose their elasticity. The symptoms of emphysema are dyspnea, coughing, and wheezing. The wheezing is usually not as prominent as it is in asthma. Often the victim develops a barrel-shaped chest as the result of repeated overexpansion of the lungs and excessive use of upper chest muscles in an attempt to provide sufficient oxygen to the body.

It is known that a relationship exists between the incidence of emphysema and air pollution and smoking. As smoking and air pollution have increased, there has been a dramatic rise in the number of cases of emphysema. Currently, chronic emphysema kills over 10,000 people in the United States each year. The disease occurs more frequently in males than in females and is more common among Caucasians than among Negroes. It is thought by some medical specialists in respiratory diseases that a defect in the elastic tissue of the lungs may make certain individuals more susceptible than others.

Bronchodilators are drugs used in the treatment of emphysema to enlarge the bronchi and provide better pathways for the air. Expectorants are administered to aid in the removal of mucus from the lungs. Postural drainage and breathing exercises may also be prescribed. In more severe cases a respirator (a machine that assists breathing) may be used.

Bronchial Hygiene for Respiratory Disorders

There are various procedures and practices that help to alleviate the health problems of persons having respiratory disorders. Two of the most effective of these bronchial hygiene measures are belly, or diaphragmatic, breathing and postural drainage.

Persons who have poor breathing habits usually do not use the diaphragm sufficiently in breathing; rather, they rely chiefly on the chest, rib, and back muscles to expand the lungs. Hence, these muscles become very tight and tense. Inefficient breathing can be corrected through specially designed exercises. Basically, the exercises assist in relaxing spasmodically contracted muscles and in decreasing the tension in rib, chest, and back muscles (the intercostals, pectoralis major and minor, and trapezius).

The basis of the exercises for diaphragmatic breathing is learning to empty the lungs more efficiently and effectively so that new air can be inhaled. The emphasis is placed upon exhalation, since, if sufficient air is expelled, an adequate amount of air will automatically return when the respiratory muscles relax. The exhalation takes place over a long period of time, taking approximately twice as long as inhalation. In the inhalation, the muscles of the abdomen are relaxed and the belly is protruded so the diaphragm can descend. The importance of extending the belly cannot be exaggerated.

With the use of the correct procedures, less effort is expended in breathing. All of the muscles are less tense. Muscles that add little to increasing the air flow in and out of the lungs, like the scalenes (neck muscles), which are frequently used in forced breathing, are not utilized. Contraction of the abdominal muscles in forced inspiration, another common error, is avoided. The net effect is improved efficiency and comfort in respiration and conservation of energy for use in other body functions.

Postural drainage is the term given to a bronchial hygenic procedure in which specific positions of the body are assumed to aid the removal of secretion from the lungs. The procedure is prescribed in conjunction with the use of bronchodilators, drugs that reduce the swelling in the lungs.

The positions for postural drainage place the chest and head lower than the rest of the body to allow the force of gravity to pull the mucus from the lungs so that it can be coughed up more easily. Recommended positions and the portion of the lungs drained in each position are shown in Figure 14–2. The treatment, which occurs three times daily, lasts for 20 to 30 minutes with three or four minutes spent in each position. It is generally recommended that the treatment sessions occur just before the three meals are taken in order to reduce the possibility of regurgitation.

Clapping on and vibration of the chest with the hands help dislodge the mucus during postural drainge. Their use requires special training and should not be practiced by the physical educator without instruction from a physician or physical therapist.

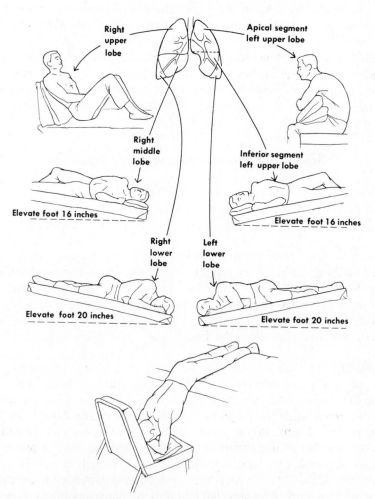

Figure 14–2. Postural drainage positions for draining various portions of the lungs. The bottom figure is in a less specific, though commonly used, position. (Miller and Keane *Encyclopedia and Dictionary of Medicine and Nursing,* p. 770.)

Needs and Adjustments for those with Respiratory Disorders

Youngsters afflicted with the more severe types of respiratory disorders are unable to participate normally in vigorous group play. Exclusion from the active games of childhood tends to produce feelings of isolation and doubts about self-worth, which if prolonged and intensified can cause serious problems of adjustment. The physical education teacher is particularly well placed to provide opportunities to fulfill these youngsters' need for social interaction by integrating them into group activities.

Lack of participation in vigorous play, which is necessary for a high level of physical fitness, produces a great need among these children for general body conditioning. Increase in strength is important, particularly the strength of the muscles of the chest and abdomen that aid in breathing. Deep breathing exercises that strengthen the muscles of respiration and develop efficient patterns of breathing can be of special benefit.

Motivating asthmatic students to engage in activities that are sufficiently vigorous to promote physical fitness presents a serious problem. The exertion of physical effort, particularly if accompanied by anxiety about doing well, tends to heighten the symptoms of respiratory diseases—breathing is more difficult, and wheezing and coughing are more pronounced. A severe attack can be a terrifying experience. Rather than risk an attack that is either frightening or embarrassing or both, the youngsters prefer not to engage in the activity. The more frequent the withdrawals from activity, the greater is the loss of tolerance for exercise. A vicious circle can become established in which the lower level of tolerance intensifies the avoidance of physical exertion that further lowers the exercise tolerance level, and so on.

For children caught in this cycle, a positive attitude toward participation in physical activity must be promoted. A good first step for the teacher is to develop social acceptance of the nose blowing, expectorating, and wheezing and coughing necessitated by the respiratory disorder. The teacher should be sure that there are paper towels or tissues (or even a receptacle for spitting) readily available and should treat the need to use them as entirely oridinary. An attitude of acceptance on the part of the teacher will do much to reassure both the afflicted youngsters and their classmates that the conduct required to attend to an ailment or a handicap is neither repulsive nor impolite.

Other steps the teacher may take depend largely upon the individual child—his interests, abilities, and adjustment. Ensuring success in his early efforts to perform an exercise or activity is, of course, the keynote of any motivational strategy.

Youngsters with a severe respiratory disorder often experience tension, owing to anxiety about performing a motor activity or owing to other causes. Consequently, it is very beneficial to them to learn the techniques of conscious relaxation. Most of the exercises for relaxation suggested in Chapter 29 make minimal demands on strength, endurance, and skill ability and so can be successfully performed by students in poor physical condition and with low tolerance for exercise. The satisfaction these students find in doing the exercises, as well as the pleasure they experience from relaxing, can provide the impetus for attempting other physical education activities.

PLANNING THE PROGRAM

For the most part, students with respiratory disorders will be able to participate in the regular physical education class. However, it may be necessary to provide rest periods of four to five minutes after several minutes of participation or to adapt the activities so that they will be less strenuous. All but a very few students can engage in non-endurance activities without modification. The few who cannot must be given special consideration.

Specific breathing exercises to increase the efficiency of respiration may be provided for those who require or may benefit from them. Because such exercises are of very little value to those who do not have breathing difficulties, they should be planned only for those who need them; the other students can spend the time more productively in other activities.

Students with breathing problems will also benefit from exercises that strengthen the muscles involved in respiration and those that generally improve physical fitness. Conditioning must be approached cautiously, however. It must be a very gradual process, beginning with mild activity and slowly increasing in strenuousness as the student is able to tolerate a greater workload. Any activity planned for the student should be checked with his physician.

It is important in planning physical education activities for students with respiratory disorders that their participation will not exceed their level of tolerance for exercise. A rule-of-thumb guide for the teacher to use in deciding when to terminate an activity is a noticeable increase in the performer's breathing rate. The breathing of air through the mouth is a good indication that the rate is increased.

In program planning, consideration must also be given to the possibility that air pollution may reach a level dangerous to health. In this event, exercises and activities requiring deep breathing should be discontinued for *all* students. Outdoor physical education classes should be terminated. If the classes are continued indoors, only those activities and games that do not require strenuous effort should be offered. Table tennis, shuffleboard, bowling, ring toss, and volleyball are among the possibilities. Students with respiratory disorders should be excused from activity, since their condition is particularly endangered by air pollution.

Suggested Activities

For older children and youths with respiratory disorders who can tolerate only minimal stress on the respiratory system, activities such as golf, archery, bowling, shuffleboard, table tennis, and weight training are usually appropriate. Of the suggested activities, weight training needs the most adaptation; the others require only the interspersion of occasional rest periods of about five minutes after every 15 to 20 minutes of participation.

Golf, archery, and weight training provide exercise to strengthen the chest muscles that aid the process of breathing. Weight training is of special value in accomplishing this objective, since the specific muscles that assist inhalation can be isolated and strengthened, applying the SAID principle (see Chapter 27).

Swimming is an activity in which nearly everyone can participate. However, some asthmatics may be sensitive to chlorine and will be unable to swim in chlorinated water. Swimming may also be contraindicated for persons with ear, nose, and throat disorders and those whose exercise-induced asthma cannot be adequately controlled with medication. For the latter, frequent rest periods during swimming, and termination of the activity before fatigue sets in are often sufficient to prevent an attack.

Trampolining is suggested, in spite of its strenuousness, as an activity for persons with cystic fibrosis or asthma. Adams and Adamson[1] have found trampolining beneficial

---

[1]R.C. Adams, and E. Adamson: "Trampoline Tumbling for Children with Chronic Lung Disease. JOHPER, *44*:4, April, 1973, pp. 86–87.

for children with accumulations of secretions in the bronchial tree; the rebounding improved drainage of the respiratory tract. However, the amount of time the participant spends on the trampoline should be strictly limited as a control on the strenuousness of the activity. The rule-of-thumb guide for cessation of exercise is useful in deciding when the activity should be terminated.

Some students with severe breathing disorders that require special consideration may be able to participate in strenuous team games with a slight modification that provides for substitute players to relieve them after two or three minutes of participation for periods of rest of five or more minutes. Volleyball and softball can often be played without adaptation, although those who are severely affected may need to have someone run bases for them in softball.

Younger children are generally able to participate in regular physical education activities. If the class is taught by the indirect method that utilizes movement exploration or problem solving, it is relatively easy to control the strenuousness of activity to the level of exertion most appropriate for each student. Many basic skill games like Pussy Wants a Corner, Circle Ball, and Red Light can be played by children with respiratory disorders because periods of rest after brief periods of movement are inherent in the game.

Other basic skill games are easily adapted to decrease the amount of energy used and so lessen in the stress upon the lungs. In most games energy requirements can be reduced by decreasing the distance required to move, slowing the tempo of movement, and interspersing milder activities or rests between periods of more strenuous play as, for example, clapping the hands or keeping time with the foot at intervals during a square dance. In the game of Red Light, any of the following suggestions may be used to decrease the strenuousness of the play: reducing the distance the players must travel, requiring players to walk rather than run, and stipulating that when the player who is Red Light turns, he must lead the group in clapping slowly in unison five to 10 times to provide a rest period. Stunt activities such as leap frog, measuring worm, and seal walk are easily modified by working with the child to set limits for himself as to how long and vigorously he is going to perform the stunt.

Children with breathing problems should begin their physical education program with breathing exercises. The techniques developed in these exercises should be learned so thoroughly that they become automatic and can be used at all times, most particularly when performing motor activity.

Children who are not accustomed to breathing exercises should be warned that in the first few seconds of the exercise, when the diaphragm is forced to do most of the work of exhaling the air, they may expect to cough and wheeze. Each child should be provided a mat to lie on, a receptacle for spitting, and a box of tissues. The children should be encouraged to cough up phlegm and to blow their noses whenever necessary. Clothing that binds the chest and waist should be loosened.

Sample exercises for improving the breathing pattern are given below.

1. Lie on the back and, employing imagery (see Chapter 29), relax the neck muscles; follow with relaxation of the chest muscles, and then the abdominal muscles.

2. Relax the neck and chest muscles and then tighten the abdomen, using any relaxation technique suggested in Chapter 29.

3. Take a supine position, with the knees bent and feet on the floor. Place the hands on the stomach just below the rib cage, fingers touching. Breathe in to the count of three. The belly should be expanded to raise the hands. Then release the air slowly through the puckered lips to a count of six, contracting the stomach muscles very slowly and pushing gently down with the fingertips. The neck muscles should be relaxed at all times.

4. Take a sitting position, with the shoulders, rib cage, and head lifted; the abdominal and neck muscles are relaxed. Inhale to the count of three. During a count of six, depress the shoulders, lower the head, tighten the stomach muscles, and expel air through the puckered lips.

Examples of Games to Develop More Efficient Breathing

For younger children with inefficient breathing patterns, games that assist in the development of control of expiration and encourage diaphragmatic breathing are recommended. The games described below may be used as models for the development of similar games.

1. One student is selected to be blindfolded. The other members of the class are divided into two groups, the membership of which is not known to the blindfolded child. One group begins to laugh and continues laughing while the child who is blindfolded calls out the name of a particular child. If the child named is in the group that is laughing, he must stop laughing; if he is not, he must begin laughing. The object is to stop all laughter by naming all those who are laughing.

2. A balloon is tossed into the air. As it descends, everyone whistles a low note until the balloon touches the floor. The player who first stops whistling before the balloon hits the floor must toss the balloon into the air for the next round.

3. Jugs and bottles of different sizes are secured as instruments for a jug band. Each child blows across the opening of his bottle to create a sound. The children are encouraged to blow low, long, steady sounds rather than short, loud ones. Homemade drums and rhythmic devices may be added to the band; these could be played by children who do not need the breathing exercises.

4. Two players stand at opposite ends of a short table. A table tennis ball is placed in the center of the table. Each player tries to blow it off the other end.

5. Two or more teams of three or four students are formed. Each team has a table tennis ball. Two lines are marked on the floor 10 to 30 feet apart, depending upon how well the ball rolls on the surface of the floor. The teams form a line behind the first player, who blows the ball to the other line and back. Each successive player in line repeats this action. The first team to complete the race is the winner.

6. Several players group around a circular table. A balloon is placed in the center and all the players try to blow it off the table. Each player attempts to prevent the balloon from going off the table on either side of him. No one is allowed to touch the balloon.

Muscles that assist in expiration can be strengthened by trunk exercises rather than breathing exercises. The iliocostalis lumborum and iliocostalis dorsi, when contracted separately, abduct and rotate the spinal column; when contracted simultaneously, they extend the spinal column. Hence any movement that rotates, abducts, or extends the trunk will strengthen these muscles if the SAID principle is applied.

Examples of exercises that might be used are given below:

1. Lie in the prone position on a bench with the trunk extended over the end. Lower the trunk toward the floor and return to the original position. Weights may be held behind the head to increase the difficulty (see Chapter 26, Weight Training).

2. Stand with the feet spread and the arms raised at the sides. Twist the trunk from one side to the other and back.

3. Stand with the feet apart and the hands on the hips. Move the trunk from side to side, lowering it as far as possible to each side.

The external and internal obliques and rectus abdominis are the muscles that bend the spinal column and the pelvis. Any exercise that flexes the spinal column or the pelvis is suitable for strengthening these muscles, applying the SAID principle. Two suitable exercises are given below:

1. Lying in the supine position on the floor, raise head and shoulders four or five inches off the floor and return to the original position. To increase the difficulty, weights may be held on the forehead.

2. Lying supine on the floor, with the knees bent and the feet on the floor, move to a sit-up position and return. Weights held behind the head increase the difficulty (see Chapter 26, Weight Training).

SELECTED READINGS

Adams, Ronald C., *et al.: Games, Sports and Exercises for the Physically Handicapped,* ed. 2. Philadelphia, Lea and Febiger, 1975.

Hinshaw, H. Corwin: *Diseases of the Chest.* Philadelphia, W. B. Saunders Co., 1969.

Krusen, Frank H., *et al.: Handbook of Physical Medicine and Rehabilitation,* ed. 2. Philadelphia, W. B. Saunders Co., 1971.

Nett, L., and Petty, T. L.: *For Those Who Live and Breathe.* Springfield, Ill., Charles C Thomas, Publ., 1969.

Chapter 15

Nutritional Disturbances

It is an alarming fact that in this country, where there is a greater abundance of food available to a larger portion of the total population than in most other countries of the world, malnourishment is an important problem. Malnourishment, or malnutrition, is a condition in which the body is not receiving the proper nutrients or is receiving them in inappropriate quantities. It may be brought about in different ways: the food intake may be inadequate or excessive in quantity or quality, or the conditions are such that the body is unable to utilize the nutrients properly. The latter is chiefly a medical problem, while the former is one of economics and education.

Malnutrition is prevalent among families of low income because they cannot afford to buy the variety of food needed for a well-balanced diet; often their incomes do not even allow a sufficient amount of food to be purchased. There are other cases in which the family income is spent unwisely and proper foods are purchased in insufficient quantities to avoid malnourishment. Consequently, in nearly every community there will be some children in the schools who are malnourished.

Among the Americans with adequate income, faulty eating habits constitute a major cause of malnourishment. Adequate amounts of the essential nutrients of a balanced diet are more likely to be obtained if a wide variety of food is eaten. Particularly important is the ingestion of fresh fruits and vegetables and milk. Some families, having failed to develop the taste for a variety of different foods, do not eat well-balanced meals. Traditions and customs of eating passed down through generations of cooks often stress one kind of food, frequently a starchy dish, which is served to the detriment of better balanced meals. Children in such families, while receiving sufficient energy-supplying foods, are likely to become malnourished because of a lack of vitamins and minerals.

Teenagers as an age group represent the segment of the population exhibiting the most faulty eating habits. Many teenagers fail to eat any breakfast; others gulp down a roll and a cup of coffee before dashing off to school. Research findings have demonstrated rather conclusively the importance of a nutritious breakfast to body efficiency; moreover, the failure to eat a good breakfast makes it more difficult for the youngster to obtain the necessary daily intake of nutrients, many of which are supplied by a balanced breakfast. Teenagers demonstrate further faulty eating habits in their selection of food for lunch. A sandwich and soft drink become a substitute for a well-balanced lunch. Although the dinner which is served to the teenager at home may represent the very best in meal planning, the appetite of the teenager is likely to have been dulled by candy bars, ice cream, and soft drinks consumed just prior to the dinner hour. Snacks of sweets, if they do not prevent the consumption of balanced meals, are useful in filling the energy requirements of those active individuals who need large amounts of foods high in calories.

Unfortunately, the poor eating habits of teenagers are sometimes carried over into adult life. High school graduates taking up new lives as college students or employees away from home do not always take up new and better eating habits. The food which they select in restaurants or choose to buy for preparing their own meals is likely to reflect their poor eating habits. For this reason considerable malnourishment may be found among young adults.

Another important factor contributing to malnourishment is the lack of knowledge about the importance of a well-balanced diet and how it may be achieved. Improper cooking methods may also have some influence.

THE NATURE AND CAUSES OF NUTRITIONAL DISTURBANCES

The most common nutritional disturbance in the United States is overweight. Its frequency among the adult population has been a recognized problem for years. The prevalence of obesity among children has come to public attention more recently.

The basic cause of overweight is that the body is taking in more energy food than it is using, and the excess energy food is stored in the body as fat. The assimilation of food, the metabolic rate, and the amount of energy used in activity are all factors that cause a difference in the amount of fat stored by two individuals who are consuming identical amounts and kinds of food.

Overeating may have a psychological origin. An individual may eat and snack repeatedly throughout the day because he is bored, is under nervous tension, or feels inadequate, and eating becomes an outlet for these anxieties and frustrations. Such "compulsive eaters" do not usually recognize the source of their problem and need help to eliminate the cause of overeating before attempting to lose excess weight.

Much overeating is a matter of habit. Food habits may be established when the energy need is high, and the habit of eating large amounts persists after the energy need has decreased.

Mayer[1] contends that the most important factor in overweight is inactivity. Activity plays an important part in the utilization of calories. His research indicates that the big difference between obese girls and normal girls of the same age group is the lack of activity on the part of the former and not the amount of food consumed. He would recommend, as one important way to control overweight, regular participation in exercises adapted to one's physical potential.

Underweight is another significant nutritional problem, but it is less prevalent than overweight. In some cases the cause is poor eating habits. In other cases the tendency to thinness appears to be hereditary. A change in fat metabolism and distribution of body fat usually occurs after pubescence, so that we often witness the filling out of the exceptionally skinny girl or the slimming down to normal proportions of the fat boy. Consequently, tendencies to slimness or stoutness in youngsters may not be permanent.

Underweight may be the indirect result of chronic infection, such as tuberculosis or diseased tonsils, or other conditions and diseases, such as hyperthyroidism or diabetes. Poor health habits, such as insufficient sleep and rest, may be a contributing cause to underweight. Loss of appetite may be a possible contributing factor in weight

---

[1]Jean Mayer: "Exercise and Weight Control," in Warren R. Johnson (Editor), *Science and Medicine of Exercise and Sports.* New York, Harper & Brothers, 1960, pp. 301–309.

loss, or it may be an indication of some underlying difficulty, usually of psychogenic origin.

PROBLEMS ASSOCIATED WITH NUTRITIONAL DISTURBANCES

The girl or boy who is not eating sufficient amounts of food to provide an adequate caloric intake will usually have other serious problems in addition to his poor nutritional state. Since he is likely to be from a family on a low socioeconomic level, he may have problems of social adjustment to face as well as personal problems arising from economic insecurity. He will be easily recognized in the physical education class because of his lack of vitality and endurance. He will usually prove to be a slow learner with no particular interest in activity. Lacking strength and skill, he is highly susceptible to injury. Because poorly nourished muscle tissue becomes flabby, poor posture is likely to result.

The malnourished student who is suffering from an inadequate consumption of *specific* mutrients, however, may be more difficult to detect. Although body efficiency may be decreased, other easily recognized symptoms of malnourishment are usually lacking in subclinical cases. Students in physical education class who evidence unexplained muscular weakness, poor coordination, and lack of vitality and interest in activity should be referred to their doctors as possible cases of malnourishment.

The extremely overweight girl or boy is at a definite disadvantage in participating in physical education activities. The fat which has accumulated in his body becomes an added weight which must be carried about in the execution of all movements. This, of course, greatly reduces speed, endurance, and some factors of coordination. To better understand the extent of the disadvantage of this additional weight in physical performance, the individual of normal weight should visualize attempting certain physical skills with a 25-pound weight strapped to his body. The difficulty in carrying this weight is not limited to the performance of sport skills for the overweight individual, but is with him throughout the routine activities of daily living, hindering him in most activities that require body movement.

The lowered efficiency contributes to the overweight individual's withdrawal from vigorous activity. This is turn fosters low physical fitness and lack of skill development. Unable to participate on an equal basis with other youngsters his age, he may turn entirely to sedentary activities to fill his leisure hours and so be denied the beneficial effects of exercise. Overweight people have a greater predisposition to diseases of the heart and circulatory system, kidney diseases, and diabetes. Although the incidence of these diseases is higher among adults than among children, a definite predisposition is evident among obese children.

The underweight boy or girl is often thought to be malnourished, but this is not always the case. The terms underweight and overweight are relative ones, used to describe a degree of variation from the average weight of individuals of certain height and structure. It is possible for an individual to be underweight—that is, below the average—without being malnourished. If, however, the underweight individual has a nutritional disturbance, this will probably be shown in his listlessness and low fatigue level.

The extremely underweight person has less than the normal amount of fatty tissue necessary for padding the body. This paddding provides protection to the nerve plexuses and affects the appearance of the body. Lacking the normal contours of the average person, the underweight person often finds himself, like his counterpart, the overweight individual, the subject of ridicule.

Table 15-1. WEIGHT-HEIGHT-AGE TABLE FOR BOYS AND GIRLS OF SCHOOL AGE

For Girls from 5-18 Years [†]

HGHT. (In.)	5 Yrs.	6 Yrs.	7 Yrs.	8 Yrs.	9 Yrs.	10 Yrs.	11 Yrs.	12 Yrs.	13 Yrs.	14 Yrs.	15 Yrs.	16 Yrs.	17 Yrs.	18 Yrs.
38	33	33												
39	34	34												
40	36	36	36											
41	37	37	37											
42	39	39	39											
43	41	41	41	41										
44	42	42	42	42										
45	45	45	45	45	45									
46	47	47	47	48	48									
47	49	50	50	50	50	50								
48			52	52	52	53								
49				55	55	56	56							
50		56		57	58	59	58	62						
51				60	61	61	61	66						
52				64	64	64	65	67						
53				67	67	67	68	71	71					
54				69	70	70	71	71	73					
55				72	72	74	74	75	77	78				
56					76	78	78	79	81	83				
57					80	82	82	82	84	88				
58						84	86	86	88	93				
59						87	90	90	92	96				
60						91	95	96	97	101	92	101		
61							99	100	101	106	106	108	104	
62							104	105	105	109	108	112	109	111
63								110	110	112	113	115	113	116
64								114	115	117	116	117	115	118
65								118	120	121	119	120	117	120
66									124	124	122	123	119	122
67									128	130	124	125	125	126
68									131	133	125	128	129	130
69										135	130	131	135	135
70										138	133	136	138	138
71											135	138	140	142
											138	140	142	144
											140	142	144	145

For Boys from 5-19 Years [†]

HGHT. (In.)	5 Yrs.	6 Yrs.	7 Yrs.	8 Yrs.	9 Yrs.	10 Yrs.	11 Yrs.	12 Yrs.	13 Yrs.	14 Yrs.	15 Yrs.	16 Yrs.	17 Yrs.	18 Yrs.	19 Yrs.
38	34	34													
39	35	35													
40	36	36	36												
41	38	38	38												
42	39	39	39	39											
43	41	41	41	41											
44	44	44	44	44											
45	46	46	46	46	46										
46	47	48	48	48	48										
47	49	50	50	50	50	50									
48			53	53	53	53									
49			55	55	55	55	55								
50		57	58	58	58	58	58	58							
51				61	61	61	61	61							
52			63	63	64	64	64	64	64						
53			66	67	67	67	67	68	68						
54				70	70	70	70	71	71						
55				72	72	73	73	74	74	72					
56				76	76	77	77	77	78	78					
57				79	79	80	81	81	82	83	80				
58					83	84	84	85	85	86	83				
59						87	88	89	89	90	87	90			
60						91	92	92	93	94	95	96			
61							96	96	97	99	100	103	106		
62							100	101	102	103	104	107	111	116	
63							105	106	107	108	110	113	118	123	
64								109		111	115	117	121	126	130
65								114	117	118	120	122	127	131	134
66									119	122	125	128	132	136	139
67									124	128	130	134	136	139	142
68										134	134	137	141	145	147
69										137	139	143	146	149	152
70										143	144	145	148	151	155
71										148	150	152	152	154	159
72											155	155	156	158	163
73											157	160	162	164	167
74											160	164	168	170	171

*Prepared by Robert M. Woodbury, Ph.D., Children's Bureau, U.S. Dept. of Labor.

†Prepared by Bird T. Baldwin, Ph.D., and Thomas D. Wood, M.D.

METROPOLITAN LIFE INSURANCE COMPANY

Determining Over- and Underweight

The correct and desirable body weight for any one person depends upon age, sex, height, bone size, and muscular development. It is, consequently, impossible to construct a table of absolutely correct weights applicable to all individuals because of the numerous possible variations in these factors. However, some basis for determining desired weight is necessary. A useful guide for estimating desirable weights for children of school age is given in Table 15–1.

PLANNING THE PROGRAM

Individuals whose extremes in weight affect their progress in physical education activities can be readily discovered. Among them will be students who could profit from special counseling and additional information concerning good nutrition, but who are able to take part in the regular physical education class. Some, however, cannot be accommodated in the regular class. For example, a student who has a problem of malnourishment due to lack of energy-supplying foods in his daily diet cannot be greatly helped in the physical education class. It may be advisable to dismiss such a student from participation in vigorous activities until such time as an improved diet effects some physiological changes which enable him to engage in sustained physical activity. Malnourishment which results from a lack of vitamins and minerals presents a similar problem in that a nutritional change which will promote greater capacity for physical performance must occur before the physical education program can be of much assistance to the individual boy or girl. If the student is not able to participate in the regular class, he may be placed in the special class. However, no greater improvement in physical proficiency can be expected until his nutritional deficiency is corrected.

The extent to which the physical educator can be of assistance in helping correct the nutritional deficiency is determined partially by the class time that can be allotted to teaching the facts of good nutrition and encouraging good nutritional habits. If nutritional information is being taught by the elementary classroom teachers and by a health or home economics teacher in the high school, the emphasis of the physical education teacher should be one of reinforcing and supplementing the classroom presentation. Where there is evidence of widespread faulty eating habits among the student body, all teachers might join together in a campaign to promote improved nutrition. Cases of nutritional disturbances which are suspected of being due to lack of food should be reported to the school authorities. Frequently, through a program of financial aid to the schools, students in actual need may eat a balanced lunch at school free of charge.

Traditionally, muscular activity has been linked with the problem of reducing excess weight. The physical education teacher has the responsibility of providing activities in which the overweight student can participate with success. He has the further responsibility of teaching the students how to secure the greatest benefit from physical activity. For the overweight, reduction of weight is one of these benefits.

Students who are only moderately overweight can, as a rule, be accommodated in the regular physical education class, but extremely overweight students cannot usually participate successfully in the regular class and should be enrolled in the special class. One of the objectives of these students will be weight reduction. This is not, however, a problem which can be solved entirely by a program of suitable exercises.

If weight reduction is to occur, more calories have to be used than are ingested. To maintain its weight the body needs from 1600 to 2800 calories per day, depending

Table 15–2. ESTIMATED CALORIC EXPENDITURES PER HOUR FOR AN INDIVIDUAL WEIGHING 150 POUNDS

Activities	Calories
Lying motionless	80
Sitting	102
Standing	112
Calisthenics, moderate	162
Walking, medium pace	172
Bowling	217
Dancing, moderate	252
Volleyball	256
Table tennis	258
Basketball	397
Swimming crawl, moderate	422
Bicycling, fast	472
Fencing	632
Parallel bar work	712
Jogging	870
Football	1002
Running, sprinting	9500

upon sex, size, and work output. Twenty-eight hundred to 3000 calories are required to add a pound of body fat; hence, to lose a pound of body fat necessitates a reduction of the same number of calories. A reduction in caloric intake plus an increase in work output will effect a loss in weight. Table 15–2 presents the caloric cost of various activities.

Changing long-established eating habits is difficult, and the student must be highly motivated. In some cases these habits have deep-rooted psychological origins beyond the scope of the physical educator. Except in these cases, students will be fairly easily motivated by their desire for improved appearance and by their wish to participate more nearly as an equal with their peers in games and sports. Before engaging in a weight reduction program, the student should secure approval from his doctor.

SUGGESTED ACTIVITIES

The activities for overweight students must be those which utilize energy but which do not require more strength and agility than the students possess. Activities in which the body weight must be lifted (for example, rope climbing and high jumping) are contraindicated both because the heavy student will probably not have sufficient strength to perform them and because of the chances of injury should he fall. Because obese students are not usually agile and cannot maneuver easily, games early in the program should not require much movement. Table tennis and light-bag punching are good in this respect. Other activities suitable for older children are:

Archery
Badminton
Football kicking for distance
   and accuracy
Basketball foul shooting
Bowling
Bowling on the green
Calisthenics

Dancing (folk, social, and modern)
Jogging short distances
Loop tennis
Shuffleboard
Tetherball
Touch football as linemen
Twenty-one
Volleyball

The selection of activities for younger obese children will not usually present much problem. During the elementary grade school years, there is less possibility weight will be so great as to restrict participation in the respects that it does the older student. The basic skill games and other activities presented in the lower elementary grades are such that a heavy child is not particularly handicapped in their performance, nor do they present any special hazards for him.

WEIGHT REDUCTION CLASSES

Special classes for older students who wish to lose weight are becoming increasingly popular and widespread. The classes may be offered within the physical education curriculum or as an after-school activity. In either case, they are more successful when conducted on a volunteer basis.

Students enrolling in such a class are highly motivated, at least at the beginning. However, because changing eating and exercise habits of long standing is not easy, the participants often need additional encouragement after the initial enthusiasm has worn off. It has been found that participation with others who share the common problem and discussion with them about the difficulties experienced in weight reduction often provide the additional encouragement and motivation needed to carry the program through to completion.

Examination.   The participants in such a class should have a physical examination before the first class session. Each should determine just how many pounds he is over the desired weight. Table 15–1 provides a guide for estimating the optimum weight. In using the tables it must be kept in mind that desired weight for any one individual must take into consideration a number of factors and that a table is, at best, only a basis for making an estimation. The family physician should be called upon to establish the optimum weight for each person.

The class usually begins each meeting with the weighing of each member and the recording of the weight on the individual charts. Weight will vary from one time to another because of such factors as the time of the last meal, the time of elimination, the amount of water lost, and the amount of work done. If the individual's daily routine does not vary substantially, his weight will be more nearly accurate than if one day he ate a meal just before class but on another day had nothing at all before coming to class. Such variations, which may influence the weight to a considerable extent, should be taken into consideration in the weighing.

Some of the class period is usually given over to a discussion of the individual diets and the problems encountered in holding to the diet. Then the class is put through the exercises. Since the class does not usually meet daily, the class members are given exercises to perform each day at home.

For general body conditioning the following are suggested:

Side-straddle hop
Running in place—knees high
Squat thrust
Twisting at hips
Side-straddle touch opposite foot
Jumping jack

For other suggestions see Chapter 27.

Some students, particularly girls, will be concerned not only with actual weight reduction but with developing a firmer and trimmer body. As muscles increase in strength they develop more tonus, and muscles with more tonus are firmer muscles.

Tonus appears in a muscle before there is much increase in muscle size as a result of exercise. Girls usually exercise to the point where tonus is developed without a great increase in muscle bulk.

Exercises for Firming the Muscles. Activities should be selected which place an overload on the muscles involved. A few simple exercises for various areas of the body are suggested below:

Arm muscles:

1. Do a modified push-up, using the knees as a fulcrum.

2. Hang by the hands and attempt to bend the elbows in a pull-up.

Chest muscles:

1. Bring the palms together in front of the chest and push against the palms.

Stomach and waist line:

1. Lie supine and lift the legs four inches off the floor and hold for 3 seconds or more (not to be done by anyone subject to hollow back).

2. Lie supine and raise the trunk to touch the toes with the fingers.

3. Lie on the side with arms overhead; while the feet are being held down, raise the upper trunk.

Hips:

1. Step up on a chair which is about knee height, first with one foot and then the other; step down again very slowly one foot at a time.

2. The third exercise for firming the stomach and waist line also forms muscles in the hip area; for a milder exercise, stand with the feet about 12 inches apart, arms overhead, and bend first to the left and then to the right.

Thighs:

1. While standing, raise one leg as high as possible in front, keeping the knee straight; repeat with the other leg.

2. Step up and down from a bench, alternating the feet.

SELECTED READINGS

Alfin-Slater, Roslyn B., and Aftergood, Lilla: *Nutrition for Today.* Dubuque, Iowa, Wm. C. Brown Co., Pub., 1973.

Beaton, George H., and McHenry, Earl W. (editors): *Nutrition: A Comprehensive Treatise,* 3 vols., New York, Academic Press, 1964.

Bogert, Jean L., *et al.: Nutrition and Physical Fitness,* ed. 9 Philadelphia, W. B. Saunders Co., 1973.

Fleck, Henrietta: *Introduction to Nutrition,* ed. 2. New York, The Macmillan Co., 1971.

Katch, Frank I., and McArdle, William D.: *Nutrition, Weight Control, and Physical Condition.* Boston, Houghton-Mifflin, 1977.

Mayer, Jean: *Overweight: Cause, Cost, and Control.* Englewood Cliffs, New Jersey, Prentice-Hall, Inc., 1968.

Morehouse, Laurence E., and Miller, Augustus T., Jr.: *Physiology of Exercise,* ed. 7. St. Louis, The C. V. Mosby Co., 1976.

Robey, Frederick B., and Davis, Russell P.: *Jogging for Fitness and Weight Control.* Philadelphia, W. B. Saunders Co., 1970.

Wilson, Eva D., *et al.: Principles of Nutrition,* ed. 3. New York, John Wiley and Sons, Inc., 1975.

Chapter 16

Other Conditions Requiring Special Consideration in Physical Education

In addition to the handicapping conditions discussed in the foregoing chapters, there are a number of other incapacitating disorders with which the teacher of physical education should be familiar. Some of these conditions, such as the various athletic injuries, are very common; others, such as blood and kidney disorders, are less common but occur frequently enough that the physical education teacher will encounter students in the physical education class having these conditions. Most of the disorders require special consideration in the programming to ensure the protection of the participant from further aggravation of the condition and from possible additional injury precipitated by overexertion and fatigue. Knowledge of the nature of these conditions and the protective and preventive measures which need to be taken during physical activity is essential to those in charge of regular work in physical education as well as to those directing the special physical education program.

NEPHRITIS

Nephritis (Bright's disease) is an inflammation of the renal capillaries (filters of the kidney responsible for the formation of urine). The inflammation may damage the renal capillaries, impairing the filtering process so that blood and proteins, such as albumen, are excreted with the urine.

The disease is classified as acute nephritis and chronic nephritis. Acute nephritis is largely a disease of childhood and youth and is the most common form of nephritis among the early age groups. The disease is apparently a reaction to an infection elsewhere in the body. Although the infection occasionally affects the skin, it is almost always in the upper respiratory tract. Common examples are scarlet fever, "strep throat," and other infections caused by streptococci. The relationship between the infection and the development of nephritis is not clearly understood; however, the disease is thought to be an antigen-antibody reaction (immune response) by the kidney to the infection. Nephritis may occur from one to three weeks after the initial infection.

Acute nephritis may vary from a very mild case to a severe attack. In milder cases, the symptoms may be unnoticeable or there may be edema (accumulation of fluid in the tissue) around the eyes, low grade fever, hematuria (passing of blood in the urine), and back pain. In severe cases, symptoms also include headaches, malaise (feelings of uneasiness), fever, hypertension (excessive pressure of the blood against blood vessels), diminution of urine excretion, and general edema. In extremely severe cases, cardiac disturbance may occur, possibly resulting in death.

Bed rest and a carefully controlled diet are the chief procedures used in treating acute nephritis. Antibiotics are frequently administered to control the streptococcal infection if it is still present. Recovery is usually complete. However, in a very few cases the disease may subside only to reappear again or to develop into chronic nephritis.

Chronic nephritis may develop from acute nephritis immediately or after the symptoms of acute nephritis have disappeared. It may also occur in those who have never had acute nephritis. Chronic nephritis differs from acute in that there is steady progressive damage of a permanent nature to the kidneys.

In most instances there are three stages of chronic nephritis. In the first stage, very few overt symptoms manifest themselves; however, blood and urine tests do reveal the presence of the disease. No special treatment is prescribed during this period except the avoidance of excessive fatigue and the maintenance of a diet that is low in sodium and high in protein.

In the second stage, general edema occurs, affecting especially the legs, arms, and face. Steroid hormones may be used to treat the disease, but maintaining a high protein, low sodium diet is the best treatment. Also, strenuous exercise is to be avoided.

In the third stage uremia (poisoning of the blood by waste products of the body) occurs. At this stage, damage to the kidneys is so great that death will result unless the kidneys are aided by the use of an artificial kidney, or unless a single kidney is removed or a transplant is accomplished.

Suggested Activities.   In developing a physical education program for those with kidney disorders, extreme care should be exercised to avoid any activities strenuous enough to cause stress to the kidneys when eliminating waste products. In severe cases all exercise is contraindicated. Those with mild acute nephritis may take part in regular physical education, avoiding any excessively strenuous activities. Competitive situations in which the student would be likely to extend himself beyond the level of activity he can comfortably tolerate should not be offered.

For children who have the disease more severely, the expenditure of energy must be drastically reduced. Because of the nature of the disease, the development of physical fitness by application of the SAID principle (see Chapter 27) must be severely limited. Concentration should be on motor skill development to decrease the use of energy in motor movement. For this purpose, the basic principles of movement and how they are utilized to make movement more efficient should be emphasized for all students old enough to comprehend their significance.

Another important goal is to provide students with severe cases of nephritis an opportunity to play with peers and to develop a feeling of belonging. Many of the less strenuous games, such as table tennis, catching and throwing, and archery, will allow the student with nephritis to integrate readily with non-affected students. In other games and activities, the regulations can be adapted to allow the child with nephritis to play with his peers. Having a teammate run the bases after the afflicted child has batted the ball is one example of an appropriate modification that can be readily made.

DIABETES MELLITUS

Diabetes mellitus is a disease in which the body exhibits an inability to properly use the starches and sugars that it ingests. The prevalence of the disease is on the rise, a fact which is partially attributable to the stress placed upon detection spearheaded by the American Diabetic Association. The highest incidence is among the late-middle-age population, although it has been estimated that about 10 per cent of the cases occur among children.

Cause. The cause of diabetes mellitus is known to be related to an improper supply of insulin, secreted by the islands of Langerhans in the pancreas and responsible for the breakdown of sugars for utilization and storage by the body. This lack of proper function is not caused by an organic defect; consequently, medical investigation of its cause is being directed toward other possible causes, such as the factors which control the production of insulin in the pancreas.

In diabetics an improper supply of insulin to act upon carbohydrates permits an excessive accumulation of sugar in the blood which is eventually eliminated from the body in the urine. The body is consequently denied the heat and energy which might have been produced by the lost sugar, and the individual begins, in severe cases, to exhibit such symptoms as loss of weight, lack of energy, and continual hunger. Other frequently experienced symptoms are unusual thirst, excessive urination, intense itching, and slow healing of injuries.

Treatment. Treatment of diabetes mellitus consists of careful diet control and the addition of insulin to the body. Insulin may be injected in carefully regulated dosages with a syringe and needle, although adults with established cases can often successfully take insulin in tablet form. The amount of exercise and physical exertion of the diabetic influences his insulin requirements because of the amount of sugar burned by the body in physical activity. A carefully established balance between food intake and insulin requirement can be upset by excessive physical activity.

When the student knows he is going to increase his activity considerably for a given day, he must decrease his insulin intake in that part of the day during which the exercise occurs; for example, if the increase in activity will be in the morning, the morning dosage is decreased, usually by about 5 to 10 per cent of the regular amount. If the insulin dosage is not decreased prior to the increase in activity, the student is in risk of an insulin shock, unless extra sugar is consumed.

Insulin shock may occur if the diabetic receives too much insulin, if his intake of food is too little, or if his participation in exercise has been too great. Feelings of hunger, trembling, perspiring, and muscular contractions are symptomatic of insulin shock. The body needs more sugar, and the eating of candy or a lump of sugar or an orange gives immediate relief.

Diabetic coma, which results from too little insulin, is a more severe condition. It is characterized by uncontrollable drowsiness or muscular pain, possibly resulting in unconsciousness. A diabetic in coma requires the immediate attention of a physician for the administration of insulin. Individuals under medical care are not likely to experience coma.

Suggested Activities. Diabetics are normal in appearance and motor function and so do not usually experience the severe emotional problems that those with more obvious handicaps frequently have. Whenever unsatisfactory adjustment is found in those suffering from diabetes, the cause can usually be found in overprotection or overindulgence by the parents during childhood.

Many doctors emphasize the importance of muscular activity in the lives of diabetics. Exercise is important not only because it decreases the need for insulin but because it contributes to general body health. Moreover, it helps to keep the body weight under control, an important problem with older diabetics, who have a tendency to obesity.

Diabetic children are usually encouraged to participate in normal play activities without restriction or adaptation. Because early fatigue is commonly associated with the disease, the physical educator planning activities for such children should take this factor into consideration. Participation in very strenuous or highly competitive games is usually contraindicated because of the greater possibility of extreme fatigue. As a general rule, diabetics should be guided into types of participation which permit them to stop when necessary to rest for a time. For young children, the games in which turns are taken and considerable time elapses between turns, as in Drop the Handkerchief, are excellent choices. Bowling, shuffleboard, swimming, and archery are examples of good activities for older students; skill in such sports should be stressed also for their value as lifetime activities.

The physical education instructor should obtain a full medical report on those students who have diabetes. Both he and the student should learn the tolerance of the student for exercise. The instructor should check on the student to make sure that he is carrying extra sugar in some form in the event of an insulin shock. He should be prepared to offer guidance and encouragement to the diabetic in observing the necessarily inflexible adherence to the regulations imposed by the treatment.

The diabetic is particularly susceptible to infection, and great care must be practiced to avoid cuts, abrasions, blisters, and fungus infections. The student in physical education should be impressed with the necessity of showering after class and of carefully drying between the toes to reduce the possibility of athlete's foot. The importance of wearing well-fitting gym shoes and lacing them carefully to avoid the rubbing which may cause blisters should also be stressed.

EPILEPSY

The incidence of epilepsy cannot be accurately determined for the general population or for the school population because only severe and uncontrolled cases come to the attention of medical and school personnel. It has been estimated that as many as one of every 200 people has some form of epilepsy; a large number of these cases are so mild as to go undetected. Many persons whose epilepsy is diagnosed respond so effectively to treatment that they live completely normal lives, and the fact that without medication they could suffer seizures is known only to their families. In others, however, the seizures are not entirely controlled. This appears to be particularly true of those with multiple handicaps who reside in institutions. The cause may be failure to follow a proper schedule in taking the medication, ineffectiveness of the medication itself, or some other, as yet undetermined, reason.

Cause. The exact cause of epilepsy is not known; it is believed that improper functioning of the brain-regulating mechanisms may cause seizures. The seizures may begin very early in life or they may not commence until adulthood. In about half of the cases in which seizures do occur, they begin before the age of 20. As age increases, the number of seizures often decreases.

Medical treatment can effectively eliminate or reduce the number of seizures. Phenobarbital and phenytoin are the drugs used most frequently to control seizures. The easing of emotional conflicts also helps to reduce the number of seizures.

Types.   Several different classifications are used for the various types of epilepsy. Generally, however, these classifications are used for the five major types: generalized motor seizure (grand mal), petit mal, psychomotor, focal (jacksonian seizure), and minor motor.

The most severe type is the generalized motor seizure. It is characterized by loss of consciousness, rigidity, and falling. Thrashing of the body, frothing at the mouth, and involuntary cries are other symptoms. The tongue may be bitten as the result of the strong contraction of the jaw muscles. Although the attack may last only a few minutes, the stuporous sleep which follows may last for several hours.

The petit mal should not be interpreted as simply a minor form of grand mal, for the difference is the kind of seizure rather than degree. It results in unconsciousness for a short duration. Mental processes cease during the attack and conscious physical activity is suspended, although automatic action may continue. Muscular twitching and rolling or blinking of the eyes or the fixing of the eyes upon some object are characteristic of this type of attack. Recovery is immediate.

Psychomotor attacks constitute another type of attack affecting a small number of epileptics. Consciousness is not lost during the attack but there is no recall of the attack afterward. The attack is characterized by extremely odd behavior in which the patient may have a temper tantrum or otherwise demonstrate unsocial behavior.

The focal or jacksonian seizure originates on one side of the body and moves to the rest of the body, although it may not encompass the entire body. Consciousness is retained unless the attack spreads to the opposite side of the body.

Minor motor seizures are manifested in several ways. There can be a sudden loss of muscle tone in the muscles of the back, causing the patient to fall forward; a sudden involuntary contraction of a group of muscles of the trunk or extremities; or a sudden contraction of most of the body musculature. The seizure is of short duration and does not result in unconsciousness unless it culminates in a grand mal seizure.

Aid to the Victim of Epilepsy During a Seizure.   Because of the success in controlling seizures with medication, a seizure is unlikely to occur in school. Nevertheless, the teacher should know the emergency care measures to be taken in the event of a seizure. He should be emotionally prepared to deal with the problem, for his conduct in the handling of the victim will greatly influence the class. Some epileptics experience warnings of an impending seizure, and in this event the teacher may possibly take the child to a quiet inconspicuous place. He should remain calm and call as little attention as possible to the administration of care to the victim.

For a child having a grand mal seizure the teacher should (1) place the victim on the floor away from all possible hazards such as hot radiators, furniture, sharp objects; and (2) loosen any restraining clothing, such as a tie or belt, if this is possible without the use of force. If the victim is hazy following the attack, he should be removed to a quiet place to rest. If he lapses into sleep, he should be kept warm and permitted to rest as long as necessary. It is important that no stimulants or depressants be administered to the victim during the attack.

Suggested Activities.   Students whose seizures are under control need no special consideration and can participate in the activities of the regular program without modification. At one time the medical profession recommended that children with epilepsy not participate in sports in which head injuries may occur. However, that attitude has been undergoing a change. Many doctors now claim that the possibility of head injury poses no special threat to children with epilepsy. It is argued that the social stigma attached to exclusion from participation is more serious than any medical problem that may be incurred.

Certain activities are contraindicated for students who are subject to seizures.

These include rope climbing and similar activities in which there is danger of injury from falling a great distance during an attack. Because of the danger of seizure underwater, diving and underwater swimming should be avoided and swimming permitted only under close supervision.

Poor development of the cardiorespiratory system from lack of exercise appears to have some relationship to the frequency of seizures. Activities that improve physical conditioning are therefore important to such students because of the possibility of reducing the number of seizures.

Multiply handicapped youngsters with a history of seizures are generally in poor physical condition and need special attention to the development of physical fitness. For these students the special programs of exercise suggested in Chapter 27, Physical Fitness, will be extremely beneficial. In addition, games that provide varied and vigorous big muscle activity are of great value.

ANEMIA

Anemia is a common defect of the blood in which there is a reduction in erythrocytes (red corpuscles) or the amount of hemoglobin they contain. Since hemoglobin carries oxygen throughout the body, a decrease in its ability to perform this function affects the amount of oxygen in the blood.

Anemia may be the result of several different conditions. The most common of these are loss of blood and nutritional deficiency. Two other conditions that are fairly prevalent in young people are defective hemoglobin synthesis and disease of the bone forming tissue. The former is the condition responsible for sickle cell anemia, and the latter for aplastic anemia and pernicious anemia. Pernicious anemia is not a common disorder among children, occurring most often after the age of 35, and so is not discussed here. Symptomatic of the presence of anemia are chronic fatigue that results from a lack of oxygen in the blood, and pallor caused by the lack of hemoglobin.

Chronic blood loss such as may occur in excessive menstruation, bleeding ulcer of the stomach, or parasitic diseases such as hookworm or malaria is treated by removing or treating the cause and by prescribing iron tablets or a diet high in foods containing iron to rebuild the hemoglobin.

Iron is the main constituent of hemoglobin, and the ingestion of a small but constant amount of iron is needed to replace the red blood cells that are destroyed by natural processes. Besides iron, vitamin B_{12} and protein are needed in the production of hemoglobin. Insufficient quantities of these in the food intake may result in anemia. Treatment consists of a diet high in the deficient nutrients.

Sickle Cell Anemia.   Defective hemoglobin synthesis causes sickle cell anemia, the name deriving from the fact that the red blood cells become crescent or sickle shaped owing to the varying portions of hemoglobin. The disorder is inherited, the trait being autosomal recessive; that is, it is not sex-linked and is incapable of expression unless it is carried by both parents. It occurs almost exclusively in the Negro race.

Sickle cell anemia may have different degrees of intensity at different times. Sickle cells have a tendency to clump together, thereby reducing the blood flow through the capillaries to the tissue. The sudden and dangerous increase in symptoms that results is called a crisis. In addition to the symptoms of weakness, pallor, and fatigue, common to anemia, during the crisis there may be attacks of fever, pain in the limbs and abdomen, severe headaches, paralysis, convulsions, or all of these.

There is no drug therapy for sickle cell anemia. Treatment is symptomatic. Anticoagulants have had some success in dislodging the clumps of sickle cells, and ice packs can relieve swelling of the joints. Some physicians recommend blood transfusions to relieve the symptoms, but relief is only temporary. Those suffering from sickle cell anemia must avoid high altitudes and other situations in which there is less available oxygen in the air than normal.

Aplastic Anemia.   Aplastic anemia is a disease of the bone marrow, where red blood corpuscles are formed. In addition to the general symptoms of anemia, in aplastic anemia there is frequently bleeding from the nose, and black and blue spots frequently form on the skin. The bone marrow's failure to effectively produce red blood cells may be caused by cancerous growth of the bone marrow or by destruction of the marrow by chemical agents, such as certain weed killers, industrial poisons, radiation, and some antibiotics.

Aplastic anemia is a serious disease and often the affected person is hospitalized until the cause has been isolated and removed. Cortisone has been effectively used to treat some cases. Blood transfusions at regular intervals are usually required. The prognosis is poor, and death often occurs at an early age.

Suggested Activities.   In any type of physical activity for the person with anemia, extreme care must be exercised to avoid excessive fatigue. Mild exercise is usually desirable and appropriate; however, in severe cases, physical activity may need to be extremely limited.

The activity program should be tailored to each student depending upon his tolerance for exercise. Each program should be checked with the student's doctor. The final decision regarding the inclusion of activities in the program must be made by medical personnel familiar with the individual's medical history and exercise tolerance level.

A carefully planned program can improve health because exercise increases the

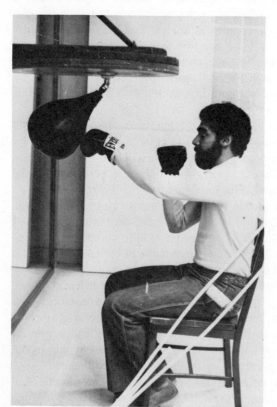

Figure 16–1. Lowering the height of the punching bag enables the student who must conserve energy to engage in appropriate exercise.

demands for oxygen and so stimulates the production of red cells. Limited exercise to increase muscle strength may also be beneficial. In general, activities should be selected from among those that can be performed without undue stress and fatigue, such as table tennis, archery, shuffleboard, bag punching, bowling, croquet, golf, foul shooting, and volleyball. Other sports may be modified to decrease their strenuousness. Swimming is recommended because of the ease with which the energy expenditure can be controlled.

In all activities, utmost care must be taken to avoid bruises and cuts, since they are likely to heal slowly. The student who suffers from sickle cell anemia may develop ulcers around the ankles, the result of vasoocclusion (closing of the blood vessels) brought about by the clumping of the red cells. When this occurs, the activity level should be reduced until the ulcers heal. Swimming is contraindicated if the ulcers are open and draining.

HERNIA

A hernia is a protrusion of a loop of an organ or tissue through an abnormal opening with the body. Hernias may occur in many different areas of the body, but the abdominal region is the most frequent. The most common hernia involves the inguinal canal, which is located in the groin and serves as the passage for the spermatic cord in the male and the round ligament in the female. In the embryo of the male the testes move down from the abdomen to the scrotum. This canal normally closes early in life but undue pressure or exertion may reopen it, resulting in a hernia or a loop of the intestine protruding through the opening.

If the protrusion remains in the canal, the hernia is called incomplete. If it leaves the canal and enters the scrotum, it is a complete hernia. In complete hernia there is a danger that it will become strangulated. The loop of the intestine becomes constricted, shutting off the blood supply to the area, which may result in the development of gangrene.

Cause and Treatment.   The frequency of inguinal hernia is higher in the male than in the female and higher among the obese. Inguinal hernia may occur where there is abdominal pressure against weak abdominal muscles. Lifting heavy weights with the epiglottis closed is a frequent cause. Blows to the abdominal region are another cause. Surgery is indicated in the cure of hernia.

Suggested Activities.   Students who have hernias should avoid such activities as weightlifting, boxing, wrestling, or football, which may cause increased pressure on the abdominal area or in which a blow to that area is likely to occur. For severe hernia cases, running games are also contraindicated. Rope climbing and activity on the bar and parallel ladders are not recommended. Games in which students may safely participate are horseshoes, swimming, bowling, casting, golf, table tennis, volleyball, and basic skill games which are not chiefly running.

Exercises to strengthen the abdominal walls are of value and offer some protection until surgery can be performed. They are also of great benefit to the patient after surgery. Added protection may be given the hernia during exercise by placing the hand over the hernia area. The breath should not be held during exercises.

DYSMENORRHEA AND MENORRHAGIA

Dysmenorrhea, or painful menstruation, occurs most frequently at the beginning of the menstrual cycle. At this time the abdominal cavity is gorged with an additional amount of blood. This produces increased pressure upon nerves and hence pain. The changes that take place during the cycle within the body may lower the threshold of pain and increase irritability. Dysmenorrhea is often due to lack of exercise, fatigue, constipation, chilling of the body, and poor posture. Sometimes an organic condition such as a displaced uterus may be the cause.

Menorrhagia is a condition of unusually heavy flow during the menstrual period. Because of the large amount of blood that is lost, the individual is likely to be tired and somewhat anemic. Exercise, which is helpful to dysmenorrhea because it increases the flow, is not desirable in cases of menorrhagia. Consequently, such girls should be excused from physical education unless permission for them to participate has been given by their physicians.

Activities and Special Exercises for Dysmenorrhea. Dysmenorrhea is frequently given as a reason by girls seeking excuse from physical education during menstruation. Most of these girls are unaware that their condition may be relieved by participation in physical education activities which are not extremely strenuous in nature. These girls should be encouraged not only to take part in their physical education classes but to participate regularly in a program of special exercises which are known to be of value in preventing and alleviating dysmenorrhea. These exercises, known as the Mosher, Billig, and Golub exercises, are beneficial because they improve circulation in the abdominal area, increase abdominal muscle tone, increase lumbopelvic flexibility, and encourage muscular relaxation.[3]

The Mosher[4] exercise is designed to relieve abdominal congestion by "abdominal pumping." To perform the exercise, a supine position is taken with the knees bent and the feet resting on the floor. One hand is placed on the abdomen. The abdominal area is then retracted or pulled in, and a deep breath is taken. The hand massages slowly and heavily from the symphysis pubis up to the sternum (approximately from the region of the pubic hair to the ribs). The abdominal area is relaxed, and the air is expelled entirely. The exercise is repeated several times.

The Billig[5] exercise is designed to stretch the fascial ligamentous bands through which the sensory nerves pass. (The fascial ligamentous bands are bands of ligaments that attach the fascia, which covers the muscle, to the bone.) It is theorized that the stretching of these bands relieves the pressure on the nerves and so reduces pain. The effectiveness of the exercise has been demonstrated in a controlled study of girls with dysmenorrhea in which 94 per cent reported their conditions alleviated to some degree by participating in the exercise.[6] To perform the exercise, the subject stands with one side of the body toward the wall, with the feet together and approximately 18 inches from the wall. With the knees locked and the hips rotated forward, the forearm is placed horizontally against the wall at shoulder height (the palm of the hand, the forearm, and the elbow should be in contact with the wall). The other hand is placed against the hollow of the hip and slowly and deliberately pushes the hips forward and toward the wall as far as possible. The return to the original position is made slowly. The exercises should be performed over a period of two or more months three times a day, three repetitions on each side.

The Golub[7] exercise stresses systematic twisting and bending of the trunk, activi-

---

[3]Eleanor Metheny: "Exercise and Menstrual Pain" *In Symposium on Dysmenorrhea.* Chicago, Phi Delta Pi Fraternity, 1950, pp. 29–32.

[4]C. D. Mosher: "Dysmenorrhea." *Journal of American Medical Association,* vol. 62, 1914, p. 1297.

[5]H. E. Billig, Jr.: "Dysmenorrhea: The Result of Postural Defect." *Archives of Surgery,* vol. 46, 1943, p. 611.

[6]Eleanor Metheny: *op. cit.,* pp. 29–32.

[7]Leib J. Golub: "A New Exercise for Dysmenorrhea." *American Journal of Obstetrics and Gynecology,* 78, July 1959, pp. 152–155.

Figure 16–2.   (A) Mosher, (B) Billig, and (C) Golub exercises for prevention of dysmenorrhea.

ties which were found to be effective in reducing the pain of dysmenorrhea in a study by Golub. The first part of the exercise is done from a standing position with the arms extended straight out from the sides. The body is bent while the knees are kept straight. One hand is lifted up, and with the other an attempt is made to reach around the outer side of the opposite foot until the heel can be touched. The exercise is repeated on the other side. In the second part of the exercise, the individual stands with the arms at the sides. The arms are then swung forward and upward, while the left leg is simultaneously raised backward vigorously. Then the exercise is repeated on the opposite foot. Each phase of the exercise is performed four times on each side.

CONVALESCENCE

Convalescence is a period of recovery from illness or injury. It can be said to begin when the acute stage of the disability has passed and to end when the patient is physically, mentally, and emotionally ready to resume the activities that he had engaged in prior to his illness or injury. The nature of the convalescence depends largely upon the nature of the illness or injury, and the types of convalescence are consequently divided into five general areas, depending upon the nature of the initial illness. The five areas are: surgery, infectious disease, constitutional disease, accidental trauma, and obstetrics.

The early stage of the convalescent period is characterized by general body weakness and low vitality which stem not so much from the illness or injury itself as from the forced inactivity during this stage. In extended bed rest, deterioration of the body functions is evident most conspicuously in the muscles. Considerable loss of muscular strength, endurance, and power occurs and there is some muscle atrophy. The patient's heart and blood vessels become less efficient in maintaining good circulation, which decreases cardiorespiratory endurance. Lack of good circulation and constant pressure on areas of the back of a patient confined to lying on his back causes bed sores. Bones decalcify from lack of muscular activity, and in very long periods of bed rest bone deterioration may be so great that strenuous muscular contraction can cause a bone to break. Appetite is affected by bed rest. Although less energy foods are required, the patient may become so finicky about eating that it becomes difficult for him to get sufficient amounts of the nutrients needed by the body. Defecation is difficult for inactive persons. Postoperative patients confined to complete bed rest are frequently bothered with distressing gas pains and difficulty in urination. Moreover, evidence indicates that postoperative patients confined to complete bed rest are more susceptible to pneumonia and thrombophlebitis (inflammation and clotting of blood in the veins).

A rehabilitation program of exercises can offset these undesirable consequences of extended confinement to bed. Participation in adapted exercises and games helps to maintain good circulation and helps prevent the deterioration of muscular strength, endurance, and coordination. Susceptibility to disease is decreased. Appetites are more likely to be stimulated because the patient is hungrier and more interested in his food. Difficulties in elimination are reduced because of the beneficial effects of the exercise.

In the late stage of convalescence, the patient is no longer confined to bed and is able to resume many of his former activities, including returning to school if he is of school age. The convalescent will experience fatigue sooner and will have less strength and endurance than before his confinement; his appetite and his capacity for restful sleep may also be less. However, all of these aspects of his health will be much improved over what they were in the early stage of convalescence, particularly if the patient has been engaging in an exercise program. Full recovery can be hastened by a carefully planned program of exercise and activities.

Some of these convalescing students who are able to return to school will have had such serious injuries or illnesses that adaptation of the physical education activities is needed not only during convalescence but for the remainder of their time as physical education students. Others will have less lasting effects but may require frequent rest periods and participation in mild forms of activities until endurance and strength begin to return.

There are some disorders that may interfere only temporarily with participation in regular physical education and so require special consideration just for the duration of the condition. Among the most common of these are athletic injuries, contagious and infectious diseases, and skin disorders.

COMMON ATHLETIC INJURIES

Certain injuries, resulting particularly from sports participation, occur more frequently than others among the school population. Because they are so common, it is desirable for the physical education teacher to have specific knowledge about these.

Ankle and Foot Injuries

The most common ankle injury is a hyperinversion sprain caused by excessive inward turning.* In this type of sprain, the collateral (situated at the sides) ligaments are stretched or torn, and immobilization of the ankle by strapping is usually necessary. The area around the ankle is tender and the patient finds it difficult to walk. As the injury heals, walking becomes easier but the injured area remains highly vulnerable to further injury from running or sudden twisting and turning.

Fractures to the ankle usually occur to the lateral malleolus. This type of fracture is often called a sprain fracture (Fig. 16–3). In the foot the most common fracture occurs to the anterior portion consisting of the metatarsals (small bones in the front of the foot) and phalanges of the foot (toes). In almost all cases, the foot or ankle fractures are immobilized by a cast. The patient may be provided with a walking cast that will bear his weight, or the cast may be such that the use of crutches is required for walking. After the cast is removed, the area needs protection from severe stress for some time.

Knee and Leg Injuries

Knee injuries that are most common are: collateral ligament sprain, cruciate ligament sprain, and meniscus tear (see Fig. 16–4). The ligament injuries result in an un-

---

*A sprain refers to the tearing or stretching of ligaments and tendons, while a strain refers to the tearing of muscles.

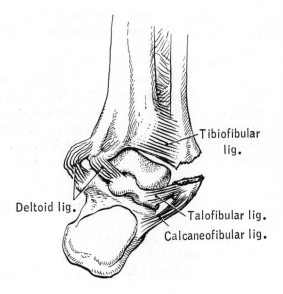

Figure 16–3. Sprain-fracture of lateral malleolus. (O'Donoghue, Don H.: Treatment of Injuries to Athletes. Philadelphia, W. B. Saunders Co., 1962, p. 557, figure 388A.)

Tibiofibular lig.

Deltoid lig.

Talofibular lig.
Calcaneofibular lig.

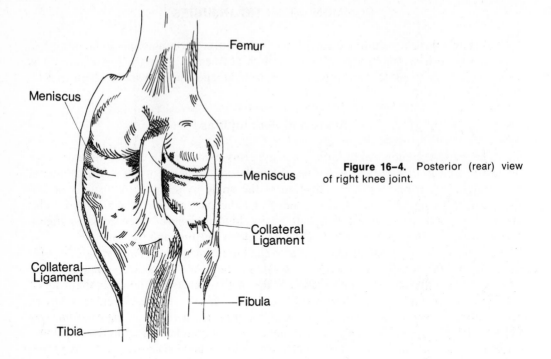

Figure 16–4. Posterior (rear) view of right knee joint.

stable knee; that is, the ligaments may not hold the femur and the tibia in proper relationship to each other. A meniscus tear may cause an inability to move the knee if the cartilage becomes misplaced, causing the locking of the joint.

If severe, these injuries to the knee cause the quadriceps extensor muscle of the thigh to atrophy and become weaker. Atrophy and accompanying weakness also occur after surgery to the knee. A specific conditioning program is necessary to prevent these results and to restore strength.

Sprains and Strains of the Spinal Column

The discussion here is concerned only with those injuries of the spine that involve muscles, ligaments, and tendons; injury to the spinal nerves is discussed in Chapter 9.

The neck area is highly vulnerable to sprain and strain. Those with a history of neck injury often experience a recurrence as the result of a sudden twist, forced hyperextension, or a quick snap of the head. Those who have experienced a lower spinal injury are also subject to a recurrence produced by suddenly twisting the trunk, bending violently from the waist, or lifting a weight while the back is bent. Youngsters with weak abdominal muscles and tight hamstring muscles that result in faulty vertebral alignment are susceptible to low back injury and low back pain.

Shoulder Girdle, Arm and Hand Injuries

Common injuries to these areas are strains to the rotator cuff (four muscles that cover the head of the humerus and attach to the scapula) in the shoulder joint, dislocation of the joint, fracture of the clavicle (collarbone), and fractures of the ulna and radius (bones in the forearm) and of the small bones of the wrist. The fractures are usually immobilized by a cast for a period of time while the strains and sprains may be partially immobilized by strapping. The injured area is tender for a period of time; and even after the cast or strapping is removed, it is highly vulnerable to re-injury by excessive force. Each time a shoulder dislocation occurs, the ligaments and tendons are stretched so that the possibility of a recurrence of the dislocation is greater. An individual with recurring dislocation must avoid all strenuous activities that necessitate raising the elbow higher than the shoulder.

CONTAGIOUS AND INFECTIOUS DISEASES

There are several contagious and infectious diseases that school children are likely to contract. Among them are influenza, pneumonia, streptococcal diseases, and infectious mononucleosis. Students returning to school* after the acute stage of illness has passed exhibit extreme fatigue and lack of endurance and strength for some time. During the completion of their convalescence, they should be placed in the special physical education program to engage in developmental activities selected for their special needs.

SKIN DISORDERS

There are several types of skin disorders that may require adaptation of the physical education activities while the student is suffering from them.

Blisters.   Blisters on the foot or certain other parts of the body may become so severe that withdrawal from certain types of physical education activities is necessitated. In a blister, pinching or continual irritation causes the epidermis to separate from the dermis, and the area between the two layers fills with fluid. If only the epidermis is involved in the injury, the area fills with the waterlike fluid of the blood to produce a water blister. If, however, the dermis is also injured, the area fills with blood, resulting in a blood blister.

Blisters occurring on the feet, usually water blisters, may cause temporary difficulty in participation in activity. First aid measures to open the blister are usually not desirable unless there is indication that the blister will be caused to break open by further irritation of the area. The opening of the blister should be done with a sterile instrument and the wound kept as sterile as possible. Proper padding around the broken or unbroken blister to reduce the pressure on the area will permit the student to participate without further irritation.

If participation in regular physical education is contraindicated because of the additional stress and strain that would be placed on the blistered area by the nature of the activities, the students may be placed in the adapted program temporarily to engage in activities which require little foot movement, such as bag punching, ring toss, table tennis, and shuffleboard. He may remove his shoes for these activities, but other activities in which running is an element should not be permitted without proper shoes because of the danger of slipping.

Corns, Calluses, Warts, and Bunions.   Students with corns, calluses, warts, or bunions may require medical attention before they are able to participate without pain

---

*No student who has had a contagious disease should be allowed to return to school until the disease is no longer contagious and permission for return has been given by the attending physician.

in unrestricted activities. Securing better fitting shoes or a better adjustment of the old shoes may relieve the condition sufficiently to permit participation. Padding to take the pressure off the area is also possible. In situations where such remedial action cannot be taken, the student may be placed in the special class for adapted activities of the same nature as those recommended above for students with blisters.

Contagious Skin Diseases.   Some communicable diseases and disturbances of the skin require dismissal from school until the condition is no longer contagious. Among these are impetigo, a dermatitis with small blisters that break and crust; pediculosis, an infection with head, body, or crab lice; and scabies, commonly called the seven-year itch, due to infestation of the skin with a very small mite that buries itself in the skin.

Athlete's Foot.   Ringworm of the foot, commonly called athlete's foot, once believed to be highly communicable, is not readily transferred. Students affected with ringworm need not be excluded from the use of the shower room and swimming pool as was once a common practice. The disease responds readily to treatment and usually does not interfere with participation. However, a severe case may be very painful, and in this event the student should be placed in activities which do not require much foot movement.

Boils.   Boils are caused by an infection produced by bacteria entering the hair follicle. Boils are readily transmitted from one part of the body to another. They should be protected with a sterile dressing in order to prevent spreading the infection. If a boil occurs in an area such as the groin or axillary region where movement might tend to irritate it, the student should not be required to participate in activities requiring the movement of the involved area but should instead be placed temporarily in the adapted program. Running activities are contraindicated for boils in the groin area, and arm movements for boils in the axillary region.

THE PROGRAM FOR CONVALESCING STUDENTS RETURNING TO SCHOOL

Convalescing students who have recuperated sufficiently to return to school should be placed in the special physical education program; during this time they may be given physical fitness or posture exercises and adapted activities as their special needs require. Participation in physical education that is suited to their special needs and abilities during the last stage of convalescence will help the students regain more quickly their former level of physical fitness; strengthen the weakened area if a particular part of the body was affected; continue their general improvement of motor skills; and achieve the feeling of well-being that is so important to complete recovery.

The physical education teacher may expect to plan activities for students in all five classifications of convalescence, including obstetrics (adolescent girls who are returning to school after having given birth or having had an abortion). In all cases medical approval for the student's participation in the adapted activities should be sought before the student begins activity. Most students who have been confined to bed in their homes will not have had convalescent exercises, will return to school with a very low level of fitness, and should not attempt the same amount of activity as they engaged in before their confinement. If there was no injury to a specific area, the exercises and activities described in Chapter 27 for low physical fitness may be used with these students. Some mild and easily regulated games in which older students may participate are:

Volleyball	Shuffleboard
Table tennis	Horseshoes
Bowling	Deck tennis
Archery	Bowling on the green

In situations where there has been injury to a specific area, a special exercise may be given to strengthen the part and to develop total body fitness. The first seven to ten days that a student is on crutches, the activity of walking is in itself sufficient overload for the upper arm area. Isometric muscular contractions can be used to exercise the muscles of the limb which is immobilized in a cast. Students with limbs in casts will want to avoid excessive perspiration in their workouts, because perspiration collects in the cast. If the activities can be performed in a cool area, undue perspiration can usually be avoided.

Games recommended for students with orthopedic handicaps are suitable for grade school and high school students with legs and arms in casts. Patients in whom a specific area of the body has been weakened by injury or infection require special precautions to protect the area from further injury during exercises which are being given to build up the strength of the area or to increase general body strength. When bones have been broken, joints sprained, or other parts of the body have suffered injuries, activities chosen for participation should be those which will not place undue stress and strain upon the area. In the cases of shoulder dislocation, knee instability, and ankle sprains, the muscles of the areas involved can be strengthened by exercise to prevent the recurrence of the injury.

To increase strength through exercise, the muscles involved must be given an overload. For a continuous increase in muscular strength, an overload must be applied to the muscle systematically. In doing so, it must be recognized that even an area of the body that may ultimately benefit from exercise may not tolerate activity during the acutely painful stage of recovering from an injury. Consequently, exercise should not be started until it is recommended by the physician of the convalescing student. The exercises, when they are initiated, must be moderate. They should not be done when the muscles are very tired and should be terminated at any time that a sharp pain occurs. If weights are used in the exercises, the load to be carried should be of an amount that is easily lifted by the injured part and yet provides a small overload.

Exercise that increases the strength of the muscles of the shoulder and shoulder girdle, especially the rotator cuff, tends to stabilize a shoulder that is susceptible to dislocation. The rotator cuff tends to hold the head of the humerus in the glenoid fossa, thus preventing displacement during abduction. It abducts and rotates the humerus. Resistance applied to the arm while abducting and laterally rotating the arm increases the strength of the muscles. All exercises that require raising the arm over the head so that there is a possibility of pressure on the arm, as in basketball, overhand swimming, and volleyball, are contraindicated. A type of belt and arm strap, shown in Figure 16–5, may be used to prevent extreme abduction of the arm and yet permit the student to engage in regular activities. Exercises and activities which may be used are the following:

> Weight lifting (avoid all lifts that raise the arm overhead)
> Pulley weights (same precaution as above)
> Heavy- and light-bag punching
> Table tennis
> Shuffleboard
> Golf
> Track
> Swimming the side stroke
> Racket games, if the weak shoulder is not involved
> Exercise on the shoulder wheel

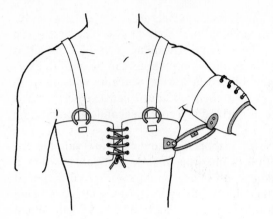

Figure 16–5. A belt with arm straps prevents extreme abduction of the arm.

Exercises that increase the strength of the quadriceps femoris of the leg tend to stabilize the knee by exerting more pull upon the patella, which in turn holds the tibia in closer contact in the joint with the femur. An exercise that is frequently used to strengthen the quadriceps femoris uses a knee exercise machine or an iron shoe strapped to the foot. The subject sits on a table, straightens the knee, and returns the leg to the original position. Individuals with unstable knees may participate in activities and games which do not place undue stress upon the knee. Among these are the following:

> Volleyball
> Shuffleboard
> Table tennis
> Bowling
> Swimming
> Bag punching

As the initial soreness of an ankle sprain decreases and walking is permitted, exercises may be given to promote healing and increase the strength of the muscles involved (peroneus longus and peroneus brevis) in preventing the foot from inverting accidentally. Forced inversion causes the majority of ankle sprains. Suggested exercises and games are the following:

> Standing and walking on tiptoes
> Toe stands with weights on back
> Exercise with ankle exerciser
> Swimming
> Bag punching
> Shuffleboard

The kind of exercise given to the back that has suffered a sprain or strain depends upon the nature and degree of injury it has sustained. In almost all cases where exercise is not contraindicated, muscular activity designed to improve the relationship of the pelvis and the sacrum with the lumbar spine, that is, to flatten out the small of the back, are appropriate. This is of special value to those with low back pain due to poor alignment of the pelvis and sacrum with the lumbar spine. The exercises are graded according to severity. In starting an exercise program for the back, the first two exercises should be given over a period of days before progressing to the more difficult ones.

1. Subject assumes a supine position on a hard surface with the hips and knees flexed. The chin is tucked to the chest by placing a pillow under the head, and the small of the back is pressed hard against the floor.

2. The same position as above is taken. One knee is brought up to the forehead in an attempt to make contact with it. The hands are wrapped around the knee to help pull it toward the forehead. The other leg maintains its original position. For the second portion of the exercise, the opposite knee is brought to the forehead.

3. The same position as above is assumed. One leg is straightened and raised straight into the air. The leg is held in this position a few seconds and then returned. The exercise is repeated with the other leg. Caution must be taken by subjects with a ruptured disc.

4. A supine position is taken on a hard surface with the legs straight. The head and shoulders are lifted slightly off the floor and held for a few seconds and then returned. To increase the strenuousness of the activity, the hips can be flexed and the feet placed flat on the surface. While the feet are held down by a helper, the subject executes a sit-up. This exercise should not be performed by one who has had a recent compression fracture or who has osteoporosis (abnormal rarefaction of bone) of the spine.

Resistive exercises to the arms and shoulders for one who has had a back injury should be performed with the back in an upright position. To supply added support to the back, the subject can be seated with his back resting against a support.

Activities for Young Children.   Elementary school children returning to school after illness or injury can be readily accommodated in the regular physical education program if the problem-solving method is being utilized, for each can work at his own capacity. This does not mean, however, that the children will not need some help from the teacher in setting up guidelines as to the kind of movement and the amount of exertion that are appropriate for their individual cases. The teacher should construct the problems to be solved in such a way as to avoid overexertion and possible harm to the area of the body that is recovering from injury. Also, the problems may be designed so that in solving them, conditioning exercises are applied to the weakened area; however, it is necessary in this situation to prevent experimentation or exploration that is likely to involve contraindicated movements.

Many of the basic skill or low organized games can be played with or without adaptation by convalescing children. The games that require only moderate expenditure of energy, such as target toss, balancing a beanbag on the head, and Circle Ball, can be performed by those who cannot engage in strenuous exercise but need moderate conditioning activity. For youngsters who require protection of an injured area, the selection of games can be made from among those that do not involve that part of the body; for example, a child recovering from a broken clavicle can participate in Line Relay or Cross Tag.

SELECTED READINGS

Boshell, Buris R.: *The Diabetic at Work and Play.* Springfield, Ill., Charles C Thomas, Publ., 1971.

Boshes, Louis D., and Gibbs, Fredric A.: *Epilepsy Handbook,* ed. 2. Springfield Ill., Charles C Thomas, Pub., 1972.

O'Donoghue, Don H.: *Treatment of Injuries to Athletes,* ed. 2. Philadelphia, W. B. Saunders Co., 1970.

Marlow, Dorothy R.: *Textbook of Pediatric Nursing.* Philadelphia, W. B. Saunders Co., 1973.

Song, J.: *Pathology of Sickle Cell Disease.* Springfield, Ill., Charles C Thomas, Pub., 1971.

Chapter 17

Mental Retardation

In the years since the turn of the century we have witnessed the development of numerous educational provisions for the mentally retarded. To speak of "educating" these individuals is significant when one realizes that only a few centuries ago society's treatment of the intellectually inferior consisted of ridicule, isolation, persecution, and for some, punishment until death. Recognition that mentally retarded persons can learn is attributed to a large extent to the work of Jean Itard, a French physician. In 1799, Itard undertook a five-year program to educate an animal-like boy of 12 who was found in the forest of Avignon, France. Although Itard considered his program a failure, others familiar with the boy observed definite improvement in the youngster's behavior. The ideas of Itard were introduced to the United States by one of his pupils, Edouard Seguin, who became superintendent of a Pennsylvania institution for the mentally retarded. During the 1800s many of the progressive ideas proposed by Seguin, such as emphasis on the whole child, individualized teaching, and good rapport between teacher and child, were incorporated into the programs of other supported institutions, which were growing rapidly in number.

The number of public school classes for the retarded, first organized in the United States in 1896, was also slowly but steadily growing. After 1930 this trend was slowed because of the effects of the depression, World War II, and the paucity of well-qualified teachers. With the end of the war and the revitalization of the economy, education for the mentally retarded was again enthusiastically supported.

Sensory-motor programs are among the oldest forms of special instructional efforts provided for the mentally retarded. Itard, Seguin, and later Maria Montessori all placed great importance on the training of the muscles, with strong reliance on gymnastic activities. Although a limited number of special educators continued this work, it was not until 1965 that physicial education for the mentally retarded became of special interest to the profession. At this time the AAHPER, in cooperation with the Joseph P. Kennedy, Jr., Foundation, established the Project on Recreation and Fitness for the Mentally Retarded to provide assistance and encouragement to schools and community agencies in the development of programs of recreation and fitness activities for the mentally retarded. The Special Olympics program, sponsored by the Joseph P. Kennedy, Jr., Foundation, has also contributed significantly in increasing the awareness of educators and the public in general to the value of physical activity for the mentally retarded.

THE NATURE OF MENTAL RETARDATION

A lack of uniformity in the use of terms describing persons who show retarded mental development has resulted in considerable confusion. No one definition of mental deficiency or retardation has been constructed that will satisfy all the professional disciplines (medical, psychological, educational, social, and legal) concerned with the problem. The most widely employed contemporary definition of mental retardation is that which appeared in a publication on terminology and classification produced by the American Association on Mental Deficiency (AAMD) in 1959 and revised in 1973: "Mental retardation refers to significantly subaverage general intellectual functioning existing concurrently with defects in adaptive behavior, and manifested during the developmental period."[1] A careful analysis of the definition clarifies some of the important considerations that must be met before classifying children as mentally retarded. Various terms used in the statement are defined as follows:

Significantly Subaverage. Intellectual functioning is determined by one or more of the standardized tests developed for that purpose. Performance on a standardized intelligence test of greater than two standard deviations below the mean is required before a score can be considered significantly subaverage. According to the definition, therefore, mentally retarded persons are those who possess an intelligence quotient (IQ)* of less than 68 if using the Stanford-Binet or less than 69 if using the Wechsler test. These are the two most frequently used tests of intelligence.

Developmental Period. The developmental period is the time during which the infant grows to maturity. The use of the term suggests that the condition of mental retardation is evident prior to the eighteenth year of age.

Adaptive Behavior. This term is defined as the ability to meet the standards of social responsibility for a particular age group. Since these expectations vary for different age groups, the defects in adaptive behavior vary according to age as well. During infancy and early childhood significant delays in the maturation areas of communication, self-help skills, and sensory-motor activities are potential indicators of mental retardation. During childhood and early adolescence primary focus is centered on the ability to learn the basic academic skills. The ability to make a living and to handle oneself and one's affairs with the prudence ordinarily expected of an adult in our society is the important determinant of the presence of mental retardation in the adult.

The American Association on Mental Deficiency definition suggests that a low IQ is not in itself sufficient evidence to make the diagnosis of mental retardation. The time of occurrence and the extent to which adaptive behavior is impaired must be determined before an individual is considered mentally retarded. The definition also provides for a dynamic concept of mental retardation, suggesting that a person may meet the criteria at one point in life but not at some other time. As explained by the American Association on Mental Deficiency, "a person may change status as a result of changes or alterations in his intellectual functioning, changes in his adaptive behaviors, changes in the expectations of the society, or for other known and unknown reasons."[2]

The terms mentally deficient, mentally retarded, and mentally handicapped are used interchangeably to designate a condition in which the individual is incapable of achieving normal mental growth. Such an individual is impaired in adaptive behavior and has an intelligence quotient of less than 70, although there are borderline cases on either side of this arbitrary number. Classification of the mentally retarded is made with tests that measure intelligence and adaptive behavior. The American Association

---

[1]Grossman, H. (Editor): *Manual on Terminology and Classification in Mental Retardation, 1973 Revision.* Washington, D.C., American Association on Mental Deficiency, 1973, p. 11.

[2]Grossman, op. cit., pp. 11–14.

*IQ is defined as mental age/chronological age × 100. Specific charts based on normative data are often used to compute this today.

on Mental Retardation classifies mental retardation as follows: mild, moderate, severe, and profound. Tests designed to determine intellectual retardation use the following scores to report the level.

Classification	Intelligence Quotients	
	Stanford-Binet	Wechsler
Mild	68–52	69–52
Moderate	51–36	54–40
Severe	32–20	39–25[a]
Profound	19 and below	24 and below[b]

a, b = Extrapolated values.

Educators frequently classify the mentally retarded into three groups. Each state has its own classification system, but most approximate the following.

Classification	Intelligence Quotient
Educable	75–50
Trainable	49–30
Totally Dependent	29 and below

Standardized tests of adaptive behavior such as the Vineland Social Maturity Scale and the American Association on Mental Deficiency Adaptive Behavior Scales are employed to determine extent of impairment in adaptive behavior. Although the relationship is not perfect, persons who score low on the intelligence tests often score low on the adaptive behavior scales and vice versa.

The Totally Dependent.   Totally dependent children are those who, because of the severeness of their mental retardation, are incapable of being trained for economic usefulness, social participation, or total self-care. These children develop at only one fourth the rate of average children. They will require nearly complete supervision and care throughout their lives, for they cannot care adequately for their personal needs, protect themselves, or communicate effectively with others.

The range of movement to be found in totally dependent children varies from random, meaningless movements to the intricate and controlled movements required by such skills as walking, running, catching, throwing, and climbing. The kinds of movements of which they are capable depend upon mental ability, absence or presence of physical handicaps, general level of physical fitness, and past experiences in physical education.

The Trainable Child.   Those mentally retarded children who have some potential for learning to care for their personal needs, for social adjustment in a group, and for economic usefulness are classified as trainable. These children can be taught enough of the self-help skills to make them generally independent of care by others. They are capable of learning to get along in the family and in a limited environment. Their mental development is approximately one fourth to one half that of the average child, and, though most trainables are able to learn a fairly wide variety of motor skills, they are not generally capable of acquiring academic skills beyond the rote learning of simple words and numbers. Nevertheless, they are capable of learning to do simple tasks around the home or for remuneration in a supervised situation outside the home. Some care, supervision, and economic support will be required throughout their lives.

The Educable Child.   Children who have difficulty learning at a rate equal to that of their peers but who are capable of learning some academic skills are classified as educable. They are generally capable of acquiring from second to fourth grade achievement in reading, writing, and arithmetic by the age of 16. Their development is approximately one half to three fourths as fast as the average child; consequently, their academic progress is also one half to three fourths the rate of the average child. Although their communication skills are definitely limited, they can be adequately developed for most situations. Most educables can learn to get along with others and can acquire enough skills to support themselves economically in adulthood. Emotional and behavior problems may limit their adaptability. The majority of these children are able to participate in the same motor activities as children of normal intelligence. Acquisition of motor skills does take longer, however.

THE EXTENT OF MENTAL RETARDATION

It is estimated that there are more than six million people in the United States who are mentally retarded. This value is close to 3 per cent of the population and approximates the number to be expected from a normal distribution of intelligence. Between 100,000 and 200,000 of the babies born each year are likely to join this group. Natural population growth can be expected to increase the total substantially, unless far-reaching preventive measures are introduced.

Of the total, approximately four million are children and young people under 20 years of age. At least 3.5 million of these children are mildly retarded, and many of them may not be singled out and identified until they enter school. Another 400,000 or more are estimated to be moderately retarded; an additional 100,000 are totally dependent.

Although a significant number of moderately, severely, and profoundly retarded children are found and given help in early childhood, many more are overlooked or not properly diagnosed. The mortality rate in this group is known to be high but is difficult to document, since frequently a baby may not show definite retardation for months or even years after birth. Usually, however, when parents of retarded children look back, they can recognize that the signs were present from infancy.

Once he has lived to the age of five or six a retarded child has a good chance of growing up. In fact, the life expectancy of the mildly retarded is probably about the same as that of other people. For the profoundly and severely retarded it is substantially less, although profoundly retarded persons have been known to live to the age of 70 to 80 years. Because the retarded adults of today were born before the introduction of antibiotics and other modern life-saving treatments, it is likely that the prevalence of moderate, severe, and profound retardation among adults will increase in the next 15 years. Statistics on survivorship among persons with Down's syndrome (mongolism), for example, indicate a much greater life expectancy for this group today than 20 or 30 years ago.

Nearly three million adults were once mildly retarded children. These are handicapped members of our society, but, to the extent that they may have been helped to achieve a satisfactory degree of "adaptive behavior" and to attain economic and social independence, they will no longer be recognized as mentally retarded. For this reason they are often not identified and counted when community surveys are made, although most of them remain potentially vulnerable to adverse social or economic pressures. Thus, the number of adults who may require help because of varying degrees of mental retardation probably is no more than one million to one and one-quarter million. Many of these persons are receiving disability or general welfare assistance or are dependent on relatives. Thus, as a cause of lifetime disability and as a medical, social, and educational problem of unique extent and complexity, mental retardation today presents an outstanding challenge to science and society in the United States and throughout the world.

THE CAUSES OF MENTAL RETARDATION

Mental retardation can be caused by any condition that hinders or interferes with development before birth (prenatal), during birth (natal), or in the early childhood years (postnatal). Well over a hundred causes have already been identified, although these account for only about one fourth of all identified cases of mental retardation.

In 1973, the American Association on Mental Deficiency, in its revised *Manual on Terminology and Classification in Mental Retardation,* grouped the causes into 10 categories.[3] The categories and a brief description of each are presented below:

Infection and Intoxication. This grouping includes maternal and child infectious diseases and intoxication. Rubella and syphilis are examples of maternal infection which are included in this category. Lead-based paints have been the most common source of poisoning among children.

Trauma or Physical Agent. This classification includes injuries to the brain from prenatal, natal, or postnatal conditions. Examples include mechanical injuries at birth or prolonged anoxia (lack of oxygen).

Metabolism or Nutrition. Disorders directly due to metabolic, nutritional, endocrine, or growth dysfunction should be classified under this category. Included are lipid (fatty acid) disorders such as Tay-Sachs disease and Hurler's disease. Phenylketonuria (PKU), a protein disorder, is also found within this grouping.

Gross Brain Disease (Postnatal). This category includes new growths and a large number of hereditary disorders in which the cause is unknown or uncertain. Examples include von Recklinghausen's disease (a nervous disorder), multiple tumors of the skin and peripheral nerves, and tumors in the central nervous system and other organs.

Unknown Prenatal Influence. This division is intended only for conditions for which no definite cause can be established but which existed at, or prior to, birth. Hydrocephalus is one of the primary examples found within this category.

Chromosomal Abnormality. Syndromes associated with chromosomal errors are included in this category. These disorders may be in the number or structure of chromosomes, or in both. Down's syndrome is one of the most common abnormalities classified under this heading.

Gestational Disorders. There is a high incidence of defects related to atypical gestation. Prematurity, low birth weight, and postmaturity are the primary subdivisions within this category.

Following Psychiatric Disorder. This category is for retardation occurring after serious mental illness when there is no evidence of cerebral disorder due to disease.

Environmental Influences. This category is for cases in which retardation is caused by a sensory handicap or by adverse environmental conditions when there is no cerebral disorder due to disease. Examples include sensory handicaps such as blindness and deafness and situations such as maternal deprivation.

Other Conditions. This category includes cases in which there is no evidence of a physical cause or structural defect, no history of subnormal functioning in parents and siblings, and no evidence of an associated psychosocial factor.

---

[3]Grossman, op. cit. pp. 49–68.

As time goes on, more people are found to have specific diagnosable causes of their mental retardation which fit neatly into the first eight categories discussed above. Nevertheless, even today, in the majority of cases, no clear diagnosis of cause can be made, and in most of these there is no demonstrable pathology of the nervous system. Therefore, most cases of mental retardation are attributed to environmental influences and other conditions. Undoubtedly among the mildly retarded there are many people whose development has been adversely affected by nonspecific influences, such as inadequate diet, inadequate prenatal and perinatal care, and lack of adequate stimulation toward growth and development through learning opportunities. Mental development, like physical development, is promoted by the right kinds of activity and stimulation and is retarded when these are lacking. Indeed, mental and physical development tend to interact. In the developmental process, the years of early childhood, when the nervous system is maturing and language is developing, are certainly very critical.

Brain Damage in Mental Retardates

The term "brain damage" has not been adequately defined and is used differently by different people. Destruction of brain tissue or interference with brain development in the infant or young child frequently produces mental retardation as well as cerebral palsy, convulsive seizures, hyperactivity, and perceptual problems. Such damage accounts for a substantial percentage of moderate, severe, and profound mental retardation. Although it may be definitely shown in some cases of mild mental retardation, the extent of its contribution is not known and expert opinion is divided. Several factors may be at work in the same individual. For example, the premature infant is more vulnerable to brain damage, prematurity is more common among mothers who receive inadequate prenatal care, and inadequate prenatal care in turn is more common in the disadvantaged groups in our society; these same children are more apt to have inadequate postnatal opportunities for growth and development and to be subject to psychological and cultural deprivation.

The extent of psychomotor, perceptual, and sensory handicaps among the retarded points to common causation in many cases. Most severely and profoundly retarded individuals have pronounced motor handicaps or impairment of hearing, vision, or speech, or a combination of several of these. Although the majority of the mildy retarded would not be readily identified as physically handicapped, their general level of motor coordination is below average, despite the occurrence among them of a few remarkable athletes.

Prevention of Mental Retardation

Progress is being made in the prevention of mental retardation, but it is proceeding, as might be expected, through a succession of small advances across the broad front rather than by any spectacular breakthrough. Each of the many contributing causes must be analyzed specifically, with specific preventive measures devised when the cause has been found. Progress is being made against some of the more serious forms by such techniques as corrective surgery for malformations of the skull and for the diversion of excess fluid in the brain. Children who have inadequate blood sugar in the first few critical days after birth are now more readily identified and given corrective treatment. Damage resulting from Rh factor incompatibility can be prevented by treatment of the mother after the birth of her first child (the first born is not vulnerable to damage). Quick treatment in cases of lead poisoning or, better yet, action to prevent children from eating paint containing lead can undoubtedly prevent some cases. The new measles vaccine can help if widely used. Some progress is being made in identifying the characteristics of mothers most likely to give birth prematurely, so that this indirect cause of mental retardation may be reduced. Thus far, however, all of these steps have been effective in eliminating only a relatively small fraction of mental retardation. Increased attention to relevant basic and applied research and to the prompt application of new discoveries is essential to carrying forward this initial progress. Moreover, some of those forms of retardation that stem from physical, emotional, or cultural deprivation will yield only to basic social reform.

NEEDS AND ADJUSTMENTS OF THE MENTALLY RETARDED

Mentally retarded children exhibit certain common characteristics, but, like their non-handicapped counterparts, they vary greatly in the extent to which they demonstrate specific characteristic behaviors. Educators must learn to recognize these common behavioral patterns while remembering, too, to search for the individual qualities that are unique to each human being, including persons who are mentally retarded.

Learning Characteristics

Essentially, the learning characteristics of the mentally retarded are similar to those of their non-retarded peers in that they follow the same developmental sequence. Primary differences are noted in the total amount of information gained and in the rate at which this material is learned. Other learning characteristics of the mentally retarded include a short attention span, difficulty in dealing with abstracts, and a limited ability to generalize information. An inability to transfer material learned, academic or social, from one situation to another is a major learning difficulty for the retarded. The primary learning deficiency, however, may be the failure of the mentally retarded person to effectively employ problem-solving strategies. Educators, therefore, must develop procedures to present information in such a fasion that retarded youngsters may attend to only relevant stimuli.

Social and Emotional Characteristics

The failure of mentally handicapped children to keep intellectual pace with normal children contributes to personality maladjustment and the development of undesirable behavior patterns. Much of the normal child's social maturity and satisfactory adjustment is acquired in play situations throughout his formative years. This is not so with the mentally retarded child, who finds himself rejected by his normal peers, or who, because of his low mentality, has no interest in group play. Retarded children, therefore, often feel inferior and then tend to devalue their skills and talents, resulting in further withdrawal and regression in ability. Understandably, these children are frustrated and develop an attitude of "I can't," which means "I have tried, I have failed, and I do not want to try again."

Some mentally retarded persons placed in circumstances in which more is expected of them than they can deliver, exhibit expressions of fear and aggression. Aggressiveness on the part of the mentally deficient child may be an attempt to cover weaknesses, to demonstrate worth, to attract attention, or to relieve tensions. Rebellious acts and other undesirable behavior are similarly motivated. On occasions the mentally retarded may use their handicap as a protective shield or in an outright bid for sympathy to compensate for their lack of social acceptance.

Physical and Motor Learning Characteristics

It is usually very apparent that mentally handicapped children need to improve in such parameters as physical fitness, motor ability, and body mechanics. Posture is usually poor and physical vitality low. A shuffling, inefficient walking gait is representative of the poorly coordinated general bodily movements. Mentally retarded persons are also more subject to other physical handicaps and neurological dysfunctions, such as cerebral palsy and epilepsy.

In comparative studies retarded children consistently score lower than normal children on measures of strength, endurance, agility, balance, running speed, flexibility, and reaction time. Generally, the motor performance of educable and trainable retarded youngsters tends to be two to four years behind normal. Some of this difference, however, may be attributed to a failure to understand the movement skill task rather than to an inability to execute the skill.

Children with Down's syndrome possess some unique physical characteristics worthy of a separate discussion. These individuals are often referred to as mongoloids because of the resemblance of their facial features to those of the Mongol race. Although these similarities have been exaggerated, children with Down's syndrome do tend to have a flat nose with eyes that appear to slant upward. Other visible characteristics include reduced head and ear size, and a small mouth with abnormal teeth and a protruding tongue. Small, square hands, and hair that is usually sparse, fine, and straight are other noticeable characteristics. Impairments in speech are quite common among this population. Physical educators should be particularly cognizant that these individuals are usually short and stocky with a tendency toward obesity. Upper respiratory infection, heart defects, and poor muscle tone are also very prevalent among individuals with Down's syndrome.

Recognition of these characteristics points to the need of educable and trainable children for successful experiences in group play. Although mentally retarded youngsters cannot generally acquire the high degree of skill of normal players, they can acquire sufficient skills to participate in enough different muscular activities to increase their physical fitness and improve their body mechanics. In addition to the physical benefits, play provides many opportunities for social development and emotional growth. Adherence to the rules of the game and to the sportsman's code of fair play provides incentive for self-discipline and self-control. Respect for one's own abilities and limitations and those of others is stimulated in the cooperation and sharing necessitated by the game situation. Many desirable learnings are claimed for sports in the training of normal youngsters. However much these have been exaggerated for normal children, they are essentially acceptable for the mentally handicapped, whose other opportunities for learning to work and play with others are considerably restricted.

The totally dependent child is in great need of personal attention in physical education; because of his physical and social limitations, he does not respond well in group play. He even experiences difficulty in relating to just one person. Serving these children effectively requires a very low teacher-pupil ratio, usually one to one.

PLANNING THE PROGRAM

Directing the play of the mentally retarded requires most careful organization on the part of the instructor. The ultimate goal is a physical activity program in which children can enjoy the experience while improving their movement proficiency. Additional planning considerations must focus on creating a program that can be conducted in an appropriate environment with suitable activities presented in a manner so that the mentally retarded can succeed.

In planning any program, particularly one funded by state and local taxes as many such programs are, it is essential that a clear statement of the rationale of the program be developed. The essential question to be answered in the statement is why this program with these activities for this group of children. This question is legitimate, and it deserves a straightforward answer that can be understood by participants, their parents, school officials, and the public.

Support of physical education for the mentally retarded often includes such justification as movement experiences improve intelligence, enhance self-concept, improve motor ability, and develop physical fitness. Although research evidence is extremely limited, support, to some extent, may be given to each of these and it would seem logical to suggest that physical education may be one of the few disciplines that contribute to all three learning domains, psychomotor, cognitive, and affective.

Nevertheless, it must be emphasized that the unique contribution physical education provides to the mentally retarded is in the area of motor development. It has been clearly established that these youngsters are deficient in motor ability and in physical fitness. Furthermore, data support conclusively the argument that improvements can be made in these areas if appropriate programs are provided.

As children experience success in physical education, they often improve in self-concept and in general emotional development. Emphasis on motor skill development also provides opportunities to reinforce the retarded youngsters' understanding of certain important concepts, such as shape, size, and color. It is important that the physical education teacher be aware of the activities that children are doing in the classroom. A coordinated curriculum is necessary for the most efficient presentation of material to the mentally retarded.

Emphasis on motor skill instruction is a must in programs for the totally dependent. Tasks such as reaching and grasping, which normally develop with maturation, will need to be taught to many of these youngsters. The value of psychomotor skills and their relationship to affective and cognitive learning will be apparent to all who work with the severely and profoundly retarded. For these reasons, school officials and parents of the children will actively seek assistance from motor development specialists. Unfortunately, in the past, too many professionals teaching the totally dependent have not had a sufficient background in motor skill development.

Class Placement

The primary purpose of educational programs for the mentally retarded is to help them to achieve at their highest possible level. Although educators are in general agreement with this statement, means to achieve this end have generated a great deal of controversy. Specifically, some feel that retarded youngsters should be taught in separate special classes and others feel that these children should receive instruction in the regular educational setting, the mainstream of education. In the field of physical education there are few studies available to support either position. It is apparent, though, that many educable mentally retarded youngsters are capable of successfully participating in regular physical education classes. Likewise most trainable and totally dependent children will require special classes that are specifically designed to meet their unique movement needs. It must not be assumed, however, that all retarded youngsters fit these general guidelines. Occasionally, trainable mentally retarded children are discovered who have the competency to participate in some or all of the regular physical education activities. Similarly, not all educable retarded students will find success in the regular class environment.

It is obvious, therefore, that placement flexibility is extremely desirable in movement programs for the mentally retarded. Some children may be placed in special classes, while others may be placed with regular classes for a small portion of every period. Some retarded children may have sufficient skill to completely integrate for an entire physical education period. Placement consideration must be based on a careful evaluation of motor skill and physical fitness performance coupled with other factors such as the child's social maturity level. Remember, too, that no placement decision is final, and periodic reviews should be made at least semi-annually.

Teaching Environment

Educators often assume that physical education activities must be taught in a gymnasium. For many children, particularly the mentally retarded, this is an incorrect assumption; conducting classes within such a large space may actually interfere with their skill development. Mentally retarded youngsters are easily distracted and the presence of permanent or temporary equipment usually found in the gymnasium will compete with the teacher's ability to hold the attention of the children. It is recommended, therefore, that instruction be confined to a small area when introducing a new skill. A distraction-free corner of the classroom will often be suitable for this purpose. As children become proficient in the skill, opportunities should be provided to utilize the new skills within the larger environment of the playground or gymnasium.

Physical education teachers should strive to maintain a class size conducive to learning. The ratio of teacher to student will vary according to the motor skill level of the youngster and the ability of the teacher. Totally dependent children will often require a one-to-one student–teacher ratio. For higher functioning retarded students, the class size may reach as high as one teacher to 10 or 12 youngsters. As a general guide, it is strongly suggested that the physical education teacher not be asked to teach more mentally retarded youngsters per class than is the classroom teacher.

Student Interest

In organizing any activity designed to assist people, it is essential to consider the interest level of the participants. Many mentally retarded youngsters will come to the physical education class with high initial interest because the change to another type of class activity is interesting in itself. Moreover, if previous physical education periods have been fun, interest is high in anticipation of more fun. If natural initial interest does not exist among the students, as is often true when new skills are introduced, it can be aroused in various ways. With educable and highly trainable students, simple, colorful pictures may be shown to introduce a game. Through cooperation with the classroom teacher, a short story related to the activity to be presented may be told. Or, if a song or music is to accompany this activity, it may be introduced in an interesting way before the actual activity is presented. While considerable student interest may be generated, it is usually not sustained because the interest span of these children is relatively short. A change to an alternate activity, designed to achieve the same purpose as the initial activity, is indicated when interest lags.

The totally dependent child does not respond well to the use of pictures, stories, or music as a means of motivation. He requires individual attention and continuous stimulation and encouragement by the teacher. The technique of behavior modification has been a most successful method for reaching these children. A complete discussion of behavior modification is found later in this chapter.

Figure 17–1. A wide variety of play equipment encourages exploration and stimulates interest.

Equipment

To maintain the interest of the mentally retarded, a wide variety of play equipment is desirable. There should be enough physical education equipment for each specific activity, so that no child need sit around idly waiting for a turn. Opportunities to explore with different items designed to achieve the same purpose, such as teaching children to throw using objects of various shapes, sizes, and substances, should be used to renew stimulation and interest.

In addition to the conventional equipment and supplies found in good physical education programs, many ordinary items can be adapted to offer variety and stimulate interest. Old tires, logs of various sizes, barrels, large pipes, boards and planks, saw horses, wooden and paper boxes, balloons, steps, and parachutes are some examples. An innovative teacher will discover many other items that can be used effectively in the program.

Teaching Methods and Techniques

The problem-solving method has limitations in teaching motor skills to mental retardates because of their general lack of imagination or innovative ability; nevertheless, exploration can be rewarding for some of them.

To increase the possibility of problem-solving being successful as a method of teaching the mentally retarded, the following suggestions are offered:

1. Select problems that have a simple solution.
2. Keep the problems few in number and related to the same area of motor skill.
3. Explain and demonstrate how moving one part of the body while in motion can change the nature of the movement. For example, in solving the problem "Can you hop like a rabbit?" demonstrate a hop on two legs and then show how, by lifting

one leg in hopping, or by raising the hands to the head to simulate bunny ears, the nature of the movement can be changed.

4. Repeat the same problem frequently, encouraging some small change in movement.

The direct method is generally very successful for helping mentally retarded students learn motor skills. Of the various techniques utilized in the method, demonstration appears to be the most effective for teaching trainable and educable mentally retarded children. These youngsters are great mimics, and much can be accomplished by encouraging them to imitate the demonstrated skill. The demonstration must necessarily be adapted to the intellectual abilities of the students. It is usually more successful when the children attempt the activity at the time it is being demonstrated. In some cases, it may be desirable to use manual kinesthesis at the time the demonstration is being made; this requires one person to demonstrate and another to lead the child's body parts through the desired movements. To avoid confusion, the instructor and child should face in the same direction when a new skill is to be demonstrated. This technique, known as mirroring, does not require the youngsters to reverse the visual image. Similarly, when giving manual guidance, the teacher should stand behind the student, reaching around him, if possible.

Manual kinesthesis is effective in many situations, such as teaching a child to ride a tricycle. Here the child may not be able to perceive the nature of the action required to pedal the tricycle until the teacher moves his feet alternately through proper movements. Manual kinesthesis is the most successful technique for teaching motor movement to the totally dependent. When working with students of this level it is important that the teacher move the parts of the body in the same way each time to avoid confusion. The hold taken on the child should be firm and reassuring to give him confidence in attempting the movement.

Verbalization can be utilized as a technique of teaching with the large majority of the mentally retarded in much the same way as with normal youngsters. However, the use of the spoken word for the totally dependent, many of whom have communication disorders, has definite limitations. It is possible to teach these children to understand and respond to a limited number of words related to the skills they are learning. Examples of such words are sit, grasp, and step over. Only one or two words should be taught during a given period. The word that is being taught should be repeated over and over as the action it describes is being demonstrated by the teacher or being performed by the student. The word should be used alone rather than in a sentence. This does not preclude speaking in sentences. Rather, it is highly desirable that such communication take place because hearing sentences is important to the potential language development of the students.

Care must be exercised not to provide the mentally retarded with more information than they can process during a given period of time. It is not uncommon to observe a response delay of several seconds in the mentally retarded, similar to that observed in very young children.[4] During this interval of inaction, it is important that the teacher not become impatient and provide additional visual or verbal cues. This extra instruction interferes with information still in the processing system, thereby confusing the mentally retarded.

In the teaching of any task it is essential for the teacher's directions to be as specific as possible. The instructor's failure to provide good visual, verbal, or manual cues often results in the mentally retarded not performing the task because of their in-

---

[4]Cratty, B. J.: *Motor Activity and the Education of Retardates,* ed. 2. Philadelphia, Lea and Febiger, 1974, p. 63.

ability to understand what is expected of them. For example, many mentally retarded children have difficulty learning the hand and foot placement required in the sprint start. Hand and foot prints cut out of cardboard or other material and placed on the floor can be invaluable aids in teaching this skill, especially if the prints are actual tracings of the children's own hands and feet. The use of various colored lines painted on the floor can help in class organization by providing the teacher and students with several specific common points of reference. One can well appreciate the confusion that can arise from an inexperienced teacher's non-specific command of "over there."

Instructional efforts should be directed toward providing success-oriented experiences for the participants. Recognition of this principle is especially critical for teachers of the mentally retarded, because so many of the retarded have failed in tasks for which they were ill-prepared. To overcome this difficulty, instructors of these children should recognize the importance of breaking skills down into minute components and listing them in a hierarchical sequence. For each component, behavioral statements with criterion levels may then be developed so that teacher and student will know when to advance to the next step. An analysis of skill in this manner provides a means for the mentally retarded to recognize success. The teacher, too, will become more cognizant that small but important improvements are being achieved.

Participation in play activities by everyone should be actively encouraged by the teacher. There should, of course, be no resort to pressure tactics. The retarded child needs and seeks approval, and he can be led to cooperate and participate if he knows that this is what the teacher wants and gives approval for. Teacher participation, when possible, in the play and fitness activities of these children is also encouraged. The mentally retarded react favorably when they see that what is asked of them is good for all, including their teacher. Because these children are easily distracted, class observers should be kept to a minimum or, perhaps best, be included in the class activities.

Praise should be offered generously for the efforts of the youngster. The attempt may not result in successful performance, but the effort that is exerted should be commended by the teacher. Sincere praise can be one of the teacher's most effective motivators and helps to create the kind of learning situation most conducive to progress.

The teacher should exercise firm discipline without resort to threats and corporal punishment. The disciplining must take a form which the group is capable of comprehending, such as withholding approval. Those who present a disruptive influence may be temporarily removed from the class and dealt with in a small group or on an individual basis.

Retarded individuals perform best the first few times they do a skill. Consequently, it is to their advantage to end the practice of any one skill before frustration at inability to master the skill sets in. After the skills of a game have been mastered over a gradual period of time, they should be reviewed briefly each time before the game is played. These drill periods should be just long enough to refresh the students' memories.

Because many retardates have low physical vitality, they fatigue easily. This has important implications for the teaching situation. First, it means that new and complex activities should be planned for the early part of the period while the students are fresh and alert. Then, too, a greater chance of injury exists after fatigue has set in, so it is extremely important for the instructor to watch for signs of fatigue.

Special efforts may be required to evoke responses from torpid youngsters. Such students are particularly in need of physical activity but show no interest in play. The physical education teacher must endeavor to arouse interest and awaken their sensibilities. To do this it may be necessary to force the torpid child to display a physical response, for example, tossing balloons at him so that he will raise his arms to protect himself or will attempt to catch or dodge the balloons. From the use of balloons, the instructor may progress to beanbags and large soft balls that would not seriously hurt the child if he failed to ward them off. Eventually the child can be taught catching, throwing, and other simple motor skills.

In some instances, physical education teachers have obtained the assistance of outstanding high school students on a volunteer basis in providing individual attention for retarded youngsters in physical activity. This has proved to be a worthwhile learning experience for both the helping student and the retarded youngsters. Parents of handicapped youngsters are often willing to volunteer their services. In such cases, it is to the benefit of both parent and child to assign to the parent a child other than the parent's own. To utilize volunteers effectively, the teacher must provide a daily written program for each child, emphasizing the skills to be learned.

The physical educator also has the opportunity of teaching the educables and highly trainables certain health and safety facts and of encouraging the development of habits pertaining to personal care and protection and in the wise use of leisure time. Specifically in the area of health are such personal hygiene matters as showering after activity, care of the feet to prevent athlete's foot, and cleanliness of gym clothes and socks. Good safety practices, such as not throwing the bat, should be clearly and firmly established so that they will be observed not only in supervised play but also in free play. By providing in the physical education curriculum opportunities to learn games that can be played during leisure hours, the wise use of such time can be encouraged. Because of their generally restricted interests and recreational opportunities, the mentally retarded often pursue undesirable leisure activities or idle the time away, which is undesirable from the standpoint of their development and may become harmful to themselves and to society.

For the low trainable and totally dependent youngster, the health and safety habits to be taught are simple and more fundamental in nature. Examples are when and where to go to the toilet, how to wash the hands, and being aware that a shoe is untied.

SUGGESTED ACTIVITIES FOR EDUCABLE AND TRAINABLE RETARDATES

The physical education program must present a variety of activities directed toward the special needs of the mentally retarded. These experiences, depending on the functioning ability of the child, range from basic motor skills to leisure activities. The discussion that follows applies primarily to the retarded youngster who, although not severely retarded, possesses movement deficiencies serious enough to exclude his successful participation in some or all of the activities of the regular physical education class. For a more complete discussion of the motor skills, games, sports, and other activities discussed within this section, the reader is referred to the chapters within this text devoted to those topics.

Basic Motor Skills

For very young children and those who cannot participate with success in more complex exercises and games, a variety of simple activities that will achieve the goal of desired physical development should be introduced. Among the very simplest of these activities are the basic motor skills of everyday living: walking, balancing, twisting, turning, bending, and climbing stairs. Slightly more involved are the basic play skills: running, hopping, jumping, skipping, kicking, hanging, catching, and throwing. Perceptual motor skills such as visually tracking a suspended ball and stepping over and under obstacles placed at various heights should also be emphasized.

The skills must be presented to the children so that they will take pleasure in performing them. Variety in presentation is also vital to achieving interest in their performance. The following suggestions are ways in which this may be accomplished:

1. Walking at varied tempos and with different sizes and kinds of steps, such as short, quick steps, slow giant strides, tiptoeing.

2. Running at varied tempos.

3. Jumping on both feet, alternating feet, one foot; attaining various heights.

4. Hopping on one foot and on alternate feet.

5. Skipping at varied tempos.

6. Marching at varied tempos; alternating with running, skipping, and jumping; accompanied by hand clapping.

7. Climbing stairs, alternating the feet.

8. Catching and throwing a large balloon.

9. Catching and bouncing a ball.

10. Throwing the ball for distance and at objects; throwing the ball to a catcher.

11. Kicking, with the leg swinging freely, at a large ball, at a small ball.

12. Hanging from a bar or the rung of a ladder, with both arms, with one arm; climbing the ladder with the hands only.

13. Balancing on a balance beam or log; walking along a chalked line; stepping on the rungs of a ladder placed on the floor.

14. Springing up and down on a jouncing board;* leaping from the board to the ground.

15. Walking on and jumping on and off tires.

16. Crawling through and over barrels or large pipes.

17. Walking on a balance beam while focusing on a fixed point at the end of the beam.

18. Walking on a balance beam while focusing on a fixed point to the side of the beam.

19. Jumping and turning to the right and then the left side.

20. Rolling on a medicine ball.

The possibilities for emphasizing the basic motor skills through mimetic play are practically limitless. Pretending they are animals, the children can waddle like ducks, hop like bunnies, leap like frogs, and walk softly (on tiptoes) like kittens. Imitating the actions of people, they may vigorously chop wood, march in a band, sweep the floor, iron clothes. At times the mimetic activities may be done to musical accompaniment, both for the added interest provided by the music and for the introduction it provides to instruction in dance.

Basic Skill Games

Activities such as relays, parachute play, and simple games may be introduced to those who have acquired some basic skill movement and can follow simple directions. The following guide is offered for the selection of simple activities. The more capable the students are of participating in complex activities, the less necessity there will be for the games to meet all of the suggested criteria. A very simple game is one in which

1. All children do the same thing.

2. The space is relatively small.

---

*A board 1 inch thick, 6 to 8 inches wide, and 6 feet long, balanced on two supports.

3. Choices which must be made are few in number.
4. Positions are fixed.
5. Quality of performance brings no penalities or privileges.
6. The possible directions of movement are restricted.
7. Personnel remain the same.
8. Motor skill requirements are limited.

Whenever possible, games that reinforce cognitive concepts such as letter, color, and symbol recognition should be incorporated into activities for the mentally retarded. In addition to the obvious value of these experiences, they are also highly motivating and are enjoyed by the children.

For the higher functioning adolescent retardate who has successfully participated in activities meeting the above criteria, opportunities to learn lead-up games, such as kickball, keep away, line soccer, twenty-one, and newcomb, should be provided.

Rhythmic Activities

The mentally deficient enjoy music and respond well to dance and rhythmic activities. Such activities are valuable in improving coordination, flexibility, and body carriage. Extensive dance activities, ranging in complexity from simple movements to musical accompaniment to folk dances of complex patterns, should be included in the physical education program. Moreover, they provide a release from tensions and anxieties, which is in itself extremely valuable for these students. The listening experience also heightens auditory perception.

Efforts at teaching rhythmic patterns should initially focus on having the children learn to keep time with one hand, then two hands, and finally, for the more advanced, incorporating the feet into the sequence as well. Mentally retarded children unable to master this sequence should be encouraged to let their bodies sway from side to side

Figure 17–2. Dance activities contribute to the development of coordination and flexibility.

with the music. Making and utilizing their own instruments to play along with the music is also an activity from which the retarded can derive much pleasure.

Physical Fitness

The mentally retarded, as a group, are deficient in all of the components of physical fitness. To a great extent this poor performance is due to a lack of opportunity for these children to participate in play activity. Therefore, if programs are well designed and administered by an enthusiastic teacher, noticeable improvements in physical fitness can be achieved. The total amount of physical education time devoted to fitness activities for the retarded need not be extensive. However, a developmental program of from five to 15 minutes that contributes to strength, flexibility, and endurance should be provided at least three times weekly.

Retarded children enjoy doing exercises with their teacher. Included in the program may be such simple activities as bending, squatting, twisting the trunk, and rotating the arms. Educable youngsters can achieve considerable skill in the performance of more complicated calisthenics, such as the push-up and squat thrust. Circuit training in which different exercises are performed at various stations in the room is highly motivating for the retarded. Charts should be provided at each station with pictures depicting the exercises to be performed and the number to be executed. For all of the physical fitness activities, records simple enough for the children to understand should be maintained to help teacher and child "see" progress.

Team Sports

As retarded children achieve success through lead-up games, additional instructional time should be directed toward teaching the various team sport activities. Most of these youngsters will be familiar with sporting events as a result of attending local contests, watching television, or looking at pictures in books describing sport activities. The retarded, like most children, thoroughly enjoy these exposures. Teachers of the mentally retarded often marvel at the number of their students who can recall the names of local and national sport heroes. Because of this high interest level, the physical education program should provide as many of these sports and games as possible. They provide the vigorous muscular activity essential to improving physical fitness in these youngsters, so many of whom are physically deficient. Besides the physical benefits are the recreational and socializing values, which have already been stressed.

Capable teachers have been able to teach the skill of team play well enough to mentally retarded students that they have been able to compete against other teams. Some residential schools field baseball and basketball teams. Many retarded children have been provided extensive opportunities to participate in competitive athletics under the auspices of the Special Olympics program sponsored by the Joseph P. Kennedy, Jr., Foundation. The mentally retarded enjoy competition of this nature and desire it for the personal satisfaction and social approval that it brings them. Competition for some, however, may promote undesirable aggressive behavior on the one hand or cause them to lose interest entirely on the other. The teacher coaching a competitive team should attempt to prevent these reactions through careful development of the best possible attitudes toward competitive play.

Leisure Skills

Within recent times the schools' responsibility for teaching students skills that they can use in later life has gained wide acceptance. For the mentally retarded, acquisition of leisure skills is particularly critical because many will have excess time available. Most important, however, is the awareness that use of these skills is a vehicle by which the retarded can lead a more normal life within the community. For the physical education teacher this means that skills such as roller skating, bicycle riding, bowling, and swimming need to be taught. Providing some of these experiences in a school district with limited equipment and facilities will require the efforts of a dedicated and resourceful teacher. One need only experience the enthusiasm and pride generated by a retarded child as he takes his first wobbly solo on a bike to make any inconveniences seem well worth the effort. Parents, seeing their children achieve vital skills, such as learning to swim, will also respond favorably to the school program. For these parents, enjoyable and relaxed "family" outings to the beach can now become a reality.

Body Mechanics

The prevalence of postural deviations among the mentally retarded appears to be quite high. Common body alignment abnormalities include forward head, sagging shoulders, and swayback and its accompanying protruding abdomen. Correcting these problems and keeping the body in balance are difficult because of the subconscious attempt to overcompensate in the other direction. This can be overcome if retarded children are encouraged to practice good postural positions in front of full length mirrors. Pictures and videotapes of the children as they walk and perform other dynamic movements can also be quite helpful in communicating information to retarded youngsters about correct and incorrect body positions. Activities in which students pair up and trace their partner's upright and supine body positions are also helpful in providing a visual image of their appearance.

Although many postural problems are directly related to inadequate amounts of strength and flexibility, frequently the key to improving the mentally retarded child's posture lies in improving his body awareness. Many times as the retarded child learns the names of the various body parts and their functions, and then is taught motor skills through which this information can be successfully used, changes in body awareness and hence improvement in posture occur. It is necessary that programs designed to remedy functional deviations be initiated prior to the child's fifteenth year of age. After this time the functional problem may become structural, with resultant changes in the skeletal design.[5] Exercises are usually not recommended for problems of this magnitude.

SUGGESTED ACTIVITIES FOR TOTALLY DEPENDENT RETARDATES

The range of activities in a physical education program for totally dependent retardates (the severely and profoundly retarded) is necessarily limited. These individuals often sit or lie for hours and appear to be totally unaware of their environment. Until recently, little attention has been devoted to the educational and motor development needs of the severely and profoundly retarded. Confined to an institution, they were frequently permitted to exist in a vegetable-like state. The lack of suitable programs may be attributed to inadequate staff-resident ratio as well as to the belief of many that the totally dependent were incapable of learning. Slight changes in this atti-

---

[5]*Program Guidelines in Physical Education for the Mentally Retarded.* Harrisburg, Pa., Pennsylvania State Department of Education, 1970, p. 96.

tude are evident today, and an increasing number of professionals are focusing on this forgotten population. Because the totally dependent exhibit numerous motor deficiencies, it is essential that attention be directed toward remedying these problems. Although little research has been conducted to provide evidence to support the choice of program content, physical education experiences for the severely and profoundly retarded have consisted primarily of sensory-motor experiences and the core movement activities of everyday skills.

Sensory-Motor Experiences

Based on information gathered from the study of infant development, sensory-motor experiences usually consist of activities to increase awareness of stimuli and to improve manipulative activity. Experiences designed to raise the severely and profoundly retarded person's level of awareness should be developed for all of the senses. Stimulation of the tactile senses may include vigorously rubbing the skin with towels and brushes of various textures to obtain a motor response. Lights and sounds of various intensities may be moved from one side to the other to elicit head turning responses. Providing opportunities for the totally dependent to discriminate between various tastes, odors, and temperatures is useful for developing avoidance (turning away) and approach (turning toward) motor responses. Combinations of various sensory stimuli may also be presented. For many severely and profoundly retarded persons, an extensive time allotment should be provided for sensory awareness activities. Without the ability to attend to relevant stimuli, further educational experiences with the totally dependent will be seriously impeded.

The skills of reaching, grasping, holding, and releasing do not develop normally for the severely and profoundly retarded. Therefore, opportunities for these individuals to play with toys of various colors and textures should be provided. Finger, hand, and arm movements may also be obtained through the use of materials such as water, sand, and clay. Efforts should also be directed toward teaching to the totally dependent child self-help skills that emphasize manipulative activities, such as eating and dressing.

Core Movement Activities

In addition to the sensory-motor experiences, the physical education curriculum for the more capable severely and profoundly retarded should include activities that develop basic, everyday skills, such as lifting the feet over objects and up steps. Additional examples of the basic activities that can be included in the program and the techniques most frequently used for teaching them are listed below. Because of the individual variation found within this population, the techniques listed are suggestions and do not preclude the use of others.

1. Crawling (arms, chest, belly, legs): demonstration, manual kinesthesis (use crawler, if necessary)

2. Creeping (hands and knees): demonstration, manual kinesthesis

3. Rolling: demonstration, manual kinesthesis

4. Sitting: demonstration, manual kinesthesis (external supports such as straps, if necessary)

5. Standing (with and without assistance): demonstration, manual kinesthesis

6. Walking: demonstration, manual kinesthesis (use parallel bars and weighted cart, if necessary)

7. Bending at the waist to pick up a favorite toy: demonstration, manual kinesthesis

8. Bending at the knees to pick up a favorite toy: demonstration, manual kinesthesis.

9. Stair climbing: demonstration, manual kinesthesis

10. Balancing: manual kinesthesis (use wide beam; assist student along beam)

11. Stepping over and into objects: manual kinesthesis (use tires, boxes, beams)

12. Bouncing: manual kinesthesis (use trampoline; start pupil by bouncing on bed; later a jouncing board may be used)

13. Jumping from object: manual kinesthesis (use object or beam no higher than one foot in the beginning; start by pulling student off balance)

14. Climbing: manual kinesthesis (use a ladder or Swedish box)

15. Running: demonstration, manual kinesthesis (pull by the hand or use rope around the waist)

16. Throwing: manual kinesthesis (use 8-inch or larger ball and a tire as a target; have student start by dropping the ball and gradually increase the distance from the tire.)

17. Catching: manual kinesthesis (use 8-inch ball; in the beginning use short distances and place the ball into the hand)

18. Kicking: demonstration, manual kinesthesis (use large soft rubber balls or heavy cardboard boxes)

The way in which these activities are presented by the teacher is extremely important in achieving good results. As pointed out above, teaching totally dependent retardates requires a very low teacher-to-pupil ratio — in most cases, one to one.

No more than two or three activities should be presented during any one class period. If a child refuses to participate in one kind of activity, he may take part in another. Participation should be of short duration. After leaving one activity the teacher may return to it in a few minutes or at some time before the period is over. The same activities should be presented every day until learned. After the skills of one activity have been mastered, new activities may be introduced; but the skills already learned should be reviewed briefly from time to time. An obstacle course in which students climb stairs, duck under bars, step over ropes, and step into and out of tires provides a good warm-up and a means of quickly reviewing important activities.

Teaching these students requires great patience and kindness. The teacher should never resort to pressure tactics to achieve improvement. His attitude must be that improvement may come very slowly, and he must work patiently with the student until it comes. All genuine effort by the student should be acknowledged with indications of approval.

Behavior Modification. Verbal praise has its limitations with totally dependent retardates because many of these children do not comprehend the spoken word; therefore, other means of rewarding successful behavior have been experimented with. One of the most effective of these is a procedure known as behavior modification. In research at Mansfield Training School in Connecticut,[6] it was demonstrated that behavior modification could be used effectively in teaching physical education activities.

Behavior modification is defined as the systematic use of selected reinforcers to weaken, maintain, or strengthen behaviors. Although there are several behavior modification techniques, the two most successfully employed with the severely and profoundly retarded are positive reinforcement and modeling. Combining these two

[6]Robert P. Ingals: *The Basic Skills Program.* Mansfield Depot, Connecticut. Unpublished, Mansfield Training School, 1969.

techniques provides a system in which a skill is demonstrated and modeled, and the student is reinforced for initiating any movement that resembles or approximates the skill. It may be necessary to shape the behavior of some totally dependent retardates by isolating and reinforcing very basic responses, such as the turning of their heads and eyes toward the demonstration. Reinforcing the severely and profoundly retarded while they are manually guided through the skill may also develop within them a sense of pleasure that over a period of time may gradually be associated with the movement. Several types of reinforcers may be employed. These include consumables such as ice cream, candy, and food treats; manipulables such as toys, trinkets, and hobby items; visual and auditory stimuli such as films, records, and animations; and social stimuli such as verbal praise and attention.[7] Selection of the appropriate reinforcer must be determined for each person. For some students, praise or knowledge that the attempt was successful is sufficient reinforcement. For others, especially those lower on the scale of retardation, a reward of candy is effective. The time between the reinforcement and the desired behavior must be as short as possible; otherwise the child is not always certain what he is being rewarded for. The reward should be given consistently and only for performance at maximum capacity.

A movement that is made up of two or more parts must be broken down into its components and each taught separately. For example, the movement pattern of reaching for and picking up a ball may be broken down into these components: (1) a movement in the direction of the ball, (2) touching the ball, (3) placing the fingers around the ball, (4) lifting the ball up. The student is first encouraged to reach for the ball; any effort to do so is rewarded with candy and words of praise. Thereafter, the reward is given when the student reaches the same distance or a greater distance than in his initial effort. Whenever he reaches a greater distance, bringing his hand closer to the ball, the new distance becomes the point of reinforcement. When the student finally touches the ball, this becomes the point of reinforcement; the same applies when he grasps it and when he picks it up. After the student has mastered the skill, the candy reinforcement is slowly withdrawn by offering it only periodically. Praise and approval continue to be given for successful effort. Often, they can eventually be used entirely as the reinforcer.

SELECTED READINGS

AAHPER: *Physical Activities for the Mentally Retarded (Ideas for Instruction)*. Washington, D.C., American Association for Health, Physical Education and Recreation, 1968.

AAHPER: *Physical and Recreational Programming for Severely and Profoundly Mentally Retarded Individuals*. Washington, D.C., American Alliance for Health, Physical Education and Recreation, 1974.

AAHPER: *Programming for the Mentally Retarded in Physical Education and Recreation*. Washington, D.C., American Association for Health, Physical Education and Recreation, 1968.

Cratty, Bryant J.: *Motor Activity and the Education of Retardates*, ed. 2. Philadelphia, Lea and Febiger, 1974.

Kolstoe, Oliver P.: *Mental Retardation: An Educational Viewpoint*. New York, Holt, Rinehart and Winston, Inc., 1972.

Robinson, Nancy M., and Robinson, Halbert B.: *The Mentally Retarded Child*, ed. 2. New York: McGraw-Hill Book Co., 1976.

Shivers, Jay S., and Fait, Hollis F.: *Therapeutic and Adapted Recreational Services*. Philadelphia, Lea and Febiger, 1975.

-----

[7]Dunn, J. M.: "Behavior Modification with Emotionally Disturbed Children." *Journal of Physical Education and Recreation*, 46, March, 1975, pp. 67–70.

Chapter 18

Learning Disabilities (Verbal and Non-verbal)

It is estimated that one out of every five children with average or above average intelligence has perceptual, cognitive, or coordinative problems of neurologic origin which seem to interfere with optimal success in the normal classroom. The United States Office of Education has suggested that one to three per cent of the school population evidence learning disabilities so severe as to need special educational provisions if they are to profit from formal instruction.

Historically, these children have been assigned such labels as perceptually handicapped, dyslexic, educationally handicapped, neurophrenic, hyperkinetic, and minimally brain-injured. Even today there is no widespread agreement with respect to terminology among the governmental agencies of the fifty states, or among the representatives of the many academic disciplines who work with learning disabilities. The formation of the Association for Children with Learning Disabilities in 1964 was, however, a major milestone in the acceptance of a single diagnostic label and the establishment of a uniform set of criteria for use in the identification of children with learning disabilities.

Foremost among these criteria is the fact that learning disabilities, whether they be disorders of listening, thinking, talking, reading, writing, spelling, or calculating, must stem from nervous system dysfunction. While environmental disadvantage, emotional disturbance, and sensory losses may serve to intensify already existing problems, they are not recognized as possible causes of learning disabilities. Because of its neurological basis, the diagnosis of learning disabilities should be made by qualified medical personnel.

Other criteria used in the identification of individuals with learning disabilities are (1) average to high intelligence — a minimum intelligence quotient of 80 on either the verbal or nonverbal part of a recognized test; (2) adequate emotional adjustment; (3) adequate hearing — a loss no greater than 30–35 decibles on the better ear; (4) adequate vision — visual impairment no greater than 20/40 when glasses are worn; and (5) absence of an orthopedic handicap or any type of cerebral palsy.

While differences still exist in the terms used to describe the various aspects of learning disability, a generally accepted definition of the condition has been supplied by the Federal Department of Health, Education and Welfare.[1] This definition

---

[1]Department of Health, Education and Welfare, Office of the Secretary: *Federal Register*, May 15, 1976, p. 20305.

describes learning disability as a disorder in understanding or using written or spoken language. In this text, learning disabilities have been divided into two categories: verbal and non-verbal. Verbal learning disabilities affect the use or comprehension of language, while non-verbal disabilities cause motor learning problems.

The relationship between verbal and non-verbal disabilities has not been clearly established. It appears to the author that the perceptual deficit that causes learning problems in language may also cause problems in motor learning. For example, it seems reasonable that a perceptual problem, such as a deficit in visual figure-ground discrimination, that interferes with the child's ability to identify a specific word from among the other printed words on a page could also hamper his ability to distinguish a target at which he is to throw a ball from other nearby targets. If a connection of this kind does exist, it might be assumed that improvement in one area effects improvement in the other. (Early theorists, as noted in Chapter 3, did make this assumption and developed perceptual-motor programs in efforts to improve academic skills through improvement of motor skills.) However, the preponderance of research evidence shows the assumption to be unfounded: no direct transfer of learning occurs between the verbal and motor skills.[2]

NON-VERBAL LEARNING DISABILITIES

Most nonverbal disabilities fall at the levels of perception and imagery or memory and hence can be more detrimental to growth and development than are specific verbal disabilities. Included in this category are such characteristics as (1) nonspecific awkwardness or cluminess, (2) problems of laterality or directionality, (3) generalized inadequacy of perceptual-motor function, (4) poorly developed body awareness, (5) poorly developed kinesthesis, and (6) fine motor incoordination.

Deficits in learning motor skills are often observable in preschool children, who are incapable of tying shoes, cutting with scissors, buttoning clothes, and performing other daily living tasks. A lack of ability to perform these common tasks that continues into the years when most other children can perform them, if not caused by loss of sensory function or paralysis, is called apraxia. Apraxic children may demonstrate inadequacies in visual perception, auditory perception, kinesthesis, and touch and pressure perception.

Visual Perception

Faulty visual perception may be due to deficiency in one or more of the following: visual discrimination, figure-ground discrimination, depth perception, object constancy, and object identification (visual agnosia).

Children whose visual perception is affected by inadequate visual discrimination have difficulty in determining the size, shape, color, and texture of an object. Very young children begin to use size, shape, and texture as aids in identifying objects. Texture is the last of these characteristics children learn to use in visual discrimination. Without special instruction in utilizing the various identifying characteristics of objects, children with impairment show little improvement in visual discrimination.

Children with faulty visual discrimination are not very successful in physical education. They are likely to be unable to distinguish a large ball from a small ball, a

---

[2]Bryant J. Cratty: *Perceptual-Motor Efficiency in Children.* Philadelphia, Lea and Febiger, 1969, p. 11.

square block from a rectangular block, a blue bean bag from a red bean bag, or rough ground from smooth. There are very few games and activities that do not require some degree of discrimination in size, form, color, and texture. Consequently, success and pleasure in play are largely denied these children.

The ability to visually differentiate a specific object from a complex background is minimal in young children and develops slowly to reach its peak during adolescence. In children with faulty visual perception due to poor figure-ground discrimination this development is retarded. Such children lack the ability to identify and focus attention upon a single object or figure in a cluttered or complex background. They may, for example, become so confused by the various players that form the background for a game of tag, that they cannot locate the one who is "it." Inability by some children to follow the aerial path of a thrown ball is another illustration of the figure-ground problem. Obviously, such children will have difficulties in the performance of many activities in the physical education program.

Depth perception is the term given to the ability to judge distances between near and far objects. Those who have problems determining how close or far away an object is have difficulty placing their bodies in the proper relationship to the object. In catching a ball, for example, they overreach or do not reach far enough, and miss the ball. Any activity that requires judgment of distances is difficult, if not impossible, for children with this visual perception deficit.

The ability to identify an object regardless of the direction from which it is viewed is termed object consistency. A youngster without this ability becomes lost in a maze of unrecognizable objects as he moves about. For example, such a child will not be able to recognize an item of play equipment when viewed from any side other than the one from whch he learned to identify it. Such a deficit in visual perception obviously creates many difficulties in physical education and in all other areas of endeavor.

Visual agnosia is a disorder that prevents the identification of objects. The underlying cause for the disorder appears to be a lesion in the cortex. As a result, the visual process is incomplete; the affected child appears to be unable to synthesize all of the visual stimuli into a unified whole, so that what he sees may lack color, form, or size. Children with this disorder have serious problems in learning any motor skills.

Auditory Perception

Like visual perception, auditory perception can be broken down into various factors: auditory discrimination of different pitches, intensities, and tonal qualities; figure-ground discrimination, directionality of sounds; and temporal or rhythmic reception. Deficiency in one or more of these detracts from successful learning but is not as detrimental to coordination of motor movement as faulty visual perception can be. The influence of faulty auditory perception will be most noticeable in rhythmic activities and in other motor activities that necessitate adequate sound perception.

Kinesthetic Perception

Kinesthetic perception is multifaceted, including such attributes as balance and laterality, orientation of the body and its parts in space, arm positioning, leg positioning, and awareness of force and extent of muscular contraction. Two of the most widely discussed aspects of kinesthesis are laterality and directionality, terms in-

Figure 18–1. Unusual playground equipment provides opportunities for the development of kinesthetic perception.

novated and made popular by Kephart[3] in the 1959s. Laterality, defined as the internal awareness of the two sides of the body and their difference, normally develops in early childhood. Well developed laterality is considered necessary by many reading specialists for success in reading and writing when left-to-right progressions across the page must be sustained. It is thought to be the vital factor underlying the ability to discriminate between such letters as *b* and *d* and *p* and *q*. Laterality is also postulated to be essential to the maintenance of balance.

Directionality, a term often used in conjunction with laterality, involves not only kinesthetic perception but also visual and auditory perception as well as such higher functions of the brain as imagery, symbolization, and conceptualization. Not only must the child be able to feel where his body is in space, but he must remember the meanings which society has attached to such words as up, down, over, under, high, and low, and acquire the ability to assign proper labels to them. Moreover, he must learn to recognize the sounds of such words and to respond correctly to instructions with respect to moving the body through space.

It is important to note that there is no general kinesthetic sense. The coordinative problems of children must be analyzed in terms of the specific factors that compose kinesthesis.

Children with perceptual-motor deficits often have a poorly developed body awareness which is manifested by difficulties in the identification of body parts and discrimination between right and left. It should be noted that an inability to identify body parts does not necessarily indicate a lack of body awareness but may be due to failure to learn the meaning of the words used for the parts of the body. The normal development of body image entails mastery of the following tasks at approximately the ages cited.

---

[3]Newell C. Kephart: *The Slow Learner in the Classroom.* Columbus, Ohio, Charles E. Merrill, 1962, *passim.*

Age 3   Ability to name one's own body parts. Somewhat later the child learns to identify the body parts of dolls, animals, and other human beings. Last in the developmental sequence, he learns to recognize body parts depicted in pictures and other unidimensional media.

Ages 6–7   Ability to understand right-left concepts in relation to space as related to own body image.

Ages 8–9   Ability to understand right-left concepts in terms of other persons.

Ages 11–12   Ability to understand right-left concepts in terms of inanimate objects.

Children with non-verbal learning disabilities may be slow in the acquisition of these abilities and may manifest confusion with respect to right-left concepts throughout life.

Other Non-verbal Disorders

Inadequacies of social perception, namely the inability to recognize the meaning and significance of the behavior of others, fall into the category of nonverbal disabilities. Illustrative of this is the child who cannot grasp the game of "Cowboys and Indians," who cannot make believe and deal with abstractions as do his playmates, and who fails to comprehend the subtleties of facial expression, tone of voice, and body language.

Behavioral characteristics such as distractibility, hyperactivity, dissociation, and perseveration influence both verbal and nonverbal learning. The management of these problems is largely controlled by physicians, often through drug therapy.

Distractibility is the inability to concentrate attention on any particular object or person in the environment. The distractible child has a short attention span and may forget completely what he was doing. He is distracted by any movement, sound, color, or smell and lacks the ability to block out irrelevant stimuli. It does little good to admonish him to "Pay attention"; he would if he could. His distractibility is of neurological origin.

Hyperactivity, or hyperkinesis, is the inability to sit or stand quietly. Hyperactive children appear driven to react to everything within an arm's reach; hence, they are always touching, bending, pulling, or twisting objects in the environment. Such children seem to have an uncanny amount of energy, and it is virtually impossible to tire them out, even through endurance-oriented big muscle activity.

Dissociation is the inability to see things as a whole. The child visualizes parts of things but cannot conceptualize the whole; he therefore often reacts only to parts, making his behavior seem inappropriate or bizarre.

Perseveration is the inability to shift with ease from one activity to another. Often mistaken for stubbornness, perseveration is of neurological origin. The child would like to follow directions but he simply cannot respond immediately and appropriately to "stop and start" type activities.

It is interesting that children with learning disabilities may exhibit any of these behavioral characteristics on some days but not on others. Inconsistency of behavior should be expected and tolerated.

VERBAL LEARNING DISABILITIES

Verbal learning disabilities usually fall at the level of symbolization, and hence they affect conceptualization. Symbolization is defined as the ability to communicate or translate visual and auditory images into meaningful symbols. It includes all of the tasks requisite to successful reading, writing, spelling, arthmetic, and speaking. Conceptualization, regarded as the highest form of intellectual activity, refers to the ability to categorize, to abstract, to critically analyze, to generalize, and to create.

The potential contributions of physical educators to the remediation of difficulties in symbolization and conceptualization are still largely unacknowledged. Movement, although widely recognized as a means of communication, is usually excluded from discussions of symbolization and conceptualization in special education textbooks.

However, for many years classroom teachers have availed themselves of the assistance of physical education specialists in using movement exploration as a means of enabling young children to feel kinesthetically language concepts related to form, size, height, distance, time, and other qualitative aspects of experience. Using the body as an instrument for making and testing initial judgments about large and small, fast and slow, high and low, circular and rectangular, and other concepts is thought by many practitioners to enhance the child's competence in symbolization and conceptualization with respect to the use of words. In addition, motivation to learn the verbal tasks is enhanced by the great interest most children have in motor movement.

Verbal learning disabilities are usually classified into the following categories; (1) inner language, (2) receptive language, and (3) expressive language. Since effective teaching is based upon adequate communication, it is imperative that physical educators be cognizant of individual differences among children in understanding and using language. Classroom teachers should be able to expect physical educators to coordinate motor activities with the teaching strategies they are employing to remedy language disorders.

Inner language processes are those that permit the transformation of experience into symbols. The first and most fundamental aspect of language to be acquired, it is greatly dependent upon the breadth and depth of experiences in infancy and early childhood. Sensory deprivation, or insufficient opportunities to see, hear, touch, smell, taste, and move in a variety of environments, is a major cause of inner language deficits. Children who read well but cannot grasp the meaning of the sentence or paragraph have inner language problems.

Receptive language is the ability to comprehend words and to remember sequences. Problems of receptive language may be either auditory or visual in nature. Children who seem to ignore or fail to follow directions often have deficits in receptive auditory language. Such youngsters find sounds in the environment confusing and frustrating. Their inability to discriminate between relevant and irrelevant sounds often helps to explain such behavioral aberrations as hyperactivity, distractibility, and short attention span. Instructing such children to "Listen" or "Pay better attention" will do little good; alternative ways of giving directions must be found. Children whose difficulties in reading are manifested by a lack of memory for words, the inability to divide words into syllables, or the inability to blend sounds into words are usually suffering from receptive visual deficits. Such individuals learn more effectively through listening than through reading.

Expressive language, or the ability to communicate, may also be either auditory or visual in nature. Auditory expressive language deficits, of course, refer to speaking and are sometimes labeled as expressive aphasias. Visual expressive language deficits encompass problems in writing and are sometimes called dysgraphias. Problems of expressive language are more easily identified and remedied than those of inner language and receptive language. Characteristics that classroom teachers often report are (1) inability to reproduce simple geometric forms; (2) persistent reversals of words, syllables or letters; (3) rotation or inversion of letters; (4) reversed sequence of letters and syllables; (5) mirror writing, and (6) transposition of numbers.

NEEDS AND ADJUSTMENTS OF CHILDREN WITH LEARNING DISABILITIES

Repeated failure on the part of the child with verbal or non-verbal learning disabilities may lead to the development of severe anxieties, frustrations, loss of self-confidence, and a tendency to either withdraw from or rebel against the educational system. These children need desperately to achieve. Children whose learning disabilities affect their ability to learn movements are often hesitant to attempt new motor skills in front of their peer group. Moreover, they generally shy away from such competitive activities as relays and softball batting in which their lack of competence may contribute to the whole team's losing.

To meet the needs of these children, the physical education setting should be structured so as to guarantee success in the initial stages of learning. It may be necessary to remove the child from the regular physical education class and substitute individualized instruction from a private tutor or paraprofessional. Arrangements should be made so that he can practice alone or with a small, understanding group in school facilities. Emphasis even in the primary grades should be upon the mastery of skills that the child will use and feels a need to acquire, such as catching, throwing, and kicking.

Because the traditional physical education or academic class rarely meets the needs of children with learning disabilities, the children often develop a variety of strategies for coping with the instructional environment, many of which are self-defeating. Foremost among these strategies are (1) attention-getting, (2) helplessness, (3) destructiveness or antisocial acts, and (4) stubbornness. Attention-getting may take the form of asking many questions, dropping objects on the floor, cute sayings, or picking on other children. On the other hand, the child may seek attention by being sweet and cooperative, shadowing the teacher, and assisting with noninstructional chores. Helplessness may be real or professed; the child who says, "I can't" generally elicits the teacher's sympathy, thereby placing her in his service. Destructiveness or antisocial acts often serve to build up the ego; the class bully is seldom ignored and often gains a small following of admirers. Stubbornness, or passive resistance, initiates a power struggle between the child and the adult. Children using this strategy purposely forget assignments, lose or hide their papers, and inevitably move at an infuriatingly slow pace.

Learning disabled children, like their normal counterparts, have the capacity to understand and show insight into the meaning of their own behavior. It is important that teachers recognize self-defeating strategies for what they are. Individual or group counseling should be made available to children who exhibit problems in classroom adjustment.

Children with learning disabilities need assistance in forming meaningful and satisfactory relationships with others. Their characteristic social immaturity often makes them victims of teasing, playful gossip, and ultimately isolation and loneliness. Both boys and girls need special guidance with respect to grooming, the development of many and varied hobbies, and the improvement of conversational skills.

PLANNING THE PROGRAM

Children with non-verbal learning disabilities demonstrate a wide range of abilities in the performance of physical education activities. While some children, particularly the younger boys and girls, are characterized by incoordination and awkwardness, others reach levels of excellence in their chosen activities. The casual observer generally cannot distinguish between children with learning disabilities and their normal counterparts in the gymnasium setting, providing the children have had equivalent instruction and opportunities for practice.

The major criteria for determining whether the child with non-verbal learning disabilities should participate in regular physical education classes or in separate classes is the type of activity conducted and the degree of success the special child can expect. When instruction is being offered in such individual and dual activities as track and field events, gymnastics, modern dance, swimming, bowling, or archery, classes should be integrated. Students who do not have figure-ground problems should be allowed the option of enrolling in classes in tennis, badminton, handball, fencing, and other lifetime sports. No child, however, should be coerced to participate in regular physical education classes. Small group instruction with familiar classmates should always be available. Scheduling should be flexible enough to allow him to go from the regular class to the special physical education class any time that he feels the need of its security or individualized program.

Most, but not all, children with non-verbal learning disabilities should not be subjected to highly organized games and team sports of an extremely competitive nature because of their perceptual defects, their difficulties in adjusting to large groups and big playing areas, and their social immaturity, unless some success can be assured.

The child with a verbal learning disability may or may not also have a non-verbal learning disability. Many children with verbal learning problems show no signs of deficiencies in motor learning, and some may actually demonstrate superior motor ability. Whether or not the child with verbal learning disability has a deficit in motor learning, he may, according to Cratty,[4] benefit from participation in selected motor activities. Cratty has found that for some children "games and game-like problem-solving situations are effective in motivating the learning of some academic competencies." The games utilized must integrate motor activity with conceptualization of selected academic skills, such as word recognition, spelling, and number combination. The physical education teacher should work closely with the classroom or special education teacher in selecting and introducing the integrated games to ensure that the motor experiences will be appropriate and successful.

Facilities and Equipment. The first, and perhaps the most important, requirement in adapting the instructional environment to the special needs of the child with severe learning disabilities is the reduction of stimuli within the gymnasium to a minimum. Reduction of extraneous stimuli may be achieved by covering windows and using artificial light. All equipment, except that which will be immediately used, can be hidden from sight. Whenever possible, noise should be minimized by soundproof walls and ceilings. Many gymnasiums designed for children with special needs now have wall-to-wall carpeting.

The number of lines on the floor and markings on the wall should also be minimized. It is recommended that "floor spots" in the form of simple geometric shapes or other relevant symbols be painted on the floor to assist young children in

[4]*Ibid.*, p. 8.

finding "their own space" and to assure that the distance between students is sufficient to eliminate body contact.

The second requirement in adapting facilities is the reduction of space in the gymnasium through the use of cubicles and partitions or the identification of small rooms within the school which can be used for physical education purposes. When children play outdoors, it is especially important that small areas be roped off and that space boundaries be carefully defined. Ideally the outdoor area should be surrounded by a high wooden fence to exclude irrelevant stimuli.

The third requirement in adapting facilities is consistency from day to day in the organization of teaching stations and the placement of equipment. Because these children are often described as "lost in space," it is recommended that the instructtional environment be highly structured with as little as possible left to chance.

In addition to the requirements of stimuli control, space reduction, and consistency in placement of equipment, the facilities for children with learning disabilities should include an adequate number of teaching stations and sufficient equipment for individualized instruction. A Learning Resources Center with tape recordings, videotapes, loop films, other audio-visual aids, and appropriate teaching machines should be established to provide opportunities for students to view themselves and others in the performance of motor skills.

Nature of Activities. Some children with learning disabilities may require specialized programs of perceptual-motor activities in addition to a well-rounded program composed of dance, aquatics, gymnastics, track and field, selected games, and individual and dual sports. It should be clearly understood, however, that perceptual-motor programs are not synonymous with and cannot be substituted for physical education programs. Some children need both kinds of programs; *all* children need physical education instruction in order to maintain and improve their physical fitness and to acquire neuromuscular skills requisite to success in the various lifetime sports.

In perceptual-motor programs, children receive training in the motor bases of behavior, such as balance in different positions and the development of laterality and directionality; training in perceptual skills, such as space discrimination, form perception, recognition of texture, size, color, and structure; and training in visual perception, auditory perception, and kinesthetic perception. At the present time well over forty perceptual-motor theories with accompanying programs of remediation have been proposed in professional literature. Those of Barsch, Cratty, Frostig, Getman, and Kephart are probably best known to physical educators who utilize an eclectic approach in planning their perceptual-motor programs, selecting the best from each school of thought.

The concept of perceptual-motor training is compatible with that of movement education. Most physical educators are now using balance beams, trampolines, vaulting boxes, and other pieces of equipment in the elementary grades as devices for gaining a better understanding of the body as an instrument for expression. Problem solving pertaining to body orientation in space, the positioning of limbs, and the improvement of balance is adding new dimensions to motor creativity.

In the perceptual-motor program, regardless of the type of activity or instructional approach, it is basic that the child develop awareness of the nature of the sensations he is receiving and of the results that occur from responses to the stimuli. Once such consciousness has been developed, the child can begin to replace the unsuccessful responses with substitutes that will result in satisfactory performance. For example, the child who has difficulty in balancing on a beam must be helped by the teacher to achieve awareness of the sensations that occur when he is losing his balance and to recognize the elements in his response to these sensations that prevent his

Figure 18-2. Work on a balance beam helps a child to become aware of the sensations of losing and regaining balance.

regaining balance. Then, with assistance from the teacher, he must analyze the motor skills involved to determine the adjustments in muscular movements he needs to make in order to regain and maintain balance. As he attempts the new movements, he must consciously associate the new responses with the stimuli. Frequent repetition of the process is required to enable the child to develop the new responses to the point that he uses them automatically in substitution for the old unsuccessful ones.

The nature of the program, whether it be perceptual-motor training or physical education instruction, must ensure success. Activities based upon a careful diagnosis of each person's needs, the use of carefully planned teaching progressions, and the avoidance of excessive competition all contribute to success.

Teaching Hints. Good teaching is based upon careful diagnosis of individual needs. With the growing popularity of the multidisciplinary approach to learning disabilities, several disciplines may share responsibility for the evaluation of the motor development of the child. Depending upon the expectations of the other academic disciplines with which he is working, the physical educator may administer standardized specific tests to assist in identifying children in need of special motor training. Some of these tests were discussed in Chapter 3. However, the most important diagnostic technique remains careful, conscientious observation of the child's motor performance over long periods of time. It cannot be overemphasized that no single test is valid and reliable enough to determine a child's needs. Nor is it possible for a child with learning disabilities to be entirely consistent in his motor performance. He may lack motivation on one day, be affected by medication on the next, and be convalescing from a cold on the next. It is important to remember that a child views his motor acts as an extension of himself and as a measure of his own worth. Therefore, the process of diagnosis and evaluation, like that of instruction, should be so presented that the child feels he is succeeding.

Effective diagnostic techniques enable the physical educator to teach to the level of involvement. It is essential to determine whether the major learning disability is auditory, visual, or kinesthetic. The accepted practice seems to be to emphasize the use of those senses which are unaffected rather than to attempt to remedy the disability. This implies that some children must be taught mainly through the visual and kinesthetic modalities while others must receive instruction chiefly via the auditory and kinesthetic modalities.

It is equally important to ascertain the level at which the child's learning is breaking down: perception, imagery or memory, symbolization, or conceptualization. The following list of questions demonstrates the application of this technique to teaching a forehand drive in tennis.

1. *Visual perception.* In viewing a demonstration, can the student discriminate between open and closed positions of the racquet face? Does he see what you think he sees? Can he organize all visual sensations of head, arms, and legs into the meaningful whole we call a forehand drive?

2. *Auditory perception.* In hearing an explanation or analysis of a skill, can the student discriminate among sounds? Does he hear what you think he hears? Can he organize all auditory sensations (words, words, and more words) into a meaningful whole?

3. *Proprioceptor perception.* Is the student aware of what the body is doing? Does he respond to the stimuli from the proprioceptor?

4. *Memory.* Is the student capable of mental practice? Can he remember the positions of joints, the rhythm of the movements, and the exact sequence in which the movements occur? Two days later is he still able to visualize the correct movements? Can he still recall the verbal analysis of the skill?

5. *Symbolization.* Can he make his body do what his mind tells him? Can he translate visual and auditory memory into an accurate reproduction of the movements viewed in the demonstration?

6. *Conceptualization.* Can he discriminate between accurate and inaccurate reproduction in movement? Can he analyze his errors in movement? Can he use problem solving to decrease the discrepancy between perceived movement, intended movement, and the actual motor performance?

One of the fundamental principles in adapting instruction is that of *structure,* a form of conditioning used with distractible children to assure appropriate responses to stimuli. Structure in the teaching situation refers to a planned routine or activities, with as little as possible left to chance, so that the child can anticipate the sequence of events and know what is expected of him. In a well-structured physical education program, the children always enter the gymnasium through the same door, go to the same floor spot, participate in warm-up activities, and start individualized instruction at the same teaching station. The direction of rotation between stations is uniform from day to day, as are the stop and start signals employed by the teacher. The structured teaching environment is adult-dominated; children are not asked to make choices and demonstrate competence in self-direction because they lack the readiness to cope with freedom and the exposure to unessential stimuli that freedom brings.

It is important to understand that in the large majority of cases some educational objectives like the development of creativity, which are important for normal children, are entirely inappropriate for boys and girls with severe motor or verbal learning disabilities. If, or when, the child learns to control his distractibility, structure is gradually lessened. The physical educator should discuss the concept of structure with the classroom teacher and ascertain that the amount of structure imposed in the gymnasium is equal to and consistent with that which is imposed in the classroom.

Many practices in physical education which traditionally have been thought of as desirable are contraindicated for children with learning disabilities. Some of these follow:

1. Opportunities to develop leadership-followership qualities through membership on many different kinds of teams with different students serving as leaders each time. Freqent changes in group structure confuse the child with learning disabilities. He should be allowed to play with the same small group throughout the year with as few changes in leadership as feasible.

2. Opportunities to "let off steam" and to develop fitness through freedom to run, jump, and shout in an optimal amount of space. While this practice may meet the needs of some children with learning disabilities, it tends to heighten the hyperactivity of others. Many special educators feel strongly that noise, as in cheering on teammates and clapping when a game is won, should be discouraged. Time should be spent on the mastery of neuromuscular skills which have carry-over value rather than upon fitness testing and activities designed primarily for cardiovascular development which may increase hyperactivity. Rather than rule out certain types of activities for *all* hyperactive children, it is desirable to experiment with variations in speed and distance to determine which kinds of fitness activities are best for each individual. Certainly not all children should be required to do the 600 yard walk-run or even the 50 yard dash simply because they are included on a standard test.

3. Emphasis upon the development of speed through awards for track and field events and the association of winning with the fastest team. Many children with learning disabilities need assistance in deceleration. For them it is recommended that the emphasis be changed to "How slowly can you dribble the ball? How slowly can you do a crab walk? How slowly can you go up and down in push-ups?" Because hyperactive children exhibit considerable muscular tension, they must be taught specific techniques for relaxation, for slowing down, and for maintaining a stationary position.

The key to successful instruction of children with learning disabilities is individualization. It is possible that no two children in the gymnasium will ever be doing the same thing simultaneously. To facilitate implementation of this principle, each child, upon entering the gymnasium, may pick up a card on which his activities for the day are printed. The nature and sequence of these activities should not change radically from week to week.

SUGGESTED ACTIVITIES

The program of physical education activities varies with age, degree of involvement, and specific type of learning disability. If the children have verbal learning disabilities, the program should be planned cooperatively by the physical educator and classroom teacher to ascertain that needs are met and that methodology is consistent.

In the primary grades, attention must be focused upon the development of basic movement patterns—running, jumping, hopping, throwing, catching, striking, and kicking. Children should explore their capability for movement on different surfaces—wood, cement, sand, pebbles, high and low grass, both wet and dry. Opportunities to experiment with different sizes, shapes, and weights of balls and sports implements should be provided. Ample time should be spent on climbing and hanging activities as well as creeping and crawling activities. Balancing activities are important provided they are varied and interesting and the child can achieve some measure of success. The gross motor activities that promote basic skill development and physical fitness can often be combined with sensory experiences to promote perceptual-motor learning; some examples may be found at the end of the chapter.

Instruction in individual and dual sports, with appropriately modified equipment, should begin as early as grade three. Competence in such activities as bowling, ballet, and swimming helps to win the admiration of the peer group, many of whom may not yet have had the opportunity to try these activities. Most important, competence in individual and dual activities enhances self-esteem and serves to compensate for the inability to participate successfully in team activities. Early acquaintance with lifetime sports also contributes to family unity and may lead to closer parent-child relationships when, for instance, the two can bowl or fish together.

In the primary grades physical education may play a major role in the development of inner language and the enrichment of vocabulary. When this is a concern, the teacher should plan contrasting activities, such as up and down, over and under, below and above, forward and backward, to enable students to experience kinesthetically the words they must recognize on paper. Likewise, appropriate time should be devoted to learning the names of body parts and the terms for different kinds of movements and positions in space.

In the intermediate and secondary grades, emphasis upon individual and dual activities should continue. Children should be introduced to mechanical principles and given special assistance in problem solving and generalizing with respect to similarities and differences in basic movements, such as, for instance, the overarm throw, the tennis serve, and the badminton smash. Because of their characteristic deficits in symbolization and conceptualization, it cannot be assumed that they will learn anything through incidental exposure.

Gross Motor Activities for Perceptual-Motor Learning

Activities Focusing on Visual Discrimination (size):

1. Tossing balls of various sizes into receptacles of appropriate size to hold them. Several receptacles of different sizes and a ball that will fit into each size will be needed. The child selects the ball that is the most appropriate size (neither too large nor too small) for the container and tosses it in.

2. Running around circles of various sizes marked on the floor. Circles of progressively larger size are painted or drawn on the floor inside a large circle. The child runs around the circle that is the size indicated by the teacher.

3. Selecting of the size indicated and running a designated distance. Needed will be an object so large that running with it is difficult, an object so small that it can be easily held in the hand, and an object of a size between these two. The child is then instructed to run to the teacher (or to some easily defined distance) with the object with which he can run the fastest; with the one which is largest, the one of middle size, and the smallest one.

4. Crawling through circular objects of various sizes. Hoops, tubes, or similar objects of various circumferences will be needed. The child crawls through the object of the size indicated by the teacher.

5. Running zigzag between chairs that are various distances apart. Several chairs are set three and five feet apart, as shown in Figure 18–3. The child runs between the chairs that are closer or farther apart as directed by the teacher.

Activities Focusing on Visual Discrimination (color):

1. Throwing balls or bean bags of different colors into containers of matching color. Balls or bean bags of various colors with receptacles to match will be needed. The child matches the colors and throws the object into the appropriate receptacle.

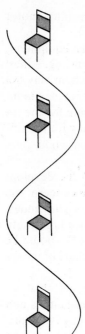

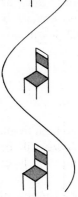

Figure 18–3.　Zigzag run using chairs set various distances apart.

2. Selecting an object of designated color from among others and running with it to another group of objects to pick the object of matching color. Two objects of each color are needed. In response to the teacher's instructions, the child picks up an object, runs with it to the location of the other objects, and matches it to one of like color.

3. Kicking balls into goals of the corresponding color. Several large balls of different colors and goals to match will be needed. (Goals can be improvised from suitably sized paper cartons from which one side is removed to allow the ball to enter.) The child kicks each of the balls into the appropriate goal.

4. Jumping into hoops of different colors after seeing a model of the color. Two hoops of each color will be needed; one set is held by the teacher and the other laid on the floor. The child is shown a hoop of a certain color and must jump into the hoop of the corresponding color. The activity can be varied by placement of other parts of the body in the hoop.

5. Striking balls with bats of the corresponding color. Several bats and balls of matching color are needed, or the bats may be tied with ribbons in matching colors. The child chooses a bat and then selects a ball of the same color for "batting practice."

Activities Focusing on Visual Discrimination (shape and form):

1. Reproducing in movement a specific shape. Several plastic, wood, or cardboard shapes will be needed. The teacher holds up a shape and the child must reproduce it by drawing in the air or walking on the floor.

2. Selecting matching shapes. Two sets of objects of various shapes will be needed. One set is placed in various locations in the room; the other remains with the teacher. When the teacher holds up one of the shapes, the child must find the one like it and run back to the teacher with it.

3. Choosing from among several objects the one best suited to an activity. Several objects such as a large block, large ball, and bean bag are needed. In response to instructions from the teacher, the child must select the object most suitable for sitting, rolling, and throwing and then use the object in the appropriate activity.

4. Matching paper shapes with objects of similar form. Shapes that resemble several of the items of furniture or equipment in the room should be cut from heavy paper. Upon being handed one of the paper shapes by the teacher, the child must locate the item that has a similar form and carry it to a designated spot. (The items will need to be ones that the child is able to carry.)

5. Reproducing shapes with the body. A child who knows the letters of the alphabet can attempt to form such letters as c, l, and y with his body, or several children may work together to reproduce in a lying position on the floor most of the letters of the alphabet.

Activities Focusing on Visual Discrimination (distance):

1. Throwing at a goal from various distances. The goal may be a box or container for younger children and a basketball hoop for older ones. Three marks are made on the floor at various distances from the goal, and the child is instructed by the teacher to shoot a ball at the goal from the mark nearest the goal, farthest from the goal, and from the mark between the two.

2. Throwing at targets of various heights. Targets are placed or drawn on a wall at three different distances from the floor. The teacher instructs the child to throw a ball or bean bag at the highest target, the lowest target, and the one at the middle distance.

3. Judging distance of an object from a given point. Several objects are placed around the room at different distances from the point where the child will stand. He is asked to estimate how many steps away each object is from him. Then he checks the accuracy of his estimates by stepping off the distance.

4. Rolling a large ball different distances. A large ball, such as a medicine ball, will be needed. Two or more sets of marks, each set placed the same distance from the starting point, but in different directions from it, are drawn or painted on the floor. From the starting point, the child must roll the ball to a set of marks that are the same distance away.

5. Tossing an object into the air at various distances. A ball or bean bag will be needed. The teacher instructs the child to throw the object a long distance into the air, a short distance, and an intermediate distance. For more acute discrimination, the child may be asked to throw the object at distances between the three; for example, to a height higher than the lowest distance but lower than the middle distance.

Activities Focusing on Visual Discrimination (speed):

1. Running at different speeds. In response to directions from the teacher, the child runs slowly, moderately, and fast.

2. Throwing objects of different kinds to compare speed of movement. Needed for the activity will be balls of various sizes, a bean bag, and a balloon. The teacher throws the objects and the child determines which ones move slower and which ones faster and which is the slowest and which the fastest.

3. Swinging a suspended ball at different rates of speed. A ball of medium size is suspended by a cord from the ceiling. The child puts the ball in motion by hitting it with his hand so that it will swing slowly, moderately, or fast in response to the instructions of the teacher.

4. Rolling a ball various distances to judge the speed of movement. Objects that will serve as backstops are placed at various distances from the starting point. The teacher rolls a ball toward each object, and the child judges the speed at which each ball travels.

5. Moving the body in various forms of locomotion to determine the speed of each. The child moves over a designated distance by hopping, crawling, jumping, and so forth, and decides which form of movement is the fastest and which the slowest, and which is faster or slower than some other one.

Activities Focusing on Figure-ground Phenomenon:

1. Catching a ball suspended in front of a distracting background. A brightly colored ball is hung from the ceiling so that it is suspended in front of other objects. When the ball is swung, the child concentrates on following it with his eyes in order to catch it.

2. Rolling a ball between objects. A tennis ball or ball of similar size will be needed, as will several objects that cannot be easily knocked over with the ball. The child rolls the ball toward the objects in an attempt to place it between two of them.

3. Locating and kicking a moving ball in a group of stationary balls. Several balls of medium size are placed on the floor a short distance from the child. One is put into motion by the teacher, and the child must move to it in order to kick it.

4. Throwing a ball at a target. A target of any kind is placed against a wall on which there are pictures or other objects. The child concentrates on the specific target and attempts to hit it with a ball thrown from several feet away.

5. Playing tag in a small space. Confining the game to a small space will make it easier for the child to keep his attention focused on the person he is trying to catch.

Activities Focusing on Auditory Discrimination:

1. Responding to different tones and frequencies with a specified motor movement. Various objects that create different tones and frequencies will be needed. The teacher works out the motor movement with the children, such as nodding the head or waving the hand, that will be used to respond when a certain tone or frequency is produced.

2. Identifying the direction of a sound. Two children work together in this activity. One child bounces a ball in various directions; the other child must determine the direction from which the sound is coming. Sight may be used to help locate the right direction.

3. Differentiating the sounds made by a ball. The child bounces a ball and describes the difference between the sound that is made when the ball is struck with the hand and that made when the ball strikes the floor.

4. Differentiating sounds made by striking objects. A short thin piece of wood or drumstick is used to strike against various objects in the room. The child listens to the sounds and tries to identify each sound with its source.

5. Isolating a sound from background noise. This activity requires that there be a number of sounds emitted from various sources in the room, such as from the play activities of several children. The teacher helps the child to isolate some of the sounds and then encourages him to try to isolate others. The child may use his vision to locate the source and identify the sound.

Activities Focusing on Balance:

1. Standing on one foot. While standing, the child lifts one foot and tries to bal-

ance himself. The difficulty of the activity can be increased by moving the raised leg to various positions and by moving one or both arms to various positions.

2. Standing on the balance beam. The child stands with one foot behind the other on the balance beam. The activity can be made more difficult by balancing only on one foot, walking on the beam, reversing direction, squatting, and so forth.

3. Walking the line. Strips several inches wide are applied or painted on the floor. The student walks along the strips, placing one foot in front of the other.

4. Balancing objects. A book or similar object is placed on the head to be balanced while walking or is placed on the feet to be balanced while holding the legs straight up from a supine position. Other parts of the body might also be used in various positions.

5. Walking on a resilient surface. The child walks around the top of a large inner tube, maintaining his balance. The trampoline may be substituted in this activity and may be used for other simple balancing stunts.

Activities Focusing on Identity of Body Parts:

1. Touching parts of the body. This activity is like a game of Simon Says, with all the activity consisting of touching parts of the body.

2. Tossing a balloon and allowing it to land on a part of the body. Each child is supplied with an air-filled balloon. The balloons are tossed into the air and the children maneuver so that the balloons land on the part of the body the teacher designates.

3. Moving a part of the body in response to its being named. The teacher or a child chosen as the leader calls out a part of the body, such as foot, arm, head, and the group responds by moving that part.

4. Naming the body part used to produce a movement. The child performs a leap or squat or picks up or throws an object and names the parts of the body involved in the action.

5. Using parts of the body to form a shape. Children are divided into pairs for this activity. One child directs the other to form his body into a certain shape by telling him which parts of the body to move.

Activities Focusing on Body Awareness:

1. Observing reflections of movements in the mirror. The child observes in a mirror the movements he makes with various parts of the body. He is encouraged to talk about what he is doing, such as by saying "My arm is moving up over my head."

2. Analyzing different kinds of locomotion. The child moves across the floor by crawling, rolling, sliding, hopping, skipping, or running. He is asked to describe the movements he made in the particular locomotion skill.

3. Describing positions of the body. The child takes a position such as the stork stand. He identifies the shape and describes the movements and parts of the body involved.

4. Performing movements of different quality. The child makes a movement that has a certain quality, such as a languid swing of the arm, and then explores other ways of making the movement to achieve other qualities, such as strength, fluidity, tenseness.

5. Performing one part of a movement pattern without engaging the rest of the parts. The child isolates one movement of a total movement pattern and performs it without moving any other part of his body.

Activities Focusing on Laterality:

1. Sliding to right and left. In response to the teacher's direction, the child slides his foot to the left or right.

2. Walking and retracing steps on the balance beam. The child walks on the balance beam and turns left or right, as indicated by the teacher, and retraces his steps.

3. Following footprints. Footprints are drawn or painted on the floor in such a

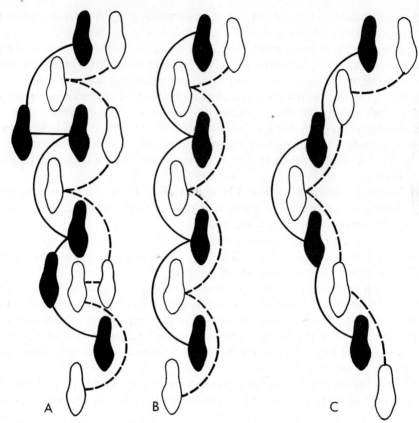

Figure 18–4. Patterns of footprints for an activity to promote laterality. (A) Simple, (B) Moderately complex, (C) Complex.

manner that the child must, in stepping on them, cross one foot over the other. (See Fig. 18–4.)

4. Crawling on alternate hands and feet. The crawl is made with the hand and the leg of opposite sides extended forward at the same time.

5. Combining arm movements with a zigzag run. The student follows a zigzag pattern, and as he turns to the left or right, he holds up the arm on that side of his body.

Activities Focusing on Directionality:

1. Passing to the left or right. The child walks toward the teacher and passes to the left or right side of the teacher as directed.

2. Matching the movements of another child. Two children work together, facing each other. One child performs a movement, such as lifting his left foot or raising his right arm, and the other child matches the movement with same side of his body.

3. Identifying the left and right sides of objects. The teacher directs the child to touch one or the other side of an object in the room, such as a chair, and the child runs to it and places his hand on the correct side.

4. Walking between objects. Large objects, such as big blocks or chairs, are placed in a row with enough space between them to allow a child to pass through. The child walks to the right or left of each chair in the row in response to the direction given by the teacher.

5. Touching the corresponding hand or foot of another child. The students work

in pairs. One child touches his right or left hand or foot to the corresponding hand or foot of the child he faces.

Activities Focusing on Rhythm and Tempo:

1. Marching to a cadence. The teacher beats a drum, increasing and decreasing the tempo to enhance the experience.

2. Keeping time with a swinging ball. A ball is suspended from the ceiling by a cord. It is swung at various speeds by the teacher, and the child swings his foot, arm, leg, head, or trunk to match the swinging of the ball.

3. Moving various parts of the body to a cadence. The cadence is supplied by a strong beat on the drum or piano. The child responds by keeping time with different parts of the body, his fingers, head, arms, legs, and so forth.

4. Jumping in rhythm to a swinging rope. The teacher and a helper swing a jump rope back and forth (not a full turn of the rope). The child jumps over the rope as it passes near his feet.

5. Performing various movements to a beat. This activity is like Number 1 except that the difficulty is increased by having the child skip, jump, or hop to the cadence.

SELECTED READING

Arnheim, Daniel D., and Sinclair, William A.: *The Clumsy Child.* St. Louis, The C. V. Mosby Co., 1975.

Cratty, Bryant J.: *Physical Expressions of Intelligence.* Englewood Cliffs, N.J., Prentice-Hall, Inc., 1975.

Cratty, Bryant J.: *Remedial Motor Activity for Children.* Philadelphia, Lea and Febiger, 1975.

Gallahue, David L., *et al*: *A Conceptual Approach to Moving and Learning.* New York, John Wiley and Sons, Inc., 1975.

Kephart, Newell C.: *The Slow Learner in the Classroom.* Columbus, Ohio, Charles E. Merrill Books, Inc., 1960.

Morris, P. R., and Whiting, H. T. A.: *Motor Impairment and Compensatory Education.* Philadelphia, Lea and Febiger, 1971.

Chapter 19

Behavioral Disorders

The problems of those in our society who deviate from normal because of their inability to adjust to the circumstances of their environment are receiving increasing attention as the sociologists, psychiatrists, psychologists, and social workers expand the body of knowledge about the causes of social maladjustment and mental illness. In former times such people were labeled criminal and insane and were considered outcasts of society. Their treatment was, until modern times, usually harsh and cruel in the extreme as was thought to befit their status as outcasts. During the ancient and medieval periods of history, the mentally ill were regarded as being possessed by the devil and were often subjected to death by slow torture. Criminals received extremely harsh penalties for even very minor offenses, and brutal treatment was frequently administered publicly as a lesson both to the prisoner and to the witnesses.

Gradually, the nature of abnormal behavior manifested by those who suffer mental illnesses and those who commit crimes against society came to be viewed differently, and a more humanitarian approach was achieved toward the problems such individuals present. Institutions and hospitals were established for the custodial care and treatment of the mentally ill. Prison conditions were improved, and punitive measures began to be replaced with a more positive approach designed to rehabilitate the offenders. The programs of rehabilitation have shown some significant success in individual cases, but the overall record has not been impressive enough to avoid calls for their abandonment by both professional and lay critics. Nevertheless, it may be said that the currently prevailing attitude toward treatment of those who demonstrate abnormal behavior is one of seeking out the causes and eliminating them; helping the individuals to achieve satisfactory adjustment and to develop normal behavior patterns; and providing the means by which they can return to society as useful, responsible, and contributing members.

In successful rehabilitation programs for the socially maladjusted and the mentally ill, the provision of opportunities for fun and exercise through games, dancing, and sports is a very important facet of the overall program, which usually also includes medical and psychiatric treatment and vocational and educational instruction. Consequently, physical educators with an understanding of the special problems and needs of those who exhibit abnormal behavior are being employed in psychiatric and penal institutions housing young people and in private and public residential schools for emotionally disturbed children. Youngsters with less severe behavior problems can attend public schools and receive physical education in the regular or special program as their needs require.

Physical education programs in schools and institutions will be examined in detail in two sections of this book. A third section will be devoted to a pattern of abnormal behavior which, while it is of less consequence to society than the other two, may nevertheless be very damaging to the individual. It is that conduct which results from extreme fear or hatred of muscular activity. Students with violent dislikes for participation in physical education activities or with great fear of certain types of muscular activities need special help from the physical education teacher to dispel these extreme emotions so that they may participate with pleasure and gain for themselves the benefits of vigorous play. Such students may profit from the greater attention and more individually planned activities of the special physical education program.

THE NATURE OF ABNORMAL BEHAVIOR

In the education profession the term abnormal behavior has largely replaced those of emotional disturbance and mental illness. However, when the latter terms are employed by educators, emotionally disturbed is used to refer to children, while mentally ill is applied to adults. Medical terminology does not make this distinction; the terms are considered to be synonymous, with preference given to mentally ill.

Medically, mental illness is classed into three major categories according to the official diagnostic manual of the American Psychiatric Association. These are the organic brain disorders, functional disorders, and mental deficiency, which was discussed in Chapter 17, Mental Retardation. Organic brain disorders are caused by injury to the brain. Most people in this group are elderly since impairment of blood circulation associated with old age is often responsible for the damage to the brain. The largest and most interesting category of mental illness, and unquestionably the most important to society in terms of human suffering and cost, is that of functional disorders. These maladies have in common the fact that no one really knows what causes them. It seems quite likely that those who display atypical or bizarre behavior do so for a wide variety of reasons.

While there are five major types of functional disorders, by far the largest number of patients in mental hospitals are diagnosed as having schizophrenia, a subgroup of the psychotic disorder. It has been estimated that one in every 100 to 200 individuals is schizophrenic. Many children of school age exhibit signs of the disorder. Over one fourth of all patients requiring hospitalization because of mental illness have schizophrenia. No other disease, medical or psychiatric, is nearly so common. Thus it becomes important to have some knowledge about schizophrenia. Actually there are nine varieties of schizophrenia recognized at the present time, although it is questionable whether all these labels are useful. In any case, there are common aspects in the history and personality of such patients, regardless of the specific label they are assigned.

Schizophrenia usually develops between the ages of 13 and 30; however, it does occur at earlier ages. The condition varies from a mild disorder, at times undetectable, to one so severe as to require long-term hospitalization.

Those who suffer from schizophrenia are usually socially withdrawn, aloof, and not easy persons with whom to interact. They tend not to form strong friendships and are likely not to date very much. Both males and females, who are found in this category in equal numbers, are less likely to be married than are normal people of comparable ages. A given person may manifest a wide variety of bizarre behaviors, including such extreme actions as eating cigarette butts or dirt and smearing walls with feces. Common symptoms include the following:

Hallucinations: perceiving something that does not exist outside the mind.

Delusions: interpreting events in a personal and unrealistic way.

Affect disturbances: displaying little or no emotion or displaying emotion inappropriate for the circumstances.

Paranoid symptomatology: developing systemized delusions of grandeur or persecution.

Motoric disturbances: inclination to assume and maintain bizarre positions or to display repetitive, ritualistic behavior. Such patients are generally labeled catatonic schizophrenic.

Schizophrenia that occurs in very young children is called autism. Although it may be present from birth, the condition is usually not diagnosed until later, generally between the ages of two and five. The autistic child responds chiefly to his inner thoughts and cannot relate to others around him or to his environment as a whole, and thus often gives the appearance of mental retardation. Frequently, he is mute and does not attempt communication of any kind and gives no indication of recognizing the presence of others. Other common characteristics that an autistic child may demonstrate at one time or another are unusual body movements and peculiar mannerisms, abnormal responses to stimuli, resistance to change, emotional outbursts, and excessive preoccupation with objects and procedures without regard to their social acceptability.

While schizophrenia is by far the most common mental illness, other types also occur often. One of these results from organic damage to the brain and falls into the category of organic brain disorders. Although many children do have organic brain disorders, the majority of persons suffering from the disorder are old and infirm. Those with organic brain damage present a special problem because of the limitations imposed by their condition. In working with them, only limited goals are likely to be achieved.

Another large group of disorders is involved with personality (character), and hence is labeled personality disorders. Individuals with this type of disorder do not become institutionalized because of bizarre behavior or inability to care for themselves, but, rather, because of behavioral patterns that are illegal or socially objectionable. In fact, they are more likely to end up in a penal institution than in a hospital. Alcoholics, sexual deviants, and overly impulsive people fall into this group. They are often vivacious and charming people, who, however, have little desire to change themselves or obey the rules and hence are unlikely to become seriously involved in therapeutic programs.

Still another fairly common mental disorder is psychoneurosis. Individuals diagnosed as being psychoneurotic may be highly anxious or depressed, and they may manifest startling and intriguing behaviors such as having two or more distinctly different personalities. Neurotics do not show the gross misperceptions and misinterpretations of reality characteristic of the psychotic disorders which include schizophrenia. They are often most eager to change themselves; they tend to respond positively to therapeutic programs and are the most rewarding to the activity leader.

In addition to the common functional disorders discussed earlier, there are several kinds of behavior recognized as symptoms of mental illness. Although they do not approximate the seriousness of most mental disorders, they are serious in children of school age to the extent that they interfere with the learning process. Consequently, teachers should be aware of them. They include hyperkinesia, characterized by excessive activity and inability to concentrate for any length of time; extreme shyness and withdrawal tendencies; chronic anxiety manifested by unrealistic fears; and overaggressiveness, in which the child is hostile and quarrelsome. Hyperkinesia, a disorder that is common among children with severe learning disabilities, is classified as a behavior disorder; but because it is so severely handicapping to learning, it is also placed in the category of learning disabilities. Hyperkinesia is discussed in Chapter 18, Learning Disabilities.

As a group, the physical condition of students with severe psychosis is poor. Physical fitness is frequently very low, particularly for those who have withdrawn from social contacts and hence from active participation in physical activities. Confinement in an institution does not permit sufficient physical activity to maintain a minimum level of physical fitness, unless special consideration is given to planning for muscular activity. Although it is not known how close the relationship may be between physical fitness and mental health, it would appear to be advantageous to the mental patient to maintain good physical fitness.

Aside from improving physical fitness, the role that meaningful activities can play in the lives of these patients is well recognized. Hospital routine which is unbroken with pleasant activities tends to produce boredom and lack of ambition. Mental patients who have no interesting activities to fill their long hours have been observed to lose all interest in their appearance, to become slovenly and untidy in their personal care, and to give little heed to the treatment and care provided for them. A program of physical education is able to provide for this dual need for vigorous muscular activity to improve physical fitness and for meaningful recreational activities which add to the zest of living.

Muscular activity following emotional stress tends to nullify some of the physiological reaction to extreme emotion. It is known that anxiety or other strong emotions cause the body to undergo certain changes preparatory to action, such as increased flow of epinephrine (excretion of the adrenal gland), change in the size of capillaries, increased rate of blood flow, and disturbances in the flow of gastric jucies. As a result, such functional disorders as indigestion and stomach upset may occur. But they are not usually evident if the strong emotions are followed by physical exertion. It would appear, then, that some of the physiological disturbances resulting from frequent emotional stress might be removed by vigorous workouts. For those who have difficulty expressing themselves to their emotional satisfaction, kinesthetic or muscular movement offers a satisfying outlet.

THE PROGRAM FOR THE MENTALLY ILL

The difference in the physical education program developed for students with mental disorders who attend regular schools and those who are in residential schools and hospital educational programs is one of scope rather than kind. Among youngsters able to attend a regular school, there is not the great variety of disorders or the severity of illness found in the residential and hospital schools. Consequently, if the physical education teacher understands the process of programming to meet the needs of students in the institutional settings, he is also prepared to develop an appropriate program for students with lesser problems in the regular school. For this reason, the discussion that follows is directed toward program planning for physical education in residential schools and in hospitals with school programs.

The kind of mental illness is not the chief factor in determining the types of activities that will be of the most value. Individual differences in abilities and interests are just as prevalent among the psychotic as among the normal. However, the classification of the disorders does provide some clue as to the type of activities which the student can engage in with success and pleasure. Information of this kind must be secured from the medical personnel involved with the student.

The activities selected for the program should include those with which the student has had experience, as their familiarity provides a sense of security. New games should be offered and can be taught successfully if properly motivated. As part of the motivating process, a wide variety of game equipment can be displayed for the students to look at and handle. When an interest in a particular piece has been kindled, the instructor may talk to the student about it and show him how to use it. As the student tries it out, he is encouraged to continue to play with it. Instructions should be simple and informal.

Group participation in play activities is highly desirable for the social contacts it makes possible. Some students may experience considerable strain in social adjustment, so it may be necessary to work gradually toward group activities, progressing from spectatorship to individual sport to dual sport and eventually to small group activity. As the youngsters become accustomed to group play, staff members and aides may be included in the group to increase the scope of social contacts. Their inclusion in the activity also provides an incentive for approved social conduct, but they should be very careful not to dominate the game or detract in any way from the successful performance of the student.

Basic skill games and exercises which do not require fine coordination are usually the most suitable. Individuals who are very regressed or experience motoric disturbances due to medication are easily frustrated by activities requiring numerous movement patterns and detailed directions. Activities of limited responses and simple structure which may be successfully used with the older school age group are shuffleboard, casting, croquet, horseshoes, ring toss, bowling, weightlifting, bag punching, and the basic sport skills of throwing, catching, dribbling, and striking a ball. A certain element of competition in the games is usually not disapproved. For most students, contact sports and highly competitive games which tend to encourage the expression of aggression directly toward others are contraindicated.

For younger children, the elementary activities utilizing the basic skills (running, throwing, catching, jumping, and so forth) are appropriate and are readily taught. More competitive activities often encourage antisocial conduct, either withdrawal or aggression; therefore, their use in the curriculum should be limited. Children who are aggressive may benefit from participation in strenuous games and activities, as vigorous exercise is helpful in reducing aggressive conduct in some persons. Some aggressive children act as they do because of a subconscious desire for attention, and it is possible to modify their behavior by giving them recognition. Making such a child a squad leader or putting him in charge of an activity can often reduce his aggressiveness.

The shy child needs special help in developing self-confidence. The teacher can help by showing confidence in the child's ability and setting goals for him that he can realistically achieve. Such a child should not be forced into any activities in which he fears to participate. This also holds true for the overanxious child. Both kinds of students should be brought to accept an activity that causes them fear and worry by very gradual exposure to parts or elements of the activity until the emotional reaction subsides.

Not all of the play activities should be organized for the students. They should be given access to equipment so they may play on their own; they should also have the chance for passive and spectator participation in sport activities. Those engaging in impromptu play must be made to understand the regulations which have been established in regard to their use of the equipment and facilities during unsupervised periods. Strict adherence to safety precautions should be expected and received. If a student must be denied permission to use the equipment or refused any other request made of the physical education instructor, this should be done upon an impersonal basis so the student will not feel hurt or discriminated against.

Co-recreational activities in which the two sexes can mingle socially should be given appropriate attention in the program. Because of the appeal of music to the emotions, one of the most successful co-recreational activities is social dancing. Square and folk dances are usually too complicated in structure for most severely disturbed students, although they are greatly enjoyed by some. Those who cannot participate in these forms of dance can be encouraged to perform simple rhythmic activities to music. Modern or interpretive dance has interesting possibilities as a therapeutic aid for mentally ill persons whose other means of expression are blocked. Because of the strong emotional involvement in this type of dance expression, it is recommended that this form of dance be approached only with the consultation of the medical personnel or dance therapist.

Swimming should be included among the activities of the program because of the desirable effects which water produces. It frequently acts as a stimulant to the depressed and encourages movement in catatonics. Hyperactive persons are often greatly relaxed by the water, particularly if it is warmer than normal.

The instructor must plan for successful participation in the activities by the students. Success is extremely important to them. To be successful does not necessitate being a winner, but it does require that the activity be fun and self-satisfying. To ensure success the instructor must consider the special needs of each person and any sports interests he had displayed; he must give him friendly, patient instruction in the skills; and he must continually encourage him toward a wider interest in play and the people who play.

Above all, the instructor must treat the mentally ill student as an individual who is deserving of respect and consideration. There is still in our society a great stigma attached to being publicly recognized as mentally ill; those who have a mental illness are regarded by far too many as misfits and failures. Of course, mental patients are well aware of these attitudes and anticipate being degraded in their dealings with others. This obviously interferes with establishing social relationships. Since most of the patients are not socially adept, having generally spent withdrawn and aloof lives, failure to treat them as deserving of the dignity accorded normal human beings is defeating to them and defeating to the success of the physical education program.

In trying to institute programs with such people, it should also be borne in mind that many of them are extremely concerned about their personal problems (some may even be pondering the desirability of death over their present life), so that games of any sort are of little interest to them. While they may participate, if forced to do so, because of their passivity, they will not enjoy the activity and will probably feel degraded and silly doing it. This is, of course, detrimental to the objectives of the program.

Many of the mentally ill desperately need help and there are few really effective techniques for helping them. The instructor in physical education, if he is sensitive and concerned, may be as able to help the mentally ill as anyone.

THE NATURE AND CAUSES OF SOCIAL MALADJUSTMENT

Social maladjustment resulting in abnormal behavior constitutes one of the greatest social problems of our day. It is not always easy to determine the dividing line between normal and abnormal behavior, although the difference at the extremes is readily observed. Abnormal conduct is antisocial, destructive to the personality, and often ends in actual criminal action. It varies in degree from very slight deviation from accepted conduct to serious breaches of the law.

When does abnormal behavior become delinquency? The National Probation and Parole Association has established these conditions as indicative of delinquent behavior: (1) violation of any laws; (2) habitual waywardness or disobedience which cannot be controlled by the parents, guardians, or custodians; and (3) conduct which injures or endangers the morals or health of the individual or others.

It is recognized that there is no one universal cause of delinquency. It is the result of many different influences of the environment upon the individual. Statistics indicate that a large majority of delinquents come from disadvantaged homes, broken homes, or homes with poor discipline (lax, overstrict, or erratic). Lack of parental love and leaving a child to his own devices without supervision or the provision for meaningful use of leisure time are other important factors in the development of delinquent behavior. At least one study has found the influence of peers to be of singular importance in delinquency at all socioeconomic levels. Considerable attention has been directed toward the violence depicted in the entertainment media as an influence upon delinquent conduct; the extent of the influence has not been established, although some authorities are inclined to feel that it may certainly tip the scale in that direction. It is also frequently stated that lack of recreational facilities is a factor, but this appears to be chiefly an excuse for delinquency rather than a basic cause.

The presence of any or all of the contributing factors in the life of any one person does not necessarily result in delinquent behavior on his part. The significance of the influence exerted by any unfavorable conditions varies from person to person, depending upon his previous background and training and his individual nature. Many children grow up under these conditions without ever exhibiting delinquent behavior, while many others become delinquents in their youth and criminals in their adult lives.

Drawing upon this evidence, it would appear that there are two motivating forces in delinquency. One of these is the adherence of the individual to group mores which do not conform to the general mores of society. The group has a distorted sense of values; its concept of right and wrong is not in agreement with generally accepted standards and with established laws and regulations. The group is likely to consist of peers but it may also be family members. Antisocial conduct is actually encouraged by some families, in which children are taught to steal and to "get by" the law, while in other families the lack of moral example and instruction contributes to the social maladjustment of the children.

The other motivating force stems from conflict. In this situation, delinquent behavior is a neurotic expression of the conflict. Early childhood conflicts resulting from unsatisfactory family relationships may develop in a person a lasting sense of hostility toward the world or toward himself. Studies comparing delinquent and nondelinquent siblings have shown that the delinquents had a very unsatisfactory relationship with their parents, while their brothers and sisters did not. Conflicts with parents in disciplinary matters and conflicts with siblings for the love and attention of the parents give rise to feelings of inadequacy and inferiority which find outlet in forms of undesirable behavior.

Peculiar characteristics of the behavior of delinquents and potential delinquents which have been noted are marked willfulness, defiance, suspicion and hostility without cause, desire to destroy and hurt others and themselves, and desire for excitement, change, or risk. Feelings of insecurity and worthlessness are common to these individuals.

Many programs are organized with the expressed purpose of combating delinquency among youngsters by providing them opportunities to gain attention and success in socially acceptable ways. It is hoped that in this way they will gain the respect for themselves and others which their home training and environment have denied them. A large part of such programs consists of sports activities designed to promote both the physical and social well-being of these youngsters, who are often as much in need of physical improvement as social rehabilitation. Numerous physical educators have found their life work as directors and instructors in such programs; many more give their free time to volunteer instruction in sport skills.

Delinquent behavior in the classrooms is a constant problem in many schools. The physical education teacher often has a better opportunity than other teachers to contribute to the solution of this problem, owing to the universal appeal of sports for young people. Using this appeal as a motivator, the teacher of physical education is often able to involve a delinquent in constructive play from which some degree of personal success is likely to result. This success, for one who has never known success, often provides the motivation and incentive for a more desirable and acceptable mode of conduct.

It is, of course, beyond the scope of his training for the physical educator to give treatment to the individual delinquent. However, his patience and understanding, his general philosophy, and his method of control may have a far-reaching effect upon such a student. Toward this end, the following suggestions are offered to the teacher.

1. Aim to understand the delinquent and his problems so that you will know why he acts as he does.

2. Isolate his chief grievance, help him to understand why it irritates him, and then help him determine acceptable ways of alleviating it.

3. Discover some things that he is able to do well, for which he will receive favorable recognition.

4. Enlist the cooperation of a small group of classmates to help develop his self-confidence.

5. Try to find a way to have any physical defects corrected, including minor ones.

6. Keep the program for helping him flexible, letting him know that it is an attempt to help him become a better person.

7. Do not become discouraged by relapses in conduct but continue to express confidence that the delinquent will improve.

8. Secure professional help when it is needed and is available.

THE PROGRAM FOR DELINQUENTS IN INSTITUTIONS

The physical education program in penal institutions is largely a recreational sports program. While it is recognized that participation in sports does not contribute directly to the control of delinquent behavior, participation may provide a certain degree of motivation and incentive for a certain mode of conduct during the game. Sometimes the desire to participate can be used to motivate desirable conduct at other times as well. If the sports program is particularly effective and enjoyed by the participants, it can be a strong incentive to better conduct so that the opportunities to play will not be jeopardized.

The sports program has benefits other than its possible influence upon behavior. It provides invigorating activity which has wide interest appeal, it makes possible social intercourse in a controlled situation, it allows strong emotions and aggressive tendencies to be expressed in a socially acceptable way, and it provides some measure of success in lives which are largely filled with failures.

Greatest benefits are secured from the sports program that offers as wide a variety of different sports and games as possible, so that all interests can be met and everyone given an opportunity to play, or learn to play, one or more games successfully. Competition should be equalized by division of players into squads of like ability. Intramural competition can be easily arranged, and a varsity team may be possible if games can be scheduled with teams in neighboring towns who are willing to come to the institution to play. Scheduling may present difficulties, but it is extremely worthwhile for the contact that it establishes with the outside world.

Any link with the world from which they have been removed is important to the morale of those confined in penal institutions. Consequently, the celebration of holidays with special sports events is desirable. Fun and activity are associated with holidays at home, and special provisions for holiday observances help to create a necessary link between home and institution.

EXTREME HATE OR FEAR OF PHYSICAL EDUCATION

Extreme hate and fear of physical education manifest themselves at all educational levels, from elementary school to college. Hatred of muscular activity can usually be traced to unfavorable experiences in physical education. Fears are most often stimulated by particular types of activities which are associated with danger in the minds of certain students, swimming being the most common. Fear of swimming ranges from a more or less normal reaction to water, because of lack of swimming skill, to aquaphobia, in which there is extreme fear of water. Contact sports elicit great fear in some students, while activities such as rope climbing, tumbling, and apparatus work may evoke fears in others.

In young children a reaction of dislike usually stems from fear of the activity or factors inherent within the situation itself. Overprotectiveness of parents and inexperience in play activities are chiefly responsible for abnormal emotional reactions to physical education activities. In older children the fears are usually more deep-seated than in the younger child. Lack of experience may be the reason, although unsatisfactory experience in such activities is the more usual cause. Fear of ridicule and continual defeat in achievement of physical performance are important contributing factors. Fear of physical injury is yet another factor.

Dislike and hate in older students may develop from a long history of continual fear as well as from experiences in poor physical education programs which promoted none of the values inherent in well-planned programs. This reason for dislike is more prevalent among high school upperclassmen and college students. In the majority of cases this dislike does not result in any great deviation in behavior; however, some students go to great lengths to avoid class participation. Malingering is the method most frequently used, in the hope of being excused from participation for physical reasons.

Students who experience extreme dislike, fear, and hate for physical education need special help in overcoming their strong emotional reactions to muscular activity. If circumstances permit, they should be placed for a time in the special program, where attention can be given to seeking out the cause which has prompted the emotion and overcoming it. When it is not possible to accommodate these students in the special program, individual conferences with the students can achieve the same objectives.

In either situation, the student should be guided toward an understanding and appreciation of the values of physical education. The facts of the physiological benefits of exercise should be described dramatically and in a vocabulary appropriate to the student's educational level. The fun of playing and the social benefits to be derived from it should be given special emphasis. If fear of injury is the basis of the strong emotional reaction, the student should be given every reassurance that the possibility of injury is minimal. All the various precautions that are exercised to ensure the safety of the players should be demonstrated to him. He should also be given instruction in falling to avoid injury to help him realize that there is little danger of personal injury even in vigorous activity. Exposure of such students to actual participation should be very gradual. The technique of helping a student overcome a fear will be described here in detail, in order to suggest ways in which a student can be led gradually into an activity that he fears.

Perhaps the most common fear of students in physical education is of water. Unless the student has an actual water phobia, he can usually overcome fear of the water through a careful process of introduction to it. A student with a phobia cannot as a rule be persuaded even to enter the pool area and will require special help from a psychiatrist or psychologist. The others should be requested to come to the pool and sit on the edge with their feet in the water. They are informed that nothing else is expected of them, but if they feel like getting into the water they may do so. After a day or two of sitting on the pool's edge it is likely that even the most reluctant student will venture into the water. From here on, the techniques are much the same as those recommended for introducing any beginner to the water; however, progress may be considerably slower and the instructor should never force or rush the students. It may, for instance, take much longer before a student who is mastering fear of the water will splash water into his face than for the normal beginner. Care must be taken to prevent splashing and commotion by experienced swimmers who may be in the pool at the same time; and, above all, no ridiculing remarks should be tolerated. It is easier, of course, if those with water fears can be alone in the pool until they overcome their fears, but this is not usually possible. Hence it is very important that careful control be exercised over the other students who are present.

Figure 19-1. Overcoming fear or anxiety about performing a motor activity necessitates a careful process of gradual exposure to build self-confidence. (Courtesy of Mansfield Training School.)

Lack of success in performance and generally unfavorable physical education experiences are the usual underlying causes of extreme dislike of physical education activities. Students who hate physical education class because they are always last in the race and repeatedly in error when playing the ball are very numerous. Subnormal strength, endurance, and flexibility are the usual basis of failure to perform well, and work in the developmental program on fitness exercises will greatly benefit these students. The instructor should also encourage these students to practice skills during their free hours. He might also refer them to visual aids and reading materials which may be used to learn more about the techniques of skill performance. He should give them as much individual instruction as possible in helping to analyze and overcome skill faults. Those whose dislike stems from former poor physical education experiences may need to be convinced of the values of physical education. Every effort should be made to arouse the interest of these students in a special game or sport which they will learn to perform with success and pleasure and which can then be used as a springboard to broader participation.

SELECTED READINGS

AAHPER: *Physical Education, Recreation, and Related Programs for Autistic and Emotionally Disturbed Children.* Washington, D.C., American Alliance for Health, Physical Education and Recreation, 1976.

Alabiso, F. P., and Hansen, J. C.: *The Hyperactive Child in the Classroom.* New York, Grune and Stratton, 1970.

Kugelmass, Newton I.: *The Autistic Child.* Springfield, Illinois, Charles C Thomas, Pub., 1974.

Long, Nicholas J., et al.: *Conflict in the Classroom.* Belmont, California, Wadsworth Publishing Co., 1971.

Polk, Kenneth, and Schafer, Walter: *Schools and Delinquency.* Englewood Cliffs, New Jersey, Prentice-Hall, 1972.

Wolman, Benjamin B.: *Children Without Childhood.* New York, Grune and Stratton, 1970.

Woody, Robert H.: *Behavioral Problem Children in the Schools.* New York, Appleton-Century-Crofts, 1969.

Section 4

Activities and Programs

The focus of this final section is on activities and programs for handicapped students. Some of the chapters provide comprehensive descriptions of adaptations for a wide variety of physical education activities to permit participation by students with handicaps. Ideas are included for modifying rules and regulations, adapting playing techniques and equipment, and devising new versions of the activities. Other chapters describe special program offerings that are particularly beneficial to handicapped students.

Chapter 20

Basic Skill (Low Organized) Games

The familiar games of childhood have a definite place in the physical education program of all elementary school children, regardless of their mental and physical capacities. Most of these activities require little or no equipment and are easily organized for play. For this reason, they are often identified as low organized. It seems fitting, however, to refer to them as basic skill activities because of the important contributions they make to the basic development of the physical, mental, and social skills of young children. To fail to provide any child with the opportunities for development engendered by play in the basic skill games is to deny him entrance to one of the best avenues to optimum growth and development.

ORGANIZING THE INSTRUCTION

Because the space required for playing the basic skill games need not be large, the games can be organized for play almost anywhere—on the playground, in the classroom, in the gymnasium or all-purpose room, even in hallways. Equipment is relatively simple and inexpensive: balls, beanbags, boxes, batons, and plastic bowling pins. Most of these items are easily obtained or readily improvised. Beanbags, for example, can be made from scrap cloth sewn into a bag and filled with dried beans or rice. Pieces of wood of suitable size and free of splinters may be substituted for batons and empty milk cartons or plastic jugs for bowling pins.

In situations where normal and handicapped children are playing together, it is usually more desirable to integrate the handicapped with their normal peers. Sometimes this will not be feasible, and then the handicapped children may be grouped separately to play one game while the other children play another game. A game to be played by the handicapped may be totally adapted or modified in part as required by the limitations of the players. For example, if no one is able to run, the game is modified to substitute a slow walk for the running. However, if, for example, only one child in the group is unable to run, the game may be adapted to permit this child to choose another child to run in his place when his turn comes.

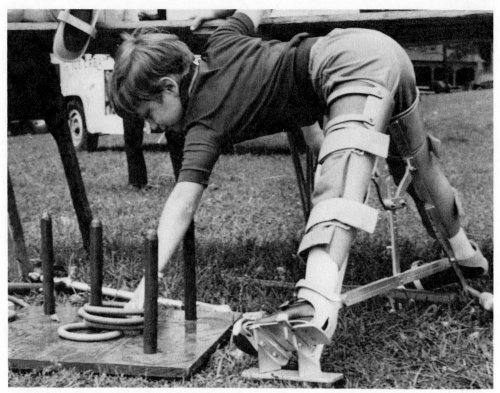

Figure 20–1. Target games usually require little adaptation for handicapped students who have the use of their upper limbs. (Courtesy Newington Children's Hospital.)

CHOOSING APPROPRIATE GAMES

The selection of games for use in the program for any given class depends upon the objectives being sought, the abilities of the children, and the space, time, and equipment available. An analysis of the nature of a game indicates which of the basic skills of running, throwing, catching, dodging, and so forth the game may be expected to accomplish. The abilities of the children can be determined both by observation and testing. Procedures for the latter are discussed in Chapter 7, Evaluation.

To facilitate the selection of appropriate games for each grade level, the games that follow, which are only representative of the vast number of existing games and stunts, have been labeled according to the levels for which they are most suited as determined by the abilities, interests, and needs of young children. It must be remembered, however, that the manner in which a game is presented has a direct bearing on its acceptance by any age group. In the case of mentally retarded children, the chronological age cannot always be relied upon as an effective guide for choosing appropriate games. Games for younger children, however, may be considered too babyish by the retarded, and they will refuse to play them or be so embarrassed while playing them that the potential value of the game is lost. Care must be exercised in selecting games that these children, particularly the older ones, are willing to accept as fitting for their age.

Ringmaster (Grades K–1).   Players form a circle, with one player called the *Ringmaster* in the center. The *Ringmaster* pretends to snap a whip and calls out the name of an animal. All those in the circle imitate the animal named. This procedure continues with different animals. Finally the *Ringmaster* calls, "We will all join in the circus parade," and everyone moves around the circle imitating any animal. *Ring-master* then picks another player to take his place.

Bouncing Ball (Grades K–1). Children choose partners, with one becoming a *ball* and the other the *bouncer*. The one who is the *bouncer* pushes on the partner's head as he would in bouncing a ball. The partner does a deep knee bend and returns to standing position.

Pussy Wants a Corner (Grades K–1). Circles are drawn on the floor for each player. One player, called *Pussy*, walks to different circles saying, "Pussy wants a corner." The player in the circle answers, "Go to my next-door neighbor." Mean-while, as *Pussy* is at other circles, the remaining players signal each other and attempt to exchange places. *Pussy* tries to occupy a circle left by another player. The one left without a circle becomes the new *Pussy*. If one player continues as *Pussy* too long, he may call "All change" and quickly find a vacant circle as everyone changes circles.

Circle Ball (Grades K–1). Players form a circle with a leader in the center. The leader tosses the ball to each player in the circle, who then tosses it back. (The teacher may serve as the leader in order to give the children practice in catching the ball at different levels, since most young children cannot throw well enough to control the heights at which the ball is to be received.)

Spider and Flies (Grades K–2). Mark off two goal lines 40 feet apart. Draw a circle between the goal lines large enough to hold all the players. One player is a *Spider* and squats in the circle while the rest of the players are *Flies* and stand behind the goal lines. All *Flies* advance toward the circle and walk around to the right. When the *Spider* jumps up, all *Flies* run toward a goal while the *Spider* tags as many *Flies* as possible before they get back behind either goal line. Those tagged join the *Spider* in the circle and help catch the remaining *Flies*. The last *Fly* caught is the *Spider* in the next game.

Jouncing on Jouncing Board (Grades K–2). A two- by eight-inch board several feet long is rested on two sturdy uprights. Participant stands in the middle of the board and jounces.

Circle Relay (Grades K–2). Players form circles of six to eight players. Number one in each circle is given a handkerchief. He runs to his right around the circle and gives the handkerchief to number two, who repeats the same procedure. The relay continues until each person has had a turn. The first circle finished is the winner.

Magic Carpet (Grades K–2). Large circles called poison spots are drawn in the play area. On signal, eight to twenty players march or skip to the right, stepping in each spot. When "stop" is called, players stop promptly in position. Players attempt to move quickly to avoid being caught on a spot.

Elephant Walk (Grades K–2). Each child stands and bends forward at the waist. He clasps his hands and lets his arms hang in imitation of an elephant's trunk. The arms are swung from side to side as the child walks with back rounded and knees slightly bent.

Bronco Relay (Grades K–2). Players form lines of even numbers of players. Each line divides into partners. The first couple, one behind the other, straddles a broomstick at the starting line. On the signal, they ride the broomstick to a specified turning line and back to the starting point, where they give the broomstick to couple number two, who repeat the same action. The line in which all the couples complete the relay first is the winner.

Midnight (Grades K–2). For this game two players are designated as *Mr. Fox* and *Mother Hen* and all the other players are called *Chickens*. The *Hen* and *Chickens* have a goal line 30 yards away from the *Fox*. *Mother Hen* leads the chickens to *Mr. Fox* and asks, "What time is it?" *Mr. Fox* replies with any time he chooses, but when he answers "Midnight" the *Hen* and *Chickens* run toward their goal with *Mr. Fox* chasing them. Those tagged become *Mr. Fox's* helpers.

Farmer and the Chickens (Grades K–2). One player, the *Farmer*, pretends to toss out seed and lead other players, the *Chickens*, away from their safety area, or *Pen*. When *Farmer* has taken them far enough from the *Pen*, he calls, "Today is Thanksgiving," and chases the *Chickens*, who run for the *Pen*. *Chickens* caught become *Farmer's* helpers.

Jumping Jack (Grades K–2). Each person squats down and crosses arms on chest. He jumps to standing position with arms out to the sides. The movements are repeated to create jumping jack. Legs may also be spread in the jump to increase the difficulty of the exercise.

Walking, Balancing Beanbag on Head (Grades K–2). Players form even-numbered teams about four feet apart. The first person in each line places a beanbag on his head and walks to a line 20 feet away. He touches the marking, walks back to the starting line, and gives the beanbag to the second player, who repeats the same procedure. Players dropping the bag must start over. The first team finished is the winner.

Target Toss (Grades K–2). Players form groups of four to eight players. Each group has a beanbag and a circle drawn on the floor. The children in each group stand in a straight line 10 feet from the circle. Each child tosses the beanbag at the target and receives one point for getting it in the circle. The group with the greatest number of points at the end of the playing time wins.

Line Relay (Grades K–2). Players form teams in parallel lines and number off. A leader calls a number, and this player steps out to the right and runs counterclockwise completely around the team, back to his original position. The player who returns first scores a point. The team with the highest score wins.

Skunk Tag (Grades K–2). Eight to ten players spread around the playing area. One person who is *It* runs around trying to tag someone. To avoid being tagged, a child must hold his nose with his right hand and hold his left foot with his left hand. If he's tagged before getting into this position, he becomes the new *It*.

Eagle and Sparrows (Grades K–3). One player is chosen as the *Eagle*. Other players, six to eight, are *Sparrows*. *Sparrows* stretch their arms to the sides and circle them up, back, down, and forward. The *Eagle* chases the *Sparrows* as they run while rotating arms in the described fahsion. *Sparrows*, when tagged, become *Eagles*.

Partner Toss (Grades K–3). Players choose partners. The pair throws the ball back and forth. Each time the ball is caught, the partners move farther apart, attempting to get as far from each other as possible. If the ball is missed, they start over at the original positions.

Wring the Dish Rag (Grades K–3). Partners stand facing each other and join hands. One raises his left hand, elevating the right hand of the other. Partners lower the other arms and turn under the raised arms ending in a back to back position. They then raise the other pair of arms, turning under them to face each other again. Repeat several times.

Cowboys and Indians (Grades K–3). Players divide into two teams called *Indians* and *Cowboys*, which stand 60 feet apart on their respective goal lines. Each team chooses a leader. All *Indians*, except the leader, turn around. The *Cowboys* walk up, and when the leader of the *Indians* thinks they're close enough he calls, "The *Cowboys* are coming!" The *Indians* chase the *Cowboys*, attempting to tag them before they reach their goal line. All *Cowboys* tagged become *Indians*. The procedure is reversed for the next game. The team having the largest number at the end of the playing time wins. If leaders are caught, the teams pick new ones.

Call Ball (Grades K–3).   Players form a circle of six to ten players. One player who is in the center is *It*. He tosses the ball into the air and calls a player's name. This player must catch the ball before it bounces more than once. If the player succeeds, he becomes the new *It*. If not, the one in the center remains until a player successfully catches the ball.

Hop Tag (Grades K–3).   Eight to ten players spread around the playing area. One player who is *It* hops around trying to tag another player who is also hopping. When another player is tagged, he becomes the new *It*.

Three Deep (Grades K–3).   Two circles of from ten to twenty players are formed, with one circle inside the other. Each child in the inside circle stands directly in front of a child in the outside circle. One child is chosen to chase another around the outside of the circles. The one being chased may step in front of a child on the inside circle to avoid being tagged. The outside player of this group then becomes the one being chased. If the runner is tagged, he turns and chases the tagger.

Simon Says (Grades K–4).   The leader performs simple activities, such as putting his hands on his shoulders, which the children imitate if the leader prefaces the activity with the words "Simon says do this." However, if the leader says only the words "Do this," the children must not execute the movement.

Drop the Handkerchief (Grades 1–2).   Eight to ten players form a circle. One player who is *It* has a handkerchief and walks around the outside of the circle. He drops the handkerchief behind a player in the circle, who picks it up and chases *It* around to the right and back to the open space. If *It* reaches the space safely, the one chasing him is the new *It*. If tagged, *It* walks around and repeats the same procedure.

Red Light (Grades 1–3).   Eight to twenty players form a line standing side by side. One player who is *It* stands about 20 yards in front of the line. *It* turns his back and rapidly counts to ten, during which the line of players runs forward to try to tag him. Upon reaching ten, *It* calls "Red Light" and all players must stop running before he turns around. If he sees anyone moving, he sends him back to the starting line. The first player to tag *It* becomes the new *It*.

Post Ball (Grades 1–4).   Two or more teams participate. They form parallel lines with each player about three feet behind the other. A leader stands facing each line 12 feet away. On signal, the leader tosses a ball to the first player in line, who catches it, throws the ball back, and squats in line. The leader repeats the same procedure with each one in the line. The team finishing first and dropping the ball the least number of times wins.

Driving Pig to Market (Grades 2–3).   Players form even-numbered lines. The first person in each line is given a wand, and a ball is placed at his feet. On signal, he pushes the ball by sliding the wand back and forth. He must go around a stool 20 feet away and return to the starting line. Here he gives the equipment to the second one in line, who repeats same action.

Stork Stand (Grades 2–4).   Child places hands on hips, raises one foot and places it against the inside of the opposite knee. To eliminate the role of the eye in achieving balance, the participant may close his eyes while he attempts to maintain balance.

Measuring Worm (Grades 2–4).   Child bends over and places his hands on the floor and extends his legs to take a front leaning position. With the hands in place, he walks up to his hands. Keeping the feet in place, he walks on the hands away from the feet. The elbows and knees remain straight as he repeats these actions several times.

Fire on the Mountain (Grades 2–4).   Players form two circles with one circle, called the *Trees*, standing inside the other circle, called *Children*. In the center is one player who is *It*. He begins clapping his hands as he calls. "Fire on the Mountain.

Run, *Children*, run!" The *Trees* remain standing while the *Children* run to the right behind the *Trees*. When *It* stops clapping, he and the *Children* run to stand in front of a *Tree*. The one who does not find a *Tree* is the new *It*. In the next game, the *Trees* and *Children* change roles.

Chain Tag (Grades 2–4).   One player is *It*. He tags another player, and the two join hands and run to tag other players. Each player who is tagged joins the chain at the end. Hands must remain joined and only the first and last players in the chain are allowed to tag.

Circle Weave Relay (Grades 2–4).   Players form circles, six to eight players to a circle. One player from each circle starts the relay by running to the outside of the player to his right, to the inside of the next, and continues weaving in this pattern around the circle to the starting position. He tags the next player to his right, who similarly runs to his right around the circle. The relay continues until everyone in the circle has had a turn. The first circle to complete the relay is the winner.

Cross Tag (Grades 3–4).   Eight to ten players scatter around the playing area. One player who is *It* runs and tries to tag another player. If another player crosses between the chased player and *It, It* must change and chase the crossing player.

Wall Ball (Grades 3–4).   Players divide into groups of four to six players. Groups form lines about four feet apart facing a wall. Distances are marked off every foot, beginning at three feet from the wall and ending at eight. Starting at the three-foot mark, the first player in each line makes three throws and catches of the ball off the wall. Upon successful completion of the three catches, he may move back to the next mark. At any time that he misses he must go to the end of the line, and the next player in line takes his turn, beginning at the three-foot mark. Each player in the line does likewise. When the first player has his turn again, he begins at the mark where he previously missed. When he successfully completes the catches at each mark, he is through. The team with all of its players completing their catches first is the winner.

Bull in the Ring (Grades 3–5).   Ten to twelve players form a circle with hands joined. One player, the *Bull*, is inside this circle. The *Bull* tries to break through the circle or slip under the hands. If he gets out, all players chase him. The player who did the tagging becomes the new *Bull*. The *Bull* is allowed three tries to break through. If he fails, he chooses a new *Bull*.

Beat Ball (Grades 4–5).   Five to ten players are on each of two teams. Bowling pins used as bases are set up in a softball or kickball formation. One team is at "bat," the other in the field. The pitcher rolls a soccer ball to the batter, who kicks it and runs to first, second, third, and home. The fielding team catches the ball and throws it to the first baseman, who knocks over the pin, throws the ball to the second baseman, who knocks over the pin, and so on. If the batter gets home before all the pins are knocked down, he scores one run—otherwise, he's out.

Outs: ball at home plate before runner; fly ball caught; batter misses kick and ball knocks over pin at home; runner knocks over any pin while running bases; or kicked ball knocks over any pin not touched by fielder first.

Runs: ball not thrown in correct order of bases; or baseman fails to knock over pin with ball before throwing to next base.

Bat Ball (Grades 4–5).   Players divide into two teams, one at bat and one in the field. A volleyball or soccer ball is used. The first player at bat hits the pitched ball into the field and runs to a base and home. If the player makes the complete trip without the fielder catching the fly or hitting him below the waist with the ball, one run is scored. Three outs and teams change. The team with the most runs wins.

Circle Kick Ball (Grades 4–5).   The players form two teams. One team stands in one half of a 25-foot circle, the other team in the remaining half. The leader rolls a ball to one team, which kicks the ball toward the opposite team, which kicks it back. One point is scored for each ball kicked out of the circle past the opponents at waist height or below. A ball kicked out above the waist scores for the opposite team. The team having the highest number of points at the end of the playing time wins.

Line Soccer (Grades 4–5). Two even-numbered teams form lines facing each other. Players stand side by side in each line. Teams count off from diagonal ends so that number one of one line faces the last number in the opposite line. A leader places the ball between the lines and calls out a number. The two players with that number rush into the center and attempt to kick the ball through the opposite line. Players in line may stop the ball from going through. A ball kicked through the line scores a point.

Leap Frog (Grades 4–6). Players take squat positions four to five feet apart in a line. One player runs toward the end of the line and leaps over each player in succession by placing his hands, fingers forward, on the player's shoulders and pushing off as he jumps. When he reaches the front of the line, he squats down. The last person in the line rises and follows the same procedure until everyone has had an opportunity to leap the entire line.

Hot Potatoes (Grades 4–6). Players form a circle with six to twenty players in each circle. Players all sit crosslegged and roll or punch balls across the circle. Three or four balls are kept going at once. Players try to knock the ball past other players through the circle. The player permitting the least number of balls to go through the circle wins. An extra player retrieves all the balls going out of the circle. No ball higher than the shoulders counts. Balls may not be bounced or thrown.

Crows and Cranes (Grades 4–6). Players divide into two groups of eight to twenty players. One group is called *Crows* and the other *Cranes*. The playing area is divided with a line in the center and a goal line at each end of the area. *Crows* and *Cranes* stand facing each other at the center. The leader calls "Crows" or "Cranes." The group called runs to the goal line behind it with the other group chasing. Players tagged go to the other group. *Crows* and *Cranes* return to the center line. The leader gives the call again. The group with the larger number of players at the end of the playing time wins.

Steal the Bacon (Grades 4–8). Players divide into two teams with the players standing side by side behind goal lines that are ten feet apart. Teams number off beginning at diagonal ends. A ball or bowling pin, called the *Bacon*, is placed on the floor midway between the lines. The leader calls any number. Both players having this number run in and attempt to steal the ball and return to own goal line before being tagged by the other player. One point is scored for each safe return. When opposing players reach the *Bacon* at the same time, they should wait for an opportune moment to steal the ball. The team scoring ten points first wins.

Frog Tip-up (Grades 4–8). Child takes a squat position with the knees apart and arms between the knees. The hands are placed on the floor with the fingers extended toward the sides and about shoulder distance apart. The knees are braced against the elbows. The child leans forward with his weight on the arms and lifts his feet off the floor. He holds this position until balance is achieved.

Seal Walk (Grades 4–8). Child puts his weight on his hands on the floor and extends legs backward. He walks forward on his hands, dragging his legs behind.

Rocker (Grades 4–8). Children lie on their stomachs and arch their backs to grasp the raised legs at the ankles with their hands. In this position, they rock forward and backward.

Walking Chairs (Grades 4–8). Children form a line standing behind each other with their hands on the waist of the one in front. All bend knees to sit on the knees of the one behind. Last person must balance himself in the sitting position. Beginning with the left foot, the line walks forward in rhythm.

Squat Thrust (Grades 4–8).   From a standing position, the participant squats and places his hands on the floor. Body weight is momentarily taken on the hands as the feet are thrown back and the participant assumes a front leaning position. He then returns to a squat position and stands.

Snail (Grades 4–8).   Children lie on their backs and raise the legs to touch the floor back of their heads with their toes. The arms are raised and the elbows bent to place the hands palms down near the shoulders.

Rocker (Dual) (Grades 4–8).   Partners take sitting positions and sit on each other's feet. One partner must bring his legs to the outside of the other's to do this. The knees must be kept bent. The partners place their hands on each other's shoulders. To create the rocking motion they alternate pulling forward on the partner's shoulders and lifting him off the floor with the feet.

Turk Stand (Grades 4–8).   Children cross feet and fold arms while standing. Keeping the arms and legs crossed, they sit. To raise themselves to the standing position, they lean forward, place weight over their feet, and lift.

Crab Walk (Grades 4–8).   Child takes a squat position. He reaches back and places his hands flat on the floor without sitting. Distributing his weight equally on all fours, he walks forward in this position.

Chinese Stand-up (Grades 4–8).   Partners stand back to back and lock elbows with each other. They push against each other's back and with small steps walk forward and sit on the floor. To stand up, the partners keep arms locked and bend the knees with the feet close to the body. They brace their feet, push against each other's back, extend legs, and come to a standing position.

Indian Wrestle (Grades 4–8).   Partners stand facing opposite directions beside each other. The outsides of the right feet are placed together. Right hands are joined. The two players push and pull until one partner's right foot is lifted from position. The one whose right foot remains in position wins.

Line Dodge Ball (Grades 4–8).   Players standing side by side form two lines 20 feet apart with a four-foot square drawn in the middle. One person stands in this box, and the other players take turns trying to hit him below the waist with the ball. The player may dodge the ball but must keep one foot in the box. When hit, the player changes places with the one who hit him.

Hand Wrestle (Grades 4–8).   Partners lie on their stomachs on the floor facing each other with their right hands grasped and right elbows together. They push on each other's hand, attempting to force the opponent's hand to the floor. The one forcing the other's hand down wins.

Grapevine (Grades 4–8).   Child bends over and places hands from front to back through the legs. The hands are wound around the legs so that the fingers of both hands touch in front of the ankles.

Wheelbarrow (Grades 4–8).   Partners stand one behind the other facing the same way. The one in front places his hands on floor while the one behind lifts his legs at the ankles. The first child walks forward on his hands with his partner holding his legs in wheelbarrow fashion.

Tug Pick-up (Grades 4–8).   Two people hold a six-foot rope at opposite ends. A block is placed six inches behind each person. On a signal, each player tries to pick up the block behind him. Releasing the rope or permitting the other player to reach the block gives one point to the winner. One match consists of three points.

Indian Leg Wrestle (Grades 4–8).   Partners lie side by side on their backs facing opposite directions. The right arms are locked together. On signal, the partners raise right legs and lock knees. They attempt to throw each other over by pushing, pulling, and so forth. Two out of three victories constitute a match.

Dodge Ball (Grades 5–8).   Players form teams. One team forms a circle; the other team stands inside the circle. The players outside try to hit the players inside below the waist with the ball. Inside players may dodge the ball. Players who are hit join the circle. When all players inside have been hit by the ball, teams change places.

Parachute Play (Grades 5–8).   To start parachute play, the chute is spread out on the floor and the students take positions around it, equidistant from each other. Twenty to 40 students can participate when a regulation size parachute is used. The students kneel on one knee and grasp the chute by its edge with both hands in any one of three ways: palms up, palms down, or one palm up and one palm down. The palms-down grasp is generally the most effective. Some parachutes have handles which make holding the chute easier for the children.

In lifting the chute into the air, height is achieved by everyone simultaneously raising the chute to the maximum of his reach. As the parachute fills with air, it rises to form a canopy above the children. A small aperture in the center of the chute permits enough air to escape in order to stabilize the parachute as it slowly descends.

Various actions are possible during the rise and descent of the parachute. Students may move to the right or to the left or in alternate directions. Their movement may be at various tempos: walking, running, galloping, skipping. Musical accompaniment may be used, if desired. Another possibility involves the use of a light ball. The chute is raised with the ball resting on top. The class attempts to bounce the ball or otherwise maneuver it about on the parachute.

There are also interesting possibilities for creative play. The parachute can be

Figure 20–2.   The creative possibilities of parachute play are not limited by restrictions on mobility.

held at waist height, and different patterns of waves and billows can be created by each child shaking the chute in independent action. Unusual patterns can be created also by small groups working together to achieve a specific motion. To facilitate this activity, the children can be separated into groups of three or four to plan the movement they will contribute to the total pattern.

ADAPTATIONS

The basic skill games can be readily modified for one youngster in the group or for an entire group. Generally, the games may be modified in one or more of the following ways:
1. Substituting walking for skipping and running.
2. Replacing throwing with underhand tossing.
3. Sitting or lying in place of standing.
4. Decreasing distances.
5. Slowing the tempo.
6. Providing more rest periods.
7. Simplifying the patterns of movement.
8. Supplying oral and kinesthetic cues to the players.

Which of these suggested adaptations is used depends, of course, upon the conditions of the children involved. In cases of limited use of the arms and legs, the adaptation may have to be made in the type of movement required by the game or in the amount of movement required. For children who lack endurance or who must not exert themselves, the games will probably need to be adapted to provide more frequent rest periods and to decrease the work involved in playing the game by slowing the tempo, reducing the distances, and so forth. Games involving complex patterns of movement may need to be simplified for mentally retarded youngsters. For these youngsters and for those who are blind and deaf, kinesthetic cues are very helpful; modifying the game to permit those who cannot perform the skills to be led through the movements kinesthetically often spells the difference between success and failure in teaching games to these youngsters.

SELECTED READINGS

Baley, James A.: *Gymnastics in the Schools*. Boston, Allyn and Bacon, 1974.
Fait, Hollis F.: *Physical Education for the Elementary School Child: Experiences in Movement,* ed. 3. Philadelphia, W. B. Saunders Co., 1976.
International Council on Health, Physical Education and Recreation: ICHPER *Book of Worldwide Games and Dances.* Washington, D.C., American Association for Health, Physical Education, and Recreation, 1967.
Kirchner, Glenn: *Physical Education for Elementary School Children,* ed. 3. Dubuque, Iowa, Wm. C. Brown Co., Publishers, 1974.
Vannier, Maryhelen, *et al.: Teaching Physical Education in the Elementary Schools,* ed. 5. Philadelphia, W. B. Saunders Co., 1973.

Chapter 21

Rhythms and Dance

Rhythm permeates the universe, and all children are capable of responding to rhythmic activity provided the stimulation exists. Basic rhythm yields simple movement patterns. Dance itself is an accumulation of various forms of movement and may be thought of as a formal composition or as a vehicle of emotional expression. Dance contains elements that can satisfy the individual's need for recognition, satisfaction, and creativity and can provide opportunities to develop a sense of belonging and of adequacy.

Rhythms and dance play an essential role in the physical education program for the handicapped child. Many such children have a basic need to develop freedom of self-expression, skill in social interaction, and fundamental movement patterns. Dance provides a medium through which these may be realized.

It is frequently observed that the handicapped child must adjust not only to problems which he has in common with other students but also to individual difficulties that stem more directly from his own disability. The teacher must continually keep in mind that these youngsters are, first, children in the dance class and, secondly, persons who are handicapped. Given the opportunity, each will benefit as well as contribute to the school dance program.

EQUIPMENT

Elaborate equipment is not necessary to provide dance activities for the handicapped child; the materials available for regular dance instruction are more than adequate. Musical accompaniment is essential. If a well-tuned piano is not at the disposal of the dance instructor, a three-speed record player is an excellent substitute.

Specially prepared records ranging from pieces with simple and definite rhythms to intricate folk and square dance melodies are available through special firms. Marking each record alphabetically and keeping a small index-card file of the records eliminates needless disorganization.

To obtain satisfying results in various dance activities, the use of individual pieces of equipment is strongly recommended. The drum, in particular, accentuates basic accents in rhythmic patterns and is a valuable dance instrument for the student who is hard of hearing. Rhythm is recognizable in terms of what it does, and its real significance on an elementary level can only be grasped by actually experiencing it. Maracas, tambourines, rhythm sticks, triangles, and homemade musical instruments are helpful. The mentally retarded child responds to the "feel" of the muscle sensations and activity aroused within his body through the use of this equipment. Movements are often awkward efforts at first, but, after timing and values of intensity are understood, efficient and more skilled movement results.

The physically handicapped child, when not involved in group-oriented activity, finds great pleasure in rhythmic muscle exercises at the dance bar. Mirrors help in stimulating self-awareness in emotionally disturbed children as well as aiding the growth of poise and unison of dance movement in other handicapped children. Heavy equipment such as the piano should be located where it will not have to be moved often; smaller instruments and dance materials should be put away after use. This allows the blind or partially sighted student full freedom of the dance area.

Equipment that provides additional expression and interpretation movement plays a vital role in rhythmic activity for the exceptional child. However, it will not take the place of the structuring and dynamic role of the dance instructor. The teacher must use these materials as tools toward a better understanding of rhythm and basic movement.

ORGANIZING THE INSTRUCTION

The development and application of teaching techniques in dance for the handicapped are much the same as in teaching children of normal capacity, because the learning process is basically the same for all individuals. However, in teaching the handicapped, the rate at which they learn and the extent to which they must adapt are more important considerations than they are with normal children.

Specific disabilities have been discussed in previous chapters. An understanding of the capabilities and limitations of each handicapped child is most valuable when considering various teaching techniques. The instructor cannot safely assume that dance fundamentals will have been previously acquired. The type and extent of the disability provide an individual guide to instruction.

Mentally Retarded Children. In many instances, educable mentally retarded children may be included in the regular dance class; they are much more like their chronological age peers than they are different from them. Naturally, particular attention must be given to appropriate placement. Motor ability and chronological age are excellent criteria.

The trainable mentally retarded child should receive his basic instruction within the special class. Progress will be slow, and stress should be placed on fundamental skills rather than complex activity. After the trainable child has successfully developed skills in following directions and rhythmic movement, he, too, should be allowed to participate in a regular dance class.

A short attention span is a known characteristic of the retarded. Dance periods, therefore, should be short and repetitive to allow for reinforcement. Techniques in teaching should be widely diversified, using, among others, mirror image, kinesthesis, and specific learning cues. Finally, little time should be given to verbal explanations of dance techniques, as these are too abstract.

Emotionally Disturbed Children. Emotionally disturbed children often have good mental ability but are unable to integrate their intellectual efforts and direct them toward realistic goals. Erratic behavior, insecurity, hostility, and withdrawal are characteristic. Rigidity of thought and insecurity of self-expression severely constrict the emotional growth of many of these children. Dance may prove most helpful in developing appropriate social adjustment.

Under the supervision of trained personnel, the dance instructor should focus the program on stimulating interaction with the environment. The disturbed child may find satisfactory emotional experiences through the medium of the dance. By identifying with objects, the child finds gratification in rhythmic movement. Later, the learning process will involve interaction with an authority figure, such as the dance instructor. Dance is then introduced in formal step sequences. Once the disturbed child has successfully mastered organized dance patterns, inclusion in the regular dance class may be considered, but it is important that care be taken to minimize frustration during this initial period.

Blind and Partially Sighted Children. Today many blind and partially sighted youngsters are attending regular public school classes. Their acute auditory skill as well as their ability to follow directions proves extremely helpful in various dance experiences.

Blind children often develop an early awareness of music and rhythmic movement because they must use auditory cues. "Blindisms" or unique mannerisms, which may take the form of rocking, twisting, or waving of the arms or fingers, are characteristic of many young blind children entering elementary school. These habits, not particularly socially acceptable, are often best controlled by calling them to the attention of the child. Interestingly enough, these very characteristics are self-expressive and almost always have a rhythmic pattern. Thus, the next obvious means of control is to convert these forms of expression into acceptable patterns of movement.

Precise verbal instruction and kinesthesis are good teaching techniques. After a basic understanding of position and formation, the blind or partially sighted student can successfully be included as an active and enthusiastic member of many folk and square dance groups.

Deaf and Hard-of-Hearing Children. Many children in the public school program have auditory deficiencies. A prime objective for these children is the utilization of residual hearing. The dance teacher is in an excellent position to provide experiences in gross discrimination through rhythm instruments and dance recordings. The child may be taught to feel vibrations from instruments and to use rhythm to develop inflection and timing in dance quality. Rhythm may be expressed in clapping activities as well as visually in an integrated group dance situation. It may first be necessary for the child who is hard-of-hearing to be conditioned by the beat of a drum or to sit close to the record player and familiarize himself with the basic rhythm being introduced.

With amplification, the hard-of-hearing are able to function in a normal group. Whenever possible, these children should be placed in a regular dance class. The teacher should position herself in such a manner that the hard-of-hearing student can see her face during the learning experience. Group dancing will prove beneficial and enjoyable if the child is appropriately placed near the music and, if necessary, accompanied by a child with normal auditory skills.

Physically Handicapped Children. Many handicaps have been found to be relative to cultural expectations. Through dance activities, the child with a physical disability can successfully fulfill various basic needs that might not be met in other areas of motor activity. Each handicapped student formulates his own response to his disability. The dance instructor may stimulate proper adjustment by providing avenues of self-expression and group interaction.

Basic rhythmic activity acts as a stimulus to control otherwise involuntary movement; however, this stimulus may also release emotional expression in free activity.

The physically handicapped child participating in an integrated dance will undoubtedly benefit more than he would if excused from such activity. Frustration can be minimized by adapting dance activities to meet the needs and capacities of these students. The teacher must use ingenuity to determine the benefits the physically handicapped may gain from dance experiences. Children in wheelchairs enjoy folk

Figure 21–1. Accenting the rhythmic pattern on the drum is helpful to the performance of other students and is a personally satisfying experience for the handicapped drummer. (Courtesy, March of Dimes.)

and square dances and can easily be propelled by other members of the class. Creative exploration utilizing upper trunk and arm movement instills physical poise and reassurance. Children with hand deficiencies can be frustrated unnecessarily when working with rhythm toys. By manipulating instruments with the knees and upper arm, these children can play successfully.

ADAPTING DANCES AND RHYTHMS

With modification, rhythmics and dancing may prove to be an enjoyable experience for the handicapped. The major objective in the adaption of dance for the handicapped is to provide experiences which allow these children to perform on a common ground with their peers. The dance instructor must select those activities that remain within the intellectual comprehension and work tolerance level of the child. The aim of instruction is to enable the child to find pleasurable and rewarding activity rather than master intricate dance techniques. The following items concerning procedure should be considered.

1. Demonstration by teacher or pupil provides the visual picture of rhythmic movement. Demonstration sets the pattern when predetermined steps are to be learned; it illustrates and stimulates the imagination when creative expression is the goal.

2. Explanations should be brief and precise. Motivation may be increased by stating a brief history of the activity. Performance should immediately follow demonstration and explanation.

3. The instructor should analyze performance and vary the method of explanation when necessary.

4. Each child should experience success. All must feel that they are dancing rather than preparing for a later performance.

5. Ample opportunity for individual practice should be provided.

6. Listening, clapping, stamping, and beating to music stimulate an understanding of tempo, accent, and phrasing.

7. For beginners in partner dancing, frequent partner change in mixer-type activities is advisable.

8. Integrating the dance program with academic and extracurricular opportunities enriches the school experience of the child.

Special methods of instruction are made necessary by the limitations imposed by specific handicaps. As pointed out in Chapter 6, verbal and visual cues and kinesthesis are vital teaching techniques in any adapted program.

Brief and precise verbal explanations are beneficial to all handicapped individuals and are essential for the blind or partially sighted.

Demonstrations and "do-as-I-do" activities are invaluable when working with the mentally retarded, and the child who is deaf or hard of hearing must also be given opportunities to watch the skill being performed.

By leading a student's arm or part of the body involved in the activity through the movement, wide avenues of understanding are opened to the handicapped child. Directing the student in this manner permits skills to be mastered and difficulties to be overcome in a pleasant and nonthreatening atmosphere. Only when the child associates the desired result with the appropriate form will be begin to "feel right" about his performance.

Rhythmic Activity. Rhythms are the basic skills of the dance. They should be an essential part of the elementary school program and occur repeatedly throughout subsequent dance activity.

With fundamental rhythms to an accompaniment, children walk, run, jump, hop, skip, and leap.

In informal rhythmic "do-as-I-do-and-say" games, children experiment with space, focus, direction of movement, levels, varying tempo, different qualities of movement.

With interpretive rhythms, children can express themselves as animals, sounds, paintings, fairy tale and story book characters.

Adapted teaching hints: Activities may be stimulated by listening to the basic beat and clapping to the rhythm. The handicapped child learns best by doing, and each student must make an effort to perform the movement within his capacity. A high degree of motivation produced and maintained by the teacher is essential. If the child is confined to a wheelchair, he can clap the basic rhythm with the class while being pushed in his chair during locomotor activity. The child with impaired hearing must use visual cues and experience the vibration of the instruments. The blind child may find great joy in marking the rhythmic beat through sound and touch.

Most children, normal or handicapped, particularly enjoy creative activity and spend much of their leisure time in imaginative play. The mentally retarded child is sometimes the exception. For him, various stimuli such as musical instruments and other toys that are easily manipulated reinforce his concentration and lead to self-expressive motor activity.

Traditional Dance Steps. Traditional dance steps have their foundation in fundamental rhythms. Folk dancing and much social dancing involve one or more traditional dance steps.

Step Point. The step point is a step on the left foot, pointing the right foot in front. This action is repeated, stepping on the right foot.

count 1	count 2	count 3	count 4
step left	point right	step right	point left

Adapted teaching hints: Floor markings prove beneficial. Teach the step first in a stationary position without music. Do the step in a circle formation later, alone, or with partners.

Step Hop. The step hop is a step on the left foot and a hop on the same foot. This action is repeated, using the right foot.

count 1	count 2	count 3	count 4
step left	hop left	step right	hop right

Adapted teaching hints: Practice entirely with one foot at first, and later alternate feet. Students in wheelchairs can enjoy the activity by moving arms on counts one and three and clapping on counts two and four.

Step Swing. The step swing is a step on the left foot followed by a swing of the right foot across in front of the left. This action is repeated, stepping on the right foot.

count 1	count 2	count 3	count 4
step left	swing right	step right	swing left

Adapted teaching hints: This step is an excellent follow-the-leader activity. The use of the dance bar as well as manual kinesthesis should be considered when introducing the "swing" technique to the blind.

Balance Step. The balance step can be done in any direction. The dancer steps left and closes right foot to left, rising on the balls of both feet.

count 1	count 2	count 3
step left	close right	rise on toes, lower

count 1	count 2	count 3
step right	close left	rise on toes, lower

Adapted teaching hint: Some handicapped children will have considerable difficulty coordinating this movement. The teacher should suggest that they gaze at a distant object at eye level to attain balance initially.

Polka. The simple polka is a step on the right, close left to right, step on right, hold. The action is repeated, using the opposite foot.

count 1	and	count 2	and
	heel		toe

count 1	and	count 2	and
step	close	step	hold

Adapted teaching hints: After listening to the music and viewing the demonstration, all children should verbally recite the action words, "heel and toe," and so forth. The steps should be practiced informally in front of the mirror to a familiar recording. The teacher can then give individual attention to each student by taking him in hand and walking through the dance pattern.

Waltz. The waltz step is a step forward left, step sideward right, and close left to right; then a step backward right, step sideward left, and close right to left.

count 1	count 2	count 3
step left (forward)	side right	close left

count 1	count 2	count 3
step right (backward)	side left	close right

Adapted teaching hints: The step should be first introduced in a line formation. Marking individual "boxes" on the floor with tape gives the students an outline to follow for a better understanding of the waltz pattern. Blind students may pass their hands over the markings on the floor to gain tactual cues.

Two-Step.   The two-step is a step forward on the left, close right to left, step left and hold. The action is repeated, beginning right.

count 1	count 2	count 3
step left	close right	step left

count 1	count 2	count 3
step right	close left	step right

Adapted teaching hints: The two-step is the foundation of social dancing and can be introduced in partner formation. The tempo should start out slowly and increase as proficiency is acquired. Practice in parallel lines, placing those having difficulty in the back line, where they can watch the successful performers in the front line, helps to promote a better understanding of the step sequence.

Folk Dances.   Folk dancing has a fascinating history that belongs to the handicapped as well as the normal child. Many of the dances done today originally stemmed from various rites that celebrated important events in men's lives — the planting of crops, weddings, and even religious sacrifices. Our heritage is rich in its variety of movement qualities, styles, and patterns. Yet with all these differences, there is a lasting universality in the social satisfaction that people derive when they move together in rhythmic harmony.

Folk and square dancing afford excellent opportunities for the handicapped to learn desirable social skills and attitudes. Much of the vigorous activity provided in this type of social dancing may be modified for the handicapped student without losing its authenticity or original sequence.

A firm understanding of basic formation and specific skills involved in various patterns are foundations for enjoyable dance experiences. Repetition and enthusiasm are tools for success. The hard-of-hearing child will learn by listening to the accompaniment and by seeing the formation in movement. The blind student may be placed with a seeing partner. With a group of partially sighted students, in dances calling for "crossing over," arch formations, or grand right and left, steps can be worked out going forward and backward instead.

The following dances are but a few examples that are easily adaptable.

The Muffin Man (English). This is an old English singing game that children enjoy greatly.

Adapted teaching hint: Walking may be substituted for skipping around the circle. Those in wheelchairs may be pushed by others or propel themselves.

Troika (Russian). Troika means three horses. The dance symbolizes the three horses which traditionally drew sleighs for noble Russian families.

Adapted teaching hints: This dance makes use of fundamental rhythms. In a formation of three, a student with a disabled arm can choose the side on which he wishes to dance. The emotionally disturbed child may find security in the middle position of the formation.

Chimes of Dunkirk (French). Here is a folk dance that delights young children. It was brought to this country by the French masters many years ago.

Adapted teaching hints: This simple activity is an enjoyable experience for the mentally retarded child. If the group is small, each handicapped student should be given the opportunity to dance with the teacher. This may stimulate the slow repetitive learning process.

Square Dances.   Folk, in the literal sense, means people. Folk dancing, therefore, is the "dance of the people." With the steady influx of people from many lands to the United States, there slowly emerged an array of international dance figures. The basic formation was the "drill of four" or the quadrille, thus leading to the name *square dance*. The following square dances are examples of easily adapted activity:

Head Two Ladies Cross Over. The four ladies are active in this exchange partner dance. A child in a wheelchair could easily be the stationary partner.

Duck for the Oyster. Duck for the Oyster is one of the oldest and most popular square dances in this country. While the square performs allemande left, grand right and left, the handicapped child with limited locomotion can circle or stamp in the center.

Virginia Reel. This contradance is an old favorite. Extensive right- and left-hand instruction may be necessary for the mentally retarded. When blind or partially sighted children are participating, clapping should be restricted to the child in the contraline who is waiting to be swung. This will enable the visually handicapped child to find more easily the one he is to swing.

Adapted teaching hints for square dances: Because of the frequent partner changes, square dancing provides unique opportunities in the school program for developing an appreciation and respect for others. It is an activity the handicapped can participate in throughout their adult years.

When a child who is hard of hearing is included, dancers should refrain from loud clapping when the dance is in progress, so that he may better follow instruction and tempo.

The walk-through method of teaching is the most profitable. Frequent repetition and an exaggeration of directional cues are necessary. Allow the children to listen to the music at first; then demonstrate, using one couple or square; complete the entire pattern with music. The blind are more successful when taught in musical phrases rather than in count. The mentally retarded achieve success when the continuity of the dance has been preserved.

The following substitutions are suggested as ways in which the regular movements of the square dance may be modified for those who must use crutches:

Honor your partner. Bow heads.

Swing your partner. Hold out one hand while balanced on crutches to partner
    who dances around. If both are on crutches, touch bottom parts of one
    crutch of each partner, forming a pivot which both partners go around.

Allemande left. Walk around to the left.

Right and left grande. Walk around first to the left and then to the right.

Promenade. Noncrippled partner places hand on partner's shoulder. If both are
    on crutches, they move their crutches in unison as they walk.

Do-si-do. Noncrippled partner may do most of the movement if it is difficult for
    the other partner to perform. If both are on crutches and movement is dif-
    ficult, the swing may be substituted.

Balance. One crutch is placed forward. If the handicapped partner has sufficient strength and skill to raise himself and balance on the crutches, as some do, this movement may be substituted for the balance.

Social Dance.   Social dance is an activity that can be engaged in with pleasure throughout life. It is a popular recreational activity among normal as well as handicapped teenagers. The courtesies and standards of social dancing can best be taught under wholesome supervision in school. Mastering these social graces will provide the handicapped student with the poise that is so important to adjustment. Self-confidence is also encouraged by the use of familiar, currently popular songs with a definite rhythm.

Modern Dance.   This type of dance derives its name from its effort to portray through movement significant ideas of current life. Modern dance represents ideas or emotions rather than some standard and traditional dance form. It is a medium of dynamic movement that releases anxieties and frustrations in a socially acceptable fashion. Modern dance is founded on techniques that develop maximum muscular strength, joint flexibility, and body coordination.

The handicapped child has a pervasive need for self-expression and harmonious utilization of the entire body that modern dance offers. The blind child dances to abstract impressions and learns to express himself through movement of his arms and hands as well as his entire body. The child with cerebral palsy can release frustrations by freely enaging in gross rhythmic movement and can actually benefit from concentrated movement, which leads to greater control of disabled limbs. The deaf or hard of hearing child seeks continuity in muscular activity. The emotionally disturbed student finds self-expressive movement a relaxing adventure. Creativity and self-awareness are developed in the mentally retarded child with the use of modern dance activities.

The program may be structured or nonstructured; the teacher must have a purpose for all activities. Scarves, pieces of rope, costumes, chairs, or other accessible materials can stimulate activity. Musical accompaniment should clearly represent various tempos or moods; many popular recordings can accomplish this goal. Narrative stories and recent happenings also provide interesting stimuli for movement.

Children should be introduced to interpretive dance first as a group and later in couples or alone. Stress should be placed on the concept that all parts of the body act as a unit and not as separate entities.

Dance Therapy

As noted in the foregoing discussion, dance activities help handicapped participants to achieve poise and confidence, to relate to others in a group, and to give expression to latent feelings. Such therapeutic benefits, while extremely important, are not the specific goal of the dance program in physical education. The utilization of dance for the promotion of mental health is the focus of the separate profession of dance therapy.

Dance therapists are primarily concerned with establishing a relationship with those in the program that permits therapeutic intervention to improve mental health. The medium for this purpose is a wide variety of dance activities adapted in style, content, form, and method of presentation to meet individual needs. Obviously, the teacher of dance to the handicapped and the dance therapist have much in common as regards knowledge of dance, information about handicapping conditions, and utilization of special teaching techniques. The important difference between the two is one of purpose: the teacher utilizes dance as a motor activity to enhance total education while the therapist seeks to improve mental health through the teaching of dance.

SELECTED READINGS

AAHPER: *Children's Dance*. Washington, D.C., American Alliance for Health, Physical Education and
    Recreation, 1973.

Fait, Hollis: *Physical Education for the Elementary School Child: Experiences in Movement,* ed. 3.
    Philadelphia, W. B. Saunders Co., 1976.

Lockhart, Aileene, and Pease, Esther: *Modern Dance: Building and Teaching Lessons,* ed. 4. Dubuque,
    Iowa, Wm. C. Brown Co., Publishers, 1973.

Mynatt, Constance V., and Kaiman, Bernard D.: *Folk Dancing for Students .and Teachers,* ed. 2.
    Dubuque, Iowa, Wm. C. Brown Co., Publishers, 1975.

Robins, Ferris and Jennet: *Educational Rhythmics for Mentally Handicapped Children.* Rapperswilz, Swit-
    zerland, Ra-Verlag, 1963.

Winters, Shirley S.: *Creative Rhythmic Movement for Children of Elementary School Age.* Dubuque,
    Iowa, Wm. C. Brown Co., Publishers, 1975.

Chapter 22

Individual Lifetime Sports

Lifetime sports is a term used to designate those sports that can generally be played for enjoyment and exercise throughout life. When these are sports in which a person may participate alone or against opponents, they are usually referred to as individual sports. Among the most widely played individual lifetime sports are archery, bowling, and golf. Participation in certain track events is also enjoyed by many long into their adult years.

Because these activities are designed for individual participation, they can be readily adapted to individual restrictions and capacities. For this reason alone, they are excellent choices for the special physical education curriculum. However, there are other important reasons for including them in the program for the handicapped. One of the most obvious of these reasons is their contribution to the physical fitness of the participants. While individual sports are not considered to be vigorous, they do place sufficient demands upon the body to encourage desirable development for handicapped players in such fitness factors as strength, flexibility, and cardiorespiratory endurance. Then, too, individual sports have high carry-over value. Because they require less organization than most other active games, they are among our most popular leisure activities. Consequently, participation in these sports virtually ensures the handicapped opportunities for good fellowship with nonhandicapped players who enjoy these sports as recreation.

ORGANIZING THE INSTRUCTION

Instruction in the individual sports requires considerable planning and organization on the part of the teacher. Because these are individual activities, each student requires considerable individual instruction, and the planning of class time must provide for this. Moreover, equipment is required by each participant, and there may not be sufficient equipment for all members of the class to practice simultaneously.

Fortunately, in most school situations the handicapped can be accommodated in the regular physical education classes. The nature of the activities is such that each participant can move at his own pace. Students who are extremely skilled and have mastered the techniques may be used by the teacher to assist in the instruction of the handicapped. If the class must be paired because of lack of equipment, it is wise to have a more skilled student with a less skilled one in the early practice sessions. Later it will prove more stimulating to the participants if they are evenly matched.

Nearly all handicapped students will require considerable experimentation to determine the best method of performing the skills of the various individual sports. It is important to help the handicapped learner to analyze the mechanics of each skill in the activity. Toward this end, audiovisual aids, and textbooks which describe the performance of the skills in detail are extremely useful, for, although in many instances the descriptions are not directly applicable, they do help the students to gain insight into the mechanics of performing the skills and thereby make possible a better understanding of how an adaptation may be made successfully.

Few schools will have their own golf courses and bowling alleys. Many aspects of these games can be taught, however, without actual use of these facilities. By utilizing plastic golf balls, golf cages, and indoor and outdoor putting areas, most of the skills of golf can be introduced to the students. Bowling skills can be taught very successfully with sets of polyethylene bowling balls and pins. If necessary, empty milk cartons and a soccer ball can be used satisfactorily as substitutes for pins and ball in teaching the fundamental skills of bowling. It is, of course, desirable to give students opportunities to play in actual game situations if at all possible. Frequently, arrangements can be made with commercial bowling alleys and golf courses to use their facilities at certain slack hours for a nominal fee. If such arrangements are to be made, they should be worked out well in advance of the teaching period in these sports and should, of course, have administrative approval.

In presenting adaptations that can be made for the handicapped in the sports discussed in this chapter, very brief descriptions of the specific skills are given to enable the reader to make a better comparison of the adaptation with normal performance and so gain a better understanding of the process of adapting skills for the handicapped. It is not the intent to provide instruction for learning to perform the skills. Those who wish this information are referred to the books in Selected Readings at the end of the chapter.

ARCHERY

Of the several forms of archery activity, shooting arrows at an upright target is the most easily adapted for most handicaps. Archery does not require vigorous movement, nor is it excessively fatiguing; consequently, it is very suitable for those who cannot participate in strenuous activities and for those with lower limb disabilities. It is also a good sport for the blind who are able to participate with slight changes in the procedure of sighting and with help in locating arrows that miss the target.

General Adaptations: For wheelchair archers and those on crutches the target should be located where there is no rise behind it to stop the arrows, because these students will have too much difficulty retrieving arrows from an elevated area.

To assist blind students in moving from the shooting area to the target, a wire may be strung from one area to the other. At the shooting area, a stick eight to 12 inches long should be placed on the ground, pointing in the direction of the target, to orient the blind archer. To help him determine the correct amount of pull on the bow, two poles are placed in the ground and aligned with the target; one pole indicates the place at which the hand of the extended arm should be, and the other the place where the back of the wrist of the hand drawing the string should be.

Stance, Nocking, and Drawing the Bow. In taking the stance, the feet are comfortably spread, with the left side of the body facing the target if the archer is right-handed. The head is turned towards the target. The bow is grasped in the left hand at the handle. It is held parallel to the ground and the target with the string toward the body and the back of the hand up. The arrow is picked up at the nock between the forefinger and thumb and placed across the bow at the arrow plate at right angles to the string. The cock feather is up. The thumb and forefinger encircle the string and hold the end of the arrow and place the nock over the bowstring.

To assume the position for shooting, the fingers of the right hand are placed under the bowstring to grasp the string with the tips of first three fingers. The arrow is held between the first and second fingers. The bow is raised with the left arm and extended toward the target.

The elbow is straight but not locked. The other arm, with fingers bent to hold the string, is raised so the arm is bent at the elbow and is parallel to the ground. The bowstring is pulled back with the right arm so that the arm, wrist, and arrow make a straight line toward the target. The bowstring is pulled back against the chin. The hand is anchored under the jaw and against the neck with the forefinger up against the chin.

Adaptations: An archer in a wheelchair will turn the chair to the side and reach over the side of the chair to draw the bow.

Those on crutches will need to prop themselves with the crutches so as to free their arms. This can be accomplished by tilting the body toward the target and putting most of the weight on the front crutch. This will hold the crutch in place, and the arm can be used to hold the bow. The other arm will have to squeeze slightly on the rear crutch to hold it in place, but the arm is freed sufficiently to draw the bowstring parallel to the ground. Another method is to maintain equal weight on both crutches and bend the extended arm at the elbow so the front crutch can be cradled in the arm pit. The back crutch is cradled in the armpit by lowering the bowstring arm. Those who have difficulty in balancing may sit in a chair for shooting.

Sighting and Releasing.   For any given bow there is a certain distance from each target at which the center can be hit by sighting over the point of the arrow to the center of the target. If the archer is closer to or farther back from the target, he must aim above or below the target to hit it.

When the bow is sighted correctly, the arrow is released by straightening the fingers quickly. No other movement of the body should occur.

Adaptations: For the blind the two poles, already described as an aid in drawing the bow, may be wound with tape at the places where the hands should be for sighting accurately. The correct location of the tape is determined by trial and error. In shooting, the blind archer knows he is sighting correctly when the backs of his hands touch the taped areas.

For those who have the use of only one arm, the bow may be anchored to a standard of the type used for supporting a volleyball net. The bow is attached in the correct position for the correct range. If the standard is portable rather than permanently fixed, it must have a sufficiently large base to enable the archer to place his foot on it to help hold it securely. Sturdy poles might be substituted for standards. If the one-armed archer is confined to a wheelchair, the bow may be strapped to the chair.

There will be little need for adaptation for those with finger amputations if at least two functional fingers remain. These fingers can then be made to perform the work oridinarily performed by the missing fingers.

The crossbow may be substituted for the standard bow for those with limited movement of the arms. The bow is cocked by the teacher and sighted and shot by the student.

BOWLING

Bowling is an extremely popular game among wheelchair patients who have the use of at least one arm. Like archery, bowling is not a vigorous game and therefore is very appropriate for those for whom strenuous activity is contraindicated. The blind usually are more successful in their efforts at bowling than at archery; they do need someone to tell them which pins are left standing after the first ball and to record their scores.

General Adaptations: In addition to providing equipment for bowling instruction when regular alleys are not available, the polyethylene pins and balls discussed in the introduction are excellent for those students who, because of their handicaps, lack the strength and coordination to use the heavier regulation bowling balls. The grip on the ball is taken at the first joints of the fingers rather than the second joints, which are used in gripping a regulation bowling ball.

A useful piece of equipment for the wheelchair bowler with limited arm movement is a light metal rack which provides a track for the ball to travel down from the lap of the holder to the floor of the alley. The ball is placed on the track and the track is aimed toward the pins. The ball is released, and it rolls down the track and onto the alley to the pins.

Approach and Delivery. The four-step approach is generally preferred. The ball is held chest high with both hands. Then, as the approach begins, the left hand (for a right-handed bowler) is withdrawn and the hand with the ball starts downward and into the backswing. The backward swing should be straight back. As the left hand is withdrawn, the first step in the approach is taken with the right foot. The second step is taken as the ball swings down. As the ball reaches the height of the backswing, the third step is taken. With the final step, the arm swings forward. The last step is a longer stride than the others. After planting the foot, the feet are allowed to slide

Figure 22–1. A, B Devices that assist delivery of the ball by a bowler with involvement of both upper and lower limbs.

forward just back of the foul line. On the last step, the body is crouched over the lead leg to enable the bowler to deliver the ball on the floor smoothly so it will not bounce.

Adaptations: To bowl from a wheelchair when the metal rack need not be used, the bowler must place the chair to face the pins. The body is leaned over the side of the chair to permit the arm to swing freely in delivering the ball. To compensate for the lack of approach in the delivery, a preliminary swing may be taken. The ball swings back, then forward without touching the floor, back again, and in the forward swing the body is leaned farther to the side so that the ball can be released smoothly on the floor.

If the wheelchair is too high for the bowler, a chair without arms may be used. A chair might also be used by bowlers on crutches or others with limited locomotion. An adaptation for those able to stand but unable to make the necessary steps in the approach is to permit them to stand at the foul line to make the delivery.

All bowlers who lack strength in the arm and shoulder should use the lighter polyethylene ball and pins. In using this ball, only the straight ball may be thrown, because the ball is not easily controlled in a spin; otherwise the ball responds similarly to the regulation bowling ball.

Blind bowlers orient themselves by feeling the sides of the alley or using a rail if one is provided. The accuracy of the aim may be determined by the number of pins knocked down, which is told to the bowler by a sighted person.

GOLF

Golf is an excellent activity for most kinds of handicapped individuals. The vigor with which the game is played is easily modified for those whose conditions do not permit strenuous workouts. Anyone with extreme limitations can play an adapted form of the game that consists of hitting balls into a golf net. Golf can also be played with considerable success by those confined to wheelchairs and crutches. Players with only one arm can become proficient enough to compete on nearly equal terms with normal players. Blind golfers are able to play without modification of the game except for the need of help in locating their balls.

It is not necessary to have a full set of clubs in order to play the game. A short set composed of the number 1 and 3 woods and the 3, 5, 7, and 9 irons plus the putter will serve adequately.

General Adaptations: Golf can be played by many handicapped players without modifications if they have sufficient stamina. Since the weather conditions and the hilliness of the course are related to the physical demands of the game, special consideration must be given to these factors if the players are convalescents, have kidney disorders or have cardiac, asthmatic, or anemic conditions.

Some handicapped players, while able to execute the strokes, are unable to do the amount of walking required by the game. The use of motor-powered carts can solve this problem if the cost of their purchase is not prohibitive. When carts cannot be provided for them, these players will need to restrict their playing to putting or shooting plastic golf balls on an available grassed area or shooting into a golf cage.

Grip. The most commonly used grip on the golf club is the overlapping grip. To take this grip, the handle of the club is placed across the fingers of the left hand (for a right-handed player) so that the shaft is angled. It should cross the index finger at the second joint and extend up to the lower part of the palm. The hand is then closed over the handle with the thumb on the top of the shaft. The right hand is placed under the shaft, with the little finger overlapping the first finger of the left hand and the left thumb fitting into the palm of the right hand. The thumb of the right hand is slightly on the left side of the shaft.

Adaptations: Students with hand or arm disabilities may require considerable adaptation of the grip on the golf club. Those with finger amputations or hand deformities may need to do extensive experimentation with gripping the club to find the grip that provides the greatest stability. For example, if the thumb is missing on the left hand of a right-handed player, instead of taking a regular grip where the palm of the right hand covers the left thumb, the right-hand grip may be taken so that the palm will come in firm contact with the base of the thumb. The interlocking grip, in which the little finger of the right hand interlocks with the forefinger of the left hand, will bring the fists closer together to make a better contact with the base of the thumb and palm.

Missing fingers other than the little finger on the right hand and forefinger on the left hand require little, if any, adjustment in the grip for a right-handed player. If the little finger of the right hand or the forefinger of the left hand is missing, the next finger may be used to make contact with the opposite hand. In this case the overlapping grip is likely to give greater stability.

A player whose left arm is missing or incapacitated must use golf clubs designed for use by left-handed players; in the use of a missing or disabled right arm, regular clubs will be used in the left hand.

With a missing hand, the stump is utilized to stabilize the club during the swing by placing it against the shaft of the club or against the arm of the hand that is grasping the club.

Players with one arm of limited function may find that the disabled arm can be used in some manner of grip to stabilize the club in the swing. Experimentation will determine if the disabled arm has a functional use in holding and swinging the club or if it will be necessary to rely entirely on one arm.

Stance, Address, and Swing.   In all strokes, the weight is distributed equally on the feet, which are spread about shoulders' width apart. The body is held partially bent at the hips with the knees flexed. There are three general types of stances used when addressing the ball preparatory to stroking it: the open stance, the closed stance, and the square stance. Each type of stance will affect the flight of the ball. In the square stance, both feet are perpendicular to the line of flight of the ball. In the open stance, the front foot is placed farther back from the intended flight; this will normally cause the ball to curve to the right. In the closed stance, the rear foot is dropped back, which causes the ball to curve to the left. The square stance is the one most frequently used.

In most shots the ball is placed in position in front of the body in line with the heel of the forward foot. The body is positioned so that the head of the golf club rests behind the ball. The swing begins by a preliminary waggle of the club head to emphasize the point of contact followed by moving the club head, hands, and arms backward in unison. The arms swing close to the body. The left arm is held straight but not rigid. The club head is carried back by rotating the body and shifting the weight to the right foot. The wrists are allowed to cock as the club reaches the waistline. The club is brought over the shoulder to a horizontal position. The head is held still throughout the swing, and the eyes are kept on the ball.

The forward swing starts with a rotation of the left hip; simultaneously the weight is transferred from the right to the left foot. This is followed immediately by a rotation of the body back to its original position. The arms are kept close to the body, and the wrists are held in the cocked position until the hands reach the level of the waist. Then wrists uncock as the club follows its arc to and through the ball. The club head should swing out along the intended line of flight, while the body rotates to permit a complete follow-through of the hands and arms.

Adaptations: For those with limitations in movement, the stance must be adjusted to create the balance necessary for swinging correctly. The distance of the feet from the ball will generally depend upon body structure (length of arms, trunk, and legs). However, players who, because of hip disabilities, cannot bend forward easily at the hips will need to stand closer to the ball or use extra long clubs.

In the case of leg impairment, the stance may need to be modified. The leg spread may be lengthened to provide a wider base for balance in the case of unilateral weight distribution caused by wearing a brace or by unequal leg lengths.

Players with crutches who cannot stand and swing a club without support can brace themselves on their left crutch, disposing of the right crutch; then, using a left-handed club in the right hand, they execute the swing with one arm. A little experimentation will determine where the left crutch should be placed on the ground to maintain the best balance for swinging; usually this will be achieved by placing the crutch slightly behind and out from the left leg.

Players who cannot maintain their balance on one crutch or are unable to stand may sit in a sturdy straight chair with a wide base to prevent tipping for such activities as driving balls into a golf cage or putting on a practice green. Those playing from a chair, as well as those in wheelchairs, must have the chair turned so they are facing the ball, with the left side (for right-handed players) in the direction of intended flight. Extra long clubs may be needed by some wheelchair players in order to reach over the foot of the chair. The wheels of the chair should be locked or blocked to prevent rolling during the swing.

Contrary to what would appear to be the case, a player with only a right arm should use left-handed clubs and one with only a left arm should use right-handed clubs. The former must make the back swing and the swing forward as if he were a normal left-handed player, while the latter makes the swing like a normal right-handed player.

Those with leg disabilities who cannot shift the weight readily from one foot to the other will need to cut down on the length of the backswing and secure force more from the rotation of the hips than from the total body, as would normally be the case.

Figure 22–2. A technique for driving balls into a golf cage, for those who cannot maintain standing balance.

Those seated in chairs or wheelchairs will shift their weight to the right of the buttocks on the backswing if they are right-handed players. The trunk will twist to the right. The head will be over the left shoulder with eyes upon the ball at the end of the backswing, as in the regular stance. The head remains stationary in the swing until after contact with the ball. As the swing is brought down, the weight is shifted to the left side and the trunk is twisted back. A follow-through is made, the trunk is twisted to the left, and the weight comes to rest on the left side.

The blind player need make no adaptation of grip, stance, or swing; but before taking the stance he may place the ball on the ground with one hand and with the other place the head of the club beside it. He then stands up and takes his stance without moving the head of his club. The preliminary waggle before stroking is eliminated because this may throw off the alignment of the club with the ball.

Most errors in stroking are the result of improper movement which causes a change in the radius of the swing. If, then, a handicapped golfer cannot make the necessary correction of his swing, he will need to make some compensation in the swing to overcome the difficulty. If, because of his disability, the player must keep his weight on the left leg in the backswing, he will need to exert conscious effort to control the arms so that, at the bottom arc of the swing, the head of the club will come where the ball is resting. A shift of the hips to the right may help to compensate for the inability to shift the weight to the right leg. In cases of an abnormal alignment of the legs, hips, or trunk the position of the left foot cannot perhaps be moved as required. Consequently, the angle of the foot will have to be adjusted so that it will allow the trunk to be parallel to the ball when addressing it.

Putting. The grip for putting differs from the grip used in other strokes. In the most commonly used grip, the whole right hand (for right-handed players) is placed on the handle and the index finger of the left hand covers the little finger of the right hand. The thumbs of both hands run straight down the top of the shaft. The left thumb is in the palm of the right hand, as in the regular grip. After the grip is taken, the head of the club is placed directly behind the ball and the stance is adjusted to center the weight opposite the ball with the eyes directly above the ball. The ball is stroked by keeping the face of the club perpendicular to the line of the putt throughout the swing. The distance of a putt is governed by the amount of backswing. The club is swung toward the cup, imparting an overspin or roll. The club should follow through for a distance greater than the backswing.

Adaptations: In cases where the thumb on either hand is missing, the forefinger may be substituted for the thumb in taking the proper grip to give stability to the club in the swing.

Wheelchair players may find the use of one arm more effective than both arms in putting. Because the wheels may cut into the greens, wide-wheeled chairs should be used; if these are not avilable, wide boards may be placed under the wheels while on the greens. Precautions against cutting into the grass are not necessary on the fairways or grassed playing fields on which wheelchair players may wish to practice.

TRACK AND FIELD

Track and field events offer many opportunities to the handicapped to participate on equal terms with their normal counterparts. Some of the events require little or no adaptation for the less disabling types of handicaps; others are readily modified to enable those with more restricted movement to participate. Even those who are prevented by their handicaps from entering competition can enjoy the personal satisfaction of achievement in competition against themselves to better their previous time or to increase the distance of their earlier effort.

The track and field events, especially the running events, are good activities for general body conditioning, which most handicapped students are in need of. Although it is not a track event, jogging should be mentioned in this connection because of its popularity as a conditioning activity among adults.

General Adaptations. In some instances the teacher's job will be one of finding an event in which the handicapped student can participate rather than adapting the performance of the skills of the event to his capabilities. For example, those with upper limb disabilities can participate in running and jumping events, while those with lower limb disabilities are able to participate in the throwing events. The blind will be able to take part in throwing events without much modification, but some modification will be needed to enable them to participate in the running events. Paraplegics and those on crutches require somewhat more adaptation of the skills since they will perform them from wheelchairs. In order to participate in jumping events, slight modifications in "style" are necessary for arm amputees.

Running Events. Common running events in track and field meets in school competition are: 100 yard dash, 220 yard run, 440 yard run, 880 yard run, one mile run, two mile run, low hurdles, high hurdles, the 880 yard relay, and the mile relay.

Adaptations. Wheelchair "running" events consist of the 50 yard and 100 yard dashes and a slalom race in which the racers must negotiate an obstacle course that tests their strength and ability to maneuver the wheelchair.

Competitive track events for blind runners are: 50 and 100 yard dashes, the mile and two mile runs, and, on occasion, cross country. In the dashes, the blind use guide wires stretched 100 yards along the track without intervening supports; or, as an alternative method of guiding them, a continuous sound is made by someone standing at the finish line to guide the runner in the right direction. In running longer distances, the sightless runner may be accompanied by a sighted partner who runs beside him or rides a bicycle just ahead of him, providing auditory clues.

When jogging is used for conditioning by those for whom strenuous activity is contraindicated, a doctor should prescribe the distance and speed of the jog for each individual. Blind joggers can be accompanied by sighted partners as suggested above for track events. If a partner is not available, jogging in place may be substituted.

Jumping Events. The two most popular events in field competition are the long jump and high jump. However, in some schools the triple jump or hop, step, and jump is also included.

Adaptations: The blind participant and the one with a single leg can perform both the high jump and the long jump from a stationary position. The former can also execute the triple jump from a stationary start. The blind participant in the high jump stations himself at the point of take-off, swings his lead leg back and forth to gain momentum, and then springs from the take-off leg. A jumper with one leg performs in the same way without the swinging of the leg to generate momentum.

Participants missing or without the use of one or both arms must alter the style of the high jump to compensate for the lack of the use of the arms in maintaining balance as they go over the bar.

Blind and one-legged performers stand at the take-off point for the standing long jump and the former would stand here as well for the triple jump.

Throwing Events. The shot put, discus, and javelin are the main field events of most track and field meets.

Adaptations: Wheelchair patients with only lower limb involvement can participate in all three of the above-mentioned field events. Each participant must adapt a style of throwing based on his capabilities. If he has trunk maneuverability, he can use the twisting of the trunk to help generate power in the throw; otherwise he must rely completely on the arm and shoulder.

The blind can participate in throwing events with little modification. In the javelin event, they must usually decrease the distance they run before making the throw to a few steps so they will not run over the foul line, or they throw from a stationary position.

SELECTED READINGS

AAHPER: *Physical Education for High School Students,* ed. 4. Washington, D.C., American Association for Health, Physical Education, and Recreation, 1970.

Cheatum, Billie Ann: *Golf,* ed. 2. Philadelphia, W. B. Saunders Co., 1975.

Kennedy, Robert E.: *Track and Field for College Men.* Philadelphia, W. B. Saunders Co., 1970.

Parker, Virginia, and Kennedy, Robert E.: *Track and Field for Girls and Women.* Philadelphia, W. B. Saunders Co., 1969.

Pszczola, Lorraine: *Archery.* Philadelphia, W. B. Saunders Co., 1971.

Schunk, Carol: *Bowling.* Philadelphia, W. B. Saunders Co., 1970.

Seaton, Don Cash, *et al.: Physical Education Handbook,* ed. 6. Englewood Cliffs, New Jersey, Prentice-Hall, Inc. 1974.

Vannier, Maryhelen, and Fait, Hollis F.: *Teaching Physical Education in Secondary Schools,* ed. 4. Philadelphia, W. B. Saunders Co., 1975.

Vannier, Maryhelen, and Poindexter, Hally Beth: *Individual and Team Sports for Girls and Women,* ed. 3. Philadelphia, W. B. Saunders Co., 1975.

Chapter 23

Dual Lifetime Sports

Dual sports are all those games in which one player engages in play with a single opponent or two players engage in play with a pair of opponents. Among the better known and most widely played dual games are tennis, badminton, and table tennis. Suitably large playing areas are required for tennis and badminton, and a special table is needed for playing table tennis. There are other dual games, however, which require much less space or special equipment; among these are loop badminton, corner ping pong, and shuffleboard. All can be considered lifetime sports, since all these sports can be played throughout life.

Some proficiency in playing all of these games can be acquired by most handicapped students, even those with severe limitations. The more simple games can, of course, be learned more easily and require less adaptation. Tennis, badminton, and table tennis require greater physical effort on the part of the learner and, consequently, usually necessitate extensive adaptations; but the rewards to the handicapped participants are so great that the games should be included in the special physical education program if at all possible.

The most obvious reward is the physiological benefit to the body resulting from the vigorous workout afforded by playing the dual games. There are other important but less tangible rewards. Because a certain amount of prestige is attached to participation in such games as tennis, playing them gives the handicapped person a real sense of achievement and the feeling of being like others. Then, too, the playing of these games opens up opportunities for social contacts with both sexes, an important consideration in selecting activities for handicapped students.

ORGANIZING THE INSTRUCTION

Those dual games played on large courts can become strenuous, and because of this they are sometimes overlooked as possibilities for adaptation for play by those whose handicaps limit the area through which they are able to move when playing. It is possible, however, to modify these games to decrease the amount of locomotion that is necessary. Most of the other games can be played with few or no adaptations by those with limited movement or by those confined to wheelchairs. All of the games discussed in this chapter can be readily modified for those with malfunction of one arm and for single-arm amputees; adaptation for these, as well as for those who have a weak shoulder on the side of the dominant arm which is subject to dislocation, consists of learning to play with the other arm.

Double-arm amputees can play all the games presented here if a functional stump remains on one arm to which the racquet or cue may be taped. In taping, padding should be placed between the handle of the equipment and the arm to prevent chafing and to ensure comfort. Enough of the handle should extend up the arm to allow two straps to encircle the arm and handle. The handle may be placed on the inside or outside of the arm, but usually the inside is preferable. The position in which the piece of equipment is taped should simulate that in which it would be held by a normal player. Two leather or cloth straps may be used to hold the handle in place. Taping makes the equipment more secure but, since this cannot be done by double-arm amputees, they may prefer to use straps which they can learn to put on themselves, using the stumps and mouth, or prostheses and mouth.

When the disability of the student is such that considerable adaptation of the playing skills is required, as in the case of the double-arm amputee, extensive experimentation is usually necessary to discover the most effective way to perform the skills. Since the process of experimenting is likely to be emotionally frustrating and physically uncomfortable, the teacher should be particularly generous with praise and encouragement during this phase of instruction.

Like the individual sports, the dual sports require careful organization of the class time to permit as much individual instruction as possible. Equally important is planning the use of the facilities to ensure as much playing of the game as possible. This is particularly applicable in games such as tennis and table tennis, where only a limited number of players can be accommodated at any one time.

In presenting adaptations that can be made for the handicapped in the sports discussed in this chapter, very brief descriptions of the specific skills are given to enable the reader to make a better comparison of the adaptation with normal performance and so gain a better understanding of the process of adapting skills for the handicapped. It is not the intent to provide instruction for learning to perform the skills. Those who wish this information are referred to the books in Selected Readings at the end of the chapter.

TENNIS

Tennis is a relatively strenuous game, but the amount of activity can be modified considerably by decreasing the size of the court. This enables those with limited leg movement and those who cannot engage in vigorous activity to play. A smaller court also allows handicapped players to participate with normal players.

General Adaptations: For individuals whose skills are inadequate to keep the ball in play for any length of time, regulation scoring may be dispensed with. As a substitution the score may be counted as the number of times the ball is successfully returned during a given period of time. The objective in this case is playing the ball so that the opponent is able to return it rather than playing so that the opponent cannot return it, as in regulation tennis. Those who have insufficient strength to hold the racquet at arm's length with a proper grip may choke up on the handle — that is, move the hand up the handle toward the head of the racquet a few inches.

Forehand and Backhand Strokes. Basic to both forehand and backhand strokes is footwork. The player must be ready to move in any direction as the ball is returned to him by his opponent. In returning the ball, the player must place his body to the side of the ball so that he may swing freely at it. The racquet is swung back while the player is moving into position, with the side of the body turned toward the net while stroking the ball.

In the forehand stroke, the left foot and shoulder are forward. When the racquet head is swung back in the backswing, the elbow is slightly bent. The weight of the body is carried well on the rear foot. A slight hesitation occurs at the end of the back swing. As the swing starts forward, the weight is shifted to the forward foot. The ball should be stroked at about waist height. The wrist is held firm as the ball is hit. After the ball is hit, the racquet continues to follow through, first following the path of the ball and then swinging in a wide arc in front of the body.

The flight of the ball is determined by how the ball is stroked and the direction the face of the racquet is at the moment of impact. With the face tilted upward the ball bounces higher into the air than if it is tilted downward. A ball going to the right or left of the intended flight may be caused by the direction the face was pointing on contact with the ball.

The backhand stroke is similar to the forehand and is used to return balls that are on the opposite side of the body from the arm that holds the racquet. For a right-handed player the right foot and the right shoulder are facing the net. The backswing is brought across the body as the weight shifts to the rear foot. Before the backswing is made, the backhand grip is taken. There is a slight pause at the end of the back-swing before the racquet is brought forward in a wide arc to meet the ball at hip level just opposite the forward foot. The racquet follows through in the direction of the ball's flight and then swings wide in front of the body.

Adaptations: By reducing the size of the court for those with some limitations in locomotion, the movement to place the body in the proper position for stroking may be achieved in no more than a single step. Reducing the court size even further enables those who cannot make the proper leg movement to achieve a satisfactory stroke by placing the body in the proper position by twisting at the hips.

A player who has the racquet strapped to his arm cannot change the position of the racquet for the backhand stroke. Therefore, he will stroke the ball in the same way as in making the forehand stroke.

Serve. In the serve, the body is turned with its side to the net as in the forehand stroke. The ball is carried in the opposite hand to that which holds the racquet. The ball is tossed at arm's length from the body high enough in the air so the racquet arm is fully extended when the ball is hit. The weight is shifted to the rear foot as the ball is tossed into the air. As the toss is begun, the racquet is swung back behind the head. As the ball drops to the correct height, the weight shifts to the forward leg and the racquet is brought up with the wrist superextended. The racquet is brought down upon the ball, driving it over the net into the opponent's right service court. The follow-through is made with a complete swing, the racquet coming to rest near the op-posite knee.

Adaptations: Individuals who lack coordination and the ability to execute the reg-ulation serve may perform the service by bringing the racquet up in front of the body as the ball is tossed into the air. The ball is stroked as it falls within reach of the racquet head. Served in this way the ball will lack speed and will make a higher arc over the net, but many players are able to learn to serve in this way who may never develop skill in serving it in the usual way.

Double-arm amputees who have the racquet taped to their arms may serve by balancing the ball on the face of the racquet. The ball is tossed into the air by a short quick upward movement of the racquet and stroked as it bounces. A loose rolling ball is brought under control by placing the racquet over the ball and pressing it to the ground. It is picked up by placing the racquet under the rolling ball and gradually brought under control by bouncing it on the face of the racquet. A stationary ball may be picked up on the racquet by placing the face of the racquet (near the handle) on the ball, drawing the racquet quickly toward the body to start the ball rolling, and slipping the head of the racquet under the rolling ball, which is brought to balance on the racquet face. A loose bouncing ball is brought under control by catching it on the racquet face and bouncing it up and down on the face until it is under control.

Players with only one arm serve by carrying the ball in the racquet hand. A regular grip is taken, and the thumb and forefinger are extended beyond the handle. The ball is grasped between these extended fingers and rests against the handle. The ball may be tossed into the air and stroked as described for players who lack coordination, or it may be tossed into the air and stroked as it bounces.

Basic Strokes and Strategy.   Volley is the term used for the act of hitting the ball after it comes over the net but before it bounces on the court. A volley is made chiefly in the forecourt position. The smash or kill is a stroke used on a high bouncing ball or a short lob. The ball is hit hard and at a sharp angle so that it will bounce above the opponent's reach. It can be made effectively between the serving line and the net. The lob is a stroke in which the ball is hit so that it is lifted above the opponent's head and falls near his base line. It is used as a defensive shot to force the opponent back to the rear court.

In singles, as soon as the ball has been stroked, the player should move to one of two places: the center of the court, three or four feet from the net, or about two feet behind the base line in the center of the court. The net position is taken when it appears that the opponent will have a difficult time returning the shot. The back court position is safer but does not allow the advantage that can be had from handling balls at the net.

The doubles game requires less speed and endurance than singles. The lob becomes one of the most important strokes to keep the opponent away from the net. It is desirable to force one of the opponents far back into the back court so that a net position can be taken by the other two players. Players should always come to the net on each serve to gain the attack. The return of the service should usually be to the deep middle court. In rallying, partners should play parallel positions. The volley and smash are used whenever possible. All lobs should be hit before they bounce, if possible, in order to keep the offensive.

Adaptations: In using one half of a single court with chops and drop shots eliminated, the player stands in the middle of the court about two feet behind the base line. The body can be positioned properly by taking one or two steps in either direction.

In the doubles game three or four players may be used on each side to decrease the amount of movement necessary to get the body or, in the case of a player in a wheelchair, the wheelchair into the proper position to stroke the ball. If three people are playing on a side, one plays at the net, the other two near the base line on each side of the court. Two players are placed on the net if four people are playing on a side.

BADMINTON

Badminton is a popular racquet game that is being used increasingly for family recreation in back yards. This is one of the important reasons for promoting it among the handicapped; having acquired the skills of the game, handicapped players can take part in one more active recreational activity with family and friends. The game is easily adapted for many types of handicaps.

General Adaptations: To decrease the amount of movement required by the game, play may be limited to half the singles court or to half the doubles court, using the back serving line of the doubles court as the back line in either case. If half the singles court is used, the players will not have to move to either right or left to return the bird. Only one or two steps will be required to return all possible placements of the bird when half a doubles court is used. To avoid the necessity of movement to and back from the net, the drop shot may be made illegal. In doubles play, a player in a wheelchair may partner a non-handicapped player on each team.

The reach of the player in a wheelchair can be extended by lengthening the handle of the racquet by splicing a length of wood to the center of the shaft as shown in Figure 23–1. To facilitate retrieval of the bird, a strip of Velcro is attached around the rim of the racquet face and around the base of the bird, so that the bird adheres to the racquet on contact and can be lifted up to the hand. (See Fig. 23–2.)

If a double-arm amputee is using a strapped-on racquet, the handle should be placed up the arm six to eight inches where it is taped or strapped to the stump. The best location must be determined for each individual through mechanical analysis combined with experimentation. Even though a large portion of the badminton stroke is made by the wrist, those with strapped-on racquets can achieve considerable success in playing the game because the racquet is relatively light. Furthermore, a good defensive game can be built around drop shots that are made effectively without wrist action.

Outdoor badminton is never very satisfactory for class work because breezes even of light velocity blow the shuttlecock off course. However, if badminton is scheduled for an outdoor court, the bird to be used can be made more stable in slight breezes by weaving copper wire between the feathers at their base.

Two players with limited mobility may work as a team to keep the bird aloft as long as possible. Consequently, instead of attempting to make the opponent miss the shot, they must attempt to place the bird so it can be stroked.

Grip. The racquet handle is grasped as if one were shaking hands with the

Figure 23–1. Splicing the handle of a badminton racquet extends the reach of a player who has limited locomotion.

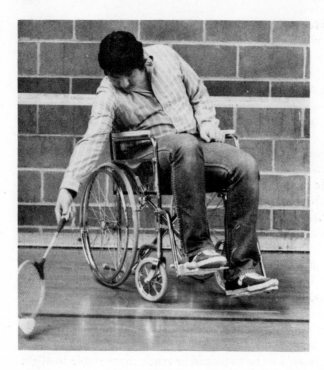

Figure 23–2. Use of Velcro on the racquet and bird facilitates retrieval of the bird.

racquet. The fingers are spread slightly. When the racquet handle is held toward the body and the racquet head is vertical to the floor, the V formed between the thumb and the forefinger is on top of the handle. The grip is taken so that the heel of the hand is flush with the end of the handle.

Adaptations: Because of the lightness of the racquet, very few players will be unable to control the racquet with the regular grip. However, in extreme cases of grip weakness, the grip may be taken higher on the handle.

Serve. The serve is made from the short service line into the service area diagonally across the net from the server.

The right-handed server stands with the left foot forward. The bird is held low in front and to the right of the body by the feathers with the thumb and forefinger. The racquet is swung back with the wrist super-extended. The racquet is brought forward and the wrist is flexed just before contact with the shuttlecock. The left hand releases the shuttlecock just before it is hit.

Adaptations: Those individuals who cannot use wrist action in serving may be allowed to serve in front of the service line so that the high serve to the back court will be effective.

Players who are unable to place their feet in the correct position for serving may manipulate the body into the proper position by twisting at the hips. Players in wheelchairs serve from the side of the chair.

Basic Strokes, Flights, and Strategy. The overhead, forehand, backhand, and underhand lift strokes are the basic strokes in badminton. The stroke used depends upon the position of the bird, the position of the opponent, and the flight or shot to be made.

The common flights are the high clear, smash, and drop shot. The high clear is a shot that is driven high and deep into the opponent's back court. The smash is a "kill" shot executed from the overhead position. The stroke is made so that the bird is driven down into the opponent's court. In the drop shot the bird is struck lightly so that it drops immediately after passing over the net.

The flight that is used will depend on the situation. The high clear is used most frequently. It is a defensive stroke used to force the opponent back. It can be used anywhere on the court. The drop shot is used when the opponent is not expecting it and is away from the net. The underhand lift is used only when the bird is falling too close to the net for any other shot. The shot is more effective if the bird is stroked so that it goes to the other side of the court as it goes over the net from where it was played. The smash is used whenever the bird is higher than the net and in the forecourt.

Adaptations: The ability to use different strokes will vary according to the nature of the handicap. Those players with limited wrist action will not be able to employ the smash as effectively as they do the drop shot. Strategy for these players will be to use chiefly the high clear and the drop shot. Those who are playing on half a singles court with the drop shot made illegal will necessarily have to rely upon the smash and high clear. Playing on the modified court, the player stands in the center of the court and merely moves the appropriate foot forward to get into position for a backhand or forehand stroke.

LOOP BADMINTON

Loop badminton is an adaptation of badminton developed by the author which is played with a badminton shuttlecock, table tennis paddles, and an upright metal loop. It is an active game, requires considerably less space than badminton, and is more adaptable to play by those who are restricted in movement than is badminton. Two players engage in play with the objective of hitting the cock legally through the loop to score.

The playing area is 10 feet by five feet with a metal loop 24 inches in diameter placed in the center of the area. The loop is strapped on an upright pole such as a badminton or volleyball standard so that the pole bisects the loop. The bottom of the loop is 46 inches from the floor. A restraining line is drawn across the court three feet from each side of the loop (Fig. 23–3).

Adaptations: The size of the loop may be increased to enable the less skilled to return the bird through the loop successfully. For those who have very poor skills, the loop may be placed on the side of the standard so that it projects from the side and is not bisected by the standard.

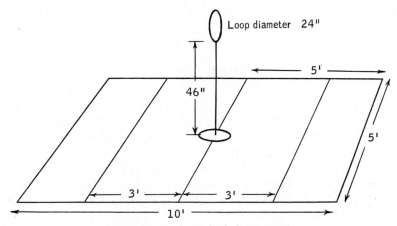

Figure 23–3. Loop badminton court.

If a standard is not available, the loop may be hung from the ceiling with a cord. To keep it from swinging, another cord must anchor it to the floor. For those who are seated either in a chair or a wheelchair while playing, the loop may be placed lower than the recommended 46 inches.

The loops may be constructed from heavy wire or from small flexible branches. The ends are brought together to form the loop and secured with wire or adhesive tape.

Playing the Game.   The game starts with an underhand service, as in badminton, behind the end line. The serve must pass through the loop without touching the loop or standard. If it touches the loop or standard, it is called a let serve and the server serves again. The bird must land beyond the opponent's restraining line and in his court. The receiver can stand anywhere behind his restraining line to receive the serve. The bird must be returned through the loop. After the serve the bird may be struck so that it lands anywhere in the opponent's court, including in front of the restraining line, as long as it passes through the loop. A bird that touches the loop or standard and goes through the loop is considered fair if it is not the serve. The bird must be struck sharply and cannot be carried momentarily on the paddle. If a player touches the loop or reaches through it or around it, he loses either a point or the serve. A player may not play the bird while standing in front of the restraining line, nor may he hold his paddle in front of the loop to prevent the bird from passing through.

Scoring is done as in badminton. Only the server can score a point. If the server makes a fault, he loses the serve. The winner of the game is the first player to get 15 points in a boy's game and 11 points in a girl's game. In boys' play, when the score has reached 13 all, the first person to reach 13 has the option of setting the game to five more points or allowing it to remain at two more. When the score is 14 all, the first player to reach the score has the option of setting the game to three more points. For girls, when the players are tied at 9 points, the first player to reach that score has the option of setting the game to three more points. At 10 all the first to reach that number has the option of setting the game to two more points.

Adaptations: If players are playing from wheelchairs or crutches, the serve is made from in front of the service line. If the player is playing from a chair that is not mobile, it is placed in the center of the court. The serve is made from this position. When the players' mobility is limited, any bird that does not land beyond the opponent's restraining line is considered a fault.

Those who are subject to chronic shoulder dislocation can usually play loop badminton using the involved arm without adverse effect, since all strokes can be made with the arm held lower than the shoulder.

TABLE TENNIS

Table tennis resembles the game of tennis, but it is far less strenuous. Consequently, many kinds of handicapped persons are able to play table tennis. By learning the skills of the game, they can participate in a popular recreational activity that provides needed exercise the year around.

General Adaptations: For play by students in wheelchairs, the table should be situated in an area with sufficient room to accommodate the movement of the chairs. The table should be made stationary by nailing or screwing the legs to the floor. This enables wheelchair players to grasp the table for support while moving their chairs into position for stroking the ball.

A paddle developed by the author, useful to blind or partially seeing players, may be constructed from a rectangular board 2 or 2½ feet by 1½ feet in size with handles attached at each end. A Space Ball net, which is made of a rectangular frame and netting and designed to be held in the hands, may also be substituted for the regulation paddle.

For blind beginning players, play may be limited to a portion of the table on each side of the net. Paper is placed on the parts of the court not being used so that players will be able to tell by the difference in the sound of the ball striking the surfaces if the ball is good or out of bounds. If a sighted player is the opponent for the beginning blind player, the former may be required to play his full court while the latter plays half of his court. Sections of plywood or finely meshed nets attached to standards may be placed along the sides of the table to help keep the ball on the table where it can be more easily located by blind players.

Another adaptation of the game for the blind is playing the ball by pushing it with a paddle so that it rolls beneath a string that is used in place of the net. Boards are attached along the sides of the table to prevent the ball from rolling off the table.

Grip. The tennis grip is the preferred grip for table tennis. The racquet is grasped as if shaking hands with the handle. The thumb and forefinger are placed on either side of the surface of the racquet. The side of the thumb rests gently on the racquet where the handle and the face meet. The forefinger is separated slightly from the rest of the fingers and extends across the face at its base. The rest of the fingers are closed around the handle.

Adaptations: Double-arm amputees will have the paddle taped to a stump. Blind players using the special paddle described previously will grasp a handle in each hand and hold the paddle in front of the body ready for play.

The pen holder grip, in which the handle is gripped as if holding a pen with the head of racquet pointing down, is preferred by some players who play from a sitting position.

Figure 23-4. Sides erected on a table and a Space Ball net, substituted for the paddle, enable a blind player to engage in modified table tennis. Paper is placed on her side of the court to provide auditory cues.

Serve. For the serve the ball is held in the open flat palm of the hand; the fingers must be held straight. The server puts the ball into play by tossing it into the air. The ball is struck with the racquet so that it bounces first into the server's court, then passes over the net and lands on the receiver's side. When the ball is struck in serving, it must be completely free of the serving hand. At the moment of impact the ball must be behind the end line and between the side lines (if they were extended beyond the end line).

Adaptations: Players who are on crutches and use the table for support are allowed to serve in front of the end line if it is necessary to maintain body balance. Players with one hand serve by grasping the ball between the extended forefinger and thumb after the grip has been taken. The ball is tossed into the air and served either before or after it bounces. The serve by a single-armed player with taped-on paddle is accomplished by balancing the ball on the face of the paddle and then tossing it into the air with an appropriate movement of the paddle. The ball is stroked after it bounces. Beginners may be permitted to hit the ball over the net without its bouncing again; skilled players may be required to allow the ball to bounce on their side of the table after it is hit and before it passes over the net.

A ball can be picked up on the face of the paddle by placing the face of the paddle on the ball. The paddle is then drawn quickly toward the player. In the same movement, the paddle is slipped under the rolling ball, which is brought to balance on the face. If the ball is resting on the table, it may be picked up by pushing it close enough to the edge of the table to be reached by the player's head. The paddle is placed parallel with the table and the ball rolled onto its face with the forehead. The ball may be carried by pressing it between the forehead and the paddle.

Blind players using the two-handled paddle may start the game by gently tossing the ball over the net to the opponent.

Forehand and Backhand. The forehand is employed for all balls that are driven more than one foot to the right side of the player (for right-handed players). As soon as it can be determined that the ball is going to land so it can be played by a forehand stroke, the backswing is made: the paddle is brought to the right side about table height, the wrist is slightly superextended, and the paddle is held so that the handle is parallel to the table and the head faces the right. As the swing forward is made, the weight shifts to the left foot. The paddle is brought forward and upward to strike the ball at its highest bounce. If top spin is desired, the face of the racquet is slanted slightly downward as it makes contact with the ball and is dragged over its top. In either case the paddle follows through forward and upward.

The backhand is used on balls that bounce on the left side of the body, in front of the body, or within one foot of the right side of the body (for a right-handed player). The paddle is turned so that the opposite face from that used in the forehand is facing the ball. If the ball is on the left side of the player, the arm crosses the body. If the ball is in front or not over one foot from the right side, the paddle is held in front of the oncoming ball. In all cases the head of the paddle points to the left and the handle is parallel to the ground. The backswing is very short, but the wrist is flexed to add power to the stroke. The backswing should bring the paddle in front of the approaching ball slightly above table height. The paddle is brought forward and upward; at the same time the wrist is superextended to meet the ball at the height of its bounce.

For a forehand or backhand chop the paddle is held above the point where the ball will reach the height of its bounce. With the paddle tilted slightly upward, the head is dragged downward on the ball as it is hit foward.

Adaptations: Beginners and those who have difficulty in making coordinated arm movements will depend chiefly upon forehand and backhand strokes without spin. If the paddle head is not dragged on the ball, the tilt of the paddle face will dictate how high the ball will go into the air. A player who consistently knocks the ball into the net will need to tilt the face up, while one who knocks the ball too high into the air will need to tilt it down.

The blind player who is using the two-handled paddle will hold the paddle in front of the body with both hands and move it to the right or left as he hears the ball bounce. If he knocks the ball consistently into the net, he will need to tilt the face of the paddle upward. Conversely, if the ball bounces too high, the board must be tilted downward. Beginners should be encouraged to bounce the ball high to make its return easier.

Playing the Ball. After moving to play a ball, the player should return to a position near the center of the table two to four feet (depending upon his ability to play the ball) from the end line. The weight should be carried on the balls of the feet, and the knees should be slightly flexed so that the body may move readily in either direction to play the ball. The ball cannot be hit until after it bounces in the receiver's court, so it is undesirable to be too close to the table as this makes it difficult to return a hard-hit ball that bounces off the table.

Adaptations: Wheelchair players will keep the center position as just described but will stay closer to the table. One hand is rested on the table to maneuver the chair into position to play the ball. Some players prefer office chairs with free-rolling casters to wheelchairs because they are more maneuverable.

A fault is not called if a blind player inadvertently holds his two-handled racquet in such a way that the ball is struck before it bounces. However, if there is intent to hit the ball, the act becomes a fault.

CORNER PING-PONG

Corner ping-pong is a game developed at the University of Connecticut by the author for use in the adapted physical education program by those who are limited in movement of the legs. The game utilizes the skills of table tennis and might be used as a practice drill as well as an adapted game.

Playing Area and Equipment. A corner area with smooth walls for a height of 6 feet by 6 feet on each side of the corner is needed. The floor and wall markings are shown in figure 23–5. Table tennis paddles and ball are used.

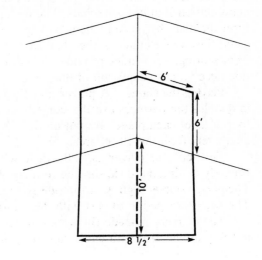

Figure 23–5. Corner ping-pong court.

Adaptations: If smooth walls are not available, plywood may be cut the required size and placed over rough walls or attached to the floor to create a corner for playing.

To decrease the amount of movement required of the players, the court size may be reduced, with the size of the wall surface kept in the same proportion to the floor area.

Playing the Game.   One player stands on each side of the center line. The ball is dropped by the server and stroked against the floor to the forward wall. The ball must rebound to the adjacent wall, then bounce onto the floor of the opponent's area. If the server fails to deliver a good serve, one point is recorded for the opponent.

The ball may bounce only once on the floor before the opponent returns it. He must stroke the ball against the forward wall in his section of the playing area so that the ball rebounds to the adjacent wall and onto the floor in the server's playing area. Failure to return the ball is scored as a point for the server.

Scoring is similar to table tennis. Each player gets five serves. A ball that is stroked out of bounds is scored as a point by the other player. Game is 21 points, and the winner must win by two points.

Adaptation: To decrease the speed of play, the served ball is required to strike the floor before it hits the wall. In each subsequent play, the ball must be hit so as to strike the floor first before it hits the wall.

SHUFFLEBOARD

Shuffleboard is readily adapted to nearly all kinds of handicapping conditions. Like the other dual sports, one of its great values is in the social contacts that it affords the handicapped whose opportunities for social interaction are so often limited.

General Adaptations: The length of the court may be shortened for those who do not have sufficient strength to propel the disks the total distance on the regulation court. It may also be shortened for mental retardates who are poorly coordinated, to ensure success in scoring.

A strip of tape placed on the floor to show the direction of the court is helpful to blind students. By feeling the tape, they are able to locate the court and to adjust their aim accordingly.

The doubles game is, of course, preferable for players with limited locomotion. If there are not enough players for a doubles game, singles may be played with opponents stationed at opposite ends. The opponent, in this case, counts the score and returns the disks by pushing them back to the other player for his next turn. Playing the game this way eliminates the challenge and excitement of preventing the opponent from scoring, but it does provide fun and exercise for those whose range of locomotion necessitates adaptation of the game.

Playing the Game.   A player in a singles game uses disks of one color only, and in doubles the partners use the same disks of one color. At the start of the game the four disks of each player are put on the side of the 10-off area. Players play the disks alternately from the 10-off area.

To shoot, the player faces the disk, with the head of the cue resting on the court squarely behind the disk, the cue forming a straight line with the disk and the target. The player stands slightly at the side so that the arm is in a straight line with the cue. The cue is grasped in the fist with the V formed by the forefinger and thumb on top.

The delivery is made (by a right-handed player) by taking a step forward on the left foot as the arm with cue swings forward, pushing the disk evenly and smoothly forward. The head of the cue slides along the floor. In the follow-through the arm is fully extended, with the cue pointing in the direction of the moving disk.

Adaptations: A wheelchair patient should place his chair facing the court and slightly to the side so that the arm with the cue can be dropped to the side of the chair to make the shot.

Players on crutches must shift the body weight to the crutch of the opposite arm to free the playing arm to make the shot.

For those seated in straight chairs for playing, it may be easier to move the disks along the 10-off line to put them in the proper position than to move the chair to place the player in the proper position for shooting.

Players who are spastic may achieve better results in playing the disk by making several repetitive movements with the cue behind the disk before actually pushing it forward. The athetoids, on the other hand, have greater success if no preliminary movements are made. They should place the cue behind the disk and push forward immediately.

To simplify scoring for the mentally retarded, the score may be based on the number of disks which land within the scoring area of the count: each disk then counts one point.

SELECTED READINGS

AAHPER: *Physical Education for High School Students,* ed. 2. Washington, D.C., American Association for Health, Physical Education, and Recreation, 1970.

Armbruster, David A., *et al.: Basic Skills in Sports for Men and Women,* ed. 6. St. Louis, The C. V. Mosby Co., 1975.

Gensmer, Robert E.: *Tennis,* ed. 2. Philadelphia, W. B. Saunders Co., 1975.

Johnson, M. L.: *Badminton.* Philadelphia, W. B. Saunders Co., 1974.

Vannier, Maryhelen, and Fait, Hollis F.: *Teaching Physical Education in Secondary Schools,* ed. 4. Philadelphia, W. B. Saunders Co., 1975.

Chapter 24

Team Games

Team games are important in the physical education program because they provide big-muscle activity necessary for developing and maintaining a desirable level of physical fitness. Since handicapped children are likely to have a low level of physical fitness, their participation in team games is especially important for this reason. Team games are important, too, for the opportunities they give these children to demonstrate their ability to contribute to the group effort. Their fellow team members are likely to gain an understanding and respect for the handicapped they would not otherwise develop, while the handicapped themselves are likely to acquire greater confidence in their abilities and to accept themselves as they really are. That some of the team games are among our most popular spectator sports is still another reason to include team games in the curriculum; in learning to play them, students become more intelligent spectators.

ORGANIZING THE INSTRUCTION

The team games, because of their vigorous nature, cannot be adapted to all types of handicapped players. However, even though the game as a whole may not be adaptable, specific skills can be adapted for play by nearly all types of handicapped students. For example, those whose locomotion is restricted because of leg disabilities may still engage in modified basketball shooting and football passing drills.

In the school situation, then, the teacher may plan to include the handicapped in the drills which are used for improving the skills of the team sports. Some slight modifications may need to be made, as, for example, in a drill which requires rapid movement from one position to another; the student who is incapable of moving rapidly may be permitted to omit this phase of the drill and continue on to his place in line.

Unless severely restricted in arm and leg movements or greatly lacking in physical fitness, handicapped students may also be included in the lead-up games and in the actual competitive play of the team sports, subject to the adaptations required by the physical condition. Frequent rest periods should be planned because the strenuousness of competitive team play may tax even the most physically fit player, and, as noted elsewhere, handicapped youngsters are likely to be lacking in physical fitness. For students unable to participate in these phases of the class instruction, the teacher may plan continued work on the drills. The drills should be varied whenever interest wanes. Injecting a competitive element into a drill makes performing the drill more interesting and often more satisfying to a handicapped student, because it provides him with a tool for evaluating his progress. Rather than drilling on passing by throwing the football to a receiver, for example, a competitive element may be introduced by drawing a target on the field at which the thrower may aim in the hope of scoring a bull's eye.

If students will be working on drills and drill-like games while the teacher is engaged in instructing and supervising the rest of the class in team play, the teacher must organize student helpers to retrieve balls and otherwise assist the handicapped players who cannot work entirely on their own. No student should be allowed to serve so frequently as a helper, however, that he is deprived of his own physical education.

In presenting adaptations that can be made for the handicapped in the sports discussed in this chapter, very brief descriptions of the specific skills are given to enable the reader to make a better comparison of the adaptation with normal performance and so gain a better understanding of the process of adapting skills for the handicapped. It is not the intent to provide instruction for learning to perform the skills. Those who wish this information are referred to the books in Selected Readings at the end of the chapter.

BASKETBALL

Because basketball is a strenuous game requiring speed and endurance, it cannot be played without considerable modification by handicapped students. For those who are able to participate in moderate exercise, however, play may be confined to half the court. The number of players per team may also be increased to reduce the physical demands upon individual players. Those for whom playing the game even with these modifications is too strenuous can usually engage in drills and games of passing, catching, and shooting.

General Adaptations. The baskets may be lowered for modified activities designed for students with restricted arm movement and for students who must shoot from a sitting position in a chair or wheelchair. A light string hung from the back side of the hoop so that it is low enough to be reached with the hand and yet high enough to be above the head is of great assistance to the blind player in determining the location of the hoop before he shoots. A bell attached to a length of twine may be hung from the hoop so that it will be made to ring when the ball enters the hoop and notify the shooter of his success.

Catching the Ball. In catching, the fingers are spread to receive the ball. When catching a high ball (above the waist), the thumbs are together. If the ball is below the waist, the little fingers are together. The ball is caught on the cushions of the finger tips, not with the heels of the hands. As the ball is caught, the arms give with the ball as the elbows are flexed. The ball is brought back toward the body. The eyes follow the ball throughout the catch.

Adaptations: A one-handed player may catch the ball by trapping it between the lower portion of the arm and the body, with the upper arm cradling the ball as it is brought into the body.

Those on crutches may find it easier to bring the ball to the side of the body rather than toward it when giving with the ball, as this permits the balance to be maintained more easily.

Blind players will catch the ball by extending both arms forward, with elbows slightly flexed. The passer must throw the ball into the open arms. The ball is cradled in the arms as the fingers come in contact with the ball to control it.

Passing. The passes most commonly used are the two-handed chest pass and overhand pass.

In the *two-handed chest pass,* the ball is brought chest high with the elbows flexed. The arms are extended sharply and the ball is released from both hands with an outward snap of the wrists. As the pass is made, the weight is brought forward.

For the *overhand pass,* the ball is brought back behind the shoulders about head high, with one arm, as in throwing a baseball. Then the arm is brought forward, and the ball is released with an abrupt snapping of the wrist. The ball should be thrown without imparting a spin, because this makes it difficult to catch.

Adaptations: One-armed players will make their passes with one arm. In long passes the overhand pass will be used, while in short passes the ball will be thrown underhanded.

Players on crutches will have to have a greater wrist snap than otherwise in making the two-handed chest pass. Generally the most effective pass for those on crutches will be the one-hand pass.

Shooting.   The two shots most used are the one-hand push shot and the two-hand set shot.

In the *one-hand push shot* (with the right hand), the ball is brought up in front of the body with both hands. The right hand is under and in back of the ball, and the left hand is under the ball. The right arm is extended up and in the direction of the basket, with the left hand holding the ball against the fingers of the right hand. As the ball is brought to shooting position in front of the right shoulder, the ball is rolled onto the right hand. The right arm is extended full length, and the left hand is removed from the ball. The ball is released with a wrist snap and leaves the hand from the finger tips. The ball must go high enough, with sufficient arch, to drop straight into the basket.

In the *two-hand set shot,* the ball is held chest high with the finger tips covering its upper portion. The knees are flexed, with the weight brought forward. The elbows are held close to the body. The wrists are straightened, the knees and the elbows extended, and the ball released toward the basket with a snap of the wrists.

Adaptations: Players on crutches are more successful with one-hand shots than with two. Most of the body weight must be taken on the crutch to free the shooting arm. A combination of one regular crutch and one Löfstrand crutch often provides sufficient means of getting around on the floor, and, with the use of the latter on the shooting arm, that arm is freed for shooting while the weight is borne on the other crutch.

Wheelchair players are usually able to make both types of shots, although they favor the two-hand shot. Power in throwing is generated by the arms.

WHEELCHAIR BASKETBALL

Wheelchair basketball is a popular sport for those who must use a wheelchair for locomotion but have active use of the arms. The game is played according to the rules of regulation basketball except for modifications necessitated by the participants' playing from wheelchairs.

For the center jump or a jump after a tie-up, the players are forbidden to raise any part of the body from the chair. The ball may be passed or dribbled. To execute a dribble, the player alternately moves his chair by pushing on the wheels and taps the ball on the floor. Taking more than two successive pushes on the wheels without tapping the ball on the floor constitutes traveling. Contacts between players and wheelchairs are treated the same as contact between players in a regular game.

Complete rules for playing wheelchair basketball may be secured from the National Wheelchair Athletic Association, 40–24 62nd St. Woodside, N.Y. 11377.

Figure 24–1. Wheelchair basketball is played on a regulation court with few modifications of the rules. (Courtesy of Spoke Benders.)

SOFTBALL

Softball can be played with only slight modification by all except the most severely handicapped. Because this is the case, mildly and moderately handicapped players are easily integrated with normal players. Others like the blind and orthopedically handicapped require radical changes in the game in order to participate.

Adaptations: The size of the diamond may be reduced and the distance of the pitching box from home plate decreased as needed to accommodate the abilities of the players.

More fielders may be added to reduce the work and the amount of movement required of any one fielder.

For blind players, the diamond should be small in size and located inside the gymnasium or within a fenced area so that balls will be more easily retrieved. Only one base is used, and a run scores when the player has run to the base and returned home safely. A large ball such as a volleyball may be substituted for the softball.

Playing the Game.   A game is divided into innings. An *inning* is completed when both teams have been up to bat and have been retired after three outs: An *out* is made at bat when:

1. The batter has three strikes (except on the third strike when the catcher fails to catch the ball and there is no one on first base).

2. A foul ball is hit and caught.

3. An infield fly is hit and there are runners at first and second base with less than two outs.

A *strike* is a ball, legally thrown above home plate in the strike zone, which the batter either fails to strike at or strikes at and misses. The *strike zone* is the area over the plate between the batter's knees and shoulders.

A batter becomes a runner when he has hit a fair ball. He is out when:

1. An opposing player reaches first base with the ball before the runner touches the base.

2. A runner is touched with the ball while going to and from any base.

3. A runner leaves the base before the ball leaves the pitcher's hand in a pitch to the batter.

4. A runner runs to the next base on a fly ball that is caught if he leaves before the ball is caught.

Pitched balls which do not legally enter the striking zone and are not struck at are called *balls*. After four balls the batter is permitted to advance to first base.

Adaptations: Strikes may be called only when the batter strikes at the ball and misses. Balls are not called, and the batter is not permitted to advance on balls.

If a batter is able to bat but unable to run bases, another player on his team may do the base running for him. Where the runner starts from will depend upon the ability of the batter. If the batter is especially good, the runner should be required to start on the opposite side of home plate from first base. For weaker batters, the runner may start closer to first base.

A blind or partially sighted player can bat from a batting tee and run the bases with assistance from the basemen, who are required to make sounds to guide the runner toward the base. If there is only one blind player in a group of normal players, he may be used as a batter for both sides to equalize play.

In play with one base and a large inflated ball, the ball is rolled to the blind batter so that it bounces on its way to home plate. The batter will depend upon hearing the ball

Figure 24–2. Softball play becomes possible for a player in a wheelchair when a teammate does the base running. (Courtesy of Newington Children's Hospital.)

in order to hit it. The batter is out after three strikes. A foul ball is counted the same as a strike except on the last strike. In this case, another ball is rolled.

If a fair hit is made, the first baseman makes an intermittent sound loud enough to be heard by the blind runner to first base and the fielders and yet not so loud as to interfere with the ability of the fielders to hear where the ball is rolling. If the ball is fielded successfully, the fielder rolls the ball to the first baseman. If it comes into the first baseman's possession before the runner gets to first base, the runner is out. If the runner gets safely to first base, his team scores and he returns to where his team is waiting to bat. Three outs retire the side.

Catching. Softball can be played without a glove, but a glove does provide protection to the hand and makes catching easier. In catching the ball, the body should be placed in line with the ball. The player should watch the ball throughout the catch. If possible, the ball should be caught in both hands. If the ball is above waist level, the thumbs will be together; if it is below the waist, the little fingers will be together. If a ball is far to the side, it may be necessary to reach with one hand to catch the ball. In either case, the ball is caught in the palm of the left hand (for right-handed players). As the ball strikes the hand, the hand should give slightly to cushion the ball. If both hands are used in catching, the right hand is brought over the top of the ball to hold it in the palm as the ball strikes the palm of the left hand.

Adaptations: In most cases, players who lack skill in catching should be provided with gloves to increase their efficiency and protect their hands.

Players with one hand can catch the ball without a glove and so be ready immediately to throw the ball; however, these players can learn to use a glove if a functional joint at the shoulder and a portion of the upper arm remains on the disabled arm. In this case, as soon as the ball is caught with the one hand, the glove with the ball in the pocket is placed under the opposite arm and the hand slipped out of the glove so that the ball stays in the pocket. In one continuous movement, the ball is grasped with the hand and thrown.

The ball may be caught by players on crutches or in wheelchairs with a little practice of the proper techniques. On crutches the body is propped in position by the crutches, with one arm bearing most of the body's weight, thereby freeing the other arm to catch the ball. The participation of players on crutches will usually be limited to throwing and catching and perhaps batting.

Blind students playing modified softball will face the direction from which the ball is coming as determined by hearing it move along the ground. The feet are spread apart to cover as much ground as feasible. The hands with fingers spread are placed between the legs. As the ball rolls forward, the hands are positioned to grasp the ball. If the ball is to be thrown through the air by seeing or partially seeing players, the catcher turns toward the thrower and extends his arms with the palms up to make a basket to catch the ball. The thrower aims for the "basket." He lets the catcher know when the ball is thrown.

Throwing. Pitching in softball is done underhanded. However, the overhand throw is used almost exclusively in the rest of the game. In making an overhand throw, the player holds the ball with the first and second fingers on top of the ball and the thumb under it. The arm is raised to the back of the head at about ear level. The wrist is superextended, and the elbow is held back on the level of the shoulder. The left foot is placed forward in the direction of the throw (for a right-handed player). The ball is brought forward past the ear until the arm is fully extended at about shoulder height. In a continuous motion, the wrist is flexed and the ball is released. The trunk is simultaneously rotated to the left. The arm follows through, coming to rest down near the knee on the opposite side of the body. The body weight shifts from the back foot to the front foot as the throw is made.

Adaptations: Very young children may need to grasp the ball by placing three fingers on top of the ball. Individuals with missing fingers will need to adjust the grip so they are able to place at least the thumb or one finger on one side of the ball and one finger on the other side.

Those players who are throwing from a sitting position or from a propped position on crutches will, of course, use the upper part of the body in throwing. The twist of the trunk will come from the hips only. Those who are unable to or should not twist in this manner will make the throw completely with the arm, keeping the body relatively motionless.

One blind player in throwing the ball to another blind player makes the throw underhanded so that it rolls along the ground, bouncing in very short bounces, and can be heard as it rolls.

Batting and Base Running.   The (right-handed) batter should grip the bat firmly near the end with his left hand, placing the right hand above and as close to the left as possible. The top hand should be aligned with the bottom hand so that the third joint of the little finger rests between the second and third joints of the index finger of the lower hand as it encircles the bat. The batter takes a position at the plate so he faces it, with his left side toward the pitcher; the corner of the plate near him splits the center of the body. The distance from the plate should be such that, when the bat is swung, the heavy part of the bat will come over the center of the plate. The bat is held back of the body and not rested on the shoulders. Both elbows and right wrist are flexed. the elbows are held away from the body, with the left elbow in line with the wrist and hand. The batter watches the ball as it leaves the pitcher's hand and continues to watch it until it is hit or has passed by the batter.

When the player swings to strike the ball, his front foot moves forward in a shuffle step. The step is completed before the ball is hit. The bat is swung parallel to the path of the oncoming ball. The ball is contacted in front of the plate, and the bat should follow the ball after it is hit until the swing of the body at the hips changes the direction of the bat. After the ball is hit, the first step toward the base is taken by the right foot with a short step. This is followed by one or two short steps to speed the acceleration, and then the runner goes into full stride toward first base. He runs through the base rather than attempting to stop exactly on it.

Adaptations: Batters on crutches will need to depend more on their arms for power in hitting than on the twist of their bodies. Consequently, they should probably concentrate more on placement than on distance. For those who are unable to run to first base, a substitute runner may be provided as described earlier in this chapter.

A blind batter in the adapted game takes a stance with the left side to the batter (if right-handed). He kneels on his left knee with his weight partially on his right foot. The left hand grasps the bat near the end. The right hand is four to five inches above the left. The bat is brought back in preparation for the swing. It is parallel to the floor and two or three inches above it. Before the pitch, the batter notifies the pitcher that he is in position to bat. As the batter hears the ball roll into the striking zone, he swings the bat forward to strike the ball, keeping the bat parallel to the floor.

FOOTBALL

Football is a strenuous competitive game in which only the handicapped who are most physically fit and skilled in the use of their bodies can participate. However, the skills of football—catching, throwing, and kicking—can be learned and enjoyed for their own sake by many types of handicapped players.

General Adaptations: Because football is a sport which requires body contact, its strenuousness cannot be modified by reducing the size of the playing area or by increasing the number of players, as is possible with the other games presented in this chapter. Consequently, only those whose handicaps do not impose restrictions on the range or amount of movement, such as the deaf* and educable mentally retarded, can participate in regulation football. For others, modifications must be made in the way the game is played. For example, arm amputees are able to play football in the position of linemen by substituting blocking for tackling. In a regular game they may be used as place kickers.

Modification of the game to eliminate end runs makes possible play by teams of blind and partially sighted players. They cannot play successfully against teams of normal players but are able to compete against other blind teams. (Partially sighted boys in a normal school situation cannot usually be worked in as players in a regulation game of football.) On the blind team, those who are totally without vision play the center, guard, and tackle positions while the partially sighted play as ends and backs. The linemen play their positions by meeting force with force. If the opponent attempts to block from a certain direction, this is taken as a cue by the linemen that the play is going in the opposite direction; and they fight their way in that direction. They grab any opponents who attempt to run by them.

Passing. In a forward pass, the ball is grasped so that the index finger is about two inches from the tip. The thumb is placed opposite the index finger, with the fingers spread. The ball is brought up and back near the ear with the end that is being grasped pointing back over the shoulder. For a right-handed thrower, the right shoulder is thrown back and the left foot is placed forward with the weight on the back foot. The arm is then brought forward close to the head. A step is taken forward in the direction of the throw. The weight is brought forward on the front foot as the arm is brought forward. The ball is released with a wrist snap, making the ball spiral as it goes forward.

Adaptations: All passes that are made to partially seeing players will of necessity be of very short distances of about four or five feet. This enables the receiver to tell where the ball is by the movement of the thrower. Passes should be thrown to the mid-section of the receiver.

For those players who because of limitations cannot participate in football but are able to throw the ball, games of accuracy can be devised for participation. Tires hung by ropes can be used as targets. The tire may be swung to increase the difficulty of the game. A pass receiver may be used to create another game of throwing accuracy. The passer's accuracy is measured by how far the receiver has to move in order to catch the ball. Throwing for distance can be used as another competitive activity.

Receiving Passes. Passes are caught on the fingers. Both hands should be used in catching the ball. The fingers are spread wide and the hands give as the ball comes in contact with the fingers. As in all catching, the ball is watched until it is caught.

Adaptations: One-arm receivers catch the ball with the palm and fingers. As the ball comes in contact with the hand, it is drawn to the body and trapped between the body and hand.

The partially seeing and the blind can catch a football thrown without great force from short distances to the receiver's mid-section. The totally blind person must be

*There is a slight modification for the deaf in that the signals are made with hand signs.

told that the ball is coming and place his arms in position with one arm above the other with the palms facing each other in readiness to catch the ball as it comes in contact with his mid-section. The ball must, of course, be thrown accurately. The player with partial sight watches the thrower, which helps in judging when the ball will arrive, even though he does not have sufficient sight to see the ball coming.

Kicking. In punting the ball is held by both hands. For a right-handed kicker, the right hand is under the ball and the left hand is on the left side. A step is taken forward with the left foot. The right foot starts the swing with the knee slightly bent. The ball is dropped so that in kicking, the ball will be partially on the instep and partially on the toe. The toe is pointed slightly inward. The foot meets the ball about knee high, continues to follow through, and rises above the head.

In the place kick, the ball is held by another player. He should be on his knees. If he is to receive the pass from center, he should be back 10 to 12 yards from the center. A mark should be made by the holder at the place where he will put the ball. If the kicker is kicking with his right foot, the holder will be on his right side. When he receives the ball, the holder places the point of the ball on the ground, with the fingers of his right hand on the top of the ball. The kicker stands in front of the ball. As the ball is placed on the ground, he steps forward with his left foot so that it is six to eight inches behind and slightly to the left of the ball. He keeps his eye on the ball at all times. He then swings his right foot forward so the toe meets the ball slightly below its center. He follows through with his leg. His head remains down, watching the ball, as he follows through.

Adaptations: One-arm amputees in kicking the football will hold the ball in one hand by placing the hand under its center and balancing it or grasping the point of the ball with the fingers and thumb. Double-arm amputees are limited to place kicking.

Students who because of physical limitations cannot play football or touch football may participate in kicking for distance contests. Contests of kicking accuracy can also be devised for these students. For this purpose, several concentric circles are laid out on the field, with each circle given a number value, much like an archery target. The points achieved by each of a designated number of kicks are totaled to determine the winner.

VOLLEYBALL

Volleyball is perhaps the most easily modified of all the team games for play by the handicapped. Even those for whom strenuous activity is contraindicated can participate if the pace of the game is moderate. Those with limited locomotion can also be successfully accommodated.

General Adaptations: The net may be lowered to less than the standard heights if the abilities of the players indicate the need for this. However, the net should be high enough so that no player is able to reach over the top of it.

On a regulation court, it is possible to increase the size of the teams to eight or 10 players. If some of the players are on crutches, the area assigned to them to defend will need to be smaller than the areas defended by players who have normal locomotion.

If wheelchair patients are playing the game, the court may be increased or decreased in size, depending upon the number of players. In any case, the area that each wheelchair player is responsible for in playing will need to be small enough so that he can readily cover it.

For the blind or partially sighted, the court may need to be larger.

Playing the Game.   In assuming playing positions, three players on each team are net players. They face the net about an arm's length from it and at equal distances from each other. The other three players are in the backcourt. The players here are directly behind the net players and about two or three strides in from the back line.

The game begins by serving the ball from anywhere behind the back boundary line. In serving, the ball is held in the open palm of one hand and struck with the closed fist of the other hand so that the ball rises into the air and goes over the net.

Each team member serves in turn and may have one trial to serve the ball over the net. The server continues to serve until his team fails to return the ball; then the serve passes to the opposing team. All offensive players rotate clockwise one position when a new player begins to serve.

In returning the ball, the player must bat it; it cannot be momentarily caught. Each team is allowed three hits to return the ball over the net. No player may hit the ball twice in succession. One point is scored if the receiving team fails to return the ball. The receiving team gets the ball to serve but does not score if the serving team fails to return the ball. Usually the game is played to 15 points, provided that the winner has won by 2 points. If such a margin does not exist, the game continues until one team wins 2 points in a row.

Adaptations: If more than six players are used, the distribution of players may be made so that they will be equally divided between the net and the backcourt, or three players may be placed at the net with three in the backcourt and three others placed in between.

Those who have insufficient power to get the ball over the net in the serve may be permitted to move up a specified distance to the net. A one-armed server must throw the ball high into the air and bat it with the same hand. An overhand stroke is made.

Players lacking sufficient coordination to strike the ball to return it over the net may be permitted to catch the ball and return it by throwing it back inbounds on the other side of the net. The net in this case should be higher than usual, and a score is made when the ball is not caught or when it is thrown out of bounds or into the net. Throwing the ball over the net may be substituted for serving, if necessary.

This adaptation may be used also by the blind with the addition of permitting the ball to bounce. A score is when:

1. The ball rolls out of bounds before it is trapped.
2. The ball is thrown and does not land in the opponents' court.
3. The ball goes into the net.

When a blind or partially sighted player is participating with normal players, he may be permitted to serve all during the game and to take part in the volleying only if he can see the ball well enough. If he is able to see the ball but not clearly enough to volley it, he may be allowed to catch the ball and play it as in the game of newcomb.

Wall volley is an activity that can be used with good results as a game for the blind and as a drill with other handicapped students learning to play volleyball. Players volley the ball against the wall. The number of times a player volleys the ball successfully constitutes the score. Blind players will need to be allowed to stand closer to the wall than other players. For sighted students, the ball is volleyed above a line six feet high which is marked on the wall. Players should control the ball on their fingers throughout the volley rather than on the palms.

Students on crutches will need to balance themselves with their crutches in such a manner as to free at least one hand for striking the ball. The ball may be served as described for the one-handed player.

The wheelchair player may serve underhand by leaning to the side of the chair, or the ball may be tossed high into the air with one hand and stroked underhand with the other. The wheelchair player will need to develop, as must the player on crutches, the ability to return the ball with one hand. However, if he skillfully maneuvers his chair, he will be able to use both hands a large portion of the time. A one-hand return executed to the side of the body, or in the case of the wheelchair player to the side of the chair, can be made by reaching straight out with the arm to the side. The ball is allowed to drop to shoulder height and the ball is struck and lifted into the air by hitting it with the palm.

SELECTED READINGS

AAHPER: *Basketball Selected Articles.* Washington, D.C., American Alliance for Health, Physical Education, and Recreation, Division for Girls' and Women's Sports, current edition.

AAHPER: *Official Basketball Rules and Guide.* Washington, D.C., American Alliance for Health, Physical Education, and Recreation, Division for Girls' and Women's Sports, current edition.

AAHPER: *Official Softball Rules and Guide.* Washington, D.C., American Alliance for Health, Physical Education, and Recreation, Division for Girls' and Women's Sports, current edition.

AAHPER: *Physical Education for High School Students,* ed. 2. Washington, D.C., American Association for Health, Physical Education, and Recreation, 1970.

Bailey, C. Ian, and Teller, Francis: *Soccer.* Philadelphia, W. B. Saunders Co., 1971.

Fait, Hollis F.: *Physical Education for the Elementary School Child: Experiences in Movement,* ed. 3. Philadelphia, W. B. Saunders Co., 1976.

National Federation of State High School Athletic Associations: *Official Basketball Rules.* Chicago, published annually.

Slaymaker, Thomas, and Brown, Virginia H.: *Power Volleyball.* Philadelphia, W. B. Saunders Co., 1970.

Vannier, Maryhelen, and Fait, Hollis F.: *Teaching Physical Education in Secondary Schools,* ed. 4. Philadelphia, W. B. Saunders Co., 1975.

Vannier, Maryhelen, and Poindexter, Holly Beth: *Individual and Team Sports for Girls and Women,* ed. 3. Philadelphia, W. B. Saunders Co., 1975.

Chapter 25

Swimming

Swimming ranks high among the physical education activities which can be most successfully taught to those who are handicapped. The success is due in large part to the buoyancy of the water, which, in providing support for the body, is both helpful and reassuring to the handicapped student engaged in learing a new skill. Sustained by the water, a crippled body can perform otherwise impossible movements; even those students who are incapable of walking, as is the case with those who have severe cerebral palsy, are frequently able to learn to swim. Mentally handicapped students find the bouyancy of the water comforting, and this fact is a great help to the teacher in allaying the fears which often prevent successful learning of an activity by the retarded.

Swimming is also high among the activities which are most beneficial to the handicapped. Swimming, of course, provides the handicapped student with important skills for his safety on, in, or near the water. It also makes possible participation in a recreational activity that is popular with the non-handicapped and so opens opportunities for socialization. In addition, the handicapped swimmer reaps important physiological benefits.

The beneficial effects upon the body result from the amount and nature of the work performed in swimming. Even mild activity in the water has a good effect upon those whose movements are severely restricted. Improved circulation and increased strength are likely to occur in most participants. Those who have restricted movements in the joints caused by pain and stiffness often benefit greatly from the increased movement of the joints made possible in the water. Likewise, cerebral palsy patients often find that because of the water's buoyancy they are able to make movements in the water that they are not otherwise able to make.

Even children with Legg-Calvé-Perthes disease, who are denied participation in so many activities, can enjoy the pleasures of swimming. While they are not encouraged to stand erect in the water, they can do so without much risk because the buoyancy of the water reduces the pressure of body weight on the head of the femur. For others, the water buoyancy makes control of the body easier by minimizing the effects of weak muscles and the lack of balance and stability which hinder or restrict movement out of the water. Appliances which must always be worn otherwise can usually be removed for swimming.

ORGANIZING THE INSTRUCTION

Swimming instruction should be scheduled regularly for students who are to be in the swimming program. Class size will vary with conditions. If the students' disabilities are not severe, the teacher will be able to handle larger numbers in a single period. Those with moderate deviations may possibly be included in a regular swimming class for normal students. When the disabilities of students are more severe, the size of the class for one teacher must be reduced proportionately to retain teaching effectiveness and maintain the safety of the participants. For some individuals with severe disabilities it may be necessary to provide individual instruction. In the school situation, individual instruction may be provided by student helpers. In a community swimming program, volunteers may be recruited from throughout the community.

For the best possible environment, the water temperature should be higher than normal to reduce tension and to prevent chilling. Nonskid material should be used around the pool area to prevent accidental falls. Ramps leading to the pool should be provided for wheelchair patients and those on crutches. Easily grasped supports should be provided on the deck and in the pool for those who have difficulty standing, handrails may be installed on the deck, and ropes or poles may be provided in the pool itself.

Before organization of the class and methods of instruction are developed, the instructor must determine for each student his present level of skill, the movements he is capable of making, and his attitude toward his handicap. Different kinds of disabilities impose different limitations. The kinds of movements an individual can make will determine the approach used by the instructor to teach him. Analysis of movement will provide information for deciding which strokes should be taught and what modifications are necessary. The student's acceptance or lack of acceptance of his disability determines to a considerable extent the way in which the instruction, particularly in its initial phase, is presented.

Consideration must also be given to provisions for those who are incontinent. Youngsters with spinal injuries, including those with spina bifida, wear a urinal bag strapped to the leg. This is not removed for swimming and can be protected from view, if desired, by wearing long pants in the pool. If a student who uses an ileostomy or colostomy bag is permitted by his doctor to swim, the bag is removed before entering the pool and the opening sealed with a watertight bandage. Mental retardates whose control is not well established can be provided with bikini diapers and rubber pants to be worn under the swimsuit. A skimmer should be readily available for dealing with the occasional emergencies when feces are deposited in the pool. Chemicals should be put into the water to prevent such an occurrence from posing a health problem.

TECHNIQUES FOR GETTING INTO AND OUT OF THE POOL

Handicapped students with limited mobility need to develop effective ways of getting into and out of the pool. Ramps and steps with handrails are helpful to those who need only such support as these provide. The techniques for using the ramps and rails need to be worked out by the teacher and the individual student. If these devices are not available or if they are insufficient, the student will need to be lifted into and out of the pool.

The usual procedure for lifting students into and out of the pool requires two people. The person who is being assisted may sit on the deck, if he is able, or be seated in a wheelchair. In the latter case, a helper stands behind the chair and reaches under the student's arms to grasp his wrists and bring them to the chest. The other helper stands in front of the wheelchair and takes hold of the student around the thighs. Together the helpers lift him free of the chair and seat him on a piece of canvas or on

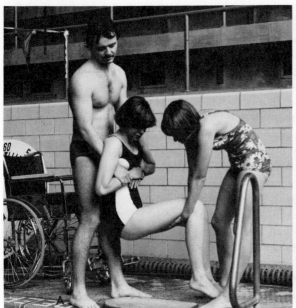

Figure 25–1. A, B Technique for lifting a student into the pool.

a kickboard that has been placed at the edge of the pool. He or she is seated parallel to the pool and supported by one helper while the other enters the water to take a position in front of the student. The helpers turn the canvas so that the student is seated with his legs hanging over the edge of the pool. The helper on the deck then gently pushes forward on the shoulders of the student while the helper in the pool takes hold at the waist to guide the body into the water. For a student who does not need to be lifted to the edge of the pool, only the techniques for lifting into and out of the water are utilized.

A hydraulic lift is sometimes available at pools to lift students in wheelchairs. In this technique canvas is placed in the seat of the wheelchair before the student occupies it. The lift is then attached to the sides of the canvas. By manipulating the handles of the lift, the student is raised from the chair and lowered into the pool.

If the pool has a ramp, an old wheelchair designated for this purpose is used to wheel the student into the water to the height of his chest. He can then be easily lifted into the water by a single helper, who places one arm under the legs and the other behind the back to make the lift.

In all these techniques, the steps for getting the handicapped student into the pool can be reversed to lift him out. It is assumed, of course, that adjustments are made as required by individual cases.

OVERCOMING FEAR OF THE WATER

Most nonswimmers feel some anxiety about entering the water in the beginning. This is especially true of handicapped nonswimmers because they lack confidence in their physical abilities. Consequently, the teacher should strive to make the introductory activities to the water as much fun as possible so that the student will begin to feel secure in the water before he has time to be frightened.

The introductory water activities can be fun if the teacher's manner is sincere and friendly, if his instructions are clearly stated and calmly spoken, if his attitude conveys understanding and appreciation of each student as an individual, and if his own enthusiasm for water activities is transmitted to the participants.

The teacher should seek to provide experiences that will lead the student from that to which he is accustomed and readily accepts to new experiences that will effect complete acceptance of the water. Sitting on the side of the pool splashing with the feet is one example of an activity that is generally accepted without anxiety and that can be directed toward the objective of complete acceptance of the water. Ambulatory students may progress from dangling the feet to standing in waist-deep water and from this to bobbing up and down to their shoulders and eventually to their chins. The final step would be ducking completely under the water and opening the eyes.

Those who are not ambulatory or have severe limitations in motor movement may need support in the water. Support may be provided by the instructor if this seems necessary or desirable. There are a number of flotation devices such as tubes, canisters, and arm bands, which may be used to support or stabilize the body in the water. The students should be held in such a manner as to relieve all fear and anxiety that may develop. Slowly, as their confidence increases, the amount of support can be reduced and finally withdrawn.

With persistent practice almost all handicapped children can learn to float, or to move in some manner to stay afloat. However, there will be a few who, because of extreme deformity or movement limitations, will always require flotation devices for support in the water.

For students with cerebral palsy it is an absolute necessity that anxiety be kept at a minimum to allow muscular relaxation. For these students, as well as for others who experience difficulty in relaxing in the water, relaxation exercises such as floating the arms and legs while in a sitting position in shallow water are very helpful. Maintaining the water temperature in the low 90s, which is somewhat higher than the 78-degree temperature recommended for normal usage, also aids in muscular relaxation.

During the introductory activities, care should be taken to prevent fearful, cautious individuals from being suddenly and unexpectedly splashed by the more adventurous. A good rule to establish firmly in everyone's mind before entering the water is no deliberate splashing of other people. Care must also be taken to prevent accidents caused by lack of concern for personal safety. Children with cerebral palsy have been observed by swimming instructors to sometimes make no effort to surface for air, after they have become familiar enough with being in the water to enjoy submerging themselves. These children must be closely watched to avert possible drowning owing to passivity to immersion; their lack of concern gives a false impression of being fully in control.

ESTABLISHING BREATHING RHYTHM

As soon as the students show sufficient confidence, they may proceed to place their face in the water while holding their breath. This is done by bending over from a standing position in chest-high water. Students should be encouraged to repeat the action until they are able to hold their face under the water 15 to 20 seconds.

The next step is to exhale through the mouth while the face is submerged. The final step is to establish a definite rhythmic pattern of breathing. To achieve this the students bob the head up and down in the water, taking air in through the mouth while the head is above the water and exhaling through the mouth while the head is down.

Those who cannot stand may take a sitting position on the bottom of the pool if the water is shallow enough. A steel chair may be used where the water is not sufficiently shallow to permit sitting on the bottom. The seated student performs the above activities in the sitting position. If a student must be wholly supported by the instructor or helper, which may be the case in muscular disorders or severe conditions of cerebral palsy, he can be introduced to the water by the instructor holding him around the waist from the back. If the pool is shallow enough, the teacher sits down in the water while supporting him with one hand. In this position the student's arms and legs can be moved alternately by the teacher in the swimming pattern, starting with raising the arms over the head and pulling them to the sides and followed by moving the legs in kicking fashion. The kinds and amount of movement that can be made by the arms and legs depend, of course, on the limitations of the individual child. As the student progresses in ability he may be held in a prone position to enable him to lift his head above and lower his face into the water at will.

Cardiacs should not be allowed to practice breath holding. For these students, instruction in how to expel air while the face is under water must accompany the instruction in how to place the face in the water. Or, if their conditions are moderate to severe, they may be taught floating and swimming techniques that do not require submersion of the face.

In presenting adaptations that can be made for the handicapped in swimming, very brief descriptions of the specific skills are given to enable the reader to make a better comparison of the adaptation with normal performance and so gain a better understanding of the process of adapting skills for the handicapped. It is not the intent to provide instruction for learning to perform the skills. Those who wish this information are referred to the books in Selected Readings at the end of the chapter.

BEGINNING SWIMMING SKILLS

The Tuck Float.   Learning the float helps greatly to promote self-confidence in the beginning swimmer. The tuck float is an easy float for the beginner to learn; moreover, in the process of learning it, the student develops the ability to regain his feet in the water. To learn the tuck float, a nonswimmer should stand in water about chest deep. A deep breath is taken and the face is placed in the water; then the knees are pulled up to the chest and gripped with the arms. Holding this position the body floats to the surface. A return to the standing position is accomplished by releasing the knees and thrusting the feet down. At the same time the head is raised. The hands push down on the water to help regain balance.

The Face Float.   The prone face or dead man's float is executed by bending at the hips and placing the face in the water. At the same time the feet are pushed against the bottom of the pool to place the body in a horizontal position face down on the surface of the water. The hands are extended in front. The return to a standing position is made by raising the head and bringing the knees up under the body. The arms are brought forcefully to the sides while at the same time the legs are extended downward into a standing position.

The Back Float.   In the back float, a position is taken by extending the head back and pushing slightly with the feet from the bottom. The hips are lifted high and the head is placed back so the ears are under the water. The arms may be held at the sides or extended to the side. A recovery to a standing position is made by bringing the knees toward the chin as the head is brought up and forward. The hands are brought down and past the hips. As the body rights itself, the legs are extended to the bottom.

Adaptations: Tuck and face floats cannot be taught to students who should not hold their breath, for example, those with cardiac disturbances. In these cases the vertical float is used as a substitution. In the vertical float, the body is at approximately a 70-degree angle with the face lifted just enough to clear the water. This will need to be done in water that is chin deep or deeper. A slight movement of the arms may be necessary to keep the chin above water. A helper may support the body until the swimmer gains confidence and skill in using his arms. To give support, the helper places one hand under the swimmer's chest.

Those who cannot support themselves in the water on their feet should be held by a helper until they have acquired sufficient confidence to use the kickboard or hang on to the gutter for support. A hand placed under the chest in the face float or under the head in the back float will provide sufficient support.

Those who do not have use of the arms will need help at first in regaining their feet from a float position, but they can learn to right themselves by a very forceful extension of the legs while simultaneously lifting the head and shoulders. If the swimmer has the use of only one arm, the arm action used to regain the feet should be executed as near to the center of the body as possible for maximum effectiveness.

The ataxic should be watched carefully during attempts to regain the standing position because of his poor sense of balance, particularly when he cannot see his feet.

The Glide and the Flutter Kick.   After the beginner has learned the face float, he may be taught how to glide in the prone position. The glide is performed much like the face float except that, instead of lifting the feet off the bottom, the feet push off from the bottom to move the body forward in a prone float position.

The flutter kick is the simplest kick to learn. The student assumes a prone position and thrashes the legs alternately up and down. The kick starts at the hip, followed by extension of the knee. The toes are extended. In the kick the feet are spread vertically from 15 to 20 inches. For younger children, the spread will be less.

Adaptations: If physical abilities permit, the kick may be introduced as a land drill; the student assumes a prone position on a bench with the legs projected beyond the bench. The kick can also be practiced while holding on to the gutter or a kickboard. After the kick is mastered, it is combined with the prone float to propel the body forward.

Anyone who cannot place his face in the water should be assisted by a helper, who takes the swimmer by his extended hands to tow him while he kicks.

Swimmers who have lost the use of one leg must learn to use the remaining leg in the flutter kick. If the leg is paralyzed, it may be helpful to put a small float under the thigh of the disabled leg.

The Dog Paddle and the Human Stroke.   In the dog paddle the head is held above the water. The arms are alternately extended forward and downward and then pulled backward under the chest. At the same time the feet are moved in the flutter kick. The human stroke is executed much like the dog paddle except that the face is in the water as in the prone float and the arms are fully extended in front of the head before pulling down and back. As in the dog paddle, the hands do not leave the water.

Adaptations: Those who are able may practice the arm stroke with the leg kick on a bench before getting into the water. Following this the arm movement is practiced while standing in chest-deep water.

Land practice of swimming strokes is not effective with cerebral palsied swimmers because of the increased tension in the muscles when they are out of the water. Consequently, their practice should all be in the water.

Swimmers who have limited movement of their limbs will need to be supported by a helper who passes a hand under the swimmer's chest. Flotation devices may also be used as supports for these students. Those who because of amputation or atrophy

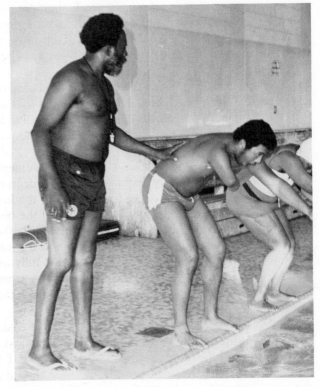

Figure 25–2. Arm amputation creates problems in body balance in swimming and diving, requiring careful movement analysis by the instructor.

of a limb have difficulty balancing in the water must make the necessary movements of the active limbs close to the center of the body to overcome the imbalance. The best placement of the limbs can be determined by movement analysis and subsequent experimentation.

Some handicapped youngsters will not be able to learn to swim or float in the prone position. For these, the progression in swimming should be from the back float to the elementary back stroke or, if this is not feasible, any movement that propels the body in any direction while supine.

INTERMEDIATE SWIMMING STROKES

The side stroke, the elementary back stroke, and the crawl are strokes that are frequently taught on the intermediate level.

The Side Stroke. The body is turned on its side with the stronger arm on top. The arm under the water is fully extended at right angles to the body while the other arm rests fully extended along the side of the body. The under arm is brought down to a nearly vertical position and then the elbow is bent. At the same time, the top arm is brought up to enter the water near the head. This arm recovers to the starting position with a downward reaching movement. Meanwhile the other arm is recovering with a pulling movement toward the body.

The kick for the side stroke is called the scissors. The legs are bent slightly at the knees as one leg (usually the top leg) is brought in front of the body and the other leg is moved to the rear. The legs are then extended fully and brought together forcefully in a movement resembling the opening and closing of a scissors.

The movements of the arms and legs are coordinated to begin and recover simultaneously. The body glides momentarily in the water before the next stroke begins.

Adaptations: Those who have weak shoulder joints subject to frequent dislocation will find the side stroke the safest stroke for swimming. It will also be the most effective stroke and the most easily learned by those who have lost one limb. When there is a disabled or missing arm, the side stroke is performed with the functional arm on the bottom.

The functional leg, when the other leg is missing or disabled, may be either on the top or bottom, whichever proves better through trial and error. If both legs have been lost, the swimmer will probably have to find a suitable modified position through experimentation; this will usually be a partially prone position rather than wholly on the side of the body.

The Elementary Back Stroke.   The arm movement for the elementary back stroke begins with the arms fully extended at a 45-degree angle between the head and shoulders. The arms are brought to the sides of the body in a sweeping arc. In the recovery the hands are brought along the sides of the body to shoulder height. They are then fully extended to begin the next downward stroke.

In the kick, the knees are brought up and out to either side of the body so the heels are touching. The legs are then extended fully and brought together forcefully.

The straightening of the legs occurs at the same time that the arms are being brought down to the sides. The arms recover along the body to the armpits before the legs start their recovery.

Adaptations: Many disabled students find it easier to swim on the back than in any other position. In the position on the back, almost any kind of movement with the arms or legs will move the body in some direction. If the swimmer does not have use of the arms, the legs may be used in a flutter kick to propel the body; conversely, if the legs cannot be used, the arms may be used as in the back stroke. Finning and sculling movements with the hands may be substituted for the arm stroke if movement of the arms is restricted.

The Crawl.   In teaching the crawl, it is necessary only to add the arm movement to the flutter kick and breathing technique introduced in the beginning skills. The arm stroke is made by extending the arm fully in front of the face and pressing downward against the water, with the hand leading the rest of the arm. When the arm is beneath the shoulder, the shoulder is lifted and the elbow is raised until it clears the water. The arm is then brought forward above the water with the fingers near the water, ready for entrance into the water for the next stroke.

The arms stroke alternately, and inhalation should occur as the shoulder is lifted in the recovery. The head may be turned to either side, depending upon which seems more natural for the swimmer. The kick is coordinated with the arms to accomplish a smooth and rhythmical stroke.

Adaptations: The crawl is the most satisfactory stroke for those with loss of movement in the legs. In some cases of leg disability, flexion and extension may be developed to compensate for lack of leg action. Hip impairment may require the swimmer to execute the flutter kick with greater knee bend.

The arm stroke may be modified for those with arm and shoulder limitations by reducing it to less than the full stroke. The crawl should not be swum by those with weak shoulder joints subject to frequent dislocation.

SELECTED READINGS

American Red Cross: *Swimming for the Handicapped—Instructor's Manual,* rev. ed. Washington, D.C., American Red Cross, 1975.
Council for National Cooperation in Aquatics and AAHPER: *A Practical Guide for Teaching the Men-*

tally Retarded to Swim. Washington, D.C., American Association for Health, Physical Education, and Recreation, 1969.

Lahoy, Laurel, *et al.: Handbook on Swimming for the Disabled.* Vancouver, B.C., Canadian Red Cross Society, (nd).

Newman, Judy: *Swimming for Children with Physical and Sensory Impairments.* Springfield, Ill., Charles C Thomas, Pub., 1976.

Reynolds, Grace Demmery (Editor): *A Swimming Program for the Handicapped.* New York, Association Press, 1973.

Richardson, Paul, and Lucas, Katie: *Aquatic Lessions for Exceptional Children.* Elwyn, Penna. Elwyn Institute, (nd).

Chapter 26

Weight Training

Weight training is the systematic exercise with weights for the purpose of developing the body; when weight training is performed competitively, it is referred to as weight-lifting. Both weight training and weight-lifting have become enormously popular with boys and young men. Part of this popularity can be attributed to the acceptance of weight training in the conditioning programs of athletes for sports competition.

Weight training for purposes of rehabilitation is a specialized activity and is usually attempted only in hospital situations under the guidance of a physician. In the school physical education program, weight training is directed toward developing and maintaining a satisfactory level of physical fitness. In addition, for the handicapped, it provides another opportunity to engage with normal peers in a popularly accepted activity.

AREA AND EQUIPMENT

Weight training requires very little space; an area as small as 100 square feet is adequate. The floor must be able to support considerable weight; therefore, a concrete floor is desirable. However, if the floor is wooden, heavy planks may be placed over it.

Equipment consists primarily of barbells and dumbbells. The barbells are used for exercises with two hands, while the dumbbells, which are shorter, are used chiefly for one-arm exercises. Weight-lifting machines like the one in Figure 26–1 eliminate the use of barbells and dumbbells; all lifts that are possible with weights can be done with the machine. In addition, some special pieces of equipment have been devised to expand the exercise possibilities; among these are head straps, iron shoes, knee exercisers, wall pulleys, wrist rollers, chest springs, inclined boards, and leg press apparatus.

ORGANIZING THE INSTRUCTION

Weight training lends itself readily to incorporation in a dual program. After initial instruction in the lifts, students may proceed on their own or in pairs. For those working alone, the use of a personal progress sheet is very helpful; on it should be recorded at the end of each class period the amount of weight lifted and the number of repetitions made. This will enable the student to know exactly where to begin at the start of the next class.

Regardless of the class organization for instruction in weight training, all students, before they begin, should have a clear understanding of the activities they must avoid, the adaptations they must make, and the safety precautions they must observe.

Safety regulations which should be stressed emphatically by the teacher are listed below. The first one applies when using either the weight-lifting machine or the barbells and dumbbells; the other three apply only to the use of the latter.

1. Warm-up exercises should be taken before attempting a heavy lift. The warm-up may consist of the side-straddle hop exercise or running in place with exaggerated arm movements.

2. In moving a heavy weight from one place to another, the lift should be made with the knees flexed and the back straight. No one, especially those with back difficulties, should ever lift heavy weights by bending at the hips with the legs straight.

3. Collars (the metal pieces which hold the weights to the bar) should be fastened securely. They should be checked before each lift is attempted.

4. A lift should never be made over someone who is sitting, squatting, or lying on the floor.

All exercises should have the approval of the handicapped student's physician. Participants with weakened or injured muscles should use light loads as prescribed by the doctor. When exercising those parts of the body which are not injured, the utmost care must be taken to prevent the injured part from being brought into action inadvertently. Special care must be taken so that the lifter will not slip or allow his load to slip, thereby bringing into action a muscle that was being protected. To be absolutely safe, a lifter with an injury should not make an all-out effort even though the injured part is not involved in the effort.

Those for whom lifting weights is contraindicated for the leg area may do their lifting while sitting or lying down, avoiding all lifts involving the legs. Students in wheelchairs can perform the lifts while seated in their wheelchairs. Some participants with minor back difficulties may be allowed to take arm and leg exercises if the back is protected against undue stress. To protect the back in such exercises as the two-arm curl, lateral raise, front raise, and military press, these lifts can be made sitting down, with the back held firmly against the back of the chair. Exercises that require heavy

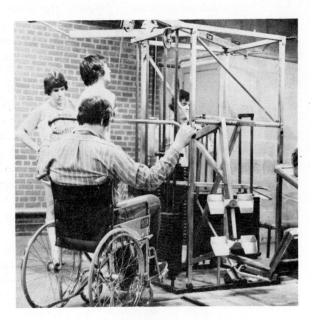

Figure 26–1. Lifts can be made while seated in the wheelchair by those with lower limb involvement.

weight on the shoulders are contraindicated for those with weak backs. Exercise with the iron shoe or leg machine is a possible substitution for the deep knee bends which require heavy weight on the shoulder to develop the quadriceps of the legs. Exercises from the prone position do not place undue stress upon the back and therefore need not be adapted. In the supine position those exercises that have a tendency to hyperextend the back, such as the leg raises and the supine pullover, are contraindicated for those with any type of back difficulties or with exceptionally weak abdominals.

In lifting heavy weights, a deep breath is taken and held to stabilize the thoracic region. When this is done, there is an extreme elevation of the arterial blood pressure because the increased pressure in the thoracic region prevents blood from returning to the heart. If the effort is prolonged, the blood pressure falls after its initial rise. This is known as the Valsalva phenomenon. Because of the increase in blood pressure caused by lifting of weights, the activity is not usually recommended for those with cardiac or circulatory disorders.

The student with the use of only one arm will perform all the lifts involving the use of an arm with this arm. The weights should be sufficiently light so that lifting them with one arm will not produce twisting of the body or bending of the spine laterally, for such movements may produce muscular development that will cause postural difficulties. Students with functional stumps may find it possible to do the lifts with a prosthesis.

In presenting adaptations that can be made for the handicapped in weight training, very brief descriptions of the specific lifts are given to enable the reader to make a better comparison of the adaptation with normal performance and so gain a better understanding of the process of adapting the lifts for the handicapped. It is not the intent to provide instruction for learning to perform the lifts. Those who wish this information are referred to the books in Selected Readings at the end of the chapter.

LIFTING TECHNIQUES

There are many different types of lifts. Many of them exercise different muscles, while others exercise muscles in different groups or exercise the same set of muscles. The muscles that are primarily involved in any given lift can be determined with some degree of accuracy even by someone who does not have a thorough knowledge of anatomy. It must be remembered that a muscle does not push but always pulls to move a joint and that a contracting muscle is harder than a muscle not being worked. Consequently, by examining the direction of movement of the part of the body involved and by palpating the muscle or muscles while the lift is being executed, the muscles being used can be located. Then, by referring to a chart of the skeletal muscles like the one in Figure 26–3, the muscles can be identified.

The lifts presented here are selected to give a fairly complete workout to the major muscle groups in a minimum number of exercises. All lifts using barbells and dumbbells are made from the standing position unless otherwise indicated. Positions for the lifts on the weight-lifting machine will vary according to the kind of machine. The lifts below are described for the barbells and dumbbells, but most of the lifts can be done on the various machines.

Neck Extension and Neck Curl. Neck extension exercises the posterior muscles of the neck (sacrospinalis, cervical muscles, trapezius). A prone position is taken on a bench or on the floor. If a bench is used, the neck extends over the end of the bench. A plate of the barbells is held with both hands on the back of the head. The head is

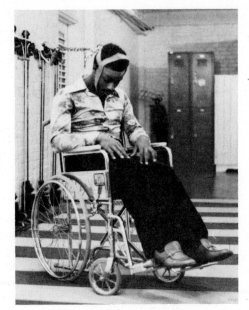

Figure 26–2. A head harness attached to a wall pulley may be used for exercise by those with movement only in the neck.

lifted backward as far as possible while the chest rests on the bench or floor. The neck is then lowered to the starting position.

The neck curl is performed in the supine position, and the weight is held on the forehead. The head is brought up and forward until the chin touches the chest.

Adaptations: The exercise may be done without the weights held to the head to decrease the strenuousness of the exercise. If there is extreme muscular weakness or cervical vertebrae injury or malfunction, the neck muscles may be exercised by tightening the flexors and extensors at the same time and holding for a few seconds, repeating until sufficient work has been given to the muscles, as a substitute for the exercise with weights.

For those in wheelchairs, a head harness may be attached to a wall pulley.

Military Press or Standing Press. The muscles involved in this lift are the deltoid, pectoralis major, and triceps. To make the lift, a pronated grip is taken on the bar. The bar is lifted and brought to rest against the chest. The bar is then raised straight over the head until the arms are fully extended. The bar is lowered to the chest position and the exercise repeated.

Adaptations: Care must be taken to keep the back straight as the weight is lifted above the head. This is especially necessary if the lifter has lower back difficulties. To avoid the tendency to hyperextend the back, the participant may sit in a chair with a high back, holding his back firmly against the chair's back.

Two-Arm Curl. The biceps and the brachialis are the primary muscles used in the two-arm curl. The supinated grip is taken. The bar is brought to the thighs. The bar is raised to the shoulders by bending the elbows. The weight is then lowered until the arms are fully extended. The lift may be done by taking a pronated grip. The extensors of the fingers and wrist can be exercised by hyperextending the wrist while lifting the weight to the shoulders.

Adaptations: Lifters with back disorders must take the utmost care to avoid pushing the hips forward to help start the lift upward. This movement hyperextends the back, thereby placing undue stress upon it. To avoid this possibility, the lifter should keep the weight light enough to be handled easily with the arms. As additional protection against hyperextension the lifter may stand with his back against the wall so that he is unable to move his hips during the lift.

Straight-Arm Pullover. The major work in this lift is performed by the pectoralis major and minor, triceps, latissimus dorsi, and serratus anterior muscles. A supine position is taken. The bar is on the floor at arm's length from the head. A grip is taken with the palms up. The bar is pulled and lifted with the arms held straight to a position above the chest. The chair is returned to the starting position and the exercise repeated.

Adaptations: To decrease the difficulty of the lift for those lacking arm strength, the pullover may be done with the arms bent until the bar is above the head, at which time the arms are extended fully. The bar is lowered in a reverse manner.

Those with weak backs should not perform the straight-arm pullover.

Straight-Leg Dead Lift. In this lift the back muscles and upper posterior leg muscles (erector spinae, gluteus maximus, and hamstrings) are used. The bar is placed near the toes. The body is bent at the hips and the upper back held straight. An alternate grip is taken on the bar (one hand pronated and the other supinated), and the bar is lifted by straightening the back. The knees are locked and the arms are kept straight. The bar is then lowered to its original position.

Adaptations: Those with back injuries should modify the lift to reduce the strain upon the back muscles and yet exercise the extensors of the back, as follows: A sitting position is taken on a bench, with a light dumbbell in each hand. The shoulders are hunched forward, and the chin rests on the chest. The head is lifted, the shoulders thrown wide, and the back straightened. Return to the original position and repeat the exercise.

Sit-ups. The major muscles involved in the sit-ups are the abdominals and the iliopsoas. A supine position is taken, with the legs straight and the toes hooked under the bar. A weight is held to the back of the head with both hands. The head is brought forward until it touches the chest and then the back is lifted off the floor in a sit-up position. The return is made to the starting position.

To make the exercise more difficult, the knees are bent rather than being held straight in the sit-up.

Adaptations: No weight is placed behind the head. The head is brought forward until the chin touches the chest. Then the shoulders start the raise from the floor. The small of the back remains in contact with the floor throughout the lift. The return is made to the supine position.

Deep Knee Bend and Heel Raise. In the deep knee bend the gastrocnemius, soleus, quadriceps, and gluteus maximus are used extensively. The bar is held across the back of the neck and shoulders, and the body is lowered to a full squat position. The return is made to the original position.

In the heel raise, the gastrocnemius, soleus, and plantar flexor of the feet are developed. The bar is carried on the shoulders as in the deep knee bend. The bar is lifted by raising the heels off the ground until the weight is resting on the balls of the feet. The heels are then lowered.

Adaptations: Some authorities feel that deep knee bends affect the ligaments of the knee to their disadvantage and therefore recommend that only a three-quarter squat be taken.

Those suffering from injured knees should substitute exercises with the iron shoe or knee exerciser for the knee bends. Students with back difficulties should not perform the lift with heavy weights on the shoulders. Those with arch problems in the feet should not do the heel raise.

Lateral, Forward, and Backward Lifts. The muscles involved in each of these lifts are: lateral lift—deltoid, supraspinatus, trapezius, serratus anterior; forward lift—deltoid, pectoralis major, coracobrachialis, serratus anterior, trapezius; backward lift—deltoid, teres major, rhomboids, trapezius.

Dumbbells are grasped in each hand with the hands at the sides of the body. In the lateral raise, the arms are lifted directly sideways to the horizontal level. For the forward raise, they are lifted forward. In the backward raise, the arms are raised backward and upward as far as possible without bending the trunk.

Adaptations: In the lateral and forward lifts, a sitting position may be taken to avoid hyperextending the back. Those with weak shoulder joints subject to dislocation should never raise the arms higher than shoulder level. As an additional safety precaution, the exercise should be performed with one arm at a time. The opposite arm is brought across the chest and the hand grasps the shoulder to pull it in toward the body during the lift. In this way it becomes impossible to raise the arm inadvertently above the desired level.

The backward lift is contraindicated for those suffering from weak shoulder joints subject to dislocation.

Prone Lateral Raise. The deltoid, pectoralis major, infraspinatus, teres minor, and trapezius muscles are brought into play in this exercise. A prone position is taken on a bench, and the hands grasp dumbbells on the floor to each side of the body. The weights are lifted toward the ceiling as far as possible, keeping the arms straight. The dumbbells are then lowered slowly to the floor.

Adaptations: No modification is required except for amputees and cardiac patients.

Supine Horizontal Arm Lift. The following muscles are used in this lift: deltoid, pectoralis major, coracobarchialis, and serratus anterior. A supine position is taken with the arms extended out from the shoulders. The dumbbells are grasped with the palms facing up. The arms are raised over the chest with the elbows locked and then returned to the original position.

Adaptations: The lift will usually not require adaptation except from amputees and cardiac patients.

Quadriceps Exercise with Iron Shoe. The lifter sits on a low table with the lower part of one leg at right angles to the thigh. An iron show is strapped to the foot. The knee is extended until it is straight and parallel to the floor. The leg is then lowered to the original position.

Adaptation: Those recuperating from knee injuries should take a much lighter load on the injured leg than they are able to lift with the normal leg; one half the weight is usually recommended. The lifter should sit so that he may be able to lower the weight to the floor rapidly at any time.

Hamstring Exercises with Iron Shoe. A prone position is taken with an iron shoe fastened to the foot. The leg is bent and the knee raised until the shoe touches the buttocks. The foot is then returned to the starting position. No adaptations are usually necessary.

Prone Arch Back. The performer lies face down on a bench, with the upper half of the body extended over the end of the bench; his ankles are held securely by a partner. Holding a dumbbell behind his head, he arches his back and holds this position for eight to 10 seconds.

Adaptations: To reduce the strain on weak extensor muscles of the back, the amount of the weight is decreased. Also, a small stool may be placed beneath the lifter's chest to prevent his going all the way to the floor.

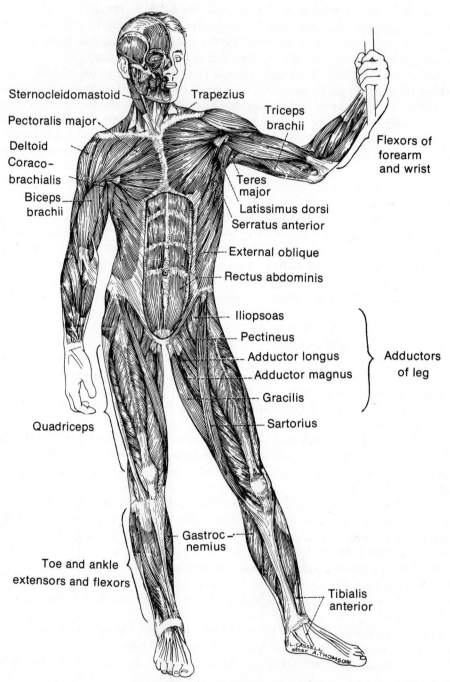

Figure 26–3. Surface muscle chart.

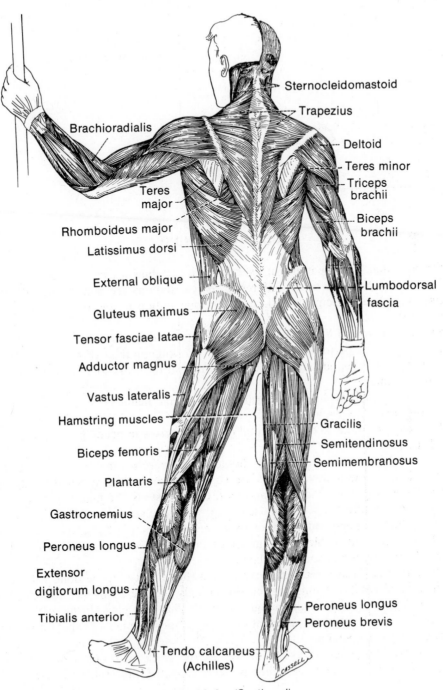

Sternocleidomastoid

Trapezius

Brachioradialis

Deltoid

Teres minor

Triceps brachii

Teres major

Biceps brachii

Rhomboideus major

Latissimus dorsi

External oblique

Lumbodorsal fascia

Gluteus maximus

Tensor fasciae latae

Adductor magnus

Vastus lateralis

Hamstring muscles

Gracilis

Biceps femoris

Semitendinosus

Semimembranosus

Plantaris

Gastrocnemius

Peroneus longus

Extensor digitorum longus

Tibialis anterior

Peroneus longus

Peroneus brevis

Tendo calcaneus (Achilles)

Figure 26–3. *(Continued)*

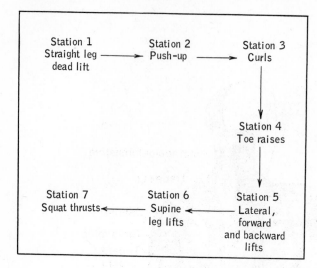

Figure 26-4. Sample circuit.

CIRCUIT TRAINING

Circuit training is a pattern of exercises that enables a large number of participants to work out at one time. Different exercise stations are placed throughout the exercise area. The participants progress from one station to the next until they have completed the circuit.

Exercises chosen for the circuit should meet the following criteria:

1. They can be performed by participants working on their own.

2. They are strenuous and of such a nature that the work load may be increased from time to time.

3. They are standardized (performed in a specific manner), so that they may be done in the same way each time.

4. They contribute to the sum total of the exercises in accomplishing the objectives of the program.

In arranging a circuit, the teacher should select exercises that develop all areas of the musculature. The following areas are suggested: arm, shoulder, and hand; neck; back; abdomen and hips; thigh, leg, and foot. Care must also be taken to select activities that exercise different sets of muscles, not the same set over and over.

The actual number and kinds of exercises which are included in a circuit will depend upon time available, body areas to be exercised or emphasized, and the amount of equipment and space available.

The number of times that each exercise in the circuit is to be done will depend upon individual ability. It must not be set so high that the performer will stop from exhaustion, but it must be high enough to ensure that it is close to the maximum of which he is capable. With experimentation the proper number of repetitions can be determined for each person.

There are two general ways of increasing the work load. One is increasing the number of repetitions, and the other is decreasing the time taken to perform the exercises.

A suggested circuit is shown in Figure 26-4.

Adaptations: If handicapped students are included with normal students in circuit training, each exercise must be analyzed to determine if it is suitable for each type of handicap. Protection from undue stress to weak areas of the body must be provided.

Adaptations must be worked out where possible. The special precautions which have been recommended for students with cardiorespiratory disorders must be observed here as well.

SELECTED READINGS

AAHPER: *Weight Training in Sports and Physical Education*. Washington, D.C., American Association for Health, Physical Education, and Recreation, 1962.
Armbruster, David A.: *Basic Skills in Sports for Men and Women,* ed. 6. St. Louis, The C. V. Mosby Co., 1975.
DeLorme, Thomas L.: *Progressive Resistance Exercises*. New York, Appleton-Century-Crofts, Inc., 1951.
Fait, Hollis F., *et al.: A Manual of Physical Education Activities,* ed. 3. Philadelphia, W. B. Saunders Co., 1967.
Rasch, Philip J.: *Weight Training*. Dubuque, Iowa, Wm. C. Brown Co., Pub., 1977.
Vannier, Maryhelen, and Fait, Hollis F.: *Teaching Physical Education in Secondary Schools,* ed. 4. Philadelphia, W. B. Saunders Co., 1975.

Chapter 27

Physical Fitness

Physical fitness as an objective of physical education has always been an important concern, but the amount of emphasis given to it in the physical education program has fluctuated with the times. Except for the war years, when physical conditioning was being stressed, physical fitness received scant attention from the turn of the century until the mid-1950s. Renewed concern about physical fitness was brought into sharp focus in 1955, when Kraus and Hirschland[1] published the results of their testing of European and American children in certain physical activities. By comparison to their European counterparts, American children were shown to be far inferior in physical performance.

The immediate response to these findings was a renewed interest in the promotion of physical fitness and a re-emphasis on physical fitness as an objective of physical education. At the instigation of then President Dwight D. Eisenhower, the President's Council on Youth Fitness was created to spearhead the promotion of physical fitness throughout the country. Successive Presidents have continued the Council and supported its work.

Today, physical fitness generally receives equal emphasis with the other objectives of the physical education program. Games and activities as well as specific exercises are offered to improve physical fitness. All youngsters, regardless of how physically fit they may be, can benefit from fitness activities offered in the regular program. Some children, however, have such a low level of physical fitness that to improve they should receive the special attention afforded by the special physical education program.

THE NATURE AND COMPONENTS OF PHYSICAL FITNESS

From the physiological viewpoint, physical fitness may be said to be the ability of the body to adapt to and recover from strenuous exercise. This definition implies a general well-being of the body and a capacity for vigorous work. In personal terms it is a reflection of one's ability to work and play with vigor and pleasure, without undue fatigue, and with sufficient energy left for meeting unforeseen emergencies.

Physical fitness level is determined by the development of each of several different components. Until recently, the main components were identified as coordina-

---

[1]Hans Kraus and Ruth P. Hirschland: "Muscular Fitness and Orthopedic Disability." *New York State Journal of Medicine*, January 15, 1954, pp. 212–215.

tion, balance, speed, muscular strength, flexibility, and cardiorespiratory and muscular endurance. Because some of these components are more closely related to physiological capacity and others to neurological aspects (skill mastery), physical educators have found it desirable to classify them separately into physical fitness and motor fitness components. The components of physical fitness, then, are muscular strength, flexibility, and cardiorespiratory and muscular endurance; and they are the components with which this discussion is concerned.

To understand the nature of each of the components of fitness and its special contribution to total physical fitness, each must be examined in detail.

Strength.   Strength is the amount of force which can be exerted by a particular muscle. In males, strength increases rapidly from the ages of 12 to 19, at a rate proportionate to the increase in weight of the body. After 19 years of age there is a decline in the acceleration of strength increase until the age of 30, after which there is a slow decrease. The growth in strength of the female parallels somewhat the growth in strength of males, except that the growth spurt starts approximately at the age of nine.[2]

Evidence indicates that the emotional state of the individual is a factor affecting the strength of muscles. Excitement may intensify the nervous discharge to the muscles, as well as liberate epinephrine (excretion of the adrenal gland), which increases the strength and endurance of the muscle. Other factors which influence the amount of strength which a muscle can exert are its mechanical advantage (attachment of the muscle to its lever) and the extent to which it is stretched.

Endurance.   There are two types of endurance components, muscular and cardiorespiratory. Endurance is the ability to persist or continue in a given effort. Muscular endurance, then, is the ability of the muscles to continue contracting or to sustain contraction over a period of time. Endurance of the muscles is measured by the number of times a contraction can be made or by the length of time a contraction can be held. The number of contractions or duration of the contraction depends upon the ability of the cells of the muscles to get and use oxygen and to rid the muscles of waste products. Such measurement of endurance is directly related to the strength of the muscle. With all other things being equal, a strong muscle can perform longer than a weak one.

Cardiorespiratory endurance is the ability of the body to process and supply oxygen to itself during work. The lungs, heart, and vascular system are involved. The greater the amount of oxygen that cardiac and respiratory systems are capable of supplying, the higher the level of muscular work the body can sustain over a period of time. As with muscular endurance, cardiorespiratory endurance is measured by how long strenuous activity can be maintained; in this case, by the entire body.

Flexibility.   Fleishman[3] in his study considered flexibility as being of two types, extent and dynamic. The former is defined as the range of movement possible in any given joint, while the latter is defined as the ability to make repeated, rapid, flexing movements.

The range of movement in a joint is determined first by bone structure; for example, the hyperextension of the joint of the elbow is limited by the bone structure. Other factors limiting range of movement are the ligaments and muscles. The effectiveness of performance in many physical activities is influenced by the degree of flex-

---

[2]Lawrence E. Morehouse and Augustus T. Miller: *Physiology of Exercise,* ed. 3. The C. V. Mosby Co., 1976, p. 59.

[3]*The Structure and Measurement of Physical Fitness.* Englewood Cliffs, N.J., Prentice-Hall Inc., 1964, p. 99.

ibility of the total body or of specific joints. A person who can exert force over a longer range, which is possible for those having more flexibility, can generate more force. Also, a more flexible person expends less energy in performing certain skills than one who has less flexibility, because energy need not be expended to overcome the limited range of motion.

The range of movement of a joint can usually be extended by forcing the joint over a wider range little by little. This is the technique utilized if muscle shortening is the chief factor in the prevention of full range of movement.

Overload or SAID Principle.   To increase physical fitness through exercise, the body must perform more work per unit of time than it is accustomed to performing. This increased work load, combined with the resultant improvement in physical fitness, is known as the overload principle. The term overload may be misleading, since it does not necessarily refer to a work load that is at or near capacity but refers to any work that is more than usual for the area of the body involved. Another term for this principle is specific adaptation to imposed demands (SAID),[4] which is more descriptive of the process.

RESULTS OF LOW PHYSICAL FITNESS

A person who is below the normal range in strength cannot perform the regular skills of his work and play because he is too weak. To take an example from play, the sub-strength tennis player cannot hold the racket with the regulation grip but must choke up on the handle because he is too weak to control the racquet otherwise.

Less than normal endurance manifests itself in the inability to carry a normal work load or to participate in normal play without undue fatigue. Lack of endurance is a contributing factor to lack of interest in vigorous activities. It is also a hindrance in other areas of endeavor, as evidenced by lack of accomplishment in academic subjects and failure to utilize opportunities to develop social skills.

Lacking normal speed and power, an individual is hindered in performing specific types of motor movements. Success in such skills as running, jumping, and throwing is dependent upon sufficient power and speed.

Without a sufficient degree of flexibility, the range of movement is limited. This may be disadvantageous when an activity requires a wide range of movement. Moreover, when the range of movement is limited, the distance over which power can be exerted is cut down, and thus less total power is generated. A thrower who has a limited range of movement in the arm will not throw the ball as far using the same amount of strength, speed, and coordination as one who has a wide range of movement. In addition, contractures (abnormal shortening of the muscle tissue) develop simultaneously with the decrease in flexibility. Increasing flexibility minimizes contractures.

Lack of flexibility and strength in the back area and lack of flexibility in the hamstrings are causes of low back pain. It had been reported that approximately 80 per cent of patients suffering from low back pain who were found free from organic diseases improved when given systematic exercise designed to increase the flexibility and strength of the back and the flexibility of the hamstrings of the legs. The patients regressed when the exercise was reduced or discontinued.[5]

---

[4]Wallis, Earl L., and Logan, Gene: *Figure Improvement and Body Conditioning Through Exercise.* Englewood Cliffs, N.J., Prentice-Hall, Inc., 1964, p. 1.

[5]Hans Kraus, *et al.: Hypokinetic Disease.* Institute for Physical Medicine and Rehabilitation, New York University, Bellevue Medical Center, 1955, *passim.*

There is evidence to indicate that students who have low scores on tests that measure factors of physical fitness have more social adjustment problems than those who have high scores. The apparent reason for this is that the lack of physical skills has caused these children to withdraw from play and sport activities, and so they have been deprived of certain types of social contacts which are valuable to social development. Such withdrawal has a further disadvantage because it fosters further decrease in physical fitness. It cannot be assumed, in all cases of poor social adjustment coupled with low physical ability, that the latter has been the contributing factor. It is possible that the reverse is true or that neither contributed to the other.

CAUSE OF LOW PHYSICAL FITNESS

There is a tendency on the part of some to think that there is only one cause of low physical fitness: lack of exercise. But there are many factors contributing to subnormal physical fitness. Among these are: physical defects or disorders; faulty nutrition; poor health practices, such as insufficient sleep and rest; psychological weakness, such as the lack of ability or desire to get optimum performance from the muscles involved; inherited factors which influence the development of physical efficiency; and lack of muscular activity due to illness, injury, or obstetrics. The physical educator must take all factors into consideration when planning a physical fitness program. Success in achieving improved physical fitness often depends upon ameliorating the influence of these factors.

TESTING FOR LOW FITNESS

Students who are handicapped frequently have lower physical fitness levels, not only in the area involved but also in total fitness, because of the tendency or necessity of withdrawal from strenuous activity. However, many students suffer from low physical fitness who are not handicapped in any other way.

Those who are in dire need of special work in components of strength and endurance frequently stand out because of poor performance in class, so that it is easy to pick them out. There is the boy who lacks the strength to lift his body, and the girl who lags far behind the others in a short distance run. Watching students attempting to use various types of skills, the teacher is able to pick out those needing special help.

Tests may be used both for determining those with generally low physical fitness and for identifying specific areas of weakness. In selecting tests it must be kept in mind that there are several factors that make up physical fitness, so the more factors that are tested, the more information can be obtained about the individual's total fitness. Also, since muscular strength, endurance, and flexibility are specific, the more areas of the body that are tested, the more complete is the total picture of fitness.

To utilize physical fitness tests adequately, the nature of the test must be understood: what it measures, the relationship of what it measures to physical fitness, and what a specific score means. Moreover, if the scores are to have meaning, the test must be given exactly the same way each time for each subject. If norms are to be used, the test must be given in exactly the same way it was given to collect data for the norms.

Measuring Strength. Strength may be measured effectively with the manuometer and the back and leg dynamometer.

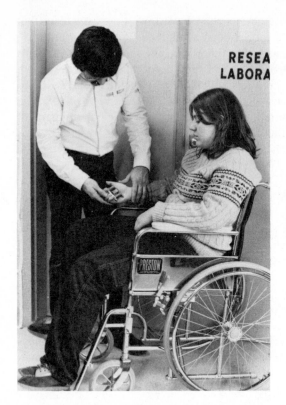

Figure 27–1. The grip strength test is useful because of its indication of strength in unaffected muscle sets of the body and because of its ease of administration to handicapped students.

The manuometer measures grip strength. In the grip strength test, the subject places the convex edge of the manuometer between the first and second joints of the fingers, with the dial toward the palm, and squeezes it. He may use any movement he wishes except supporting the fist against an object.

To measure the static strength of the back extensors, the subject stands on the dynamometer with the feet parallel, about six inches apart, and the toes about one inch from the front of the stand. To secure the proper adjustment of the bar, the subject stands erect with the hands hanging loosely in front of the thighs. The bar is connected to the chain at the tip of the subject's fingers. The subject bends forward slightly and grips the bar with one hand forward and the other backward. He lifts straight up, keeping the knees straight throughout the lift. The tester may place his hands over the subject's to prevent their slipping on the bar.

For the leg lift, the subject assumes the same position as for the back lift. A belt is used around the subject's hips to stabilize the bar. The grip is taken at the center of the bar with the palms down at a level just above the pubic bone. As the subject faces the tester in this position, the tester brings the belt around the lower portion of the sacrum to be attached to the right end of the handle and then brought back under the portion of the belt that is in the back. The subject, keeping the head up and the back straight, bends at the knees. The handle is hooked to the chain while the knees are flexed at about 135 degrees. The subject may grip the bar in the middle or at the ends of the bar. He lifts straight up.

Lifting the weight of the body in pull-ups, push-ups, sit-ups, dips, reverse sit-ups, and leg lifts can be used as a rough measurement of the static strength of the muscle group involved.

Measuring Muscular Endurance.   Endurance of the muscles is frequently measured by pull-ups, dips, push-ups, leg lifts, and reverse sit-ups.

Pull-ups: To execute a pull-up, a bar which is at a height above the reach of the subject is grasped with the hands and the arms are completely extended, letting the body hang free. Taking the grip while standing on a stool and then stepping off it places the body in the right position. The bar can be grasped with the reverse or regular grip. In the reverse grip the palms face the head; in the regular grip the knuckles are toward the head. When the reverse grip is used, pull-ups are easier; approximately two and one-half more pull-ups can be made. The reverse grip should be used by younger children. The American Alliance for Health, Physical Education and Recreation[6] norms established for the pull-ups show that over 25 per cent of the boys under 10 are unable to do one pull-up with a regular grip. The use of the reverse grip would reduce the number of failures, and hence the test would have greater discriminatory value. If rings are used instead of a bar, the arms will automatically twist to the most efficient position.

In doing the pull-up, the body is pulled up until the chin touches the bar or is even with the bar. The subject may not use his feet to kick up. The body is then lowered until the arms are straight. The subject continues raising and lowering his body until he can no longer continue. One point is scored for each pull-up.

A modified pull-up is sometimes used for girls. In a modified pull-up, the bar is lowered to chest height, so that in gripping the bar the body can be placed at a 45-degree angle to the floor with the arms fully extended. The knees and hips must remain straight during the pull-up. A bent-arm endurance hang has been used as a substitute for the modified pull-up, since the latter has lower objectivity and reliability and is not discriminating. For the bent-arm endurance hang, a stool for the student to stand on is placed under the bar. A grip is taken on the bar with the palms out. The head is brought to the bar at the bridge of the nose just below the eyebrows and held there as the stool is removed. The score is the number of seconds that the subject is able to hold the position. Sometimes the hairline, chin, eyebrows, or end of the nose is used as the anchor point for the bar.

Studies by Fait[7] in developing a test for the Connecticut Association for Health, Physical Education and Recreation fitness battery indicated that anchoring at the forehead increased the number of failures by approximately 10 per cent, thereby decreasing the discriminating value of the test. Furthermore, placing the bar at the hairline was difficult because of the many different types of hair styles that girls wear. When the bar was anchored at the chin, the test had less reliability, owing to an inability to keep the head level and at the same angle in repetitions of the test. Anchoring at the tip of the nose was rejected because of possible unsanitary conditions created by testing one person after the other on the same bar.

Dips: Dips also measure arm and shoulder endurance but do not measure the same muscles which are measured in pull-ups. The dips measure the antagonistic muscles of those involved in pull-ups. Consequently, the dips can be given in the same testing period as the pull-up or hang tests because the muscle involved will not be fatigued. However, since there is a high relationship between the flexors and extensors of the arm, it is not necessary to give both tests. Generally dips can be executed only by older boys. For the test, parallel bars are used, and the bars should be shoulder high. The subject mounts by grasping the bars and jumping up to take the weight on his

---

[6]American Alliance for Health, Physical Education, and Recreation, *Youth Fitness Test Manual,* rev. ed., Washington, D.C., 1975, p. 34.

[7]Hollis F. Fait: "The Endurance Hang." Unpublished study, Storrs, Conn., Physical Efficiency Laboratory, University of Connecticut, 1962.

arms. One point is scored for mounting successfully. He then dips to lower his body until the elbows of both arms form right angles. The point is noted by having a helper place his fist at the location. The subject must touch the fist each time he dips. One point is scored for each raising and lowering of the body.

Push-ups: The push-ups test approximately the same muscles involved in the dips. The subject performs the push-up in a prone position with his hands at least shoulder distance apart. The body is lowered, keeping a straight line from head to foot. Only the chin touches the floor. No sagging of any part of the body is permitted. Each full dip scores one point.

Girls who are very strong are able to do this type of push-up. For the other girls and for very young boys, a modification is made by making the knees the fulcrum rather than the toes. This is too easy for many girls and so may not be sufficiently selective. A second modification is possible with the use of a stall bar bench. The techniques of the regular push-up are used except the hands are placed on the bench and the chest is lowered to the bench. This test is more difficult, and many girls will be unable to score in this performance.

Sit-ups: The sit-up test is performed the same by both boys and girls. The subject is supine with the legs straight and the feet slightly apart. The hands are clasped behind the head and the feet are held down. The subject rolls up to touch the right elbow to the left knee and then lowers the trunk to the floor. The trunk is raised again to touch the left elbow to the right knee. One point is counted for each time the subject sits up and touches the elbow to the knee. The knees may be bent if necessary to touch the elbows.

Sometimes sit-ups are given by having the subject cross his arms across the chest and bring his body up to a 90-degree angle. This makes the sit-up easier to perform. Sit-ups are made more difficult by having the subject bend his knees. The feet are held by the tester while the legs are in the bent position.

Leg Lift: The subject lies on his back, hands behind his neck, with his elbows held to the floor by an assistant. He raises his legs until they are vertical and then lowers them to the floor. The tester may hold his hand above the subject at ankle height when the legs are held vertically to keep the subject from bending his legs or failing to bring them completely to a vertical position. In the leg lift the hips maintain contact with the floor at all times. This test is usually timed for 20 seconds, and the number of times the legs are lifted during that time is the score.

Leg Raise: The subject is supine, with the hands behind the neck and the legs extended. He lifts his legs 10 inches off the floor with the knees held straight. The tester may hold his hands at a point 10 inches above the floor as a guide to the subject. The score is the number of seconds the subject holds his legs in this position.

Reverse Sit-ups: The subject is prone with his hands behind his neck. An assistant holds the subject's feet down. The subject raises his head and chest and shoulders as far as possible. The height is noted, and the subject returns to the original position. On the command "Go," the subject makes as many reverse sit-ups as possible in 20 seconds. The tester may hold his hand at the height the subject reached in the trial to ensure that the subject lifts to his limit of flexibility each time. The score is the number of lifts in 20 seconds.

In Fleishman's study[8] it was pointed out that the ability to perform a muscular endurance test as fast as possible for 20 seconds depends on the same factor as that which determines the ability to hold a position as long as possible or do as many repetitions as possible. Therefore the three types of tests could be used interchangeably.

---

[8]Fleishman: *op. cit.,* p. 64.

Measuring Power or Explosive Strength.   Power, or explosive strength, is the ability to release force at a specific moment. This ability is influenced by muscular strength and speed. Even though power is a factor in motor fitness rather than physical fitness, a discussion of the measurement of power is appropriate because of the relationship between muscular strength and power. Also, tests of the kind described below are frequently included in physical fitness test batteries.

The power of leg muscles relative to body weight can be measured by a vertical jump or a standing broad jump or short dashes; the power of arm and shoulder muscles by the softball throw.

Vertical Jump: For the vertical jump the subject faces the wall and reaches over his head with both hands. The height of his reach is marked. The subject then turns his side to the wall, crouches, and jumps as high as possible with one hand touching the wall at the height of his jump. The difference between the reaching and jumping heights is the score. To eliminate the effects of coordination of the arm in the jump, the first measurement may be taken at the height of the head while the subject stands against the wall. The subject then jumps without the use of the arm in a preliminary jump. The tester places a yardstick vertically to the wall at the height of the jump. On subsequent jumps the tester adjusts the stick to the highest point reached. The score is taken when an accurate measurement is achieved.

Standing Broad Jump: The subject puts his toes on the line and then without preliminary movement of the feet jumps forward as far as possible. The score is the length of the jump measured from the line to the point nearest to where the subject landed.

Softball Throw: The power of certain muscles of the arm and shoulders is sometimes measured by the softball throw. It appears that skill is a more important factor in getting a good score in the softball throw than it is in the tests measuring explosive power that have already been described. However, Fleishman[9] found that the softball throw using a 15-inch ball and requiring the subject to keep his feet in place while throwing was highly related to the factor of explosive strength that was isolated in his study. Fleishman's subjects were males, and among boys throwing is such a universally well-developed skill that it is likely that the power of the arm was more dominant in determining the distance thrown than the skill level attained. If this assumption is correct, the softball throw would not be as good a measurement for girls, since their skill in throwing is usually not as well developed.

There are two common ways of administering the softball throw. In one, the participant throws from between two lines six feet apart. The subject is allowed to run from the back line to the forward line while throwing. In the other method, the throw is made from a stationary position. The subject must keep his feet in place throughout the throw; no follow-through with the feet is allowed. The score in both cases is the distance the ball is thrown.

In his factor analysis, Fleishman[10] found no factor of agility or running speed as such; movements that require change of direction or short bursts of speed were highly related to explosive power. If this is true, the AAHPER shuttle run and the short dashes can be used as a measurement of explosive power.

Shuttle Run: For the shuttle run, two parallel lines are marked on the floor 30 feet apart. Two wooden blocks are placed behind one of the lines. The subject starts from behind the other line, runs to the blocks, picks up one, runs back to the starting line, and puts the block behind the line. He then runs back and picks up the second

---

[9]*Ibid.,* pp. 67, 72.
[10]*Ibid.,* p. 99

block, which he carries back across the starting line. The score is the time it takes to carry the two blocks over the starting line.

Short Dashes: In administering the 35-, 50-, or 60-yard dash a standardized starting technique should be used to eliminate the influence of skill in starting, as follows: The back foot is placed parallel to a wall, or to a board 2 inches by 4 inches by 3 feet secured to the ground, if outdoors. The forward foot and the upper body are turned in the direction of the run. The knees are slightly bent, and the hands rest gently on the knees. The time as measured by a stop watch is the score.

Measuring Flexibility. The flexibility test most frequently administered is toe touching with knees straight, which measures the flexibility of the hamstring muscles. The subject stands erect, hands at his sides. With the feet together and the knees straight, he bends down slowly in an attempt to touch the floor with his finger tips. The subject is not permitted to bounce. The tester places his hands on the subject's knees to detect bending. A modification of this test which affords greater discrimination is placement of the subject on a stall bar bench to perform the test. This permits measurement of the distance beyond the toes which the subject can reach.

A flexibility test recommended by Fleishman[11] is the twist and touch. This test measures how far the subject can rotate his spine. The subject stands with his side toward the wall, an arm's length away with the fist closed. His feet are together, and his toes touch a line drawn perpendicular to the wall. A horizontal scale marked off from 0 to 30 inches extends on either side of a line on the wall which is drawn perpendicular to the line on the floor. Keeping his feet in place, the subject twists back around as far as possible and touches the wall, with his hand at shoulder height and the palm facing the floor. The tester helps the subject keep his feet from moving by placing his own foot against the subject's foot. The subject's score is the farthest point on the scale reached and held for at least two seconds.

Fleishman's[12] test for dynamic flexibility is the bend, twist, and touch. This test measures the speed with which the subject can flex, extend, and rotate his spine. The subject stands with his back to the wall, far enough from the wall so that he can bend over. His feet are approximately shoulder width apart. A mark is placed on the wall in chalk directly behind the middle of the subject's back and at shoulder height. Another mark is made on the floor between the subject's feet. On the signal "Go," the subject bends forward, touches the mark between his feet with both hands, and then straightens up, twists, and touches the mark on the wall with both hands. He then repeats by touching the floor and turning the other way to touch the wall. The score is the number of complete cycles made in 20 seconds.

Measuring Cardiorespiratory Endurance. Distance runs of 300, 440, or 600 yards are frequently used to measure this factor. A drop-off score or endurance ratio may be used, the formula for which is the time of the distance run of 300 yards divided by the time of the 60-yard dash. The smaller the quotient, the greater is the endurance, the rationale being that the 60-yard run represents the subject's speed of running. If cardiorespiratory endurance does not affect running time for the 300 yards, the time for the total should be only five times greater than the time for 60 yards.

The Kraus-Weber Test. A once-popular physical fitness test is the Kraus-Weber battery, which consists of six test items measuring the strength of the abdominal and psoas muscles, certain back muscles, and the flexibility of the back and hamstrings.

For testing the abdominals plus the psoas, the subject is supine with the hands behind the neck; his feet are held down. Holding his hands behind his neck, the sub-

---

[11]*Ibid.,* p. 130.
[12]*Ibid.,* p. 130.

ject attempts to roll up into a sitting position; he must not perform a stiff back sit-up. If the subject is unable to perform the test, he has very weak abdominals. A twisting of the upper body during the sit-up may indicate an unequal development of the back muscles.

To test the strength of the abdominals without the psoas, the subject is supine with the hands behind the neck and the knees bent. The feet are held down during the test. The subject rolls up to the sitting position as in the first test item.

For the testing of the psoas, the subject is in a supine position with the hands behind the neck and the legs extended. He lifts the legs 10 inches off the floor and holds for 10 seconds. The knees are straight. If the subject arches his back extremely in performing the test, this may indicate very weak abdominal muscles. It may also be an indication of postural habits contributing to lordosis.

In the test for strength of the back, the subject is prone with a pillow under his abdomen. The pillow must be large enough to supply actual support to the body, and it must be placed so that it becomes a fulcrum for the body. The subject places his hands behind the neck and raises his chest, head, and shoulders while his feet are being held down. He holds the position for 10 seconds. The observer should check for pronounced muscular development on one side of the spinal column, as this is possible evidence of the development of scoliosis.

For another test of the back area, the subject assumes the same position as above except that the hands are placed so the head can rest on them. With his chest held down, the subject attempts to raise his legs without bending the knees and to hold them in the raised position for the count of 10 seconds. Failure to do so indicates a weak back area.

In the test of the flexibility of the back and hamstrings, the subject stands erect with the hands at the sides. He should not wear shoes. With the feet together and the knees straight, he bends down slowly in an attempt to touch the floor with his finger tips. He remains as far down as it is possible for him to reach for the count of three. The subject is not permitted to bounce. The tester places his hands on the subject's knees to detect bending. Inability to touch the floor indicates short hamstrings and an inflexible spinal column.

Recovery Index Test. The recovery index test attempts to measure the cardiorespiratory resources of the individual. The final score obtained is a rough indication of the efficiency of these resources.

For giving the test, a sturdy platform or box 14 inches high is required. To start the test, the student steps with either foot onto the box at the command of "one." At the command of "two" he steps up with the other foot. He steps down with the first foot and then the other foot at the commands of "three" and "four." The cadence of the count should be such that the steps up and the steps down are done in two seconds. The test continues for four minutes, after which the student stops, sits down, and rests. One minute later, his pulse rate is taken for 30 seconds. One minute after the first measurement, the pulse is taken again for 30 seconds. It is taken the third time one minute after the second measurement, for 30 seconds. The three rates are added for a total score. The result can be compared to pulse count totals in Table 27–1 for interpretation. Anyone scoring "poor" should be referred to his physician.

AAHPER Fitness Test. The American Alliance for Health, Physical Education and Recreation includes six items[13] in its physical fitness test battery. The items follow, with any variations or special directions required by the battery.

---

[13]American Alliance for Health, Physical Education, and Recreation: *op. cit., passim.*

Table 27-1. EVALUATION OF RECOVERY INDEX TEST SCORES

Total of the Three 30-Second Pulse Counts	Rating
200 or more	Poor
171 to 199	Fair
150 to 170	Good
133 to 149	Very Good
132 or less	Excellent

1. Pull-ups for boys (regular grip); flexed arm hang for girls (the chin is brought above the bar).

2. Sit-ups for 60 seconds (hands behind the head; when the body is brought up to the 90-degree angle, the trunk is turned and the right elbow is brought to the left knee; a return is made to the supine position and the trunk raised to touch the left elbow to the right knee).

3. Shuttle run (lines 30 feet apart).

4. Standing broad jump.

5. Fifty-yard dash.

6. Six-hundred-yard run-walk (running may be interspersed with walking at subject's discretion).

See Table 27-2 for an evaluation of fitness test scores.

Fleishman's Fitness Test. Based upon his scientific analysis of the physical fitness factors, Fleishman[14] recommends the following tests. Any variations or special methods of performance are noted.

1. Twist and touch.

2. Bend, twist, and touch.

3. Shuttle run (between two parallel lines 20 yards apart; the runner runs to the opposite line, touches the ground on the far side of it with either foot, returns to the starting line, and repeats; on the last lap he is to go all out to cross the finish line standing up).

4. Softball throw (from a stationary position; no follow-through with the feet is allowed).

5. Hand grip on the manuometer.

6. Pull-ups (reverse grip).

7. Leg lifts.

8. Cable jump test (a rope about 20 inches in length is held in front by the subject, who must jump over it without losing his grip; the score is the number of correct jumps out of five attempts).

9. Balance (one foot is placed lengthwise on beam 1 1/2 inches high by 3/4 inch wide by 24 inches long).

10. Six-hundred-yard run-walk.

It is difficult for children below the fifth grade to maintain interest in the testing and to exert maximum effort. However, if an evaluation is greatly desired, a suitable battery could be composed from the appropriate items of the Youth Fitness Test. Included would be the sit-up, broad jump, and a dash of 30 yards instead of 50 yards. Table 27-3 presents standards for judging the performance in these events of children in grades one to five.

---

[14] Edwin A. Fleishman: *Examiner's Manual for the Basic Fitness Tests.* Englewood Cliffs, N.J., Prentice-Hall, Inc., 1964, *passim.*

Table 27-2. EVALUATION OF AAHPER TEST SCORES (AGES 10-13)

	Age	Poor	Average	Good
Flexed-Arm Hang				
Girls	10–11	3	7	15
Girls	12–13	2	6	13
Pull-ups for Boys				
Boys	10–11	0	1	4
Boys	12–13	0	1	5
Sit-ups				
Girls	10–11	15	22	29
Boys	10–11	25	43	68
Girls	12–13	22	30	36
Boys	12–13	34	55	96
Shuttle Run (Seconds)				
Girls	10–11	12.5	11.8	11.0
Boys	10–11	12.4	11.2	10.6
Girls	12–13	12.2	11.5	10.9
Boys	12–13	11.4	10.8	10.2
Standing Broad Jump (Feet and Inches)				
Girls	10–11	4'3"	4'8"	5'2"
Boys	10–11	4'7"	5'1"	5'6"
Girls	12–13	4'5"	5'0"	5'6"
Boys	12–13	5'2"	5'8"	6'2"
50-Yard Dash (Seconds)				
Girls	10–11	9.0	8.5	7.9
Boys	10–11	8.7	8.1	7.6
Girls	12–13	8.9	8.2	7.8
Boys	12–13	8.2	7.7	7.2
600-Yard Run-Walk (Minutes and Seconds)				
Girls	10–11	3'11"	2'48"	2'31"
Boys	10–11	2'46"	2'30"	2'16"
Girls	12–13	3'13"	2'50"	2'32"
Boys	12–13	2'33"	2'17"	2'4"

Table 27–3. EVALUATION OF FITNESS TEST SCORES (AGES 6 TO 9)

Age	Poor	Average	Good
		Sit-up	
Girls 6	2	4	6
Boys 6	2	4	6
Girls 7	3	5	7
Boys 7	3	5	7
Girls 8	5	8	10
Boys 8	6	9	11
Girls 9	9	15	25
Boys 9	14	20	30
		Standing Broad Jump *(feet and inches)*	
Girls 6	2'10"	3'5"	4'0"
Boys 6	2'10"	3'5"	4'0"
Girls 7	3'0"	3'7"	4'2"
Boys 7	3'4"	3'9"	4'4"
Girls 8	3'6"	4'0"	4'7"
Boys 8	3'7"	4'2"	4'10"
Girls 9	3'8"	4'3"	4'8"
Boys 9	4'0"	4'5"	5'0"
		30 Yard Dash *(seconds)*	
Girls 6	10.0	9.5	9.3
Boys 6	10.0	9.5	9.3
Girls 7	8.8	8.6	8.4
Boys 7	8.7	8.5	8.3
Girls 8	7.7	7.4	7.1
Boys 8	7.2	6.8	6.5
Girls 9	7.0	6.7	6.4
Boys 9	6.8	6.4	6.1

PHYSICAL FITNESS TESTING OF THE PHYSICALLY AND MENTALLY HANDICAPPED

Tests for Physically Handicapped Children. Some students cannot be given physical fitness tests, either because their disabilities render them incapable of performing the tests or because their conditions may be aggravated in attempting them. However, many of the handicapped can be included in the testing if proper precautions are taken. In some instances, this will mean eliminating those tests which involve the part of the body which is injured or disabled. A subject with only one arm, for example, would not be required to do pull-ups but could be expected to take the running tests, as these would not be dangerous for him. In certain cases, the nature of the disability will not be such that safety is a major factor of concern. For example, missing fingers on a hand will not prevent safe participation in the pull-ups. It would not be meaningful, however, to make an evaluation of this subject's score by comparing it to scores achieved by students able to take a normal grip. His score is likely to be less because he has less grip strength and not because of less muscular endurance of the arms, as would be indicated by a low score by non-handicapped students. A meaningful measurement for each handicapped individual can be devised, however, by using a progress chart on which scores are recorded each time the test is taken.

Tests for Mildly Mentally Retarded Children. Physical fitness tests designed for non-handicapped youngsters are not valid measurements of physical fitness for the mentally retarded because they are for the most part too complex, and many times the scores are lowered because of the subjects' inability to comprehend and respond immediately with the proper muscular movements. This contention is supported by studies which show that when physical fitness tests commonly given to normal children are given to mentally retarded subjects, the scores demonstrate a positive relationship to the IQ scores of the subject.[15] Fait and Kupferer[16] demonstrated that when the physical fitness test items were simplified, the relationship of the scores to the IQ score was greatly diminished. The Burpee or squat thrust test serves as a good illustration. The scores of retarded children, when given a modified Burpee test which required them to squat and return without thrusting, fitted a fairly normal curve comparable to normal children, whereas the scores from the performance of the full squat thrust test produced a curve skewed to the left comparable to the curve of their IQ scores. The inability of the mentally retarded to perform well on the Burpee test appears to be caused more by their inability to remember the movement sequence than by poor agility.

Subsequent to this study, Fait adapted physical fitness tests for the mentally retarded from those given to non-handicapped children. Although most of the original tests indicated a positive relationship to IQ, the correlations between IQ and the adapted tests were near zero. The adapted tests and the original tests were both given to normal youngsters. A high correlation was shown to exist, indicating that the adapted tests were measuring the same factors of fitness as the original tests. The adapted tests are used as test items in the following battery of physical fitness tests for the mentally retarded.[17]

These tests may be used for the educable and for a majority of the medium and high trainables, if the youngsters do not have other handicaps which prevent safe performance of the test. (See Chapter 17 for discussion of educable and trainable.)

Description of Test Items

Twenty-Five Yard Run. (Measures the speed of running short distances). The subject places either foot against the wall (or block) with the foot parallel to it. He then takes a semi-crouch position with the hands resting lightly on the knees. His forward foot and trunk are turned in the direction he is to run. His head is held up so that he is looking toward the finish line. At the command of "Ready: go!" the subject begins the run. The watch is started on the "Go" and is stopped as the subject passes the finish line. However, the subject is directed to run to a second line which is about five feet beyond the finish line to prevent his slowing down as he approaches the true finish line. The time of the run is recorded to the nearest one-tenth of a second.

Bent Arm Hang. (Measures static muscular endurance of the arm and shoulder girdle). A horizontal bar or doorway bar may be used for this test. A stool approximately 12 inches high is placed under the bar. The subject steps onto the stool and takes

[15]Lawrence Rarick and Robert J. Francis: "Motor Characteristics of the Mentally Retarded." *Competitive Research Monograph*, No. 1, OE-35005, U.S. Office of Education, 1960, *passim*.

[16]Hollis F. Fait and Harriet Kupferer: "A Study of Two Motor Achievement Tests and Its Implications in Planning Physical Education Activities for the Mentally Retarded." *American Journal of Mental Deficiency*, Vol. 60, 1956, pp. 728–732.

[17]Research study, financed by the Joseph P. Kennedy, Jr., Foundation made at the Physical Efficiency Laboratory at the University of Connecticut under the direction of Hollis Fait in conjunction with the Mansfield State Training School.

Table 27–4. SCORE CARD FOR PHYSICAL FITNESS TEST FOR THE MENTALLY RETARDED

25 Yard Run

Boys
(Score in Seconds)

Age	Low	Trainable Av.	Good	Low	Educable Av.	Good
9–12	7	6	5.2	6.2	5.2	4.4
13–16	6.5	5.5	4.7	5.4	4.7	4.2
17–20	6	5	4.2	5.1	4.4	3.9

Girls

Age	Low	Trainable Av.	Good	Low	Educable Av.	Good
9–12	7.4	6.3	5.3	5.8	5.4	5.2
13–16	6.7	5.6	4.7	6.1	5.2	4.3
17–20	7.3	6.1	5.1	6.4	5.4	4.7

Bent Arm Hang

Boys
(Score in Seconds)

Age	Low	Trainable Av.	Good	Low	Educable Av.	Good
9–12	2	10	16	3	19	33
13–16	11.2	22	30.2	5	25	43
17–20	23	23	31	8	30	50

Girls

Age	Low	Trainable Av.	Good	Low	Educable Av.	Good
9–12	2	8	12	3	9	13
13–16	4	14	22	5	15	23
17–20	3	9	13	4	12	18

Leg Lift

Boys

Age	Low	Trainable Av.	Good	Low	Educable Av.	Good
9–12	6	9	12	7	10	13
13–16	6	9	12	8	11	14
17–20	7	10	13	8	11	14

Girls

Age	Low	Trainable Av.	Good	Low	Educable Av.	Good
9–12	6	10	14	6	10	14
13–16	7	11	15	7	11	15
17–20	6	10	14	6	10	14

Table 27–4. SCORE CARD FOR PHYSICAL FITNESS TEST
FOR THE MENTALLY RETARDED (*Continued*)

Static Balance

Boys
(Score in Seconds)

Age	Low	Trainable Av.	Good	Low	Educable Av.	Good
9–12	3	4.4	5.8	4	5	6
13–16	3.1	4.5	5.9	5	6	7
17–20	3.2	4.6	6	5	10	15

Girls

Age	Low	Trainable Av.	Good	Low	Educable Av.	Good
9–12	2.2	3.2	4.2	2.5	3.5	4.5
13–16	5.1	6.1	7.1	8.6	9.6	10.6
17–20	4.9	5.9	6.9	5.2	6.2	7.2

Thrust

Boys

Age	Low	Trainable Av.	Good	Low	Educable Av.	Good
9–12	4	8	10	6	12	14
13–16	4	8	10	8	14	16
17–20	5	9	11	8	14	16

Girls

Age	Low	Trainable Av.	Good	Low	Educable Av.	Good
9–12	4	8	10	5	9	11
13–16	4	8	10	8	12	14
17–20	5	9	11	5	9	11

300 Yard Run-Walk

Boys
(Score in Seconds)

Age	Low	Trainable Av.	Good	Low	Educable Av.	Good
9–12	145	115	95	105	80	60
13–16	111	86	66	95	75	55
17–20	104	79	59	74	59	39

Girls
(Score in Seconds)

Age	Low	Trainable Av.	Good	Low	Educable Av.	Good
9–12	198	148	108	143	113	83
13–16	158	108	65	125	91	61
17–20	159	107	66	142	102	71

hold of the bar with both hands, using a reverse grip (palms toward the face). The hands are shoulders' width apart. The subject brings his head to the bar, presses the bridge of the nose to the bar, and steps off the stool. He holds this position as long as possible. The timer starts the watch as the subject's nose presses to bar and the body weight is taken on the arms. The watch is stopped when the subject drops away from the bar. The tester should be ready to catch the subject in the event that he falls. The number of seconds the subject held the position is recorded on the score card.

Leg Lift (Measures dynamic muscular endurance of the flexor muscles of the leg and of the abdominal muscles). The subject lies flat on his back with his hands clasped behind the neck. A helper should hold the subject's elbows to the mat. The subject raises his legs, keeping the knees straight until they are at a 90-degree angle. Another helper, who stands to the side of the subject, extends one hand over the subject's abdomen at the height of the ankles when the legs are fully lifted. This serves as a guide to the subject in achieving the desired angle and encourages him to keep the legs straight. He should be instructed to touch the shins against the helper's arm. The subject is to do as many leg lifts as possible in the 20-second time limit. He begins on the command of "Go" and ceases on the command of "Stop." The score is the number of leg lifts performed during the 20 seconds.

Static Balance Test (Measures ability to maintain balance in a stationary position). The subject places his hands on his hips, lifts one leg, and places the foot on the inside of the knee of the other leg. He then closes his eyes and maintains his balance in this position as long as he can. The watch is started the moment he closes his eyes. As soon as the subject loses his balance, the watch is stopped. The score is the number of seconds to the nearest one-tenth of a second.

Thrusts (Measures the specific type of agility that is measured by the Squat Thrust or Burpee). The subject takes a squatting position with the feet and hands flat on the floor. The knees should make contact with the arms. At the command "Go," the stop watch is started. The subject takes the weight upon his hands so that he may thrust his legs straight out behind him. The legs are returned to the original position. The score is the number of complete thrusts the subject is able to perform in 20 seconds. One-half point is awarded for completing half of the thrust.

300 Yard Run-Walk (Measures cardiorespiratory endurance). If the run is to be given outside on a track, it can be administered to large numbers at one time by placing the runners in one long straight row or in two rows with one behind the other. The runners in taking a starting position should place one foot comfortably ahead of the other. A semi-crouch position with the hands resting lightly on the knees is taken. At the command to go, the stop watch is started. The subject runs the prescribed course. He is allowed to walk part of the distance if he is unable to run the total distance. As each runner crosses the finish line, the timer calls off the time to a recorder who makes a check beside the corresponding time on a prepared sheet. As the timer continues to call off the times as the runners pass the finish line, the recorder goes down the line of times and checks the times called. If two runners cross the line at the same time, two checks are placed beside the appropriate time on the sheet. As the runners finish, they line up according to the order in which they finished. One person will be needed to help the runners stay in correct order. When the runners are all in line, the name of the runner and the time it took him to complete the race can be matched and placed on his score card by comparing the order of runners to the order of times as they appear on the sheet.

A score card for comparison of the results of the test items is presented in Table 27-4.

Following the development of the physical fitness test discussed above, a modification of the AAHPER Youth Fitness Test was published in the *Special Fitness Test Manual for Mildly Mentally Retarded Persons.*[18] This test consists of seven items: flexed arm hang, sit-ups, standing long jump, 50-yard dash, softball throw for distance, shuttle run, and 300-yard run. All the test items show very low relationship between score on the item and IQ measurement, except the shuttle run. Approximately 25 per cent of the factors measured by the shuttle run test are also measured by IQ tests.

THE PROGRAM FOR THOSE WITH EXTREMELY LOW PHYSICAL FITNESS

The development of physical fitness is limited by the structure of the organism. Inheritance may establish a certain capacity for an individual. Accidental injury, disease, or other debilitating factors further influence the limitations for the development of total fitness. Such students require special concentration and attention to their needs and should be placed in the special physical education class for activities that are planned to build up specific factors of physical fitness. Included among those who are to be placed in the special class should be those who because of their inability to participate successfully in the regular class have withdrawn or desire to withdraw from activity and those who owing to general low fitness are unable to keep up with class instruction.

Those who are only slightly handicapped by their lack of fitness or are low in just one factor may be included in the regular class if certain modifications are made to give special emphasis to strengthening the weak areas and, if necessary, to offer protection to these areas of weakness.

In the special class emphasis is given to the areas that need work. This does not mean that the physical education program must consist only of activities designed to overcome deficiency, for the program should provide activities that will aid in the achieving of the broad general objectives of physical education.

Before much improvement can be expected in strengthening specific weak areas, the students must be convinced of the values of such improvement. Students may be motivated by helping them establish goals that can be obtained and are desirable for the age in question. Such goals as a better-looking body, more efficient performance of everyday working skills, or an improvement in sports skills may act as motivators.

Increasing Strength.   Special exercises and activities to increase strength may be given to those who are in special need of such a program. The most effective way to build strength is to apply the SAID principle by resistive exercises or by participation in games that require an additional work load to be carried.

In setting a work load for the student who has below normal strength, the teacher must take initial capacity into consideration and adjust the work load accordingly. Any area of the body that has a past history of injury should be protected, and the overload given this area should be very slight initially and slowly increased over a period of time. Students who have no organic lesions or history of injury but who are generally weak exhibit a tendency to select too small a work load and need to be encouraged to take more in order to achieve the desired results.

Weight training is a good activity for applying the correct amount of overload to

---

[18]American Alliance for Health, Physical Education, and Recreation: *Special Fitness Test Manual for Mildly Mentally Retarded Persons*, rev. ed., Washington, D.C. 1976, *passim.*

any set of muscles. However, if the size of the group working on strength improvement is rather large, weight training may be contraindicated because of lack of space and available weights.

Another activity for promoting the development of strength, especially suitable for large classes, is the dual resisting exercises, in which two people work together giving resistance to each other. Some examples of exercises that can be utilized are given below; others can be worked out using the same basic principles.

1. Students face each other, upper arms against the body with elbows bent and forearms extended to the front. They place their palms against each other and push. One person exercises the triceps; the other, the biceps.

2. Students face each other with arms fully extended and proceed as above.

3. Facing each other, the students extend their arms forward and upward with the fingers interlocked with each other. The hands are brought down, keeping the arms straight and flexing the wrists in an attempt to force the opponent to superextend his wrists.

4. One student carries the other piggyback and takes quarter or half squats, depending upon his strength.

5. Contests such as leg wrestle, arm wrestle, or Indian arm wrestle can be utilized to apply overload.

Increase in muscular strength will also increase muscular endurance and power. General muscular strength increase will influence scores on the pull-ups, push-ups, dips, sit-ups, and vertical jump tests.

There is insufficient evidence to indicate one special way to train for muscular endurance, explosive power, or strength. It is the general practice at this time to develop explosive power by increasing the static strength by means of overloading the muscle, using a heavy load with a fewer number of repetitions. In increasing muscular endurance, it is the common practice to use a smaller weight and a greater number of repetitions. However, since there is a proven relationship between muscular strength and muscular endurance, as they are commonly measured, exercise that increases muscular strength also increases muscular endurance.

Increasing Cardiorespiratory Endurance.   Those who are below par in strength, even though they are free from pathological disturbances, are also often very low in cardiorespiratory endurance; therefore, activities designed to develop cardiorespiratory endurance should be given along with those designed especially for increasing strength. The body appears to respond to an "overload" upon the cardiorespiratory system by improving the function, as it does when an overload is applied to a muscle.

Those with low endurance levels who have been selected from the regular class for special work will need to be introduced very slowly to endurance activities, since their lack of endurance is frequently connected with an attitude that has made them shun such activities. If there are no pathological causes present, there is little physical danger of giving too much work. However, more can usually be accomplished with this group by starting out very slowly and increasing the length of time of participation in the activity at a slow rate.

Games and sports that require running are excellent for developing endurance. However, with this group, interest may be very low because of past unsuccessful experiences in these activities. If games are used, modifications may be necessary so as to make the participation within the range of their abilities.

Some examples of modified games and activities related to team sports are listed below:

1. Three-court basketball
2. Line soccer with distance between goal line shortened
3. Basketball dribble relays

4. Dribble length of basketball floor and shoot

5. Football throw over goal post (Thrower throws high enough so he can run forward and catch ball; score is distance run if ball is caught.)

The work load that affects endurance can be more easily controlled when giving specific exercises than in game situations. Exercises such as side-straddle hop, squat thrusts, and rope jumping are ones in which the work load is easily regulated.

The pulse provides information about how the cardiorespiratory system is responding to the severity of the exercise. The pulse can either be taken at the radial artery at the wrist or at the carotid artery at the neck. In using the pulse to determine body response, a basal measurement must be established to determine the pulse rate when the body is at rest. At a predetermined time, the pulse is taken again. Based on studies of cardiorespiratory fitness in healthy male subjects, Cooper[19] found that an exercise must raise the pulse to at least 150 beats per minute and the exercise must be sustained for five minutes before substantial cardiorespiratory benefits occur. However, those who have a pathological condition of the cardiorespiratory system should not use 150 beats per minute as their goal. For information in setting targets for heart rates during exercise, refer to Chapter 13.

Increasing Flexibility. Flexibility can be increased by extending the range of motion. If there is no pathological reason for lack of flexibility, exercises that require stretching can be given. Each time the exercise is given, the joint should be moved in a wider range. Usually it is not desirable to segregate those who lack flexibility, because this usually does not hinder them to the extent that they cannot participate successfully with the other students. Flexibility exercises that are given to the entire regular class are appropriate for those who lack a wide range of movement. Such exercises are usually given as warm-up exercises preceding more strenuous activity. Some suggestions are:

1. Touch floor without bending knees.

2. Raise arms laterally and rotate at the shoulder in as wide an arc as possible.

3. With hands on hips, rotate trunk in as wide a circle as possible (same procedure for the head).

4. Hold arms in front of body, crossed at wrists and at belt level, then throw arms upward and backward as far as possible.

SPECIAL ELEMENTARY SCHOOL ACTIVITIES

In the elementary school it is usually not desirable to place the children with low physical fitness in the special program. As a rule, unless there are pathological disturbances, the difference between the normal group and the less physically fit group is relatively small compared to the difference in these groups in older children. Moreover, segregation at this age level may have psychological repercussions that may be difficult for the teacher to minimize. The most satisfactory method of teaching such children appears to be to keep them with the regular class and to include numerous games and activities which will encourage an improved condition of physical fitness.

Many of the activities already discussed are good for young children, but some will be too difficult for them to perform or too complex for their comprehension. Certain special exercises are valuable in the physical education program for the young child. Hanging, walking with the hands on a low parallel ladder, and climbing should be included in the elementary program to increase shoulder and arm strength. However, when the desired movements and exercises are incorporated into games and activi-

---

[19]Cooper, Kenneth: *The Aerobics*, New York, Bantam Books, Inc., 1970, *passim.*

ties, they become more meaningful to the child and more fun for him to do. The dual resisting exercises can be used effectively as games and contests with children beyond the second grade, although some are appropriate only to boys. The piggyback-ride exercise should be used with discretion, since it may be too strenuous for many.

The teacher must keep in mind that the sub-strength child should not be placed in game situations where he is always last. An attempt should be made to equalize the competition so that he can achieve some success. Attitudes of the class should be so shaped that any member of the team is readily accepted for the contributions he can make, even though he is not as strong or as efficient in the performance of skills as others on the team.

Following are some suggested activities for use in increasing muscular strength and endurance, cardiorespiratory endurance, and flexibility. Most of the activities contribute to more than one factor of physical fitness, but they are listed here under the factor to which they appear to make the greatest contribution. The lists are not intended to be exhaustive; they are, rather, suggestions for planning the program on the elementary level. The activities are listed according to their degree of difficulty and interest appeal.

Activities for Increasing Muscular Strength and Endurance

Race on tiptoes	Chinese stand-up
Seal walk	Walking chairs
Jumping jack	Wheelbarrow
Crab walk	Tug pick-up
Squat thrust	Hand wrestle
Modified push-up	Indian wrestle
Leap frog	Indian leg wrestle
Dual rocker	Frog tip-up

Activities for Increasing Cardiorespiratory Endurance

Midnight	Line relay
Drop the handkerchief	Cross tag
Bronco relay	Chain tag
Circle relay	Rope-jumping contest
Cowboys and Indians	Post ball

Activities for Increasing Flexibility

Bird flying	
Dry-land swimming	Measuring worm
Snail	Elephant walk
Rocker	Touch floor, knees straight
Twisting at hips	Sit-up, touch toes
Bending at hips, forward,	Grape vine
backward and to the sides	Forward roll
Wring the dish rag	Backward roll

SELECTED READINGS

AAHPER: *Testing for Impaired, Disabled and Handicapped Individuals.* Washington, D.C., American Alliance for Health, Physical Education, and Recreation, 1975.

Allsen, Phillip E., *et al.: Fitness for Life: An Individualized Approach.* Dubuque, Iowa, Wm. C. Brown Co., Pub., 1976.

Cooper, Kenneth H. : *The Aerobics.* New York, Bantam Books, Inc., 1970.

Fox, Edward L., and Mathews, Donald K.: *Interval Training: Conditioning for Sports and Physical Fitness.* Philadelphia, W. B. Saunders Co., 1974.

Raick, G. Lawrence, *et al.: The Motor Domain and Its Correlates in Educationally Handicapped Children.* Englewood Cliffs, N.J., Prentice-Hall, Inc., 1976.

Chapter 28

Posture and Body Awareness

Concepts of good posture have undergone numerous changes throughout history. At times the exaggerated styles of women's clothing have influenced the concept of good posture, as in the days of the bustle. The ramrod-straight position of the soldier at attention influenced for many years the idea of good body carriage. There is no doubt that the physical education teacher concerned with promoting good posture must take into consideration the esthetics of certain positions, and these, of course, are dictated by custom and tradition. But he should not ignore the effects that a specific posture will have upon the efficiency of the body.

Mastering efficient walking, sitting, and standing postures makes these movements more beautiful as well as more practical from the standpoint of preventing fatigue. Achieving this efficient, graceful posture involves body mechanics. This term refers to the alignment of the various segments of the body. Achievement of good body mechanics is dependent upon well-developed body awareness; that is, consciousness of how the body moves in space and what space it occupies. Developing this awareness is prerequisite to the most efficient use of the muscles to ensure the most effective alignment for the position desired.

Posture cannot be thought of as a single static position, for it changes continually with each movement. Moving the shoulders forward while leaning over from the hips to pick up a small object may be very good posture for that activity, but it is not effective for walking or standing. Consequently, we may say that posture depends upon the type of activity which the body is being called upon to perform.

Good posture also depends upon the structure of the body, which is determined by the relationship of the parts of the body to each other—that is, the relationship of the head to the spinal column and shoulder girdle, and so on. The relationship of the parts, how they fit together, is a determining factor in what constitutes good posture for the individual. People are not built alike, and to force everyone into the same mold of a preconceived idea of good posture is useless. An individual who, because of his body structure, is more round-shouldered than others should not be forced to stand with his shoulders thrust back to the same extent as one whose bone structure permits him to do this without strain. To do so will lower his body efficiency rather than raise it.

The incidence of poor body alignment is difficult to determine, since no standard of good posture can be universally applied. It is estimated that from 75 to 80 per cent of the population have some postural deficiency.

Only about 1 per cent can be classified as having such good body mechanics that no improvement is possible. Nearly 5 per cent have very marked postural deviations. Consequently, the physical education instructor may expect to find a large number of students in the total enrollment who may profit from instruction in good body mechanics and a small percentage in definite need of such instruction.

The teaching unit for developing good posture should stress awareness of how the parts of the body work together to obtain and maintain the relationship that produces the best posture for the individual. Awareness is developed in students by helping them to assume positions of efficient posture and noting how the body segments relate to achieve each position. Practice is afforded by specific corrective exercises, which subsequently become more meaningful to the students because of their awareness of how the body must move in order to achieve efficient posture.

BODY STRUCTURE

The body is held erect by the spinal column. The spinal column of the normal adult is a segmented structure consisting of four curves: the cervical, dorsal or thoracic, lumbar, and sacral. The cervical curve is the curve at the neck; the convex of this curve is forward. The dorsal curve is the curve of the upper back, and the convex of its curve is backward. The lumbar curve is the curve in the small of the back, and the sacral curve is the curve in the inferior (lower) extremity of the spinal column. The convex of the lumbar curve is forward, while in the sacral it is backward.

At birth the spinal column has a single curve, with its convex to the back. During the early months of life, when the baby starts to raise its head and kick its legs, the spine becomes relatively straight. The cervical curvature develops at the time when the infant sits upright. Later, when the child starts to support his weight on his feet and begins to walk, the lumbar curve comes gradually into prominence. This is accompanied by development of the other curves until the spine adopts the normal curves of an adult. The normal development of the curves is dependent in part upon whether the child is well and active during his early years.

Alignment.   The upper segment of the body, when in an upright position, must be in alignment with the base of the body (the feet). In perfect alignment the center of gravity of the head, upper trunk, lower trunk, and legs is in a straight line. Looking at the side view, if a plumb line is dropped even with the lobe of the ear, it will pass through the middle of the shoulder, through the middle of the hip, to the side and slightly behind the patella, and fall in front of the outer malleolus. As seen from the back, a line drawn through the body showing the center of gravity would bisect the head and neck and follow the spinal column down between the cleft of the buttocks. The spine should be straight and the shoulders and hips even, but slight variations will occur, depending upon individual differences. The more the body deviates from this alignment, the more energy is needed to hold the body erect because the postural muscles will have less mechanical advantage in maintaining balance. However, in certain cases the structure of the body may be such that there will be more energy expended in forcing the body into the alignment described above than in a less erect position.

Standing Posture.   There has been a tendency to portray good posture as the proper body alignment for the average body build and to expect all "good" posture to resemble this. Such expectation fails to take into consideration the difference in bone structure and body build.

Body builds are usually classified into three categories: Ectomorphy, slender; mesomorphy, medium stature with predominance of bone and muscle; and endomorphy, fat and bulky with no muscle definition. Most individuals are predominantly one type or the other; however, most people have characteristics of more than one type. One segment of the body may be predominantly in one classification while another segment will have more characteristics of another type. This sometimes causes the individual to appear to have poor posture while actually his body alignment is the most efficient for his body structure. For example, a person who has a deep, thick chest with a heavy dorsal area and relatively slender hip area will appear to have kyphosis (round upper back). To eliminate this condition would require an exaggerated posture that could be maintained only by tremendous contraction of the sacrospinalis muscles. This would entail considerable expenditure of energy and would therefore be a much less efficient posture than the original one.

The length of the clavicle influences the degree of erectness at which the shoulders will be held habitually by the individual. A relatively long clavicle will force the shoulder girdle back, while a relatively short one will require the scapulae to lie forward and to the side and will cause the shoulders to be brought forward.

The curves of the spine are also influenced by its structure. If the borders of the body of a single vertebra are thicker on one side than on the other, the curve in that area of the spinal column will tend to be increased. There is considerable variation in the thickness of the borders of vertebral bodies in individuals. The difference in thickness will produce a greater or lesser spinal curve than in the average person. To force a person whose curve deviates from normal to assume a very erect position may actually reduce the efficiency of the support of the spinal column. If the vertebrae are in alignment and the edges of the vertebrae cause a larger curve, an attempt to straighten the curve will spread the vertebrae farther apart, causing a probable instability. This cannot be determined by observation of the back, but it can be shown by x-ray.

Differences in the location of the acetabula (cavities in the pelvis receiving the heads of the femurs) influence the degree to which the pelvis is tilted, and the tilt of the pelvis determines the size of the angle in the lumbar curve. The acetabula form the pivotal point of balance of the pelvis and the spinal column because of the column's relationship to the pelvis. If the acetabula are situated slightly more to the front than usual, there will be a tendency for the posterior area to drop because of imbalance. The pelvic area rotates upward, causing the lumbar to flatten. If the anterior area drops, the pelvis will rotate downward and the lumbar curve is increased.

Walking Posture. The mechanics of efficient walking involve a basic pattern, but, like standing posture, the best pattern for any individual is dictated in part by body structure, particularly leg alignment, and variations within limits may be expressions of individual structure and not actual walking faults. Excessive variations which are caused by improper use of the muscles will, in most cases, warrant efforts to modify them. Common walking errors which are frequently caused by improper use of the muscles are the following:

1. Leaning forward before the lead foot strikes the ground.
2. Carrying the weight on the rear foot until after the lead foot strikes the ground.
3. Exaggerated shifting of the weight to the supporting foot.
4. Swinging the arms in too wide an arc.
5. Exerting force straight up from the rear foot as the step is made.
6. Failing to swing the arms at the shoulders.
7. Looking at the feet.
8. Toeing in or out.

Sitting Posture. A good sitting posture should permit some relaxation, whether one is seated for work or for rest. When sitting in a chair for the purpose of resting, as much of the chair as possible should be used to support the body. A slumping posture which does not utilize fully the support of the chair will be more fatiguing than an erect sitting position. Sitting far back in the chair, with the entire back resting against its contours, permits the chair to aid in holding the body, thereby allowing some muscular relaxation.

For desk work, it is usually necessary to bring the head and eyes over the work; consequently, the back of the chair cannot be used for support. The buttocks are placed far back in the chair, and the weight of the trunk is distributed over the entire area of the buttocks. The trunk leans forward slightly from the hips, and head, neck, and trunk are kept in a relatively straight line. When it is not necessary for the head to be over the working area, the back of the body may be in contact with the back of the chair for support.

The most common errors in sitting are as follows:

1. Failure to place the buttocks against the back of the chair.
2. Permitting the shoulders and back to slump.
3. Shifting the weight of the body to one side.
4. Sitting on one foot.

Lifting Posture. Lifting heavy objects from the floor or ground incorrectly is a common cause of back strain. When lifting heavy objects, the object should be placed as near to the center of the body as possible, as this increases the mechanical advantage in lifting. To pick up the load, the legs should be bent and the lift made by extending the legs with the back held relatively straight. If the object being lifted has a handle, it is possible to keep the back entirely straight during the lift. However, when it is necessary to put the hands under the heavy object on the floor, the trunk may be bent while the hold is being taken. The knees will be flexed during this process. The back is then straightened and the object lifted by extending the knees. In holding a heavy object, the knees should not be locked, as this position has a tendency to cause an exaggeration of the lumbar curve which may place undue stress upon the muscles of this region.

Light objects may be lifted by bending at the hips. However, anyone who has a history of lower back disorder should use the technique for lifting heavy objects in order to protect the back from possible strain.

CAUSES OF POOR POSTURE

It is frequently difficult to attribute poor posture to any single cause; in most cases a combination of two or more factors has produced it. For purposes of this discussion, the causes will be divided into two classes: those which are closely associated with fields such as medicine and psychiatry, and those which can be corrected by remedial work in physical education. It is recognized that no hard and fast demarcation can be established between the two because of factors which overlap; however, a rough line can be drawn between (1) poor posture attributed to such conditions as illness, infection, injury, malnourishment, a feeling of inadequacy, and deformities which are chiefly medical or psychiatric; and (2) faulty mechanics caused by poor neuromuscular habits of the postural muscles, weak musculature, overdevelopment of one set of muscles at the expense of another, and lack of body awareness, which are more nearly physical education problems.

Medical or Psychiatric Problems.   Accidents and illnesses frequently cause deformities which are conducive to incorrect use of the body. Students who suffer from such conditions should be under the care of an orthopedic physician, and postural work with such cases should be under the direct supervision of the physician and the physical therapist. However, in the later stages of recovery, the physical educator may be able to recommend games and activities that will complement the work of the medical team. Such activities need the approval of the physician before the student begins participation.

Injuries which cause a person to shift his weight to avoid pain or ease his work often encourage the development of poor posture. The treatment of the injury must be made by the physician, but the re-learning of postural skills after the healing of the injury may be directed by the physical education teacher in many cases. A missing limb creates problems in aligning the body correctly because of the shift in the body's center of gravity. A student who has lost an arm or a leg will need special assistance in learning to achieve and maintain the most efficient alignment of body parts.

Illness often causes an over-all body weakness which lowers the threshold of fatigue. General fatigue is often a contributing factor to poor posture. The fatigued individual doesn't have the energy necessary to hold his body in its proper alignment. The postural muscles are allowed to relax partially, and the various segments of the body gravitate out of alignment (body slump). The longer the fatigue continues, the more habitual the slump becomes. The slumping of the body would appear to be a means of conserving energy. Actually, however, this is not true, for in most cases when the body slumps, the center of gravity is no longer in a straight line; and the force of gravity will make certain muscles work harder to maintain balance.

Emotions and attitudes influence muscular movement and postural stance. This is readily observed in the child jumping with joy upon receiving a pleasant surprise or the adolescent slumping in the seat with boredom or dejection. There is evidence to support the contention that a habitual feeling of inadequacy and defeat, especially during childhood, encourages postural slumping. In such cases, if the desired outcome is to be achieved from postural training, it is first necessary to rebuild the individual's self-esteem.

Physical Education Problems.   The reasons for neuromuscular habits of the postural muscles which have no pathological basis are difficult to ascertain. It would appear that in some cases the cause is improper use of the muscles: the individual just learned to hold his body incorrectly in much the same way as one sometimes learns a sport skill wrong through trial and error. Just as the error in the sport skill is corrected by a re-learning process, the correction of faulty body mechanics requires a process of re-learning.

Lack of use of the postural muscles contributes to their weakness. Weak muscles, because they are weak, will not be used greatly in maintaining posture; this lack of use contributes further to their weakness. If the muscles are weak, there is greater difficulty in maintaining good body alignment.

In cases where the antagonistic muscles are much stronger than the agonists, there is a tendency for the stronger muscles to pull the body out of alignment. It is possible that a contributing factor to the overdevelopment of one set of muscles is an overspecialization in sports that develop this set of muscles. Evidence for this may be seen in athletes who participate exclusively in sports which require extensive use of the muscles of the chest but little of the back muscles. They may be round-shouldered to some degree because the weak muscles of the back are unable to perform their share of the work in maintaining equilibrium.

Failure to develop body awareness can cause poor posture. A child who does not know how his body moves and what space it occupies as it moves cannot tell when he is utilizing good body mechanics. Consequently, he is likely to develop poor postural habits. For such a child the posture improvement program must deal extensively with creating awareness of the body.

POSTURAL DEVIATIONS

There is no precise standard of erectness for measuring normal or abnormal posture. The only possible definition of the normal, or most desired, posture is that it is one in which the center of gravity of each segment of the body is kept in an approximately straight line without decreasing the efficiency of the body elsewhere. The frequently heard postural directive to "stand straight" has given rise to some confusion regarding the position of the spine. The spine is, of course, not straight; it has distinct curves. In some cases in which the curves are too marked, it may be advisable to straighten the curves; but a certain amount of curve is normal and natural. Marked increase in the curvature of the spine does not necessarily indicate a serious handicap. If the various segments of the body are balanced properly, a spine with moderately increased curves may be considered normal for some individuals.

Postural deviations are classified as structural or functional. In the *structural* deviation, the bony structure has changed. A structural deviation is a permanent condition. Because of the change in the bone structure, the deviation cannot be corrected short of surgery or placing the involved area in a cast. Corrective exercise is of little use in this situation. A *functional* disorder refers to a condition in which only the soft tissue such as muscles and ligaments are primarily involved. Functional disorders respond to exercise, and the disorder can be overcome. It should be remembered that it is not always easy to determine the difference between a structural and a functional disorder. Some cases involve a degree of fixation. In the early stages the disturbance may be in the soft tissues alone, but, as the condition persists, bone changes gradually take place.

Forward Head.   Forward head is a term used to describe a position in which the neck is flexed and the head is held forward and downward, usually with the chin dropped. The condition in which the head and chin are not dropped, frequently called "poke neck" or cervical lordosis, has a high incidence among the nearsighted. It is frequently accompanied by the inability to extend the cervical area and hence does not respond well to postural exercise.

In most cases, forward head accompanies an increased thoracic curve. However, if the thoracic curve remains normal, the efficiency of the body will not be decreased to a great extent, although the neck muscles will of necessity do more work to hold the head in position since it is not well balanced on the neck and shoulders. The chief disadvantage is in appearance. Sometimes a twisting of the neck or lateral flexion accompanies the forward head.

Round Shoulders.   The term round shoulders describes the position that occurs when the scapulae are held to the side toward the axillary area and forward. This is almost always accompanied by an increased thoracic curve. The majority of cases respond well to postural exercises. Some cases of round shoulders, as was pointed out earlier, are not a postural fault in the true sense since they are due to structural differences.

Protruding Shoulder Blades.   In the young child protruding shoulder blades or "angel wings" are common. The condition may accompany round shoulders and back. Lack of muscular strength in the back area is a frequent contributor to protruding shoulder blades. Muscles involved in holding the scapulae flat also aid in pulling the shoulders into correct standing posture. Besides the exercises prescribed for the correction of round back and shoulders, hanging and climbing exercises and games are excellent activities to strengthen these muscles in children.

Round Upper Back.   An increased curve in the upper back causes a round upper back. This is called thoracic or dorsal kyphosis. It is frequently the result of fatigue or inadequate muscular strength in the extensors of the spine. When the upper back is rounded, the sternum is depressed and the rib cage is lowered, resulting in a decrease of chest cavity that may result in distortion of the normal position of the vital organs. It is not known what effects this may have upon health, although it appears that the normal functions of the vital organs might be restricted. The condition responds well to exercises that strengthen the muscles involved in holding the spine more erect and that stretch their antagonists.

Lumbar Lordosis.   An exaggeration of the lumbar curve is called lumbar lordosis. A functional exaggeration of this curve is caused by increasing the tilt of the pelvic girdle. As the pelvic area is tilted, the symphysis pubis is lowered in front, followed by a forward movement of the lumbar area of the spine, causing an increase in the lumbar curve.

Sometimes lordosis accompanies kyphosis, as an attempt to balance the shift of the center of weight caused by the increased thoracic curve. With the increase of the lumbar curve, the center of gravity in that area is shifted to the back, thus compensating for the shifting of the weight forward in the upper trunk caused by the increased thoracic curve. Also accompanying the increased lumbar curve is the hyperextension of the knees. It is thought that this often precipitates the development of lordosis.

When the lumbar curve is increased, the center of gravity is shifted from near the center onto the back part of the vertebrae, bringing the spinous processes closer together and decreasing the size of the foramina (openings between the vertebrae through which the spinal nerves pass). This decrease in the size of the opening may cause a pressure upon the nerves.

Flat Back.   A large decrease in the normal lumbar curve causes a flat back. The action involved in the rotation of the pelvic girdle is the opposite of that in the condition of swayback.

It is difficult to determine just how much a flat back decreases body efficiency. It has been pointed out by some authorities that the extremely straight condition of the back reduces the shock-absorbing mechanism of the spine and causes disturbance in the function of the viscera because of changes in the size of the cavity and in the position of the viscera within the cavity. A flat back does decrease the esthetics of the body.

Scoliosis.   When the body is viewed from the back, the right and left sides of the body should be symmetrical, both shoulders and hips at the same level with the spinal column straight. Most individuals will show a very slight deviation in the spinal column. A slight deviation is usually not noticeable in casual observation and, if it does not become progressively worse, is of no consequence. However, a lateral curvature that is obvious must be considered as an abnormal condition.

Scoliosis, which is definitely a medical problem, is discussed in detail in Chapter 9, Orthopedic Handicaps. The special exercises needed by persons with this condition should be prescribed by medical personnel.

Severe Abdominal Muscle Weakness.   The abdominal wall comprises four sets of muscles: external and internal obliques, rectus abdominis, and transversus abdominis

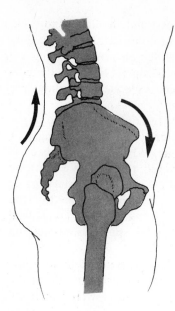

Figure 28–1. An increase in the lumbar curve results from rotating the pelvic area downward.

(see Fig. 26–3). The external oblique muscles are closest to the surface, while the transversus abdominis is the deepest muscle; the rectus abdominis and internal obliques are in the middle. Some of the muscles run parallel to each other while others run obliquely. Together they work to compress the abdomen into its roughly cylindrical shape to maintain body form, to change the intra-abdominal pressure in the visceral functions of breathing, defecation, urination, coughing, and vomiting, and to stabilize the pelvis.

Strong muscles tend to shorten, hence strong abdominal muscles tend to flatten the abdomen. Weakness of the abdominal muscles permits the abdomen to protrude, increases the lumbar curve, and, as explained in Chapter 14, makes breathing difficult for those with cardiorespiratory problems. Also, weak muscles allow the hip flexors and lumbar extensors to rotate the pelvic area downward, which increases the lumbar curve (Fig. 28–1). Such an increase causes undue stress to the lumbar spine. In school children, however, an exaggeration is common and is not considered abnormal, because it disappears with maturation.

Tight Hamstrings. The hamstring muscles are three muscles on the posterior of the thigh having a common origin on the tuberosity of the ischium (lower projection of the hip bone) and insertions at different places on the distal (far) end of the tibia. Tightness of these muscles is characterized by the inability to reach down and touch the toes without bending the knees. Otherwise undiagnosed low back pain has been attributed to tightness of the hamstrings. Frequently, if no organic lesion exists, lengthening the hamstrings through stretching exercises eliminates the pain.

Leg Alignment. People do not all walk or stand in the same way because of such differences in basic structure of the body as size, weight distribution, length and shape of the legs, and structure of the pelvic girdle. Leg and foot alignment is said to be proper when a line drawn from the anterior inferior iliac spine bisects the knee cap, ankle joint, and second toe. Some variation will occur due to structure. The location of the acetabulum determines to some extent the alignment. If the acetabulum is located to the front of the center of pelvic gravity, there is a tendency for the person to toe in. Often knock knees accompany this tendency. With the acetabulum to the rear, there is a tendency to toe out. To force one with this structure to toe straight ahead would be to decrease the efficiency in the hip area since the head of the femur would have to change from its customary position in the acetabulum.

FOOT MECHANICS

The feet are the base of the body and bear the entire weight of the body in an upright position. Since the foot is made up of several segments, it is subject to misalignment. The bones for the foot are so constructed as to form two arches: the longitudinal arch and the transverse arch.

The highest part of the longitudinal arch is on the inner side of the foot. On the inside of the foot the arch extends from the calcaneus to the first, second, or third metatarsal (near the ball of the foot). The longitudinal arch is supported by the shape of the bones that fit together, the ligaments, and the muscles.

The chief factor in the stability of the foot is how well the bones involved fit into each other. For example, the calcaneus gives the best support to the talus if its contact point with the talus is flat (horizontal) rather than slanting. If it slopes forward and downward, as it does in some individuals, the body weight pushes the talus down the slope of calcaneus, causing a broken arch or flat foot. Muscles involved in maintaining the longitudinal arch of the foot include the plantar muscles of the foot, that have their origin and insertion on the foot, as well as the deep muscles of the calf that pass under the foot and insert in the toes. Variations in bone structure in individuals account for varying degrees of the height of the arch. The highest arch is not necessarily the strongest arch.

The transverse arch extends across the foot in the area of the ball of the foot. The five metatarsals form the arch. The fifth and first metatarsals are the base for the arch. It is thought by some authorities that a dropping of this arch occurs when the second and third metatarsals drop down and become weight-bearing. A callus develops under the second metatarsal as a result. There is some disagreement among authorities about the importance of the transverse arch and the part it plays in creating the callus. Some point out that the callus and pain occur in this area when the second metatarsal is longer than the first and becomes the weight-bearing bone. In either case the problem is accentuated when a person wears high heels, and it occurs less frequently when low heels are worn.

Figure 28–2. A forward sloping of the calcaneus affects foot stability.

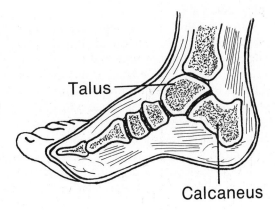

Position of the Feet. The preferred foot position with normal structure of the feet and legs is that in which the toes are pointing straight ahead or only slightly abducted. When the feet are abducted to any great extent, the weight of the body is forced over the longitudinal arch instead of over the outer borders of the feet with their stable structure.

Pronation is a movement in which the ankle rolls inward and the body weight is thrown over the longitudinal arch, causing the depressing and lowering of the arch. Pronation is brought about frequently by inadequate muscle strength and improper bony structure. Accompanying this is the abduction of the feet (turning the toes out).

Supination is the opposite condition of pronation. The ankle rolls outward, with the body weight falling on the outer borders of the feet.

Overweight and Flat Feet. Extreme overweight is often a causative factor in flat feet. A person who puts on weight too quickly often overloads foot muscles that have not been strengthened sufficiently over a period of time and cannot do the job of maintaining the arch. Placing a load upon the feet that they are not capable of handling will cause arches to fall. Weak and painful arches are common to the overweight individual.

POSTURE EVALUATION

To develop sufficient muscular strength, endurance, and skill in maintaining the best posture for the individual body structure is an objective of the physical education program. Whenever an individual deviates so much that he cannot participate in the regular program to his greatest advantage, or requires special attention to his needs which cannot be given him in the regular class, he should be placed in the special physical education class.

Screening Tests. Some schools administer screening tests to select those who require a more extensive examination to determine if they are in need of special consideration in postural education. Every physical education program should provide for some type of screening if it is at all feasible.

There are several different techniques that may be utilized in screening, but subjective evaluation is the one most frequently used. It is less expensive and less time-consuming than other methods. Subjective ratings are made by the examiner of anteroposterior and lateral balance and the alignment of the feet and legs in the standing position. To increase the validity of the observation, the body mechanics of walking can be examined. Students should be dressed in swimming suits to provide a view of the spinal column.

For the test, the students are lined up facing the examiner. The students are asked to turn to the left and right and to the back to give the examiner a view of all sides in a minimum of time and to enable the students to change positions frequently to avoid fatigue. The examiner moves along the line about eight or 10 feet from the subjects to make his observations. It should be mentioned that those with poor static posture usually overcompensate when attempting to assume good posture for the examination. Those who have fatigue slump with the rounded shoulders and forward head will throw their shoulders too far back and tilt the head up with the chin slightly elevated, resembling somewhat the "poke head."

As the subject faces the examiner, leg alignment, head and neck alignment, shoulder imbalance, transmission of the body weight to feet, and foot mechanics should be noticed. The feet of the subject are then placed with the heels about two inches apart, and each subject in turn curls the trunk forward with the head, shoulders, and arms relaxed. He reaches down until his fingers are about two feet from the floor and then returns slowly to standing position. The examiner should keep his eyes on a level with the back of the subject, noting any protrusions of one side of the rib cage or a twisting of the back. Either of these indicates muscular imbalance of the back.

As the subject turns to the left and right, notice is taken of evidence of kyphosis, lordosis, flat back, head misalignment, and hyperextension of the knees. The back view should be checked for evidence of hip imbalance and another check made for shoulder imbalance, neck and head misalignment, and faulty foot mechanics.

To make an evaluation of the walking mechanics, the examiner should observe the subjects walking toward him, away from him, and parallel to him. Observations should be made of toeing, leg alignment, use of the foot in heel-ball-toe action, pronation, and movements of the trunk.

New York Posture Rating Chart.   This chart effectively measures and records posture and postural changes that may occur in students. The chart is constructed so that measurements can be recorded each year for a period of nine years, from the time the child is in the fourth grade until he graduates from the twelfth grade. The grade numbers four through 12 at the top of the chart (see Fig. 28–3) head the column of each grade. The numbered boxes set in diagonals on the right side of each set of three pictures are spaces for recording the judgment of the examiner. Each row of pictures diagrammatically shows the "good" posture and the deviation from that in a specific portion of the body. The examiner is to decide which picture best represents the posture of the child being examined. He then places the number of the picture, which is printed in the picture's left-hand corner, in the appropriate box on the right. For example, if the child is a fourth grader who holds his head as shown in the picture on the extreme right of the first row, the score of 1 is recorded in the box labeled 4. The next year, when the student is in the fifth grade, his score will be placed in the box labeled 5. For a child who does not pass into the next grade, an extra box can be drawn on the chart and an appropriate note made. The final score for the student at each grade level is the sum of all the numbers in the boxes.

Diagnostic Posture Test.   Those who are screened out as needing postural work beyond that given in regular class should be examined by a physician before the remedial exercises begin. To assist the doctor in making his recommendations for the kind and extent of activity, diagnostic posture tests may be administered. There are several types. Two of the most effective are the evaluation of postural photographs and anthropometric measurements of the body. Procedures for these tests may be found in test and measurement textbooks. The tests are relatively complex and not recommended for general class testing.

Some schools make a silhouette of each student as a graphic record of his posture. The silhouette, because it shows the student so well his own postural errors, can be a very successful motivator for posture improvement. A series of silhouettes make an excellent record of progress.

The teacher may be able to secure the assistance of the school photography club in making the silhouettes. The process is relatively simple. A bed sheet or similar large piece of material is tacked to a frame to form a screen about 7½ by 3 feet. In a semidark room a light is placed behind the screen so that it will focus on the back of the screen. The subject stands in front of the screen wearing a swimming suit. The picture is taken against the screen.

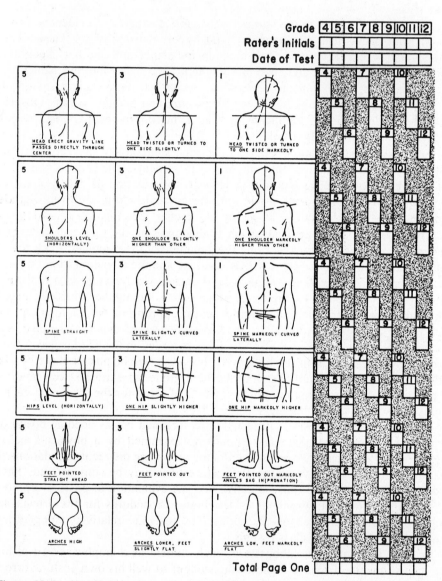

Figure 28–3. New York posture rating chart. (Vannier and Fait, *Teaching Physical Education in Secondary Schools*, 3rd Ed.)

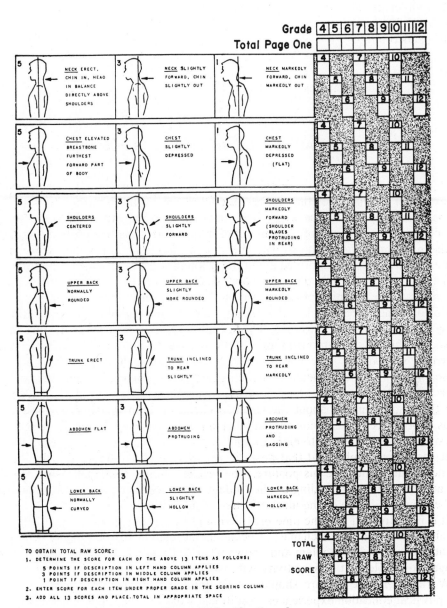

Figure 28-3. *(Continued)*

EQUIPMENT

The following items are extremely useful in presenting exercises and activities for the improvement of body mechanics:
1. Free wall space (to flatten the back in standing position)
2. Full-length mirrors
3. Individual mats
4. Padded plinths
5. Pulley weights
6. Weights
7. Stall bars and benches

THE PROGRAM FOR THOSE WITH POOR POSTURE

After the students have been selected and the medical diagnosis and recommendations are in the hands of the teacher, a conference should be arranged with each student. The body mechanics which need improvement are explained to the student and a clear indication made of the amount of improvement that may be expected. The exercise program is then planned with the student, based upon his special needs and his interests. He must be informed about the amount of exercise which is required and the danger signals of too much or improper kinds of exercise. The limitations placed upon him by the examining physician should be explained to him.

For older age groups, a list of activities can be mimeographed, with descriptions of how the activities are performed. The specific exercises for each individual can be checked on this list. A demonstration of the exercises should be given and the possible errors pointed out. The use of special equipment such as mirrors, stall bars, weights, and wall pulleys should be demonstrated and explained. Students above the junior high school level may be permitted to work on their own after this briefing, while the teacher moves about the room to check on individuals. For younger age groups, more direct supervision should be given. For the best possible instruction, the class size should be limited to eight to 10.

It should be emphasized that postural exercises are of little avail if the student does not want to improve his posture. The teacher should continually seek ways to motivate him. An understanding by the student of his needs and the improvement that may be expected is one of the most effective of all motivators.

It is not expected that the time provided in physical education classes is sufficient to enable much significant change to occur in the quality of the posture. Once the student is aware of his problem and knows what can be done for it, he should be encouraged to supplement class activity with work outside the class.

Work to improve posture should not be done at the expense of participation in other physical education experiences. Additional work in other physical education activities is a necessity in many cases to ensure optimum development in organic efficiency and social adjustment. The activities must, of course, be selected with care, particularly for those with severe problems.

For a person to assume good posture, he must first know what constitutes good posture for him. In attempting to assume good posture, one who has poor posture is likely to throw his head and shoulders too far back. This is a strained position, and it is no wonder that he cannot maintain it. Before he can achieve a better position, he must first be taught the proper body alignment for his body build. To introduce the student to the new position he should be shown how to assume the desired standing posture with the following:

1. The head balanced on neck, neither thrown back nor thrust out, chin slightly tucked in;
2. The shoulders spread as wide as possible, not thrown back;
3. The breast bone held up rather than the chest thrown out;
4. The pelvis placed under the trunk;
5. The knees slightly bent, not locked.

This standing position should be one of ease; it should not be strained or difficult to maintain. This position should be assumed frequently and checked for the ease with which it is held.

Postural exercises are designed to strengthen the muscles that are involved in maintaining the desired posture and in stretching their antagonists. Exercise is, of course, to be undertaken only after determining that the deviation is functional and all pathological causes have been overruled.

Exercise should be moderate in the beginning and the work load gradually increased, until the desired results are achieved or it has become obvious that exercise is not going to be effective. Weak muscles must initially be protected from overwork while their antagonists, that have shortened and so will not allow a wide range of movement, should not be overly stretched in the beginning.

As has been pointed out, the spinal column may compensate for an overcurve by curving in the opposite direction in another area of the spine. In the case of kyphosis, there is usually an increased curve in the lumbar area. When this is so and exercise is given for the round back, care should be taken that the movement does not increase the size of the lumbar curve. The same precaution must be taken with the exercises that are given for forward head and round shoulders and back to avoid increasing the lumbar curve.

The preventive and corrective exercises that follow are frequently suggested for use in postural work. They are divided into three groups: mild, moderate, and strenuous. These are very broad categories, and some exercises do not belong exclusively to any one group because so much depends on how vigorously the individual performs them. *Those exercises for scoliosis that are asymmetrical (exercising only one side of the body) should not be given except under the direction of a physician; they are identified with an asterisk.*

Prevention and Correction of the Forward Head

Mild Exercises

1. Assume correct standing position and place light object on head. Walk with weight balanced on head and chin held in as much as possible.
2. Rotate head in circle with chin held in. The forward movement is relatively passive; backward movement is more forceful.
3. Lie supine on mat; force head down on mat while chin is held in. Do not increase the lumbar curve.
4. Stand with back to wall, heels two to three inches from the wall. Press the back of the head against the wall with chin held down. Do not increase the amount of curve in the lumbar area.

Moderate Exercises

1. Interlace fingers behind head, pull down with arms, and push back with head.

2. Tighten the muscles of the back of the neck, keeping chin in contact with the chest.

3. Lying in prone position, clasp hands behind the back, raise head as high as possible, keeping chin tucked to chest. (Not recommended when lordosis is present.)

Strenuous Exercises

1. On the back in a reverse hook position with the feet on the floor, arch up on back of neck, bearing weight upon the head and feet. (Not recommended when lordosis is present.)

2. A helper stands in front and locks his hands around subject's head. Helper pulls the head down while subject attempts to push the head back.

3. See exercise for neck extensor with the use of weights (Chapter 26). In using this exercise for the forward head, keep the chin tucked as much as possible.

Prevention and Correction of Round Shoulders, Round Back, and Protruding Shoulder Blades

Mild Exercises

1. Stand with feet slightly apart and fists clenched. Cross the arms in front and fling them upward and backward behind the head. Raise up on toes as arms are flung backward to prevent the arching of the back.

2. Raise the arms at the sides until they are parallel to the floor. Hold the palms up. Move the arms with moderate speed so that the hands describe a small circle backward, downward, forward, and upward.

3. Raise elbows to shoulder level, clasp hands and pull, with each arm resisting the other.

4. Lying supine on a narrow bench with knees bent, feet on floor, grasp dumbbell or weight in each hand. Extend arms sideward, allowing weight of dumbbells to stretch muscles of chest. Bend elbows and return to original position. Do not increase the amount of curve in the lumbar area.

5. Stand in a corner and place a hand on each side of the corner, shoulder height, with arms parallel to floor. Try to touch nose to corner, keeping back straight and feet flat on floor but allowing elbows to bend.

6. On the back, with the knees bent, the feet on the floor, and the hands at the sides, palms up, move the arms horizontally to a position over the head and return to original position. Do not increase the curve in the lumbar area.

Moderate Exercises

1. Lying prone, hands clasped behind the back, raise the head and shoulders off the mat. Keep lower back straight.

2. Lying prone, extend arms over head. Raise head, trunk, and arms, arching upper back. Keep lower back straight.

3. Interlock fingers behind back in lumbar area. Press elbows down and back, trying to bring elbows together. Head is held up. Do not sway lower back.

4. With hands well spread, grasping wand, raise hands overhead. Wand is moved back over the head as far as possible while the arms are kept straight. Do not sway lower back.

5. Lie supine on mat with pad under shoulders and fingers laced behind neck. Helper kneels at the head, grasps subject's elbows, and presses downward slowly.

6. Standing with arms at sides, move shoulders in circle by first shrugging them, then forcing them backward, and finally dropping them to original position.

Strenuous Exercises

1. Lie supine and place the hands under the neck; inhale and raise the shoulders off the floor. The head, elbows, hips, and legs remain in contact with the floor. Avoid arching the small of the back. Exhale and return to original position.

2. Sit on the floor. Place the feet in front and the hands behind the body. Raise the weight of the body on the hands and feet and walk forward, backward, or sideways.

3. Sitting on the floor, interlock fingers behind the neck, arms parallel with the floor. Helper places knee in back, grasps elbows, and pulls.

4. Perform straight-arm hang on bar or rings. (Exercise is mild, moderate, or strenuous depending on the length of time position is held.)

5. With a dumbbell or weight in each hand, bend at the waist, extend the arms to the sides, and raise as far as possible. Return to original position.

6. Lying in supine position with helper holding feet, clasp hands at the small of the back, raise trunk, while pushing on back with hands. (Not recommended when lordosis is present.)

7. See exercises for trapezius, serratus anterior, and rhomboids with weights (Chapter 26).

Prevention and Correction of Lordosis

Mild Exercises

1. Standing with feet spread, bend forward at the hips, keeping knees straight with arms hanging down between legs. Relax with bouncing movement; bob the trunk up and down.

2. Tilt the pelvis backward; rotate around and around as in hula dancing. Make a rather passive movement in tilting the pelvis forward since this will increase the lumbar curve.

3. Lie in the supine position. Attempt to force the small of the back to the floor by rotating the lower part of the pelvis forward.

4. In hook position on back, contract abdominal muscles and press lumbar region to the floor.

Moderate Exercises

1. Stand as in above with feet spread. Touch first between legs, return to original position, then touch on the outside of right foot and then outside of left foot.

2. With feet together, bend forward at the hips, keeping knees straight with arms hanging down between the legs. Bouncing from hips, touch floor. Hold three seconds.

3. In supine position, raise knees to chest.

4. On hands and knees, tuck pelvic area in so as to flatten the back. Hold for count of five. Return to original position. Avoid extreme arching of the back when returning to original position.

Strenuous Exercises

1. Lying in supine position, raise both knees to chest. Stretch both legs into the air. Return to knees on chest position.

2. Lying on the back, draw knees up to chest, grasp shins, and pull. Hold for three counts.

3. In a sitting position with knees straight and feet apart, reach forward and grasp ankles and pull trunk forward several times.

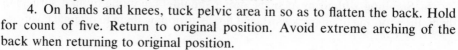

4. In a prone position, arms extended to the sides with palms up, raise head and shoulders. At the same time forcibly contract abdominal muscles to prevent lumbar curve from increasing.

Note: Exercises that exaggerate the lumbar curve should be avoided by those with lordosis.[1] Exercises such as back bending, leg raises (lying on the back and lifting both legs), and the straight-arm pullover in weight training are contraindicated for those with weak abdominals who are subject to hollow back.

Exercises for those with low back pain due to poor alignment of the pelvis and sacrum with the lumbar spine are found in Chapter 16.

Prevention and Correction of Flat Back

Mild Exercises

1. On knees, place forehead on floor; rotate hips to increase lumbar curve.

2. Tilt the pelvis backward; rotate around. Make a rather passive movement in tilting the pelvis forward and forceful in tilting backward.

Moderate Exercises

1. Stand with back against wall; push shoulders against wall and force hips away from wall.

2. Interlock fingers behind back in lumbar area. Press elbows down and back, trying to bring elbows together. Sway in at the back.

Strenuous Exercises

1. Lie prone and place the hands behind the neck; raise the shoulders off the floor. Arch the back, keeping hips in contact with floor.

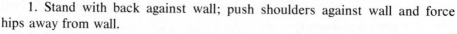

---

[1]Charles L. Lowman and Carl H. Young: *op. cit.,* pp. 173–176.

2. Lying on the back with the feet on the floor, arch the back taking the weight on the head and feet.

Correction of Scoliosis: C Curve

Note: These exercises are for C curve to the left; if curve is to the right the exercises should be reversed.

Mild Exercises

1. Hang from a bar or rings by the hands with the arms fully extended. (This exercise is mild, moderate, or strenuous, depending upon the time the position is held.)

*2. Standing with hands on hips, raise the right arm forward, upward, and overhead; raise the left arm sideward to shoulder height. Then raise on tiptoe and lift leg sideward and stretch the whole body. Return to original position.

*3. Standing with hands on hips, stretch the left arm down at the side and push down hard. Avoid bending body toward left side.

*4. Standing, facing the stall bars, stretch left arm forward and grasp the opposite stall bar. Raise the right arm overhead and stretch.

*5. Standing with hands on hips, stretch the right arm up overhead and press the left hand against ribs at side of body at point which forces the spine into a straighter position.

Moderate Exercises

*1. Stand with feet slightly apart. Trunk should be inclined forward. Place the right hand back of the neck and the left hand well up against ribs. Bend to left and push in with left hand. Avoid letting right elbow come forward.

*2. Sit on stool with hands on hips. Stretch right leg back of stool, resting foot on toes. Stretch right arm up and left arm back. Keep trunk on line with right leg.

*3. Standing with hands on hips, charge forward with the left foot, keeping right foot back and slightly turned out. The sole rests on the floor. Raise right arm forward and upward. Stretch left arm back. Do not drop the head. Keep trunk in a line with the rear leg.

*4. Standing with hands on hips, charge forward with the left foot. Turn right foot and keep it on the floor. Raise right arm forward and upward. Stretch left arm down and back. Bend forward and touch the floor with the right hand as far out in front of the left foot as can be reached. Keep trunk in a line with the rear foot.

Hint to instructor: Exercise 4 is very much like the preceding one, but the final stretch to touch the floor makes it more difficult. Give exercise 3 first, and when that can be done easily, go on to 4.

Strenuous Exercises

*1. Face the stall bars, the right hand grasping the top bar, the left hand the second bar, the feet resting on a stool or lower bar. Hang down on the arms and stretch right leg over stool or bar.

*2. Lie on plinth or table with right knee bent over end, left knee bent, and left foot on plinth; left arm is under the back, right arm bent with elbow at waist. Helper grasps wrist of student's right arm pulling sideward while student resists. When arm is up, student must relax and helper stretches to count of five. Student then brings arm to first position while helper resists.

*3. Hanging with back to stall with right arm high, bend and raise left knee.

*4. Hang on stall bars with face toward bars and right arm high.

Exercises for Scoliosis: S Curve

Note: These exercises are for S curve with left dorsal and right lumbar curve; if curves are opposite, exercise positions should be reversed.

Mild Exercises

1. Hang from a bar or rings by the hands with the arms fully extended. (This exercise is mild, moderate, or strenuous, depending upon the time the position is held.)

2. Sit on floor with legs straight, keeping back erect. Sit in this position for a short time, relax, assume it again.

3. Lying on floor draw knees up to chest. Clasp hands firmly around knees and hold this position for one minute.

4. With hands on hips, bend forward from hips until back is flat. Hold head up.

*5. Sit astride chair facing back, hands on neck. Bend to left side and come to straight position. Bend only in the dorsal area.

*6. In a supine position with hands on neck, extend right arm upward and at same time stretch left leg across body.

*7. Lying prone, stretch right arm over head and at the same time stretch left arm downward and across back. Hold this position one minute.

*8. Place hands on hips, shift weight to right leg, and at the same time stretch up as far as possible.

Moderate Exercises

1. Lying prone on table, feet held firmly by helper, clasp hands behind back, straighten arms by sliding the hands down the back, at the same time raise body from the table as far as possible.

*2. Place pad under each knee. Assume position for creeping on hands and knees. Stretch the right arm forward and at the same time slide left knee forward. Stretch left arm forward and slide the right knee forward. Creep in a circle to the left.

*3. Stand erect with feet apart, arms extended sideward. Twist trunk backward to right, trying to touch right toe with left hand. Keep knees straight and return to erect position each time.

*4. Sit astride chair facing back, hands on neck. As helper places knee on convexity of upper curve and grasps elbow, bend sideward over helper's knee.

*5. Same as exercise 4 but against lower curve on the other side.

Strenuous Exercises

1. Stand at bar which comes just to hips. Place hands on bar, push down, stretch spine as much as possible. If possible, lift body weight off floor.
2. Lying supine, feet held firmly by a partner, clasp hands in front. Slowly come to the sitting position.
*3. Facing stall bars, grasp bars firmly with both hands with right hand two bars above left hand. Slide feet slowly to right side until body hangs in a curved position.

Correction of Misalignment of Feet and Weak Arches.

In most cases of weak arches, the condition has been developing over a period of time. Poor standing and walking habits may be so thoroughly ingrained into the movement pattern that it will take a period of time to develop the strength of the muscles and relearn proper skills of standing and walking. Furthermore, the plantar muscles of the feet are difficult to provide adequate exercises for, and so the feet respond slowly to corrective exercise. Any exercise program undertaken must be continued over a period of time to be of any value.

Prevention of foot problems by exercises is much easier than the correction of foot deviation. The following exercises are for strengthening the muscles that aid in maintaining the longitudinal arch. A transverse arch disorder does not generally respond to exercise and should be treated by the proper medical personnel.

Foot exercises that consist of rising on the toes or walking on the toes should not be performed by those who have weak arches because this kind of exercise shortens the calf muscles and throws additional stress on the balls of the feet.

Mild Exercises

1. Stand with feet slightly apart, press toes against floor, and attempt to rotate the knees inwardly to lift the arches of the feet. (Inside of foot should rise.)
2. In a sitting position, cross one leg over the other. Circle foot, first in, then up, out, and down.

Moderate Exercises

1. In standing or sitting position, curl the toes as if to grasp the floor. Hold in isometric contraction for a brief period of time. The base of the first phalange (big toe) is not lifted off the floor.

Strenuous Exercises

1. In a sitting position, place the toes on the edge of a towel. Curl the toes so as to pull the towel under the feet. Do not raise the heel, and keep the base of the big toe on the floor throughout the exercise.
2. Sit on the floor with the knees bent and the balls of the feet touching each other, with the heels slightly apart. Draw the feet toward the body keeping the balls of the feet together and the heels apart.

Note: Exercises should not be given to those with painful feet. These students should be referred to the proper medical personnel.

ELEMENTARY SCHOOL ACTIVITIES

Posture difficulties owing to the improper use of muscles are not as prevalent or obvious in children of elementary school age as in older children. However, exercises are much more effective in overcoming postural deviations if they are given before the improper posture becomes well established. Consequently posture exercises should be included in the physical education program for young children.

As with children who have less than normal physical fitness, it is usually wiser not to segregate from the regular class those who need special posture exercises. Such students can usually be accommodated in the regular class by providing special activity designed to meet their special needs. The best method of doing this is through the use of games* that require those who need special exercises to perform types of movements that are beneficial to them. Games, contests, and relays have the additional advantage of providing the strong motivation so often lacking in the performance of exercises as such. A few activities are presented here as examples of games or contests that provide beneficial exercises.

1. Mimicking the giraffe. The children stretch their bodies to make them tall like the giraffe by reaching high with the arms and rising on tiptoes. Purpose: to strengthen postural muscles generally (not to be used by those with arch difficulties).

2. Eagle and mice. One student is chosen as the eagle; the others are mice. The eagle spreads his arms to the sides and rotates them back, then up and forward. He pursues the mice, trying to catch them while rotating the arms in this manner. The game may be modified so that all must "fly" in which case the mice become sparrows. Purpose: to strengthen muscles in upper back and stretch chest muscles.

3. Follow the leader. The leader executes various exercises for improving posture. Purpose: see exercises for specific postural difficulties.

4. Seesaw. Two students face each other in a sitting position with the legs extended. They grasp each other's hands and place their feet together. Keeping the knees straight, one pulls the other until he is raised off the floor. Then the procedure is reversed. Purpose: to strengthen muscles of the upper back.

5. Relays using the crab walk (walking on hands and feet with back to the floor), seal walk (walking on hands with legs dragging along floor), or measuring worm walk (walking on hands and feet by first moving forward on the hands and then bringing feet up to hands). The class is divided into two or more separate lines. The first one in each line "walks" to specified goal and returns to his line, where he touches the first one in line and then goes to the end of the line. The one who has been touched takes his turn and so on through the entire line. The line which finishes first is the winner. Purpose: crab walk—to strengthen back muscles; seal walk—to increase lumbar curve in flat back; measuring worm walk—to decrease curve in lumbar area.

6. Crab-walk ball. Using the rules of kick ball with the distances between goals shortened, the ball is played with the feet while all players are using the crab walk. Purpose: to strengthen muscles of the upper back.

7. Basketball with the feet. Using a wastebasket or similar receptacle as the basket, the students attempt to toss a basketball or volleyball into the basket with their feet from a sitting position on the floor six to 10 feet from the basket. The ball must be grasped by the soles of the feet. Purpose: to strengthen muscles of the longitudinal arch.

8. Ball-passing overhead relay. Two or more teams can participate. Teams form a straight line by sitting cross-legged on the floor. The first player in line passes a

---

*For description of games see Chapter 20.

basketball over his head with his two hands, keeping his elbows as straight as possible. The next one in line receives and pass it on. The last one in the line runs forward with the ball and, sitting down, passes the ball back. When the one who started the game again becomes the first in line, the game is completed. The first team to complete the game is the winner. Purpose: to strengthen muscles of the upper back.

9. Over and under ball-passing relay. Two or more teams can participate. The teams form a straight line. The first one in line passes the ball between his legs to the second person who receives it and passes it over his head to the next one in line. The ball is passed, alternating the over and under pass. The first line to complete the relay is the winner. Purpose: to strengthen muscles of the upper back and decrease curve in lumbar area. (Those with exaggerated lumbar curve should not pass the ball overhead.)

10. Overhead ball passing with the feet. Two or more teams may be formed, with the members of each team in a straight line, sitting down with the legs extended. The first player in line takes the volleyball between the feet and rolling backward, keeping the knees straight, passes the ball to the person behind him, who takes it in his hands and places it between his feet and passes it back in the same manner. The last person in line receives the ball, runs forward to the front of the line, sits down, and passes the ball with his feet to the one behind. The game is completed when the one who started the game returns to the head of the line. Purpose: to decrease curve in lumbar area.

SELECTED READINGS

Arnheim, Daniel D.: *Principles and Methods of Adapted Physical Education and Recreation,* ed. 3. St. Louis, The C. V. Mosby Co., 1977.

Fait, Hollis F.: *Experiences in Movement: Physical Education for the Elementary School Child.* Philadelphia, W. B. Saunders Co., 1976.

Lindsey, Ruth, *et al.: Body Mechanics: Posture, Figure, Fitness.* Dubuque, Iowa, Wm. C. Brown Co., Pub., 1974.

Sherrill, Claudine: *Adapted Physical Education and Recreation.* Dubuque, Iowa, Wm. C. Brown Co., Pub., 1976.

Vodola, Thomas M: *Individualized Physical Education Program for the Handicapped Child.* Englewood Cliffs, N. J., Prentice-Hall, Inc., 1973.

Chapter 29

Relaxation

Muscular relaxation is the opposite of muscular contraction or tension. Muscles contract in response to stimuli from the central nervous system. In muscular relaxation, the muscles receive minimal innervation, and their fibers become longer and less thick than in contraction. In appearance the relaxed muscle is smaller in circumference around its belly (largest part), and to the touch it feels less tense, softer, and more pliable. It is an erroneous assumption that when a muscle is not in complete contraction it is relaxed. A muscle need not be completely tensed to be in a state of contraction. A certain amount of contraction is always present, but more than normal tonus can be detrimental to health and well-being.

THE VALUES OF RELAXATION

In the relaxation of overly tense muscles, certain positive changes take place in the body. The blood, which is impeded in its flow by the constriction of the blood vessels in tense muscles, circulates more freely, and the work of the heart and the stress on the blood vessels is reduced. It has been reported that the pulse rate can be lowered five beats or more per minute by participation in a specific relaxation program.[1] Because of the salutary effects on the circulatory system, a program of relaxation may be particularly beneficial to those with elevated blood pressure and heart problems.

Because relaxation conserves energy, it prevents undue fatigue. Energy is consumed by muscular contraction, producing waste products that must be removed promptly and efficiently in order to prevent fatigue. The increased consumption of energy brought about by excessive muscular tension produces great amounts of waste that cannot be effectively removed by normal processes, owing to the greater volume of the waste and the impeded circulation of the blood. As a result, fatigue develops more rapidly and is more prolonged. Fatigue can usually be relieved by relaxation; exercises for this purpose are generally helpful to those who tire easily, are chronically fatigued, and have trouble falling asleep.

Another positive effect of relaxation is that breathing becomes easier. Since lung capacity is greater when the chest muscles are relaxed, the breathing rate is decreased. A program of activities to develop slower, more relaxed inhalation and exhalation is often advantageous to those with breathing disorders.

Muscular relaxation has beneficial effects related to such disorders as diarrhea,

---

[1]Laurence E. Morehouse and Augustus T. Miller, Jr.: *Physiology of Exercises.* St. Louis, The C. V. Mosby Co., 1976, p. 304.

constipation, stomach upset, non-specific muscle pain and headaches, and skin irritations. It has been established that frequently at the root of these health problems is an extreme or prolonged psychological response, such as fear, anger, or frustration. Muscular tension caused by an emotional reaction is one of the precursors of all of the disorders mentioned above; other precursors vary according to the nature of the condition. Relaxation tends to restore calm after emotional outbreaks and, of course, decreases the tension within the muscles which, in turn, helps to diminish the symptoms of the disorder.

Recent research[2] provides evidence that training in relaxation can be helpful to children with learning problems. Subjects in the research studies demonstrated reduced levels of anxiety, increased attentiveness, and possibly higher scholastic achievement. Evidence is not conclusive on the relationship between relaxation and improvement in scholastic achievement, but it seems likely that freedom from anxiety and tension permits greater concentration on the academic material and, therefore, achievement would be improved.

Because of the positive effects of relaxation on the body, the ability to relax consciously is valuable to nearly everyone. Periods of greater than normal tension are experienced by most people, and for many the periods are prolonged and intense. Handicapped children, especially, often have a high degree of tension, engendered both by the physical pain and problems associated with their condition and by the negative social situation in which they find themselves. For these children relaxation is prophylactic (tending to ward off disease). Moreover, relaxation promotes feelings of well-being and, in some instances, such as in asthma and neurological hyperactivity, provides direct relief from some of the symptoms of the condition. It is important, then, for the physical education teacher to understand the significance of relaxation and to be able to teach the skills of conscious relaxation. Knowledge of the importance of and the means to achieve relaxation in effective performance of motor skills, which is a basic in the training of physical educators, provides a good foundation for teaching conscious total body relaxation to all students, handicapped or non-handicapped, who exhibit signs of hypertonicity.

SIGNS OF TENSION

Muscular tension can be determined by several simple tests, which will be described later in connection with evaluation for program planning. There are numerous overt signs that indicate hypertonicity. In some people these take the form of displays of excessive annoyance and overanxiousness, inability to remain motionless, or excessive, rapid, and loud conversation, or all of these. Other people display an appearance of great calmness. They seem to be entirely immobile; however, close observation generally reveals signs of muscular tension and physical strain such as rigidity of posture and lack of facial expressiveness. Abnormal perspiration, uncontrollable crying, and irregular breathing (hyperventilation or hypoventilation) are other common signs of neuromuscular tension.

It should be noted that where extreme anxiety and annoyance are evident, it is often difficult to determine if these responses are the results of excessive muscular tension or the causes of it. Actually, they are both cause and result. Someone with

---

[2]Bryant J. Cratty: *Physical Expressions of Intelligence.* Englewood Cliffs, N.J., Prentice-Hall, Inc., 1972, p. 183.

hypertonicity becomes annoyed or angered by trivial matters that he could ignore if he were not in a state of tenseness. On the other hand, if a person is anxious or angry, he becomes more tense than he would otherwise be. Actually, emotional responses can be controlled to some degree by decreasing the tension in the muscles. The reverse is also true, but more often it is harder to decrease anxiety and anger than to reduce excessive muscular tension because decreasing anxiety and anger involves discovering the cause from which these emotions spring. The cause may be so obscure and deep-seated as to require professional help in finding and alleviating it.

The Difference between Tension and Relaxation. The process of learning to relax begins with becoming aware of the difference between tension and relaxation. Since relaxation is the opposite of tension, the difference can be perceived in activity that contrasts the two. The muscles in a segment of the body, such as in the arm, are contracted with great force, and thought is concentrated on the contraction. The muscles are then relaxed completely, and the difference between the relaxation and contraction is mentally noted. Alternate contracting and relaxing are continued with an attempt to increase the difference between the two conditions each time.

The contracted muscle is firmer and less flexible and produces a feeling of tenseness and tightness. In contrast, the relaxed muscle is loose and soft. Vigorous contraction followed by relaxation produces a sensation of heaviness and warmth in the muscle. (This phenomenon has significance when using imagery to develop a relaxed state, which will be discussed later in the chapter).

METHODS OF RELAXATION

The program to teach conscious relaxation may be based entirely on the techniques of one of several methods currently favored by sizeable groups of ahderents, or it may incorporate the techniques of two or more of these. Techniques and activities of several of the widely known methods that appear to be most useful to the physical educator in helping handicapped and non-handicapped students to achieve relaxation are described briefly below.

Progressive Relaxation. The method called progressive relaxation was developed during the 1920s and 30s by Edmund Jacobson, a medical doctor who was greatly concerned about the management of neuromuscular tension. Because Dr. Jacobson tested his method with laboratory procedures, his publications on the subject were, and are, highly regarded, and his method widely practiced in its original and more recently adapted forms.

The basis of the Jacobson method is the development of the ability to "localize tensions when they occur during nervous irritability and excitement and to relax them away."[3] Such ability is achieved, in general, by first learning to recognize muscular contraction and to reduce the tension by relaxing the muscles; this is followed by practice in relaxing major muscle groups, one at a time in a prescribed order. As relaxation of each new group is attempted, all of the groups previously practiced should be relaxed simultaneously. The number of muscle sets included, the duration of the practice, and the specific form of the technique employed depend upon the condition (degree of tension, aptitude, and so forth) of the learner.

When the relaxation techniques are to be used for inducing sleep, Jacobson recommends that auxiliary objects be used to relieve tension at body points where

---

[3]Edmund, Jacobson: *Progressive Relaxation,* ed. 2. Chicago, The University of Chicago Press, 1938, p. 40.

muscular contraction occurs in the supine position. He suggests that a pillow be placed beneath the back of the neck to relieve strain on the shoulders. A pillow should also be placed under the knees to release tension on the hamstring muscles. When a comfortable position is achieved, the individual consciously relaxes various parts of the body progressively, beginning at the head and going down toward the feet.

Yoga. Yoga is a system of mental and physical disciplines by which man seeks to attain union with the supreme being or ultimate principle. Originating in ancient India. Yoga has had a strong following through the centuries, which continues to the present day. In the United States there is much current interest in the physical discipline known as Hatha Yoga, which offers forms of exercise that are particularly effective in learning to relax.

One form is the âsana, which can be described as a held position or pose. The âsana is performed by moving the body slowly into the prescribed position, stretching each segment of the body that is brought into the movement as far as it can comfortably be stretched. No movement is ever forced and excessive stretching that can cause pain is avoided. The number of repetitions of the âsana exercise is not increased; however, the length of time the position is held may be increased as greater ease is achieved in holding it. The distance over which the body is stretched in the movement increases with practice.

A breathing exercise called pranayma is another form of Hatha Yoga. The objective of the pranayama is to slow the breathing process. This is achieved by gradually increasing the amount of air in each inhalation and exhalation.

Static Stretching. One of the earliest proponents of the teaching of techniques of relaxation in physical education and recreation was Josephine Rathbone of Columbia University. Her views on relaxation were influenced by her study of Hatha Yoga in India during the 1930s, and some of the exercises she recommends for relaxation are adaptations of Yogic exercises.

In a recent book, she suggests relaxation exercises to increase flexibility in the joints in order to free the muscles of excessive tension.[4] Basically these exercises are of two types: one in which a stretch is placed on the muscle and then released, and the other in which a position is held for several minutes. All movements are performed in a slow and deliberate manner. The reason for this manner of movement in the flexibility exercises, and in other exercises that promote relaxation, is that ballistic or jerky movements tend to increase the tension of the muscle.

Rhythmic Exercises. Rathbone has also suggested the use of rhythmic exercises to encourage the development of a relaxed state.[5] It has been her experience that individuals who were observed to be tense responded well and reported less tension after participating in such exercises. She believes that the feeling of relaxation is the result of improved circulation brought about by performing the rhythmic activities.

The exercises she has developed for this purpose involve the legs, arms, and trunk and consist of swinging and swaying movements. Each exercise is performed for 30 to 60 seconds. Jerky and uncertain movements are avoided. Rhythm is inherent in the natural swinging movements, but music may be used to help establish the rhythmic pattern.

Imagery. Imagery is the formation of mental pictures; the process may be invoked internally without outside stimulation, but often it is encouraged by an external stimulus such as the spoken word or musical mood. Physical education teachers of

---

[4]Josephine L. Rathbone: *Relaxation*. Philadelphia, Lea and Febiger, 1969, p. 83.
[5]*Ibid.*, p. 81.

young children have found imagery extremely helpful in teaching quality of movement. Imagery can also help young children understand the nature of relaxation and how it is achieved. The theoretical basis for the use of imagery to this end is that the formation of certain mental pictures helps students to match movements with their perception of relaxation. Empirical evidence would indicate that mind-set and feelings have a strong influence on the tonus of the muscles; imagery assists the process of changing the mind-set or of establishing feelings that are compatible with relaxation.

Imagery is also used to induce autogenous (self-produced) control over certain involuntary functions of the body, such as the rate of the heart beat. The relationship of the use of imagery in relaxation to its use in autogenous control has not been well established. It is recommended that autogenous control not be used with involuntary functions of the body or in conjunction with hypnosis by anyone except a psychiatrist or qualified physician.

Impulse Control. Controlling the impulse to move at a normal rate of speed in the performance of a motor movement has been found to decrease muscular tension in some people. Cratty has found it a useful relaxation technique for hyperactive children.[6]

In impulse control activities the student tries to move as slowly as he can in the performance of a designated motor task. For example, he may be directed to walk as slowly as possible along a line, catch a balloon with the slowest possible movement, or push a large ball across the floor in slow motion. These activities are similar in the quality of movement to those used with the imagery technique. However, the objectives of the activities are different: in imagery the goal is to achieve a quality of movement that is like that of some object, such as a rag doll, while in impulse control the objective is to perform a given movement as slowly as possible.

PLANNING THE PROGRAM

Although a total class period could be used to teach relaxation techniques to students, in most instances the results are better when the instruction is integrated or alternated with the teaching of the regular activities of the program. The way in which the teaching of relaxation is worked into the program depends upon the nature of the physical education activity being presented and the background and experience of the students.

Relaxation activities can be readily integrated with motor exploration activities. Exploration of movement leads easily into discovering the differences between muscular relaxation and contraction. The use of imagery in exploration can lead to an understanding of the quality of the relaxed state and can promote conscious relaxation.

Relaxation activities may be incorporated into warm-up exercises by stressing the difference between contraction and relaxation. Relaxation activities may be done after an active game or at the end of the period to calm the children for their return to classroom work. Use at the end of the period or after any vigorous activity may be of special value to hyperactive children. Preferably, the children should lie down in a quiet semi-dark environment that is conducive to practicing relaxation techniques on their own. For very young children, such an environment can be provided by placing large paper boxes in the quietest area of the room. It should never appear that the child who goes to the resting place is being set apart from the rest of the class. Since

---

[6]Bryant J. Cratty: *op. cit.*, pp. 183–85.

every young child benefits from occasional rest, all children might take a turn resting in the box, thereby avoiding any stigma being attached to the procedure.

Participation in strenuous motor activities provides an outlet for releasing excessive tension for some children. Such children are generally those who are successful in the activities; even though fatigued, they feel relaxed and comfortable after a hard fought competitive game or other activity requiring physical skill and stamina. However, for many others, especially the mentally retarded, hyperactive, or emotionally disturbed children who have not experienced success in the activity, strenuous motor effort leads to increased tension that persists long after the activity has concluded. Time devoted to relaxation after the activity is very beneficial to these children.

Students who demonstrate no inability to relax will not need extensive work on relaxation, but they should be given some experience in relaxing for possible future use. They may be introduced to the techniques of discovering the difference between muscular relaxation and contraction and have the experience of trying the various techniques on several different muscle groups of their bodies. The students who do show excessive muscular tension will need special help and considerable time in actual practice of relaxation. Contrary to the popular notion, it often takes as much practice to learn to relax the muscles as it does to learn to contract them for proper performance of a motor skill.

The instruction can proceed in a number of ways. Impulse control or imagery may be introduced when students are participating in another activity. For example, if the children are exploring ways of throwing a ball (overhand, underhand, and so forth), they can also try throwing the ball so slowly that it barely reaches the target or as if it were an egg that must not be broken. Or students may be asked to assume a random formation on the floor to perform relaxation exercises or movements. The teacher may start with the group standing to practice alternate contraction and relaxation of their facial, neck, arm, and finger muscles. Then they sit or lie down to practice relaxing other muscles.

The actual teaching of relaxation may commence with evaluation of the students' ability to relax, using both subjective observation and any of the tests described below. If the students are few, testing may be accomplished by the teacher alone. With larger classes the teacher will need to instruct the students in the techniques of giving the tests. Then, with the class divided into pairs, the students can give the tests to one another. If the number who are tested at any time is limited to five or six, the teacher will be able to assist the students who are administering the tests in making a determination of the presence of muscular tension.

Arm Test of Relaxation. The subject being tested sits in a chair at a desk with his arm resting on the desk. He is instructed to relax his arm and shoulder but to maintain his balance. The tester lifts the forearm a few inches (the elbow remains on the desk). The arm is then released. If the arm drops without control back to the desk, this is evidence of the subject's being able to relax his arm. If, however, the subject contracts the muscles of the arm to assist in raising it, to hold the arm, or to lower the arm when it is dropped, or if he resists the lifting action, tension in the arm is indicated.

The test may also be given using the total arm at the shoulder or the hand at the wrist.

Lower Limb Test of Relaxation. The subject sits on a chair with both feet on the floor and the legs comfortably spread. He is directed by the tester to relax his legs but to maintain his balance. The tester pushes the legs to the center and then to the side, one leg at a time and then both together. If the legs are relaxed, they will push easily to the side and then spring back to the original position, bouncing back and forth slightly as they return. Tension is present if the legs remain in the position in which they have been pushed or if they resist the push. Muscular relaxation tests are often performed with the subject lying down. However, this position is not as conducive to detection of muscular tension as a sitting position, because relaxation is more difficult when seated. Greater muscular contraction is required to hold the body in a sitting position, hence an inability to relax is more easily detected.

SUGGESTED ACTIVITIES

The following activities are eclectic, having been chosen from among the various methods for developing the ability to relax the body at will. The activities may be used in the form described or adapted to fit the specific situation as will be required for students with restricted mobility or deficits in motor learning. The activities presented need not be from only one category; some from several categories may be combined for a meaningful lesson in relaxation. The selection of activities should be made in accordance with the age level and experience of the students.

Exercises for Feeling the Difference Between Relaxation and Tension

In these exercises the student is directed to make a mental note of the difference between relaxation and tension. Each time he contracts or relaxes the muscles, he is to try to make the difference greater. Muscles not involved should be relaxed during the contraction.

1. Make an ugly face by tensing the muscles of the face and neck; then relax the muscles.

2. With the arms hanging loosely at the sides of the body, tighten the muscles of the arms and fingers without bending the arms and fingers; then relax them.

3. Tighten the muscles of the abdomen and relax them.

4. Contract the muscles of the leg while standing. Do not bend the leg. Relax the muscles while maintaining balance.

5. In a supine position with the arms beside the body and palms on the floor, press forcibly against the floor; then hyperextend the wrists and follow with relaxation of the wrists.

6. In a supine position with the knees slightly bent and the feet raised so that only the heels remain in contact with the floor, curl the toes down as far as possible; curl them up and relax.

7. In a supine position with the knees slightly bent, rotate the thighs outward as far as possible, draw the thighs up with the knees bent until the heels are raised two or three inches from the floor or mat. Then relax and return to original position.

8. Sit in a chair with a partner standing behind. Place your hands behind your neck and interlace the fingers. The partner grasps your elbows and pulls back. Resist the pull for a few moments after which, the partner releases his hold on the elbows and you relax your arms. (The pull back should be made slowly and steadily to avoid injury.)

9. Sit in a chair. A partner, who stands in front of the chair, interlocks his fingers behind your head and, placing his elbows on your chest, uses them as fulcrums to pull your head forward. Resist the pull. Upon the partner's release of his grasp, relax your neck.

10. Stand in front of a partner who encircles your waist with his arms, pinning your arms to the sides of your body. Try to lift the arms straight up from the sides. Upon the partner's release of his grip, relax your arms.

Relaxation Exercises Using Imagery

The students are asked to imagine the objects specified in the exercises and then to move as they imagine they would move in the described circumstances. All of the activities are suitable for young children; items 7 through 10 are also appropriate for older students. Since feelings of heaviness and warmth in the muscles accompany relaxation, the imagery related to these feelings suggested in items 7, 8, and 9 is especially helpful in inducing relaxation.

1. Move like a rag doll.
2. Fall slowly to the floor like a balloon that is floating to the ground.
3. Move like a flag waving in a gentle breeze.
4. Be a soft, fluffy kitten curling up its body on the rug.
5. Sway like a slender flower in a gentle breeze.
6. Lie on the floor like a wet towel.
7. Lying on your back, think that your eyelids are getting heavier and heavier; then close the eyelids and relax the entire body.
8. Lying on your back on a mat, think that your arms and legs are heavy like iron and are sinking slowly, slowly into the mat.
9. Lying on your back on the mat, think that your entire body is pleasantly warm and comfortable and is sinking deeper and deeper into a soft, soft mattress.
10. Combine 7, 8, and 9. (Some students may go to sleep if they engage in the combined activity for a sufficiently long period of time.)

Static Stretching of Muscles

All of these activities are performed very slowly and deliberately. Positions obtained should be held for several seconds, followed by relaxation of all muscles involved.

1. Lower the head forward as far as possible, move it to the right and touch the chin to the collarbone and then to the left, touching the collarbone on that side.
2. Bend at the hips and reach to the floor without bending the knees.
3. With the arms hanging loosely at the sides of the body, bend to each side as far as possible.
4. Stand on tip-toes and raise the arms at the sides and parallel to the ground. Move the arms backward as far as possible.
5. Sit on floor with the legs bent and crossed so that the heel of one foot is under the calf of the opposite leg and the toe of that leg is under the calf of the other leg. Place the hands on the knees and push them toward the floor.
6. Lie on the back and bring the knees to the chest with the arms at the sides, palms on the mat or floor. Holding the palms and shoulders on the floor, lower the legs to one side and then to the other until the thighs touch the floor.
7. Lie on the back with the arms stretched to the sides. Raise one leg in the air and bring it over to touch the opposite hand. Hold the position briefly and then return to the original position. Repeat, using the opposite leg and hand.
8. Stand with one foot on the floor and the other on the seat of a chair. Bring the trunk forward in an attempt to place it on the knee.
9. Stand with the arms raised at the sides. Turn the body to the right as far as possible; then to the left as far as possible.
10. Lie on the back and spread the legs as far possible.

Rhythmic Exercises

These exercises can be performed to music or counted cadence or without either. The movement should be executed in a smooth and easy manner.

1. Stand and swing one arm back and forth. Swing one arm forward; swing the other backward. Swing both arms together.

2. Move the head in rhythmic motion from side to side very slowly.

3. Sitting in a chair, clench the fist and swing one arm forcibly in a circle. Repeat using the other arm.

4. Sitting either in a chair or on the floor, swing the trunk from side to side in time to a very slow count.

5. Sitting on a high table so the feet do not touch the floor, swing one leg back and forth and then the other. Swing both at the same time.

6. Using the back of a chair for support, stand on one leg and swing the opposite leg back and forth.

7. Select any part of the body and move it back and forth at a slow tempo.

8. Kneel on all fours and sway slowly forward and backward.

9. Walk very slowly forward, moving the arms in an exaggerated swing in rhythm to the walking cadence.

10. With the hands clasped in front of the chest, rock the arms back and forth as if rocking a baby.

Impulse Control Activities

These exercises are done as slowly as possible. The performance of a given activity may be timed with a stop watch to provide students with a definite goal to match or to better in the next performance of the activity. (In these exercises, a better time is a slower time.)

1. Walk as slowly as possible on a balance beam or along a straight or circular line drawn on the floor.

2. Pretend to throw, bat, or kick a ball in slow motion.

3. Catch a thrown ballon and match the catching movement to the speed of the balloon.

4. Take side-steps as slowly as possible.

5. Sway the body from side to side as slowly as possible.

6. Clap hands in slow motion.

7. Stand on one foot, swing the opposite foot back and forth as slowly as possible; repeat, using opposite feet; swing an arm and leg on the same side of the body.

8. Sit down as slowly as possible; rise equally slowly.

9. Roll over and over on the mat as slowly as possible.

10. Skip as slowly as possible.

Yoga Exercises

The first three of the following activities are âsanas, while the last two are pranayamas. The latter are performed to a count by the performer. All movements in both kinds of activities are slow and deliberate.

1. To assume the position, lie on the back with the arms to the sides. Slowly raise the legs, keeping them straight, and bring them over the head until the feet touch the floor above the head. To increase the difficulty, the hands are removed from the sides and locked above the head. This position is called plowshares.

2. To assume the position referred to as the cobra, lie face down with the forehead on the floor or mat. The hands are placed on the floor on either side of the chest. The head is raised with the chest held against the mat. Then the chest is raised. In the first attempts, the hands may be used to help raise the chest, but as skill is increased, the use of the hands is discontinued.

3. A sitting position is taken with the legs straight out. The right leg is bent and turned outward so the thigh touches the floor or mat. The heel is brought up to the crotch with the sole of the foot touching the left thigh. The left foot is then placed on the right thigh. (This is the lotus position.) The right arm is placed to encircle the knee coming over the top so the right shoulder can be placed on the knee. The right hand extends across the body and grasps the left foot. The right shoulder must be firmly set against the knee to avoid injury to the elbow joint.* The reverse position may be taken by starting with the left leg.

4. The pulse is taken at rest to establish the cadence for breathing. A reclining position is taken on the back with the knees slightly bent. Inhale slowly for four counts and then exhale for four counts. The exercise continues for several minutes.

5. Sit on the floor with the legs crossed as in number 5 of the static stretching exercises. Hold the spine erect and take a deep breath and hold for six counts. (The rhythm is the same as in item 4.) Exhale at the count of six. Continue the exercise for several minutes.

---

*The addition to the lotus position was adapted from an exercise by Rathbone.

SELECTED READINGS

Hittleman, Richard: *Introduction to Yoga*. New York, Bantam Books, 1969.
Jacobson, E. O.: *Modern Treatment of Tense Patients*. Springfield, Ill., Charles C Thomas, Pub., 1970.
Jacobson, Edmund: *Progressive Relaxation*, ed. 2. Chicago, The University of Chicago Press, 1938.
Mackey, R. T.: *Exercise, Rest, and Relaxation*. Dubuque, Iowa, Wm. C. Brown Co., Pub., 1970.
Rathbone, Josephine: *Relaxation*. Philadelphia, Lea and Febiger, 1969.
Selye, Hans: *Stress Without Distress*. Philadelphia, J. B. Lippincott Co., 1974.

Chapter 30

Outdoor Education and Camping

Broadly stated, outdoor education embraces all of the learning activities which deal directly with the wise utilization and appreciation of the natural environment. It consists of learning by actual performance in the natural laboratory out of doors.

More specifically, however, for purposes of this discussion, outdoor education is defined as one specialized aspect of general education. As such, it is an integral part of the school curriculum. Identified in this way, outdoor education enhances every field in the modern curriculum from pre-school through college.

Outdoor education has been part of human experience since human society began. In primitive cultures almost all learning took place in and was directly related to the natural environment. As civilization developed and human knowledge expanded, learning experiences necessarily became less direct. Inevitably, it was determined that a combination of direct and indirect learning was required if man was to develop culturally, socially, and physically. Educators came to accept the view that both direct experiences — learning through working with real things in life situations — and textbook and laboratory materials are essential for the best possible education.

One phase of outdoor education, camping, has a long history. Camping was fairly well established as an organized activity for normal children by the end of the 19th century. Children who suffered physical and mental disabilities, however, were generally denied admittance to camps, both because those in charge were unable to cope with their disabilities and because the values of camping for the handicapped had not been fully realized. The establishment of camps especially for handicapped children began with what were generally referred to as "summer homes" along the eastern seaboard. The first actual camp appears to have been established around 1900 through the efforts of two Chicago teachers of crippled children. The success of this initial effort led to the establishment of more camps. Today, camping facilities are available to thousands of handicapped children.

VALUES OF OUTDOOR EDUCATION

Outdoor education, particularly that phase of it known as camping, offers excellent living experiences to those handicapped participants who might be stifled in a less permissive atmosphere. Here the individual is, for a little while, taken away from the normal routine of school or home and placed in a dynamic situation under the guidance of professional personnel who have an understanding of the psychological problems faced by those who are handicapped.

In an outdoor environment the individual is able to express himself freely. There are no distractions, no noisome cities, no densely populated neighborhoods, no loneliness bred of isolation from one's peers. Here the needs of the individual are satisfied. The child or adult has an opportunity to live close to nature and in so doing acquires an appreciation of the resources of the land.

Luther Burbank once said:

> Every child should have mud pies, grasshoppers, water-bugs, tadpoles, frogs, mud-turtles, elderberries, wild strawberries, acorns, chestnuts, trees to climb, brooks to wade in, water-lilies, woodchucks, bats, bees, butterflies, various animals to pet, hay fields, pine cones, rocks to roll, sand, snakes, huckleberries and hornets; and any child who has been deprived of these has been deprived of the best part of his education.

If the experiences described by Burbank are so vital to the normal child, how infinitely more important they are for the handicapped child. The healing magic of nature's world may not cure a cardiac condition or alleviate rheumatoid arthritis, but it can do much to soothe an aching spirit, quiet an emotionally disturbed child, and offer a new world to the blind, deaf, or mentally retarded. The therapeutic value of outdoor education comes from simply being out of doors, living at an unhurried and unharried pace, learning whatever new skills one is capable of performing, experiencing an entirely new series of activities, or re-learning valuable skills which have been forgotten through disuse.

THE OUTDOOR EDUCATION PROGRAM

Direct learning in an outdoor environment should be part of the regular school curriculum; particularly is this true for those special classes designed for exceptional children. Short walking tours on the school site may be worthwhile, if the school is located in a rural area, but of more significance is the planned trip to nearby parks, zoos, museums, planetariums, farms, reservations, aquatic areas, or other nature resources of the community. Some schools have a sufficiently large site or have acquired enough additional land that it is possible to create an outdoor nature laboratory. Here students can be taught nature study, horticulture, floriculture, conservation, and earth sciences. A gardening activity begun in the spring can be carried on through the summer months and related to several aspects of the curriculum. Such an experience usually correlates with entomology, ecology, biology, and other sciences. A school fortunate enough to have a heavily wooded area combined with a farm has an ideal setting for instruction, for then it is possible to plan many more experiences, including care of animals, forestry practices, conservation methods, and land use, and to relate these to every phase of the curriculum from mathematics, social studies, and crafts to the earth sciences, health, and physical education.

Whatever the normal child can learn, the handicapped child can learn unless he is handicapped by mental inability. In consequence, there need be no educational adaptation of the programmed learning; adaptations will occur only in those educational activities which preclude participation by the handicapped. The environment may need to be modified to meet the needs of the orthopedically handicapped, the blind, and so forth; but few of the nature-oriented activities will have to undergo change. Certain outdoor activities such as mountain climbing, spelunking, or tree climbing are obviously going to be beyond the capacities of most handicapped individuals. There are, however, many other activities which can be adapted, so that even those whose handicaps prevent their leaving the wheelchair or stretcher can be included.

Gardening.   Gardening is an outdoor education activity particularly adaptable for the handicapped. Nonambulatory persons may garden without bending or leaving the bed, stretcher, or wheelchair if light longhandled tools are provided. The bed-ridden patient can have a windowsill or dish garden to bring the outdoors inside.

Nature Studies.   Bird watching, astronomical observations, and the classification of minerals, flora, fauna, and other natural specimens do not require extensive movement. They may be performed by the nonambulatory in sitting, lying, or reclining positions. The materials for classification may be brought by others for manipulation, mounting, or taxonomy. However, if the handicapped person can be provided with a lightweight tool with a long handle and a cutting edge, much like that used by a pruner, he will be able to gather some types of specimens for himself.

Fishing.   Fishing is easily adapted to meet the physical limitations of participants. In the extreme case of a double-arm amputee, the fishing rod may be attached to his waist and harnessed around his upper back so that the rod is at the correct angle. A volunteer will be needed to pull in and unhook the catch. The helper should remain nearby at all times to give assistance if needed.

Field Trips and Hikes.   A field trip, as the name implies, is a walk taken to explore a field or outdoor area. Its purpose may be simply to enjoy the surroundings,

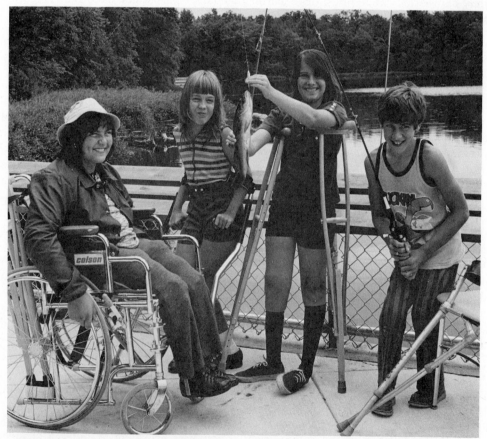

Figure 30–1.   Fishing is easily adapted to meet the physical limitations of campers. (Courtesy of The Easter Seal Society for Crippled Children and Adults of Connecticut, Inc.)

or it may be to search for wildflowers, rocks, or other nature objects or to find materials for use in crafts. Because the pace of a field trip is slow and leisurely, even the most disabled can participate. The distance can be readily adjusted to the physical abilities and endurance of the group.

Hikes are more extensive than field trips and frequently have a specific destination, but this does not mean that anyone need be excluded. Those whose disabilities or lack of stamina prevent their hiking the entire distance may be transported part of the way or the entire distance if the condition requires. Even those who are unable to hike even a short distance enjoy being at the destination when the others arrive, sharing the end-of-the-hike activities and discussions with the hikers. Everyone should be included in the planning and preparations for the hike. Those being transported can be asked to bring the cold drinks for the others or in other ways made to feel they are a part of the entire expedition.

Depending upon the physical conditions of the handicapped, it may be necessary to provide periods of rest during the hike. If only a portion of the hikers will require rest along the way, this group can start earlier and stop to rest when the need becomes apparent.

These are just a few examples of the hundreds of activities which may be adapted to meet the limitations imposed by physical handicaps. A few experiences must be omitted because of environmental impossibility, but for the most part every tool,

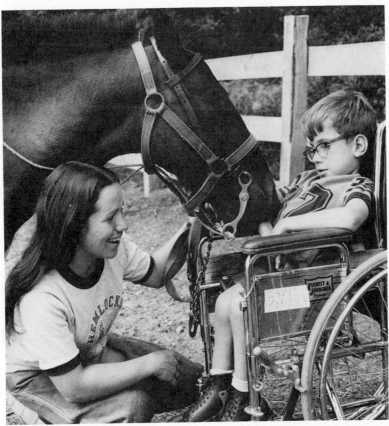

Figure 30–2. Field trips offer opportunities to make new discoveries and new acquaintances, including some from the animal world. (Courtesy of The Easter Seal Society for Crippled Children and Adults of Connecticut, Inc.)

device, or activity may be modified in some way to enable the handicapped individual to share in the self-fulfillment of outdoor education.

CAMPING

Camping provides, in addition to the values inherent in any outdoor education activity, a unique experience in group living. In the ideal camp situation the child learns to relax and have fun, to work in harmony with others, to broaden his skills and interests, to develop his own initiative and resourcefulness, and to expand his awareness of himself and the world in which he lives. By camping a youngster may gain skills, interests, and appreciations which will enrich his entire life.

Day and Residential Camps.   Day camps are those which campers attend for the day, returning home at night. The day camp is an ideal arrangement for youngsters who are not ambulatory, who require exceptional help with their braces or with their personal needs, or who for medical or other reasons cannot leave home for extended periods. Residential camps are those in which the campers spend the day and night for a span of several days, usually a week or longer. The obvious advantage of the residential camp for those who are able to participate is the added experience of being completely away from the home environment.

School Camps.   Closely allied to the outdoor educational opportunities described previously is the school-sponsored camping program. The school camp may be one of two distinct operations. As a summer camp, it represents an operation of the school system during the months when the school is closed. In this situation (the operation of the camp by the school throughout the summer), the camp becomes by extension a part of the curriculum. The second operational aspect is the year-round school camp. Here the camp is, indeed, an integral part of a curriculum which recognizes that many learning experiences can best be undertaken out of doors. It provides first-hand learning experiences close to a natural environment.

The teacher occupies a central position in the school camp program. Through classroom instruction before the class moves into the camp situation, he stimulates his pupils to look forward to the entire outdoor educational experience. He does much to make camping meaningful and serves as a coordinator for relating the camp program to the entire curriculum.

The camping program is generally enriched and comprehensive, specifically suited to meet the needs of the handicapped children who are involved. Months may be spent in planning for the occasion. The school camp is a student's community and all of the usual hazards and problems of sanitation, safety, health, and maintenance of public property are involved. The camper is confronted not only by curriculum subjects but also by the countless offerings of a bountiful nature.

The concepts basic to design, location, and operation of other publicly operated camping facilities apply to school camp properties. In selecting the camp site the following must be considered:

1. Availability of a safe and adequate supply of water;
2. Safe disposal of all sewage and garbage;
3. Climate, topographic features, and general environment;
4. Sources of food supply;
5. Accessibility to good transportation and communication;
6. Natural resources of the camp site;
7. Fire-fighting and protective devices;
8. Adequate cabins and shelters for campers;

9. Facilities for operating a comprehensive camp activities program;
10. Aquatic facilities;
11. Health facilities; and
12. Special facilities for maintenance operations.

All facilities of the school camp should be in accordance with state and local health department rules, ordinances, and regulations. Local building and zoning codes apply to the camp facility and must be followed.

With the camp facility as a base of operations, many experiences proper to the locale can be arranged to offer a meaningful and developmental series of activities. An essential part of programming is that these activities be fun, with plenty of time allowed to complete them. In order to build intellectual appreciation and appropriate skills for lifetime use, the camp should avoid the formal and sometimes regimented procedures of school by offering the most permissive atmosphere possible without anarchy.

Special Camps. Camps for handicapped children are usually not geared for the medical or therapeutic treatment of the handicap except in special instances. Camps for diabetics and epileptics are examples of the camps established expressly for assisting these conditions medically. Most other camps, but not all, are organized for specific types of disabilities, such as the camps for crippled children. In these camps, although the personnel is trained in the understanding of the physical debilitating aspects and the mental and emotional stresses of the young campers, the primary aim is to provide camping fun rather than treatment. This is not to say, however, that the therapeutic effects which result from a good camping program are neglected in either the planning or practice.

In addition to those camps organized to provide medical treatment and those designed specifically for one type of handicap or another, there are many camps attended primarily by non-handicapped children which also accept children with less severe types of disabilities. In this situation, the child may simply be a handicapped individual going to camp with physically normal children, or he may be one of a group of handicapped attending the same camp as the non-handicapped but participating in a separate or slightly modified program.

CAMPS FOR THE CRIPPLED. Under this heading are included camps for the orthopedically and neurologically incapacitated and for cardiacs. These camps have been established and maintained throughout the country largely through the efforts of the National Easter Seal Society for Crippled Children and Adults. The camps have tried to provide an introductory experience in camping which enables the camper to attend a regular camp after his initial experience in the special camp. In this way the facilities of the special camp can be extended to other crippled children.

A few camps have been established for severely disabled adults, with the program and environment adapted to their special needs. Because such campers have spent much of their lives in hospitals receiving treatment and rehabilitation services, the camp program is deliberately void of medical and vocational therapy. Its aim is rather to provide recreation in a relaxed, friendly atmosphere. There is an emphasis on physical activity in the program offerings because so many disabled adults have given up the thought of ever again participating in active games and dances. The campers are encouraged to get into the water for swimming or just splashing around and to play the adapted sports and games which are offered.

CAMPS FOR THE DIABETIC. In special camps for those who have diabetes mellitus, medical treatment and observation are an essential part of the camping experience. Under the direction of a physician a careful check is made of the diet, exercise, and medication of the camper. The diabetic does, in effect, receive the same careful observation and care that he would receive in a hospital at approximately comparable costs but with the tremendous advantage of the relaxed and pleasant surroundings.

In many areas where there is no special diabetic camp, regular camps have arranged to accommodate a group of diabetics in their programs. These camps make available a physician who directs the diet and insulin dosage of the campers and visits them daily. A nurse experienced in handling diabetic cases is on the camp staff and laboratory facilities are provided for the necessary tests.

CAMPS FOR THE EPILEPTIC. Epileptic children profit greatly from camping experiences. An increasing number of regular camps are providing opportunities for epileptic children to participate in camping activities under the supervision of medical personnel. The children admitted to regular camps are carefully screened, as it has been demonstrated that successful participation is related to personal adjustment to the illness and control of seizures. Those epileptics with serious maladjustments need and deserve the more individual attention which is given at special camps for epileptics. Reasonably good control of seizures appears necessary for satisfactory camping experience with normal youngsters although complete freedom from attacks is not essential unless the camp is totally unprepared for epileptic campers.

CAMPS FOR THE BLIND. Camping for blind children and adults is well established. Special camps have been operated successfully for many years, and in more recent years many regular camps have taken blind children into their programs. Blind campers when given a good program of orientation in carefully planned facilities are able to participate in all camp activities, including boating and swimming.

CAMPS FOR THE DEAF. Regular camps accept deaf children unless their communication skills or personality adjustment decidedly unfits them for successful participation in the program. Special camps for the deaf are operated by many schools for the deaf.

CAMPS FOR THE MENTALLY RETARDED. Camps for the mentally handicapped represent another development in the ever-increasing scope of camping for the handicapped. Camping is a particularly enjoyable experience for these youngsters whose participation in so many of the enriching experiences of childhood is limited. The typical program offers all types of waterfront activities, simple recreational games, crafts, group singing, dancing, and story reading. Time is allotted for relaxation and informal get-togethers and for definite periods of rest, all of which are essential to the welfare of the retarded camper.

CAMPS FOR THE OVERWEIGHT. The concern about overweight has, in recent years, prompted the development of summer camps where children may enroll to lose weight under medical supervision. Weight reduction is effected through carefully controlled diet and a vigorous exercise program. Effort is made by camp personnel to keep the morale of the dieters high, and, toward this end, an interesting schedule of activities is maintained.

Referring Students to Camps. Careful consideration must be given to several factors in recommending students for a nonspecialized camp. A youngster is generally considered to be ready for camping experiences when he can perform the following:

1. He can take care of his toilet and other personal care needs as well as other youngsters his age.

2. He is able to care for and put on and remove the braces or appliances which he must use.

3. He understands the limitations which his handicap imposes and the safety precautions which are entailed.

4. He has made a reasonable adjustment to his condition.

5. He possesses enough physical stamina to go through the camping period without undue fatigue or recurrent illness.

The type of camp which any particular youngsters should attend may be determined by availability, family finances, and other considerations. A few specific suggestions can be made by the physical education teacher, however, based upon his observation and work with the youngster as a student in his program. Children with severe disabilities or personality problems will probably profit most, particularly the first year, from a day camp or specialized camp which is prepared to give special help to those unable to take charge of their personal needs. Wherever the circumstances are favorable, however, the child should be recommended for enrollment in a camp that integrates the handicapped with the non-handicapped because of the opportunities for social growth in an atmosphere of acceptance which such a camp cultivates.

The youngster must, of course, be examined and judged able to attend camp by his doctor. The camp will request a medical history of the disability as well as a social history describing his adjustment and personality problems. Recommendations of the kinds of activities which may prove most physiologically and psychologically beneficial may be requested. The medical report should list the activities in which the youngster may not engage and any special precautions which should be exercised. All of this information will serve the camp officials as a medical guide and as a program guide. The care and thoroughness with which the requested information is supplied will determine to a great extent the success with which the camping experience can be directed to meet the needs of the camper.

Camp Personnel. There are many opportunities for physical education teachers trained to provide for the special needs of the handicapped to find summer employment in camps for disabled youngsters and adults.

The administrative personnel, more or less standard in all camps for the handicapped, consists of a director, medical staff, counselors, and activity supervisors and instructors. The director is usually responsible for establishing the policies and procedures of the camp as they are set forth by the sponsoring agency. He must have a sound philosophy of camping and understand the goals which the camp is attempting to reach for exceptional children. Among the skills, talents, and knowledge that the camp director must possess are those related to site selection and development, accounting, budget making, selection and education of the camp staff, insurance, construction, maintenance, equipment, program, legal responsibilities, and above all, supervision. The camp director is primarily and directly responsible for everything that happens at the camp and for the health and safety of all the campers.

An understanding of the nature of the handicap and the problems in adjustment which it has presented to the youngster is essential for the counselor or instructor in the special camp. This is no less true of those working with handicapped children within the regular camp situation. The specific duties of the cabin counselor are outlined by the director. Often the instructor of a phase of the program, such as crafts or swimming, will also serve as a cabin counselor. The counselor must be prepared to deal with homesickness, failure to conform to the regulations, and similar problems common to any child in an unfamiliar situation, in addition to which he must be equal to the problems, both physical and psychological, arising from the handicap.

The activity instructor (such as the instructor in charge of sports and games) must be ready and willing to meet the challenges of providing a program in which the handicapped campers can participate with success and pleasure. He must learn how to help these children fulfill their needs, how to direct their energies, and how to help them develop their potential within the bounds of their limitations.

Special Facilities. The physical facilities which must be provided for handicapped campers are not extensive. Ramps at entrances to buildings are necessary for children who cannot readily negotiate steps. Obstacles should be removed if they necessitate special assistance to handicapped campers or require considerable effort on their part in overcoming them. However, a limited number of obstacles to overcome can prove stimulating to the disabled campers. Pathways, buildings, and activity areas must be made easily identifiable for those with visual handicaps. For campers who have difficulty standing unassisted while showering, seats may be provided in the shower stalls. Some special medical and therapeutic facilities and equipment may need to be supplied so that the infirmary is prepared to cope with emergencies arising from a specific disability.

The Camp Program. Camps which provide the best possible environment and experience for the handicapped are those which carefully plan and administer their program. Comprehensive and varied nature-oriented activites should be a fundamental part of the program offered in the camp setting; among them are aquatics, astronomy, agriculture, archery, art, crafts, ceremonials, scouting, exploring, hiking, boating, tripping, dances, games, conservation, lapidary work, geology, ecology, hobbies, dramatics, tournaments, music, reading, motor skills, meteorology, pomology, and entomology. There should be both highly organized and free-play experiences for passive and active recreational experiences. There must be opportunities for self-expression through leadership as well as conformity through followership. To the extent that they are capable, the campers should be allowed to plan and assume responsibilities for the success of the program. There should be guidance, counseling, unobtrusive supervision, and enthusiastic leadership. There should also be a minimum of essential regulation and no dogmatism or slavish devotion to a single method of activity presentation.

The program of the school camp for the handicapped must attempt to improve the quality of the camper's educational experiences as well as to provide an environment that is conducive to healthful living. The program must be soundly based upon the abilities of the campers to participate, and their interests should be the guidelines for choosing effective activities.

Adaptations. While every effort should be made to offer handicapped campers "normal" games, dances, sports, and camp activities, some modifications are necessitated by the nature of their disabilities. In the special day and residential camps, the activities can be adapted in a general way for everyone, with such attention as is required directed toward individual needs other than the specific handicap. The program activities for the integrated camp will require more careful planning to ensure nearly equal participation by the able-bodied and the handicapped. The same considerations which govern successful integration of the handicapped into the regular physical education program will apply in the camp situation. It must be remembered that the handicapped camper has the same basic needs as normal youngsters but some needs are more pronounced than others because of his disability.

A general guide for planning and conducting a program of physical activities for handicapped campers is offered here:

1. Safety precautions must be strictly adhered to, even though the handicapped camper is so anxious to try all the new experiences that he may prefer to ignore restrictions.

2. Lead-up skills must be well mastered before complicated feats are attempted.

3. Campers must be closely observed for early signs of fatigue because handicapped youngsters usually tire easily. Rest periods should be provided as needed.

4. The program should be kept relaxed and unhurried to avoid unnecessary frustrations and anxieties. Competitive events should be prevented from becoming highly emotional.

5. The camper's relationship to others and his acceptance by them should be closely observed, with guidance offered unobtrusively.

6. The camper should be helped to establish realistic goals for his physical development and skill achievement, with full recognition of his potential as well as his limitations.

7. Help should be readily given when actually needed; however, when confidence rather than skill is lacking, the camper should be encouraged to try to do things himself rather than having them done for him.

The camp activities should not follow along the same lines as the city or school recreational program for the handicapped. The campers will, of course, want to play individual and team sports to which they have been introduced in their school and town recreational programs, but these should not form the core of the program.

SELECTED REFERENCES

AAHPER: *Involving Impaired, Disabled, and Handicapped Persons in Regular Camp Programs*. Washington, D.C., American Alliance for Health, Physical Education and Recreation, 1976.

Croucher, Norman: *Outdoor Pursuits for Disabled People*. London, Disabled Living Foundation, 1974.

Nesbitt, John A., *et al.* (Editors): *Training Needs and Strategies in Camping for the Handicapped*. Eugene, Ore., Center of Leisure Studies, University of Oregon, 1972.

Shea, Thomas M.: *Camping for Special Children*. St. Louis, The C. V. Mosby Co., 1977.

Shivers, Jay S.: *Camping: Administration, Counseling, Programming*. New York, Appleton-Century-Crofts, 1971.

Special Studies Institute: *Outdoor Education Experiences for Emotionally Handicapped Children and Youth*. Plattsburgh, N.Y., State University College of Arts and Science, 1972.

Index of Activities

Subject Index